ENGLISH CATHOLIC BOOKS 1701-1800

A BIBLIOGRAPHY

English Catholic Books
1701-1800

A Bibliography

Compiled by

F. Blom
J. Blom
F. Korsten
G. Scott

SCOLAR
PRESS

Published by
SCOLAR PRESS
Gower House
Croft Road
Aldershot
Hants GU11 3HR
England

Ashgate Publishing Company
Old Post Road
Brookfield
Vermont 05036-9704
USA

British Library Cataloguing-in-Publication data.

English Catholic Books, 1701–1800: a bibliography
  I. Blom, F.
  016.8209935282

Library of Congress Cataloging-in-Publication data.

English Catholic books, 1701–1800 : a bibliography / compiled by
  F. Blom ... [et al.].
     p. cm.
   Includes indexes.
   ISBN 1-85928-148-6
   1. Catholic Church—England—Bibliography. 2. Catholic
literature—Bibliography. 3. Bibliography—Great Britain—Early
printed books—18th century. 4. Theology, Catholic—Bibliography.
5. English imprints. I. Blom, Frans.
Z7837.7.G7E44 1996
[BX1492]
016.282'41—dc20   95-36772
                    CIP

ISBN 1 85928 148 6

Printed in Great Britain by Antony Rowe Ltd, Chippenham, Wiltshire

Contents

Acknowledgements

We wish to thank the following libraries for permission to examine printed books and archives in their possession.

St. Alban's College (Valladolid); the American Antiquarian Society; Ampleforth Abbey; Bar Convent (York); St. Andrew's Cathedral (Dundee); Biblioteca Apostolica Vaticana; Arundel Castle; Baltimore Catholic Archives; Bibliothèque Nationale; Birmingham Archdiocesan Archives; Bishop's House (Newcastle); Bodleian Library; Diocese of Brentwood, Archives Office; British Library; California University Library, Special Collections; Cambridge University Library; Catholic University of America, Mullen Library; Chicago University Library, Special Collections; Collegio di San Clemente dei Dominicani Irlandesi (Rome); Colwich Abbey; Diocese of Clifton (Bristol); Clongowes Wood College; Biblioteca Dominicana (Gent); Bibliothèque Municipale de Douai; Douai Abbey; Downside Abbey Library; Dublin Diocesan Archives; St. Edmund's College (Ware); the English Convent (Bruges); Archives of the English Province of the Order of Preachers (Edinburgh); Essex Record Office; Farm Street (London); Fernham Priory; Franciscan Library (Killiney); Georgetown University Library; Harry Ransom Humanities Research Center, University of Texas at Austin; Hendred House; Heythrop College; the Houghton Library (Cambridge, Mass.); University of Illinois Library; Bibliothèque de l'Institut de France; Collège des Irlandais (Paris); Collegio di San Isidoro dei Franciscani Irlandesi (Rome); John Carter Brown Library (Providence); Koninklijke Bibliotheek (The Hague); Lancashire Record Office; Leeds Diocesan Archives; Library Company of Philadelphia; Lille, Archives du Nord; London Oratory; Université Catholique de Louvain, Bibliothèque Générale et de Sciences Humaines; Mapledurham House; St. Mary's College (Oscott); Milltown Park; National Library of Scotland; National Library of Ireland; National Library of Wales; New York Public Library; Universiteitsbibliotheek Nijmegen; Pontifico Collegio Beda (Rome); Pontifico Collegio Scozzese (Rome); Presbyterian Church (Philadelphia); Princeton Theological Seminary, Speer Library; Real Colegio de Escoceses (Salamanca); Bibliothèque Municipale de Rouen; Russell Library, St. Patrick's College (Maynooth); St. Benedict's Abbey, Fort Augustus; Bibliothèque Sainte-Geneviève; St. Mary's Priory (Tallaght); Scottish Catholic Archives (Edinburgh); Scotus College; Stanbrook Abbey; Stonyhurst College; Talbot Library (Preston); Traquair House; Trinity College Library (Dublin); Ushaw College; Abdij St. Benedictusberg (Vaals); Venerable English College (Rome); Warwickshire Record Office; Westminster Diocesan Archives; William L. Clements Library; Yale University Library.

We are grateful to the librarians and staffs of the libraries mentioned above for the trouble they have taken over answering our queries and for the time a number of them have had to spend explaining to us the workings of catalogues that they inherited from their predecessors. Special thanks are due to Father Bede Bailey, O.P.; Mr C. Benson; Dr K. Bishop; Dame Gertrude Brown; Dr Maurice Caillet; Dr T.A.F. Cherry; Father Dermot Cox; Dom Anselm Cramer; Father

Ian Dickie; D. W. Doughty (Over, Cambridge); George Every; Mark A. Hackson; Mr K. Hall; Geoffrey Holt, S.J.; Father Petroc Howell; Thomas M. McCoog, S.J.; Mgr Ian Murray; Karen Nipps; Charles Parry; Mr Nicolas Petit; Dom Daniel Rees; John Martin Robinson; Dom Ben Schlatmann; James R. South; Lady Maxwell Stuart; Rev. Paul K. Thomas: Michael Walsh; David Walters; Sister Katharine Williams.

At crucial moments during the past years we received grants from Dutch foundations and institutions that enabled us to travel to important libraries. We are grateful to the Nederlandse Provincie van de Jezuïeten, the Mr Paul De Gruyter Stichting and the Stichting Sormanifonds.

During the various stages of this bibliography a great many people contributed to the work in all kinds of different ways. It is impossible to mention them all by name, but we want to explicitly express our gratitude to the following persons: John Bevan, bookseller and expert in the field of English Catholic books, who was kind enough to inform us extensively about his past and present stock; Frank Carleton, who volunteered information about Australian books; Dr Edward Corp who helped us with information about the printer W. Weston; Michael Crump, managing editor of ESTC, who allowed us free access to ESTC computer files in a completely unbureaucratic way and who put up with two of us occupying places in the overcrowded ESTC London office for a week; Father Ignatius Fennessy, O.F.M., for being one of the kindest librarians we ever met and for not believing in business hours; Bishop B. Foley for his help with J. P. Coghlan and the *Laity's Directory*; Dr Elizabeth Leedham-Green for replying to our many queries swiftly and efficiently; Dr Jan Rhodes, who was an invaluable help during our stay at Ushaw; Maartje Rondeboom for her extensive report on the progress of ESTC in Australia; Jan Steenbrink, who volunteered to assist us in working our way through ESTC; Father F.J. Turner, S.J., for his efficiency in making available Stonyhurst books to us; Penelope Woods for allowing us to make the most of our research visit to Maynooth.

We are grateful to the Benedictine communities of Downside, Ealing and Cockforsters' for putting us up during various visits, and to Liesbeth van de Arend, Anita Boerakker, Nigel Browne, Odin Dekkers, Henk Dijkgraaf, Martine Swennen and Thea Steeghs for help with collecting information, typing, filing, indexing and proof-reading. Astrid van Hoek was a great help during the final stages of our research. Karin Bosveld assisted with all aspects of the work from the beginning and cheerfully put up with overworked researchers at impossible times.

In the notes to the various entries in our bibliography three names keep cropping up followed by the statement '(personal communication)': the names are those of Hugh Fenning, O.P., Thomas Clancy, S.J., and Dr David Rogers. All three of them have played a crucial role in our researches. Hugh Fenning and Thomas Clancy, with the characteristic generosity of bibliographers, both unselfishly shared with us information from their forthcoming books. Fenning's information about Ireland and Clancy's advice about American holdings were essential to us. Clancy, author of *English Catholic Books 1641-1700. A Bibliography*, was, moreover, an inspiration for our own book. While we were proofreading the final pages of our bibliography news came of David Rogers's death. Together with Antony Allison, David Rogers was the pioneer of English Roman Catholic bibliography. His expertise - not only in his own period, but also in the eighteenth century - was unrivalled and during long days at his house in Blewbury he freely gave detailed answers to innumerable queries as well as access to material, such as eighteenth-century booksellers' catalogues, that he had been been collecting during a lifetime.

And finally we would like to express our gratitude to Tom Birrell, one of the few people who enjoys catalogues as bedside reading. Apart from the fact that he taught three of us the principles of bibliography, he was the one to suggest the subject of this book. His involvement is characterized by the fact that he was checking incomplete entries for us in the Bodleian Library two days before our manuscript was due at the Scolar Press.

Jos Blom
Frans Blom
Frans Korsten
Geoffrey Scott

Background

It is nearly forty years since the first general bibliography of English Catholic books appeared in the form of A.F. Allison and D.M. Roger's *A Catalogue of Catholic books in English Printed Abroad or Secretly in England 1558-1640* (Bognor Regis 1956). Since then, there have been two further major contributions. T.H. Clancy published an extension of the work of Allison and Rogers in his *English Catholic Books 1641-1700: A Bibliography* (Chicago 1974). Meanwhile, Allison and Rogers continued to refine and add to their earliest provisional bibliographical lists, a task which they pursued for over thirty years and which culminated in their monumentally thorough *The Contemporary Printed Literature of the English Counter Reformation* (Aldershot 1989, 1994). Chronologically, the 18th century needed tackling next. Over recent years, studies of 18th century English Catholicism have made considerable advances. Much of the work pursued at a local level has been centered on this period, and the recent celebration of some notable bi-centenaries, such as the death of Bishop Richard Challoner in 1781 and the expulsion of the English Catholic colleges and religious communities from the Continent in the 1790s in the aftermath of the French Revolution, has also heightenend contemporary interest in the period and generated some published work. The discovery of archival material relative to 18th century English Catholic publishers and a number of recent detailed studies on them and their work has, in turn, helped to open up the shadowy world of Catholic publishing which served an expanding circle of readers in the United Kingdom, Ireland and America. Possibly the greatest incentive to this bibliography came with the establishment of the *Eighteenth Century Short Title Catalogue* (ESTC) at the British Library in 1977. The ESTC has given immediate access to 18th century holdings in scores of major libraries and has provided the compilers of this catalogue with a tool not hitherto available to earlier Catholic bibliographers.

1. Eighteenth Century Catholic Publishers

Among historians of the English Catholic community, the 18th century has traditionally been neglected as something of a backwater stagnating between the heroic age of martyrs and missionaries of the 17th century and the emancipated community of the 19th century marching forwards self-confidently to full maturity. The single most important contribution which this bibliography will make will be to modify this judgement. The great increase in Catholic publishing during these years and the wide variety in the type of material published are indications of a community increasingly settled, conscious of its own traditions and willing to share them within a society where tolerance generally triumphed over the occasional bouts of anti-popery. Many of the books, pamphlets and ephemera in our list are to be found in private and inaccessible collections, and by listing them here, this bibliography constitutes a useful adjunct to the ESTC.

It has been our aim, therefore, to establish the foundations for a Roman Catholic ESTC.

There were to be some major developments in English Catholic publishing during the 18th century. The long tradition of Catholic books published abroad for English use disappeared. False continental imprints continued to appear, however, until after mid-century, when they gradually declined. The same pattern is apparent in books actually published in Europe, although there still appeared the occasional volume published in the Austrian Netherlands in the 1780s and 1790s. In England, Catholic publishers had no grounds to fear censorship after the decision in 1695 not to renew the Licensing Act, but the existence of the Penal Laws still made Catholic writers and publishers liable to charges of treason, and the 1709 Copyright Act prevented the import of Catholic books from abroad. Thus, Thomas Meighan's edition of Robert Manning's *England's Conversion*, published in London with the false imprint of Antwerp, was seized by the authorities in 1726 as 'seditious and impious'. In 1737 Meighan was arrested for publishing one of Challoner's polemical works, and in 1747 he was imprisoned for allegedly selling copies of the dying speeches of Jacobites involved in the '45. Yet despite these setbacks a small number of Catholic publishers succeeded in firmly establishing themselves, and in acquiring a virtual monopoly over works published for their co-religionists. It is striking that compared to the late 17th century, such publishers were fewer in number but more prolific.

Catholic publishing in London was almost entirely on the presses of a handful of well-known names, Thomas Meighan (died 1753), James Marmaduke (died 1788), and James Peter Coghlan (died 1800). It was typical also of the printing trade generally that these publishers too established a line of descent in the 18th century, one firm often succeeding the other. Meighan, 'the father of the modern Catholic bookselling trade in England' succeeded Thomas Metcalfe, the London Catholic publisher, between 1711 and 1715, and remained in business until his death in 1753. Meighan seems to have been an enthusiastic apologist of the English Catholic cause. He had numerous brushes with the civil authorities, patronized key apologetical authors like Robert Manning and Edward Hawarden, and was the first openly to 'puff' his Catholic books by distributing his catalogues from his shop or binding them into the backs of his volumes. These Catholic booklists were an 18th century innovation and belonged to that flood of Catholic ephemera which included episcopal, pastoral and encyclical letters, obit notices, school prospectuses, and appeal leaflets, all of which reflect an effectively governed church with its own corporate life, pride, and sense of purpose. Thomas Meighan's business was continued by his wife Martha, who published an edition of the *Manual* in 1755, and then by his son, the younger Thomas. After the latter's death in 1774, the stock was bought by James Peter Coghlan, and so the tradition was continued.

James Marmaduke seems to have entered Catholic publishing about 1741, and was particularly interested in the publication of liturgical works. It was Marmaduke who was the inspiration behind the *Laity's Directory*, which appeared first in 1758. This was an annual publication for the Catholic laity, at first mainly instructional and devotional, but gradually also developing into a domestic bulletin for the Catholic community. Coghlan at first competed with Marmaduke by publishing his rival *Laity's Directory*, 'By permission and with approbation', and the edition for 1764 is the first listed here. Coghlan continued the series after Marmaduke's death in 1788. After his own death in 1800, the *Directory* was taken over by Keating, Brown and Keating, Richard Brown being Coghlan's wife's nephew.

Coghlan's contribution to Catholic publishing was more enterprising than any of his predecessors or rivals. He benefited not only from the thirst for books among the increasingly literate Catholic middle classes, but also from the optimism generated by the Catholic Relief Acts of 1778 and 1791. Coghlan acquired the types of John Baskerville just before the latter's death in 1775, proudly announcing at the time that his was the only London press to use them. In the last decade of the century, he exploited the émigré traffic created by the French Revolution and thus became the chief London publisher for the droves of Catholic émigrés swarming into the capital and country. Coghlan's range of subjects was wider than any of his predecessors. Besides maintaining the tradition of liturgical 'black book' publishing and being responsible for the *Laity's Directory*, he was closely involved in the affairs of the Catholic Committee, and published Roman official documents and letters of the English Vicars Apostolic. Unofficially he thus became publisher by appointment to the Catholic community in England, but in other respects he was a typical 18th century London bookman, combining in one the trades of publisher, printer, binder, bookseller, stationer, and purveyor of such patent medicines as 'Jesuits' Nervous Pills'. Apart from his professional activities, Coghlan played an important part as an intermediary in the Catholic community of his day.

In Ireland and Scotland, Catholic publishing developed apace during the century. Irish printers and publishers suffered certain restrictions until the end of the century, and the civil authorities were constantly vigilant to prevent the publication of religious books which might carry a subversive political message. Still, in Cork, Dublin and elsewhere, publishers were involved throughout the period in aiding the Catholic nation's march towards civil liberties, besides maintaining their usual stock-in-trade of devotional books. There was a degree of collaboration between Catholic Irish and English publishers, one example being the close co-operation between Thomas Meighan the elder and Richard Fitzsimons of Dublin. It became customary for books printed in England to be reprinted later in Ireland, and there are many examples of Irish imprints following on from the publication of a work in England. Coghlan was in the habit of sending sheets of the books he was printing to Dublin for them to be published by Irish colleagues. In Scotland, Catholic books were fewer and publishers seemed less enthusiastic about revealing their identities, at least not until the end of the century. One striking feature of the period is the emergence of Catholic publishing in the provinces. Catholic books tended to be published in areas like northern England where Catholics were more numerous than elsewhere. John Ferguson of Wigan and later of Liverpool, John Sadler of Liverpool, John Sharrock of Walton-le-Dale were all publishing in the last decades of the century.

Many questions surrounding the financing of 18th century Catholic books still need clearer answers. Most publishers diversified their business to ensure survival. Coghlan issued a 'General Catalogue' besides his list of Catholic books. Sadler made his reputation, with another Catholic printer, Guy Green, by the invention of a method for printing on earthenware. Ferguson went even further and brought out Anglican and Nonconformist commentaries and manuals simultaneously with his Catholic publications. Such a practice presumably helped to focus on any common ground the different denominations might share, and there is clear evidence that certain spiritual classics continued to remain popular across the denominational divide throughout the century. Given the extent of the English Catholic community in the 18th century it is very likely that a book like Challoner's *The garden of the soul* with more than thirty known impressions, will have found many non-Catholic buyers. On the other hand editions of the devotional writings of Thomas à Kempis and Fénelon came off Protestant as well as Catholic presses and found their way into many Catholic homes. The attempt to reach a religious inclusivity can be illustrated as far as publishing is concerned in the 1798 edition of the popular *Daily Companion* for 'all Christians' not just 'all Catholicks' as earlier editions were entitled.

2. Devotional Works

Devotional works form the single largest group of books within the bibliography, and a striking characteristic of 18th century English Catholic publishing is the profusion of small private prayer manuals and 'companions' for daily, weekly, or monthly devotional exercises. These were produced in ever larger numbers as the century progressed. Hence the presence of so many editions of the *Primer* and the *Manual of devout prayers* - especially popular with the laity - in our list. The many instructions for a pious life written by the secular priest, John Gother, whose wisdom had been attested in the previous century, were now re-edited and the different parts published separately. The beginning of the century witnessed Gother's accolade when his spiritual works, collected by the secular priest William Crathorne, were published, and its end saw Coghlan continuing to edit the more popular volumes. Bishop Richard Challoner, the other great spiritual luminary, launched in 1740 his famous *Garden of the soul, a manual of spiritual exercises for those Christians who living in the world aspire to devotion.* Thirty-one impressions of it are recorded in this bibliography, including examples from presses in Dublin, Kilkenny, Baltimore, Philadelphia, as well as from provincial presses in Preston, Newcastle, Stockport and Wolverhampton. Challoner also edited some versions of the *Manual* and this and the large number of other popular 18th century manuals such as *The poor man's companion*, *The poor man's manual of devotions* and *The poor man's posey of prayers* clearly served the needs of English Catholics of 'the middling and common sort'.

In the 18th century, Jesuit books from an earlier period were adopted for publication either because they seemed to reflect current tastes in spirituality or because the Society used the press as a method of deliberately influencing Catholic opinion. The expulsion and suppression of the Jesuits in the 1760s and

1770s does not seem to have halted the flow of their books which began to be published in more sympathetic centres like Bruges, Liège and Prague. If there is any single common theme linking many of the Jesuit publications of the period, it is a sense of missionary endeavour against the forces of unorthodoxy, heresy and rationalism. Thus frequent communion and the cult of the Sacred Heart were fostered so as to act as a foil to Jansenism, the labours of Jesuit saints like St Francis Regis among the Huguenots were narrated to provide models for Catholic missionaries in Protestant England, and an answer to Rousseau was attempted in Jean-Nicolas Grou's *Morality, extracted from the Confessions of Saint Austin*.

Some of the greatest of the Jesuit missionary preachers had their works translated in the 18th century. The attraction of Giovanni Pietro Pinamonti and his companion, Paolo Segneri the elder, lay in the simple direct approach they used on their preaching missions in the Italian countryside. Their stark treatment of the Four Last Things was as popular among English Catholic readers as another Jesuit's, Jean Croiset's, meditation at the hour of death. This fear of an unprovided death is also clearly seen in the immense popularity of the *Bona Mors* manual which had attained sixteen editions by 1796. The Bona Mors Confraternity had also been sponsored by the Jesuits who were doubtless the inspiration behind the editions of *A pious association ... for the obtaining a happy death*.

If the Jesuits stood for evangelism, many of the works of devotion associated with the secular clergy came from the pens of those concerned with catechesis. This involved the reform of dioceses, the advancement of the secular clergy in regular discipline as well as instruction of the laity in the catechism. Among such were translations of Henri-Marie Boudon (by Challoner), Antoine Godeau, and the Mexican archbishop, Juan de Palafox y Mendoza, a scourge of the Jesuits. The accusation by the Jesuits that the English secular clergy at the beginning of the 18th century were tainted with Jansenism has encouraged historians to treat the spirituality of both groups as distinct, but this can be qualified by analysing some of the devotional books emanating from the secular clergy. While it is true that some of the authors whose works were translated by the secular clergy were, like Simon-Michel Treuvé, sympathetic to Jansenism and that the writings of others might be interpreted in a Jansenist sense, several other authors, like Jean-Joseph Languet, were opposed to that religion of fear and that rigorism with which Jansenism was usually identified. Finally, it must be emphasized that there was a spiritual tradition which both had in common, for many Jesuit and secular authors, as well as their translators, looked for inspiration to St Francis de Sales. His practical and optimistic spirituality and his doctrine of the love of God appealed to the 18th century clergy and laity alike.

During the century, the other religious orders propagated their traditional devotions, the Dominicans publishing works on the Rosary, the Franciscans, manuals on the confraternity of the cord and crosses of St Francis. But the Benedictines seem to have fought shy of such particularism and, leaving their monastic inheritance to one side, concentrated instead on publishing devotional tracts for general use which served the needs of small household congregations at the beginning of the century and larger urban communities at its end. In contrast to the 17th century, the religious orders published more on presses in the United Kingdom and Ireland than they did on the Continent where lay their colleges and monasteries. Many books printed in Douai, St Omers and elsewhere on the Continent, were for internal use. These included constitutions, mass supplements and catalogues of religious, but there were also biographies of superiors published out of a sense of *pietas*, and *paeans* celebrating jubilees, clothings and professions. The publication of these latter might be funded by a benefactor, as in the case of the publisher J.P. Coghlan himself, who had two daughters Poor Clares at Aire. Among the religious abroad, one figure stands out whose devotional writings were published in England and on the Continent, and whose popularity spanned most of the century. Lady Lucy Herbert (1669-1744), daughter of the Marquess of Powis and prioress of the Austin Canonesses in Bruges, is the only authoress of any weight found in this bibliography, which lists fifteen impressions of her spiritual works.

Hagiography had been a popular aid to edification during the 17th century when martyrologies of the penal times had circulated. In the 18th century, this genre was kept alive by the secular priests, Richard Challoner and Alban Butler, who both exploited the apologetical value of the English pre-Reformation saints' lives by demonstrating that contemporary Catholicism was part of that inheritance. It is likely that biographies of national patrons and heroes like Fisher and More attracted a more general readership, while Cornelius Murphy's account of the execution of two martyrs in 1628 must have appeared rather anachronistic when it was published in 1737. The Jesuits remained the most zealous hagiographers and published numerous lives of, and prayers to, Jesuit saints and others with whom they had a special relationship: Barbara (patroness against an unprovided death), Winifred (whose shrine adjoined a Jesuit mission), and Edward the Confessor (whose *Life* was interpolated in a Jacobite sense). Bizarre miracles and extreme asceticism were anathema to the rationalist 18th century mind, so some authors exercised a degree of caution. The secular priest Charles Fell's comprehensive *Lives of the Saints* was denounced for its dilution of the miraculous and even Challoner, in attempting to absolve Catholicism of charges of 'enthusiasm', apologized for some of the practices of the desert fathers which were 'more to be admired than imitated'. Given the spirit of the age, then, it was inevitable that the contemporary fanaticism of Benedict Labre, detailed in the translations of his biography, should be a source of such fascination at the end of the century.

3. The Mission at Home

a. Instruction and Apologetics

Preaching was another feature of English Catholic life which was performed more openly in the 18th century. There were virtually no published Catholic sermons before 1780, but thanks to the Relief Acts and lesser factors like the immigration of French refugees and the abandonment of a clerical education abroad which was thought to hinder training in English oratory, the number of printed sermons increased rapidly in the last two decades of the century. During these years, the number of published Irish sermons preponderate over those from England, doubtless because of the need to preach to the large established congregations in Ireland. By the 1790s in England, the custom had developed of preaching set sermons on important occasions such as days of General Fasting and at funeral masses. London was the main forum for Catholic sermons which were delivered by visiting preachers in the embassy chapels and new churches. Collections of model sermons for training in 'sacred eloquence' were published, and the golden age of French pulpit oratory was recognised by the publication of Bourdaloue's sermons in translation.

Catechisms, however, remained the most popular method of instructing in the faith. Their pedigree has been thoroughly researched by bibliographers, who have acknowledged the debt which the English Catholic catechism owes to Henry Turberville's Douai Catechism, or *An abridgment of Christian doctrine* (Douai 1649). This book maintained its pre-eminence throughout the 18th century, and on it was modelled a large number of other catechisms. This bibliography reveals that the catechism during the century became the undisputed preserve of the secular clergy, an essential tool for its apostolate. Not only are the catechisms of Gother and Challoner - themselves based on earlier exemplars - present here, but there are also secular catechisms approved by various Vicars Apostolic for use in their districts, catechisms in Irish, Welsh and French, as well as in verse, translations and commentaries on famous French catechisms, and abstracts of the catechisms of Trent and Cardinal Bellarmine.

In the previous century, many Catholic apologetical works had been concerned with the defence of the Church from Protestant attacks, and this struggle continued in the 18th century in books which vaunted Catholic claims and doctrines like transubstantiation. Edward Hawarden, his ally Robert Manning, and Challoner himself were the most industrious and widely read defenders of Catholicism, although earlier responses written by Heigham, Gother and Bossuet continued to find favour. In the 1720s a few Catholic writers joined in the debate about the validity of Anglican ordinations and sought to limit the damage caused by Pierre François Le Courayer. It cannot be said that there was any sign of a flood of genuine and prestigious conversions to Catholicism during the century; if anything, the traffic was the other way, and apostate priests' apologias had to be answered by Catholic replies. The dearth of notable converts was partially satisfied by ten editions of Anthony Ulrick, the convert Duke of Brunswick's, *Fifty reasons*, which traversed the century. Robust debates in print about the value of Catholicism continued throughout the century, and were now generally conducted by 'gentlemen'. Meanwhile, apologists sought to prove the reasonableness of Catholicism and the fervent patriotism of Catholics, especially at times of heightened antipathy to the Church, as during the period of the '45 Rebellion. The later Cisalpines were to draw some inspiration from these attempts to calm Protestant fears.

During the 18th century apologists had to contend with the more damaging and more fundamental attacks of enlightened rationalism on the Church, and in its early decades, such authors published convincing statements of

Christian belief against some of the leading Anglican divines who appeared to have been tainted by the new philosophies and had veered towards scepticism, deism and Arianism. Thus a number of books reasserted the orthodox belief in miracles against Conyers Middleton, one of its opponents. As the century progressed, authors broadened their front to answer the onslaughts of the *philosophes* on Christianity. A powerful impulse here came from the European émigrés, who in the 1790s brought with them some examples of major French Catholic apologists whose work was to be rapidly published in England and Ireland. History seemed to offer unassailable evidence for vindicating Christianity's and Catholicism's claims against Protestant and rationalist opponents, and this explains the appearance of some histories of the Church during the 18th century, which rested on a powerful apologetical foundation, as well as some 'scripture histories' which argued that there was agreement between the claims of biblical and natural history.

The 18th century Catholic community was also prepared to use scripture as an anchor for its claims as well as a quarry for its devotions. The century thus saw important advances in the field of scriptural scholarship. The first editions of the Bible and the New Testament for over a century appeared, beginning with Cornelius Nary's translation of the New Testament from the Vulgate, which established new principles for translation. It was followed by a series of revisions and, later, translations of the 1582 Rheims New Testament, which were the work of Robert Witham and Richard Challoner, who was aided by Francis Blyth. Challoner's revision of the Douai Bible's Old Testament appeared in 1750 and 1763. The numerous editions and adaptations which were based on Challoner's books indicate the popularity of and need for cheap and up-to-date versions of the scriptures. The originality of Alexander Geddes's methods of textual biblical criticism at the end of the century was, however, too advanced for most Catholics, and his bible remained condemned and unfinished at the time of his death in 1802. Geddes, who was closely identified with Cisalpine circles, had an international reputation as a founder of higher biblical criticism.

b. Issues

The overarching concerns of religious toleration and security so dominated British and Irish Catholics in the 18th century that other issues, which might be of concern to the British abroad, hardly intruded. In the early 18th century Jacobitism gradually disappeared as a factor in English Catholicism, and by the time of the '45, English Catholic authors were inclined to profess their loyalty to the House of Hanover.

At the beginning of the century, there had been accusations of Jansenism levelled at some of the secular clergy who served the Stuart Court, and this coincided with a renewed outbreak of the deeply ingrained hostility between the English secular clergy and the Jesuits. In part, this was the result of the instability affecting the English Church after the Glorious Revolution, which encouraged suspicion and rumours of conspiracy to circulate, but the traditional antipathy went much further back, finding its basis in mutually opposed views regarding the English mission, and was exacerbated by differences in Jesuit and secular theological training. It was this last which sparked off the storm in the first decade of the 18th century. A pamphlet war arose when English Jesuits like Thomas Fairfax and William Darrell depicted the English secular college at Douai as a hotbed of Jansenism since it had allegedly defended the 1701 *Cas de Conscience*. Douai's professors and past students, notably Sylvester Jenks, strongly rebutted the charges and exposed the evil intentions of their opponents in books like Hugh Tootell's *The secret policy of the English Society of Jesus*. The controversy might have remained behind closed academic doors on the Continent had not the Pope refuelled fears of Jansenism by ordering the adherence of the English Vicars Apostolic and religious superiors to the anti-Jansenist bull, *Vineam Domini*, in 1709 and promulgating the bull *Unigenitus* in 1713 which condemned the Jansenist Pasquier Quesnel's *Moral reflections*. In England, the Jesuits criticized the circumspect procrastination of the Vicars Apostolic in subscribing to the anti-Jansenist formulary, which served to heighten the divisions on the English mission. Thus for decades there remained an animosity between seculars and Jesuits discernible in many of the books of both groups and especially in the historical works of the secular priest Hugh Tootell *alias* Charles Dodd, which deliberately played down the Society's contribution to the post-Reformation Church.

The 18th century saw major encroachments by ecclesiastical and political hierarchies on the privileges and status of the regular clergy. In England, the demands of the Vicars Apostolic for more jurisdiction over the regular missioners can be charted in the publication of Roman decrees in mid-century to settle the dispute in favour of the bishops, whose enhanced status is illustrated by the general introduction from the 1750s of annually published pastoral letters and instructions. In Europe, it was not in any way easier for the religious orders. In France they were forced to bring their constitutions in line with the recommendations of the *Commission des Réguliers* appointed in 1768. The Jesuits suffered most. Their expulsion from various countries in the 1760s was followed by the Society's suppression by Pope Clement XIV (Ganganelli) in 1773. The crisis of expulsion and suppression produced a considerable number of books. Those inspired by the Jesuits sought to damage the reputation of Clement XIV, to justify the Society's past record in the countries from which it was expelled, and to compliment those which offered a refuge to its members. The Society's opponents defended Ganganelli from the libels and approved the confiscation of ex-Jesuit property like the college at St Omers. Significantly, the major polemical works, published during the Jesuit-Jansenist stirs at the beginning of the century, were re-published in the 1760s.

4. The Mission Abroad

Just as the later Jansenist controversy became embroiled in questions over interpretation, so too the other great conflict which engaged the Jesuits at this time, the Chinese Rites question, also centred upon questions of interpretation. Half a dozen works, published in the first decade of the century, reveal a degree of interest in this remote oriental controversy which gave a perspective to current European questions about orthodoxy and jurisdiction. The first published accounts were sympathetic to the Jesuits' attempt at syncretism, and included a few of Charles Le Gobien's large collections of *Edifying letters* from Jesuit missionaries in the Orient. Later, the papal legate, Maillard de Tournon's justification for his condemnation of the Chinese Rites, as well as Clement XI's supportive decree of 1709, were also supplied to English audiences. There was, of course, an 18th century fascination for exotic cultures and explorers' heroics which fired a general interest in distant civilizations over and above a taste for theological debate, and this partly explains the popularity of editions of the Jesuit Jean Crasset's history of the Church in Japan and the earlier Portuguese Balthasar Teles's (Tellez) travelogues describing Jesuit voyages to the Orient, America and Africa. Information about a contemporary missionary enterprise was made available in 1759 through Muratori's defence of the famous Jesuit experiments in Paraguay.

Publication of English Catholic books in America effectively began in 1784 when John Carroll was appointed superior of the United States mission. The few books appearing prior to this date tended to be the work of Jesuit missionaries like Robert Molyneux of Philadelphia. English-speaking Catholics mostly settled in Maryland and Philadelphia, where the first Catholic presses began to operate. For the French-speaking community, the Quebec Act of 1774 provided the necessary kick-start to launch an expansion of Catholic books. In 1789, Carroll was consecrated Bishop of Baltimore, and works appearing from the presses from that time accompanied the development of his pastoral charge: in 1790 his profession of loyalty to President Washington on behalf of American Catholics was published, the seminary at Georgetown was opened in 1791, and there followed proposals for building a cathedral, and the publication of pastoral letters, liturgical books and translations of scripture. Much of the published material of the Carroll period reflected devotional concerns shared by Catholics in England. The catechisms of George Hay and Jean-Joseph Languet, together with Challoner's *Garden of the Soul*, were republished across the Atlantic. Carroll used arguments found in the works of the Cisalpine Joseph Berington, to refute in 1784 the allegations of the apostate priest, Charles Henry Wharton, once a missioner in Worcester, and he corrected his English Jesuit friend Charles Plowden's account of the see of Baltimore before it reached the press. The bitter contest between Jesuit and secular clergy, endemic in England, was also highlighted in the United States through Patrick Smyth's vituperative pamphlet of 1788. The problem of lay trustees, emerging in England during the 1790s was identified in Carroll's warning to the congregation of Holy Trinity Church, Boston. But the Church in the United States was a young Church and still uncertain of itself; it thus found it necessary to publish as widely as possible the conversion story of the Congregationalist minister, John Thayer, and to deal with troublesome clergymen like Claude de la Poterie as quickly as possible.

5. Emancipation and Emigration

As the century drew to its close, so did the clamour for civil and political liberties for Catholics increase. The struggle for emancipation generated a vast amount of printed material in the last two decades of the century. The volume of published minutes and statements emanating from the Catholic Committee and other groups sympathetic to its aims indicates the maturing of an English Catholic literate class able to hold its own in the public forum and aware of its civil and religious rights. The story can be traced through this bibliography. As early as the 1760s, during a period of persecution, printed works sought to demonstrate the innocuity of Catholicism in England, Ireland and North America, and urged a reconsideration of the value of the penal laws. In the next decade, the various published addresses demonstrated the Catholic laity's support for the Relief Act of 1778. The Catholic response to the Gordon Riots can be measured in Scotland through Bishop George Hay's pamphlets, and in England by Lord Petre's address to the Protestant Association and the publication - by Coghlan in 1782 - of accounts of the trials ten years earlier at which two priests were acquitted. The period leading up to the passing of the second Relief Act in July 1791 was one of intense debate between the Catholic Committee and some of the Vicars Apostolic over the forms which the Protestation and Oath of Allegiance should take. The number of pamphlets and broadsheets, with the sophisticated legal reasoning contained in them, made this debate conducted in public a unique phenomenon in the history of English Catholicism. It demonstrated how far public opinion had come in its toleration of Catholicism and how far Catholics were prepared to go in their determination to adjust to English society. The controversy helped to bring some leading Catholic authors to the public's attention: Joseph Berington, Charles Butler, Alexander Geddes, John Milner, and Charles and Robert Plowden. The resolution of some of the outstanding issues which had agitated the Committee formed the main task of its successor, the Cisalpine Club, which met for the first time in April 1792.

In Ireland, the campaign for Catholic Emancipation forced religion and politics to be even more entwined. The basis of the movement for emancipation was established at the beginning of the century by the publication of new editions of earlier historical studies of Catholic Ireland. The severe 1704 Act 'to prevent the further growth of popery' seems to have stimulated the new edition of Nicholas French's 1668 work on 'the sale of Ireland'. It was followed in the 1740s and later by numerous editions of Hugh Reilly's very popular *Impartial history* which catalogued the neglect of the Catholic Irish by past British governments. The founders of the first General Committee of the Irish Catholics (1759), which aimed to remove political disabilities, included authors like the antiquary Charles O'Conor, and Dr John Curry, both of whom published books during the 1740s and 1750s which also had arguments based on past sufferings. They were, however, moderate in tone, and Curry's work was used by the Protestant Henry Brooke, once critical of Catholics but later employed by them to advocate the relaxation of the penal laws, to compile *The tryal of the Roman Catholics* in 1761. By the time of the 1774 and 1778 Relief Acts, the movement for emancipation was well established and had brilliant spokesmen in the figures of Edmund Burke and Henry Grattan. A new Catholic General Committee was established in 1773 and claimed to have national representation; its agents were to include Richard Burke and Theobald Wolfe Tone who himself helped to found the United Irishmen Society in 1791. The Committee was to be responsible for further petitions for relief sent directly to the king, which were partly satisfied by the 1793 Irish Relief Act. The latter part of the decade was, however, very disturbed. Besides the violence of a Protestant backlash, the Catholics were divided among themselves. On the one hand there were the supporters of moderate reform and the maintenance of the Union, and they were favoured by Pitt, who encouraged the foundation of the seminary at Maynooth in 1795; on the other hand there were those Catholics in societies like the United Irishmen who supported violence, separatism, republicanism and France. Both sides had their advocates in print: Theobald MacKenna for the moderates and William James McNeven for the extremists. The 1800 Act of Union was an attempt to prevent further violence and bound the Irish Catholics closer to England. It had the support of the Protestant ascendancy as well as that of the Irish Catholic leaders won over by Pitt promising emancipation in its wake.

The effects of Catholic emancipation in Ireland and England are immediately apparent from the works published in the 1790s. During this last decade of the century, the newly emancipated congregations published appeals to build or complete their legalised chapels, and evidence for the strength of lay 'trusteeism' can be found in the published rules governing congregations in Cork and Limerick, as well as in Raymund Harris's appeal in regard to the mission in Liverpool. Finally, emancipation allowed refinements in liturgical practice. Although parts of the Divine Office and the *Ordo* regulating it had been published at the beginning of the century, in the 1790s there was a rapid increase in the number of books published in Dublin and London dealing with Gregorian chant and ecclesiastical music.

The effects of the French Revolution did as much to enhance the prospects of the Catholic community on the other side of the Channel as did creeping Catholic emancipation. The Revolution thrust back into their native land a large number of religious communities and their schools. Some preserved a sense of continuity with the past by publishing the traditional school text books and teaching the same ecclesiastical courses as they had done on the Continent, but these were now published in London, Preston, Blackburn or Newcastle, rather than in Paris, Douai or Liège. Nevertheless, new schools and seminaries with new curricula (French was a major subject), new rules and printed prospectuses were a feature of the 1790s. The other palpable effect of the Revolution was the huge number of French émigré clergy who swarmed into England and Ireland. They brought with them their own subculture and like in so many expatriate minorities, the printed word was deemed vital for preserving native beliefs and customs. Indeed, the number of French émigré religious works published was out of proportion to the émigrés' influence in British society. Few French authors were reckoned to be sufficiently acclimatised to have their books translated into English, Augustin Barruel and Jean-Nicolas Grou being notable exceptions. In their enclave, the émigrés read French spirituality, were directed by French manuals, heard French pastoral letters from émigré bishops, conducted obsequies for the French royal family, and rejoiced at news of the Revolution's failures. Coghlan published several of their works, but books also came from presses in Winchester, Guernsey, Ireland and the United States. The uncompromising St Cyprian, who had directed his weak and cowardly flock from exile, was their patron. Like him, most ultimately returned to their homeland.

6. Conclusion

As far as Catholic publishing was concerned, the 18th century fashioned the patterns which the following century would follow and develop. Eighteenth-century catechisms, bibles, directories and spiritual classics, as well as new translations of the works of the French émigrés were published after 1800 for an increasingly literate community by new firms like Keating, Brown and Keating which inherited Coghlan's mantle. The incipient ultramontanism which had sprung up in the last decade of the century rapidly reached maturity at the beginning of the 19th century. Catholic publishers now felt confident enough to launch Catholic periodicals, which provided a forum for controversial debate. For a bibliographical study of the 19th century one could think of 1789 rather than 1800 as a starting date, for by then Catholic emancipation was actively underway and discussions on the nature of ecclesiastical authority and jurisdiction were well advanced. Between 1789 and 1815, the turbulence caused by the Revolutionary and Napoleonic wars created new challenges for the Church and contributed towards the fighting spirit and optimism which pervaded many of the Catholic books of this period. If the grant of Catholic Emancipation in 1829 marked for these the beginning of the new age, it was also the reward of a struggle which had endured throughout the 18th century.

Definition, scope and form of items

This introduction consists of four parts: the definition of an 18th century English Catholic book, the ways in which the catalogue has been composed, the arrangement of the catalogue and the description of an individual item.

First the four constituent terms of the definition - 18th century, English, Catholic and book - will each of them be discussed. With regard to the period we have conformed to the ESTC boundaries of 1701 and 1800. It would have been conceivable to take 1829, the year of the Catholic Emancipation Bill as the termination point, but we decided against this because both the quantity and the nature of the extra material would have made the catalogue lop-sided. Many publications of the last decade of the 18th century already suggest something of the major changes that were to take place in the Catholic Church in England during the first quarter of the 19th century.

The term 'English' refers to the place of publication and to the language used. All the Catholic books written in English and published in England, Scotland, Wales, Ireland and the colonies are included, plus all the books in English published abroad, mainly in such 'Catholic' places as Rome, Paris, Douai, St. Omers and Bruges. Also Catholic books written in languages other than English are present if published in England or in territory officially regarded as English. The latter category mainly comprises Latin and French publications. The bulk of the works in Latin is formed by publications for the clergy such as *Officia*, *Ordo recitandi* and *Tabula congregationis*. The French items consist of the numerous publications that appeared in London in the last years of the century and were intended for the French refugees then residing in England, and of the books published in Canada in the last quarter of the century. Besides the Latin and French books, there is a small number of publications in Irish, Welsh, German, Italian, Portuguese, and even one of the Indian languages of North America. A book like *Regulae observandae in Anglicanis missionibus* published at Rome in 1753, does not, strictly speaking, fit the above definition, but it has been included because it was clearly meant primarily for an English Catholic audience. Books in Latin and other foreign languages, written by English Catholics and published abroad, have been excluded, unless these books were specifically intended for the English Catholic market. That is why Latin theses by British and Irish students at foreign universities and seminaries have not found a place in our list. It could be argued that several of these theses reflect the wider, international context of Catholicism, and that some of them had an impact on English Catholicism. Yet the theses were first and foremost part of the curriculum of the specific universities and seminaries, and they were often not more than obligatory exercises, not in any way intended for the English Catholic community in Britain or Ireland. Thus Challoner's theological thesis, *De veritate religionis Christianae & Catholicae* which appeared at Douai in 1727, is not present. Late 18th century Latin theses published in Britain and Ireland have been included.

The crucial part of the definition is of course the qualification 'Catholic'.

The term refers both to the nature of the contents and to the authorship. Only those books are listed that are specifically religious; that is to say that Alexander Pope's and Edward Jerningham's poems do not qualify, but certain 18th century editions of Dryden's *The Hind and the Panther* do. The criterion 'religious' is clearly not always unproblematical. With travel-accounts by missionaries one moves into a border-area, and historical works can also present problems. The close connection between politics and religion in Ireland, especially in the later 18th century, makes it often hard to arrive at a satisfactory demarcation, but if the work in question is sufficiently 'religious' and published in the Catholic interest, it qualifies for inclusion. In case of doubt we adopt the policy of listing one edition and referring to other editions in a note. Many originally Catholic publications, especially works of devotion, underwent a 'protestantisation' or a 'neutralisation' in the 17th and 18th centuries, in that they were purged of all-too Catholic elements, and provided with an introduction warning the Protestant reader. Protestant editions of, for instance, St. Augustine, Thomas à Kempis and Robert Parsons's *A Christian Directory* are left out. Also a book like the 1715 edition of Sir Richard Bulstrode's *Miscellaneous essays with the life and conversion of Mary Magdalen*, with an introduction by his non-R.C. son Whitelock Bulstrode, intended to 'soften' the Catholic nature of the work, is not present because the book was not published under Catholic auspices. With respect to the requirement of a 'Catholic' content an exception has been made for a number of grammars, in English, designed or adapted for use at Catholic educational institutions in England and abroad. This leaves us with all the religious works written, compiled, edited and translated by English, Irish, Scottish, Welsh and North-American Catholics, published in the Catholic interest and under Catholic auspices. Occasionally a non-R.C. author is present with one item, when the author is clearly sympathetic to the Catholic cause and the work in question promoted the Catholic interest. Hence the presence of books like Henry Brooke's *The tryal of the Roman Catholics* and Edmund Burke's *The humble address and petition of the Roman Catholics of Ireland* in our list. On the other hand, only one work by the French priest Pierre François Le Courayer - the first edition of the English translation of his book on the validity of the Anglican ordinations - is included because Le Courayer, who claimed that he never gave up being a Catholic, was regarded as a traitor by the English Catholics, and because the English translations of his works were evidently not published in the Catholic interest. With some anonymous works an investigation of the contents did not prove conclusive, and then the involvement of a Catholic printer or publisher has sometimes been decisive in establishing the book as Catholic. Finally, it will be clear that the criterion of 'Catholic auspices' has been applied with the necessary caution. In the course of the 18th century certain evidently Catholic books were brought out by neutral publishers and towards the end of the century this criterion, understandably tended to lose much of its validity.

The last term of the definition - book - is on the whole not a problematical category. We include all independent publications, in which the printed text forms a substantial part of the whole; this rules out such 'hybrid' productions as altar-charts and many church-music books, but it means the inclusion of ephemera such as separately published obituary-notices and printed forms. Unlike ESTC we do not include book-lists, because they in almost all cases form part of other books. We have made an exception for *A catalogue of all the Catholic books now in print amongst which are those purchased from the stock of Mr Thomas Meighan deceased; with all new publications up to the 30th of October, 1776*, issued by J.P. Coghlan, late in 1776. This catalogue, combining the stock of two major Catholic printers and publishers, is a central document in 18th century English Catholic book-history. A new phenomenon towards the end of the century was the magazine-article by a Catholic author. Although from the point of view of the contents a number of these articles would have qualified for inclusion, this type of publication is excluded. Alexander Geddes wrote articles on a variety of subjects for several magazines. Thus, at the height of the internal divisions within the English Catholic Church in 1790 and 1791, he wrote a series of articles for *The Analytical Review* under the title 'Review of various pamphlets and printed papers, relative to the present controversy among the English Catholics &c.'

We are aware that the definition adopted by us can never be watertight, and that occasionally other inclusions or exclusions might arguably have been made. Yet in all bordercases, and also when we deviate from our own definition, we try to provide arguments in the accompanying notes.

ESTC, the major bibliographical research instrument at our disposal, naturally forms the basis of our list. Approximately two-thirds of our catalogue is in ESTC, which means that we present about 1,000 new items. Moreover the R.C. books are not of course neatly arranged in a 'Catholic' block, and several of the anonymous publications, or those with a false or no imprint, are not easily recognisable as Catholic, and hence hard to retrieve. The London ESTC team was kind enough to allow us access to their complete files, to which new items are being added every day. Inevitably we had to call a halt at some point; our cut-off date for ESTC was July/August 1994. We started many years ago with a systematic investigation of the relevant biographical and bibliographical reference works, and in the course of our researches we paid visits, not only to the major libraries in Great Britain and Ireland, but to a number of specifically Catholic libraries and archives - most of them not covered in ESTC - in England, Scotland, Ireland, Belgium, France, Italy and the Netherlands. The already-mentioned booklists also yielded much, although the information provided is not always clear or reliable, because brief and inadequate descriptions of books are given, and one cannot be always sure that the publications announced were actually brought out. In order to avoid the creation of ghosts we have not included books from these booklists that have not otherwise been traced. Part of our search was carried out through correspondence, and especially for books in American collections we corresponded extensively - after having checked our provisional list against NUC. Not surprisingly, we found that the coverage by ESTC of American collections - and for that matter several English ones as well - is far from complete.

The bibliography itself will be preceded by a list of of locations. The publications are arranged alphabetically. No attempt at categorisation has been made - 'the holy bible' comes under 'holy' and 'the new testament' under 'new' - but a short title/author index and cross-referencing in the catalogue itself will indicate ways of grouping. The order is alphabetical per word-unit, so that 'We beg' comes before 'Webbe'. The description of the items has been standardised as much as possible. Lower case has been used for the titles, excepting proper names and words like 'Christian', 'Catholic' and 'Protestant', and large discrepancies in the length of titles have been avoided, wherever possible. Yet, in the case of books not actually seen by us, the information was not always provided uniformly, so that at times there is some unevenness in the presentation of the individual items. Some items are incomplete because the necessary information could not be acquired. All the names of foreign places of publication have been 'Englished'. In the case of a consecutive series such as the *Laity's Directory* or the Franciscan *Tabula Congregationis* slight alphabetical differences are ignored and the chronological order is adhered to. The numerous editions of works by John Gother are a real bibliographer's nightmare. We have come across Gother's works in such a bewildering variety of editions and issues, separately and in various combined forms, that we present our findings with due caution. The bibliography itself will be followed by three indexes, the already-mentioned short title/author index, an index of names of persons occurring in the titles and notes, and an index of printers, publishers and booksellers.

For each separately numbered publication there is a maximum of fourteen entries in the order given below.

1. number
2. author: in the case of collective publications with a long list of signatories, such as most letters and addresses of the Catholic Committee, the publications are listed under title, unless there is clear evidence of one particular author; pastoral letters issued by more than one of the vicars apostolic are given under the name of the first signer, or - if unsigned - of the vicar apostolic of the specific district mentioned; when the author is unknown the work appears under its title.
3. title: with English translations of foreign works, the original title - if traced - is given in square brackets, but only for the edition listed first; if there is no proper title-page the heading or opening words of the publication are given.
4. edition
5. anonymous
6. number of volumes
7. place of publication
8. year of publication
9. format
10. pagination: with more-volume works ESTC does not give pagination; we provide the exact pagination if we have seen the work ourselves; 's.s.' indicates single sheet.

11. printer, publisher, bookseller: sometimes it is impossible to decide to which of the three categories the name mentioned in the imprint belongs; in those cases the person is given as the publisher.

12. ESTC number or other source of identification: occasionally the only source for a publication is a reference-work like Sommervogel, Gillow, Kirk, Burton or Byrns; in these cases the publication is only included in our list when the reference is sufficiently specific, that is, if information is provided about format, printer or publisher, or pagination; the publications thus excluded from our list - possibly 'ghosts', possibly very rare books - are referred to in the notes, in order not to lose them.

13. location: the location-symbols, given in alphabetical order are preceded by an asterisk; there is a maximum of twenty-five locations, always including the copies we have examined ourselves and the copies at the major libraries in England, Scotland, Ireland and North-America.

14. note: a note contains information on the author, editor or translator, on material and non-material aspects of the publication, and on the context of the work; the notes are also used for cross-referencing.

Any information about imprint or title not actually found on the title-page and supplied by us, appears in square brackets.

References and Abbreviations

Abercrombie, Nigel J., 'The Early Life of Charles Butler (1750-1783)', *Recusant History,* vol. 14, no. 4, Oct. 1978, pp. 281-292.

Abercrombie, Nigel J., 'Charles Butler and the English Jesuits, 1770-1823', *Recusant History*, vol. 15, no. 4, Oct. 1980, pp. 283-301.

Allison, A.F., 'John Heigham of S. Omer (c.1568-c.1632)', *Recusant History,* vol. 4, no. 6, Oct. 1958, pp. 226-242.

Allison, A.F., and D.M Rogers, *A Catalogue of Catholic Books in English Printed Abroad or Secretly in England 1558-1640*, Bognor Regis 1956.

Allison, A.F., and D.M. Rogers, *The Contemporary Printed Literature of the English Counter-Reformation between 1558 and 1640*, vol. 1, Aldershot 1989.

Allison, A.F. and D.M. Rogers, *The Contemporary Printed Literature of the English Counter-Reformation between 1558 and 1640,* vol. 2, Aldershot 1994.

Alston, R.C. and M.J. Crump (eds), *The Eighteenth Century Short Title Catalogue* (Microfiche edition), London 1983 (first ed.); London 1990, 2 vols. (second ed.).

Amherst, W.J., *The History of Catholic Emancipation and the Progress of the Catholic church in the British Isles ... from 1771 to 1829,* 2 vols., London 1886.

Anson, Peter F., *Underground Catholicism in Scotland*, Montrose 1970.

Anstruther, Godfrey, *The Seminary Priests. Vol. 4: 1716-1800,* Great Wakering 1977.

ARCR, see Allison, A.F.

Astbury, R., 'The Renewal of the Licensing Act in 1693 and its Lapse in 1695', *The Library*, 33, 1978, pp. 296-322.

Aveling, J.C.H., 'The Eighteenth-Century English Benedictines', in Eamon Duffy (ed.) *Challoner & his Church. A Catholic Bishop in Georgian England,* London 1981, pp. 152-173.

Barclay Squire, W., *Catalogue of Printed Music Published Between 1487 and 1800 Now in the British Library*, 2 vols, London 1912.

Barnard, E.A.B., *The Sheldons,* Cambridge 1936.

Bellenger, Dominic, 'The English Catholics and the French Exiled Clergy', *Recusant History,* vol. 15, no. 6, Oct. 1981, pp. 433-451.

Bellenger, Dominic, *The French Exiled Clergy*, Downside Abbey 1986.

Bevan, J.F.X., 'Joseph Gillow and his Dictionary of the English Catholics', *North West Catholic History*, vol. 13, 1986, pp. 14-17.

Bevan, John, *Bishop Challoner 1691-1781. Anniversary Catalogue of Books & Pamphlets*, Ross-on-Wye 1981.

Bevan, John, *Three Centuries of English Catholic Books*, Ross-on-Wye 1986.

Bevan, John, *A Catalogue of Books Relating to the Catholic Church*, Ross-on-Wye 1993 (Pentecost).

Bevan, John, *A Catalogue of Books Relating to the Catholic Church*, Ross-on-Wye 1993 (St. Michael).

Bevan, John, *Three Centuries of English Catholic Books*, Ross-on-Wye 1993 (Advent).

Bevan, John (1995). Note that 'Bevan 1995' indicates books in the possession of the bookseller John Bevan; when our bibliography went to press these books had not yet been catalogued.

Blom, J.M., *The Post-Tridentine English Primer*, Catholic Records Society, Monograph 3, London 1982.

Bossy, J., *The English Catholic Community, 1570-1850*, London 1975.

Bowe, Forest B., 'Some Corrections and Additions to *Early Catholic Americana*',

Catholic Historical Review, vol. 28, July 1942, 249-257.

Brady, John, 'Catholics and Catholicism in the Eighteenth-Century Press', *Archivum Hibernicum,* vol. 16, 1951.

Brenan, M.J., *An Ecclesiastical History of Ireland, from the Introduction of Christianity into that Country, to the year MDCCXXIX,* Dublin 1864.

Burton, E.H., *The life and Times of Bishop Challoner (1691-1781),* 2 vols, London 1909.

Byrns, L., *Recusant Books in America 1700-1829,* New York 1964.

Carleton, F.,'Catholic Libraries and the Early Imprints Project in New South Wales', *Bibliographical Society of Australia and New Zealand Bulletin,* 6, 1982.

Chinnici, Joseph P., *The English Catholic Enlightenment. John Lingard and the Cisalpine Movement 1780-1850,* Shepherdstown 1980.

Clancy, T.H., *English Catholic Books 1641-1700. A Bibliography,* Chicago 1974.

Cole, Richard Cargill, *Irish Booksellers and English Writers 1740-1800,* Atlantic Highlands/London 1986.

Crichton, J.D. 'Challoner and the "Penny Catechism"', *Recusant History,* vol. 15, no. 6, Oct. 1981, pp. 425-432.

Crichton, J.D., 'Challoner's "Catechism"', *Clergy Review,* vol. 63, 4, April 1978, pp. 140-46.

Crichton, J.D., 'Richard Challoner: catechist and spiritual writer', *Clergy Review,* vol. 66, 1981, pp. 269-75.

Crichton, J.D., *Worship in a Hidden Church,* Blackrock 1988.

D & M, see Darlow, T.H.

Darlow, T.H., and H.F. Moule, *Historical Catalogue of the Printed Editions of Holy Scripture in the Library of the British and Foreign Bible Society,* 2 vols, London 1903-11 (see also Herbert, A.S.).

Dix, E.R.McC., and Seamus Cassidy, *List of Books, Pamphlets &c Printed Wholly, or Partly, in Irish, from the Earliest Period to 1820,* Dublin 1905.

Duffy, Eamon (ed.), *Challoner & His Church. A Catholic Bishop in Georgian England,* London 1981.

Duffy, Eamon, 'Ecclesiastical Democracy Detected I (1779-1787)', *Recusant History,* vol. 10, no. 4, Jan. 1970, pp. 193-209.

Duffy, Eamon, 'Ecclesiastical Democracy Detected II (1787-1796)', *Recusant History,* vol. 10, no. 6, Oct. 1970, pp. 309-331.

Duffy, Eamon, 'Richard Challoner and the English Salesian Tradition', *Clergy Review,* vol. 66, 1981, pp. 449-55.

Duffy, Eamon, 'A Rubb-up for Old Soares: Jesuits, Jansenists, and the English Secular Clergy 1705-1715', *Journal of Ecclesiastical History,* vol. 28, no. 3, July 1977, pp. 291-317.

English, Adrian T., 'The Historiography of American Catholic History (1785-1884)', *The Catholic Historical Review,* New Series vol. 5, Jan. 1926, pp. 561-598.

ESTC, see Alston, R.C.

Fagan, Patrick, *An Irish Bishop of Penal Times. The Chequered Career of Sylvester Lloyd O.F.M. 1680-1747,* Blackrock 1993.

Faulkner, Anselm, O.F.M., *Liber Dubliniensis. Chapter Documents of the Irish Franciscans 1719-1875,* Killiney 1978.

Feather, John, *A History of English Publishing,* London 1984.

Feather, John, *The Provincial Book Trade in Eighteenth-Century England,* Cambridge 1985.

Fenning, Hugh, *Publications of Irish Catholic Interest 1700-1800: An Experimental Check-List,* Rome 1973.

Finotti, J.M., *Bibliographia Catholica Americana*, New York 1872.

Firth, Francis J., *English Recusant Literature and Other Religious Polemical Tracts: A Catalogue*, Ampleforth Abbey 1986.

Foley, H., *Records of the English Province of the Society of Jesus*, 7 vols, London 1875-83.

Foxon, D.F., *English Verse 1701-1750. A Catalogue of Separately Printed Poems with Notes on Contemporary Collected Editions*, 2 vols, Cambridge 1975

Fuller, Reginald C., *Alexander Geddes 1737-1802. A Pioneer of Biblical Criticism*, Sheffield 1984.

Gillow, J., *A Literary and Biographical History or Bibliographical Dictionary of the English Catholics*, 5 vols, London and New York 1885.

Gordon, J.F.S., *The Catholic Church in Scotland from the Suppression of the Hierarchy till the Present Time*, Glasgow 1869.

Greer, Germaine et al, *Kissing the Rod*, London 1988.

Guilday, Peter, 'Arthur O'Leary', *Catholic Historical Review*, New Series vol. 3, Jan. 1924, pp. 530-545.

Guilday, Peter. *The English Catholic Refugees on the Continent 1558-1795: Vol. 1., The English Catholic Colleges and Convents in the Catholic Low Countries, 1558-1795*, London 1914.

Guilday, Peter, *The Life and Times of John Carroll*, New York 1922.

Guilday, Peter, *National Pastorals of the American Hierarchy, 1792-1919*, Washington 1923.

Gumbley, Walter, see Jarrett, Bede

Hanley, L., 'John Sadler: An Eighteenth-century Liverpool Catholic', *North West Catholic History*, vol. 8, 1981, pp. 16-24.

Hansom, Joseph S. (ed.), 'Obituaries for the "Laity's Directory", 1773-1839', *Catholic Record Society*, vol. 12, London 1913.

Hawkes, Arthur John, *Lancashire Printed Books. A Bibliography of all the Books printed in Lancashire down to the year 1800*, Wigan 1925.

Herbert, A.S., *Historical Catalogue of Printed Editions of the English Bible 1525-1961. Revised and expanded from the Edition of T.H. Darlow and H.F. Moule*, London and New York 1968.

Howell and Co., *A Catalogue of Books, exclusively relating to the Church of Rome: Her Doctrines, Worship, Discipline ... On Sale by Howell and Co., Successors to Ogle, Duncan and Co.*, 1829.

Hughes, Thomas, *The History of the Society of Jesus in North America*, 4 vols, London and New York 1907.

Hyde, Douglas and D.J. O'Donoghue, *Catalogue of the books and manuscripts ... of the late Sir John T. Gilbert*, Dublin 1918.

Jarrett, Bede (revised by Walter Gumbley), *The English Dominicans*, London 1937.

Kirk, J. (edited by J.H. Pollen and E. Burton), *Biographies of English Catholics in the Eighteenth Century*, London 1909.

Merrill, W.S., 'Catholic Authorship in the American Colonies before 1784', *Catholic Historical Review*, vol. 3, 1917-18, pp. 308-325.

Mitchell, C.J., 'Thomas Meighan: Notes on the Father of Catholic Bookselling in England', *Publishing History*, vol. 19, Cambridge 1981, pp. 51-58.

Mitchell, C.J., 'The Other Thomas Stapleton', *Recusant History*, vol. 15, no. 6, Oct. 1981, pp. 423-424.

Mitchell, C.J., 'Robert Manning and Thomas Howlatt: English Catholic Printing in the Early Eighteenth Century', *Recusant History*, vol. 17, no. 1, May 1984, pp. 38-47.

Morison, Stanley, *English Prayerbooks*, Cambridge 1945.

Morison, Stanley, 'The Writings of Challoner', *Richard Challoner 1691-1781, Westminster Cathedral Chronicle*, 1946, pp. 25-32.

Munter, R.L., *A History of the Print Trade in Ireland 1550-1775*, New York 1988.

Munter, R.L., *A Dictionary of the Print Trade in Ireland 1550-1775*, New York 1988.

Nixon, Howard M., 'The Memorandum Book of James Coghlan. The Stock of an 18th-Century printer and binder', *Journal of the Printing Historical Society*, no. 6, 1970, pp. 33-52.

Nolan, Hugh (ed.), *Pastoral Letters of the American Hierarchy, 1792-1970*, Huntington 1971.

Norman, Marion, 'John Gother and the English way of spirituality', *Recusant History*, vol. 11, 1972, pp. 306-14.

National Union Catalogue Pre-1956 Imprints, London/Chicago 1968- (NUC).

The Old Brotherhood of the English Secular Clergy: Catalogue of Part of the Archives. Published for the Old Brotherhood by the Catholic Record Society, London 1968

Parsons, Wilfrid, *Early Catholic Americana. A List of Books and Other Works by Catholic Authors in the United States 1729-1830*, New York 1939 (repr. Boston 1977).

Pickering, Bernard, 'Bishop Challoner and Teaching of the Faith', *The Clergy Review*, vol. 65, no. 1, Jan. 1980, pp. 6-15.

Pope, Hugh, *A Brief History of the English Version of the New Testament first published at Rheims in 1582, continued down to the present day*, London 1940 (repr. from the *Transactions of the Bibliographical Society, The Library*, vol. 20, no. 4, March 1940, pp. 351-376 and pp. 44-77).

Pope, Hugh, *English Versions of the Bible*, London 1952.

Pullen, G.F. (ed.), *Catalogue of the Bible Collections in the Old Library at St. Mary's, Oscott c.1472-c.1850*, New Oscott 1971.

Pullen, G.F. (ed.), *Recusant Books at St. Mary's, Oscott. Part II: 1641-1830 (with a supplement to Part I: to 1687)*, New Oscott 1966.

Rees, Eiluned, *Libri Walliae: A Catalogue of Welsh Books and Books Printed in Wales, 1546-1820*, Aberystwyth 1987.

Robinson F.J.G., and P.J. Wallis, *Book Subscription Lists. A Revised Guide*, Newcastle upon Tyne 1975 (with supplements 1976, 1977, 1980, 1981).

Ronan, Myles V. *An Apostle of Catholic Dublin. Father Henry Young*, Dublin 1944.

Schmandt, Raymond H., 'A Checklist of Eighteenth and Nineteenth Century Pamphlets in the Library of the American Catholic Historical Society', *Records of the American Catholic Historical Society of Philadelphia*, vol. 81, June, September, December, 1970, pp. 89-122, 131-175, 214-247; vol. 82, March, December, 1971, pp. 6-46, 195-264.

Schroth, R.A., 'The Excommunication of Reverend John Baptist Causse', *Records of the American Historical Society of Philadelphia*, vol. 81, 1970, pp. 42-56.

Scott, Geoffrey, *Gothic Rage Undone. English Monks in the Age of Enlightenment*, Downside Abbey 1992.

Shea, J.D.G., *A Bibliographical Account of Catholic Bibles, Testaments, and Other Portions of Scripture Printed in the United States of America*, New York 1859.

Shea, J.D.G., *The Catholic Church in Colonial Days*, New York 1892

Sommervogel, C., *Bibliothèque de la Compagnie de Jésus* (originally published by A. and A. de Backer), Brussels-Paris [1890-1932], repr. 1960.

Sutcliffe, E.G., *Bibliography of the English Province of the Society of Jesus, 1773-1953*, London 1957.

Thurston, Herbert, 'An Old-Established Periodical', *The Month*, vol. 44, February 1882, pp. 153-166.

Tremaine, Marie, *A Bibliography of Canadian Imprints 1751-1800,* Toronto 1952.

Tynan, Michael, *Catholic Instruction in Ireland 1720-1950. The O'Reilly/Donlevy Catechetical Tradition,* Blackrock 1985.

Wall, Thomas, *The Sign of Doctor Hay's Head, being some account of the hazards and fortunes of Catholic printers and publishers in Dublin from the later penal times to the present day,* Dublin 1955.

Walsh, M.J., 'An Eighteenth-century Jesuit Bibliography', *The Heythrop Journal,* vol. 20, 1979, pp. 44-56.

Ward, Bernard, *The Dawn of the Catholic Revival in England 1781-1803,* 2 vols, London 1909.

Williams, J. Anthony, 'Change or Decay? The Provincial Laity 1691-1781', in Eamon Duffy (ed.) *Challoner & His Church. A Provincial Bishop in Georgian England,* London 1981, pp. 27-54.

Wiseman, Nicholas, 'Catholic versions of Scripture', *Dublin Review,* April 1837, pp. 475-92.

Zon, Bennett Mitchell, *Plainchant in the Eighteenth-century Roman Catholic Church in England (1737-1834): An Examination of Surviving Printed and Manuscript Sources, with Particular Reference to the Work of John F. Wade,* University of Oxford D. Phil. thesis, 1993.

Zon, Bennett Mitchell, 'Plainchant in the eighteenth-century English Catholic Church', *Recusant History,* vol. 21, no. 3, 1993, pp. 361-80.

Key to Library Symbols

Note that, whenever possible, the ESTC library symbols have been adopted

ABu: Aberdeen, University Library
Amp: Ampleforth Abbey
AMu: Amsterdam, Universiteits-bibliotheek
AR: Arundel Castle
AWn: National Library of Wales
AWu: University College of Wales, Hugh Owen Library
AzTeS: Arizona State University
AzU: University of Arizona

BAA: Birmingham Archdiocesan Archives
BB: Blom private library, Nijmegen
BCA: Baltimore Catholic Archives
Bevan: see 'References and Abbreviations'
BFq: Queen's University of Belfast
BHN: Bishop's House, Newcastle
BIC: Bradshaw Irish College
BMp: Birmingham, Central Library
BMs: Birmingham, Selly Oak Colleges, Central Library
BMu: Birmingham, University Library
BPL: Boston Public Library
BRG: Brighton, Central Library
BRp: Bristol, Central Library
BRu: Bristol, University Library
BRw: Bristol, Wesley College
BUYs: Suffolk Record Office

C: Cambridge, University Library
CaAEU: University of Alberta
CaBVaS: Simon Fraser University, British Columbia
CaBVaU: University of British Columbia
CAI: Cork Archives Institute
CAL: Colwich Abbey Library
CaMWU: University of Manitoba, Dafoe Library
CaNBFMM: Christ Church Cathedral Archives, Fredericton
CaNBFU: University of New Brunswick
CaNfSM: Memorial University of Newfoundland

CaNSHD: Dalhousie University
CaNSHK: University of King's College, Nova Scotia
CaNSHPH: Atlantic School of Theology, Nova Scotia
CaNSWA: Acadia University, Vaughan Memorial Library, Nova Scotia
CaOHM: McMaster University, Mills Memorial Library
CaOKQ: Queen's University, Douglas Library
CaOLU: University of Western Ontario
CaOOA: Public Archives of Canada, Ontario
CaOONL: National Library of Canada
CaOOP: Library of Parliament, Ottawa
CaOTMC: Massey College, University of Toronto
CaOTP: Toronto Public Library
CaOTU: University of Toronto
CaOTV: Victoria University, Ontario
CaOWtU: University of Waterloo, Ontario
CaQMBM: Bibliothèque de la Ville de Montréal
CaQMBN: Bibliothèque Nationale du Québec
CaQMC: Collège de Montréal
CaQMJ: Ecole Normale Jacques Cartier, Montréal
CaQMM: McGill University
CaQMMD: Religious Studies Library, McGill University
CaQMS: Bibliothèque de St. Sulpice, Montréal
CaQMUC: Université du Québec à Montréal
CaQNicS: Séminaire de Nicolet, Quebec
CaQQLa: Université Laval Bibliothèque
CaSRU: University of Regina, Saskatchewan
CaSSU: University of Saskatchewan
Ce: Cambridge, Emmanuel College
Cha: Chapeltown Library
Cj: Cambridge, Jesus College

CKcl: Cork City Library
CKu: Cork, University College, Boole Library
CL: Los Angeles Public Library
Cli: Archives of the Diocese of Clifton, Bristol
CLobS: California State University
CLSU: University of Southern California
CLU: University of California, Los Angeles
CLU-C: William Andrews Clark Memorial Library, University of California
CLU-S/C: University of California, Los Angeles, Special Collections
Cm: Cambridge, Magdalene College
CME: Canterbury Mendham Collection, University of Kent at Canterbury
CNoS: California State University, Northridge
COA: Coalville, Mount St. Bernard Abbey
COCu: Colchester, University of Essex, Albert Sloman Library
COMC: Mills College, California
CoU: University of Colorado at Boulder
COVu: University of Warwick
Cpl: Cambridge, Central Library
C-S: Sutro Library, San Francisco
CSd: San Diego Public Library
CSdS: San Diego State University
Csj: Cambridge, St. John's College
CSL: California State University
CSmH: Henry E. Huntington Library
CSt: Stanford University
CStclU: University of Santa Clara, Orradre Library
Ct: Cambridge, Trinity College
CtHI: Institute of Living Medical Library, Connecticut
CtHT: Trinity College, Connecticut
CtHT-W: Watkinson Collection, Trinity College, Connecticut
CtSoP: Pequot Library, Southport, Connecticut
CtU: University of Connecticut
CtW: Wesleyan University, Olin Library, Connecticut
CtY: Yale University
CtY-BR: Beinecke Rare Books Library, Yale University
CtY-D: Divinity Library, Yale University
CtY-Mus: Music Library, Yale University
CU: University of California, Berkeley
CU-A: University of California, Davis
CU-BANC: Bancroft Library, University of California, Berkeley
CU-L: Law Library, University of California, Berkeley
CU-Riv: University of California, Riverside, Rivera Library
CU-S: University of California, San Diego
CU-SB: University of California, Santa Barbara
CYc: Canterbury, Cathedral Library

D: National Library of Ireland
DAE: Dominican Archives, Edinburgh
DB: American Antiquarian Society, Mass.
DCU: Catholic University of America
DE: Howard University, Washington D.C./U.S. Office of Education Library
De: Delaware Department of Community Affairs and Economic Development, Division of Libraries
DeGE: Hagley Museum and Library, Delaware
DeU: University of Delaware
DFo: Folger Shakespeare Library
DGU: Georgetown University
DGU-W: Woodstock Theological Center, Georgetown University
DGW: George Washington University
Di: Dublin, Royal Irish Academy
Dk: Kings Inn Library, Dublin
DLC: Library of Congress
DMR: D. M. Rogers, private library.
Do: Downside Abbey
DoA: Douai Abbey
Dobm: Douai Bibliothèque Municipale
DowA: Downside Archives
DP: United States Patent Office, Arlington
Dp: Dublin Public Libraries, Central Public Library
DT: United States Department of the

Treasury
Dt: Dublin, Trinity College Library
DU: Dartmouth College, New Hampshire
Du: Dublin, University College Library
DuA: St. Andrews Cathedral, Dundee
DUc: Durham, Cathedral Library
DUC: University Club, Washington D.C.
DUN: Dundee, Central Library
Dun: Dundee, Cathedral Library
DUu: Durham, University Library

E: National Library of Scotland
ECB: English Convent, Bruges
ECR: English College, Rome
ECW: St. Edmund's College, Ware
ET: Eton College Library
Eu: Edinburgh, University Library
EXp: Exeter, Central Library
EXu: Exeter, University Library

F: Florida State Library
FA: St. Benedict's Abbey, Fort Augustus
FK: F.J.M. Korsten, private library, Nijmegen
FLK: Franciscan Library, Killiney
FMU: University of Miami
Foley: Bishop B. C. Foley, private library, Preston
FP: Fernham Priory
FU: University of Florida

GeBS: Bisschoppelijk Seminarie, Gent
GEU: Emory University, Woodruff Library
GEU-T: Candler School of Theology Library, Emory University
Gi: Gillow Collection, Downside Abbey
GOT: Göttingen, Niedersächsische Staats- und Universitätsbibliothek
Gp: Glasgow, Mitchell Library
Gron: Groningen, Universiteitsbibliotheek
GU: University of Georgia
Gu: Glasgow, University Library

Harris: Rev. Peter Harris, private collection, London
HC: Harvard University

Hen: Hendred House, East Hendred
HLp: Hull, Central Library
HLu: University of Hull, Brynmor Jones Library
HLue: University of Hull, Institute of Education Library
Hor: Catholic Church, Hornby, Lancashire
Howell: see 'References and Abbreviations'

IAPA: Irish Augustinian Provincial Archives
IaU: University of Iowa
ICIU: University of Illinois at Chicago Circle
ICN: Newberry Library
ICR: Irish College, Rome
ICRL: Center for Research Libraries, Illinois
ICU: University of Chicago, Regenstein Library
IDA: Irish Dominican Archives
IEN: Northwestern University
IEN-M: Church Medical Library, Northwestern University
IES: Garrett-Evangelical Theological Seminary, Illinois
IISHA: International Institute for Social History, Amsterdam
IMunS: Saint Mary of the Lake Seminary, Illinois
InLP: Purdue University, Indiana
InNd: University of Notre Dame, Indiana
InU: Indiana University, Bloomington
InU-Li: Lilly Library, Indiana University
IObT: Bethany and Northern Baptist Theological Seminaries, Illinois
IU: University of Illinois, Urbana-Champaign

KAS: St. Benedict's College, Atchison, Kansas
KBH: Koninklijke Bibliotheek, Den Haag
KDA: Killarney Diocesan Archives
KMK: Kansas State University
KU: University of Kansas
KU-S: University of Kansas, Spencer

Research Library
KyU: University of Kentucky

L: London, British Library
LAM: Lampeter, St. David's University College, University Library
LANre: Lancaster Record Office
LANu: Lancaster, University Library
Lca: London, Camden Libraries
LCp: Leicester, Central Library
LDA: Leeds Diocesan Archives
Ldw: London, Dr. Williams's Library
Leeuw: Leeuwarden, Provinciale Bibliotheek Friesland
Leid: Leiden, Universiteitsbibliotheek
LEp: Leeds, Central Library
LEu: University of Leeds, Brotherton Library
Lfa: Jesuits, Farm Street, London
LfaA: Jesuit Archives, Farm Street, London
Lfs: London, University College, Folklore Society Library
Lg: London, Guildhall Library
Lhe: London, Heythrop College Library
Lhl: London, House of Lords Library
Lil: Lille, Archives du Nord
Ljc: London, Jews' College Library
Llp: London, Lambeth Palace Library
Lmc: London, Mercers' Company
Lmh: London, Congregational Library
Lnat: The National Trust, England
LNT: Tulane University
LO: London Oratory
LONu: Londonderry, University of Ulster at Magee College Library
LONU: Louisiana State University in New Orleans
LOU: Universiteitsbibliotheek, Leuven
Lpr: London, Post Office Archives
Lpro: London, Public Record Office
Lras: London, Royal Asiatic Society Library
Lsb: London, St. Bride Printing Library
Lse: London School of Economics, British Library of Political and Economic Science
Lsn: London, Hackney Libraries, Stoke Newington Library
Lu: University of London Library, Senate House

LU: Louisiana State University, Middleton Library
LU-HLS: Henry L. Snyder, private collection, now in Riverside, California
Luk: University of London, King's College London Library
Luu: University of London, University College London Library
LVp: Liverpool, Central Libraries
LVu: Liverpool, University Library

M: State Library of Massachusetts
Maas: Maastricht, Universiteitsbibliotheek
MAJ: Jones Library of Amherst, Mass.
Map: Mapledurham House
MB: Boston Public Library
MBAt: Boston Athenaeum
MBC: American Congregational Association
MBNEH: New England Historic Genealogical Society
MBtS: St. John's Seminary Library, Brighton, Mass.
MChB: Boston College, Chestnut Hill
MChB-W: Weston School of Theology, Cambridge, Mass.
MCR-S: Radcliffe College, Schlesinger Library, Mass.
MdBJ: Johns Hopkins University
MdBJ-G: John Work Garrett Library, Johns Hopkins University
MdBP: George Peabody Library, Johns Hopkins University
MdE: Mount St. Mary's College, Phillips Library, Maryland
MdHi: Maryland Historical Society
MdU: University of Maryland
MdW: Woodstock College, Maryland
MeB: Bowdoin College, Maine
MeHi: Maine Historical Society
MH: Harvard University
MH-AH: Andover-Harvard Theological Library, Harvard University
MH-BA: Graduate School of Business Administration, Baker Library, Harvard University
MH-H: Houghton Library, Harvard University
MHi: Massachusetts Historical Society

MH-L: Law School Library, Harvard University

MiDW: Wayne State University

MiEM: Michigan State University

MiKCS: Institute of Cistercian Studies, Western Michigan University

Mil: Miltown Park, Dublin

MiU: University of Michigan

MiU-C: William L. Clements Library, University of Michigan

MNS: Smith College, Northampton, Mass.

MnU: University of Minnesota, Meredith Wilson and James Ford Bell Libraries

MoLiWJ: William Jewell College, Missouri

MoSM: St. Louis Mercantile Library Association

MoSU-D: School of Divinity Library, St. Louis University

MoSW: Washington University

MoU: University of Missouri, Ellis Library

MRc: Manchester, Chetham's Library

MRp: Manchester, Central Library

MRu: Manchester, John Rylands University Library

MSaE: Essex Institute, Salem, Mass.

MWA: American Antiquarian Society, Worcester, Mass.

MWH: College of the Holy Cross, Worcester, Mass.

MY: Maynooth, St. Patrick's College, Russell Library

Nancy: Nancy, Archives Merthe-et-Moselle

NBi: Binghamton Public Library

NBiSU: State University of New York at Binghamton

NbOC: Creighton University, Omaha

NBu: Buffalo and Erie County Public Library

NcA: Pack Memorial Public Library, Ashville

NcA-S: Pack Memorial Public Library, Sondley Reference Library, Ashville

NcD: Duke University, William R. Perkins Library, North Carolina

NcGU: University of North Carolina at Greensboro, Jackson Library

NCp: Newcastle upon Tyne, Central Library

NcU: University of North Carolina at Chapel Hill, Wilson Library

NHi: New York Historical Society

NIC: Cornell University

Nijm: Nijmegen, Universiteitsbibliotheek

NjP: Princeton University

NjPT: Princeton Theological Seminary

NjR: Rutgers - The State University, New Brunswick

NN: New York Public Library

NNAB: American Bible Society, New York

NNC: Columbia University

NNC-T: Teachers College, Columbia University

NNF: Fordham University, Duane Library

NNG: General Theological Seminary of the Protestant Episcopal Church, New York

NNGr: Grolier Club Library, New York

NNMan: Manhattan College, Hayes Library

NNPM: Pierpont Morgan Library, New York

NNS: New York Society Library

NNStJ: St. John's University, New York

NNU: New York University

NNUT: Union Theological Seminary, New York

NOp: Nottingham, County Library

NOW: Norwich, Central Library

NPV: Vassar College, Poughkeepsie

NRAB: American Baptist Historical Society, Rochester

NRCR: Colgate Rochester Divinity School, Swasey Library, New York

NRU: University of Rochester, Rush Rhees Library

NRU-Mus: Eastman School of Music, Sibley Library, University of Rochester

NSbSU: State University of New York at Stony Brook

NSCH: Sisters of Charity Archives,

Sydney

NSchU: Union College, Schaffer Library, New York

NSIC: New South Wales, St. Ignatius' College

NSJH: New South Wales, St. Joseph's College

NSPM: New South Wales, St. Patrick's College

NSPN: New South Wales, St. Paul's National Seminary

NSyU: Syracuse University

NU: University of Sydney

NUN: University of New South Wales Libraries

NYPL: New York Public Library

O: Oxford, Bodleian Library

Oa: Oxford, All Souls College

OAkU: University of Akron, Ohio

OAU: Ohio University, Athens

Ob: Oxford, Balliol College

OBA: Old Brotherhood Archives (Westminster Diocesan Archives, London)

Obl: Oxford, Blackfriars

Oc: Oxford, Christ Church

Occ: Oxford, Corpus Christi College

OCH: Hebrew Union College - Jewish Institute of Religion, Cincinnati

OCl: Cleveland Public Library

OClW: Case Western Reserve University, Cleveland

ODaU: University of Dayton, Ohio

Oe: Oxford, Exeter College

OKentU: Kent State University

OkTU: University of Tulsa, McFarlin Library, Oklahoma

OkU: University of Oklahoma

Ol: Oxford, Lincoln College

Om: Oxford, Merton College

Oma: Oxford, Magdalen College

OMC: Marietta College, Dawes Memorial Library

OMc: Herbert Wescoat Memorial Library, Mc Arthur, Ohio

Omc: Oxford, Manchester College

OO: Oberlin College, Mudd Learning Center, Ohio

OOxM: Miami University

Op: Oxford, Pembroke College

Opl: Oxford, Central Library

Or: Oxford, Regent's Park College

OrPU: University of Portland

OrU: University of Oregon

Osc: St. Mary's College, Oscott

Ot: Oxford, Trinity College

Ou: Oxford, University College

OU: Ohio State University

Owa: Oxford, Wadham College

Owo: Oxford, Worcester College

P: Note that ESTC uses 'P' for 'Paris, Bibliothèque Nationale' as well as for 'Pennsylvania State Library'

Parsons: see 'References and Abbreviations'

PAtM: Muhlenburg College, Pennsylvania

PcA: American Baptist Historical Society, Rochester

Pci: Paris, Collège des Irlandais

PHC: Haverford College, Pennsylvania

PHi: Historical Society of Pennsylvania

PIF: Paris, Institute de France

PLatS: St. Vincent College, Latrobe, Pennsylvania

Pm: Paris, Bibliothèque Mazarine

PP: Free Library of Philadelphia

PPAmP: American Philosophical Society, Pennsylvania

PPCCH: Chestnut Hill College, Philadelphia

PPiPT: Pittsburgh Theological Seminary, Barbour Library

PPL: Library Company of Philadelphia

PPPrHi: Presbyterian Historical Society, Pennsylvania

PPRF: Rosenbach Museum Library, Pennsylvania

PPStCh: Saint Charles Borromeo Seminary, Overbrook, Philadelphia

PPULC: Union Library Catalogue of Pennsylvania, Philadelphia

PPWa: Wagner Free Institute of Science, on deposit at Temple University, Pennsylvania

PRTus: Pretoria, University of South Africa Library

PSC: Swarthmore College, Pennsylvania

Psg: Paris, Saint Geneviève

PSt: Pennsylvania State University, Pattee Library
PU: University of Pennsylvania
PV: Villanova University, Pennsylvania

RBM: Bibliothèque Municipale, Rouen
RHi: Rhode Island Historical Society, Providence
ROHp: Rochester, Kent County Library, Rochester Library
RP: Providence Public Library
RPB: Brown University, Rhode Island
RPJCB: John Carter Brown Library, Brown University
RPPC: Providence College, Phillips Memorial Library
RY: Ryde, Quarr Abbey

Sal: Salamanca, Scotch College
SAN: St. Andrews, University Library
SAW: Essex County Library, Saffron Walden Library
SCA: Scottish Catholic Archives, Edinburgh
ScCleU: Clemson University, Cooper Library
ScCM: Medical University of South Carolina
ScCR: Scotch College, Rome
Sco: Scotus College, Glasgow
SCR: San Clemente, Rome
ScU: University of South Carolina
SHp: Sheffield, Central Library
SHu: Sheffield, University Library
SIR: San Isidore, Rome
SPu: Southampton, University Library
STA: Stafford, William Salt Library
Stan: Stanbrook Abbey
StD: St. Deiniol's Library, Hawarden
Sto: Stonyhurst College
SWNu: University College of Swansea Library

TAB: T. A. Birrell, private library
TAUa: Taunton, Somerset Archaeological and Natural History Society
TGrT: Tusculum College, Tennessee
TH: Traquair House
Tilb: Tilburg, Universiteitsbibliotheek
TLP: Talbot Library, Preston
TMM: Memphis State University

TNJ: Joint University Libraries, Nashville
TU: University of Tennessee, James D. Hoskins Library
TxDaM-P: Bridwell Library, Perkins School of Theology, Southern Methodist University, Texas
TxH: Houston Public Library
TxHR: Rice University, Fondren Library, Texas
TxU: University of Texas at Austin, Humanities Research Center
Tynan: see 'References and Abbreviations'

UGL: Upholland Gradwell Library
UPB: Brigham Young University, Lee Library, Utah
Ush: Ushaw College
UshA: Ushaw College Archives
UshL: Ushaw College, Lisbon Collection
Utr: Utrecht, Universiteitsbibliotheek

Vat: Vatican Library
Vi: Virginia State Library
ViRUT: Union Theological Seminary Library, Richmond
ViU: University of Virginia
ViW: College of William and Mary, Swem Library, Virginia
ViWC: Colonial Williamsburg Foundation, Virginia
VtMiM: Middlebury College
VUA: Vrije Universiteit, Amsterdam

WaPS: Washington State University
WaSpG: Gonzaga University, Crosby Library, Spokane
WaSpStM: St. Michael's Institute, Spokane
WaU: University of Washington
WAu: Warsaw, Biblioteka Uniwersytecka
WDA: Westminster Diocesan Archives, London
WHi: State Historical Society of Wisconsin, Madison
WIW: Johannesburg, University of the Witwatersrand Library
WMM: Marquette University

WMUW: University of Wisconsin

WNp: Hampshire County Library, Winchester Library

WNs: Winchester College, Fellows' Library

WOV: Wolverhampton, Central Library

WRW: Warwickshire Record Office

WvBeC: Bethany College, Phillips Memorial Library, West Virginia

Yb: Bar Convent, York

ZAP: Auckland Public Library, New Zealand

ZWTU: Alexander Turnbull Library, Wellington, New Zealand

Catalogue

1. *An abridgement of Christian doctrine: newly revised and enlarged by R.C.* [London?]. 1755. 12°. 28 p. ESTC t193901. * DUc; ECR.

> 'R.C.' is Richard Challoner. For the intricate relationship between this work and the 'Abridgement' by Henry Turberville (cf. nos 2801ff.) see Pickering. See also next 3 items.

2. *An abridgment of Christian doctrine: revised and enlarged by R.C. and published for the use of the L...n district.* Anon. [London]. 1759. 12°. 28 p. ESTC t134112. * ECW; L; O.

3. *An abridgment of Christian doctrine: revised and enlarged by R.C. and published for the use of the L...n district.* [London?]. 1767. 18°. 28 p. ESTC t203422. * E.

4. *An abridgment of Christian doctrine. Revised and enlarged by R.C.* Anon. St. Omers. 1772. 8°. 32 p. Printed by: Boubers, H.F. ESTC t083402. * L.

> Burton (II, 337) also mentions a 1775 and a 1777 ed. both issued by Coghlan.

5. *An abridgment of the life of blessed Joh. Fran. Regis, of the Society of Jesus. Translated out of French into English, by N.N. of the same society.* London. 1718. 8°. [12], 65, [5] p. * LfaA.

> LfaA suggests Lewis Sabran S.J. as the translator and St. Omers as the place of publication. Bevan (Advent 1993, no. 10) has a copy with viii, 65, [1] p.

6. *An abridgment of the rules of the English sodality, of our blessed lady. Under the charge of the Society of Jesus in S. Omers.* St. Omers. 1726. 12°. 24 p. Printed by: Le Febvre, N.J. * ICN.

> Bound up with *Libellus precum et piarum exercitationum*, 1730 (no. 1662).

7. *An abstract of the catechism, or abridgment of the Christian doctrine. With proofs of holy scripture.* [Edinburgh?]. [1776?]. 12°. 97, [1] p. ESTC t200819. * E.

> A catechism including Scots days of obligation, possibly compiled by George Hay.

8. *An abstract of the Douay catechism. To which is added instructions for confirmation.* Paris. 1703. 12°. [2], 58, [2], 89, [5] p. Sold by: Debats, I.; Chavepeyre, J. (St. Germain en Laye). ESTC t188033. * P.

> 'Sometime in the 1680s an unknown writer issued a shorter version of Turberville's work [*Abridgment of Christian doctrine*, also referred to as the Doway Catechism] under the title *An abstract of the Douay catechism*' (Pickering, p. 7). See also next 8 items.

9. *An abstract of the Douay catechism ... To which is added instructions for confirmation.* Paris. 1715. 12°. [2], 152, [2], p. Published by: Debats, I. ESTC t153024. * DoA; Gi; Lhe; P.

10. *An abstract of the Douay catechism. Published with allowance.* Douai. 1716. 12°. 233, [1] p. Printed by: Mairesse, M. ESTC t124212. * Dobm; Gi; L; Pm.

11. *An abstract of the Douay catechism.* London. 1748. 12°. 57, [1] p. Published by: Goddard, T. * ECR.
> With one page of Goddard adverts.

12. *An abstract of the Douay catechism.* London. 1762. 12°. 48 p. * Lfa.

13. *An abstract of the Dowai catechism. For the use of children, and ignorant people. Published with allowance.* Cork. 1774. 12°. 60 p. Printed by: Flyn, W. ESTC t183672. * D; P.
> With a final page of adverts.

14. *An abstract of the Douay catechism. Published with permission of the Lord Bishop of Quebec.* Quebec. 1778. 18°. 75, [1] p. Printed by: Brown, W. * CaOOA; CaQMS; CaOOP; P.

15. *An abstract of the Douay catechism.* London. 1792. 32°. 126 p. Printed by: Coghlan, J.P. ESTC t119117. * L.

16. *An abstract of the Douay catechism. Published with allowance.* Preston. 1795. 18°. 54 p. Printed by: Sergent, E. * Ush.

17. *Abstract of the rules and regulations for the students in the college of Aquhorties.* Edinburgh. [1799]. s.s. Printed by: Moir, J. ESTC t183603. * E.
> Abstracted for display from Bishop Hay's *Regulations* drawn up for the new college after the closure of Scalan (no. 1415).

18. *An abstract of what is necessary to be known concerning the constitution Unigenitus ... Translated from the ... copy printed at Luxembourg, 1719 [Abrégé de ce qu'il faut sçavoir touchant ... Unigenitus].* [Amsterdam or Antwerp?]. 1724. 12°. [12], 56 p. ESTC t065119. * Do(2); DoA; ECW; ICN; L; LfaA; Lhe; Osc; TxU; Ush; Yb.
> Translated by Thomas Percy Plowden. Dedication signed 'D.***'. The text is in the form of a catechism. The two Do copies have variant tps. Ush bound up with no. 718.

An account of some of the sufferings. This pamphlet is occasionally found by itself (ESTC mentions two instances; see below) but was basically printed in various editions in order to be bound with various editions of Ordo recitandi and Laity's directory (s.v.).

19. *An account of some of the sufferings of his holiness Pius VI. Immediately previous to his being forced from Rome. With other interesting matter.* London. 1798. 8°. 15, [1] p. Printed by: Coghlan, J.P. ESTC t163518. * L.

20. *An account of some of the sufferings of his holiness Pius VI. Immediately previous to his being forced from Rome; with other interesting matter.* Dublin. 1799. 12°. 20 p. Printed by: Fitzpatrick, H. ESTC t183331. * D.

21. *An account of the funeral ceremonies perform'd at Rome, in honour of the Princess Clementina Sobieski. Translated from the Roman Journal of Jan. 29. 1735. No. 2729.* [Dublin?]. 1735. 8°. [2], 16 p. ESTC t095412. * ABu; CSt; E;

L; O; TxU.

22. *An account of the miraculous cure, wrought by the intercession of the Blessed Virgin Mary, in the person of sister Jane Weardon, a nun of the English Benedictin Convent in Ghent, on the 28th Jan. 1783.* London. 1785. 12°. 10 p. Printed by: Coghlan, J.P. * Sto.

> The account by Jane Weardon was recorded and sent on by the mother superior Teresa Hodgson O.S.B.

23. *An account of the obsequies for the late King of France, in the Spanish Chapel, London, on Monday, January 28, 1793.* London. 1793. 4°. [2], 12 p. Printed by: Coghlan, J.P. Sold by: Debrett, J.; Booker; Keating; Lewis; Robinsons; Robins (Winchester). ESTC t148379. * CYc; LU; TxU; WDA.

> Cf. no. 24, which seems to be another edition.

24. *An account of the obsequies for the late King of France, in the Spanish Chapel, London, on Monday, January 28th, 1793.* London. 1793. 4°. 2, [9], 1 p. Printed by: Coghlan, J.P. Sold by: Debrett; Booker, J.; Keating; Lewis; Robinsons; Robins (Winchester). * Ush.

> Cf. no. 23, which seems to be another edition.

25. *An act for the better education of persons professing the popish or Roman Catholic religion.* [London]. [1795]. fol. 2 p. Printed by: Coghlan, J.P. * Ush.

26. *An act for the relief of his majesty's popish or Roman Catholic subjects of Ireland.* [London]. [1793]. fol. 4 p. Printed by: Coghlan, J.P. * Ush; WDA.

27. *An act to incorporate the members of the religious society of German Roman Catholics, of the church called The Holy Trinity, in the city of Philadelphia.* [Philadelphia]. 1788. 8 p.

> See Schmandt (p. 92, no. 17). See also Schroth (Vol. 81, 1970, pp. 42-56) for the general background to this pamphlet and other pamphlets concerning Trinity church.

28. *An act to remove certain restraints and disabilities therein mentioned, to which his majesty's subjects, professing the popish religion are now subject.* [London]. [1792]. 8°. 3, [1] p. Printed by: Coghlan, J.P. * WDA.

> Headed 'Dublin, April 20, 1792'.

29. *Acts of faith, hope and charity recommended to the frequent use of the faithful, living amongst hereticks and infidels.* [1772?]. 12°. [2] p. * DAE; ECB.

> On p. [2] there is a prayer dated 'April 5, 1772'.

30. *Acts of the three theological virtues and contrition absolutely necessary to salvation ... Gniomhartha na ntri subhailce diadha agus croidh-hruighidh ro riachtanacha chum slainte.* Dublin. [1770]. 12°. 23, [1] p. Printed by: Corcoran, B. ESTC t086893. * L.

> In English and Irish. On last page 2 Latin imprimaturs.

31. Adams, James. *A sermon preached at the Catholic Chapel of S. Patrick, Sutton Street, Soho Square, on Wednesday, the seventh of March, the day of public fast ... By the rev. James Adams, S.R.E.S.* London. 1798. 8°. [2], 33, [1] p. Printed by: Adams, J. Published by: Adams, J. Sold by: Keating, P.; Booker; author. ESTC t175137. * D; ECW; Lfa; MY; Sto.

ESTC gives the author's dates as 1737-1802 in order to distinguish him from James B. Adams (fl. 1770-1820).

32. Adams, James B. *A selection from the new version of psalms, for the use of Brompton-Chapel.* London. 1791. 12°. [4], vii, [1], 71, [1] p. Sold by: Brompton Chapel; Editor. ESTC t092076. * L.

The author is James B. Adams, organist (fl. 1770-1820).

33. *An address from the general committee of Roman Catholics, to their Protestant fellow subjects, and to the public in general, respecting the calumnies and misrepresentations.* Dublin. 1792. 8°. viii, 45, [1] p. Printed by: Byrne, P. ESTC t020359. * CaOTU; CoU; CSmH; D; Dt; Du; IU; L; Lhl; MChB; MRu; MY; Oc; PP; PPL; Sto.

34. *An address from the general committee of Roman Catholics, to their Protestant fellow subjects, and to the public in general, respecting the calumnies and misrepresentations.* London repr. [Dublin]. 1792. 8°. viii, 45, [3] p. Published by: Debrett, J. ESTC t012299. * CaOTU; CLU-S/C; CSmH; CtY; DLC; Dt; ICU; L; LfaA; Lmh; Lu; MChB; MoU; MRu; NN; NSbSU; O; PPL; RP; Sto; Ush.

With a final advertisement leaf.

35. *An address from the Roman Catholic nobility, clergy & gentry of Ireland, presented to his excellency, the lord lieutenant May 30, 1798, with his excellency's answer.* London. 1798. 12°. [4], 60 p. Printed by: Coghlan, J.P. ESTC t088089. * D (-ht); DUc; ECW; L; Llp; Ush.

Half-title: 'Address and remonstrances of the Roman Catholics of Ireland'. Coghlan and others also published a French translation of this work by abbé de Champeaux (no. 51). See also next item.

36. *An address from the Roman Catholic nobility, clergy and gentry of Ireland, presented to his excellency the lord lieutenant, May 30, 1798 ... To which is added, The excommunication.* London. [1798]. 12°. [2], 86 p. Printed by: Coghlan, J.P. Sold by: Coghlan, J.P.; Debrett; Booker, E.; Keating, P.; Robinson. ESTC t215179. * Di; Osc; Ush.

'The excommunication' is *The excommunication of the rev. Robert M'Evoy* by John Troy (no. 2783).

37. *The address of the Catholics of Dublin to the right hon. Henry Grattan, presented to him by the gentlemen appointed for that purpose ... on the 27th February, 1795. With his answer.* [Dublin]. [1795]. s.s. Printed by: Bates, T.M. ESTC t020375. * L.

For another edition see no. 482.

38. *The address of the Catholics of Dublin, to the right honourable Henry Grattan, presented to him ... on the twenty-seventh of February, MDCCXCV. With his answer.* Dublin. 1798. 8°. 44 p. Published by: Milliken, J. ESTC t117677. * BFq; L; Lhl (imp.); MY; O (imp.); SIR.

This work is bound up with the 4th ed. of Patrick Duigenan's *An answer to the address of the Rt. Hon. Henry Grattan*, Dublin, 1799.

39. *The address of the Catholics of Dublin, to the right honourable Henry*

Grattan, presented to him ... on the twenty-seventh of February, MDCCXCV. With his answer. Dublin. 1798. 8°. 42 p. Published by: Milliken, J. ESTC t165074. * BMp (imp.); C; CaOTU; Dt; KU-S; Lhl; Mil (imp.); MY; PP.

40. *Address of the Catholics of Ireland to the people of England.* Dublin and London. 4 p. Printed by: Grace, R. * Amp; Ush.

41. *Address of the Catholics of the city of Dublin, to the right honorable Henry Grattan, presented by the gentlemen appointed for that purpose at the meeting in Francis Street Chapel, Feb. the 27th, 1795.* Dublin. [1795]. s.s. Printed by: Fitzpatrick, H. ESTC n045330. * Lpro.
> Includes Grattan's answer.

42. *Address to his excellency John, Earl of Westmorland, lord lieutenant general and general governor of Ireland. We the undernamed his majesty's most dutiful and loyal subjects, Roman Catholics.* [1791]. 8°. 8 p. * WDA.
> Signed by John Troy and many others.

43. *An address to the abettors and well-wishers of the late attempt at a revolution in this kingdom: particularly to those among them who are of the old religion. By Father D-y, P.P. of K-y.* Dublin. 1800. 8°. 16 p. Printed by: Porter, W. ESTC n029271. * D; PP.

44. *An address to the Catholic clergy of England, by their brethren of the county of Stafford.* [London]. [1792]. 4°. 7, [1] p. * BAA; P; SIR; Sto; Ush.
> This concerns the case of Joseph Wilks. Signed and dated by Thomas Flynn and 12 others 'Jan. 26, 1792'.

45. *An address to the Catholic clergy of England, by their brethren of the county of Stafford.* London. 1792. 4°. 24 p. Printed by: Swinney & Walker. Published by: Booker, T.; Coghlan, J.P. ESTC t187776. * BAA; BMp (imp.); DUc; ECW; Lfa; LfaA; Lhe; Osc.

46. *An address to the president of the Protestant association; including remarks on strictures lately published on The state and behaviour of English Catholics.* Anon. London. 1782. 8°. [2], 72 p. Published by: Faulder, R. ESTC n029418. * BMu; C; CaOKQ; E; ECW; ICN; Llp; MdBJ-P; Osc; P; Ush.
> Chinnici (p. 229) attributes the work to J. Berington. The President of the Protestant association was Lord George Gordon.

47. *An address to the public, on the expediency of building a chapel for the use of his majesty's soldiers, mariners, sailors, labourers ... professing the Roman Catholic religion, in Chatham Barracks.* [London?]. [1800?]. s.s. ESTC t020489. * L.

48. *An address to the public, on the expediency of supporting Saint Patrick's Chapel, Sutton-street, Soho.* [London]. 1792. 8°. 10, [2] p. Published by: Keating, P. ESTC t121213. * L; MB; Sto; Ush.
> Sometimes attributed to Arthur O'Leary.

49. *An address to the right. hon. Henry Grattan, on the present state of the Roman Catholics of Ireland. By one of that body.* Dublin. 1791. 8°. 16 p. Printed by: Byrne, P. ESTC t109874. * CSmH; D; L; NIC.

50. *Address to the subscribers for the Doway translation of the Vulgate Bible.* [Philadelphia]. [1790]. 8°. 4 p. Published by: [Carey, Stewart & Co.]. ESTC w035264. * DP; MWA.

> Dated on p. 3 'Philadelphia, Sept. 24, 1790'. Also issued as the first 4 pages of *The American museum; or, Universal Magazine*, no. 45, (Sept. 1790), published by Carey, Stewart & Co.

51. *Adresse de la noblesse, du clergé et des gentils-hommes d'Irlande Catholiques Romains, présentée à Son Excellence le Lord Lieutenant, le 30 May, 1798, avec la réponse de Son Excellence.* London. 1798. 8°. vii, [1], 70 p. Sold by: Coghlan, J.P.; Dulau & Co.; Boffe, J. de; Boosey, T.; L'Homme, L.; Bené. ESTC n030129. * MY; PPL.

> A translation of no. 35/36, made by abbé de Champeaux who signs the dedication.

52. Agard de Champs, Etienne. *A brief abstract of the memorial, concerning the state and progress of Jansenism in Holland.* [London?]. 1703. 8°. 34 p. ESTC t217853. * Lfa; Lhe; O; Ush.

> Walsh (p. 50), who assigns the book to Louis Ducin, gives Thomas Coxon (1676-1735) as the translator. Also issued as part of *The secret policy of the Jansenists* (no. 54).

53. Agard de Champs, Etienne. *The secret policy of the Jansenists, and the present state of the Sorbon, discovered by a doctour of that faculty [Secrète politique des Jansénistes et l'estat présent].* Anon. [1703?]. 8°. 72 p. * Lfa; Lhe; Ush.

> This was one of the most violent attacks on Jansenism; it is a reprint, with some additions, of the 1667 ed. (Clancy no. 15.3). According to Kirk (p. 77) translated by Th. Fairfax. Osc (see next item) gives Richard Thimelby, alias Ashby, as translator. Tp gives 'Troyes, 1667 printed by C. Roman', but a ms note in Lfa suggests that this refers to a French ed. Lfa bound with *A brief abstract*, 1703 (no. 52). See also next item.

54. Agard de Champs, Etienne. *The secret policy of the Jansenists; and the present state of the Sorbon, discover'd by a converted doctor of that faculty.* 2nd ed. [London?]. 1703. 8°. 184, [2] p. ESTC t083101. * Amp; DFo; E; ECW; Gi; L; Lfa; LfaA; O; Osc; StD; Ush.

55. Alegani, J.B. *The life of the servant of God Benedict Joseph Labre ... Translated from the third edition of the French [Vie de Bénoît-Joseph Labre].* London. 1785. 12°. 75, [1] p. Printed by: Marmaduke, J. * Yb.

56. *An teagasg Cristny; agus U'rnihe na mainne, agus trahno'na.* Cork. 1774. 12°. 58 p. Printed by: O'Donnoghue, D. * Tynan pp. 19 and 51.

57. *An angelical exercise for every day in the week. Composed by a father of the Society of Jesus.* St. Omers. 1729. 12°. 120 p. Printed by: Le Febvre, N.J. * Do (imp.); DoA.

58. *An angelical exercise. With other devout prayers. Composed by a father of the Society of Jesus.* Bruges. [1763]. 12°. 143, [1] p. Printed by: Praet, J. van. ESTC t118303. * Do; FP; Gi; L; Sto; Ush.

Imprimatur on final leaf dated 'Aug. 1763' lacking in Sto.

59. *Anno à verbi incarnatione 1770, die 1a mensis Decembris, in collegio Anglorum Duaci.* [1770]. s.s. * UshA.

> Obit notice for William Green, president of Douai College.

60. *Anno ab incarnatione Dominica 1762, die 26 mensis Januarii, in collegio Anglorum.* [1762]. s.s. * UshA.

> Obit notice for Francis Petre, vice-president of Douai College.

61. *An answer to a paper bearing the following title; The relations of Mr T[albot], of L[onglf[or]d, against the J[esui]ts.* [London?]. [1745?]. 4°. ii, 26 p. ESTC t074426. * L; Lfa; LfaA; Lhe; NNU; STA.

> Ascribed by ESTC to Philip Carteret S.J. The case concerns the right of religious to inherit estates and relates specifically to Gilbert Talbot. See also nos 103, 763, 2455 and the next 2 items.

62. *An answer to a paper bearing the following title; The relations of Mr T[al]B[o]T, of L[onglf[or]d, against the J[esui]ts.* [London?]. [1745?]. 4°. ii, 35, [1] p. * Stan; Sto; Ush.

63. *An answer to a reply in vindication of Mr T[albot]'s Relations.* [1745?]. 4°. 28 p. ESTC t218294. * Pm; Ush.

64. *An answer to Mr. Podmore's letter against transubstantiation by J*** P***.* [London]. [1748?]. 8°. 36 p. ESTC t191538. * DoA; ECW; Lhe; TLP; Ush.

> Dated 'July 28, 1748'.

65. *An answer to so much of a certain treatise that has lately appear'd in print, as relates to the law.* [London?]. [1745?]. 4°. 12 p. ESTC t218293. * Pm; Sto.

66. *Anthems, hymns, &c. usually sung at the Catholick church in Boston.* Boston. 1800. 16°. 72 p. Printed by: Manning & Loring. ESTC w000454. * BPL; CL; DCU; DGU; GU; HC; MBAt; MBC; MH; NN; NYPL.

67. *Antiphons which are sung whilst the blessed sacrament is exposed in the Church of the English Dames of St. Clare, at Aire in Artois.* London. 1783. 8°. [2], 6 p. Printed by: Coghlan, J.P. ESTC t065391. * CtY-Mus; Dt; ICN; L; Lhe; O; Ush.

68. Antonelli, Leonardo. *Copy of a letter from Rome. Illustrissimis et reverendissimis dominis, uti fratribus, dominis episcopis et vicariis apostolicis regni Angliae.* [London?]. [1795]. fol. 2 p. ESTC t034105. * Cli; ICN; L.

> The letter is signed 'L. Card. Antonellus, praefectus, A. Archip. Adanen, secretarius'.

69. Antonelli, Leonardo. *Copy of a letter written by express order of his holiness in answer to that which we addressed to the apostolic see.* [London]. [1791]. s.s. Printed by: Coghlan, J.Pt [sic]. ESTC t034135. * DowA; Hor; L; Ush; WDA.

> The head-note is signed 'James Barnard, V.G.' The letter is dated and signed 'Romae, 30 Septembris, 1791 ... L. Cardinalis Antonellus praefectus, A. Archiepiscopus Adanensis secretarius'.

70. Antonelli, Leonardo. *Letters from Cardinal Antonelli ... to their lordships the bishops, vicars apostolic, etc. of the Church of Rome.* London. 1796. 8°. [2], 31,

[1] p. Printed by: Coghlan, J.P. Sold by: Booker; Keating; Lewis; Debrett; Robinsons. ESTC n046046. * CSmH; Sto; Ush.

> The letters are in English, Latin and Italian. Cf. also no. 2291.

71. *An apology for Roman Catholics. In a letter to a Member of Parliament.* [London?]. 1703. 4°. 26 p. ESTC n030142. * O; TxU.

72. *An apology for the Catholics of Great Britain and Ireland: humbly offered to the consideration of the king's most excellent majesty, and both Houses of Parliament.* London. 1767. 12°. viii, 172 p. ESTC t120196. * E; L; Ush.

> Sometimes attributed to 'Mrs Patsall' (see also next 2 items). Gillow (I, 198) states that this work was written and published by Simon Berington, who died in 1755.

73. *An apology for the Catholics of Great Britain and Ireland: humbly offered to the consideration of the king's most excellent majesty, and both Houses of Parliament.* London. 1768. 12°. viii, 172, [2], 175-196 p. Published by: Author. Sold by: Peat, T. ESTC t133328. * Amp; Do (imp.); ICU; L; Ldw; Lhe; Lu; MB; MH-H; O; StD.

> A reissue of the 1767 ed., with a reset tp and the addition of pp. 175-196. Do lacks pp. 175-196.

74. *An apology for the Catholics of Gteat [sic] Britain and Ireland: humbly offered to the consideration of the king's most excellent majesty and both Houses of Parliament.* Dublin repr. [London]. 1768. 12°. viii, 172 p. ESTC t124590. * D; ECW; KU-S; L; Lfa (imp.); Lhe; MY; Ush.

75. *Apparatus ad clericorum institutionem. Permissu superiorum.* Cork. 1764. 12°. [2], v, [1], 160 p. Printed by: Swiney, E. ESTC t083117. * D; FLK; L.

76. *An appeal to his grace the Lord P...te of all I...d; being a short vindication of the political principles of Roman Catholics, in answer to the calumnies contained in two late pamphlets.* Dublin. 1757. 12°. [2], 14 p. ESTC n049197. * CSmH.

> Signed 'A.B.' The Lord Primate is George Stone. The book argues for R.C. emancipation and defends R.C. religious and political convictions. See also next item and nos 2507 and 2699.

77. *An appeal to his grace the Lord P...te of all I...d; being a short vindication of the political principles of Roman Catholics, in answer to the calumnies contained in two late pamphlets.* Dublin. 1757. 8°. 22 p. Sold by: [Lord, P.]. ESTC t022268. * D; InU; L.

78. *An appeal to the Catholics of England. By the Catholic clergy of the county of Stafford.* Wolverhampton. 1792. 8°. 30, [2] p. Printed by: Smart, J. Published by: Booker, T. ESTC t163713. * Amp; BAA; BMp; CSmH; DUc; ECW; Gi; ICN; L; Lfa; LfaA; MoU; Osc; STA; Sto; TLP; Ush.

> According to Chinnici (p. 229) the work of Joseph Berington. Osc cat. adds 'With the "Queries proposed to Charles Butler Esq., secretary to the Catholic Committee, and his answers"'.

79. *An appeal to the people; or, a political olio. Made up of the following ingredients ... Catholic Committee.* Dublin. 1792. 8°. vii, [1], 153, [1] p.

Printed by: Murphy, J. ESTC n016626. * Dt; InU-Li; PP; Sto.
> A mainly political tract in favour of the Catholic cause.

80. *[Appendix. The constitution Unigenitus. Clement Bishop, servant of the servants of God; to all the faithful of Christ.]* 30 p. [rest missing]. * Ush (-tp).

81. *An appendix to the ritual, containing instructions and exhortations, proper to be made by priests in the administration of the sacraments and other ecclesiastical offices.* [London?]. 1759. 8°. 47, [1] p. ESTC n030892. * CLU; E; GEU-T; ICN; L; Lhe; LO; NSPM; Stan; Sto; TLP; Ush.
> LO, NSPM, Stan, Sto and Ush bound up with *Ordo administrandi sacramenta* (no. 2104).

82. Appleton, James. *A collection of discourses, on the various duties of religion, as taught by the Catholic Church.* 3 vols. Reading. 1786. 8°. [12], 327, [3]; [6], 390, [2]; [8], 347, [7] p. Printed by: Smart, A.M.; Cowslade, T. Published by: Author. Sold by: Coghlan, J.P. ESTC t104762. * CSt; Do; DoA (vol. 1); ECW; L; Map; NNUT; O; TxU; Ush.
> With a list of subscribers. Appleton was chaplain at Mapledurham House, Reading.

83. Appleton, James. *A collection of discourses, on the various duties of religion, as taught by the Catholic Church; comprizing all the Sundays and festivals of the year.* Dublin. 1790. 8°. xv, [1], 472 p. Published by: Wogan, P. ESTC n005608. * FLK; IDA; Lhe; MChB; Mil; NSPM; O; SIR; Yb.
> Gillow (I, 54) also gives a London 1800 ed.

84. *An approved manual of Christian devotions, fitted for all persons and occasions.* London. 1760. 12°. 286, [2] p. * ECW.
> Inserted card says '1766'. For a general treatment of the manual see Blom (chapter 6).

85. *An approved manual of devout prayers, and other Christian devotions. Permissu superiorum.* London. 1753. 12°. 285, [3] p. * Gi.

86. *An approved manual of devout prayers, and other Christian devotions, fitted for all persons and occasions ... With a new version of Dies irae.* London. 1769. 18°. 285, [3] p. ESTC t079986. * L.

87. Archer, James. *A sermon on the love of our country, preached at the Catholic Chapel, White Street, Little Moor Fields ... for a general fast.* [London]. 1799. 8°. 28 p. Printed by: Low, S. Published by: Booker, E.; Keating, P. * Osc.

88. Archer, James. *A sermon, preached at Saint Patrick's Chapel, Sutton-Stree [sic], Soho-Square, on Monday, the eighteenth of March, M.DCC.XCIII.* London. [1793]. 8°. 30 p. Printed by: Keating, P. Published by: Keating, P. Sold by: Coghlan, J.P.; Booker; Lewis. ESTC t084379. * BAA; C; ECW (imp.); L; Lhe; Stan; Sto; ViW.
> With a final advertisement leaf. Sto has a variant tp on which 'Sutton Street' is spelt correctly. Stan has no adverts.

89. Archer, James. *Sermons on various moral and religious subjects, for all the Sundays, and some of the principal festivals of the year.* 4 vols. London.

1785-86. 8°. viii, 407, [1]; iv, 380; iv, 369, [1]; iv, 414 p. Published by: Author. Sold by: Booker, T. ESTC a005169. * DAE; Do; ECR; ECW; Hen; Map; NSPM (vols 1,3); O (vol. 2); Stan (vol. 2).

> Vol. 1 has the date 1785, vols 2-4, 1786. Vols 1 & 2 are listed in ESTC as t195797. NSPM adds 'page nos in round brackets'.

90. Archer, James. *Sermons on various moral and religious subjects, for all the Sundays, and some of the principal festivals of the year.* 5 vols. London. 1786. 8°. Published by: Author. Sold by: Booker, T. ESTC a005168. * Hor (vol. 2); NSPM (vols 1, 2 (-tp), 4 (-tp), 5).

> Tp of vol. 5 bears the imprint 'Printed by J.P. Coghlan; and sold by T. Booker; P. Keating; and T. Lewis'. This might be another issue of no. 89.

91. Archer, James. *Sermons on various moral and religious subjects for all the Sundays, and some of the principal festivals of the year.* Dublin. 1788. 8°. x, 613, [1] p. Printed by: Byrne, P. ESTC t207393. * D; FLK; IDA.

92. Archer, James. *Sermons on various moral and religious subjects, for all the Sundays and some of the principal festivals of the year.* London. 1789. 8°. vii, [1], 319. [1] p. Printed by: Coghlan, J.P. Sold by: Booker, T.; Keating, P.; Lewis, T. ESTC t084371. * CaOHM; E; ECR; ECW; Hen; ICN; L; Lhe; NSPM; TxU.

> With final advertisement leaf lacking in Lhe. NSPM states that the book is part of a 5-volume ed. of which vols 1-4 are missing.

93. Archer, James. *Sermons on various moral and religious subjects, for all the Sundays, and some of the principal festivals of the year.* 2nd ed. 4 vols. London. 1794. 12°. Printed by: Low, S. Published by: Booker, E. ESTC t084370. * CaOHM; E; ECW (vols 1-3); Hen; L; Lfa; SIR; Yb.

94. Archer, James. *Sermons on various moral and religious subjects for all the Sundays and some of the principal festivals of the year.* 3rd ed. 2 vols. Dublin. 1799. 12°. viii, 498; vi, 476 p. Printed by: Byrne, P. ESTC n024127. * Dt; Du; FLK; IObT; Lhe; NNUT; SIR.

95. Arnauld, Antoine and Pierre Nicole. *The constant belief of the Catholick church in all ages, concerning the eucharist. Done into English [Perpétuité de la foy de l'église Catholique sur l'eucharistie].* London. 1710. 8°. [8], 78 p. ESTC t132417. * Do; ECW; ICN; KU-S; L; Lhe; Llp; MRu; O; PP; Stan; Ush.

96. Arnauld, Antoine and Pierre Nicole. *The constant belief of the Catholick church in all ages, concerning the eucharist. Done into English.* [London]. 1719. 8°. [6], 78 p. Published by: [Meighan, T.]. * Lfa; Osc; Stan; Ush.

97. *The art of singing: or, a short and easy method, for obtaining a perfect knowledge of the Gregorian note.* London. 1748. 12°. 24 p. Published by: Meighan, T. ESTC t191344. * DMR; Map; O; Stan (imp.); TH.

> DMR, Map, Stan, and TH are bound up with *The evening-office*, 1748 (no. 996). With some Meighan adverts.

98. *The art of singing, or a short and easy method for obtaining a perfect knowledge of the Gregorian note.* Dublin. 1754. 12°. 22, [2] p. Published by: Kelly, E. ESTC t181886. * D(2); IDA; Map.

10

One of the D copies has an advertisement leaf. IDA is bound up with *The evening-office*, 1754 (no. 997); Map with *The evening-office*, 1748 (no. 995).

99. Arvisenet, Claude. *Memoriale vitae sacerdotalis a sacerdote Gallicano, dioecesis Lingonensis exule redactum.* Anon. London. 1795. 8°. 318, [6] p. Printed by: Dulonchamp, J. ESTC t172072. * DoA; E; Hen; Lfa; Lhe; MRu; O.
> 'Sacerdote Gallicano' refers to Claude Arvisenet. See also next 2 items.

100. Arvisenet, Claude. *Memoriale vitae sacerdotalis, a sacerdote Gallicano, dioecesis Linconensis exule redactum ... aucta psalmis et orationibus consuetis ante et post missam.* 2nd ed. [Anon.] London. 1795. 12°. 214, [2] p. Printed by: Clarke, C. ESTC t124426. * L; Lfa.

101. Arvisenet, Claude. *Memoriale vitae sacerdotalis, a sacerdote Gallicano, dioecesis Lingonensis exule redactum.* Anon. Dublin. 1797. 8°. [3], iv-vi, [1], 8-248, [4] p. Printed by: Fitzpatrick, H. ESTC t212703. * Dt; FLK; MY; Osc.
> With 2 pages of adverts.

102. *As it is very well known that many inconveniences attend the Bell Tree House ... it is hoped that the proposal of a subscription ... will meet with the approbation of the gentlemen.* [Bath]. [1777]. fol. s.s. * DowA; Lil.
> A list of 69 subscribers to the new chapel proposed at Bath, dated 'Bath, March 14, 1777'. This chapel was later destroyed in the Gordon Riots.

103. *As the following piece is frequently quoted ... in ... The relations of Mr Talbot ... it has been thought proper to have this also printed. Answer to a paper called The reply.* 4°. 11, [1] p. * LfaA.
> See note to no. 61.

104. *At a general meeting of Catholics held at Free-Masons Tavern, on Thursday the 21st instant.* [1793]. s.s. * BAA.
> Draft of an address to the King. Signed and dated 'Henry Clifford, 1793 February 22, Lincoln's Inn'.

105. *At a general meeting of English Catholics, at the Crown and Anchor Tavern in the Strand. The right honourable Lord Petre in the chair.* [London]. [1791]. fol. 3, [1] p. ESTC t022592. * BAA; Cli; DowA; L; SIR; Sto.
> Dated 'June 9, 1791'. The text concerns the question of the oath and ends with a letter from Charles Butler, the secretary Catholic Committee.

106. *At a general meeting of the English Catholics at Free-Masons Hall, Great Queen Street.* [London]. [1787]. fol. 2 p. * Ush.
> Dated 'May 3, 1787'.

107. *At a general meeting of the English Catholics, held at Free Mason's Hall, May 15, 1788. John Throckmorton Esq. in the chair.* [London]. [1788]. fol. [2] p. * O; Sto; Ush.

108. *At a general meeting of the Roman Catholics of the county and city of Cork, convened by public advertisements, held at the Cork Tavern, the 15th October, 1792.* [Cork]. 1792. fol. s.s. Printed by: Flyn, W. ESTC n033349. * CSmH.
> Signed 'Justin McCarthy, chairman'.

109. *At a meeting held at the Crown and Anchor in the Strand, on the 1st of*

May, 1794. The right honorable Lord Stourton in the chair. [1794]. fol. 3, [1] p. * Cli; O; Sto.

> Signed 'William Havers, secretary'.

110. *At a meeting held on the 15th of January, 1787. To consider of the most proper means to be adopted for the support of the Catholic Chapel in Bath.* [1787]. fol. s.s. * Cli.

111. *At a meeting of gentlemen educated at Old Hall Green, held at the Shakespear Tavern, in Covent Garden, on Thursday the 28th instant, present, Henry Clifford, Esq. in the chair.* [London?]. [1796]. 4°. [2] p. * Sto.

> Dated 'April 30th, 1796'.

112. *At a meeting of the general committee of the Catholics of Ireland. The resolutions and instructions transmitted from various parts of the kingdom ... having been read.* [Dublin]. [1791]. fol. 3, [1] p. ESTC n043690. * Lpro.

> Dated 'Dublin, 10th February 1791'.

113. *At a meeting of the general committee of Roman Catholics, it was resolved, that the following letter should be addressed to the different committees, and to the principal persons of our persuasion.* [Dublin?]. [1792]. fol. 2, [2] p. ESTC n043711. * Lpro.

> Signed and dated 'Edward Byrne, chairman, Dublin, 14 January, 1792'.

114. *At a meeting of the sub-committee of the Catholics of Ireland, Edward Byrne, Esq. in the chair, resolved - that the following letter be signed by our chairman.* [Londonderry]. [1792]. fol. 3, [1] p. Printed by: Glen, S. ESTC n043670. * Lpro.

> Signed and dated 'Edward Byrne. May 26th, 1792'. Imprint from colophon.

115. *At a meeting of the sub-committee of the Catholics of Ireland, Edward Byrne, Esq. in the chair, resolved - that the following letter be signed by our chairman.* [Dublin]. [1792]. fol. 3, [1] p. Printed by: Fitzpatrick, H. ESTC n043677. * Lpr.

> Dated 'May 26th, 1792'.

116. *At a meeting of the sub-committee of the Catholics of Ireland, Edward Byrne, Esq. in the chair, resolved - that the following letter be circulated.* [Dublin?]. [1792?]. 4°. 3, [1] p. ESTC n014668. * CSmH.

> Signed 'Richard McCormick, secretary'. A declaration of unity among Irish Catholics in support of emancipation.

117. *At a meeting of the sub-committee of the Catholics of Ireland, Edward Byrne, Esq. in the chair. Resolved - that the following letter be signed by our chairman.* [Dublin?]. [1792?]. fol. 4 p. ESTC n043672. * Lpro.

> Signed 'Edward Byrne'.

118. *At a special meeting of the English Catholics, held for the purpose of taking into consideration the propriety of establishing a school.* [1787]. fol. s.s. * Ush.

> Dated 'May 15, 1787'. The meeting itself took place on May 7, 1787.

119. *At an adjourned general meeting of the Roman Catholic nobility and gentry assembled at the Crown and Anchor Tavern ... 5th of February 1795.* [1795]. 4°. 4 p. * Cli.

Signed 'William Havers, secretary'.

120. *At the annual assembly of the Roman Catholic clergy of the county of Lancaster held the 30th day of August 1791, at Preston ... was resolved.* [London]. [1791]. s.s. Printed by: Coghlan, J.P. ESTC t022664. * BAA; L; Sto; Ush.

>The Latin part of the text signed 'Gul. Dun, S. Th. Gul. Fisher' and 28 others.

121. *At the general meeting of the Roman Catholic clergy of the county of Lancaster, held the 30th day of August 1791 at Preston.* London. fol. s.s. Published by: Coghlan, J.P. * Cli.

>Address from the Lancaster clergy to 3 vicars apostolic expressing support. Cf. no. 120. Latin and English.

122. Augustine, Saint. *The manual of the glorious doctor St. Augustine.* 2nd ed. Dublin. 1760. 16°. 126, [2] p. Printed by: Hoey, J. ESTC t172662. * D.

>Not in fact by Augustine. With a final advertisement leaf.

123. Augustine, Saint. *The meditations of St. Augustine. Permissu superiorum [De meditatione].* 2nd ed. Dublin. 1760. 18°. xiii, [1], 242 p. Printed by: Hoey, J. * O.

>This and the next item not in fact by Augustine.

124. Augustine, Saint. *The meditations of Saint Augustine, from the Latin original. By the rev. J. Martin, O.S.A.* Dublin. 1798. 12°. [10], 183, [7] p. Printed by: Fitzpatrick, H. Published by: Author. ESTC t124470. * IDA; IU; L; Lhe; Yb.

125. Augustine, Saint. *The rule of S. Augustin, as also the statutes & constitutions of the English regular canonesses of the order of St. Augustin established at Bridges in Flanders.* 1717. 4°. [6], 17, [1], 131, [5] p. * ECB(2).

>One copy has the ms note 'Given to us by the Bishop of Bruges'.

126. Augustine, Saint. *The rule of the glorious doctor of the church, our holy father S. Augustine, originally drawn up for the use of the nuns instituted by him.* 1768. 12°. 34 p. * ECB.

>'Preface to the rule of S. Augustine, compiled by ... Nicholas Loes, Lord Bishop of Bois-le-Duc'. According to ms note this was translated from Latin into English by Alban Butler.

127. Augustine, Saint. *St. Augustine's confessions; or praises of God. In ten books. Newly translated into English from the original Latin [Confessiones].* [London]. 1739. 12°. [4], 390, [18] p. Published by: Meighan, T. ESTC t097729. * CAL; CLU-C; Do; DoA; E; ECB; ECW; FK; GEU-T; ICN; L; Map; O; P; Stan; TLP; TxU; Ush.

>Translated by Challoner (see also next 3 items). Copies vary as to the number of advert pages. Some copies have Meighan adverts only, others have also adverts for Marmaduke and Needham.

128. Augustine, Saint. *St. Augustine's confessions; or, praises of God. In ten books. Newly translated into English from the original Latin.* Dublin. 1746. 12°. [4], 415, [17] p. Printed by: Bate, E. Published by: Connor, C. ESTC t082142. * D; Dt; ECW (imp.); L; PU.

Gillow (I, 453) also mentions a 1762 ed.

129. Augustine, Saint. *St. Augustine's confessions: or, praises of God. In ten books. Newly translated into English from the original Latin.* Dublin. 1770. 12°. [4], 411, [17] p. Printed by: Kiernan, F. Published by: Cross, R. ESTC t178751. * CStclU; D; IDA; O.

130. Augustine, Saint. *St. Augustine's confessions: or, praises of God. In ten books. Newly translated into English, from the original Latin.* Dublin. 1795. 12°. [4], 411, [17] p. Printed by: Wogan, P. ESTC t160321. * C; CAL; DoA; ICN; O; TxU.

131. Augustine, Saint. *The soliloquies of the glorious doctor, Saint Augustine: being the secret discourses and conferences of his soul with God [Soliloquia animae ad Deum].* Dublin. 1747. 18°. 143, [1] p. Published by: Lamb, J. ESTC t097726. * L; TxU.
This and the next item not in fact by Augustine.

132. Augustine, Saint. *The soliloquies of the glorious doctor, Saint Augustine: being the secret discourses and conferences of his soul with God.* Dublin. 1774. 18°. 143, [1] p. Published by: Wogan, P. ESTC t178675. * D.

133. Austin, John. *Devotions in the ancient way of offices; containing exercises for every day in the week, and every holiday in the year.* Edinburgh. 1789. 8°. vii, [1], 555, [1] p. Printed by: Mundell and Son. Sold by: Coghlan, J.P. (London); Downie, D. (Edinburgh). ESTC t079358. * Do; E; Gi; L; Lhe; Llp; O; TH; Ush.

134. *Authentic statement of the proceedings of the Roman Catholics of Dublin, April 9, 1795, on receiving the report of Baron Hussey, of Galtrim, Edward Byrne, Esq. and Bryan Keogh.* London. [1795]. 8°. [4], 38, [2] p. Printed by: Debrett, J. ESTC n033346. * D; MChB; RP.
With a final advertisement leaf.

135. Baker, Pacificus. *A brief essay on the confraternity of the cord of the seraphical father St. Francis. With instructions and devotions for those who wear the cord. Permissu superiorum. By P.B. Ord. S.P.F.* [London]. 1752. 12°. 31, [1] p. Printed by: Marmaduke, J. Published by: Marmaduke, J. * Map; WDA.
With 1½ pages of Marmaduke adverts.

136. Baker, Pacificus. *The Christian Advent, or entertainments for that holy season: in moral reflections and pious thoughts and aspirations ... By P.B. O.S.F.* London. 1755. 12°. viii, 9-184 p. Printed by: Marmaduke, J. Sold by: Marmaduke, J. ESTC t132768. * CLU; DMR; Do; E (imp.); ECW; FLK; Hen; L; Lfa; Map; O; PcA.

137. Baker, Pacificus. *The Christian Advent, or, entertainments for that holy season: in moral reflections and pious thoughts and aspirations ... By P.B.* 2nd ed. London. 1759. 12°. viii, [3], 10-270, [2] p. Sold by: Marmaduke, J.; Needham, W. ESTC t115863. * DAE; Do; DoA; E; ECW; Gi; Hor; L; Lhe; LO; O; Sal; TLP; Yb.
Copies vary as to the place of the contents leaf.

138. Baker, Pacificus. *The Christian Advent, or, entertainments for that holy season: in moral reflections and pious thoughts and aspirations ... By P.B.* 3rd ed. London. 1768. 12°. viii, 9-270, [2] p. Sold by: Meighan, T.; Coghlan, J.P. * Amp; Do; DoA; Lhe.

139. Baker, Pacificus. *The Christian Advent, or, entertainments for that holy season: in moral reflections and pious thoughts and aspirations on the gospel.* 3rd ed. London. 1782. 12°. xi, [1], 242, [2] p. Printed by: Coghlan, J.P. ESTC t115751. * Do; E; ECB; FLK; Gi; L; Lhe; MWH; Stan; Sto; TxU.
> With a final leaf of Coghlan adverts. For another issue see *The works*, vol. 1 (no. 164). This is the second '3rd' ed.

140. Baker, Pacificus. *The devout Christian's companion for holy-days; or pious reflections and aspirations on the gospels for the festivals of our blessed Lord ... By P.B. O.S.F.* London. 1757. 12°. xx, 484 p. Printed by: Marmaduke, J. Sold by: Marmaduke, J. ESTC t131493. * DMR; Do; DoA; E; ECW; FLK; Gi; Hen; Hor; L; LO; Map; O; TLP; Ush.

141. Baker, Pacificus. *The devout Christian's companion for holy-days; or pious reflections and aspirations on the gospels for the festivals of our blessed Lord ... By P.B. O.S.F.* 2nd ed. London. 1765. 12°. [2], xxv, [1], 484 p. Published by: Meighan, T.; Coghlan, J.P. Sold by: Meighan, T.; Coghlan, J.P. ESTC t185867. * CAL; DMR; Do; ECW; FLK; Gi; Lhe; O; Ush.

142. Baker, Pacificus. *The devout Christian's companion for holy-days; or pious reflections and aspirations on the gospels for the festivals of our blessed Lord ... By P.B. O.S.F.* 3rd ed. London. 1773. 12°. [4], xxv, [1], 484 p. Printed by: Coghlan, J.P. Sold by: Coghlan, J.P. ESTC t185865. * Do; ECW; O; Stan; Yb.
> For another issue see *The works*, vol. 3 (no. 164).

143. Baker, Pacificus. *The devout Christian's companion for holy days; or, pious reflections and aspirations on the gospels for the festivals of our blessed Lord.* 4th ed. London. 1799. 12°. xx, 432 p. Printed by: Coghlan, J.P. ESTC n030994. * CLU; Do; E; ECW; Lhe; MY; Stan; Sto; TxU.

144. Baker, Pacificus. *The devout communicant; or, spiritual entertainments before and after communion. In pious meditations, aspirations ... By P.B. O.S.F.* London. 1761. 12°. x, 166 p. Sold by: Gibson, N.; Needham, W. ESTC t218875. * Amp; Do; Map; P.

145. Baker, Pacificus. *The devout communicant; or, spiritual entertainments before and after communion. In pious meditations, aspirations ... By P.B. O.S.F.* 2nd ed. London. 1765. 12°. xii, 214 p. Printed by: Balfe, R. * CAL; LO.

146. Baker, Pacificus. *The devout communicant; or, spiritual entertainments before and after communion. In pious meditations, aspirations ... By P.B. O.S.F.* 3rd ed. London. 1768. 12°. xii, 13-213, [1] p. Printed by: Balfe, R. Sold by: Meighan, T.; Lewis, T.; Coghlan, J.; Marmaduke, J. * Do.

147. Baker, Pacificus. *The devout communicant: or, spiritual entertainments before and after communion. In pious meditations, aspirations.* 4th ed. London. 1779. 12°. xii, 206, [10] p. Printed by: Coghlan, J.P. ESTC t185050. * Do;

ECW; O.

> With 6 pages of Coghlan adverts. For another issue see *The works*, vol. 4 (no. 164).

148. Baker, Pacificus. *The devout communicant; or, spiritual entertainments before and after communion. In pious meditations.* 5th ed. London. 1794. 12°. 203, [1] p. Printed by: Coghlan, J.P. ESTC t164989. * BMp; ECW; Lhe; TxU.

> Gillow (I, 118) also mentions a 6th ed., London 1798.

149. Baker, Pacificus. *The devout communicant; or, spiritual entertainments ... With a devout method of visiting the blessed sacrament ... The whole revised and enlarged, by ... William Gahan.* Anon. Dublin. 1794. 12°. 192 p. Printed by: M'Donnell, T. ESTC t164990. * D; Du.

150. Baker, Pacificus. *The devout communicant or spiritual entertainments ... With a devout method of visiting the blessed sacrament ... revised and enlarged by William Gahan.* 2nd ed. Dublin. 1794. 12°. xii, 13-192 p. Printed by: M'Donnell, T. * FLK; IDA; Mil.

151. Baker, Pacificus. *The devout communicant; or, spiritual entertainments ... With a devout method of visiting the blessed sacrament ... To which is added an appendix ... revised and enlarged by William Gahan.* Anon. Cork. 1794. 12°. xii, 13-190 p. Printed by: Haly, J. ESTC t167493. * D.

> The preface refers to the 'editor of this first Dublin edition'. The author is identified on p. iii.

152. Baker, Pacificus. *The devout communicant; or, spiritual entertainments ... With a devout method of visiting the blessed sacrament ... revised and enlarged by the rev. William Gahan.* 3rd ed. Anon. Dublin. 1798. 18°. xii, 204 p. Printed by: M'Donnell, T. ESTC t201439. * D; Dt.

153. Baker, Pacificus. *Holy altar and sacrifice explained: in some familiar dialogues on the mass, and what may appertain to it. By P.B. O.S.F.* London. 1768. 12°. iv, 167, [1] p. * BB; Do; ECW; Gi; Lhe; Map.

> An abridgment of Richard Mason's *Liturgical discourse of the holy sacrifice of the mass* (Clancy nos 647-9).

154. Baker, Pacificus. *Holy altar and sacrifice explain'd: in some familiar dialogues on the mass, and what may appertain to it: ... With an appendix, concerning saying mass in Latin ... By P.B. O.S.F.* London. 1768. 12°. vi, 258 p. Sold by: Lewis, T.; Meighan, T.; Coghlan, J.P.; Marmaduke, J. ESTC t088943. * Do; E; ECW; FLK; L; O; OrPU; TxU; Yb.

> The appendix is Gother's *Instructions and devotions for hearing mass*, 1767 (no. 1236).

155. Baker, Pacificus. *Holy altar and sacrifice explained: in some familiar dialogues on the mass, and what may appertain to it. By P.B. O.S.F.* London. 1792. 12°. viii, 208 p. Printed by: Coghlan, J.P. ESTC t204735. * Amp; Do; E; ECW; Lhe; LO; ScCR.

> With 2 pages of Coghlan adverts. For another issue see *The works*, vol. 5 (no. 164).

156. Baker, Pacificus. *A lenten monitor to Christians, in pious thoughts, moral* *reflections, and devout aspirations, on the gospels, for every day in Lent ... By P.B. O.S.F.* London. 1755. 12°. xii, 364, [4] p. Printed by: Marmaduke, J. Sold by: Marmaduke, J. ESTC t194622. * ECW; FLK; Lhe; Map; Nijm; O; Yb.

> With 4½ pages of Marmaduke adverts.

157. Baker, Pacificus. *A lenten monitor, to Christians, in pious thoughts, moral reflections, and devout aspirations on the gospels for every day in Lent ... By P.B. O.S.F.* 2nd ed. London. 1760. 12°. [2], xii, 432 p. Sold by: Marmaduke, J.; Needham, W. ESTC n019455. * Do; DoA; ECW; IES; L; NSPM; TLP; TxU; Ush; Yb.

158. Baker, Pacificus. *A lenten monitor to Christians, in pious thoughts, moral reflections, and devout aspirations on the gospels, for every day in Lent ... By P.B. O.S.F.* 3rd ed. London. 1769. 12°. [2], xii, 432 p. Sold by: Meighan, T.; Lewis, T.; Marmaduke, J.; Coghlan, J.P. ESTC t194605. * DMR; ECB; ECW; Gi; Lhe; LO; O; Ush.

159. Baker, Pacificus. *A lenten monitor to Christians, in pious thoughts, moral reflections, and devout aspirations on the gospels, for every day in Lent.* 3rd ed. London. 1792. 12°. xi, [1], 372 p. Printed by: Coghlan, J.P. ESTC t089935. * CLU; Do (-tp); ICN; L; Lhe; O; Stan; TLP; TxU.

> This is the second '3rd' ed. For another issue see *The works*, vol. 2 (no. 164).

160. Baker, Pacificus. *A sermon on the parable of the grain of mustard-seed, by P.B., O.F.M.* [London]. 1753. 8°. [1], 27 p. Printed by: [Marmaduke, J.]. * Do; Map; Osc; Ush.

> With a final page of Marmaduke adverts.

161. Baker, Pacificus. *Sundays kept holy; in moral reflections, pious thoughts, and devout aspirations ... Being a supplement to the Christian Advent and lenten monitor ... By P.B. O.S.F.* London. 1760. 12°. xii, 279, [1] p. Sold by: Marmaduke, J.; Needham, W. ESTC n037627. * CAL; ECW; Hen; Lhe; Map; O; TLP; TxU; Yb.

162. Baker, Pacificus. *Sundays kept holy; in moral reflections, pious thoughts, and devout aspirations, on the gospels ... Being a supplement to the Christian Advent and lenten monitor ... By P.B. O.S.F.* 2nd ed. London. 1772. 12°. xii, 13-288 p. Published by: Author; Coghlan, J.P. ESTC t131505. * Do; L; Lhe.

163. Baker, Pacificus. *Sundays kept holy; in moral reflections, pious thoughts and devout aspirations on the gospels ... To which is added, a discourse on the grain of mustard seed.* 2nd ed. London. 1792. 12°. xii, 268 p. Printed by: Coghlan, J.P. ESTC n037628. * DMR; ECW; FLK; Lhe; LO; Stan; Sto; TxU.

> For another issue see *The works*, vol. 1 (no. 164).

164. Baker, Pacificus. *The works of the reverend father Pacificus Baker.* 5 vols. London. [1792]. 12°. [2], xii, 265-8, 264, xi, [1], 242, [2]; [2], xi, [1], 372; [6], xxv, [1], 484; [2], 206, 10; [2], viii, 208 p. Published by: Coghlan, J.P. * Do (vol. 1); ECW.

> Vol. 4 has 5 pages of Coghlan adverts. The series in fact consists of reissues of other works by Baker, previously published by Coghlan. See nos 139, 142, 147, 155, 159, 163.

165. Bandot, Seraphin. *Discours prononcé le 4 Juillet, jour de l'anniversaire de l'indépendance, dans l'église Catholique, par le reverend père Seraphin Bandot.* Philadelphia. [1779]. s.s. Printed by: Steiner & Cist. ESTC w015044. * PPL.

> Bandot was chaplain to the French plenipotentiary in the United States.

166. Barbandt, Charles. *Sacred hymns, anthems and versicles, for morning and evening service, on all Sundays and festivals throughout the year, taken out of the public liturgy of the Church, and set to music.* London. 1766. 4°. [2], iv, 87, [1], iv, 108 p. Published by: Author. ESTC n017478. * CaOHM; Ct.

> With tp in Latin, English and French.

167. Bareau de Girac, François. *Lettre de mgr. l'évêque de Rennes, aux prêtres de son diocèse, exilés pour la cause de la foi.* London. 1796. 8°. 30 p. Printed by: Baylis. ESTC t079446. * CSmH; L; P.

> Dated 'Königsworth, le 15 octobre 1795'.

168. Barnard, James. *A catechism. Or collection of some points of Christian faith and morality, composed in verse.* London. 1786. 12°. vi, 84 p. Printed by: Coghlan, J.P. ESTC t079784. * E; ECW; Gi; L; Lfa; TxU; Ush; UshL.

> For critical reactions on this work see Gillow (I, 137); James Barnard was vicar general of the London district.

169. Barnard, James. *The dignity, labours and reward of apostolick missionaries proposed in a sermon preached March the twelfth, 1781 ... at Lisbon ... Together with a short exhortation.* London. 1782. 12°. 93, [1], p. Printed by: Coghlan, J.P. ESTC t185449. * Do; E; ECW; MY; O; Sco; UshL.

> Gillow (I, 137) also gives a London 1786 ed.

170. Barnard, James. *The divinity of our Lord Jesus Christ demonstrated from the holy scriptures, and from the doctrine of the primitive church ... in a series of letters ... to the rev. Dr. Joseph Priestley.* London. 1789. 12°. xxii, [2], 371, [1] p. Printed by: Coghlan, J.P. Sold by: Robinsons, Messrs. ESTC t082003. * C; CLU; Do; E; ECW; Gu; IU; L; Lhe; MH; MWH; O; P; PU; Sto; TxU; Ush; UshL; Vat.

171. Barnard, James. *A general view of the arguments for the divinity of Christ, and plurality of persons in God. From the holy scriptures.* London. 1793. 12°. 30, ii, p. Published by: Barnard, J. Sold by: Coghlan, J.P.; Robinsons, Messrs. ESTC t061764. * C; E; ECW; Gu; L; Lhe; Ush.

> With a final leaf of advertisements.

172. Barnard, James. *The life of the venerable and right reverend Richard Challoner, D.D. Bishop of Debra, and V.A. Collected from his writings.* London. 1784. 8°. xii, 284 p. Printed by: Coghlan, J.P. ESTC t068579. * C; DAE; DoA; ECR; ECW; Gi; Hor; ICN; L; Lfa; Lhe; LO; Map; MRu; NSPM; O(2); SIR; Stan; Sto; TLP; TxU; Ush.

> The two O copies represent two different issues with different frontispieces.

173. Barnard, James. *The life of the venerable and right reverend Richard Challoner ... Collected from his writings.* Dublin. 1793. 12°. xix, [1], 234, [2] p. Printed by: Fitzpatrick, H. ESTC t130536. * D; Dt; FLK; ICR; IDA; L; LfaA; Map; MY; SIR.

With a list of subscribers. SIR has an issue with pagination iv, [2], 234, while the pagination of FLK is xvi, [2], 234 p.

174. Barnardin, Father. *A discourse delivered in the church of the English dames of St. Clare, at Air in Artois, on the admission and cloathing sister Mary-Elizabeth of Jesus, the 25th of May, 1783.* 6th impression. Anon. Douai. [1783]. 12°. 11, (1) p. ESTC n046094. * Amp; CSmH.

This and the following two discourses by Barnardin were delivered on the occasion of the clothings of two of the daughters of the publisher J.P. Coghlan and the profession of one of them.

175. Barnardin, Father. *A second discourse in the church of the English dames of St. Clare, at Aire in Artois, on the solemn profession of sister Mary-Elizabeth of Jesus, on the fourth day of October, 1784.* [Douai?]. 1785. 12°. 15, [1] p. * Amp; Osc.

Coghlan's personal involvement might also suggest London as the place of publication. See also next item.

176. Barnardin, Father. *A third discourse delivered in the church of the English dames of St. Clare ... on the cloathing and admitting to the noviceship of sister Mary-Anne-Joseph of Jesus, on the twenty-fifth of July, 1785.* [Douai?]. 1785. 12°. 14 p. * Amp; Osc.

177. Barral, Louis Matthias de. *Réponse à une brochure intitulée: Véritable état de la question de la promesse de fidélité à la constitution, demandée aux pretres.* London. 1800. 12°. 96, [2] p. * Map.

A reply to a pamphlet by Henri Benoit Jules de Bethisy de Mézières, Bishop of Uzès. See also no. 2525.

178. Barruel, Augustin. *A l'anonyme, auteur du soi-disant véritable état de la question de la promesse de fidélité, l'abbé Barruel.* London. 1800. 12°. [2], 9, [1] p. Printed by: [Dulau, A. & Co.; Nardini, L]. ESTC t080001. * L; TxU.

Dated '19 Sept. 1800'. The 'anonymous author' is Bethisy de Mézières.

179. Barruel, Augustin. *Abrégé des mémoires pour servir à l'histoire du Jacobinisme.* London. 1798. 8°. [4], iv, [2], xv, [1], 456 p. Published by: Boussonnier, P. le, & Co. Sold by: Boffe; Boosey; Booker; Fauche, P. (Hamburg). ESTC t080473. * CaAEU; CaOTU (imp.); CaQMBN; CaQQLa; E; L; Maas; MChB; MRu; NIC.

180. Barruel, Augustin. *Abrégé des mémoires pour servir à l'histoire du Jacobinisme.* London. 1799. 8°. [4], iv, xvi, 424 p. Published by: Boussonnier, P. le, & Co. Sold by: Fauche, P. (Hamburg and Brunswick). ESTC t080474. * AMu; CaAEU; Gron; L; Maas; MiEM.

Probably printed in Germany.

181. Barruel, Augustin. *Abstract of the history of the clergy during the revolution in France. Dedicated to the English nation [Histoire du clergé].* London. 1794. 8°. viii, 53, [1] p. Printed by: Nichols, J. Sold by: Robinson, G.G. and J. ESTC n043146. * MB.

182. Barruel, Augustin. *Détail des raisons péremptoires qui ont déterminé le clergé de Paris et d'autres dioceses à faire la déclaration de fidélité exigée par la* *république.* London. 1800. 12°. [2], 23, [1] p. Printed by: Dulau, A.; Nardini, L. ESTC t080003. * L; Lhe.

> Signed and dated 'l'abbé Barruel Londres le 8 juillet'. Printers' names from colophon and verso of tp.

183. Barruel, Augustin. *A dissertation on ecclesiastical jurisdiction in the Catholic church.* London. 1794. 8°. vii, [1], 130, [2] p. Printed by: Coghlan, J.P. Sold by: Debrett, J.; Booker; Keating; Lewis; De Boffe; Robinsons; Robins (Winchester); Gregory (Brighton); Leger (Dover); Watts (Gosport). ESTC n028572. * E; ECW; ICN; L; Lfa; Lhe; Llp; MRu; PP; SIR; Sto; TxU; Ush.

> With a final advertisement leaf. Lhe is bound up with nos 2314 and 2744.

184. Barruel, Augustin. *L'évangile et le clergé François, sur la soumission des pasteurs, dans les révolutions des empires.* London. 1800. 12°. 87, [1] p. Printed by: Dulau, A.; Nardini, L. ESTC t080006. * L; MH.

> L has 66 pages of ms note in reply to the above, entitled 'De la soumission passive'.

185. Barruel, Augustin. *Histoire du clergé pendant la révolution Françoise ouvrage dédié à la nation Angloise.* London. 1793. 8°. x, 414 p. Printed by: Coghlan, J.P. Sold by: Lemaire (Brussels). ESTC n003647. * CAL; LOU; WaSpG.

> CAL and WaSpG lack the third part (pp. 231-414).

186. Barruel, Augustin. *Histoire du clergé pendant la révolution Françoise; ouvrage dédié à la nation Angloise.* London. 1793. 8°. [2], ix, [1], 601, [3] p. Printed by: Coghlan, J.P. Sold by: Debrett, J. [and 4 others in London]; Robins (Winchester); Gregory (Brighton); Leger (Dover); Watts (Gosport). ESTC t080487. * C; CaQMM; E; ICIU; ICN; L; Leid; Lfa (imp.); Lhe; Llp; MChB; MRu; O; Tilb; Ush.

187. Barruel, Augustin. *Histoire du clergé, pendant la révolution Françoise.* 2nd ed. London. 1794. 8°. viii, 376 p. Sold by: De Vos, C.H. ESTC t190672. * Leeuw; MRu; Nijm; P; Utr.

> Probably printed in Antwerp.

188. Barruel, Augustin. *Histoire du clergé, pendant la révolution Française.* 2 vols. London. 1797. 12°. Sold by: The Paris booksellers. ESTC n003156. * InU-Li; P.

> Probably printed in Paris. See also next 2 items.

189. Barruel, Augustin. *Histoire du clergé, pendant la révolution Française.* London. 1797. 8°. xvi, 344 p. Sold by: The Paris booksellers. ESTC n017706. * MH; MiEM; P.

190. Barruel, Augustin. *Histoire du clergé, pendant la révolution Française.* 2 vols. London. 1797. 12°. Sold by: The Paris booksellers. ESTC n028934. * MH.

191. Barruel, Augustin. *Histoire du clergé, pendant la révolution Française.* 2 vols. London. 1800. 12°. Printed by: Baylis. ESTC t190674. * C.

192. Barruel, Augustin. *The history of the clergy during the French Revolution. A* *work dedicated to the English nation.* 3 pts. London. 1794. 8°. [4], vii, [1], vi, [2], xvi, 160, 170, 249, [1] p. Printed by: Coghlan, J.P. Sold by: Debrett, J.; Booker; Keating; Lewis; De Boffe; Robinsons; Robins (Winchester); Gregory (Brighton); Leger (Dover); Watts (Gosport). ESTC t080488. * BRp; CaOHM; D; DMR; E; ECB; ECW; GU; Gu; Hen; ICN; InU-Li; L; O; OAU; OU; PPL; TLP; Ush.

The dedication is dated 'May 10, 1793'.

193. Barruel, Augustin. *The history of the clergy during the French Revolution.* 3rd ed. 3 pts. Burlington [N.J.]. 1794. 12°. xii, [1], 4-13, [2], 14-289, 330-423, [1] p. Printed by: Neale, I.; Kammerer, H. ESTC w012727. * CNoS; DB; DGU-W; DLC; IaU; IObT; MH-H; MWA; NjR; NN; OKentU.

The odd pagination is partly due to errors in paging. This is the first American ed.

194. Barruel, Augustin. *The history of the clergy during the French Revolution. A work dedicated to the English nation.* Dublin. 1794. 8°. xxvi, 396 p. Printed by: Fitzpatrick, H. Published by: Wogan, P.; Colbert, H.; Fitzpatrick, H. ESTC t078036. * C; CaBVaS; CU-SB; D; DLC; Dt; ECR; FLK; IDA; IU; L; LEu; Llp; MAJ; MdBJ-P; MY; NbOC; PU; Yb.

195. Barruel, Augustin. *The history of the clergy during the French Revolution. A work dedicated to the English nation.* 3rd ed. Dublin. 1795. 12°. xvi, 344 p. Printed by: Fitzpatrick, H. Published by: Wogan, P.; Fitzpatrick, H. ESTC n008425. * C; CaQMBN; FLK; ICN; IDA; OKentU; PPiPT; SIR.

Note: This is the second '3rd ed.'

196. Barruel, Augustin. *Lettres d'un voyageur à l'abbé Barruel ou nouveaux documens pour ses memoires, nouvelles découvertes faites en Allemagne, anecdotes sur quelques grands personnages de ce pays, chronique de la secte.* [London]. 1800. 8°. [2], iv, [2], 191, [1] p. Printed by: [Dulau & Co.; Nardini, L.]. Sold by: Dulau & Co.; De Boffe; Boosey; Booker; L'Homme. ESTC t080011. * L; MH-H; MiDW; O.

'Un voyageur' is probably Barruel himself. With an advert.

197. Barruel, Augustin. *Mémoires pour servir à l'histoire du Jacobinisme.* 4 vols. London. 1797-1798. 8°. Printed by: Le Boussonnier, P. Sold by: Dulau & Co; de Boffe; Boosey; Booker; Fauche, P. (Hamburg). ESTC t080525. * C; CaOLU (vols 1-3); CaQMBN (vols 3, 4); CaQMM; CU-Riv; DLC; E; GEU; ICU; InU-Li; L; Maas; MRu; Nijm; Oe; Tilb.

Vol. 4 dated 1798.

198. Barruel, Augustin. *Memoirs, illustrating the antichristian conspiracy. A translation from the French of the abbé Barruel [Mémoires pour servir à l'histoire du Jacobinisme. part 1].* Dublin. 1798. 8°. xxiii, [1], 387, [1] p. Printed by: Watson, W., and Son. ESTC t080527. * C; D; Di; DLC; Dt; NNUT; FLK; IDA; L; MY; O; PPAmP; SIR.

Translated by Robert Clifford. See also next three items.

199. Barruel, Augustin. *Memoirs, illustrating the history of Jacobinism [Mémoires pour servir à l'histoire du Jacobinisme].* 4 vols. London. 1797-1798.

8°. Printed by: Burton, T. & Co. Published by: Author. Sold by: Booker, E. ESTC t080526. * BMp; C; CaOHM; Ct; CtY-D; DLC; Dt; Du; E; ICN; IU; L; MRu; NHi; NRU; O.

> Vols 3 and 4 dated 1798.

200. Barruel, Augustin. *Memoirs, illustrating the history of Jacobinism.* 2nd ed. 4 vols. London. 1798. 8°. Printed by: Burton, T. & Co. Published by: Translator. Sold by: Booker, E. ESTC t080528. * CaOTU; CU-S; D; DeGE; E; ICN; InNd; L; MChB; MH-H; MiEM; NBiSU; NIC; O; OU; PPiPT.

201. Barruel, Augustin. *Memoirs illustrating the history of Jacobinism.* 4 vols. New York. 1799. 8°. xviii, 226; viii, v, [1], 264, [2]; xii, 256, [2]; xi, [2], 14-16, [3], 18-400, [2] p. Printed by: Hudson & Goodwin. Published by: Davis, C. ESTC w026110. * CaOLU; CSdS; DB; DLC; MeB; MH-AH; MH-H; MWA; MWH; NjR; NN; TGrT; VtMiM.

> First American ed. from the 2nd London ed. Tp of vol. 4 varies. There are some errors in pagination.

202. Barruel, Augustin. *Réponse de m. l'abbé Barruel a une lettre de M. l'abbé Lambert. Imprimée a Londres en date du 22 Juillet.* London. 1800. 12°. 11, [1] p. Printed by: [Dulau, A. & Co.; Nardini, L.]. Sold by: Dulau, A. & Co. ESTC t080328. * L.

203. Basset, Joshua. *Ecclesiae theoria nova Dodwelliana exposita. Cui accessit rerum, quae indiligentes lectores fugiant, indiculus.* London. 1713. 8°. [14], 152 p. Printed by: Osborne, T. ESTC t089359. * Csj; DUu; L; Ush.

204. Basset, Joshua. *An essay towards a proposal for catholick communion ... By a minister of the Church of England.* London. 1704. 8°. [14], 248 p. Sold by: Nutt, J. ESTC t005919. * C; CaQMM; CSmH; Do; E; ECW; ICN; L; Lhe; Llp; LVu; O; ScCR; Ush.

> In fact a 'pretended' minister (see also next 2 items). Basset's book called forth reactions by Nathaniel Spinckes, Edward Stephens and Samuel Grascome.

205. Basset, Joshua. *An essay towards a proposal for catholic communion ... By a minister of the Church of England.* London. 1705. 8°. [14], 248 p. * Do; Lhe; Ush.

206. Basset, Joshua. *An essay towards a proposal for catholic communion ... By a minister of the Church of England.* Dublin repr. [London]. 1781. 12°. 292 p. Printed by: Bonham, G. Published by: Walker, T. Sold by: Cross, R.; Wogan, P. ESTC t119106. * DU; ICR; L; NNUT (imp.).

207. Batthyany, Jozsef. *A letter from Cardinal Bathiani, primate of Hungary, to the Emperor Joseph II. Translated from the original.* London. 1782. 8°. [2], 70 p. Printed by: Coghlan, J.P. Sold by: Wilkie, G.; Stockdale, J. ESTC t148195. * CSmH; Lu; O; P; Sto (imp.); Ush.

208. Baudrand, Barthélemy. *The elevation of the soul to God, by means of spiritual considerations and affections, translated from the French of Mons. l'abbé B. by R.P. [Ame élevée à Dieu].* 2 vols. Exeter. [1786]. 8°. [4], iii, [5], 310; [8], 299, [1] p. Printed by: Thorn, B., & Son. Sold by: Thorn, B., & Son;

Coghlan, J.P.; Booker, J. * Do; DoA; ECW (vol. 2); Gi (vol. 1); Lhe; LO; Osc; Yb.

> 'R.P.' is Robert Plowden (see also next 3 items). Sommervogel (VI, 907) mentions a 1793 ed.

209. Baudrand, Barthélemy. *The elevation of the soul to God, by means of spiritual considerations and affections. Translated from the French of l'abbé B. by R.P.* 2nd ed. 2 vols in one. Edinburgh. 1792. 8°. [2], [6], 488 p. Printed by: Grant and Moir. Published by: The select library Black-Friars Wynd. Sold by: Booker, T. * Sco.

210. Baudrand, Barthélemy. *The elevation of the soul to God, by means of spiritual considerations and affections. Translated from the French of l'abbé B. by R.P.* 3rd ed. 2 vols. Dublin. 1795. 12°. Printed by: Wogan, P. ESTC t119089. * L; NIC.

211. Baudrand, Barthélemy. *The religious soul elevated to perfection, by the exercises of an interior life; translated from the French op [sic] the abbé Baudrand, by J.P. [sic] [Ame élevée à Dieu].* London. 1786. 12°. xi, [1], 234, [4] p. Printed by: Coghlan, J.P. ESTC t076262. * CAL; DAE; DMR; Do; DoA; ECB; ECW; Gi; ICN; IU; L; Lhe; O; Stan; ViU; Yb.

212. Bayly, Thomas. *The life and death of the renowned John Fisher, Bishop of Rochester, who was beheaded ... 22nd of June, 1535 ... Carefully selected from several ancient records.* London. 1739. 12°. [2], 267, [1] p. Published by: Meighan, P. ESTC t138969. * BB; C; CLU-C; Csj; CtHT-W; Do; DoA; ECW; L; Lfa; Lhe; Sto.

> Edited by (the non-R.C.) T. Coxeter (see also next 2 items). Some copies have a dedication 'To my honoured kinsman Mr. John Questall'. Do and BB have 8 preliminary pages. DoA has a variant with '1739' in ms.

213. Bayly, Thomas. *The life and death of the renowned John Fisher, Bishop of Rochester, who was beheaded ... 22nd of June, 1535 ... Carefully selected from several ancient records.* 3rd ed. Dublin. 1740. 12°. [20], 25-202, 233-298 p. Published by: Keating, J. ESTC t138968. * C; IU; L; P; Sto.

> With a list of subscribers.

214. Bayly, Thomas. *The life and death of the renowned John Fisher, Bishop of Rochester, who was beheaded ... 22nd of June, 1535 ... Carefully selected from several ancient records.* 3rd ed. London. 1740. 12°. [6], 267, [1] p. Published by: Meighan, P. ESTC t138970. * C; CLU-C; Ct; DFo; DMR; DUN; E; ECW; Gi; ICN; KU-S; L; LO; MH; MRu; NcD; ROHp; TxU.

> A reissue of the 1739 ed; this is another '3rd' ed.

215. Bayly, Thomas. *The life and death of the renowned John Fisher, Bishop of Rochester, who was beheaded ... 22nd of June, 1535 ... Carefully selected from several antients [sic] records.* 6th ed. Dublin. 1765. 12°. [2], 169, [1] p. Published by: Lord, P.; Fitzsimmons, R.; Kelly, D. ESTC t119003. * L; MY.

> An issue of the second part of *The lives and deaths of Sir Thomas More ... and of John Fisher* by Thomas Bayly and William Roper, Dublin 1765 (no. 217).

216. Bayly, Thomas and William Roper. *The lives and deaths of Sir Thomas*

More ... and of John Fisher, Bishop of Rochester: who were both beheaded in the reign of H. VIII. 6th ed. Dublin. 1765. 12°. 12, 163, [1], [2], 169, [1] p. Published by: Lord, P.; Fitzsimons, R.; Kylly [sic], D. ESTC t119035. * C; FLK; L; Mil; PHC; StC.

> On tp William Roper is given as Thomas Roper. In 2 parts each with separate pagination and register; part 2 has a separate, dated tp. See also next item.

217. Bayly, Thomas and William Roper. *The lives and deaths of Sir Thomas More ... and of John Fisher, Bishop of Rochester; who were both beheaded in the reign of H. VIII.* 6th ed. Dublin. 1765. 12°. 12, 163, [1], 169, [1] p. Published by: Lord, P.; Fitzsimons, R. ESTC t173527. * D; IDA.

> This is another '6th' ed.

218. Bede, the Venerable. *The ecclesiastical history of the English nation ... Written in Latin by Venerable Bede, translated into English from Dr. Smith's edition [Historia ecclesiastica gentis Anglorum].* London. 1723. 8°. [48], 479, [1] p. Printed by: [Meighan, T.]. Published by: Batley, J.; Meighan, T. ESTC t111716. * AWn; C; CLU-C; Cpl; CU-SB; CYc; DFo; E; Hor; ICN; L; LCp; Ldw; Lfa (-tp); Luk; NOW; O; RPPC; SAW; UGL; UPB; Ush; Yb.

> The book was the result of a cooperation between a Protestant and a Catholic publisher. The notes are by the R.C. Captain John Stevens, who was a prolific translator and editor (d. 1726). The preliminaries include 2 pages of adverts.

219. Bede, the Venerable Saint. *The ecclesiastical history of the English nation ... Written in Latin by Venerable Bede ... and now translated into English by John Stevens gent.* London. 1723. 8°. [44], 479, [5] p. Published by: Meighan, T. ESTC n009064. * CtHT-W; DMR; E; ECW; EXu; Lhe; Luk; MH-L; SIR; TLP; TxU.

> In this ed. Batley's name does not occur in the imprint; with 5 pages of adverts for Batley and Meighan.

220. Bedingfeld, Edward. *A hymn to the Blessed Virgin Mary.* York. 1792. 4°. 12 p. * Lhe; Sto.

221. Bedingfeld, Edward. *A hymn to the Blessed Virgin Mary.* York. 1796. 4°. 10 p. ESTC n003423. * MH-H.

222. Bedingfield, Anne. *A short account of the life and virtues of the venerable and religious mother, Mary of the Holy Cross, abbess of the English Poor Clares at Rouen ... by A.B.* London. 1767. 12°. [2], xix, [1], 21-205, [1] p. ESTC t069975. * AR; BB; C; CAL; CLU; DAE; Do; DoA; ECB; ECW; FLK; Hor; ICN; L; Lhe; LO; Map; MChB; O; Osc; Stan; TLP; TxU; Ush; UshL; Yb.

> Gillow and ms note in Yb attribute this work to Alban Butler. Mother Mary of the Holy Cross was a Howard.

223. Bell, Robert. *Proposals for printing by subscription The Catholic Christian instructed. In the sacraments, sacrifice, ceremonies and observances of the church. By way of question and answer. By R. C.* Philadelphia. [1774]. 12°. [4] p. Printed by: Bell, R. ESTC w001262. * DGU.

> Prospectus for Richard Challoner's *The Catholic Christian*. 'Subscriptions are received by Robert Bell, bookseller, Third-Street ...' The work was apparently never published by Bell.

224. Belsunce de Castelmoron, Henri. *The mandate of the Bishop of Marseilles, concerning the plague in France. Faithfully translated into English, from the original French, printed at Marseilles.* [London?]. 1721. 8°. 13, [1] p. ESTC n034865. * Ct; MY.

225. Ben-Yizaakeer, Abraham. *A second address humbly presented to the reverend, pious and learned D****r G****s, on his late edifying publications, and especially on the first volume of his excellent translation of the holy bible.* London. 1794. 4°. 58 p. Published by: Ephraim Levi. Sold by: Robinsons and Debrett. * Osc.
> A burlesque on Geddes's bible translation. Lhe cat. also lists *The first address*, 1791, of which no further data were available.

226. Benedetti da Todi, Giacopone de'. *Hymn to the Virgin Mary. Set to music by Baron D'Astorga [Stabat mater dolorosa].* Anon. [Oxford?]. [1753?]. 8°. 7, [1] p. ESTC t095186. * ICN; IU; L.
> Perhaps wrongly attributed to G. de Benedetti da Todi. Parallel English and Latin texts, without the music (see also next item).

227. Benedetti da Todi, Giacopone de'. *The plaint of the Blessed Virgin, in Latin and English. The musick composed by Signor Pergolesi [Stabat mater dolorosa].* Dublin. 1749. 4°. 7, [1] p. Printed by: Hoey, J. ESTC t095187. * L.

228. Benedict XIV. *Instructions for gaining the jubily [sic] of the holy year, as extended to the whole Catholick world by our holy father Benedict XIV. Anno 1751.* Dublin. 1751. 12°. 22, [2] p. Published by: Kelly, I. ESTC t188748. * D.
> With a final advertisement leaf.

229. Benedict XIV. *A papal brief, dated 2 September, 1745, confirming the decrees of propaganda concerning the dispute between the vicars apostolic and the regular clergy of the Catholic Church in England.* [London]. [1748]. fol. [4] p. ESTC t085896. * BAA; L; TxU; UshA.
> Signed and dated 'Joannis Thespiensis ... Benjamin Prusen ... Eduardus Mallen ... 1748, August 23'. The papal brief is entitled 'Benedictus P.P. XIV. Ad futuram rei memoriam, emanavit nuper'.

230. Bergier, Nicolas Sylvestre. *Deism self-refuted; or an examination of the principles of infidelity ... throughout the ... works of Mons. Rousseau ... Translated from the fourth edition [Déisme réfuté par lui-même].* 2 vols. [London?]. 1775. 12°. xii, [3], 4-228; [3], 4-214, [2] p. ESTC t119559. * Amp; C; CaQMM; Du; E; ECW; Hor; L; LAM; NSPM (vol. 1); Osc; Ou; Sal; Yb.
> According to Gillow (I, 566) and Kirk (p. 58) translated by Charles Cordell. Gillow and Dr D.M. Rogers suggest Newcastle as place of publication (see also next item).

231. Bergier, Nicolas Sylvestre. *Deism self-refuted; or, an examination of the principles of infidelity ... throughout the ... works of Mons. Rousseau ... Translated from the Paris edition.* 2 vols. Newcastle. Published by: Coates, F. Sold by: Booker, T.; Keating, P. (London); Mehain, J.; Fitzpatrick, H. (Dublin). ESTC t201330. * Amp; Lhe; MY; NCp.

232. Berington, Charles. *To all the faithful of the Midland district. Dearly* *beloved brethren, the season is again returned of proclaiming the annual fast of Christians.* Anon. [1796]. 4°. 3, [1] p. * BAA; Sto.

A lenten pastoral, signed and dated 'Carolus Hiero-Caes. 1796, January 26th'.

233. Berington, Charles. *To all the faithful of the Midland district... Dearly beloved brethren. In these solemn words of a prophet and of an apostle, is the Catholic Church accustomed to proclaim her annual fast of Lent.* [Longbirch?]. [1797]. fol. 3, [1] p. * WDA.

Dated and signed 'Longbirch, Feb. 12, 1797 Car. Hiero-Caes. V.A.'.

234. Berington, Charles. *To all the faithful of the Midland district. Dearly beloved brethren, you have read in the book of Exodus.* [1798]. fol. 3, [1] p. * BAA; Cli.

Dated 'Long-birch, February 9, 1798'.

235. Berington, Charles. *To all the faithful of the Midland district. Dearly beloved brethren, in the present scenes of trouble which continue to disturb the nations of Europe.* [1798]. s.s. * BAA.

Dated '1798, 5 May, Longbirch'.

236. Berington, Charles. *To the clergy of the London district. Gentlemen, the dissensions which have lately prevailed amongst us.* [1790?]. fol. s.s. * Cli; O.

Dated 'Oscot, November 4, 1790'. Berington here gives up his pretensions to the post of V.A. of the London district.

237. Berington, Joseph. *An address to the Protestant dissenters, who have lately petitioned for a repeal of the corporation and test acts.* Birmingham. 1787. 8°. [4], 56 p. Printed by: Swinney, M. Published by: Robinson, G.G.J; Robinson, J.; Faulder, R. ESTC t140599. * BMp; C; CaOHM; Ct; ECW; L; LfaA; Lhe; LU; MBAt; NjR; Oe; Osc; Ush.

238. Berington, Joseph. *An address to the Protestant dissenters.* 2nd ed. Birmingham. 1787. 8°. [2], 61, [1] p. Printed by: Swinney, M. Published by: Robinson, G.G.J. and J.; Faulder, R. ESTC t140600. * BMp; C; L; Ldw; Lhe; Lmh; PU; Sto.

A reissue of the first ed., with a different tp and the addition of pages 57-61, containing a letter by Joseph Priestley.

239. Berington, Joseph. *An essay on the depravity of the nation, with a view to the promotion of Sunday schools, &c. of which a more extended plan is proposed.* Birmingham. 1788. 8°. [4], 50 p. Printed by: Swinney, M. Sold by: Swinney, M.; Robinson, G.G.J. and J. ESTC n016886. * BMp; C; CtY-BR; HLue; KU-S; Ldw; Lhe; Sto; Ush.

A proposal for the foundation of oecumenical Sunday schools. Gillow (I, 193) mentions a London ed. of 1788, and a Birmingham ed. of 1789.

240. Berington, Joseph. *An examination of events, termed miraculous, as reported in letters from Italy.* Oxford. 1796. 8°. 31, [1] p. Printed by: Dawson, W. and Co. Sold by: Cooke, J.; Booker, E. (London). ESTC n007512. * C; DUc; ECW; IU; LfaA; PPL; Sto.

For comments on this publication see George Bruning's *Remarks* (no. 374), and see also nos 247 and 1046.

241. Berington, Joseph. *The history of the lives of Abeillard and Heloisa, comprising a period ... from 1079 to 1163.* Birmingham. 1788. 4°. xxxii, 398, [5], 400-498, [2] p. Printed by: Swinney, M. Published by: Robinson, G.G.J. and J.; Faulder, R. (London). ESTC n008544. * BMp; CaOHM; CLU-S/C; CSt; DLC; E; F; ICN; MiEM; NIC; NNU; PU; TxU.

> Although the work is of a generally historical nature we have decided to include the 1st ed. because of its relevance for the internal Catholic controversy. In Eamon Duffy's words: 'The anti-Roman, anti-papistical polemic of the Cisalpines [is here] enshrined in medieval historiography.' (Duffy, 1970, p. 207). See also no. 249.

242. Berington, Joseph. *The history of the reign of Henry the Second, and of Richard and John, his sons; with the events of the period from 1154 to 1216. In which the character of Thomas a Becket is vindicated.* Birmingham. 1790. 4°. [2], xxxvi, 683, [3] p. Printed by: Swinney, M. Published by: Robinson, G.G.J. and J.; Faulder, R. (London). ESTC t078379. * C; C-S; Ct; Dt; DUc; E; GOT; L; Lfa; Lhe; MB; MiEM; MRu; NNU; NSPM; O; Osc; OU; P; PIF; ScCleU; TxU; Vat; WMUW.

> With 2 pages of adverts. The book is a reply to George Baron Lyttleton's *The history of the life of King Henry the Second*, 1767-1771. See also next 2 items.

243. Berington, Joseph. *The history of the reign of Henry the Second, and of Richard and John, his sons; with the events of the period, from 1154 to 1216. In which the character of Thomas a Becket is vindicated.* 2 vols. Dublin. 1790. 8°. Printed by: White, L.; Byrne, P.; Moore, J.; Grueber; Mc'Allister; Jones, W.; Draper, G.; White, R. ESTC n007468. * BFq; CSmH; D; DLC; Du; MB; MWA; NjR; NNS; P; PPL; Sco.

244. Berington, Joseph. *The history of the reign of Henry the Second, and of Richard and John, his sons; with the events of the period from 1154 to 1216. In which the character of Thomas a Becket is vindicated.* 3 vols. Basil. 1793. 8°. Printed by: Tourneisen, J.J. Published by: Tourneisen, J.J. ESTC n007467. * C; CaOTU; DLC; Du; GOT; ICU; NSyU; P; Vat.

245. Berington, Joseph. *Immaterialism delineated: or, a view of the first principles of things.* London. 1779. 8°. viii, 438 p. Published by: Robinson, G.; Fisk, J. ESTC t154506. * C; CtY; DLC; ECW; Gi; Gu; Lhe; TxU; Ush.

246. Berington, Joseph. *A letter to Dr. Fordyce, in answer to his sermon on the delusive and persecuting spirit of popery.* Anon. London. 1779. 8°. [2], 68 p. Published by: Robinson, G.; Fisk, J. ESTC t027917. * E; ECW; L; Sto; TxU; Ush.

247. Berington, Joseph. *A letter to the right reverend John Douglass.* London. 1797. 8°. [4], 23, [1] p. Published by: Booker, E. ESTC n033768. * DUc; ECW; LfaA; MH; Sto; Ush; WDA.

> This letter, dated Feb. 25, was an answer to Bishop Douglass's reaction to Berington's *An examination of events* (see Gillow I, 194 and see also no. 240).

248. Berington, Joseph. *Letters on materialism and Hartley's theory of the human mind, addressed to Dr. Priestley, F.R.S.* London. 1776. 8°. [8], 225 [i.e. 229], [1], p. Published by: Robinson, G.; Swinney, M. (Birmingham). ESTC t106878.

* BMp; CSmH; CtY; ICN; L; LAM; Ldw; Lhe; Lu; O; Osc; Sto; Ush.
> Pages 224 and 229 are misnumbered 214, 225. Sto has the correct page numbers. The dedication is dated 'Winsley, August 12'.

249. Berington, Joseph. *The memoirs of Gregorio Panzani; giving an account of his agency in England, in the years 1634, 1635, 1636. Translated from the Italian original, and now first published.* Birmingham. 1793. 8°. [2], v-xliii, 473 p. Printed by: Swinney & Walker. Published by: Robinson, G.G.J. and J.; Faulder, R. (London). ESTC t153540. * BB; C; CSt; DFo; ECR; ECW; IaU; ICU; L; LEu; LfaA; Lhe; Lpro; MH; MiU; MnU; MY; O; Osc; ScCR; Sto.
> The Gillow library has this ed. with a tp dated 1813; 'in effect the standard Cisalpine history of English Catholicism' (Duffy 1970, p.324). Charles Plowden, S.J. published *Remarks* on Berington's publication (Liege, 1794; see no. 2309) in which he questions the authenticity of the memoirs.

250. Berington, Joseph. *Reflections addressed to the rev. John Hawkins. To which is added, an exposition of Roman Catholic principles in reference to God and the country.* Birmingham. 1785. 8°. xiv, 121, [1] p. Printed by: Swinney, M. Published by: Booker, T. ESTC t149882. * Amp; BMp; C; COA; DoA; ECW; Gi; Hen; ICN; LfaA; Lhe; MY; Osc; StD; Sto; TLP; Ush; Vat.
> With one page of adverts. One of the several replies to the apostates John Hawkins and Charles Henry Wharton. The *Principles* were by James Maurus Corker (Clancy no. 248ff. and see also no. 794). Gillow (I, 192) also gives eds in 1787 and 1788.

251. Berington, Joseph. *The rights of dissenters from the established church, in relation, principally, to English Catholics.* Birmingham. 1789. 8°. xii, 66, [2] p. Printed by: Swinney, M. Sold by: Swinney, M.; Robinson, G.G.J. and J.; Faulder, R. ESTC t144401. * BB; BFq; BMp; C; CaQMM; DoA; E; Hen; L; Ldw; LfaA; Lhe; Lse; Lu; O; Sto; Ush (2).
> With 2 pages of adverts for works by Berington; one of the Ush copies lacks the adverts.

252. Berington, Joseph. *The rights of dissenters from the established church, in relation, principally, to English Catholics.* Dublin. 1790. 8°. viii, 53, [1] p. Printed by: Byrne, P.; Jones, W. ESTC t144387. * C; Dt; KU-S; L; MChB; MY; O; OkU; PP.

253. Berington, Joseph. *The state and behaviour of English Catholics, from the Reformation to the year 1780. With a view of their present number, wealth, character; &c. In two parts.* Anon. London. 1780. 8°. [2], xiii, [1], 190, [2] p. Published by: Faulder, R. ESTC t048568. * BB; BFq; CLU; CoU; CSmH; CU-A; DoA; ECW; Eu; ICN; IES; KU-S; L (imp.); Lhe; MB; MChB; MoU; MRu; O; Sto; TxDaM-P; TxU; Ush.
> With one page of adverts for works by Berington.

254. Berington, Joseph. *The state and behaviour of English Catholics, from the Reformation to the year 1781. With a view of their present number, wealth, character, &c. In two parts.* 2nd ed. Anon. London. 1781. 8°. [2], xxxvii, [1], 199, [1] p. Published by: Faulder, R. ESTC t048569. * CLU; CSmH; Ct; Dt; DUc; ICN; ICU; L; Lfa; Lhe; MB; MnU; Owo; StD; TxDaM-P; TxU; Ush.

255. Berington, Simon. *Dissertations on the Mosaical creation, deluge, building of Babel, and confusion of tongues, &c.* London. 1750. 8°. [14], 466 p. Published by: Author. Sold by: Davis, C.; Osborne, T. ESTC t104363. * BRu; C; CLU-C; CYc; Du; E; ECW; GEU-T; GOT; ICN; ICU; L; Lhe; Llp; Map; MoLiWJ; NIC; NNUT; P; PU.

> Gillow (I, 199): 'In these dissertations the author combats infidels and Hutchinsonians, La Pluche, Woodward, Sir Isaac Newton, and many other writers'.

256. Berington, Simon. *The great duties of life. In three parts. I. With respect to the supreme being. II. With respect to the laws of morality. III. With respect to the law of Christ ... By S.B. Gent.* London. 1738. 8°. xxxviii, [4], 378 p. Printed by: Ackers, C. Published by: Author. Sold by: Innys and Manby; Meadows; Meighan; Lewis. ESTC t071866. * C; Du; E; ECW; GEU-T; Gi; L; Ldw; Lhe; Map; TxH; UPB; ViU.

257. Berington, Simon. *The great duties of life. In three parts. I. With respect to the supreme being. II. With respect to the laws of morality. III. With respect to the law of Christ ... By S.B. Gent.* 2nd ed. London. 1750. 8°. xxxviii, [4], 378 p. Published by: Meighan, T. ESTC t072168. * C; E; ECW; L; Lhe; Ush.

> A reissue of the sheets of the first ed., with a cancel tp.

258. Berington, Simon. *The memoirs of Sigr. Gaudentio di Lucca: taken from his confession and examination before the fathers of the inquisition at Bologna in Italy ... Faithfully translated from the Italian, by E.T. gent.* London. 1737. 8°. xiii, [3], 335, [1] p. Published by: Cooper, T. ESTC t059628. * C; CaOHM; CaOTU; CLU-C; CLU-C/S; C-S; CSmH; CtY; D; DFo; DLC; ICN; ICU; IU; L; LEu; Lfs; Mil; MRu; NjP; O; Owo; Ush.

> This work, called by Kirk (p. 20) a 'moral and excellent romance' does not really come within the terms of our bibliography. For the many eds meant for the general public, see ESTC.

259. Berington, Simon. *A modest enquiry how far Catholics are guilty of the horrid tenets laid to their charge. By S. B.* London. 1749. 8°. x, [2], 163, [1] p. ESTC t061461. * C; CL-U; Do; Dt; E; ECW; Gi; KU-S; L; LAM; Lfa; Lhe; O; Ush; ViU; Yb.

260. Berington, Simon. *A popish pagan the fiction of a Protestant heathen. In a conversation betwixt a gentleman of the states of Holland ... and a doctor of heathen mythology.* Anon. London. 1743. 8°. ix, [1], 244 p. ESTC t094015. * C; CaOTU; CLU-C; CSt; Ct; CU-A; DMR; Do; E; ECW; GEU; GEU-T; Gi; GOT; IEN; KBH; L; Lhe; Map; MRu; O; PU; TH; Ush; Utr.

> Gillow (I, 198): 'This was an answer to Dr Conyers Middleton's *Letter from Rome*'. Gillow (IV, 332) attributes the work to Philip Lorraine O.S.F.

261. Berington, Simon. *To his most excellent majesty James III. King of England, Scotland, France, and Ireland. Defender of the faith &c.* [Douai]. [1715?]. 4°. [8] p. ESTC t125216. * L; O.

> Signed 'Simon Berington priest & present professour of poetry in the English Colledge at Doway'. Gillow (I, 198): 'A moral and encomiastic poem ... in

which a new Utopia is described'. Foxon B199.

262. Berkeley, Robert. *Considerations on the declaration against transubstantiation, in a letter to a friend.* Anon. 1778. 8°. [2], 29, [1] p. ESTC t031498. * ECW; KU-S; L; LfaA; Osc; Ush.

>Kirk (p. 23) and Gillow (I, 201-2) attribute this work to Robert Berkeley (see Gillow for a biographical account).

263. Berkeley, Robert. *Considerations on the oath of supremacy, in two letters to a friend.* Anon. London. 1778. 8°. [2], 46 p. ESTC n027655. * KU-S; Lfa; LfaA; Osc; Sto; TxDaM-P; Ush.

>Kirk, Sto and ms note in Lfa attribute this work to Robert Berkeley. It is a plea for toleration of Catholicism.

264. Bertier, Charles. *An account of the miracle wrought on the 31st of May, the feast of Corpus Christi, in ... 1725 ... at Paris [Relation du miracle arrivé le 31 mai 1725].* 2nd. ed. Anon. London. 1727. 8°. 85, [3] p. Published by: Meighn [sic], T. ESTC t164102. * Lhe.

>Gillow (I, 588) attributes the translation to William Crathorne.

265. Bertier, Charles. *An account of the miracle wrought on the 31st of May, the feast of Corpus Christi, in ... 1725 ... at Paris.* Anon. London. 1728. 8°. 58 p. Printed by: Roberts, J. Sold by: Roberts, J. ESTC t110718. * DLC; E; L; Ush.

>Roberts uses the same sheets as the Meighan ed. (no. 264), minus the prayer at the end (pp. 59-84) and with a different tp.

266. Bertier, Charles. *An account of the miracle wrought on the 31st of May, the feast of Corpus Christi, in ... 1725 ... at Paris.* Anon. London. 1728. 8°. 85, [3] p. Printed by: Roberts, J. Published by: Roberts, J. * ECW.

>With one page of Meighan adverts.

267. Bertier, Charles. *An account of the miracle wrought on the 31st of May, the feast of Corpus Christi, in ... 1725 ... at Paris.* 2nd ed. Anon. London. 1728. 8°. 85, [3] p. Published by: Meighan, T. ESTC t205265. * Do; ECW; Lhe; O.

>This is the second '2nd' ed. With one page of Meighan adverts.

268. Bew, John. *Copy of a letter from Dr Bew at Paris. March the 16th, 1790.* 1790. fol. s.s. * BAA.

>Bew asks for the advice of the clergy and of Bishop Talbot on mission funds and property in Paris in view of the troubled situation. Dated 'March 16th, 1790'.

269. Bill. *A bill, intituled an act for relieving his majesty's subjects professing the popish religion ... 1778.* fol. 5, [3] p. * Sto.

>It is not clear under whose auspices this bill was published.

270. Blanchard, Pierre Louis. *Précis historique de la vie et du pontificat de Pie VI.* London. 1800. 8°. [2], 218, [2] p. Printed by: Boussonnier, Ph. le & Co. Sold by: Author; Dulau, A. & Co. ESTC t114894. * CaQMBN; E; GOT; L; Ush.

271. Blanchard, Pierre Louis. *Précis historique de la vie et du pontificat de Pie VI.* 2nd ed. London. 1800. 12°. [4], 251, [1] p. Printed by: Boussonnier, Ph. le et C.e [sic]. ESTC t120521. * L.

272. Blois, Louis de. *Meditations on the life and death of the holy Jesus; by the abbot Blosius. And two discourses by the Archbishop of Cambray.* Edinburgh. 1730. 12°. [2], 127, [1] p. Printed by: Catanach, J. Published by: Robertson, J. ESTC t200884. * E; ECW; Sto.

> The Archbishop of Cambray is François de Salignac Fénelon.

273. Blount, Michael. *A congratulatory poem presented to the right reverend lady Mary Crispe of the Isle of Tenet, abbess of the RR Benedictin dames at Brussells on the occasion of celebrating her jubilie, June 5th, 1737.* Brussels. 1737. s.s. Printed by: Foppens, P. * Map.

274. Blyth, Francis. *Appendix to the discourses on the four last things of man: containing two discourses on a middle state.* Anon. London. 1763. 8°. 59, [1] p. ESTC t102865. * BB; L; OrPU; UshL.

> This is an appendix to *The streams of eternity, or, the mystical waters of life and death*, London, 1763 (no. 289), with which it is bound up. With one page of adverts.

275. Blyth, Francis. *A caution against prejudice, particularly in matters which concern our devotions. In a pastoral letter from a missioner in town to his penitent in the country.* Anon. [London?]. 1740. 12°. [4], 57, [3] p. Published by: [Meighan, T.]. ESTC t162998. * ECW; Lhe; TxU.

> Kirk (p. 30) and ESTC attribute this work to Francis Blyth.

276. Blyth, Francis. *A devout paraphrase on the seven penitential psalms; or, a practical guide to repentance.* Anon. [London?]. 1741. 12°. [4], 103, [1] p. ESTC t142177. * CAL; CaOHM; CLU-C; DGU; Do; DoA; E; ECW; Gi; InNd; L; Lhe; Map; NN; O; Ush.

> With initial and final advertisement leaf. The preface states: 'For the text of the Psalms I have rather followed the Manual than the Douay version'.

277. Blyth, Francis. *A devout paraphrase on the seven penitential psalms: or, a practical guide to repentance. By F. Bl*th.* 2nd ed. London. 1742. 8°. [6], xix, [1], 123, [1], 61, [3] p. Printed by: Hoyles, J. Published by: Author. ESTC n030064. * BB; DMR; E; ECW; Lhe; MoLiWJ; O; Osc; TH; TxU.

> O has [8] instead of [6] preliminary pages. With an advert for Blyth's sermons.

278. Blyth, Francis. *A devout paraphrase on the seven penitential psalms; or, a practical guide to repentance. With approbation.* 3rd ed. Dublin. 1749. 8°. [2], xiv, 78, 50 p. Published by: Lamb, J. ESTC t133061. * D; Dt; FLK; L; MY; PPULC; PV.

> The last 50 pages are an 'Appendix'.

279. Blyth, Francis. *A devout paraphrase on the seven penitential psalms.* 7th ed. Leyden. 1751. 8°. [4], xix, [1], 124, 61, [1] p. Published by: Author. * DoA.

280. Blyth, Francis. *Eternal misery the necessary consequence of infinite mercy abused. A sermon.* Anon. London. 1740. 8°. [4], 68 p. Published by: Cooper, T. ESTC t068776. * CLU-C; L; MRu.

> Gillow (I, 253): 'In reply to William Whiston's *Eternity of hell torments considered* [London 1740]'.

281. Blyth, Francis. *Eternal misery the necessary consequence of infinit mercy* *abused. A sermon. By F. Bl*th.* 2nd ed. London. 1742. 8°. 107, [1] p. ESTC t069197. * L.

282. Blyth, Francis. *Eternal misery the necessary consequence of infinit mercy abused. A sermon ... Printed for the first time separately in the year MDCCXL.* 3rd ed. Anon. London. 1745. 8°. 107, [1] p. ESTC n007114. * E; MnU; Ush.

283. Blyth, Francis. *An explanation of the adoration of the holy cross.* [London]. 1766. 8°. [4], 27, [1] p. Published by: [Coghlan, J.P.]. ESTC t175656. * ECW; MBAt; MBU-T; O; Osc.

> Place of publication and name of publisher are suggested by an advert in no. 1473 where the book is listed as 'just published by J.P. Coghlan'.

284. Blyth, Francis. *An explanation of the adoration of the holy cross.* London. [1785?]. 12°. 24 p. Printed by: Coghlan, J.P. ESTC t183516. * Lmh; Ush.

285. Blyth, Francis. *Passion of our Lord and Saviour Jesus Christ: a sermon on Good Friday. Preach'd by the late rev. Mr. Blyth.* London. 1775. 8°. iv, 134 p. * Do; Ush; Yb.

286. Blyth, Francis. *Sermons for every Sunday in the year ... By F. BL*TH Disc. Car. --- S.T.P.* 4 vols. London. 1742-43. 8°. [8], 488, [2]; [1], 499, [3]; [8], 392, [2]; [8], 263, [75]. Printed by: Hoyles, J. Published by: Author. ESTC t105035. * Amp; Do; E; ECW; L; Lhe; O; TH; TxU; UGL (vols 1, 2); Ush.

287. Blyth, Francis. *Sermons for every Sunday in the year ... By F. BL*TH, Disc. Car. ---S.T.P.* 4 vols. Dublin. 1762-63. 12°. [8], 348; viii, 351, [1]; viii, 275, [1]; viii, 208, [70] p. Printed by: Corcoran, B. ESTC t212623. * Dt; FLK; IDA (vols 1 & 3).

> The final 70 pages in vol. 4 are a general index.

288. Blyth, Francis. *Sermons for every Sunday in the year ... By F. BL*TH, Disc. Car. --- S.T.P.* 2 vols. Dublin. 1763. 4°. [6], 234; vi, 140, 72, [24] p. Printed by: Corcoran, B. Published by: Corcoran, B. ESTC t104914. * FLK; L; Lhe; MY; Sto.

> The final 72, [24] pages are an appendix and a general index.

289. Blyth, Francis. *The streams of eternity, or, the mystical waters of life and death: in twelve discourses.* Anon. London. 1763. 8°. xvi, xliii, [1], 245, [3], 59, [1] p. Printed by: Dixwell, J. Published by: Author. ESTC t102864. * BB; ECW; L; OrPU; PHi; PPULC; Ush; UshL.

> Bound up with *Appendix to the discourses on the four last things of man* (no. 274).

290. Boisgelin de Cucé, Jean de Dieu R. *Discours pour la bénédiction de la chapelle de King Street, Portman-Square.* London. 1799. 8°. 16 p. Printed by: Baylis. Sold by: Dulau & Co. ESTC t185213. * CaQMBN; O; Sto.

291. Boisgelin de Cucé, Jean de Dieu R. *Discours pour la première communion à la chapelle de King-Street, Portman-Square.* London. 1799. 8°. 31, [1] p. Printed by: Baylis. Published by: Dulan [sic], A. & Co.; Booker; L'Homme; Huard; Fougères; Bené. ESTC t122030. * E; L; O; Sto; WDA.

> WDA is a variant with 'Dulau' in the imprint. Pages 25-31 contain a 'Discours

pour la rénovation des voeux du baptème'.

292. Boisgelin de Cucé, Jean de Dieu R. *Discours prononcé, par mgr l'Archevêque d'Aix pour la bénédiction de la chapelle de King-Street, Portman-Square.* London. 1799. 8°. [2], 2-9, [1] p. Printed by: Baylis, T. * Harris.

293. Boisgelin de Cucé, Jean de Dieu R. *Le psalmiste. Précedé d'un discours préliminaire sur la poésie sacrée.* London. 1799. 8°. [6], xxxi, [1], 119, [1] p. Printed by: Baylis. Published by: Dulau & Co. ESTC t124006. * CaQMBM; L; O.

294. Bona, Giovanni. *De sacrificio missae tractatus asceticus, continens praxim attente, devote, et reverenter celebrandi.* London. 1798. 12°. [2], 168, 9, [3] p. Printed by: Baylis, T. ESTC n003500. * LONu; MiKCS; Ush.

295. Bona, Giovanni. *A guide to heaven: or moral instructions compiled partly out of the maxims of holy fathers, and partly out of the sentences of antient philosophers [Manuductio ad coelum].* Dublin. 1755. 12°. [2], xviii, [17], 38-262 p. Published by: Buck, J. ESTC t166435. * D; MY.
Translated by James Price. With a list of subscribers.

296. *Bona mors: or, a preparation for a happy death.* 1737. 8°. 40 p. ESTC t209480. * E; Gi (imp.); Hen.

297. *Bona mors. Or, the art of dying happily in the congregation, of Jesus Christ crucify'd and of his condoling mother.* [London?]. 1706. 8°. [16], 124 p. ESTC t115499. * CU-SB; DFo; Do; Gi; Hen; L; Lhe; Stan (imp.); Sto; Ush; Yb.
Gi, Hen, Stan, Ush and Yb have a 4-page postscript. Sto cat. suggests St. Omers as the place of publication. Hen has a 4-page list of books lately bought from Holland.

298. *Bona mors. Or, the art of dying happily in the congregation of Jesus Christ crucify'd, and of his condoling mother.* 1709. 12°. 70 p. * Do; DoA.

299. *Bona mors. Or, the art of dying happily in the congregation, of Jesus Christ crucify'd and of his condoling mother.* 2nd ed. [London?]. 1709. 12°. [16], 104 p. ESTC t115500. * ECW; L; Lfa; Lhe; Mil.

300. *Bona mors: or, the art of dying happily, in the congregation of Jesus Christ crucify'd and of his condoling mother.* 3rd ed. [London?]. 1713. 12°. 72 p. ESTC t166371. * Lhe.

301. *Bona mors, or, the art of dying happily in the congregation of Jesus Christ crucify'd and of his condoling mother.* 4th ed. 1717. 12°. 72 p. * Osc.

302. *Bona mors: or, the art of dying happily in the congregation of Jesus Christ crucify'd and of his condoling mother.* 5th ed. [London?]. 1722. 12°. 72 p. ESTC t166372. * LANu; Lhe.

303. *Bona mors: or, the art of dying happily in the congregation of Jesus Christ crucify'd and of his condoling mother.* 6th ed. 1726. 12°. 71, [1]. * Do.

304. *Bona mors: or, the art of dying happily, in the congregation of Jesus Christ crucify'd, and of his condoling mother.* 7th ed. [London]. 1736. 12°. 71, [1].

Published by: [Meighan, T.]. * Do.
> With one page of Meighan adverts.

305. *Bona mors: or, the art of dying happily in the congregation of Jesus Christ crucify'd, and of his condoling mother.* 8th ed. London. 1745. 12°. 71, [1] p. Published by: Meighan, T. ESTC t166373. * Gi; Lhe; Map.

306. *Bona mors: or, the art of dying happily in the congregation of Jesus Christ, and of his condoling mother.* 9th ed. London. 1754. 12°. 72 p. Published by: Meighan, T. ESTC t166374. * C; Do; Lfa; Lhe; Map.

307. *Bona mors: or, the art of dying happily in the congregation of Jesus Christ crucify'd, and of his condoling mother.* 8th ed. Liverpool. [1765]. 24°. 72 p. Printed by: [Sadler, J.?]. Sold by: Green, G. ESTC t167260. * LVp.
> Printer's name and date from Hawkes. This is the second '8th' ed.

308. *Bona mors: or, the art of dying happily in the congregation of Jesus Christ crucify'd, and of his condoling mother. To which is annex'd the rosary of our blessed Lady.* 10th ed. Preston. 1766. 12°. 70, 24 p. Printed by: Stuart, W. ESTC t115501. * DoA; L.
> *The method of saying the rosary* (21st ed.) has a separate tp, dated 1767, and separate pagination, but the signatures are continuous.

309. *Bona mors: or the art of dying happily in the congregation of Jesus Christ crucify'd, and of his condoling mother. To which is annex'd the rosary of our blessed Lady.* 10th ed. York. 1766. 12°. 70, 24 p. ESTC t115497. * L.
> *The method of saying the rosary* (21st ed.) has a separate tp, dated 1776 [i.e. 1766 or 1767?], and separate pagination, but the signatures are continuous. This is another '10th' ed.

310. *Bona mors: or, the art of dying happily in the congregation of Jesus Christ crucified, and of his condoling mother, to which is annex'd the rosary of our blessed Lady.* 13th ed. London. 1776. 12°. 96 p. ESTC t166375. * Lhe.

311. *Bona mors: or, the art of dying happily in the congregation of Jesus Christ crucified, and of his condoling mother; to which is annexed the rosary of our blessed Lady.* 12th ed. London. [1777]. 72, 24 p. Printed by: Coghlan, J.P. * Do.
> Although the signatures are continuous, the 'Rosary' has a separate tp stating '22nd ed. Printed and sold by J.P. Coghlan, 1777'.

312. *Bona mors: or the art of dying happily in the congregation of Jesus Christ crucified.* 14th ed. Preston. 1788. 8°. 97, [1] p. Printed by: Binns, N. * Gi.

313. *Bona mors: or the art of dying happily to which is annexed the rosary, the crosses of St. Francis and the thirty day prayer.* 14th ed. London. 1788. 12°. 96 p. Printed by: Coghlan, J.P. * ECB.
> This is another '14th' ed.

314. *Bona mors, or the art of dying happily in the congregation of Jesus Christ crucified, and of his condoling mother.* 15th ed. Preston. 1789. 12°. 95, [1] p. Printed by: Sergent, E. * DoA.

315. *Bona mors: or the art of dying happily. To which is annexed the rosary, the*

crosses of St. Francis, and the thirty days prayer. 15th ed. London. 1792. 12°.
96 p. Printed by: Coghlan, J.P. * Stan; Ush.
> This is another '15th' ed.

316. *Bona mors: or the art of dying happily.. To which is annexed, the rosary,
the crosses of St. Francis, and the thirty days Sprayer [sic].* 16th ed. London.
1796. 12°. 96 p. Printed by: Coghlan, J.P. * Stan.

317. Bonaventura, Saint. *The life of our Lord and Saviour Jesus Christ.
Translated by Edward Yates [Meditationes vitae Christi].* London. 1739. 8°. [4],
364 p. Printed by: [Meighan, T.?]. ESTC t105809. * ECW; L; Map.
> Not in fact by Saint Bonaventura (see also next 3 items). In a list of adverts in
> no. 996 this book is listed as 'printed for T. Meighan'. The preface is signed by
> the translator.

318. Bonaventura, Saint. *The life of our Lord and Saviour Jesus Christ. Written
in Latin in the thirteenth century by S. Bonaventure. And translated into English
by Mr. Edward Yates.* London. 1773. 8°. [27], 4-421, [1], 26 p. Printed by:
Coghlan, J.P. Sold by: Coghlan, J.P. ESTC t062248. * DAE; Do; ECW (imp.);
Hor; L; Map; TLP; TxU; Yb.
> With 'Some account of the life of St. Bonaventura' separately paginated (see also
> next item). Do has [18], 421, [1], 26, [8] p., i.e. the table of contents [8] is
> bound in at the end. According to Gillow (I, 253) this and the following two eds
> were edited by Francis Blyth.

319. Bonaventura, Saint. *The life of our Lord and Saviour Jesus Christ. In a
series of devout meditations. Translated by the rev. Edward Yates.* London. 1774.
8°. [18], 421, [1], 26, [8] p. Published by: Snagg, R. ESTC t194617. * DAE;
O; Stan; Yb.

320. Bonaventura, Saint. *The life of our Lord and Saviour Jesus Christ. Written
in Latin in the thirteenth century. And translated into English by Edward Yates.*
London. [1774]. 8°. [18], 421, [1], 26, [8] p. * Do.
> An issue of no. 319 with a different tp.

321. Bonnefons, Amable. *Le petit livre de vie, qui apprend à bien vivre et bien
prier Dieu. A l'usage de diocèse de Quebec.* Montreal. 1777. [2], [xxii], 456, [4]
p. Printed by: Mesplet, F.; Berger, C. * CaQMS.
> Standard devotional work used by Catholics in French Canada.

322. Bonnefons, Amable. *Le petit livre de vie, qui apprend a bien vivre et a bien
prier Dieu, contenant plusieurs offices, litanies, exercices de dévotion.* Quebec.
1796. xii, 431, [3] p. Printed by: Germain, L. ESTC w016699. * CaQMM.

323. Bonnefons, Amable. *Le petit livre de vie; qui apprend à bien vivre et à bien
prier Dieu, contenant plusieurs offices, litanies, exercices de dévotion.* Quebec.
1798. 12°. xvi, 498, [6] p. Sold by: Huot, F. ESTC w016700. * CaOTP (imp.);
CaQMM; CaQQLa (imp.).

324. Bonnefons, Amable. *Le petit livre de vie qui apprend à bien vivre et a bien
prier Dieu. Contient plusieurs offices, litanies, indulgences, exercices de
devotion.* Quebec. 1800. 12°. 546, [6] p. ESTC t104412. * CaQQLa; L.
> Part of the text is in Latin.

325. Bossuet, Jacques Bénigne. *Exposition of the doctrine of the Catholic Church in matters of controversie [Exposition de la doctrine de l'église Catholique].* Paris. 1729. 12°. 281, [7] p. Printed by: Delusseux, J. ESTC t194760. * O; P.

> With regard to our selection of works by Bossuet it must be noted that only those works and eds published under R.C. auspices have been included.

326. Bossuet, Jacques Bénigne. *An exposition of the doctrine of the Catholic Church in matters of controversie ... Done into English from the fifth edition.* 3rd ed. London. 1735. 12°. [2], 224, [2] p. ESTC t107631. * DMR; Dt; FLK; ICIU; L.

327. Bossuet, Jacques Bénigne. *An exposition of the doctrine of the Catholic Church, in matters of controversy.* London. 1753. 12°. 144 p. ESTC t107632. * CAL; DoA; Gi; ICN; L; Lhe; O.

328. Bossuet, Jacques Bénigne. *An exposition of the doctrine of the Catholic Church, in matters of controversy. To which is added, the approbation of ... Pope Innocent XI.* [London?]. [1785?]. 8°. viii, 112 p. ESTC t106709. * Do; E; GEU-T; L; Lhe; O.

329. Bossuet, Jacques Bénigne. *An exposition of the doctrine of the Catholic Church, in matters of controversy ... Translated from the French by W.C.* Cork. 1789. 18°. 122, [1], 15, iv p. Printed by: Cronin, J. ESTC t184036. * D.

> 'The principles of Roman Catholics', written by the translator, William Coppinger, is here inserted between Bossuet's book and its index. For works by Coppinger see nos 781 and 782.

330. Bossuet, Jacques Bénigne. *An exposition of the doctrine of the Catholic Church, in matters of controversy. With the approbation of ... Pope Innocent XI.* London. 1790. 8°. [4], xxxv, [1], viii, 112 p. Printed by: Coghlan, J.P. Sold by: Robinsons, Messrs. ESTC t139978. * E; ECW; L; Lhe; Osc; Ush.

> According to ESTC translated by J. Johnston O.S.B. There is a long introduction providing a theological and literary commentary on Bossuet's work.

331. Bossuet, Jacques Bénigne. *An exposition of the doctrine of the Catholic Church, in matters of controversy ... Translated ... by the right rev. William Coppinger.* 2nd ed. Cork. 1798. 18°. 144, 18, v, [1] p. Printed by: Cronin, J. ESTC n009559. * C; IU; Yb.

332. Bossuet, Jacques Bénigne. *An exposition of the doctrine of the Catholic Church, with respect to controverted points.* Preston. [1800?]. 8°. 25, [1] p. Printed by: Newby's office. ESTC t012320. * L.

333. Bossuet, Jacques Bénigne. *The history of the variations of the Protestant churches ... In two parts. Translated from the sixth edition ... printed at Paris, MDCCXVIII [Histoire des variations des églises protestantes].* 2 vols. Antwerp. 1742. 8°. xxxii, 480, [36]; [2], 493, [35] p. ESTC n018682. * CLU; CLU-C; DAE (imp.); ECW; GEU-T; Hen; KU-S; LEu; Lfa; Lhe; LONu; MSaE; O; P; TxU; UGL; Ush; Yb.

> This translation is generally attributed to Levinius Brown, *vere* Samuel Musson S.J. (1686-1769). See also next item.

334. Bossuet, Jacques Bénigne. *The history of the variations of the Protestant* *churches ... Translated from the sixth edition ... printed at Paris, MDCCXVIII.* 2 vols. Antwerp [Dublin]. 1745. 12°. xxi, [1], 441, [41]; 450, [42] p. Published by: [Kelly, I]. ESTC n018683. * DFo; ECW (vol. 2); FLK; IDA; L; SIR.

'Antwerp' is in fact Dublin according to a ms note in FLK; moreover, IDA and FLK have adverts for I. Kelly in both vols.

335. Boudon, Henri Marie. *God everywhere present. Written in French by ... Dr. Henry Mary Boudon, archdeacon of Evreuse, who died in the odour of sanctity, August 31, 1702. Translated by R.C. [Dieu présent partout].* London. 1766. 12°. [1], 8-52 p. Published by: Meighan, T. * BB; DMR; Map; Sto; Ush.

'R.C.' is Richard Challoner (see also next 3 items).

336. Boudon, Henri Marie. *God every where present. Written in French by ... Dr. Henry Mary Boudon, archdeacon of Evreuse, who died in the odour of sanctity, August 31, 1702. Translated by R.C.* London. 1766. 24°. [3], iv-vi, [1], 8-62 p. Published by: Meighan, T. ESTC t204278. * Amp; DMR; DoA; E; ECB; Map.

337. Boudon, Henri Marie. *God every where present. Translated from the French ... Published as a new year's gift for 1784.* 4th ed. London. 1787. 12°. 46, [2] p. Printed by: Coghlan, J.P. * Amp.; ECW; Ush; Yb.

Bevan (Summer 1986, no. 121) has 36 p.

338. Boudon, Henri Marie. *God everywhere present ... Translated from the French, by ... Richard Challoner ... published as a new year's gift for MDCCLXXXIV. By his successor ... James Talbot.* 5th ed. London. 1792. 12°. 36 p. Printed by: Coghlan, J.P. * CAL; ECW; Stan; Yb.

339. Bouhours, Dominique. *Christian thoughts for every day of the month, with a prayer [Pensées Chrétiennes pour tous les jours du mois].* Anon. London. 1705. 12°. [12], 132 p. Published by: Pawlet, E. ESTC t116134. * CLU-C; L; MChB.

Translated by the 17th century R.C. Edward Sheldon (see Barnard, pp. 46-7).

340. Bouhours, Dominique. *Christian thoughts for every day of the month. Done out of the French.* Anon. 1727. 12°. [6], 88, [2] p. * Do.

341. Bouhours, Dominique. *The life of Saint Francis Xavier, of the Society of Jesus ... Translated by John Dryden [Vie de Saint François Xavier].* Dublin. 1743. 8°. [24], 376 p. Published by: Kelly, I. ESTC t105366. * CaQMM; CLU-C; D; L.

With a list of subscribers. John Dryden is the son of the poet.

342. Bouhours, Dominique. *The life of Francis Xavier, of the Society of Jesus.* London. 1764. 12°. 155, [1] p. Printed by: Cooke, J. Sold by: Cooke, J. ESTC t168473. * Amp; GEU-T; MRu; NcD; Ush.

This is an abridged version.

343. Bouhours, Dominique. *Pious meditations for every day in the month, a new translation from the French [Pensées Chrétiennes pour tous les jours du mois].* Manchester. 1800. 12°. iv, [1], 6-38, [4] p. Printed by: Dean, R. & W. Published by: Haydock, T. * Osc; Ush.

Cf. also no. 1041.

344. Bourdaloue, Louis. *Bourdaloue's sermon on Ash-Wednesday.* London. 1776. 12°. 65, [3] p. Printed by: Coghlan, J.P. ESTC n046557. * CSmH; Do; Osc; Ush.

345. Bourdaloue, Louis. *Bourdaloue's sermon on Ash-Wednesday.* London. 1786. 12°. 65, [1] p. * Amp.

346. Bourdaloue, Louis. *Practical divinity: being a regular series of sermons translated from the French of Bourdaloue ... by A. C.* 4 vols. 1776. 12°. [2], viii, [2], 324; [2], 352; [2], 312; [2], 341, [1] p. Printed by: Faden, W. Sold by: Marmaduke, J. ESTC t206650. * E; L; Lhe; PRTus; TLP; Ush; Yb.

> 'A.C.' is Anthony Carroll. For Carroll (1722-1794), cousin of John Carroll, Archbishop of Baltimore, see DNB.

347. Bourdaloue, Louis. *Practical theology in a regular series of sermons, selected from Bourdaloue's. Translated from French by the rev. A. Carroll ... Revised and corrected by the rev. B. MacMahon.* 2nd ed. 2 vols. Dublin. 1794. 8°. [4], iv, [10], 3-421, [1]; [4], 400 p. Printed by: Mehain, J. ESTC t212129. * FLK; IDA; MRu (vol. 1); PLatS.

> Bernard MacMahon was a prolific editor; among his eds are *The key of paradise* (nos 1540-1542) and works by Gobinet. MRu pagination is [12], iv, 3-421, [1] p. See also next item.

348. Bourdaloue, Louis. *Practical theology in a regular series of sermons selected from Bourdaloue's: translated from French by the rev. A. Carroll ... Revised and corrected by the reverend B. MacMahon.* 2nd ed. 2 vols. Dublin. 1797. 8°. [10], ii, 3-421, [1]; [2], 400 p. Printed by: Wogan, P. ESTC t201170. * FLK; NSPM; NSPN; SIR.

> With a 6-page list of subscribers. NSPM and FLK have a pasted label 'H. Fitzpatrick, printer and bookseller to ... St.Patrick'. This is the second '2nd' ed.

349. Boutauld, Michel. *The counsels of wisdom or, a collection of the maxims of Solomon ... with reflexions upon the maxims. Faithfully translated out of the French [Conseils de la sagesse].* 2nd ed. Anon. London. 1735. 12°. [12], 276 p. Published by: Meighan, T. ESTC t121995. * L.

> The translator's dedication is signed 'E.S.', i.e. Edward Sheldon. For Sheldon see Barnard, pp. 46-7.

350. Boutauld, Michel. *A method of conversing with God. Translated from the French by J.W. of the Society of Jesus [Méthode pour converser avec Dieu].* Anon. 1778. 12°. 71, [1] p. * DoA; Gi; Lfa; Stan.

> 'J.W.' is John Warner. Warner was a well-known 17th century author and translator (cf. e.g. Clancy nos 1481Y-1489X). See also next 3 items.

351. Boutauld, Michel. *A method of conversing with God, translated from the French, by J.W. of the Society of Jesus.* Anon. Dublin. 1789. 16°. 79, [1] p. Printed by: Wogan, P. ESTC t220151. * D; Lfa; MY.

352. Boutauld, Michel. *A method of conversing with God ... Translated out of the French by I.W. of the Society of Jesus.* 2nd ed. Anon. Liege. 1789. 12°. 143, [1] p. Printed by: Dessain, H. and sisters. ESTC t092149. * DMR; Gi; L; Yb.

353. Boutauld, Michel. *A method of conversing with God ... Translated out of* *the French of M. Boutauld by I.W. of the Society of Jesus.* London. 1792. 12°. vi, 135, [1] p. * P.

354. Bowes, Robert. *Practical reflections for every day thro'out the year.* 2nd ed. Anon. 1710. 12°. 379, [5] p. * Lhe; Sto; UGL.

> For Robert Bowes, alias Lane, priest, 1673-1735 see Kirk, p. 32. See also next 6 items.

355. Bowes, Robert. *Practical reflections for every day thro'out the year.* 3rd ed. Anon. 1722. 12°. 329, [5] p. * Lhe; Yb.

356. Bowes, Robert. *Practical reflections for every day throughout the year.* 4th ed. Anon. [London]. 1736. 12°. 403, [5] p. Published by: Meighan, T. ESTC t206554. * E; Osc; TLP.

357. Bowes, Robert. *Practical reflections for every day throughout the year.* 5th ed. Anon. [London]. 1752. 12°. iv, [8], 391, [9] p. Published by: Meighan, T. ESTC n024482. * Do; DoA; ECW; TxU.

> According to Kirk (pp. 32, 60) this and earlier versions were edited by William Crathorne.

358. Bowes, Robert. *Practical reflections for every day throughout the year ... to which is added, A brief method of meditation.* 7th ed. Anon. London. 1768. 8°. 403, [5] p. ESTC t109811. * Amp; ECW; L; Lhe; O.

359. Bowes, Robert. *Practical reflections for every day throughout the year ... to which is added, A brief method of meditation.* 7th ed. Preston. 1768. 8°. 403, [7] p. Printed by: Stuart, W. Sold by: Stuart, W. ESTC t222185. * BMu; Nijm.

> With 6 pages of adverts. This is another 7th ed.

360. Bowes, Robert. *Practical reflections for every day throughout the year ... To which is added A brief method of meditation.* 8th ed. Anon. London. 1792. 12°. xxxi, [1], 334, [6] p. Printed by: Coghlan, J.P. ESTC t200650. * Amp; Do; NSCH; Ush.

361. Brancadoro, Caesar. *Oration delivered at the funeral obsequies of the Pontiff Pius VI. October 31, 1799 ... Translated ... by William Henry Coombes [Parentalibus Pii Sexti pontificis optimi maximi oratio].* London. 1800. 4°. [4], vii, [1], 66 p. Printed by: Brown, R. Published by: Brown, R. * Ush.

> Printed and published by Brown for the executors of the late J.P. Coghlan. With 2 pages of adverts. In English only (cf. no. 362). For Coombes, see Anstruther, vol. 4, p. 70.

362. Brancadoro, Caesar. *Oration delivered at the funeral obsequies of the Pontiff Pius VI, October 31, 1799. Translated by William Henry Coombes.* London. 1800. 8°. 4, vii, 129, [1] p. Printed by: Brown, R. Published by: Brown, R. ESTC t200976. * ECW; Lhe; Sto; Ush.

> Latin and English.

363. Brancas, Henri Ignace de. *Love and charity the basis of religion. A sermon preached before the parliament of Normandy ... the 30th day of December, 1753 ... Translated by John Vailiant.* London. 1754. 8°. iv, 27, [1] p. Published by: Carpenter, H. ESTC n019049. * CYc; MBAt; MH-H; MRu; NIC.

John Vailiant, LL.D. of Lincoln's Inn, is the non-R.C. translator of this heavily anti-Jesuit sermon by the Bishop of Lisieux. There are two more 1754 Dublin eds.

364. Briand, Jean Olivier. *Lettre circulaire de Monseigneur l'Evêque, au clergé du diocèse de Quebec.* [Quebec]. [1777]. fol. s.s. * CaOOA; CaOOP; CaQQL.

> A circular letter prepared to accompany *Missa in festo* (no. 1887) and *Officium in honorem D.N.J.C.* (no. 2046).

365. *A brief account of the general meeting of Catholic delegates, held in Dublin, December 1792 ... with the speeches of doctors McNeven and McDermot.* Dublin. 1793. 8°. [2], 10; 33, [1] p. Printed by: Fitzpatrick. H. ESTC t087741. * CLU-S/C; CSmH; D; Gi; L; Lhe; Lhl; Mil; MY.

366. *A brief account of the manner of life which is practised in the monastery of the House-of-God of the Holy-Vale of our Blessed Lady of La Grappe in the canton of Friburg in Switzerland.* London. 1794. 12°. 12 p. Printed by: Coghlan, J.P. ESTC t192549. * Lhe; O.

367. Brittain, Lewis. *Principles of the Christian religion and Catholic faith investigated.* London. 1790. 12°. xi, [1], 253 [i.e 353], [3] p. Printed by: Coghlan, J.P. ESTC t124558. * Amp; CSt; DAE; Do; E; ECB; ECW; Hen; L; Lhe; MRu; NSPM; O; Osc; TLP; TxU; Ush.

> With a final advertisement leaf. The Dominican Lewis Brittain was Regent of the English College at Bornheim.

368. Brooke, Henry. *The tryal of the cause of the Roman Catholics ... August 5th, 1761.* 1st ed. Dublin. 1761. 8°. [4], 304 p. Printed by: Faulkner, G. ESTC t115812. * BMp; CSmH; D; Dt; ECR; FLK; ICN; ICU; IDA; KU-S; L; Mil; MRu; NBu; O.

> Written by the non-R.C. Henry Brooke in the R.C. interest. There are at least seven more eds of this work, brought out by non-R.C. publishers. Other books by Brooke are outside the terms of our bibliography.

369. Brosius, Francis Xavier. *Antwort eines römisch-catholischen Priesters an einen friedensliebenden Prediger der lutherischen Kirche.* Lancäster. 1796. 8°. 8, 196, [2] p. Printed by: Albrecht, J., und Comp. ESTC w018446. * DGU-W; PAtM; PHi.

> Addressed to Frederick Valentine Melsheimer, who wrote a reply in the same year (see ESTC w035479).

370. Brosius, Francis Xavier. *Reply of a Roman Catholic priest to a peace-loving preacher of the Lutheran church.* Lancaster. 1796. 16°. 196 p. Printed by: Albrecht, J., & Co. *Evans 30125.

371. Browne, Levinius. *The Protestant's tryal (in controverted points of faith) by the written word.* Brussels. 1745. 12°. xxviii, [4], 220 p. ESTC t133743. * CLU-C; COA; Do; E; ECW; FLK; Gi; L; Lhe; LO; MChB; StD; TxU;Ush.

> The book is advertised in no. 996. This suggests Meighan as publisher and London rather than Brussels as place of publication.

372. Browne, Levinius. *The Protestant's tryal (in controverted points of faith) by the written word.* Brussels. 1771. 12°. xxv, [5], 219, [1] p. ESTC t133740. *

Amp; Dt; E; Gi; Hor; L; Map; Sal; Sco; TH; UshL; Yb.

373. Bruning, George. *The divine economy of Christ in his kingdom or church.* London. 1791. 8°. xvi, 139, [1] p. Printed by: Coghlan, J.P. Sold by: Booker; Keating; Lewis; Robinsons. ESTC t185186. * D; E; Lfa; Lhe; O; P.

> In Kirk (p. 61) and Gillow (II, 13) Edward Daniel (1749-1819) is given as the author of a work with this title.

374. Bruning, George. *Remarks on the rev. Joseph Berington's examination of events termed miraculous as reported in letters from Italy addressed to the public.* London. [1796?]. 12°. xi, 43, [1] p. Printed by: Coghlan, J.P. ESTC t169053. * Lfa; Lhe; Ush.

> The date occurs on p. 43 in Lhe and Ush. Lfa has 1796 on tp. For Berington's *Examination* see no. 240.

375. *Brunswick-Street Academy, (licensed according to act of Parliament). The rev. Edmond Keating ... has opened an academy.* Cork. [1783]. s.s. Printed by: Flyn, W. * IAPA.

> The Augustinians of Cork announce the opening of a school on 2 April 1783.

376. *The bull, Unigenitus, clear'd from innovation and immorality.* London. 1729. 8°. [2], vi, [1], 40 p. ESTC t167961. * Amp; E; Ush.

377. Burgis, Edward Ambrose. *The annals of the church from the death of Christ.* Anon. London. 1712. 8°. [6], 326 p. Printed by: T.H. Sold by: Booksellers of London and Westminster. ESTC t193559. * DFo; Do; ECB; MB; O; Pci; TxU; Yb.

> For Burgis see also no. 2957.

378. Burgis, Edward Ambrose. *The annals of the church from the death of Christ.* Anon. 4 vols. London. 1737-38. 8°. [4], 82, [12], 532; [2], 83-182, 546; [2], 183-226, 480; [2], 227-280, 347, [1] p. Published by: Meighan, T.; Lewis, W. ESTC t090078. * E; L; Lhe; O; ODaU; Ush.

> With a list of subscribers. Vol. 2 is dated 1738. Each volume is preceded by notes, continuously paginated from volume to volume. L has a 5th volume which is in fact a combination of the notes of the first four volumes.

379. Burgis, Edward Ambrose. *The annals of the church from the death of Christ.* Anon. 5 vols. London. 1738. 8°. Published by: Meighan, T. ESTC t149055. * Cha (vols 4-5); CLU-C; DAE (vols 1-4); ECB; FU; GOT; ICU; MChB; MY (vols 1, 2, & 4); TxU.

> With a list of subscribers.

380. *The burial service, according to the Roman ritual.* Baltimore. 1797. [2], 21, [1] p. Printed by: Hayes, J. ESTC w009056. * DGU-W; MdW.

> Latin and English.

381. Burke, Edmund, O.P. *The rosary's of the B. Virgin Mary, and of the ... name of Jesus re-printed. Answers to three curious letters. I. Of the infallibility ... II. Of Easter-Confession. III. Of Holy-Communion. By E.B. D.D.* Louvain. 1725. 8°. [8], 40, 8, 78, [2] p. Printed by: Denique, A. ESTC t193195. * DMR; Dt; IDA; SIR; StD; UshL.

> ESTC, basing itself on Dt, has 8, 78, [2] p. According to Hugh Fenning O.P.

(personal communication) in fact printed at Dublin (cf. Thomas M. Burke *Hibernia Dominicana*, p. 549; no. 389).

382. Burke, Edmund. *The case of the suffering clergy of France, refugees in the British dominions.* Anon. [London]. [1793?]. fol. 3, [1] p. Published by: [Coghlan, J.P.?]. ESTC t198805. * O.

> An appeal for financial support for the French clergy, first printed the *Evening Mail*, 17-19 Sept. 1792. Burke, although non-R.C. was in favour of Catholic emancipation. The pamphlet mentions the names of Catholic bankers. The style of the ornament suggests J.P. Coghlan.

383. Burke, Edmund. *The humble address, and petition of the Roman Catholics of Ireland ... presented ... on 27th day of October, by the Earl of Fingal, the hon. James Preston, and Anthony Dermot.* [1774]. fol. 2 p. Printed by: Coghlan, J.P. * BAA; Map; SCA; Ush; WDA.

> Signed by the Earl of Fingal and many others. The address was written by Edmund Burke at the request of the Irish Catholics (see Amherst, I, 57).

384. Burke, Edmund. *A letter from the right hon. Edmund Burke, M.P. ... to Sir Hercules Langrishe, Bart M.P. on the subject of the Roman Catholics of Ireland, and the propriety of admitting them to the elective franchise.* Dublin. 1792. 8°. iv, 27, [1] p. Printed by: Byrne, P. ESTC t037951. * CSmH; D; DLC; Du; IU; L; LNT; MdU; MY; O; PPL; RP.

> The present letter was edited in the form of an advertisement (p.iii-iv) by someone who was clearly R.C. There is one more ed. of this letter (ESTC t037950) and there are many other publications by Burke which have not been included in our list.

385. Burke, Richard. *A letter from Richard Burke, Esq. to ... Esq. of Cork ... together with some observations on a measure proposed by a friend to be substituted in the place of the Catholic Committee.* Dublin. 1792. 8°. [4], 46 p. Printed by: Byrne, P. ESTC t087913. * C; CSmH; D; DLC; Dt; Du; L; Lhl; Mil; Sto.

> Richard Burke was probably not R.C. but wrote in favour of the Catholic cause (see also next item).

386. Burke, Richard. *A letter from Richard Burke, Esq; to a gentleman of the city of Cork, upon the utility of a Catholic Committee, as recommended by Mr. Byrne, and upon the substitution of another measure in the place of it.* Cork. 1792. 8°. [2], 26 p. Printed by: Flyn, W. ESTC t196283. * CKu; O.

387. Burke, Thomas Myles. *A catechism moral and controversial proper for such as are already advanced to some knowledge of the Christian doctrine ... By T...s M...s B...ke O.P.* Lisbon [Kilkenny?]. 1752. 16°. [24], 416 p. Printed by: [Finn, E.?]. ESTC t028889. * Amp; DT; Du; IDA; L; MRu; Sto.

> Final page wrongly numbered 446. Sto has a variant tp without place of publication. ESTC suggests Kilkenny; however, Burke was regent of the college at Lisbon (see also next item).

388. Burke, Thomas Myles. *A catechism moral and controversial proper for such as are already advanced to some knowledge of the Christian doctrine. By T...s M...s B...ke O.P.* Lisbon. 1753. 16°. [24], 416 p. * IDA.

389. Burke, Thomas Myles. *Hibernia Dominicana. Sive historiae provinciae Hiberniae ordinis praedicatorum, per P. Thomam de Burgo.* Cologne [Kilkenny]. 1762. 4°. xvi, 949, [1] p. Printed by: Metternich. ESTC t036179. * Di; ECR; L; MH-H; NNUT; SIR (-Suppl.); TxU.

> According to ESTC a copy exists with the imprint of Jacobus Stokes of Kilkenny. The supplement has a separate tp dated 1772. See no. 392.

390. Burke, Thomas Myles. *Officia propria sanctorum Hiberniae, ab omnibus utriusque sexus, qui ad horas canonicas tenentur, tam in memorato regno, quam in conventibus, & collegiis extranationalibus ... Procurante Thoma de Burgo.* Dublin. 1751. 12°. [4], 127, [5] p. Printed by: Kelly, I. ESTC t196527. * CME; FLK; ICR; IDA; MY; O; SCR; SIR.

> With a Kelly advert at end.

391. Burke, Thomas Myles. *Officia propria sanctorum Hiberniae, ab omnibus utriusque sexus, qui ad horas canonicas tenentur ... recitanda procurante A.R.P. Thoma de Burgo ... postea E[piscopo] O[ssoriensi].* 2nd ed. Dublin. 1767. 12°. [4], 127, [1] p. Printed by: Gorman, B. ESTC t209565. * Dk; Dt; FLK; IDA; LANu; MY.

392. Burke, Thomas Myles. *Supplementum Hiberniae Dominicanae, varia virorum generum complectens additamenta, juxta memorati operis seriem; disposita, per eundem auctorem P. Thomam de Burgo, O.P. Ep-sc-p-m Oss-r-ns-m.* 1772. 4°. [2], 801-949, [1] p. * SCR.

> This publication was meant to be bound up with *Hibernia Dominicana.* (no. 389).

393. Butler, Alban. *An appendix to Butler's Lives of the saints: containing the life of the author: a chronological table ... a general index ... Adapted to the Dublin edition of 1799.* Edinburgh and London. 1799-1800. 8°. [6], 96, 32, 62 p. Printed by: Moir, J. Published by: Keatings [sic]; Brown; Booker, E.; Coates, F. (Newcastle). ESTC t105831. * DMR; E; IU; L; Ush; Yb.

> This appendix contains nos 394 and 413, which were also issued separately.

394. Butler, Alban. *A chronological index for the rev. Alban Butler's Lives of the saints.* Edinburgh. 1798-1800. 8°. 96 p. Printed by: Moir, J. Published by: Keatings [sic]; Brown; Booker, E.; Coates, F. (Newcastle). ESTC t128418. * DAE; DMR; E; ECW; L; Lhe; LO; Ush; Yb.

> Also issued as part of no. 393.

395. Butler, Alban. *The life of Sir Tobie Matthews. Being a posthumous work of the rev. Alban Butler.* London. 1795. 8°. [2], 37, [1] p. Printed by: Coghlan, J.P. ESTC t088091. * DFo; E; ECW; Hen; L; Lhe; LO; O; SIR; Sto; Ush; Yb.

396. Butler, Alban. *The life of St Teresa of Jesus; virgin, foundress of the Discalced Carmelites.* Anon. 12°. 60 p. * Ush.

> Page 3 misnumbered 2. Robinson & Wallis (p. 48) list a 1794 Dublin ed. at D.

397. Butler, Alban. *Lives of saints, by the rev. Alban Butler, illustrated with engravings from G.M. Brighty, Esqr.* 3 vols. [Dublin]. [1799]. 8°. Published by: Cumming, J. ESTC n055443. * GEU.

An abridgement of Butler's *Lives of the fathers*.

398. Butler, Alban. *Lives of saints, selected and abridged from the original work of the rev. Alban Butler [Lives of the fathers, martyrs and other principal saints].* 2 vols. Newcastle upon Tyne. 1799. 8°. xiii, [1], 550; [2], 461, [1], xii p. Printed by: Walker, E. ESTC t105234. * DMR; Do (imp.); Hen (vol. 1); L; LEu; NSPM; O; TLP; Ush; WNp.

> The editor was John Bell (d. 1854), priest, prefect-general and later professor of rhetoric and poetry at Crook Hall (Ushaw).

399. Butler, Alban. *The lives of the fathers, martyrs, and other principal saints: compiled from original monuments, and other authentick records.* 4 vols. London. 1756-59. 8°. [1116] p. ESTC t147377. * AR; C; CLU-C; Csj; Do; DoA (imp.); Du; ECB; ECR; ECW; GEU-T; L; Lhe; Map; MH-AH; P; Pci (imp.); TH; TLP (imp.); UGL (imp.); Utr.

> In fact 4 parts in a varying number of vols. Thus Do has 12, AR 6, ECW 7, and ECB 5 vols.

400. Butler, Alban. *The lives of the fathers, martyrs, and other principal saints: compiled from original monuments, and other authentic records. Vol I.* Dublin. 1766. 8°. [2], xxii, [2], iv, 561, [3] p. Printed by: Hoey, J. Published by: Hoey, J. * FLK; MY.

> With a final page inviting subscription to vol. II.

401. Butler, Alban. *The lives of the fathers, martyrs, and other principal saints: compiled from original monuments, and other authentic records.* 2nd ed. 12 vols. Dublin. 1779-80. 8°. Printed by: Chambers, J.; Exshaw, J. Published by: Morris, J. ESTC n033655. * DoA; O; OO; Ush.

> Tps to vols 3-12 bear the imprint 'Dublin, printed by John Exshaw for John Morris'; vols 5-12 are dated 1780. There are more issues of this work with varying imprints. See nos 402 and 403.

402. Butler, Alban. *The lives of the fathers, martyrs, and other principal saints: compiled from original monuments, and other authentic records.* 2nd ed. 12 vols Dublin. 1779-80. 8°. Printed by: Chambers, J.; Exshaw, J. Published by: Morris, J. ESTC t131324. * CaOHM; CSmH; IDA (5 vols); L; Lca; Nijm; O; P; TxU; Vat; Yb.

> Vols 3-9 and 11-12 are printed by John Exshaw and dated 1780. With a list of subscribers. There are more issues of this work with varying imprints. See nos 401 and 403.

403. Butler, Alban. *The lives of the fathers, martyrs, and other principal saints: compiled from original monuments, and other authentic records.* 2nd ed. 12 vols. Dublin. 1779-80. 8°. Printed by: Exshaw, J. Published by: Morris, J. ESTC n047526. * CaOHM; Ce; CSmH; FLK; Lpro; Oc; OO; TxU.

> Vols 5-12 are dated 1780. There are more issues of this work with varying imprints. See nos 401 and 402.

404. Butler, Alban. *The lives of the primitive fathers, martyrs, and other principal saints: compiled from original monuments, and other authentic records.* 3rd ed. 12 vols. London, Edinburgh, Newcastle. 1798-1800. 8°. Printed by: Moir, J. Published by: Coghlan, J.P.; Keating, P.; Booker, E.; Coates, F.

(Newcastle). ESTC t105829. * AR; CSj; DAE; ECW (imp.); Hen; L; Lhe; LO; NjR; O; ODaU; Stan; TLP (imp); Ush.

> Vols 1-4 bear the imprint date 1798, vols 5-11 1799 and vol. 12 1800.

405. Butler, Alban. *The lives of the principal fathers, martyrs and saints: compiled from original monuments and other ancient records.* Dublin. 1797. 8°. vi, 400 p. Printed by: M'Donald, R. ESTC n019189. * IU; OMC.

406. Butler, Alban. *Meditations and discourses on the sublime truths and important duties of Christianity. Being a posthumous work.* 3 vols. London. 1791-93. 8°. viii, 369, [1]; 396; [4], 362 p. Printed by: Coghlan, J.P. ESTC t088092. * DoA (vols 2, 3); Du; DUN; E; ECB; ECW; ICN; L; Lfa; Lhe; LO; MWH; NSJH; O; Osc; P (vol. 1); SIR; TxU; UGL (vols 1, 2); Ush.

> Vols 2 and 3 are entitled 'Discourses on the sublime truths and important duties of Christianity'. The three vols are dated 1791, 1792 and 1793, respectively. Edited by Charles Butler and the rev. Philip Jones.

407. Butler, Alban. *The moveable feasts, fasts, and other annual observances of the Catholic Church; a posthumous work.* London. 1774. 8°. viii, 658, [2] p. Printed by: Kiernan, C. Sold by: Lewis, T. ESTC t120651. * AR; C; CAL; CaOHM; Cha; DAE; DFo; Do; DoA; E; ECB; ECR; GEU-T; GOT; Hen; L; Lfa; Lhe; LO; Map; O; TH; Ush; Yb.

> Probably revised by Richard Challoner. Do has pagination iv, 658. Cargill Cole (Appendix I) mentions a 1755 ed. See also next 2 items.

408. Butler, Alban. *The moveable feasts, fasts, and other annual observances of the Catholic church; a posthumous work.* Dublin. 1775. 8°. [8], 523, [1] p. Printed by: Morris, J. ESTC t170301. * D; Dt; ECW; FLK; IDA; Mil; NN; P.

> With a list of subscribers.

409. Butler, Alban. *The moveable feasts, fasts, and other observances of the Catholic church.* Dublin. 1795. 8°. [8], 523, [1] p. Printed by: Wogan, P. * FLK.

> With a list of subscribers.

410. Butler, Alban. *Remarks on Bower's Lives of the popes, in a series of letters.* Dublin. 1778. 8°. [2], 120 p. Printed by: Talbot, C.; Morris, J. Published by: Talbot, C.; Morris, J. ESTC t122291. * C; D; FLK; IDA; L; Mil; MY.

> Written against the apostate Jesuit Archibald Bower, whose *Lives of the popes* (1748-1766) gave rise to much controversy. See also next item.

411. Butler, Alban. *Remarks on the two first volumes of the late Lives of the popes. In letters, from a gentleman to a friend in the country.* Douai. 1754. 8°. 100 p. Published by: Derbaix, L. ESTC t087672. * Cha; CLU-C; Do; Dt; E; ECW; ICN; L; Lfa; Lhe; NIC; NSPM; O; Sto; TH; Ush; WDA.

412. Butler, Charles. *An account of the life and writings of the rev. Alban Butler: interspersed with observations on some subjects of sacred and profane literature.* Anon. London. 1799. 8°. [4], 158, [2] p. Printed by: Coghlan, J.P. ESTC t131467. * CaOTV; DoA; ECB; ECW; ICR; L; Lfa; Lhe; LVu; O; OMc; SIR; STA; Stan; StD.

413. Butler, Charles. *An account of the life and writings of the rev. Alban Butler:*

interspersed with observations on some subjects of sacred and profane literature. Edinburgh. 1800. 8°. [4], 60 p. Printed by: Moir, J. Published by: Keating; Brown; Booker, E. (London); Coates, F. (Newcastle). ESTC t088254. * DMR; DoA; E; ECW; L; LO; O.

> Also issued - together with no. 394 - as part of *An appendix to Butler's lives of the saints* (no. 393).

414. Butler, Charles. *An account of the life and writings of the rev. Alban Butler: interspersed with observations on some subjects of sacred and profane literature.* Edinburgh. 1800. 8°. [4], 60 p. Printed by: Moir, J. Published by: Coghlan, J.P.; Keating, P.; Booker, E.; Coates, F. (Newcastle). ESTC t217226. * Du; Lhe.

415. Butler, Charles. *Horae biblicae.* [London?]. 1797. 8°. [4], 109, [1] p. ESTC t116281. * C; DMR; DUu; ICR; IObT; L; Lfa; Lhe; Lu; Luk; MB; NjR; O; Ush.

> Gillow (I, 358): '[this] was not sold, but printed for the author's friends and dedicated to Sir John Courtenay Throckmorton'. L is bound up with *Horae biblicae part the second*, dated 1802.

416. Butler, Charles. *Horae biblicae, being a connected series of miscellaneous notes on the original text, early versions, and printed editions of the old and new testament.* Oxford. 1799. 8°. [4], 270, [2] p. Sold by: White, J. ESTC t144807. * BRp; CaNSHK; Csj; CSmH; Ct; E; L; LAM; Ldw; Lsb; MH; MRp; NNGr; NNUT; NSPM; O; Pci; PPL; ViU; VUA.

> BN cat. mentions a 1799 ed. numbering 367 pages.

417. Butler, Charles. *Horae biblicae, being a connected series of miscellaneous notes on the original text, early versions, and printed editions of the old and new testament.* 3rd ed. Dublin. 1799. 8°. viii, 168 p. Printed by: Mercier, R.E. and Co. Published by: Mercier, R.E. and Co. ESTC t116287. * CaQMM; ICR; IDA; L; NSPM; SIR; WvBeC.

418. Butler, James. *A justification of the tenets of the Roman Catholic religion; and a refutation of the charges brought against its clergy by the right reverend the Lord Bishop of Cloyne. In two parts.* Dublin. 1787. 8°. vii, [3], 98, [2], 88 p. Printed by: Byrne, P. ESTC t107908. * C; CtY; CU-SB; D; Dt; Du; E; FLK; ICR; ICU; IDA; L; MdBP; Mil; MY; O; SCR.

> An answer to *The present state of the Church of Ireland* by Richard Woodward, Bishop of Cloyne (see also next item). The second part is the appendix.

419. Butler, James. *A justification of the tenets of the Roman Catholic religion; and a refutation of the charges brought against its clrgy [sic], by the Bishop of Cloyne.* London. 1787. 8°. 182, [2] p. Printed by: Coghlan, J.P.; Robinsons; Richardson; Faulder. ESTC t122232. * CSmH; E; ECW; ICR; IDA; L; Lu; MBAt; MHi; MRu; MY; O; SCR; Ush.

> With a final advertisement leaf.

420. Butler, James. *A letter from the most reverend doctor Butler, titular Archbishop of Cashel, to the right honourable Lord Viscount Kenmare.* Dublin. 1787. 8°. 15, [1] p. Printed by: Byrne, P. ESTC t121321. * C; CtY; D; ICR; IU; L; Lhl; LONu; MdBJ-P; Mil; MY.

A criticism of Woodward's *The present state of the Church of Ireland* (see also next 2 items).

421. Butler, James. *A letter from the most reverend doctor Butler, titular Archbishop of Cashel, to the right honourable Lord Viscount Kenmare.* Kilkenny. 1787. 8°. 8 p. Printed by: Finn, C. ESTC t077137. * D; DLC; L; SCR.

422. Butler, James. *A letter from the most reverend doctor Butler, titular Archbishop of Cashel, to the right honourable Lord Viscount Kenmare.* London repr. [Dublin]. 1787. 8°. [4], 20 p. Printed by: Coghlan, J.P. [reprinted]. ESTC t174889. * Ct; O; Sto; Ush.

423. Butler, James. *An teagasg Criosduidhe, do reir cheist agus freagradh.* Anon. Cork. 1796. 12°. 24 p. Printed by: Harris, M. * MY.

424. Butler, James. *An teagusg Crèesdéegh, chun aós óg, no Leanavh do heagusg. Re M.R. Dr Sheúmus Bulheár. Agus aisdrighe a Béurla, go Gaólige, le muirertach Bán O'Céiliochair.* Cork. 1792. 8°. 56 p. Printed by: White, T.; O'Haly, J. ESTC t126494. * D; Di; L; Mil; MY.

425. Butler, James. *Suim athgar an teagasg Criosduighe.* Anon. Dublin. 1784. 18°. 78 p. Printed by: Boyce, J. Sold by: Everard, N. ESTC t086853. * Dt; L.

426. *By order of the Catholics of the town and neighbourhood of Wexford, assembled in Wexford on Tuesday, the 30th July, 1793, I have the honour of transmitting to you their resolutions.* [Wexford]. [1793]. s.s. * MY.
      Signed 'J. E. Devereux'.

427. Caimo, John Robert. *The mandate of the right reverend father in God the Lord Bishop of Bruges to the English regular canonesses of the holy order of S. Augustine in the monastery of ... Mary of Nazareth in ... Bruges.* St. Omers. 1768. 12°. 186, [4] p. Printed by: Boubers, H.F. * ECB.

428. *Calendarium a congregatione Anglicana ordinis S. Benedicti.* Paris. 1784. 12°. [3], 4-25, [1] p. * DoA; DowA; ECR.

429. *Calendarium congregationis Anglo-Benedictinae.* Douai. 1755. 12°. 268, [6], [24] p. Printed by: Derbaix. * Amp; DoA; Stan.
      The last 24 pages are a 'supplement' from an undated Spanish/English Benedictine breviary, which may also have been printed in 1755. Amp has 268, [8], 22, [2] p.

430. *Calendrier Français, pour l'année commune.* Newport. [1780]. [2], 44 p. ESTC w001748. * RHi.
      The first French almanac published in Rhode Island and possibly the first Roman Catholic almanac printed on the American Continent.

431. *A candid enquiry, whether the Roman Catholics of Ireland, ought or ought not to be admitted to the rights of subjects; with observations on their political and religious conduct.* Dublin. 1792. 8°. [2], 37, [1] p. Published by: Boyce, J. ESTC t186593. * D; MY.

432. *Cantiques Francaises a l'usage du catéchisme de l'église de Saint-Patrice de Baltimore.* Baltimore. 1798. 12°. 108 p. Printed by: Hayes, J. Published by: Rice, J., & Co. ESTC w030210. * DB; DGU-W; LNT; MWA; RPJCB.

433. Caperan, Arnauld Thomas. *Sense prophétique de l'exurgat Deus, ou, le psaume LXVII, suivant la Vulgate.* London. 1800. 8°. xxxii, 165, [1], 2 p. Printed by: Wilson, A. Sold by: Dulau, A.; Payne, T.; White, J.; Evans, J. et al. ESTC t047450. * C; ECW; L; O.

434. Caraccioli, Louis-Antoine. *Interesting letters of Pope Clement XIV. (Ganganelli.) To which are prefixed, anecdotes of his life. Translated from the French edition.* 3 vols. London. 1777. 12°. Published by: Becket, T. ESTC t102749. * AWn; AzU; BUYs; C; CaOHM; CLU; COCu; E; GEU-T; Gp; KU-S; L; LEu; Lhe; Lu; MChB; MiU; MnU; MrU; O; OAU; SAN.

> This book was sufficiently spectacular to be aimed at the general public. This is the first of 13 separate eds (10 of which in 1777) in which both R.C. and non-R.C. publishers were involved.

435. Caraccioli, Louis-Antoine. *The life of Pope Clement XIV (Ganganelli). Translated from the French of Monsieur Caraccioli.* London. 1776. 8°. vi, 181, [1], lxxxiv, [2] p. Published by: Johnson, J.; Coghlan, J.P. ESTC t105328. * C; CaQMM; CSmH; E; ECW; GEU-T; Gu; ICN; ICU; L; Lhe; Lu; Mil; MRp; NNC; O; P; PPiPT; RY; SAN; TNJ; TxU.

> First English ed. According to Bevan (Summer 1986, no. 130) the translator is Charles Cordell (see also next item). The second sequence of roman page numbers contains 'An Appendix to the Life of Clement XIV'.

436. Caraccioli, Louis-Antoine. *The life of Pope Clement XIV (Ganganelli) ... Carefully compared with the third edition published at Paris, by the Marquis Caraccioli.* 2nd ed. London. 1778. 8°. vi, 182, ix, [5], xciii, [1] p. Published by: Johnson, J.; Goghlan, J.P. [sic]; Charnley, W.; Vesey & Whitfield (Newcastle). ESTC t105310. * CLU-C; D; ECR; ECW; KU-S; L; LANu; Lfa; MChB; NNMan; NNS; NNUT; PPL; TxU.

437. Carey, Mathew. *Philadelphia, August 15, 1789. To the Roman Catholics of America ... proposals for printing by subscription ... holy bible.* Philadelphia. 1789. 8°. [4] p. Printed by: Carey, M. ESTC w008997. * PPL.

> Prospectus for the first Douai version of the bible printed in America.

438. Carey, Mathew. *Reverend Sir, the opportunity afforded by the present meeting is so favourable, that I will avail myself of it, to call your attention to the institution for printing Roman Catholic books.* [Philadelphia]. 1791. s.s. Printed by: Carey, M. ESTC w009002. * PPL.

> Signed and dated 'Matthew Carey, Philadelphia, Nov. 7, 1791'.

439. Carnegy, Ja[mes]. *Instructions and prayers for children.* Anon. [London?]. 1725. 8°. [8], 48 p. ESTC t060054. * L.

> Dedication signed 'Ja. Carnegy'.

440. Carroll, John. *Address from the Roman Catholics of America, to George Washington, Esq. President of the United States.* Anon. London. 1790. fol. 8 p. Printed by: Coghlan, J.P. Sold by: Robinsons, Messrs. ESTC n042269. * BAA; Cli; NN; NNPM; RPJCB; Ush.

441. Carroll, John. *Address to the inhabitants of Philadelphia ... Bishop Carroll ... has recommended to the reverend Mr. Carr, superior of the Augustinian order* *in Dublin [to settle in Philadelphia] ... Willing's Alley.* [Philadelphia?]. [1796]. s.s. * PHi.

>In the title the date 'May 29th, 1796' is given.

442. Carroll, John. *An address to the Roman Catholics of the United States of America. By a Catholic clergyman.* Annapolis. 1784. 8°. 116 p. Printed by: Green, F. ESTC w009039. * CSmH; DGU-W; DLC; Lfa; Lhe; M; NjP; NN; PU; RPJCB; Sto (imp.).

>A reply to *A letter to the Roman Catholics of the city of Worcester* by the apostate Charles Henry Wharton (see also next 3 items and no. 1045).

443. Carroll, John. *An address to the Roman Catholics of the United States of America. By a Catholic clergyman.* Worcester repr. [Annapolis]. 1785. 8°. 120 p. Printed by: Tymbs, J. repr. [Green, F.]. ESTC t163555. * Do; ECW; L; Lhe; O; Osc; Sto; TxU; Ush.

444. Carroll, John. *An address to the Roman Catholics of the United States of America. Occasioned by a letter addressed to the Catholics of Worcester, by Mr Wharton.* 2nd ed. London. 1785. 12°. [2], 115, [3] p. Published by: Keating, P. Sold by: Keating, P. ESTC t129426. * CSmH; Do; DoA; L; LONu; O; Ush.

445. Carroll, John. *An address to the Roman Catholics of the United States of America. Occasioned by a letter addressed to the Catholics of Worcester, by Mr Wharton, their late chaplain.* Dublin repr. [Annapolis]. 1785. 8°. 88 p. Printed by: Wogan, P. ESTC t059862. * L; Mil; MY.

446. Carroll, John. *An answer to strictures on an extraordinary signature.* [1792]. 4°. 4 p. * BCA; Sto.

>A reply to a letter by a Presbyterian minister of Baltimore who protests against the custom of Catholic bishops styling themselves 'John, Bishop of Baltimore'. Dated 'November 21, 1792'.

447. Carroll, John. *Baltimore, December 29, 1799. Rev. Sir: We, Roman Catholics, in common with our fellow citizens.* [Baltimore]. [1799]. s.s. * Parsons no. 208.

>Letter to the clergy on the death of George Washington.

448. Carroll, John. *A discourse on General Washington; delivered in the Catholic church of St. Peter, in Baltimore. Feb. 22d. 1800.* Baltimore. [1800]. 8°. 24 p. Printed by: Warner & Hanna. ESTC w030836. * CtSoP; DGU-W; DLC; GU; MB; MH-H; PPL.

449. Carroll, John. *Jean, par la permission de Dieu ... La grande entendu de mon diocèse, et la nécessité de regler.* 1792. 15, [1] p. * InNd.

>Dated 'May 28, 1792'.

450. Carroll, John. *John, by divine permission and with the approbation of the holy see, Bishop of Baltimore, to my dearly-beloved brethren, the faithful of my diocese, health and the blessing of our Lord. The approaching season of our solemn yearly Lent.* [Baltimore]. [1792]. [4] p. * BCA.

>The date is supplied in ms.

451. Carroll, John. *John, by divine permission, and with the approbation of the* *holy see, Bishop of Baltimore, to my dearly beloved brethren, the members of the Catholic Church in this diocese, health and blessing.* [Baltimore]. [1792]. 6 p. ESTC w009060. * BCA; DGU-W.

> Dated 'May 28, 1792'. A pastoral on the first National Synod of Baltimore (Nov. 7-10, 1791).

452. Carroll, John. *John, by the grace of God, and with the approbation of the holy see, Bishop of Baltimore, to my beloved brethren, of the congregation of Trinity Church, Philadelphia.* [Baltimore]. [1797]. 19, [1] p. * Amp; BCA.

> Dated 'Feb. 22, 1797'. This and the next item concern the schism of the rev. J. N. Goetz (see also nos 1211, 1212).

453. Carroll, John. *John, by the grace of God, and with the approbation of the holy see, Bishop of Baltimore, to my beloved brethren, of the congregation of Trinity Church, Philadelphia.* [Baltimore]. [1797]. 8 p. Printed by: Hayes, J. ESTC w033921. * BCA; DGU; MdW; PHi.

> Dated 'Feb. 22, 1797'.

454. Carroll, John. *[Letter of July 7th].* 10 p. * Amp (imp.).

> Tp missing.

455. Carroll, John. *My dear brethren and children in Jesus Christ of the Catholic congregation of Baltimore.* Washington. 1800. * Parsons no. 214.

> Pastoral on the yellow fever epidemic in Baltimore, dated and signed 'City of Washington, Aug. 26, 1800. John, Bishop of Baltimore'. There is a ms copy at BCA.

456. Carroll, John. *A pastoral letter from the right rev. Dr. John Carroll ... On the prostitution of the rights, and the usurpation of church authority, by two prevaricating priests, and some misinformed laicks.* London. 1798. 12°. [2], 19, [3], 10, [4] p. Printed by: Coghlan, J.P. ESTC t196799. * Lhe; O; Ush (imp.); WDA.

> The two 'prevaricating priests' are Johann Nepomuck Goetz and William Elling (see also nos 452, 1211 and 1212). With 2 final advertisement leaves.

457. Carroll, John. *A pastoral letter from the right rev. Dr. John Carroll ... On the prostitution of the rights, and the usurpation of church authority, by two prevaricating priests, and some misinformed laicks.* London. 1798. 12°. [2], 19, [7] p. Printed by: Coghlan, J.P. ESTC t193903. * DUc; Lhe; O; Ush.

> With some pages of Coghlan adverts.

458. Carroll, John. *Proposals for a subscription, to build a Cathedral Church at Baltimore.* Anon. [1795?]. fol. [6] p. Printed by: Pechin & Co. * BCA; DGU; MdW.

459. Carron, Guy Toussaint Julien. *L'ecclesiastique accompli, ou plan d'une vie vraiment sacerdotale, par l'auteur des pensées ecclesiastiques.* London. 1799. 12°. viii, 183, [1] p. Printed by: Baylis. Sold by: Author; Dulau, A. & Co.; Huard, P.; Fougère. ESTC t111717. * DoA; E; ECW; L.

460. Carron, Guy Toussaint Julien. *L'ecclesiastique accompli, ou plan d'une vie vraiment sacerdotale.* 2nd ed. London. 1800. 12°. 342 p. Printed by: Baylis, T. * Lhe; Nijm.

461. Carron, Guy Toussaint Julien. *Exercice public qui ouvrira a une heure, dans la chapelle Françoise de London-Street.* London. 1799. 4°. [2], ii, 16 p. Printed by: Baylis. * Ush.

462. Carron, Guy Toussaint Julien. *Pensées ecclésiastiques pour tous les jours de l'année: recueillies par un prêtre François exilé pour la foi.* 3 vols. London. 1799. 12°. xii, 348; [2], 406; [2], 370 p. Printed by: Baylis. Sold by: Author; Dulau, A., & Co.; Huard, P.; Fougère. ESTC t114348. * E; L; Lhe.

463. Carron, Guy Toussaint Julien. *Pensées ecclésiastiques pour tous les jours de l'année: recueillies par un prêtre François exilé pour la foi.* 2nd ed. 4 vols. London. 1800. 12°. Printed by: Baylis, T. Sold by: Author; Dulau; Keating; Brown; Fauche (Hamburg). ESTC t197466. * Lhe (in 6 vols); NSPM (vols 1, 4).

464. Carron, Guy Toussaint Julien. *Reflexions Chretiennes pour tous les jours de l'annee. Puisées dans les pères, dans l'histoire de l'eglise.* Winchester. 1796. 12°. v, [1], 555, [1] p. Printed by: Robbins. ESTC t115165. * L; Lhe; O; Ush.

465. *A case of conscience ... decided by forty doctors of the faculty at Paris, in favour of Jansenism. As also what has been done on this occasion by the Pope, Archbishop of Paris, and the King.* [London?]. 1703. 8°. [8], 136 p. Published by: A.B. * DFo; E; ECW; IaU; ICN; L; Lhe; NCp; NIC; TxU.

> Gillow (II, 222) states that S. Jenks attributed this translation to Thomas Fairfax S.J., 'one of the chief anti-Jansenists'; Gillow (IV, 209) gives Louis Ellis Du Pin as the author of this work.

466. *The case of the English Catholic dissenters. The laws in force against the English Catholic dissenters may be ranged under four heads.* [London]. 1789. fol. 3, [1] p. ESTC t203967. * CYc; DowA; Ldw; Sto; WDA.

467. *The case of the English Catholic dissenters. The laws in force against the English Catholic dissenters may be ranged under four heads.* [London?] 1791. fol. 4 p. ESTC t020192. * BAA; L; O; Sto; TxU; WDA; WRW.

468. *[Catalogue of professed monks. English Benedictine congregation].* 1713. s.s. * Nancy.

> A list of 118 names of English Benedictines.

469. *[Catalogue of professed monks. English Benedictine congregation].* London. 1777. s.s. Printed by: Coghlan, J.P. * DowA.

> A list of 95 names.

470. *[Catalogue of professed monks. English Benedictine congregation.].* 1785. fol. s.s. * DoA; DowA.

> A list of 95 names published after the 1785 General Chapter.

471. *[Catalogue of professed monks. English Benedictine congregation.].* 1798. fol. s.s. * DoA; DowA.

> A list of 87 names published after the 1798 General Chapter.

Catechism. See also Abstract and Doway.

472. *Catechism for first communicants. Or instructions for the worthy making and* *preserving the fruits of the first communion ... to which is added instructions for indulgences.* 2nd ed. London. 1781. 12°. [2], 22 p. Printed by: Coghlan, J.P. ESTC t096558. * L.

>The instructions for indulgences are by Charles Walmesley. Cf. no. 2892.

473. *Catechism; or, abridgement of the Christian doctrine.* Newcastle upon Tyne. 1790. 12°. 35, [1] p. Printed by: Hall; Elliot. ESTC t204446. * DoA; Gi; NCp; Ush.

>According to Gillow, edited by Charles Cordell.

474. *Catechisme a l'usage du diocese de Quebec. Imprimé par l'ordre de monseigneur Jean Olivier Briand, Evêque de Quebec.* Montreal. 1777. 12°. [12], 7-59, [3], 61-205, [3] p. Printed by: Mesplet, F.;Berger, C. ESTC w016640. * CaOOA; CaOONL; CaQMBN.

>The third ed. of the Catholic Catechism printed in Canada and the first ed. of the Quebec use.

475. *Catechisme a l'usage du diocese de Québec. Imprimé par l'ordre de monseigneur Jean Olivier Briand, Evêque de Quebec.* 2nd ed. Quebec. [1783?] 12°. [10], 7-59, [3], 61-205, [3] p. Printed by: Brown, G. ESTC w016641. * CaQMM.

476. *Catechisme a l'usage du diocese de Québec. Imprimé par l'ordre de monseigneur Jean Olivier Briand, Evêque de Quebec.* 3rd ed. Quebec. [1791]. 12°. [2], 210, [4] p. Printed by: Neilson, S. Sold by: Germain, L. ESTC w016642. * CaQMBM; CaQMM; CaQQLa.

477. *Catechisme a l'usage du diocese de Québec. Imprimé par l'ordre de monseigneur Jean Olivier Briand, Evêque de Quebec.* 3rd ed. Quebec. [1791]. 12°. [2], 210, [4] p. Printed by: Neilson, S. Sold by: Germain, L. * CaQQLa; MBAt.

>According to Tremaine (699, 670) this is another '3rd' ed. printed from newer type on better paper. Differences include the frame (rule) on tp.

478. *Catechisme à l'usage du diocese de Quebec. Imprimé par l'ordre de monseigneur Jean Olivier Briand, Evêque de Quebec.* 4th ed. Quebec. 1796. 12°. [2], 2-60, [2] p. Printed by: Vondenvelden, W. Published by: Germain, L. Sold by: Germain, L. * CaQMS.

>In spite of the imprint this is probably the 5th or a later ed.

479. *Catechisme a l'usage du diocese de Quebec. Imprimé par l'ordre de monseigneur Jean Olivier Briand, Evêque de Quebec.* 5th ed. Quebec. 1798. 12°. [8], 52 p. Sold by: Huot, F. * CaQQLa (imp.).

480. *Catechisme ou abrégé de la foi Catholique, publié par l'ordre de mgr. l'Archevêque de Paris pour les fideles de son diocese.* Baltimore. 1796. 12°. [4], 113, [1], 12 p. Printed by: Sower, S. ESTC w034926. * DGU; MWA.

481. *Catechistical instructions upon the chief mysteries of faith, and Christian duties.* 1728. 440 p. * Amp (-tp); ECW (-tp and last 6 p.)

>Title and year from Amp catalogue.

482. *Catholic address to Mr. Grattan, with his answer. The following address of* *the Catholics of Dublin, was presented to Mr. Grattan by the gentlemen appointed for that purpose.* [Dublin]. [1795]. fol. s.s. ESTC t207343. * D.

> Address signed 'Thomas Braughall, chairman. John Sweetman, secretary'. Printed in two columns; a note at the foot of the second column reports a resolution of St. Catherine's Parish on Sunday, March 15th, 1795. This concerns Grattan's Catholic Relief Bill. See also no. 37ff.

483. *The Catholic question considered: in a letter addressed to the editor of the Anti-Jacobin review and magazine.* London. 1800. 8°. [4], 52 p. Printed by: Low, S. Sold by: Booker, E.; Hurst, T. ESTC t018212. * CSmH; CYc; E; ECW; KU-S; L; O.

484. *The Catholick question considered: in a letter addressed to the editor of the Anti-Jacobin review and magazine.* Dublin. 1800. 8°. 39, [1] p. Printed by: Fitzpatrick, H. * UshL.

485. *A Catholick answer to Mr. Barrett's sermon. Preach'd at Midhurst July 29th 1722.* [London?]. 1724. 8°. 72 p. ESTC n030672. * Do; InU-Li; Lhe.

486. *The Catholick answer to the seeker's request; in a letter directed to the seeker: proving the real presence, by the scripture only.* 1750. 8°. 8 p. * Ush.

487. *The Catholick's letter to the Roman Catholicks of Ireland, on the late French invasion.* Dublin. [1760]. 8°. 23, [1] p. ESTC t192106. * C; MBAt.
> The imprint gives 'MDCCXL', erroneously according to ESTC.

488. *Catholisches Gebät-buch.* Baltimore. 1795. 18°. 269, [1] p. Printed by: Saur, S. ESTC w018556. * PPL (imp.); ViRUT.

489. Caussin, Nicolas. *Entertainments for Lent ... translated into English by Sir B.B. [Sagesse évangelique pour les sacrez entretiens du caresme].* London. 1741. 12°. [8], 244 p. Published by: Meighan, T. ESTC t103912. * ECW; InNd; L; Lfa.
> 'Sir B.B.' is the 17th century R.C. Sir Basil Brook (1576-1646?). See also next 5 items.

490. Caussin, Nicolas. *Entertainments for Lent ... Translated into English by Sir Basil Brook.* Liverpool. 1755. 18°. 248, [4] p. Printed by: Sadler, J. ESTC t103913. * BRG; CaNSHD; D; DFo; E; Gi; InNd; L; Lhe; LVp; MWH; O; Stan.

491. Caussin, Nicolas. *Entertainments for Lent ... translated into English by Sir B.B.* Dublin. 1765. 8°. 224 p. Printed by: Gorman, B.; Kelly, D. ESTC t210252. * Di.

492. Caussin, Nicolas. *Entertainments for Lent ... Translated into English by Sir Basil Brook.* Preston. 1768. 12°. 248, [4] p. Printed by: Stuart, W. * Ush.

493. Caussin, Nicolas. *Entertainment for Lent ... translated into English by Sir B.B.* Dublin. 1778. 12°. [6], 3-258, [2] p. Printed by: Corcoran, B. ESTC t185451. * O.
> With a final advertisement leaf.

494. Caussin, Nicolas. *Entertainments for Lent ... Translated into English by Sir*

Basil Brook. Wigan. 1785. 12°. viii, 279, [1] p. Printed by: Bancks, W. ESTC t103914. * L; NSPM; Ush.

495. Caussin, Nicolas. *The holy court, in five books. Translated into English by Sir T.H. and others.* Cork. 1767. fol. [10], 869, [1] p. Printed by: Swiney, E. Sold by: Swiney, E. ESTC n009938. * CaOHM; D; IDA; MdW; MY; WaSpG; WaSpStM.
> 'Sir T.H.' is the 17th century R.C. translator Sir Thomas Hawkins (d. 1640)

496. Caussin, Nicolas. *The holy court, in five books; with the lives of the most illustrious courtiers, taken from the old and new testament, and from modern authors.* London. 1767. * MChB-W; MdW; PPL; PPULC; WaSpG.

497. Caussin, Nicolas. *The penitent: or, entertainments for Lent ... Translated into English by Sir B.B [Sagesse évangelique pour les sacrez entretiens du caresme].* London. 1714. 12°. [10], 244. Published by: Gosling, R. ESTC n038514. * Gi; Sal; TxU.
> 'Sir B.B.' is the 17th century R.C. Sir Basil Brook (1576-1646?).

498. *The ceremonies observed in saying mass. Represented in thirty five compartments; with their mistical allusion to the death and passion of our blessed Saviour.* [London?]. [1730?]. 12°. [72] p. ESTC t131016. * L.
> The book consists of 34 copperplates with a few explanatory words each.

499. *Chaine des preuves de la religion.* London. 1798. 8°. 15, [1] p. Printed by: [Baylis, T.]. * ECW.
> The name of the printer occurs on p. 15.

500. Challoner, Richard. *An abstract of the history of the bible: or, a short account of the most remarkable things that have happened to the people of God. By R.C.* 2 vols. London. [1767?]. 12°. 127, [1]; 184 p. Published by: Meighan, T. ESTC t163505. * L; Map.
> The second vol. has a tp reading 'An abstract of the history of the new testament'.

501. Challoner, Richard. *An abstract of the history of the new testament.* 4th ed. London. 1800. 12°. 228 p. Printed by: Coghlan, J.P. * Ush.

502. Challoner, Richard. *An abstract of the history of the old and new testament. Divided into three parts. By R.C.* 2nd ed. London. 1779. 12°. [2], 242, 10 p. Printed by: Coghlan, J.P. ESTC t203588. * DMR; E.

503. Challoner, Richard. *Breve istoria del primo principo e del progresso della religione protestante [A short history of the first beginning and progress of the Protestant religion. English and Italian].* Arezzo. 1767. 8°. xv, [1], 315, [1] p. Published by: Bellotti, M. ESTC t133742. * DLC; ICU; L.
> The translator is Francesco Maria Soldini (see also next item).

504. Challoner, Richard. *Breve storia a favore della chiesa cattolica del primo incominciamento [A short history of the first beginning and progress of the Protestant religion. English and Italian].* Siena. 1790. 12°. [4], 183, [1] p. Printed by: Carli, P. ESTC t133741. * Eu; L.

505. Challoner, Richard. *Britannia sancta, or, the lives of the most celebrated*

British, English, Scottish, and Irish saints ... from the earliest times of Christianity, down to the change. Anon. 2 vols. London. 1745. 4°. v, [3], 388; [4], 335, [1] p. Published by: Meighan, T. ESTC t090074. * ABu; CAL; D; DFo; DLC; DoA; E; ECR; Eu; GOT; HLu; L; Lfa; Lhe; LO; Map; MChB; MRu; MY; NOp; TAUa; TH; UGL; Ush; Yb.

506. Challoner, Richard. *Britannia sancta: or, the lives of the most celebrated British, English, Scottish, and Irish saints ... from the earliest times of Christianity, down to the change.* Anon. 2 vols. London. 1745. 4°. Published by: Meighan, T. ESTC t090075. * CaBVaU; CaOHM; ECB; ECW; L; Nijm; TLP; TxU.

> Large paper issue of no. 505.

507. Challoner, Richard. *A call to a godly life; a discourse on the name of Jesus, and other New year's gifts formerly published by R.C.* London. 8°. [80] p. Printed by: Coghlan, J.P. * ECW.

> Among the 'New year's gifts' are those for 1772, 1773, 1774 and 1776.

508. Challoner, Richard. *The Catholick Christian instructed in the sacraments, sacrifice, ceremonies, and observances of the church. By way of question and answer. By R. C.* London. 1737. 12°. xxiv, 261, [3] p. Printed by: [Meighan, T.?]. ESTC t072815. * BB; C; CLU-C; CU-A; Do; DoA; Dt; ECW; GEU-T; GOT; ICN; ICR; L; Ldw; Lhe; Llp; LO; Map; MRu; NSPM; O; TH; TLP; TxU; Ush.

> The preface of this and the next items contains an answer to C. Middleton's *A letter from Rome* (1729). See also next 10 items.

509. Challoner, Richard. *The Catholic Christian instructed, in the sacraments, sacrifice, ceremonies, and observances of the church. By R- C-.* London. 1738. 12°. xx, 227, [3] p. * CME.

510. Challoner, Richard. *The Catholic Christian instructed in the sacraments, sacrifice, ceremonies, and observances of the church, by way of question and answer.* London. 1747. 12°. xx, 227, [3] p. * CtY.

511. Challoner, Richard. *The Catholick Christian instructed in the sacraments, sacrifice, ceremonies, and observances of the church. By way of question and answer. By R. C.* London. 1753. 12°. xxiv, 261, [3] p. Printed by: [Meighan, T.?]. ESTC t072816. * CAL; Do; Dt; E; ECW; FLK; FU; GeBS; Gi; IDA; L; Lfa; LfaA; Map; NIC; NSIC; O; P; TxU; Ush.

512. Challoner, Richard. *The Catholic Christian instructed, in the sacraments, sacrifice, ceremonies, and observances of the church. By way of question and answer. By R- C-.* London. 1768. 12°. xx, 227, [3] p. ESTC t200861. * Du; FLK.

513. Challoner, Richard. *The Catholic Christian instructed, in the sacraments, sacrifice, ceremonies and observances of the church. By way of question and answer. By R.C.* London. 1769. 12°. xx, 227, [3] p. ESTC t184491. * LfaA; Lhe; Llp.

514. Challoner, Richard. *The Catholic Christian instructed in the sacraments,* *sacrifice, ceremonies, and observances of the church. By way of question and answer. By R. C.* London. 1770. 12°. xxiv, 261, [3] p. Published by: [Meighan, T.?]. ESTC t129231. * BB; ICR; L; Sal.

> Ms note in L states that this is the '3rd ed.' With a Meighan advert at the end of the preface.

515. Challoner, Richard. *The Catholick Christian instructed in the sacraments, sacrifice, ceremonies, and observances of the church. By way of question and answer.* Philadelphia. 1786. 12°. [4], 264 p. Printed by: Talbot, C. Published by: Talbot, C. ESTC w026648. * DB; MWA.

> Parsons (p. 16) suggests the rev. Robert Molyneux, S.J. as editor. See also Shea (p. 375).

516. Challoner, Richard. *The Catholic Christian instructed, in the sacraments, sacrifice, ceremonies, and observances of the church. By way of question and answer.* 12th ed. London. 1788. 12°. xxiv, 237, [3] p. Printed by: [Coghlan, J.P.]. Published by: [Coghlan, J.P.]. * CME; ECR.

> See Coghlan's letters to John Geddes of Jan., March and May 1788 (SCA).

517. Challoner, Richard. *The Catholic Christian instructed in the sacraments, sacrifice, ceremonies, and observances of the church. By way of question and answer.* 13th ed. London. 1793. 12°. xxiv, 237, [3] p. Printed by: Coghlan, J.P. ESTC t120627. * AWn; C; L; Lhe.

518. Challoner, Richard. *The Catholic Christian instructed in the sacraments, sacrifice, ceremonies and observances of the church.* 14th ed. London. 1798. 12°. xxiv, 237, [3] p. Printed by: Coghlan, J.P. ESTC t061344. * Do; E; L.

519. Challoner, Richard. *A caveat against the Methodists. Shewing how unsafe it is for any Christian to join himself to their society, or to adhere to their teachers.* Anon. London. 1760. 12°. 46 p. Published by: Cooper, M. ESTC t092150. * E; L; MRu.

520. Challoner, Richard. *A caveat against the Methodists. Shewing how unsafe it is for any Christian to join himself to their society, or to adhere to their teachers.* Anon. London. 1760. 12°. 46 p. Published by: Needham, W. ESTC t163049. * CaQMM; ICN; Lhe; TxDaM-P; TxU; Ush.

521. Challoner, Richard. *A caveat against the Methodists, showing how unsafe it is for any Christian to join himself to their teachers ... to which is added, the Catholic devotion to the Blessed Virgin Mary.* 3rd ed. London. 1787. 12°. 45, [1] p. Printed by: Coghlan, J.P. ESTC t163051. * BRw; Osc.

522. Challoner, Richard. *A caveat against the Methodists. Shewing how unsafe it is for any Christian to join himself to their society ... To which is added the Catholic devotion to the Blessed Virgin Mary.* 4th ed. London. 1792. 12°. 48 p. Printed by: Coghlan, J.P. ESTC n033504. * CLU; ECR; MoU; O; TLP.

523. Challoner, Richard. *The city of God of the new testament; or a short abstract of the history of the church of Christ.* Anon. London. 1760. 12°. 60 p. Published by: Needham, W. ESTC t162145. * BB; E; ECW; Lfa; Lhe; O; Osc; Sto; TxU; Ush; UshL.

BB and UshL bound up with no. 608.

524. Challoner, Richard. *The city of God of the new testament: or a short abstract of the history of the church of Christ.* 3rd ed. London. 1787. 12°. 60 p. Printed by: Coghlan, J.P. ESTC t014219. * L; Lfa; MBAt; O; Ush.

> Burton (II, 334) gives date of 3rd ed. as '1788'. Page 27 is misnumbered 7.

525. Challoner, Richard. *The city of God of the new testament; or, a short abstract of the history of the church of Christ.* 4th ed. London. 1799. 12°. 56 p. Printed by: Coghlan, J.P. ESTC t185622. * ECW; O; Sal.

526. Challoner, Richard. *A collection of controversial tracts, published by R.C., D.D.* [London]. [1735]. 8°. Printed by: [Meighan, T.]. * Osc.

> Contains 7 tracts beginning with *A plain answer to Dr. Conyers Middleton's Letter from Rome* (cf. nos 622 and 623). The date '1735' probably does not apply to the whole collection but to one of the tracts it contains. Osc copy was reported missing in 1995.

527. Challoner, Richard. *A collection of controversial tracts. Publish'd by R.C.D.D.* London. [1742-48]. 8°. [2], 24, 60, 24, 34, [2], 12, 47, [1], 77, [3] p. Published by: [Meighan, T.]. * Do; ECW; Hen; Lhe.

> The Do pagination is 24, 60, 24, 34, 12, 80. Although the general tp has the date '1747', the dates on the individual tracts range from 1742 to 1748. With 3 pages of Meighan adverts.

528. Challoner, Richard. *A collection of the new year's gifts; which have been published by R.C.* London. 1777. 8°. 27, [1], 19, [1], 2, 2, 18, 15, [1], 9, [3], 25, [1], 13, [2], 26-36 p. Printed by: Coghlan, J.P. * Ush.

> This book mainly consists of separately paginated versions of the new year's gifts for 1773 to 1780. There are several pages of adverts for Coghlan, who states that he has acquired Meighan's stock.

529. Challoner, Richard. *Considerations upon Christian truths and Christian duties digested into meditations for every day in the year. Part I. for the first six months.* Anon. [London?]. [1753]. 12°. [2], x, viii, 387, [1] p. ESTC t165705. * MRu.

> ESTC attribution of date comes from Gillow.

530. Challoner, Richard. *Considerations upon Christian truths and Christian duties digested into meditations for every day in the year.* Anon. 2 vols. [London?]. 1754. 12°. [2], x, viii, 387 [1]; viii, 422 p. ESTC n027886. * CLU-C; DAE (vol. 1); Do (vol. 1); DoA; E; ECW; Gi (vol. 1); IU; Map; O; TxU; UGL (vol. 1); UshL (vol. 1).

> UshL is presentation copy by author.

531. Challoner, Richard. *Considerations upon Christian truths and Christian duties digested into meditations for every day in the year.* Anon. 2 vols. [London?]. 1759. 12°. [2], x, viii, 387, [1]; [2], viii, 422 p. ESTC t129088. * CU-A; Do; DoA; E; ECW; ICN; L; Lhe; Map; TLP.

> Ms attribution on tp of L (vol. 1) and a ms note stating that this is the '2nd ed.'

532. Challoner, Richard. *Considerations upon Christian truths and Christian duties digested into meditations for every day in the year.* Anon. 2 vols.

[London?]. 1767. 12°. [2], x, viii, 387, [1]; [2], viii, 422 p. ESTC t119082. *
DMR; Do (vol. 2); E; FLK; Gi (vol. 2); L (vol. 1); Lhe; P; Sal; Sto.

533. Challoner, Richard. *Considerations upon Christian truths and Christian
duties digested into meditations for every day in the year.* 2 vols. Dublin. 1772.
12°. [14], v, [1], 377, [1]; [3], iv-viii, 422 p. Printed by: Morris, J. * FLK;
IDA; Yb.
> Published by subscription. IDA has first volume with pagination [18], 377, [1].

534. Challoner, Richard. *Considerations upon Christian truths and Christian
duties digested into meditations for every day in the year.* 2 vols. Cork. 1773.
12°. xii, 455, [1]; viii, 482 p. Printed by: Flynn, W. ESTC t221720. * D (vol.
2); Bevan (Summer 1986, no. 103).
> ESTC gives [1780?] on the basis of the incomplete D copy. Bevan lists both
> vols. With two lists of subscribers.

535. Challoner, Richard. *Considerations upon Christian truths and Christian
duties; digested into meditations for every day in the year.* 5th ed. 4 vols.
London. 1784. 12°. Printed by: Coghlan, J.P. ESTC t120570. * DoA (vol. 2);
E; ECW; L; O; TLP; Ush; Vat.

536. Challoner, Richard. *Considerations upon Christian truths and Christian
duties, digested into meditations for every day in the year.* Dublin. 1791. *
PPULC.

537. Challoner, Richard. *Considerations upon Christian truths and Christian
duties digested into meditations for every day in the year.* 2 vols. Dublin. 1795.
12°. viii, 438 p. (vol. 2). Printed by: Wogan, P. ESTC n027887. * Lhe (vol. 2);
RPPC.

538. Challoner, Richard. *Considerations upon Christian truths and Christian
duties, digested into meditations for every day in the year. In two parts.* 2 vols.
Dublin. 1795. 12°. vii, [8], [13], 358; viii, 379, [1] p. Printed by: Jones, W.
Sold by: Jones, W. ESTC n027889. * PPL; SIR.

539. Challoner, Richard. *Considerations upon Christian truths and Christian
duties; digested into meditations for every day in the year ... A new edition.* 2
vols. London. 1796. 12°. [4], iv, 183, [1], [4], iv, 220; xii, 165, [1], viii, 179,
[1] p. Printed by: Coghlan, J.P. ESTC t165277. * DAE (vol. 1); Do; DoA; Du;
Lfa; Stan; TLP; Yb.

540. Challoner, Richard. *The devotion of Catholicks by the Blessed Virgin truly
represented.* [1764]. 8°. 8 p. * Ush.
> Signed 'R.C. E.D. September 29, 1764'.

541. Challoner, Richard. *An exhortation to a thorough conversion from sin to
God: with regulations for Lent, 1762.* Anon. [1762]. 8°. 8 p. * ECW.
> Burton (II, 336), probably following Gillow (I, 457), mentions a 1767 ed. of
> 'Exhortations for paschal communion' which is probably another ed. of this
> book.

542. Challoner, Richard. *An exhortation to a thorough conversion from sin to
God: with regulations for Lent, 1773.* Anon. [1773]. 8°. 15, [1] p. * BAA.

543. Challoner, Richard. *An exhortation to a thorough conversion from sin to God: with regulations for Lent, 1775.* Anon. [1775]. 8°. 15, [1] p. * ECW; Ush.

On tp and on p. 15 of ECW the date 1775 has been changed into 1777.

544. Challoner, Richard. *The garden of the soul: or, a manual of spiritual exercises and instructions for Christians who living in the world aspire to devotion.* [London]. 1740. 12°. [2], 293, [5] p. Published by: [Meighan, T.] . * BB; Do; ECW; Sto.

Do and ECW have 2 pages of Meighan adverts.

545. Challoner, Richard. *The garden of the soul: or, a manual of spiritual exercises and instructions for Christians who living in the world aspire to devotion.* 2nd ed. 1741. [2], 293, [5] p. Published by: [Meighan, T.]. * C; Do; ECW (imp.).

Do has 2 pages of Meighan adverts.

546. Challoner, Richard. *The garden of the soul: or, a manual of spiritual exercises and instructions for Christians who living in the world aspire to devotion.* 3rd ed. 1743. 12°. [2], 294, [4] p. Published by: [Meighan, T.] . * Stan.

With some pages of Meighan adverts. Burton (II, 328) also lists a 1746 ed.

547. Challoner, Richard. *The garden of the soul: or, a manual of spiritual exercises and instructions for Christians who (living in the world) aspire to devotion.* 4th ed. London. 1747. 12°. [2], 294, 6 p. Published by: Meighan, T. * ECW.

With 3 pages of Meighan adverts.

548. Challoner, Richard. *The garden of the soul: or, a manual of spiritual exercises and instructions for Christians who (living in the world) aspire to devotion.* 6th ed. London. 1751. 12°. 327, [3?] p. Published by: Meighan, T. * FLK; Map.

Final pages (contents) of FLK are missing.

549. Challoner, Richard. *The garden of the soul: or, a manual of spiritual exercises and instructions for Christians who (living in the world) aspire to devotion.* 6th ed. Anon. London. 1751. 12°. [2], 40, 307, [3] p. Published by: Meighan, T. ESTC t185008. * ECW; Lhe.

This is another '6th' ed. with different pagination.

550. Challoner, Richard. *The garden of the soul: or, a manual of spiritual exercises and instructions for Christians who (living in the world) aspire to devotion.* Anon. London. 1755. 12°. 317, [7] p. ESTC t190656. * O; Stan (imp.).

With 2 final advertisement leaves. Page 317 misnumbered 217.

551. Challoner, Richard. *The garden of the soul: or, a manual of spiritual exercises and instructions for Christians who living in the world aspire to devotion.* 7th ed. London. 1757. 12°. Published by: Needham, W. * Map; P.

552. Challoner, Richard. *The garden of the soul: or, a manual of spiritual exercises and instructions for Christians.* 8th ed. London. 1759. 12°. 314, [18]

p. Published by: Meighan, T. * ECW; Gi (-tp).
See no. 555 for another '8th' ed.

553. Challoner, Richard. *The garden of the soul: or, a manual of spiritual exercises and instructions for Christians ... From the London copy, neatly corrected and enlarged.* Dublin. 1759. 12°. 336 p. Published by: Executors of the late widow Kelly. ESTC t105943. * L.

554. Challoner, Richard. *The garden of the soul: or, a manual of spiritual exercises and instructions for Christians who living in the world aspire to devotion.* 9th ed. London. 1764. 12°. 314, [16], [4] p. Published by: Meighan, T. * Do; TAB.
With 4 pages of adverts for books by Challoner and Gother.

555. Challoner, Richard. *The garden of the soul: or, a manual of spiritual exercises and instructions for Christians who living in the world aspire to devotion.* 8th ed. Anon. Preston. 1765. 12°. 333, [3] p. Published by: Stewart, W. ESTC t203567. * Do; E; ICN; MRc; Stan.
See no. 552 for another '8th' ed. Burton (II, 328-9) mentions further eds in 1769 and 1775.

556. Challoner, Richard. *The garden of the soul: or, a manual of spiritual exercises and instructions for Christians, who (living in the world) aspire to devotion.* 7th ed. Philadelphia repr. [London]. [1773?]. 24°. 362 p. Printed by: Crukshank, J. * DGU; ICN; MiU-C.
The first Roman Catholic prayer-book printed in English in America.

557. Challoner, Richard. *The garden of the soul: or, a manual of spiritual exercises and instructions for Christians who living in the world aspire to devotion.* 10th ed. Preston. 1777. * TLP.
Burton (II, 329) mentions a '10th ed.' published in 1778.

558. Challoner, Richard. *The garden of the soul: or, a manual of spiritual exercises and instructions for Christians ... To which are added, the vespers for Sundays, not in any former edition.* Kilkenny. 1779. 12°. xx, 305, [1] p. Printed by: Finn, C. ESTC t129802. * L (imp.).
Engr. tp and 10 plates from an ed. of *A manual of devout prayers and other Christian devotions*, Dublin 1742, sold by Ignatius Kelly (see no. 1787).

559. Challoner, Richard. *The garden of the soul, or a manual of spiritual exercises and instructions for Christians.* London. 1782. 24°. 353, iv p. Printed by: Coghlan, J.P. * P.
In the Coghlan correspondence at Edinburgh (SCA BL 3/354/6, 3/354/7 and 3/354/10) Coghlan mentions that he has just (July-October 1782) reprinted *The garden of the soul*.

560. Challoner, Richard. *The garden of the soul: or, a manual of spiritual exercises and instructions for Christians, who living in the world aspire to devotion.* London. 1787. 12°. 360 p. Published by: Coghlan, J.P. * ECW.

561. Challoner, Richard. *The garden of the soul: or, a manual of spiritual exercises and instructions for Christians, who (living in the world) aspire to devotion.* Newcastle. 1789. 12°. [2], 357, [3] p. Printed by: Hall; Elliott. * Gi.

562. Challoner, Richard. *The garden of the soul: or a manual of spiritual exercises and instructions for Christians, who, living in the world, aspire to devotion.* London. 1791. 12°. 360 p. Printed by: Coghlan, J.P. * Map; TxU.

563. Challoner, Richard. *The garden of the soul: or, a manual of spiritual exercises and instructions for Christians who (living in the world) aspire to devotion.* Anon. Philadelphia. [1792]. 357, [3] p. Printed by: Carey, M. ESTC w030133. * DGU-W; ICN.

564. Challoner, Richard. *The garden of the soul: or, a manual of spiritual exercises and instructions for Christians.* London. 1793. 12°. 320, [4] p. * Do; ECW.

565. Challoner, Richard. *The garden of the soul: or, a manual of spiritual exercises and instructions, for Christians.* London. 1793. 12°. xii, 60, xlviii, 61-326, [2] p. Printed by: Coghlan, J.P. ESTC t105169. * L; TLP (imp.); Ush.
    The mass in Latin and English has separate pagination and register.

566. Challoner, Richard. *The garden of the soul: or, a manual of spiritual exercises and instructions, for Christians.* London. 1794. 24°. 360 p. Printed by: Coghlan, J.P. * Utr.

567. Challoner, Richard. *The garden of the soul: or, a manual of spiritual exercises and instructions for Christians ... To which are added, the vespers for Sundays.* 2nd Am. ed. Baltimore. 1796. 18°. 313, [3] p. Printed by: Rice, J. & Co. ESTC w030626. * DB; MWA.
    With 3 pages of adverts.

568. Challoner, Richard. *The garden of the soul: or, a manual of spiritual exercises and instructions for Christians.* [London]. 1796. 24°. 360 p. Printed by: Coghlan, J.P. ESTC t203565. * E; Lnat.

569. Challoner, Richard. *The garden of the soul: or, a manual of spiritual exercises and instructions for Christians ... To which are added the vespers for Sundays.* Dublin. 1798. 12°. 356, [4] p. Printed by: Cross, R. ESTC t105942. * L.
    Page 356 misnumbered 256.

570. Challoner, Richard. *The garden of the soul: or, a manual of spiritual exercises and instructions for Christians.* London. 1798. 12°. 360 p. Printed by: Coghlan, J.P. ESTC t185872. * DoA; ECW; O.

571. Challoner, Richard. *The garden of the soul; or, a manual of spiritual exercises and instructions for Christians.* Anon. London. 1799. 12°. 360 p. Printed by: Coghlan, J.P. * Do.

572. Challoner, Richard. *The garden of the soul; or, a manual of spiritual exercises and instructions for Christians, who, living in the world, aspire to devotion.* Anon. Stockport. 1799. 18°. 355, v p. Printed by: Clarke, J. Published by: Haydock, T. (Manchester). ESTC t116009. * BB; Do; ECR; L; Lhe; Map.
    With 2 pages of Haydock adverts.

573. Challoner, Richard. *The garden of the soul: or, a manual of spiritual* *exercises and instructions for Christians who living in the world aspire to devotion.* Wolverhampton. 1800. [6], 338 p. Printed by: Smart, J. Sold by: Smart, J.; Booker (London). * ECW.

'For the use of Sedgley Park School'.

574. Challoner, Richard. *The garden of the soul; or, a manual of spiritual exercises and instructions for Christians who living in the world aspire to devotion.* London. 1800. 8°. xii, 60, xlviii, 61-326, [2] p. Printed by: Coghlan, J.P. Published by: Keating; Brown & Keating. ESTC t199144. * MRu; TLP.

575. Challoner, Richard. *The grounds of the Catholick doctrine contained in the profession of the faith, publish'd by Pope Pius the Fourth. By way of question and answer.* 5th ed. Anon. [London]. 1735. 12°. 60 p. * L.

The first 4 eds were entitled *A profession of Catholick faith.*

576. Challoner, Richard. *The grounds of the Catholick doctrine contained in the profession of the faith, publish'd by Pope Pius the Fourth, by way of question and answer.* 5th ed. Anon. [London]. 1736. 12°. 60 p. ESTC t062231. * BB; CLU-C; DoA; E; ECW; Gi; L; Lhe; MUN; O; TxU; UGL.

This is the second '5th' ed.

577. Challoner, Richard. *The grounds of the Catholick doctrine, contained in the profession of faith, publish'd by Pope Pius the Fourth, by way of question and answer.* 6th ed. Anon. [London]. 1747. 12°. 60 p. Published by: [Meighan, T.]. ESTC t014629. * Do; DoA; L; MRu; SIR; TxU.

The book is advertised by Meighan in no. 996.

578. Challoner, Richard. *The grounds of the Catholick doctrine, contained in the profession of faith, publish'd by Pope Pius the Fourth, by way of question and answer.* 7th ed. Anon. [Dublin?]. 1752. 12°. 60 p. ESTC t014631. * Do [?]; ECW; L; Map; P; Sto; TxU.

There are four '7th' eds, two of them '[Dublin?]'. In this ed. the headpiece is a framed bowl of fruit. It is not clear whether Do is no. 578 or 579.

579. Challoner, Richard. *The grounds of the Catholick doctrine, contained in the profession of faith, publish'd by Pope Pius the Fourth, by way of question and answer.* 7th ed. Anon. [Dublin?]. 1752. 12°. 60 p. ESTC t089739. * Do [?]; ECW; L; LO; O.

In this ed. the headpiece is an unframed angel with lute. It is not clear whether Do is no. 578 or 579.

580. Challoner, Richard. *The grounds of the Catholick doctrine, contained in the profession of faith, published by Pope Pius the Fourth, by way of question and answer.* 7th ed. Anon. London. 1753. 12°. 60 p. ESTC t014632. * L.

This might be Burton's 8th ed. (Burton II, 324). For other '7th' eds, see nos 578, 579 and 585.

581. Challoner, Richard. *The grounds of the Catholick doctrine contained in the profession of faith publish'd by Pope Pius the Fourth by way of question and answer.* 10th ed. 1771. 12°. 60 p. * DoA; Lhe; Osc; Sto; Ush.

582. Challoner, Richard. *The grounds of the Catholick doctrine contained in the profession of faith publish'd by Pope Pius the Fourth by way of question and* *answer.* 8th ed. Preston. 1775. 12°. 60 p. Published by: Stuart, W. * NN.

For other '8th' eds see nos 583 and 587.

583. Challoner, Richard. *The grounds of the Catholic doctrine, contained in the profession of faith published by Pope Pius the Fourth by way of question and answer.* 8th ed. London. 1779. 8°. 60 p. Printed by: Coghlan, J.P. * ECW.

For other '8th' eds see nos 582 and 587.

584. Challoner, Richard. *The grounds of the Catholic doctrine, contained in the profession of faith published by Pope Pius the IVth ... To which are added, reasons why a Roman Catholic cannot conform.* 9th ed. Anon. Dublin. 1779. 18°. 108 p. ESTC t204171. * D.

585. Challoner, Richard. *The grounds of the Catholick doctrine, contained in the profession of faith, published by Pope Pius the Fourth; by way of question and answer.* 7th ed. London. 1790. 12°. 58 p. Printed by: Coghlan, J.P. ESTC t014633. * L; P.

According to Burton (II, 324) 'wrongly called 7th edition'; see also nos 578, 579, and 580.

586. Challoner, Richard. *The grounds of the Catholic doctrine, contained in the profession of faith published by Pope Pius the IVth.* 10th ed. Anon. Dublin. 1792. 12°. 108 p. Printed by: Cross, R. ESTC t213622. * ZAP.

587. Challoner, Richard. *The grounds of the Catholick doctrine, contained in the profession of faith, published by Pope Pius the Fourth; by way of question and answer.* 8th ed. London. 1796. 12°. 53, [1] p. Printed by: Coghlan, J.P. ESTC t185737. * ECR; Lhe; O.

588. Challoner, Richard. *The grounds of the old religion: or, some general arguments in favour of the Catholick, apostolick, Roman communion. Collected from both ancient and modern controvertists. By a convert.* Augusta [i.e. London]. 1742. 12°. [2], v, [7], 213, [1] p. ESTC t095748. * BB; C; CAL; CaOHM; CU-BANC; Do; E; ECW; FU; Hen; ICN; L; Lfa; Lhe; Map; MRu; MY; O; PPL; TLP; TxU; Ush; Yb.

589. Challoner, Richard. *The grounds of the old religion: or, some general arguments in favour of the Catholick, apostolick, Roman communion. By a convert.* Augusta [i.e. London]. 1742. 12°. vii, 182 p. * Do (Dom Maidlow-Davis).

590. Challoner, Richard. *The grounds of the old religion: or, some general arguments in favour of the Catholick, apostolick, Roman communion. Collected from both ancient and modern controvertists. By a convert.* Augusta [i.e. London]. 1746. 12°. 194, [6] p. ESTC t095744. * Dt; Gi; L; MWH; P.

591. Challoner, Richard. *The grounds of the old religion: or, some general arguments in favour of the Catholick, apostolick, Roman communion. Collected from both ancient and modern controvertists ... By a convert.* Augusta [i.e. London]. 1751. 12°. vii, [7], 182 p. ESTC t061532. * Do; DoA; E; ECW; Gi; L; Lhe; LO; Map; MRu; MY; NNF; O; Sto; Ush; UshL.

The pagination of Do, Sto and UshL is vii, [1], 183, [6]; this is due to the table of contents being placed differently. LO has vii, [1], 182, [6].

592. Challoner, Richard. *The grounds of the old religion, or, some general arguments in favour of the Catholic, apostolick, Roman communion. Collected from both ancient and modern controvertists.* 4th ed. London. 1781. 12°. v, [1], 169, [5] p. Published by: [Coghlan, J.P.?]. ESTC n017963. * DUu; E; ECW; Lhe; MRu; O; Sal; Sco; StD; Vat.

Burton (II, 330) gives Coghlan as publisher.

593. Challoner, Richard. *The grounds of the old religion; or, some general arguments in favour of the Catholic, apostolic, Roman communion.* London. 1797. Published by: Coghlan, J.P. *Gillow I, 454.

'With beautiful medallion head executed by J. Nagle, and a short sketch of the life of the author by Dr. Milner'.

594. Challoner, Richard. *Grounds of the old religion, or, general arguments in favour of the Catholic, apostolic, Roman communion. Collected from both ancient and modern controvertists.* 5th ed. London. 1798. 12°. [4], 50, iv, 1-36, 49-230, 6 p. Printed by: Coghlan, J.P. ESTC t061345. * CLU; DMR; Do; DoA; Dt; DUu; E; ECW; L; Lhe; NN; Sal; Stan; TLP; TxU.

With a second tp 'A brief account of the life of ... Challoner' by John Milner (see no. 1865). Do pagination is [2], iv, [4], 50, 230, [6].

595. Challoner, Richard. *Instructions and advice to Catholicks, upon occasion of the late earthquakes.* Anon. [London?]. 1750. 8°. 8 p. ESTC t066561. * CtY; ECW; L; Map; O; Ush.

A pastoral letter by Bishop Petre and his coadjutor Richard Challoner, but in fact written by Challoner.

596. Challoner, Richard. *Instructions and advice to Catholicks upon occasion of the late dreadful earthquakes together with thirty meditations.* Anon. [London?]. 1755. 12°. 106, [2] p. ESTC t210182. * DUc; ECR; ICN; TxU.

The *Instructions and advice* was originally published separately (see previous item).

597. Challoner, Richard. *Instructions and directions for gaining the grand jubilee of the holy year, celebrated at Rome anno 1775, and extended to the universal church anno 1776, by his holiness Pius VI.* Anon. London. [1775?]. 12°. 17, [1] p. Printed by: Coghlan, J.P. ESTC t184693. * O; Ush.

598. Challoner, Richard. *Instructions and directions for gaining the grand jubilee.* London. [1776]. 17, [3], 84 p. Printed by: Coghlan, J.P. * Do; Lhe; Ush.

599. Challoner, Richard. *Instructions and directions for the jubilee, 1770.* [1770]. 12°. [2], 9, [1] p. * ECW; WDA.

Dated and signed 'February 28, 1770. R.D.V.A.'; see also no. 603.

600. Challoner, Richard. *Instructions and regulations for the fast of Lent, 1757. Addressed to the faithful of the London district.* Anon. [1757]. 8°. 8 p. * BAA; ECW; Ush.

Ms note in BAA suggests that this work was written by Richard Challoner as coadjutor to Bishop Petre.

601. Challoner, Richard. *Instructions for the time of the jubilee anno 1751, with meditations, in order to determine the soul to turn from sin to God.* Anon. [London?]. 1751. 18°. xii, 95, [1] p. ESTC t119605. * CLU-C; DoA; ECW; Gi; IU; L; Lfa; Lhe; LO; Map; O; Sto; TxU; Ush.

602. Challoner, Richard. *[Instructions for the time of the jubilee anno 1751, with meditations, in order to determine the soul to turn from sin to God].* Anon. [London?]. [1760?]. 12°. 3-92 p. ESTC t134111. * L (-tp).

603. Challoner, Richard. *Instructions for the time of the jubilee anno 1770, with meditations, in order to determine the soul to turn from sin to God.* 2nd ed. [London?]. 1770. 12°. [2], 9, [1], 84 p. ESTC t037305. * ECW (-tp); L; Ush.
> Signed 'R.D.V.A.'

604. Challoner, Richard. *A letter to a friend. Concerning the infallibility of the church of Christ. In answer to a late pamphlet, entitled, An humble address to the Jesuits.* London. 1743. 12°. 47, [1] p. ESTC t014213. * BB; CLU-C; COA; Do; E; ECW; L; Lhe; LO; Map; NNF; O; StD; Sto; TLP; Ush.
> Also issued as part of *A collection of controversial tracts,* 1747 (no. 527).

605. Challoner, Richard. *London district. Regulations for Lent, 1778.* [1778]. 8°. 2 p. * Cli; ECW.

606. Challoner, Richard. *A mandate to the clergy, Oct. 5, 1753, on occasion of a breve pontificium of Benedict XIV.* 1753. *Burton, II, 333.
> See also Gillow (I, 455).

607. Challoner, Richard. *Memoirs of missionary priests, as well secular as regular; and of other Catholics, of both sexes, that have suffered death in England.* Anon. 2 vols. [London]. 1741-42. 8°. [26], 450; [14], 496. Sold by: [Needham, F.] ESTC t125100. * AR; C; CAL; CME; DAE; DFo; Do; Dt; E; ECW; FLK; FP; Gi (vol. 2); L; Lfa; Lhe; Map; Pci; Sal; SIR; Stan (vol. 2); TH; TLP; Ush; Yb.
> CME pagination is [28], 450; [16], 496; the extra pages contain errata and adverts for F. Needham. ECW is an interleaved copy annotated by Challoner himself.

608. Challoner, Richard. *A memorial of ancient British piety: or, a British martyrology. Giving a short account of all such Britons as have been honoured of old amongst the saints.* Anon. London. 1761. 12°. 216, 50 p. Published by: Needham, W. ESTC t143957. * BB; C; CAL; CtY; D; Do; DoA; E; ECB (-tp); ECW; ICN; L; Lfa; LO; MRu; MY; O; Osc; SIR; STA; Sto; TxU; UGL; Ush; UshL.
> BB and UshL lack the 50-page supplement (about Saxon manuscripts), but are bound up with *The city of God,* 1760 (no. 523).

609. Challoner, Richard. *The morality of the bible: extracted from all the canonical books, both of the old and of the new testament: for the use of such pious Christians as desire to nourish their souls to eternal life. By R.C.* London. 1762. 12°. 466, xiv p. ESTC t170174. * CLU; DMR; DoA; ECW; Gi; Hor; Map; NSPM; O; Osc; P; Ush.
> The selections are from the Douai Bible (see also next item).

610. Challoner, Richard. *The morality of the bible; extracted from all the canonical books, both of the old and of the new testament.* Dublin repr. [London]. 1765. 12°. v, [11], 377, [1], xiv p. Printed by: Byrn, J. Published by: Bowes, P. Sold by: Bowes, P.; Kelly, D. ESTC t132776. * D; FLK; IDA; InNd; L; Lhe; Mil; O.

> With a list of subscribers.

611. Challoner, Richard. *A new year's gift, containing rules of life for a Christian who desires to live holily: and to die happily, collected by R.C.* [c.1770]. 8°. 25-33 p. * Osc.

> *New year's gifts* tended to appear as part of *Laity's directories*, hence the unusual pagination of some of these items. Of this and the following 3 items the corresponding *Directory* has not been found and therefore they are listed separately.

612. Challoner, Richard. *A new year's gift for 1766.* 8°. 8 p. * Ush (imp. lacks pp. 3-6).

613. Challoner, Richard. *A new-year's gift for the year 1771. Some thoughts on the great concern of eternity; and on the means of securing to our souls a happy eternity.* 12°. 27-36 p. * ECW.

614. Challoner, Richard. *A new-year's gift for the year 1773: a call to a godly life ... The life of faith, with acts of faith, hope and charity, translated from the French, printed at Lille, 1771.* Anon. [1773]. 8°. 11 p. * Osc.

615. Challoner, Richard. *A pastoral instruction for the apostolic fast of Lent. By R.C.* [London]. [1767?]. 8°. [2], 36 p. Printed by: Coghlan, J.P. * ECW.

> According to ECW cat. this is the 1st ed.

616. Challoner, Richard. *A pastoral instruction for the apostolic fast of Lent. By R.C.* [London]. [1767?]. 12°. 28 p. Published by: Coghlan, J.P. * Ush.

> Ush suggests '1767'.

617. Challoner, Richard. *A pastoral instruction for the apostolic fast of Lent. By R.C.* 2nd ed. [London]. [1767?]. 8°. [4], 36 p. Printed by: Coghlan, J.P. * ECW; Ush.

> Ush suggests '1767'.

618. Challoner, Richard. *A pastoral instruction for the apostolic fast of Lent.* 4th ed. London. 1786. 12°. 35, [1] p. Printed by: Coghlan, J.P. * Amp.

619. Challoner, Richard. *A pastoral letter addressed to the Catholicks of the British islands in the West-Indies.* [London]. [1770]. 8°. 8 p. * Ush.

> Signed and dated 'R.C. B.D.V.A. December 19th, 1770'.

620. Challoner, Richard. *A pastoral letter addressed to the Catholicks of the British islands in the West-Indies.* [London]. [1770]. 8°. 12 p. * WDA.

> Signed and dated 'R.C. B.D.V.A. December 19th, 1770'.

621. Challoner, Richard. *Pious reflections on patient sufferings, collected from the lives of the fathers, martyrs and other saints.* Anon. [1767] 12°. 48 p. * Osc; Ush.

> In an advert in Luis de Granada's *An exhortation to alms-deeds*, 1775 (no.

1682), Alban Butler is given as the author of this work.

622. Challoner, Richard. *A plain answer to Dr. Middleton's letter from Rome: in which the gross misrepresentations contained therein are exposed ... By a friend to truth.* London. 1741. 8°. [2], 22 p. Published by: Huggonson, J. ESTC t011586. * Ct; CtHT-W; E; IU; L; LVu; Map; MoU; O.

> The text of this work forms the preface of *The Catholick Christian instructed* (no. 508ff.); see also next item. 'C-s M-n' is Conyers Middleton, for whose *A letter from Rome* (1729) see ESTC.

623. Challoner, Richard. *A plain answer to Dr. C-s M-n's letter from Rome.* Anon. London. 1742. 12°. 24 p. ESTC n038439. * Do; Lhe; Map; MdU.

624. Challoner, Richard. *A profession of Catholick faith, extracted out of the Council of Trent by Pope Pius IV.* Anon. [London?]. 1732. 12°. 48 p. Published by: [Meighan, T.?]. ESTC t176375. * CU-BANC; ECW; Lhe.

625. Challoner, Richard. *A profession of Catholick faith, extracted out of the Council of Trent by Pope Pius IV.* 4th ed. Anon. [London?]. 1734. 12°. 60 p. ESTC t014628. * C; Do; ECW; FLK; L; Ldw; Lhe; Omc.

> From the 5th ed. onward, this work was published as *The grounds of the Catholick doctrine* (no. 575ff.).

626. Challoner, Richard. *A profession of Catholick faith.* Anon. [London?]. [1750?]. 12°. [1], 4-60 p. ESTC t014630. * L (-tp).

> ESTC's suggestion of 1750 as date of publication seems unlikely in view of the fact that the book had a different title from 1736 onwards. See note to no. 625.

627. Challoner, Richard. *Regulations for Lent, 1780.* [1780]. 8°. 3, [1] p. Printed by: Coghlan, J.P. * Ush.

> Signed and dated 'Richard Deboren, James Birthan. London, 29 Jan. 1780'.

628. Challoner, Richard. *Regulations for the fast of Lent 1766 for the L... district. In consideration of the hardness of the times.* Anon. [1766?]. 8°. 2 p. * ECW.

> On tp of ECW 1766 has been changed in pen to '1767'.

629. Challoner, Richard. *Regulations for the fast of Lent, 1772. For the L... district. In consideration of the hardness of the times.* Anon. [1772]. 8°. 7-8 p. * ECW.

630. Challoner, Richard. *Regulations for the fast of Lent, 1773. For the L... district.* Anon. [1773]. 8°. 2 p. * ECW.

631. Challoner, Richard. *Remarks on two letters against popery, pretended to be written by a Protestant lady and first published in the year 1727 upon the recommendation of Dr. Samuel Clarke, in a letter to a friend.* [London?]. 1751. 12°. 47, [1] p. ESTC t168994. * ICN; Lhe; Osc.

> Signed on verso D3 'R.C.'.

632. Challoner, Richard. *A Roman Catholick's reasons why he cannot conform to the Protestant religion.* Anon. 1734. 12°. 12 p. * Do; ECW [?]; Map.

> ECW has 2 copies without tp. They could be this, or one of the 5 following eds. In 1748 an ed. of this book was advertised by Thomas Meighan in no. 996.

633. Challoner, Richard. *A Roman Catholick's reasons why he cannot conform to the Protestant religion.* Anon. [London?]. [1735?]. 12°. 12 p. ESTC t014177. * CLU-C; Do (-tp); L; Lhe.

    The first leaf is unsigned.

634. Challoner, Richard. *A Roman Catholick's reasons why he cannot conform to the Protestant religion.* Anon. [London]. [1735?]. 12°. 12 p. ESTC t014178. * E; ECW; L; MRu; TLP; Ush.

    The first leaf is signed 'A'.

635. Challoner, Richard. *A Roman Catholick's reasons why he cannot conform to the Protestant religion.* Anon. [London?]. [1736?]. 12°. 12 p. ESTC t014179. * BB; DoA; L.

    An illustrated letter B on page 1.

636. Challoner, Richard. *A Roman Catholick's reasons why he cannot conform to the Protestant religion.* Anon. [London?]. [1736?]. 12°. 12 p. * Ush.

    An illustrated letter B on page 1 and the first leaf is signed 'A'.

637. Challoner, Richard. *A Roman Catholick's reasons why he cannot conform to the Protestant religion.* Anon. [London?]. [1740?]. 12°. 12 p. Published by: [Meighan, T.] ESTC t014180. * Do (-tp); ECW; L; ; Map (imp.); O.

    There is a factotum on page 1 round the letter B.

638. Challoner, Richard. *A Romam [sic] Catholick's reasons why he cannot conform to the Protestant religion.* Anon. [London?]. [1750?]. 12°. 12 p. ESTC t014181. * L; Lhe.

    There is a plain capital B on page 1.

639. Challoner, Richard. *A Roman Catholick's reasons why he cannot conform to the Protestant religion.* [Baltimore]. [1790?]. [8] p. Printed by: Adams, S. & J. Published by: Adams, S. & J. * CtY.

    'Lately distributed among the Roman Catholicks of Baltimore town, by their newly consecrated bishop ... now re-published. Printed by S. & J. Adams' (Note 'To the public' at head of title).

640. Challoner, Richard. *A Roman Catholick's reasons why he cannot conform to the Protestant religion.* Anon. [London]. [1796]. 12°. 12 p. Printed by: Coghlan, J.P. ESTC t014182. * L.

    Imprint from colophon.

641. Challoner, Richard. *Rules of life for a Christian, who desires to live holily, and to die happily. Collected by R.C.* London. 1766. 24°. [3], 4-52 p. Published by: Meighan, T. ESTC t206733. * DMR; DoA; E; ECB; LOU; Map; Ush.

642. Challoner, Richard. *Rules of life for a Christian who desires to live holily and to die happily.* 3rd ed. London. 1788. 12°. 35, [1] p. Printed by: Coghlan, J.P. * ECW.

643. Challoner, Richard. *Sail yr athrawiaeth Gatholic, gynnwysedig mewn profess ffydd a gyhoeddwyd gan Bab Piws y Bedwerydd [A profession of Catholick faith].* Anon. London. 1764. 12°. vi, [2], 87, [1] p. Printed by: Balfe, R. ESTC t116295. * AWn; AWu; L.

The translator's preface is signed 'Grigor ap Joan' [i.e. David Powell].

644. Challoner, Richard. *The scripture doctrine of the church.* [London?]. [1740?]. 12°. 34, [2] p. ESTC t062270. * BB; COA; Do (-tp); E; L; Lhe; O; TxU; Ush (-tp).

    The final leaf has a catalogue of books by Challoner.

645. Challoner, Richard. *Scripture sentences for the encouragement and comfort of such as suffer from conscience.* Anon. London. 1744. 12°. 12 p. Published by: Needham, F. ESTC n037285. * BB; ECW; MBAt; TLP.

    BB gives Challoner as author.

646. Challoner, Richard. *A short daily exercise with devotions for mass, confession and communion; abridged from The garden of the soul.* [London?]. 1760. 12°. 285, [3] p. * C.

    Burton (II, 337) claims that the 1st ed. came out in 1767.

647. Challoner, Richard. *A short daily exercise with devotions for mass, confession and communion; abridged from The garden of the soul. By R.C. D.D.* 3rd ed. [London]. 1769. 12°. 285, [3] p. Published by: Meighan, T. * Gi.

648. Challoner, Richard. *A short daily exercise, with devotions for mass, confession and communion: abridged from The garden of the soul, and published for the use of the poor.* 3rd ed. [London?]. 1770. 12°. 285, [3] p. * Amp.

    This is the second '3rd' ed.

649. Challoner, Richard. *A short explanation of indulgences, grounded upon holy scriptures from the authority of popes and general-councils. By a lover of souls.* London. 1742. 12°. 93, [3] p. Printed by: [Hoyles, J.]. ESTC t118197. * L; Lhe; TxU.

    With 2 pages of Hoyles adverts.

650. Challoner, Richard. *A short history of the beginning and progress of the Protestant religion. Gathered out of the best Protestant writers. By way of question and answer.* Anon. London. 1735. 12°. 78 p. Published by: Brabham, H. ESTC t014159. * Do; ECW; ICN; L; TxU.

    This title also occurs with the word 'first' before 'beginning' (see next 10 items). Burton (I, 92) also lists a 1733 ed.

651. Challoner, Richard. *A short history of the first beginning and progress of the Protestant religion. Gathered out of the best Protestant writers. By way of question and answer.* Anon. London. 1735. 12°. 78 p. Published by: Brabham, H. ESTC n024877. * ICN; TxU.

    It is not unlikely that this is an issue of no. 650 with a different tp.

652. Challoner, Richard. *A short history of the first beginning and progress of the Protestant religion. Gathered out of the best Protestant writers. By way of question and answer.* Anon. London. 1735. 12°. 93, [1] p. ESTC t172725. * Dt.

653. Challoner, Richard. *A short history of the first beginning and progress of the Protestant religion, gather'd out of the best Protestant writers, by way of question and answer.* Anon. 3rd ed. London. 1736. 12°. 76, [2] p. Published by:

Meighan, T. ESTC t179853. * CLU-C; DoA; ECW; O; Ush.

654. Challoner, Richard. *A short history of the first beginning and progress of the Protestant religion, gather'd out of the best Protestant writers, by way of question and answer.* Anon. London. 1736. 12°. 76 p. Published by: Meighan, T. * ECW; Lhe.

655. Challoner, Richard. *A short history of the first beginning and progress of the Protestant religion, gather'd out of the best Protestant writers, by way of question and answer.* Anon. London. 1742. 12°. 77, [3] p. Published by: Meighan, T. ESTC t014160. * Do; Gi; L; Lhe; Oc; TLP; TxU.
Do, Gi and TLP have 3 pages of Meighan adverts.

656. Challoner, Richard. *A short history of the first beginning and progress of the Protestant religion, gather'd out of the best Protestant writers. By way of question and answer.* Anon. London. 1753. 12°. 77, [3] p. Published by: Meighan, T. ESTC t059215. * DFo; Do; L; Lhe; Map.
Burton (II, 325) mentions a 6th and a 7th ed. in 1753 (see also next item) and Gillow (I, 452) also mentions a 1767 ed.

657. Challoner, Richard. *A short history of the first beginning and progress of the Protestant religion, gather'd out of the best Protestant writers, by way of question and answer.* Anon. London. 1753. 12°. 72 p. ESTC t014161. * CtY; D; L.

658. Challoner, Richard. *A short history of the first beginning and progress of the Protestant religion, gathered out of the best Protestant writers.* 10th ed. London. 1781. 12°. 59, [1] p. Printed by: Coghlan, J.P. * MY; Ush.

659. Challoner, Richard. *A short history of the first beginning and progress of the Protestant religion, gathered out of the best Protestant writers. By way of question and answer.* 11th ed. London. 1789. 12°. 59, [1] p. Printed by: Coghlan, J.P. ESTC n022762. * CSmH; MBAt; MHi.

660. Challoner, Richard. *A short history of the first beginning and progress of the Protestant religion, gathered out of the best Protestant writers, by way of question and answer.* 12th ed. Anon. London. 1795. 12°. 59, [1] p. Printed by: Coghlan, J.P. ESTC t014162. * ECR; L; O; Osc.

661. Challoner, Richard. *A specimen of the spirit of the dissenting teachers in their sermons lately preach'd at Salters-Hall; or some remarks upon Mr. John Barker's sermon against popery ... By Philalethes.* London. 1736. 12°. [2], 226 p. Published by: Meighan, T. ESTC n023926. * CLU-C; COA; Do; ECW; KU-S; Lhe; LO; MRu; MY; Osc; Pci; Sto; TLP; TxU.
Against John Barker's *Popery the great corruption* and Samuel Chandler's *The notes of the church* (ESTC t054745 and t028379); see also next item.

662. Challoner, Richard. *A specimen of the spirit of the dissenting teachers in their sermons lately preach'd at Salters-Hall; or some remarks upon Mr. John Barker's sermon on popery ... By Philalethes.* London. 1736. 12°. [2], 226 p. Printed by: [Meighan, T.]. ESTC t086314. * BB; C; Do; E; ECW; Gi; Hen; ICU; L; Lhe; NIC; O; Pci; Stan; TxDaM-P; UGL; Ush; UshL.

Bevan (Advent 1993, no. 69) suggests Thomas Meighan as printer.

663. Challoner, Richard. *Think well on't; or, reflections on the great truths of the Christian religion. For every day in the month.* 2nd ed. Anon. London. 1734. 18°. 190, [2] p. Published by: Meigham [sic], T. ESTC t103915. * L.
> Morison (p. 26) gives 1728 as date of the 1st ed.

664. Challoner, Richard. *Think well on't; or, reflections on the great truths of the Christian religion. For every day in the month.* 3rd ed. Anon. London. 1736. 18°. 190, [2] p. Published by: Meighan, T. ESTC t118429. * L.

665. Challoner, Richard. *Think well on't; or, reflections on the great truths of the Christian religion. For every day in the month.* 4th ed. Anon. London. 1744. 24°. 190, [2] p. Published by: Meighan, T. ESTC t104421. * E; Gi; L.

666. Challoner, Richard. *Think well on't; or, reflections on the great truths of the Christian religion. For every day in the month.* 5th ed. Anon. London. 1749. 12°. 190, [2] p. Published by: Meighan, T. ESTC t179770. * ECW; Lfa; Lhe; O; Sto; TxU.

667. Challoner, Richard. *Think well on't: or reflections on the great truths of the Christian religion.* Dublin. 1749. 8°. 144 p. Published by: Kelly, I. * P.

668. Challoner, Richard. *Think well on't; or, reflections on the great truths of the Christian religion. For every day in the month.* 5th ed. corr. Anon. Liverpool. 1751. 12°. 190, [2] p. Printed by: Sadler, J. ESTC t118371. * L.
> This is the second '5th' ed.

669. Challoner, Richard. *Think well on't; or, reflections on the great truths of the Christian religion.* 6th ed. London. 1768. 24°. 180 p. Printed by: Meighan, T. * Map; Sal; Ush.

670. Challoner, Richard. *Think well on't: or, reflections on the great truths of the Christian religion.* 8th ed. London. 1781. 12°. 221, [1] p. Printed by: Coghlan, J.P. * Lfa; Yb.

671. Challoner, Richard. *Think well on't: or reflections on the great truths of the Christian religion.* Dublin. 1784. 8°. 143, [1] p. Printed by: Cross, R. * P.

672. Challoner, Richard. *Think well on't: or, reflections on the great truths of the Christian religion for every day in the month.* 9th ed. London. 1785. 12°. 213, [3] p. Printed by: Coghlan, J.P. * Lfa.
> With 2 pages of adverts.

673. Challoner, Richard. *Think well on't: or, reflections on the great truths of the Christian religion for every day in the month.* 10th ed. London. 1789. 12°. [6], 213, [1] p. Printed by: Coghlan, J.P. * Amp.

674. Challoner, Richard. *Think well on't: or, reflections on the great truths of the Christian religion. For every day of the month.* 1st Am. ed. Philadelphia. [1791]. 18°. 143, [1] p. Printed by: Carey, Stewart & Co. ESTC w030627. * DGU-W; MWA.
> According to Finotti (p. 85ff.) this is the 34th ed. On tp the author is given as 'Chalenor'. Byrns (p. 22) lists a 30th ed. (Dublin 1795) with a copy at the

71

675. Challoner, Richard. *Think well on't; or reflections on the great truths of the Christian religion. For every day in the month.* 12th ed. London. 1798. 12°. 214 p. Printed by: Coghlan, J.P. ESTC t208488. * Lhe.

676. Challoner, Richard. *Think well on't: or, reflections on the great truths of the Christian religion. For every day of the month.* 32nd ed. Philadelphia. 1800. 18°. 136, [4] p. Printed by: Bioren, J. Published by: Carey, M. ESTC w030628. * IObT; MWA.

677. Challoner, Richard. *Think well on't; or, reflections on the great truths of the Christian religion. For every day of the month.* [Manchester]. 12°. ii, 107, [1] p. Printed by: [Dean, R. & W.]. * Lfa (-tp).
'Manchester. Printed by R. & W. Dean & Co.' (p. 107).

678. Challoner, Richard. *To all the Catholic clergy, both secular and regular, residing in the southern district.* [London]. [1778]. fol. 2 p. Printed by: [Coghlan, J.P.]. * Map; Ush; UshA.
Dated and signed '4th June, 1778, Richard Deboren, James Birthan ... John Philomel, Thomas Aeon, William Trachon, Charles Ramaten'.

679. Challoner, Richard. *To the faithful of the L- district. This is to acquaint you, dearly beloved, that we have lately received from the holy apostolic see, a grant of the reduction of a greater part of our holydays.* [London]. [1777]. 4°. s.s. ESTC t051197. * L; Llp; Ush; UshA (imp.); WDA.
Signed 'Richard Deboren and James Birthan'. Ms note in WDA states 'March 1777, London'.

680. Challoner, Richard. *To the faithful of the L... district. We have lately acquainted you, dearly beloved, that the holy see apostolic, in consideration of the circumstances of the faithful.* [London?]. [1777?]. fol. s.s. ESTC t051198. * L; Llp; Ush.
Signed 'Richard Deboren and James Birthan'.

681. Challoner, Richard. *The touchstone of the new religion: or, sixty assertions of Protestants, try'd by their own rule of scripture alone, and condemn'd by clear and express texts of their own bible.* Anon. London. 1735. 12°. 32 p. ESTC n027597. * Amp; CLU-C; Do; DoA; ECW; ICN; Lhe; MUN; Ush.
Byrns (p. 19) and Burton (II, 325) list a 1734 ed. with, according to Byrns, a copy at Yale. Do has half a page of adverts.

682. Challoner, Richard. *The touchstone of the new religion: or, sixty assertions of Protestants try'd by their own rule of scripture alone, and condemn'd by clear and express texts of their own bible.* Anon. London. 1735. 12°. 70 p. * NjPT.

683. Challoner, Richard. *The touchstone of the new religion: or, sixty assertions of Protestants try'd by their own rule of scripture alone, and condemn'd by clear and express texts of their own bible.* 2nd ed. Anon. London. 1735. 12°. 76 p. * Ush.

684. Challoner, Richard. *The touchstone of the new religion: or, sixty assertions of Protestants, try'd by their own rule of scripture alone, and condemn'd by clear* *and express texts of their own bible.* Anon. London. 1741. 12°. 24 p. ESTC t062269. * BB; COA; Do; E; ECW; L; TLP; Ush.

> In the title the word 'scripture' is divided as 'scri-pture'. Do, Ush and ECW are either this or the next item.

685. Challoner, Richard. *The touchstone of the new religion: or, sixty assertions of Protestants, try'd by their own rule of scripture alone, and condemned by clear and express texts of their own bible.* Anon. London. 1741. 12°. 24 p. ESTC t014169. * L; O.

> In the title the word 'scripture' is divided as 'scrip-ture'.

686. Challoner, Richard. *The touchstone of the new religion: or, sixty assertions of Protestants, try'd by their own rule of scripture alone, and condemn'd by clear and express texts of their own bible.* Anon. London. 1748. 12°. 24 p. ESTC t014170. * Do; L; Lhe; Map; MRu.

> Gillow (I, 452) also mentions a 1788 ed.

687. Challoner, Richard. *The touchstone of the new religion: or sixty assertions of Protestants, tried by their own rule of scripture alone ... To which is added the true principles of a Catholic.* 7th ed. London. 1795. 12°. 24 p. Printed by: Coghlan, J.P. ESTC t014168. * CAL; ECR; L; O; Ush.

688. Challoner, Richard. *The true principles of a Catholic. Written in the year 1780.* Anon. 12°. 21-24 p. Printed by: Coghlan, J.P. * Amp; Lhe; Ush.

> As the odd pagination suggests this pamphlet also forms part of several eds of *The touchstone*.

689. Challoner, Richard. *The true principles of a Catholic.* Anon. 12°. 11, [1] p. Printed by: Coghlan, J.P. * ECW; Sto; Ush.

690. Challoner, Richard. *The true principles of a Catholic. Written in the beginning of the year, 1780.* 3rd ed. Anon. London. 1786. 12°. 2, [12] p. Printed by: Coghlan, J.P. * Ush.

691. Challoner, Richard. *The true principles of a Catholic ... To which is added, an exposition of the commandments.* Philadelphia. [1789]. 12°. 12 p. Printed by: Carey, M. ESTC w009070. * DGU-W; MBAt; NN.

> The author is given as 'Chalenor' on tp. With one page of Carey adverts.

692. Challoner, Richard. *The unerring authority of the Catholick church, in matters of faith, maintain'd against the exceptions of a late author, in his answer to a letter on the subject of infallibility.* Anon. [Dublin?]. 1732. 12°. xvi, 221, [3] p. ESTC t119663. * C; CLU-C; CU-BANC; Do; DoA; E; ECW; Gi; ICN; InNd; L; Lhe; MRu; Osc; Sco; Stan; Ush; UshL.

> A reply to *An humble address to the Jesuits* by a 'Mr. J.R.', a Lincolnshire minister. For a discussion of this case see Burton (I, 88ff.). See also next 2 items. Burton (II, 123) states that the 1st ed. came out without the publisher's name, but that it was in fact published by Thomas Meighan.

693. Challoner, Richard. *The unerring authority of the Catholick church, in matters of faith: maintain'd against the exceptions of a late author, in his answer to a letter on the subject of infallibility.* Anon. [London?]. 1735. 12°. xvi, [4], 220 p. Printed by: [Meighan, T.]. ESTC t145006. * BB; CaOHM; CLU-C; Do;

E; ECR; ECW; Gi; Hen; ICN; InNd; L; LAM; Lfa; Lhe; Map; MRu; MUN; StD; TLP; TxU; UGL.

> Burton (II, 323) states that this is the 2nd ed., printed by T. Meighan and also claims that there is a 3rd ed., dated 1736, printed by T. Meighan.

694. Challoner, Richard. *The unerring authority of the Catholick church, in matters of faith. Maintained against the exceptions of a late author, in his answer to a letter on the subject of infallibility.* Anon. Philadelphia repr. [London]. [1789]. 12°. 203, [9] p. Published by: Lloyd, T. ESTC w002439. * CaQQLa; DGU-W; ECW; KyU; MWA; MWH; NN.

695. Challoner, Richard. *The wonders of God in the wilderness; or the lives of the most celebrated saints of the oriental desarts.* London. 1755. 8°. vi, [2], 363, [19] p. Published by: Needham, W. ESTC t083953. * CLU-C; CSmH; DAE; Do; DoA; ECB; ECW; L; Ldw; Lfa; LO; TLP; TxU; UGL; Yb.

> Burton and ESTC state that Challoner is the editor; Do attributes the book to John Mannock.

696. Challoner, Richard. *The wonders of God in the wilderness; or the lives of the most celebrated saints of the oriental desarts; faithfully collected out of the genuine works of the holy fathers.* Manchester. 1786. 8°. vi, 282, 289-356, [4] p. Printed by: Swindells, G. & Co. ESTC t121693. * ICN; L; TxU; Ush.

697. Challoner, Richard. *The young gentleman instructed in the grounds of the Christian religion. In three dialogues, between a young gentleman and his tutor.* Anon. London. 1735. 12°. xi, [1], 155, [1] p. Published by: Meighan, T. Sold by: Wilford, J. ESTC t195041. * Lhe.

698. Challoner, Richard. *The young gentleman instructed in the grounds of the Christian religion. In three dialogues, between a young gentleman and his tutor.* Anon. London. 1735. 12°. xi, [1], 155, [1] p. Published by: Meighan, T. ESTC t014208. * BB; C; CLU-C; Do; DoA; E; ECW; ICN; L; Lhe; MChB; MRu; MUN; O; Osc; TLP; Ush.

> With one page of adverts.

699. Challoner, Richard. *The young gentleman instructed in the grounds of the Christian religion. In three dialogues, between a young gentleman and his tutor.* Anon. Dublin repr. [London]. 1736. 12°. xi, [1], 155, [1] p. Sold by: Browne, T.; Hoey, J. ESTC n048427. * PPL.

700. Challoner, Richard. *The young gentleman instructed in the grounds of the Christian religion. In three dialogues, between a young gentleman and his tutor.* 3rd ed. Anon. London. 1755. 12°. [2], xx, [14], 196 p. Published by: Needham, W. ESTC t014207. * CLU-C; E; ECW; Gi; ICN; L; Lhe; Map; P; Sal; TxU; UshL; ViU.

701. *Charitable society, for the purpose of putting out apprentices such poor boys as have no relations, or whose relations are in circumstances which render them incapable of putting out their children apprentices.* [London]. [1784]. fol. 4 p. * WDA.

> 'Subscriptions and benefactions are received by Mr. Halford, no. 130 opposite Newton-Street, High Holborn; Mr. Hutchinson, no. 248, opposite Dean-Street,

High Holborn; and by Mr. Carpue, of Dukestreet, Lincoln's-Inn-Fields, Treasurer to this Society.'

702. *Charity for the dead: or, a method of hearing and applying the holy sacrifice of the mass. For the benefit of the souls departed.* [London]. 1755. 12°. 12 p. Printed by: [Marmaduke, J.?]. ESTC n047361. * ICN; Lhe.

703. *Charity for the dead: or, a method of hearing and applying the holy sacrifice of the mass ... by the English Poor Clares at Air.* London. 1783. 12°. 47, [1] p. Printed by: Coghlan, J.P. * Ush.

704. *A choice collection of prayers &c. Divided into two parts. Part I containing a manual of devout prayers ... Part II. The holy mass in Latin and English ... the method of saying the rosary.* [London]. 1728. 12°. [12], 271, [5], 284, [4] p. Printed by: [Meighan, T.]. ESTC t116584. * KU-S; L (imp.); Ush.
> With one page of Meighan adverts in part 1. The table of moveable feasts covers 1735-1762. Part 2 is dated 1727. Versions of the manual of devout prayers, the holy mass in Latin and English and the method of saying the rosary were also published independently or as part of other compilations (see also next 4 items).

705. *A choice collection of prayers, &c. Divided into two parts. Part I. containing a manual of devout prayers ... Part II. The holy mass in Latin and English... the method of saying the rosary.* 1729. 12°. x, 173, iii, 262, ii p. * Bevan (Advent 1993, no. 106).

706. *A choice collection of prayers, &c. Divided into two parts. Part I. Containing a manual of devout prayers ... Part II. The holy mass in Latin and English ... the method of saying the rosary.* [London]. 1737. 12°. [12], 271, [5], 285, [3] p. Published by: [Meighan, T.] . * Amp.
> With one page of Meighan adverts in part 1.

707. *A choice collection of prayers, &c. Divided into two parts. Part I. Containing, a manual of devout prayers. Part II. The holy mass in Latin and English ... the method of saying the rosary.* 2 vols. [London]. 1751. 12°. Published by: [Meighan, T.]. ESTC t220541. * P.
> Each vol. has a separate tp dated 1750, and contains adverts for Meighan.

708. *A choice collection of prayers, &c. Divided into two parts. Part I. Containing, a manual of devout prayers ... Part II. The holy mass in Latin and English ... the method of saying the rosary.* [London]. 1755. 18°. Published by: [Meighan, T.]. [12], 234, [6], 318, [6] p. ESTC t184354. * O.
> With one page of Meighan adverts in both part 1 and part 2.

709. *The Christian sacrifice; with its office and ceremonies explained, by G.C.* 1704. 12°. [4], 9-111, [1] p. * Stan; TLP; TxU.
> According to Clancy and Stan this is an abstract of Richard Mason's *Liturgical discourse* (see Clancy nos 647-9).

710. *The Christian's companion. Being a choice-manual.* Vienna. 1795. 12°. [2], vii, [13], 403, [7] p. Published by: Sammer, R. * Gi.

711. *The Christian's guide to heaven, or a manual of Catholic piety.* London. 1794. 12°. [2], 360 p. Printed by: Keating. Published by: Keating. * ECB; ECW; Gi; Hen; Stan.

Ms note in Gi suggests that it was translated and edited from the French by the rev. W. Gahan O.S.A. ECW is bound up with *The prayers of St. Brigitte* (no. 2371).

712. Chrysostome de Saint-Lô, Jean. *A short treatise on the method and advantage of withdrawing the soul from being employed on creatures, in order to occupy it on God alone. Translated from the French by R. C.* [London]. 1765. 18°. 55, [1] p. Published by: Meighan, T. ESTC t207197. * Amp; DMR; DoA; Du; E; ECB; Map; Ush.

>'R.C.' is Richard Challoner. Burton (II, 336) and Gillow (I, 456) also mention a 1769 ed.

713. Chrysostome de Saint-Lô, Jean. *A short treatise on the method and advantages of withdrawing the soul from being employed on creatures, in order to occupy it on God alone. Translated from the French by Richard Challoner.* 3rd ed. London. 1788. 12°. 23, [1] p. Printed by: Coghlan, J.P. ESTC t212793. * Do; ECW; Lhe; Yb.

714. *Cisalpine Club, Freemason's Tavern, June 4, 1793 ... Resolved unanimously.* [London]. [1793]. 4°. 2, [2] p. * Cli; Ush.

>Signed and dated 'Henry Clifford, Secretary. Lincoln's-Inn, June 17th, 1793'.

715. *Cisalpine Club. The secretary having communicated to the law members of the Club, a letter which he received from the reverend Mr. Charles Plowden.* [London]. [1795]. fol. 3, [1] p. ESTC t146865. * L.

>Signed and dated 'Charles Butler, Wm. Cruise, Henry Clifford, Wm. Throckmorton. May 12, 1795'; a comment on the protestation of the Committee of English Catholics.

716. Clarkson, John. *An introduction to the celebrated devotion of the most holy rosary. To which is annex'd a method of saying it, according to the form prescribed by his holiness Pope Pius V.* London. 1737. 12°. xii, 144 p. Published by: Meighan, T. ESTC t112630. * CLU-C; L; Lhe; TxU (imp.).

>The dedication is signed 'John Clarkson, O.P.', who was provincial from 1758 to 1762.

717. Clarkson, John. *An introduction to the celebrated devotion of the most holy rosary. To which is annex'd, a method of saying it, according to the form prescribed by his holiness Pope Pius V.* Anon. London. 1737. 12°. xii, 144 p. Published by: Meighan, T. ESTC t183440. * DAE; Do; DoA; Gi; ICN; O; Osc; Stan; Ush.

>The dedication is signed 'J.C.O.P.' Gumbley gives two other eds, Dublin 1772 and 1778.

718. Clement XI. *The constitution of his holiness Pope Clement XI. Condemning a great number of propositions taken out of a book printed in French.* Rome [i.e. London]. 1713. 12°. [2], 47, [1] p. Printed by: Printing house of the Camera Apostolica. ESTC t113247. * CU-Riv; L; Ldw; LVu; MRu; Oc; Osc; Owo; Ush.

>English and Latin. This concerns the bull 'Unigenitus'. Ush is bound up with *Abstract* (no. 18).

719. Clement XI. *Homilia sanctiss. domini nostri Clementis XI. pont. max.*

habita in die natali Christi ... anno MDCCII. A homily spoken by his holiness Pope Clement XI ... 1702. Florence. 1703. 4°. 12 p. Printed by: Brigonci, P. A. ESTC n017346. * C; CLU-C; L; MoU; O.

> Latin and English text in parallel columns, also on tp, which has an additional imprint in English: 'Florence, printed at the Great Duke's printing-house, by A. Brigonci, 1703'.

720. Clement XI. *A homily of Pope Clement XI. As deliver'd by him in St. Peter's in the Vatican. On the feast of the holy apostles, St. Peter and St. Paul ... upon occasion of the pretender's being there.* [London]. 1717. 8°. 23, [1] p. Sold by: Warner, T. ESTC t199260. * Hen; O.

> Latin and English text in parallel columns, also on tp. Translated from the copy printed in Rome, 1717. T. Warner was a miscellaneous publisher, who here offers for sale a straightforward printing of a pious homily by Clement XI.

721. Clement XI. *A homily spoken by his holyness, Pope Clement XII [sic]. Upon Christmas Day ... in the Cathedral Church of St. Peter, in the year 1702.* [London?]. [1703?]. 4°. [4] p. ESTC n017348. * E; Gu; TxU.

722. Clement XII. *To his beloved children, all the Catholicks dwelling in the United Netherlands.* [Rome?]. [1741?]. fol. s.s. * Ush.

> A warning against Johannes Petrus Meindarts, who was deposed as Archbishop of Utrecht but refused to go. There are similar letters in French, Dutch and Latin, all printed in Rome.

723. Clement XIII. *A brief of our holy father the pope, to the King of Poland, and Duke of Lorraine. To our most dearly beloved son Stanislaus, King of Poland, and Duke of Lorraine. Greeting and apostolic benediction.* [London?]. [1763]. 12°. 16 p. * Lhe; NN.

724. Clement XIII. *His holin-ss, P-pe Clem-t the XIIIth's constitution dated the 7th of January, 1765 by which the institute of the S. of J. is again approved.* [London?]. [1765?]. 12°. 23, [1] p. * E; Lhe; Ush; UshA.

> English and Latin.

725. Clement XIV. *The circular letter of our most holy father and lord in Christ Clement XIV by divine providence, pope. To the patriarchs, primates, archbishops, and bishops of the whole Catholic Church.* London. 1770. 8°. [3], 4-20 p. ESTC t218011. * MY.

726. Clement XIV. *Instructions for gaining the jubilee granted by his holiness Pope Clement XIV. soon after his election ... Revised by several eminent clergymen.* Dublin. 1770. 12°. 22 p. Printed by: Corcoran, B. ESTC t189022. * D.

727. Clifford, Henry. *Reflections on the appointment of a Catholic bishop to the London district. In a letter to the Catholic laity of the said district.* London. 1791. 8°. [4], 91, [1] p. Published by: Messrs. Robinsons; Faulder, R. ESTC t149983. * ECW; ICN; Ldw; Lhe; Osc; Ush.

728. Clifford, Henry. *Reflections on the appointment of a Catholic bishop to the London district. In a letter to the Catholic laity of the said district.* Dublin. 1791. 8°. [4], 60 p. Printed by: Corbet, W. Published by: Byrne, P. ESTC t122236. *

C; D; Dt; L; Lhl; Ush.

729. Clifford, William. *A little manual of the poor man's daily devotion, collected out of several pious and approved authors. By W.C. In which are added, the Jesus-Psalter, with a litany of our saviour's passion.* 5th ed. London. 1705. 12°. [12], 420 p. ESTC t104451. * C; DoA; ECW; L; Osc; Ush.

> The book was written while the author was resident in the Hospital for Incurables in Paris, where he died in 1670. It was first published in 1669. Cf. Clancy nos 230-3. See also next item.

730. Clifford, William. *A little manual of the poor man's daily devotion, collected out of several pious and approved authors.* 6th ed. London. 1735. 12°. [12], 347, [1] p. Published by: Dempsy, J. * Do.

731. Clinch, J. B. *A vindication of the Roman Catholic clergy of the town of Wexford, during the late unhappy rebellion, from the groundless charges and illiberal insinuations of an anonymous writer, signed Verax. By Veritas.* London repr. (Dublin). 1798. 12°. [2], 25, [1] p. Printed by: Coghlan, J.P. (repr.). * CtY; Ush.

> 'Veritas' was the pseudonym of J.B. Clinch, lay professor of rhetoric at Maynooth. See also next 4 items.

732. Clinch, J. B. *A vindication of the Roman Catholic clergy of the town of Wexford, during the late unhappy rebellion, from the groundless charges and illiberal insinuations of an anonymous writer, signed Verax. By Veritas.* 2nd ed. Dublin. 1798. 8°. 31, [1] p. Printed by: Fitzpatrick, H. ESTC t178972. * BFq; C; D; Di; FLK; IU; MY; PP.

733. Clinch, J. B. *A vindication of the Roman Catholic clergy of the town of Wexford, during the late unhappy rebellion, from the groundless charges and illiberal insinuations of an anonymous writer, signed Verax. By Veritas.* 2nd ed. Dublin. 1798. 8°. 29, [1] p. Printed by: Fitzpatrick, H. ESTC t178973. * D; Dt; MY.

> For another '2nd' ed. see no. 732.

734. Clinch, J. B. *A vindication of the Roman Catholic clergy of the town of Wexford, during the late unhappy rebellion, from the groundless charges and illiberal insinuations of an anonymous writer, signed Verax. By Veritas.* 3rd ed. Dublin. 1798. 8°. 31, [1] p. Printed by: Fitzpatrick, H. ESTC t175610. * D; Di; ICU; KU-S; MnU; MY; O; Ush.

735. Clinch, J. B. *A vindication of the Roman Catholic clergy of the town of Wexford, during the late unhappy rebellion, from the groundless charges and illiberal insinuations of an anonymous writer, signed Verax. By Veritas.* 3rd ed. Dublin. 1798. 8°. 29, [1] p. Printed by: Fitzpatrick, H. ESTC t202853. * Du; MY.

> For another '3rd' ed. see no. 734.

Clinton, Alexander. See MacKenzie, Alexander.

736. Coghlan, James Peter. *A catalogue of a library, which has been above two hundred years collecting by a society of gentlemen, who have distinguished themselves for their literary abilities, consisting of Hebrew, Greek, Latin, French,*

Spanish, Portuguese, German, Dutch, Italian, English, and a great number of manuscripts in various languages ... being the second part of that collection, which was purchased, and began selling, for ready money only, this day 1781, by J.P. Coghlan. [London]. [1781]. Printed by: [Coghlan, J.P.]. Published by: [Coghlan, J.P.].

> In the spring of 1777 Coghlan purchased a Jesuit library of 14,000 volumes. He intended to sell them off in batches of 2,000 volumes each, and had catalogues printed for the first two batches; he asked several of his friends to disperse these catalogues and to advertise the books in various newspapers. It is not clear whether any catalogues were ever made of the remaining books. No copies of the two catalogues have been traced so far (see letter Coghlan to George Hay, 20 April 1777, SCA; the first catalogue is advertised in the *Ordo recitandi* for 1782). For the catalogue of the first batch see no. 739.

737. Coghlan, James Peter. *A catalogue of all the Catholic books now in print amongst which are those purchased from the stock of Mr. Thomas Meighan, deceased; with all the new publications up to the 30th of October 1776.* [London]. [1776]. 12°. 22 p. Printed by: Coghlan, J.P. Published by: Coghlan, J.P. * Ush; WDA.

> Bound up with *Ordo recitandi* for 1777 (no. 2165). Page 22 mentions a catalogue of thousands of volumes, of several persons and in different languages, which is being prepared for the press (see nos 736 and 739).

738. Coghlan, James Peter. *A catalogue of the several parcels of books belonging to Mr. Errington of Gloucester-Street, deceased and Mr. T. M-N.* London. 1770. 8°. Printed by: Kiernan, C. Published by: Coghlan, J.P. Sold by: Coghlan, J.P. * P.

> William Errington (1716-1768) was a Roman Catholic priest.

739. Coghlan, James Peter. *The first part of the catalogue of a library, which has been almost two hundred years collecting, by a society of gentlemen, who have distinguished themselves for their literary abilities, consisting of manuscript, black letter and other valuable books, in the different branches of literature, and in various languages, lately purchased, and are selling for ready money only, by J.P. Coghlan.* [London]. [1778]. Printed by: [Coghlan, J.P.]. Published by: [Coghlan, J.P.].

> This catalogue is advertised in the *Ordo recitandi* for 1778 (no. 2166). See also no. 736.

740. Coghlan, R.B. *An apology for Catholic faith, morality and loyalty. Addressed to the Countess Dowager of Huntington. Occasioned by a late publication, entitled Interesting facts concerning popery. By the rev. Peckwell.* London. 1779. 12°. [2], 58 p. Printed by: Coghlan, J.P. Sold by: Faulder, R.; Payne, H.; Wilkie, J. ESTC n043338. * Ct; ECW; Ush.

> There were at least four eds of *Interesting facts concerning popery* - by Henry Peckwell (1747-1787) - in 1779, the year preceding the Gordon riots.

741. Coghlan, William. *Rev. William Coghlan begs leave to express his grateful acknowledgements.* [London]. 1800. s.s. * Cli.

> This is a notice from William Coghlan thanking friends for their condolences on the death of his father J.P. Coghlan and announcing that the business will be

carried on by Keating and Brown.

742. Coleny, Thomas. *A small book intituled England, & the other northern reformed countries reconciled to Rome. Presented chiefly to the people of England.* Coimbra. 1730. 8°. xvi, 400 p. ESTC t101698. * DMR; L; Lhe; O; StD.

743. *A collection of sacred music, as used in the chapel of the King of Sardinia.* London. 1785. fol. Printed by: Longman & Broderick. Published by: Author. * L.

744. *College of Scholes, near Prescott, for the education of young Catholic gentlemen.* [1796]. 12°. s.s. * Cli.
    A prospectus.

745. *A companion to the altar, or compact pocket missal, for all the Sundays, the holydays, the days of devotion etc. Throughout the year.* London. 1791. 12°. xi, [1], 396, lxxix, [1] p. Printed by: Keating, P. Published by: Keating, P. * Do; Gi.
    With one page of Keating adverts.

746. *A companion to the altar or compact pocket missal, for all the Sundays, festivals of obligation & devotion &c. &c. in the year.* 2nd ed. London. 1796. 12°. xiv, 15-505, [1] p. Published by: Keating, P. * UGL.

747. *A compendious history of the life and principal actions of our Lord and Saviour Jesus Christ. For the use of schools.* Dublin. 1792. 12°. xiii, [1], 15-197, [7] p. Printed by: M'Donnel, T. * ECR.

748. *A compilation of the litanies and vespers hymns and anthems as they are sung in the Catholic Church and adapted to the voice or organ by John Aitken.* Philadelphia. 1787 [1788]. 4°. [7], 136, [1] p. Published by: Aitken, J. ESTC w035378. * DGU; ICN; MWA; PPL.
    The first collection of Catholic church music published in America.

749. *A compilation of the litanies vespers hymns & anthems as they are sung in the Catholic Church.* Philadelphia. 1791. [4], 181, [1] p. Printed by: Aitken, J. Sold by: Aitken, J. ESTC w009194. * RPJCB.

750. *The complete Catholic manual: containing morning and evening prayers for the use of Catholic families.* 1770. 8°. [16], xxxiv, 224 p. * Gi; Ush.
    The editor is Charles Cordell.

751. *The complete pocket manual containing all the essential duties of a Catholic Christian.* London. 1760. 12°. vii, 316, 118, p. Published by: Lewis, T. * Do.
    2 vols in 1; vol. 2 is *Morning and night prayers*, 1766 (see no. 1904).

752. *Complin, or night office.* [c.1790]. 8°. 167, [1], 72 p. * Osc.
    Based largely on Challoner and Gother; Latin and English on facing pages. The final 72 pages are in English and contain various prayers by Hay, Challoner and others and 20 pages of 'Additions recommended by a person who chuses to be unknown'.

753. *Conceduntur [blank] facultates sequentes in districtu [blank] exercendae, ad [blank].* [London?]. [1748?]. 8°. s.s. ESTC n055979. * TxU.

Faculties for missionaries. Spaces have been left for ms insertions. See also next 3 items.

754. *Conceduntur [blank] facultates sequentes in districtu [blank] exercendae, ad [blank].* [1753]. 4 p. * UshA.
UshA dated in ms '1753'.

755. *Conceduntur [blank] facultates sequentes in districtu [blank] excercendae, ad [blank].* [1768?]. [2] p. * UshA.
UshA dated in ms '1768'.

756. *Conceduntur [blank] facultates sequentes in districtu [blank] exercendae, ad [blank]. 1. Administrandi sacramentum poenitentiae, & omnia munia parochialia exercendi.* [London?]. [1789?]. 8°. s.s. ESTC t108352. * ECW; L; Lpro; TxU.
ECW and L have blanks filled and form signed in ms by resp. 'William Walton' and 'John Douglas'.

757. *Conclusiones ex universa theologia, quas, in collegio Saxo-sylvensi, (vulgo Stonyhurst) ... defendet D. Gualterus Clifford ... anno domini M.DCC.XCVII.* Preston. [1797]. 4°. 16 p. Printed by: Newby, P. ESTC t124167. * L; Lhe.

758. *Conclusiones theologicae de Deo uno quas in seminario Saxo-sylvensi (vulgo Stonyhurst). Propugnabit dominus Gualterus Clifford ... mense junio die xxii hora tertia postmeridiem A.D. MDCCXCVI.* Blackburn. [1796]. 4°. 8 p. Printed by: Waterworth, J. ESTC t163352. * Lhe; WDA.

759. *Conditions for gaining the present jubilee. Together with prayers at large.* Dublin. 1759. 8°. 8 p. Printed by: Harrison, G. * SCR.

760. *A conference between a Roman Catholic gentleman, and some divines of the Church of England, about the meaning of the word transubstantiation.* [Dublin?]. 1729. 4°. [2], 6 p. ESTC n044604. * CaQMM.

761. *A conference between J.M. a Roman Catholic gentleman, and some divines of the Church of England, about the meaning of the word transubstantiation.* [Dublin?]. 1730. 12°. 8 p. ESTC t153305. * Dt; L.

762. *A conference between J.M. a Roman Catholic gentleman, and some divines of the Church of England, about the meaning of the word transubstantiation.* Dublin. 1730. 8°. 8 p. ESTC t162383. * Dt.

763. *A confutation from the general canon law ... and the constitution of the order of Jesuits, of the argument ... in maintenance of their pretensions to ... the personal estate of ... Mr Talbot.* 4°. 11, [1] p. * LfaA.
Drophead title 'The relations of the late Mr Talbot of Longford, against the Jesuits'. Ms note states that it was written by Bishop Stonor. See also nos 61-63, 103, 2453, 2455, 2616.

764. *The conscientious difficulties of different Roman Catholics in regard to the proposed form of oath to be introduced into the bill for their relief.* [1791]. fol. [2] p. * Sto.

765. *Considerations addressed to the French bishops and clergy now residing in England.* London. 1796. 8°. [4], 72 p. Published by: Debrett, J. ESTC n002042. * Ldw; LEu; Lu; Osc; PPL; Sto.

Osc tentatively ascribes the book to Charles Butler.

766. *Considerations on the penal laws against Roman Catholics in England, and the new acquired colonies in America. In a letter to a noble lord. By a country gentleman.* London. 1764. 8°. [2], 70 p. Published by: Dodsley, R. & J. ESTC t062790. * C; CaSSU; CtY; IES; L; Map; MdBJ-P; MnU; NNC; O; Ush; ViU.

Gillow (V, 184) attributes this to Charles Howard, 10th Duke of Norfolk.

767. *Considerations on the state of the Roman Catholics in Scotland.* London. 1779. 8°. [2], 21, [1] p. Printed by: Coghlan, J.P. Sold by: Coghlan, J.P. ESTC t079509. * AWn; CLU-C; CSmH; CtHT-W; CtY; CU-BANC; E; GU; InU-Li; L; Lhe; Llp; MnU; MRu; O; SHp; Sto; TLP.

768. *Considerations on the state of the Roman Catholics in Scotland.* 2nd ed. London. 1779. 8°. [2], 21, [1] p. Printed by: Coghlan, J.P. Sold by: Coghlan, J.P. * Sto; Ush.

769. *Considerations upon the establishment of an university in Ireland, for the educating of Roman Catholics.* Dublin. 1784. 8°. 54 p. Printed by: Graisberry, D. Sold by: All booksellers. ESTC t165280. * D; Dt; IU; Mil.

770. Constable, John. *Deism and Christianity fairly consider'd, in four dialogues. To which is added a fifth upon latitudinarian Christianity. And two letters to a friend upon a book intitled, The moral philosopher.* Anon. London. 1739. 12°. vi, [6], 320, [2] p. Printed by: Hoyles, J. Sold by: Booksellers of London and Westminster. ESTC t057972. * CaQMBN; E; ICU; L; Lfa; Lhe; Llp; O; TxU; Ush.

The moral philosopher is by Thomas Morgan (d. 1743).

771. Constable, John. *The doctrine of antiquity concerning the most blessed eucharist, plainly shewed, in remarks written, some years since, upon Mr Johnson's book, of the unbloody sacrifice ... By Clerophilus Alethes.* London. 1736. 8°. [2], v, [9], 153, [1] p. ESTC t121198. * CLU-C; DAE; Do; DoA; E; ECW; Gi; ICN; L; Lfa; Lhe; MChB; NSPM; O; Osc; P; Sal; StD; Sto; Ush; Yb.

John Johnson (1662-1725) published *The unbloody sacrifice* in 1714-1718.

772. Constable, John. *Practical methods of performing the ordinary actions of a religious life with fervour of spirit.* Anon. London [i.e. St. Omers]. 1718. 8°. 311 [i.e. 301], [1] p. Printed by: Bonvall, L. ESTC t092135. * C; CAL; Do; DoA; E; ECB; ECW; Gi; ICN; L; Lfa; Lhe; LO; O; Sto.

Do, Gi and Sommervogel (VI, 906) state that this book is by Thomas Percy Plowden S.J. (1672-1745).

773. Constable, John. *Remarks upon F. Le Courayer's book in defence of the English ordinations. Wherein all his arguments are ... answered, and the invalidity of the English ordinations is fairly considered and fully proved.* [London?]. [1727?]. 8°. [8], 384 p. ESTC t086357. * C; CLU-C; Do; Dt; E; ECW; Gi; ICN; L; Lfa; Lhe; MChB; MY; O; Osc; P; Pci; SIR; TLP; Ush; Yb.

The author is given as Clerophilus Alethes. The first English ed. of Le Courayer's *Defence* was published in 1725 (no. 1625). For the controversy see Gillow (I, 552-4). Sommervogel (II, 1374) and Kirk (p. 55) mention another, as yet untraced, contribution by Constable to this controversy, entitled 'The stratagem discovered' (1727).

774. Constable, John. *A specimen of amendments candidly proposed; to the compiler of a work, which he calls, The church history of England from the year 1500, to the year 1688. By Clerophilus Alethes.* London. 1741. 12°. [14], 244, [4] p. Published by: [Hoyles, J.]. ESTC t086345. * BB; C; CLU; CSmH; Du; ECR; ECW; Eu; Gi; L; Lfa; LfaA; Lhe; Map; MH; Mil; O; Osc; Pci; SIR; Sto; TxU; Ush; Yb.

> With 2 pages of Hoyles adverts. The author of *The church history* is Hugh Tootell (see nos 2767 and 2769).

775. *Constitutiones congregationis Anglicanae Ordinis Sancti Benedicti.* Paris. 1784. 12°. xi, [1], 271, lxiii p. Printed by: Lambert, M. * DoA.

776. *Constitutiones ecclesiasticae pro unitis dioecesibus Ardfertensi & Aghadoensi, in duodecim capita distributae.* Waterford. [1747]. 8°. 125, [3] p. Printed by: Calwell, J. ESTC t167596. * C; FLK; IDA; L.

> With a final advertisement leaf. Dated '15. mensis Julij ... 1747'.

777. *Constitutiones provinciales et synodales ecclaesiae metropolitanae et primatialis Dubliniensis.* [Dublin]. 1770. 12°. 148, 121-122 p. ESTC t146876. * C; Dt; IDA; L; O.

> The final leaf, paginated 121-122, contains 'Statuta facta ... Dom Ricardo Lincoln [the Archbishop of Dublin]'.

778. *Constitutions of the English nunnes of the immaculate conception of our Lady. Established in this city of Paris.* 1721. 12°. 165, [1] p. * DoA.

779. *A continuation of the account of British subjects who have suffered by the French Revolution. 1795.* London. [1795]. 12°. 40 p. Printed by: Coghlan, J.P. ESTC t114518. * L; MB; O; TxU.

> This is a sequel to *Some account* (no. 2572). See also *The establishment* (no. 987). This material also formed part of eds of the *Laity's directory* and the *Ordo*.

780. Coombes, William Henry. *Sacred eloquence: or discourses selected from the writings of St. Basil the Great, and St. John Chrysostom; with the letter of St. Eucherius Bishop of Lyons to his kinsman Valerian.* London. 1798. 8°. [8], xvi, 343, [3] p. Printed by: Coghlan, J.P. Sold by: Booker; Cook; Keating; Lewis; Robinsons; Barratt (Bath); Edwards (Bristol); Gamage (Worcester); Grafton and Co. (Birmingham); Robins (Winchester); Smart and Co. (Reading); Sharrock (Preston); Wilson (Ecclestone, Lancs.); Coates (Newcastle); North, Todd and Tessyman (York); Wogan, P. (Dublin). ESTC t177008. * Du; ECW; IDA; Lhe; NSPM; O; Osc; TAUa; TxU.

> The book is dedicated to Bishops Walmesley and Milner. Coombes also wrote an account of his escape from France, which is found in the *Ordo* for 1800 (no. 2189).

781. Coppinger, William. *The life of miss Nano Nagle, as sketched by the right rev. Dr. Coppinger in a funeral sermon preached by him in Cork, on the anniversary of her death.* Cork. 1794. 8°. 31, [1] p. Printed by: Haly, J. Sold by: Haly, J. ESTC t124315. * D; L.

> Miss Nano Nagle (d. 1784) established both the Ursulines and the Presentation Sisters in Cork.

782. Coppinger, William. *A remonstrance addressed to the lower order of Roman Catholics, in the diocess of Cloyne and Ross, by the rev. doctor Coppinger.* [Cork]. [1798]. 8°. 8 p. Printed by: [Harris]. ESTC t108347. * D; L; MRu; MY.

> Place, and name of printer in colophon only. L copy has ms note beneath the imprint stating 'May 1798'; MRu has the date 1799 in ms.

783. *Copy. Declaration and protestation of English Catholics. We, whose names are hereunto subscribed.* fol. 2 p. * Sto; Ush.

> This concerns the oath controversy. Both Ush and Sto have ms note 'Stella Hall 2d April 89 Matthew Gibson. N.B. This is the true copy signed by Matthew Gibson'.

784. *Copy of a letter to the right reverend Mr. Charles Berington. Dear sir, you request to know our opinion ... Longbirch, Feb. 15, 1791.* [1791]. 4°. s.s. * WDA.

> Signed 'Anthony Clough, Thomas Flyn, George Beeston, Joseph Berington, Edward Eyre'.

785. *Copy of the sentence given by the rev. doctor Brewer, on the appeal made to him by the rev. doctor Joseph Wilks; and of the correspondence relating thereto.* 1799. fol. 3, [1] p. * DowA; WRW.

> John Brewer O.S.B. was president of the English Benedictine Congregation from 1799 to 1822.

786. Cordell, Charles. *The Catholic layman's companion: containing morning and evening prayers for families. The ordinary of the holy sacrifice of the mass, and vespers and complin ... By the compiler of The divine office.* Newcastle upon Tyne. [1790?]. 8°. [14], 20, xxxiv, 224, 72 p. Published by: Coates, F. Sold by: Wogan, P.; Fitzpatrick, H.; M'Donnell, T.; Mehain, J. ESTC t204448. * NCp.

> The compiler of *The divine office* is Charles Cordell. See also next 4 items.

787. Cordell, Charles. *The Catholick layman's companion. Designed chiefly for the use of the poor. By the compiler of The divine office for the use of the laity.* 1766. 12°. xxxiv, 224 p. * TLP.

788. Cordell, Charles. *[The divine office for the use of the laity].* [London]. 12°. x, 484, [8] p. Sold by: Meighan, T. * Amp (-tp).

> With a final advertisement leaf. Amp cat. suggests '1738' but that must be incorrect. It is conceivable that this copy is part of the 2-vol. 1780 ed. (no. 790).

789. Cordell, Charles. *The divine office for the use of the laity.* 4 vols. [London?]. 1763. 12°. 260, cccxlii, [4]; 228, cccxx, [4]; 325, [1], ccciv, [6]; 353, [3], cccxlvi, [6] p. ESTC t129283. * Do; DoA; Du; ICN; L; LO; NSCH; O; Osc; Stan (vol. 2); Sto; TH; TLP; UGL (vol. 4).

> The author signs himself 'C.C.C.A-D.A' [i.e. Car. Cordell Coll. Angl. Duacen. Alumn.]. Bossy (p. 368) mentions a 4-vol. 1768 ed.

790. Cordell, Charles. *The divine office for the use of the laity.* 2 vols.

[Newcastle?]. 1780. 12°. [2], 510, cxlvii, [3]; 484, cl, [4] p. * Do; NSCH; Stan; TLP (vol. 2); Ush; Yb.

> Dr D.M. Rogers suggests 'Newcastle' as place of publication. Cordell worked in Newcastle.

791. Cordell, Charles. *A letter to the author of a book, called. A candid and impartial sketch of the life and government of Pope Clement XIV.* Anon. 1785. 8°. 32 p. Published by: Author. * Osc; Ush.

> For *A candid and impartial sketch* see no. 2301. Kirk (p. 58) identifies the author of the present work, which defends Clement XIV, as Cordell, whereas ESTC attributes the work to John Milner. See also next item.

792. Cordell, Charles. *A letter to the author of a book, called. A candid and impartial sketch of the life and government of Pope Clement XIV.* Anon. London. 1785. 8°. [2], 32 p. Published by: Author. ESTC t222180. * BMu; ECW; Lfa; Osc.

> This ed. differs from no. 791 in that it gives the place of publication.

793. Corker, James Maurus. *Queries to Dr. Sacheverell from North-Britain.* [c.1710]. 8°. 6 p. * DowA.

794. Corker, James Maurus. *Roman Catholic principles in reference to God and the country.* Anon. [London]. [1760?]. 8°. [2], 12 p. ESTC t124169. * BAA; CaAEU; L (-tp); Lhe; MBAt.

> BAA gives '1785' as date.

795. Cowley, William Gregory. *Elements of French grammar, as taught at Vernon Hall.* Anon. Liverpool. 1797. 8°. 146 p. Printed by: M'Creery, J. * DoA.

> Cowley began a school at the mission in Vernon Hall.

796. Coyle, Anthony. *Collectanea sacra; or pious miscellany. In verse and prose. In six books.* 2 vols. Strabane. 1788. 8°. Printed by: Bellew, J. ESTC t106101. * Dt; L; O.

> Tp of vol. 1 is dated 1788; the first item in vol. 2, which has no separate tp, 'Plain reason ... By the Chev. O'Dunn.' is dated '1787' and seems a reissue. Coyle was the R.C. Bishop of Raphoe.

797. Crasset, Jean. *The history of the church of Japan. Written originally in French by Monsieur l'abbe de T. And now translated into English. By N.N. [Histoire de l'eglise du Japon].* 2 vols. London. 1705-1707. 4°. [24], 544, [8]; [12], 549, [7] p. ESTC t094112. * CSmH; CtY-D; D (vol. 1); DFo; DLC; DoA; ECW; Eu; ICN; L; Lfa; LfaA; Lhe; MH; MH-AH (vol. 1); NBu (vol. 1); NN; NNUT; NSPM; Yb.

> 'Monsieur l'abbé de T.' is Jean Crasset; ESTC identifies N.N. as 'Webb'. Walsh (p. 54) attributes the translation to William Riddell S.J. (1669/1670-1711).

798. Crathorne, William. *A Catholick's resolution, shewing his reasons, for not being a Protestant.* Anon. [London?]. 1717. 12°. 72 p. ESTC t192101. * E.

799. Crathorne, William. *A Catholic's resolution shewing his reasons, for not being a Protestant.* Anon. Bruges. [1763]. 12°. 84 p. Printed by: Praet, J. van.

ESTC t142065. * L.

800. Crathorne, William. *Lessons for Lent; or instructions on the two sacraments of penance, and the b. eucharist.* Anon. [London]. 1718. 12°. [2], 148, [5] p. Published by: [Meighan, T.?]. Sold by: [Meighan, T.?]. ESTC t171510. * DMR; Do; DoA; ECW; Hen; Lhe.

801. Crathorne, William. *Lessons for Lent: or, instructions on the two sacraments of penance, and the b. eucharist.* 2nd ed. Anon. London. 1789. 12°. 155, [1] p. Published by: Keating, P. ESTC t076303. * L; O; Yb.

> Ms note in O suggests 'the rev. Mr Shepherd' as editor; probably John Shepherd, 1714-1789 (see Kirk p. 207).

802. Crathorne, William. *A practical catechism upon the Sundays, feasts and fasts of the whole year.* Anon. [London?]. 1711. 12°. [8], 239, [17] p. ESTC n024476. * DoA; ECW; TxU; Ush.

803. Crathorne, William. *A practical catechism on the Sundays, feasts and fasts of the whole year.* 2nd ed. Anon. [London]. 1749. 12°. iv, [8], 252, [12] p. Published by: Meighan, T. ESTC t114567. * CaOONL; Do; E; ECW; Hen; L; LO; Map; TLP; TxU; Yb.

804. Crathorne, William. *A practical catechism on the Sundays, feasts and fasts of the whole year.* 3rd ed. Anon. London. 1774. 12°. [8], 244 p. Published by: Meighan, T. ESTC t173891. * DoA; ECW; ICN; Lhe; Map; MRu; Sal; TxU; Ush.

805. Crathorne, William. *A practical catechism on the Sundays, feasts and fasts of the whole year ... The first edition in this kingdom, with considerable additions.* Anon. Dublin. 1775. 12°. [12], 13-300 p. Printed by: Cross, R. ESTC t173893. * Dt (imp.); FLK; Lhe; MY.

806. Crathorne, William. *A practical catechism upon the Sundays, feasts, and fasts, of the whole year.* 2nd ed. Anon. Liverpool. 1799. 8°. 183, [1] p. Printed by: M'Creery. ESTC t118924. * L; LVp; UGL.

> This is the second '2nd' ed.

807. Crawley, James. *A sermon against popery, preached in the Catholic chapel of - on the twentithird [sic] day of February, 1786.* Anon. [Armagh?]. 1786. 8°. [2], 40 p. ESTC t173085. * D.

> There is a half-title 'A sermon preached in the Catholic chapel of A---m---h, by the rev. Dr. C-w-y, parish priest'. The author is identified by Hugh Fenning O.P. (personal communication). This sermon was answered by the 'Parish clerk' in a letter (ESTC t169983).

808. *A critical review of the B. of Cloyne's publication; with occasional remarks on the production of some other writers, particularly those of Trinity College, and on the conduct of the present ministry.* Dublin. 1787. 8°. 101, [1] p. Printed by: Chambers, J. ESTC t192038. * Du; Lhl; SIR.

> 'The B. of Cloyne's publication' is *The present state of the Church of Ireland* by Richard Woodward (Dublin, 1787). See also next item.

809. *A critical review of the B. of Cloyne's publication; with occasional remarks on the production of some other writers.* 2nd ed. Dublin. 1788. 8°. 112 p.

Printed by: Chambers, J. ESTC t192039. * Du.

810. Croiset, Jean. *A spiritual retreat for one day in every month. Written in French by a father of the Society of Jesus [Retraite spirituelle pour un jour chaque mois].* Anon. London. 1703. 12°. [8], 304 p. [i.e. 302; 265-266 omitted]. Printed by: Hales, T. ESTC n046277. * ICN; Lfa; Sto.

> Ms note in Sto suggests St. Omers as place of publication.

811. Croiset, Jean. *A spiritual retreat for one day in every month. By a priest of the Society of Jesus.* Anon. [London?]. 1704. 12°. [12], 263, [1] p. Published by: [Metcalfe, T.]. ESTC t160356. * ICN; Lfa; Lhe; Sal; TxU; Yb(2).

> One of the Yb copies has an additional 3-page catalogue of Metcalfe adverts.

812. Croiset, Jean. *A spiritual retreat for one day in every month. By a priest of the Society of Jesus. Translated out of French.* Anon. [London?]. 1710. 12°. [12], 263, [1] p. ESTC t131185. * CaOHM; DFo; Do; DoA; Dt; L; LO; Map; O; TLP; Ush.

813. Croiset, Jean. *A spiritual retreat for one day in every month. Translated from the French. By a priest of the Society of Jesus.* Anon. Cork. 1800. 18°. 350 p. Printed by: Haly, J. ESTC t160357. * D; Do; IDA; Sal; Ush.

> Ush has [2], 353-356, 3-350 p.; Do and IDA have [2], 3-350, 353-356 p. The difference is due to the place of the table of contents.

814. Crowther, A. and T.V. Sadler. *A daily exercise, of the devout Christian: containing several moving practises of piety; in order to live holily, and die happily ... By T.V.* 7th ed. London. [1727?]. 12°. [40], 453, [3], 56 p. Published by: Turner, M. Sold by: Dillon, L. ESTC t204620. * Do; E.

> Although the initials in the title only refer to Thomas Vincent Sadler, the book was written by Sadler together with Arthur Anselm Crowther. Cf. Clancy for 17th century eds and see also the next 10 items. ESTC deduces the possible date of this ed. from the table of moveable feasts. In view of the dates of publication of the 6th and the 8th eds (see nos 815 and 816) a later date is more likely. The 'M. Turner' in the imprint probably refers to the 17th century publisher.

815. Crowther, A. and T.V. Sadler. *A daily exercise of the devout Christian ... Publish'd by T.V. monk of the holy order of St. Benedict.* 6th ed. Dublin. 1743. 12°. 482, [12] p. Published by [Meighan, T.]. ESTC t190527. * C; CAL; Do; ECW; FLK; Gi; Stan (imp.); TxU.

> There is an engraved frontispiece stating 'sold by Thomas Meighan in Drury Lane'.

816. Crowther, A. and T.V. Sadler. *A daily exercise of the devout Christian ... Publish'd by T.V. monk of the holy order of St. Benedict.* 8th ed. Dublin. 1763. 12°. [22], 520, [10] p. Printed by: Executors of the late widow Kelly. ESTC n033302. * KU-S.

817. Crowther, A. and T.V. Sadler. *A daily exercise of the devout Christian ... Publish'd by T.V. monk of the holy order of St. Benedict.* 9th ed. Cork. 1766. 12°. [10], 520, [10] p. Published by: Swiney, E. ESTC t208749. * D; Stan; Yb.

818. Crowther, A. and T.V. Sadler. *A daily exercise of the devout Christian ...*

Published by T.V. monk of the holy order of St. Benedict. 8th ed. Cork. 1770. 12°. [22], 520, [10] p. Printed by: Swiney, E. * Gi; IDA.

    This is the second '8th' ed.

819. Crowther, A. and T.V. Sadler. *A daily exercise of the devout Christian ... Published by T.V. monk of the holy order of St. Benedict.* 9th ed. Cork. 1770. 12°. [24], 520, [10] p. Printed by: Swiney, E. * Amp.

    This is the second '9th' ed.

820. Crowther, A. and T.V. Sadler. *A daily exercise, of the devout Christian ... Published by T.V. monk of the holy order of St. Benedict.* 10th ed. Cork. 1780. 12°. [20], 520, [10] p. Printed by: White, T.; Flyn, W. ESTC t190529. * D; FLK (-tp).

821. Crowther, A. and T.V. Sadler. *A daily exercise of the devout Christian ... Published by T.V. monk of the holy order of St. Benedict.* 14th ed. Dublin. 1785. 12°. [27], 28-517, [11] p. Printed by: Hoey, P. * FLK.

    There are three '14th' eds (cf. nos 822 and 823).

822. Crowther, A. and T.V. Sadler. *A daily exercise of the devout Christian ... Published by T.V. monk of the holy order of St. Benedict.* 14th ed. Dublin. 1789. 12°. 540, [12] p. Printed by: Hoey, P. * Do.

    There are three '14th' eds (cf. nos 821 and 823).

823. Crowther, A. and T.V. Sadler. *A daily exercise of the devout Christian ... Published by T.V. monk of the holy order of St. Benedict.* 14th ed. Dublin. 1793. 12°. [24], 517, [1] p. Printed by: Hoey, P. ESTC t190528. * NSPM.

    There are three '14th' eds (cf. nos 821 and 822).

824. Crowther, A. and T.V. Sadler. *A daily exercise of the devout Christian ... Published by T.V. monk of the holy order of St. Benedict.* 15th ed. Dublin. 1793. 12°. 168, 139-174, 225-420, [10] p. Printed by: Jones, W. ESTC n028384. * Do; IES; MB; PU.

    Text continuous despite pagination.

825. Cullin, Michael. *Remarks upon the introduction to a devout life. In which the errors of the English translation are set forth.* Dublin. 1742. 8°. 18 p. * SIR.

    The writer criticizes a hasty translation of the book by St. Francis de Sales.

Curry, John, see also O'Conor, Charles.

826. Curry, John. *A brief account from the most authentic Protestant writers of the causes, motives, and mischiefs, of the Irish rebellion.* London. 1747. 8°. [4], 62 [i.e. 162] p. ESTC t064962. * CSmH; D; Di; ICU; IU; KU-S; L; OCl.

    See also no. 836.

827. Curry, John. *An historical and critical review of the civil wars in Ireland, from the reign of Queen Elizabeth, to the settlement under King William. By J.C. M.D.* Dublin. 1775. 4°. [4], xxi, [3], 447, [7] p. Printed by: Hoey, J.; Faulkner, T.T.; Burnet, G.; Morris, J. Sold by: Hoey, J.; Faulkner, T.T.; Burnet, G.; Morris, J. ESTC t072428. * C; CLU; COVu; CtY; CU-A; D; DFo; Di; FU; GOT; ICN; ICU; IDA; IU; L; MChB; MY; Osc; SIR.

828. Curry, John. *An historical and critical review of the civil wars in Ireland,* *from the reign of Queen Elizabeth, to the settlement under King William.* 2 vols. Dublin. 1786. 8°. xiii, [3], 400; vi, 400, [12] p. Published by: White, L. ESTC t110536. * C; CSmH; D; DLC; Du; GOT; ICN; L; MChB; MH; MiU; MoSM; NIC; OCl; P; SCR; SPu; Ush; Vi.

    According to NUC edited by Charles O'Conor (see also next 2 items).

829. Curry, John. *An historical and critical review of the civil wars in Ireland, from the reign of Queen Elizabeth, to the settlement under King William.* 2 vols. London. 1786. 8°. xxiii, [1], 400; [8], v-vi, 400, [8] p. Published by: Robinson, G.G.J. and J.; Murray, J. ESTC t131404. * C; CaNfSM; CaOHM; CtHT; Di; E; FU; KU-S; L; MChB; MiEM; MRu; O; Pci; PPWa; PSt.

830. Curry, John. *An historical and critical review of the civil wars in Ireland, from the reign of Queen Elizabeth, to the settlement under King William.* 2 vols. Dublin. 1793. 8°. xiii, [3], 400; vi, 400, [12] p. Published by: Wogan, P. ESTC t204484. * D; Mil.

831. Curry, John. *Historical memoirs of the Irish rebellion in the year, 1641; extracted from parliamentary journals ... and the most eminent Protestant historians ... In a letter to Walter Harris.* Anon. London. 1758. 8°. xiv, ix-316 p. ESTC t146947. * D; DFo; Di; Dt; Du; HLp; L; MdBJ-P; NIC; Osc.

    In answer to W. Harris's *Fiction unmasked; or an answer to ... a popish physician,* Dublin, 1752. See also next 4 items.

832. Curry, John. *Historical memoirs of the Irish rebellion, in the year, 1641; extracted from parliamentary journals ... and the most eminent Protestant historians ... In a letter to Walter Harris.* Anon. London. 1765. 12°. iv, 279, [1] p. ESTC t146948. * E; KU-S; L; MY; O; PPL; Sto; Ush.

833. Curry, John. *Historical memoirs of the Irish rebellion, in the year, 1641; extracted from parliamentary journals ... and the most eminent Protestant historians ... In a letter to Walter Harris.* Anon. London. 1767. 12°. iv, 279, [1] p. Published by: Williams, J.; Lewis, T. ESTC t146949. * C; Di; E; L; Llp; NOp.

834. Curry, John. *Historical memoirs of the Irish rebellion, in the year, 1641; extracted from parliamentary journals ... and the most eminent Protestant historians ... In a letter to Walter Harris.* Anon. Dublin. 1770. 12°. 288 p. Published by: Hoey, J. jun. ESTC t113786. * AzTeS; Csj; CSmH; D; Di; ICU; IDA; IU; L.

835. Curry, John. *Historical memoirs of the Irish rebellion, in the year 1641. Extracted from parliamentary journals ... and the most eminent Protestant historians ... In a letter to Walter Harris.* Anon. London. [1770?]. 12°. 288 p. Published by: Williams, J.; Lewis, T. ESTC n017894. * MiU; MoU.

836. Curry, John. *A letter from an English gentleman, to a Member of Parliament. Shewing the hardships, cruelties and severe usage with which the Irish nation has been treated.* London. 1751. 12°. 85, [1], 87-172 p. Published by: Hill, T. ESTC t083635. * D; Dt; IDA; KU-S; L; N.

    The second part (signatures and pagination are continuous) is 'A brief account from the most authentic Protestant writers', London, 1751 (see no. 826).

837. Cyprian, Saint. *Sanctus Cyprianus ad martyres & confsssores [sic]. Ad usum confessorum ecclesiæ gallicanæ.* London. 1794. 12°. xx, 120 p. Published by: Coghlan, J.P.; Booker, E. ESTC t124222. * DMR; E; ECW; Hen; L; Lfa; MChB; MH; MY; O; Osc; Ush; UshL.

> With a 7-page 'Address to the French clergy' by Coghlan.

838. *The daily companion: or, a little pocket-manual: containing those devotions which are necessary to be perform'd every day by all Catholicks who have opportunity and leisure.* 2nd ed. London. 1737. 12°. viii, 87, [1] p. Published by: Meighan, T. * DoA.

> With one page of Meighan adverts. Gillow (I, 588) and ms note in Gi copy of the 4th ed. (no. 840) suggest William Crathorne as the author of this work. See also next 7 items.

839. *The daily companion: or, a little pocket-manual: containing those devotions which are necessary to be perform'd every day by all Catholicks.* 3rd ed. London. 1743. 12°. ix, [1], 87, [2] p. Published by: Meighan, T. * Ush.

> With 2 pages of Meighan adverts.

840. *The daily companion: or a little pocket-manual: containing those devotions necessary to be performed daily, with litanies and prayers recommended to Catholic families, and the universal prayer.* 4th ed. London. 1752. 12°. x, 85 p. Published by: Meighan, T. * Do; Gi; Lhe.

> Page 34 occurs twice.

841. *The daily companion: or, a little pocket-manual: containing those devotions which are necessary to be perform'd every day by all Catholicks who have opportunity and leisure.* 5th ed. London. 1761. 12°. ix, [1], 86 p. Published by: Meighan, T. ESTC t185913. * O.

842. *The daily companion: or, a little pocket-manual: containing those devotions which are necessary to be performed every day by all Catholics who have leisure.* 7th ed. Liverpool. 1765. 24°. viii, 112 p. Printed by: Sadler, J. Sold by: Sadler, J. ESTC t190520. * LVp.

> Place of publication and printer from half-title.

843. *The daily companion. Or, a little pocket-manual; containing those devotions which are necessary to be perform'd every day by all Catholicks who have opportunity and leisure.* 9th ed. 1768. 24°. x, 142 p. * Stan.

> Cf. also no. 844 which has Meighan's name in the imprint.

844. *The daily companion: or, a little pocket-manual: containing those devotions which are necessary to be perform'd every day by all Catholicks who have opportunity and leisure.* 9th ed. London. 1768. 24°. x, 142, [8] p. Published by: Meighan, T. * DoA; Stan.

> Cf. also no. 843 for an issue without Meighan's name in the imprint.

845. *The daily companion; or, a little pocket manual: containing such devotions as are necessary to be performed daily by all Christians.* 6th ed. London. 1798. 12°. 204, [4] p. Published by: Booker, E. * Stan.

> With 4 pages of Booker adverts.

846. *Daily devotions, or the most profitable manner of hearing mass very necessary for all Roman Catholics.* London. 1722. 24°. [2], 71, [1] p. Published by: [Meighan, T.?]. ESTC t092183. * L.

> Advertised in no. 991.

847. *Daily devotions, or the most profitable manner of hearing mass. Very necessary for all Roman Catholics, for the better understanding thereof.* Dublin. 1777. 12°. 72 p. ESTC t118276. * L; MY.

848. *Daily devotions, or the most profitable manner of hearing mass. Very necessary for all Roman Catholics, for the better understanding thereof.* Dublin. 1800. 12°. 72 p. Printed by: Wogan, P. * Do.

> Do bound up with *The poor man's manual* of 1797 (no. 2337).

849. *The daily duty of a pious Christian.* Hereford. 1777. 12°. viii, 78 p. Printed by: Pugh, C. * ECB.

> 'The prayers contained in this last part are chiefly collected out of M. Gother' (p. 78). In view of the date and the place of publication the compiler might be Michael Benedict Pembridge (see also Gillow, V, 254).

850. *A daily exercise, and devotions, for the young ladies, and gentlewomen pensioners at the monastery of the English canonesses regulars of the holy order of S. Augustin, at Bruges.* Douai. 1712. 12°. 249, [3] p. Printed by: Mairesse, M. ESTC t144085. * BB; C; DFo; DoA; ECB; ECW; Gi; L; Lfa; O; Stan; TxU.

851. *A daily exercise, and devotions, for the young ladies, and gentlewomen pensioners at the monastery of the English canonesses regulars of the holy order of S. Augustin, at Bruges.* Douai. 1748. 12°. 249, [3] p. Printed by: Willerval, J.F. ESTC t118322. * CLU-C; Do; ECW; Gi; Hen; L; O.

> Page 249 is misnumbered 245.

852. *A daily exercise, and devotions, for the young ladies, and gentlewomen pensioners at the monastery of the English canonesses regulars of the holy order of S. Augustin, at Bruges.* Bruges. 1766. 8°. 210, [2] p. Printed by: Roose, P. ESTC t144086. * ECB; L; O.

853. *A daily exercise, and devotions, for the young ladies, and gentlewomen pensioners at the monastery of the English canonesses regulars of the holy order of S. Augustin, at Bruges.* Bruges. 1786. 8°. 214, [2] p. Printed by: Moor, C. de. ESTC t144084. * BB (-tp); DMR; ECB; ECW; L; Lhe; NSPM; O.

854. *Daily pious practices and prayers in honour of the adorable sacrament of the altar.* London. 1781. 8°. viii, 94, [2], 14 p. Printed by: Coghlan, J.P. ESTC t119859. * ECW; Hen; L; Llp; O; TxU; Ush.

855. Daniel, Edward. *Ode to St. Winefride, patroness of Wales and her holy well. By E.D.* Liverpool. 1793. 12°. [2], 12 p. Printed by: Nevett, W. & Son. * Ush.

856. Daniel, Gabriel. *The discourses of Cleander and Eudoxus upon the Provincial letters. By a lover of peace and concord. Translated out of a French copy [Entretiens de Cleandre et d'Eudoxe].* Cullen [i.e. St. Omers]. 1701. 8°.

[4], 431, [1] p. Printed by: [English College Press]. ESTC t122034. * L; TxU.

Translated by William Darrell (see also next 2 items).

857. Daniel, Gabriel. *The discourses of Cleander and Eudoxus upon the Provincial letters. By a lover of peace and concord. Translated out of a French copy.* Cullen [i.e. St. Omers]. [1701?]. 8°. [4], 431, [1] p. Printed by: [English College Press]. ESTC t122033. * Do; L.

Another issue of this work (no. 856) has the year 1701 in the imprint. Tp of present ed. gives 1694, the date of the original French ed.

858. Daniel, Gabriel. *The discourses of Cleander and Eudoxe. Upon the Provincial letters. To which is added, an answer to the apology for the Provincial letters.* London. 1704. 8°. [34], 526 p. ESTC t101404. * C; CLU-C; DFo; Do; ECW; GEU-T; Gi; ICN; L(2); Lfa; LfaA; Llp; MH; Mil; MRu (2); O; Sto; TU; TxU; Ush; Yb.

One L copy and one MRu copy have a variant tp.

859. Darrell, William. *The case review'd, or, an answer to The case stated, by Mr. L--y. In which it is clearly shew'd that he has stated the case wrong between the Church of Rome and the Church of England.* [St. Omers]. 1715. 8°. [28], 402, [6], 24 p. Printed by: [English College Press]. ESTC t183418. * BB; DoA; DT; ECR; Lfa; Lhe; O.

A reply to Charles Leslie's *The case stated.* Tp states 'by the author of The gentleman instructed'. We do not include the eds of Darrell's *The gentleman instructed* in view of its neutral character. See also next item.

860. Darrell, William. *The case review'd, or, an answer to The case stated, by Mr. L...y. In which it is clearly shewed, that he had stated the case wrong between the Church of Rome, and the Church of England.* 2nd ed. London [i.e. St. Omers]. 1717. 8°. [20], 350, [6], 20 p. Printed by: [English College Press]. ESTC t106612. * Do; E; ECW; Gi; L; Lfa; LfaA; Lhe; P; TH.

861. Darrell, William. *Moral reflections on the epistles, and gospels of every Sunday, throughout the whole year. Divided into four parts.* Anon. London. 1711. 12°. [12], 344, [4] p. ESTC t170134. * Lhe; Ush.

Parts 2, 3 and 4 were separately published (see also next 5 items).

862. Darrell, William. *Moral reflections on the epistles and gospels of every Sunday, throughout the whole year. The second part.* Anon. London. 1713. 12°. 201, [1] p. ESTC t170135. * ECW; Hen; Lhe; Stan.

863. Darrell, William. *Moral reflections on the epistles and gospels of every Sunday throughout the whole year. The third part ... By the author of The gentleman instructed.* London. 1732. 12°. 261, [9] p. Published by: Meighan, T. ESTC t170138. * Do; ECW; Lfa; Lhe.

864. Darrell, William. *Moral reflections on the epistles and gospels of every Sunday throughout the whole year. The fourth part ... By the author of The gentleman instructed.* London. 1732. 12°. 204, [4] p. Published by: Meighan, T. ESTC t170139. * DoA; ECW; Lfa; Lhe.

865. Darrell, William. *Moral reflections on the epistles and gospels of every Sunday, throughout the whole year. The second part ... By the author of the* *gentleman instructed.* 2nd ed. London. 1733. 12°. 201, [3] p. Published by: Lewis, W. ESTC t170136. * Cha; ECB; Lfa; Lhe; PcA.

866. Darrell, William. *Moral reflections on the epistles and gospels of every Sunday, throughout the whole year. First part ... By the author of The gentleman instructed.* 2nd ed. Anon. London. 1734. 12°. [16], 290, [6] p. Printed by: Meighan, T. Published by: Meighan, T. ESTC t205921. * Do; E; ECW; Hen.

867. Darrell, William. *Moral reflections on the epistles and gospels of every Sunday; throughout the whole year.* 3rd ed. 4 vols. Dublin. 1740. 12°. [16], 290, [6] p. (vol. 1); 201, [3] p. (vol. 2). Published by: Kelly, I. * FLK (vols 1, 2).

868. Darrell, William. *Moral reflections on the epistles and gospels of every Sunday throughout the whole year.* 4th ed. 4 vols. Dublin. 1748. 12°. [16], 290, [6]; 201, [3]; 261, [7]; 204, 4 p. Published by: Kelly, I. * FLK.
   With respectively 1, 1 and 4 pages of Kelly adverts at end of vols 1, 3 and 4.

869. Darrell, William. *Moral reflections on the epistles and gospels of every Sunday, throughout the whole year. By Mr. Dorrell [sic].* 5th ed. 4 vols [bound in 2]. Dublin. 1767. 12°. [2], xii, 404; [3], 4-390, [16] p. Published by: Walsh, E. ESTC t107588. * FLK; L.
   Vols 1 & 2, and 3 & 4 respectively are continuously paginated and have a continuous register. See also next item. Sommervogel (II, 1826) also mentions a 1772 Dublin ed. printed by Byrne.

870. Darrell, William. *Moral reflections on the epistles and gospels of every Sunday, throughout the whole year. By W. Dorrell [sic].* 6th ed. 4 vols. Dublin. 1794. 12°. Published by: Cross, R.; Wogan, P. ESTC t170133. * Du; FLK (vol. 3); SIR.
   Sommervogel (II, 1826) also mentions a 1797 Dublin ed. printed by Wogan.

871. Darrell, William. *A treatise of the real presence; in answer to the author of, The case stated ... The second part. By the author of The gentleman instructed.* London [i.e. St. Omers]. 1721. 8°. [14], 400, [2] p. Printed by: [English College Press]. ESTC t117822. * Gi; L; Lfa; Lhe.
   A continuation of the author's *The case review'd* (nos 859-860) against Charles Leslie.

872. Daubenton, Guillaume. *The life of St. John Francis Regis, of the Society of Jesus. Translated into English by C. M. [La vie de S. Jean-François Régis].* London. 1734. 8°. viii, 368 p. * Do.
   'C. M.' is Cornelius Murphy (see also next item).

873. Daubenton, Guillaume. *The life of St. John Francis Regis, of the Society of Jesus. Translated into English by C*** M***.* London. 1738. 8°. viii, 368 p. Printed by: Hoyles, J. Sold by: Meighan, T. ESTC t085772. * C; CLU-C; DAE; Do; Dt; ECB; ECW; L; Lfa; Lhe; Map; NbOC; O; Osc; Stan (imp.); TxU.

874. *The debates, at large, on the Catholic Bill, in the Irish House of Commons, on Monday 4, 1795; to which is prefixed, the bill itself, as introduced by the right hon. Henry Grattan.* Cork. 1795. 8°. 88 p. Printed by: Haly, J. Sold by: Haly, J. ESTC t183956. * C; CSmH; D; Dt; Du; IU.

The book was edited under R.C. auspices.

875. *A declaration of political sentiments published by the Roman Catholics, of the city and vicinity of Waterford, in answer to the resolutions entered into by the different grand juries.* [Waterford?]. [1792]. 8°. [2], 93, [1] p. ESTC t185334. * D.

876. *Declaration of the Catholic Society of Dublin; resolutions and oath of United Irishmen; Phelan's letter; and Kenmare's address.* Dublin. 1791. 8°. 84 p. Published by: White, R. ESTC n028904. * Llp; O; PP.
> A collection of documents: the 'Declaration' by Theobald McKenna; the resolutions of the United Irishmen by James Napper Tandy; a circular letter by James Phelan, etc. See also next 2 items.

877. *Declaration of the Catholic Society of Dublin; resolutions and oath of United Irishmen; Phelan's letter, and Kenmare's address.* Dublin. 1791. 8°. 22 p. Published by: White, R. ESTC t033129. * CSmH; D; Du; IU; KU-S; L; PP.

878. *Declaration of the Catholic Society of Dublin; resolutions and oath of United Irishmen; Phelan's letter, and Kenmare's address.* Dublin. 1791. 8°. 24, [1], 80-84 p. Published by: White, R. ESTC t179901. * C; Dt; Sto.

879. *Declaration of the Catholic Society of Dublin.* Dublin. [1791]. 4°. x p. Printed by: Hoey, P. ESTC n043712. * BB; KU-S; Lpro; O.
> Dated and signed 'Dublin, October 21st 1791. By order of the society, Theobald McKenna secretary'.

880. *Declaration of the Society instituted for the purpose of promoting unanimity amongst Irishmen, and removing religious prejudices.* [Dublin]. [1791]. 4°. x p. ESTC n043679. * Lpro.
> Dated 'Dublin, October 21st, 1791'. This ed. is unsigned. With a letter signed by order of the Catholic Society of Dublin by James Phelan.

881. *Declaration of the Society instituted for the purpose of promoting unanimity amongst Irishmen, and removing religious prejudices.* [Dublin]. [1791]. 4°. x p. ESTC n043689. * Lpro.
> Signed 'Theo. M'Kenna'.

882. *Declarations of the parochial Roman Catholic clergy of the diocesses of Kilmacduagh and Kilfenora, September 10, 1798.* London. 1798. 8°. 8 p. Printed by: Coghlan, J.P. ESTC t201384. * E; WDA.
> Signed and dated 'James Burke [and 20 others]. Ardrahan, Sept. 10, 1798'.

883. *Decretum feria quinta die 25 sept. 1710.* 6 p. * OBA.
> Three pages in Latin followed by three pages with an English translation.

884. *A defence of the character of the reverend Mr. Hussey, against the aspersions contained in the Narrative of Mr. O'Leary, (with the narrative at large.) By a friend to the reverend Mr. Hussey.* London. 1791. 8°. [4], 32 p. Published by: Ridgway, J. ESTC t186853. * Du; DUc; ECW; Lfa.
> A reply to *A narrative of the misunderstanding between the rev. Arthur O'Leary and the rev. Mr. Hussey*, which is possibly by O'Leary himself (cf. nos 2075 and 1924).

885. *Defence of the sub-committee of the Catholics of Ireland, from the* *imputations attempted to be thrown on that body, particularly from the charge of supporting the defenders.* Dublin. 1793. 8°. [4], 12 p. Printed by: Fitzpatrick, H. ESTC t087739. * C; CLU-S/C; CSmH; D; L; Lhe; Lhl; Mil; MoSW; MY; NU.

886. Denaut, Pierre. *Mandement de Monseigneur l'Evêque de Québec, pour des actions de graces publiques.* [Quebec]. [1798]. fol. [4] p. Printed by: Lelievre, R.; Desbarats, P.E. ESTC w016679. * CaOOA; CaOOP; CaQMM; CaQQLa.
> Conveying the bishop's orders for thanksgiving on Jan. 10, 1799 for Nelson's victory over the French.

887. Denaut, Pierre. *Pierre Denaut ... Evêque de Quebec &c. &c. A tous les prêtres, curés, vicaires, missionaires et à tous les fidèles de notre diocèse salut et bénédiction.* [Quebec]. [1800]. 4°. [4] p. * CaOOP; CaQQLa.
> Signed and dated 'Donné à Quebec ... 7 Juillet 1800. J.O. Plessis Vic. Gen.'

888. Denaut, Pierre. *Pierre Denaut, par la miséricorde de Dieu, & la grace du St. Siège Apostolique, Evêque de Quebec, &c. &c. &c. à tous les curés, vicaires, missionaires, et à tous les fidèles de ce diocèse.* [Quebec]. [1800]. fol. [4] p. * CaQQLa.
> This circular letter gives instructions for the bishop's visitation. Dated and signed in ms '9 mai 1800. P. Evêque de Québec. J.J. Lartique'.

889. Denhoff, Jan Kazimierz. *The letter of the Lord Cardinal Denhoff Bp. of Cesene. Directed to the pastors and confessors of his diocess [sic] [Instruzione pastorale sopra il sagramento della penitenza].* [London?]. 1709. 12°. 228 p. ESTC t082730. * CLU-C; CSmH; DMR; Do; DoA; E; ECW; Hen; L; Lhe; O; TLP; Ush; Yb.

890. Denhoff, Jan Kazimierz. *Pastoral instructions proper for penitents as well as confessors. Wherein are to be seen all the faults committed by penitents.* 2nd ed. London. 1720. 12°. 228 p. Published by: Meighan, T. ESTC t101382. * CLU-C; Do; E; Gi; L; Lfa; LO; NPV; O; TLP; TxU; Ush.
> A reissue of no. 889, under a different title.

891. Denhoff, Jan Kazimierz. *The poor man's library: or, guide to salvation. Containing I. A short historical catechism ... II. An enlargement thereof ... III. Prayers and meditations. By the author of the Pastoral instructions.* London. 1730. 12°. [18], 483, [1] p. Printed by: M[eighan], P. Sold by: M[eighan], P. ESTC t177726. * Amp; Gi; O.

892. Denhoff, Jan Kazimierz. *A short historical catechism, collected from the holy scriptures. With an enlargement ... in most controverted points, about faith and God's worship. By the author of the Pastoral instructions.* London. 1732. 12°. [20], 483, [9] p. Printed by: Meighan, T. Sold by: Meighan, T. ESTC t124472. * L.
> With 2 pages of Meighan adverts.

893. *Description of the solemn obsequies of Pope Pius VI.* [London?]. [1799?]. 8°. [1], 4-18 p. ESTC t108337. * C (-tp); L (imp.); MY.

894. *La devotion aux ss. anges gardiens.* Montreal. 1783. 16°. 77, [3] p. Printed by: Mesplet, F. ESTC w016656. * CaOONL; CaQMM; CaQQLa.

895. *A devotion to the sacred heart of our Saviour Jesus Christ. Collected from the French.* [London?]. 1711. 12°. [6], 53, [1] p. ESTC t123724. * L; Lhe; Yb.
Dedication signed 'R.B.'i.e. Robert Beeston S.J.

896. *A devotion to the sacred heart of our Saviour Jesus Christ.* 1733. 12°. [4], 56 p. * CAL.
Bound up with the *Litany of St. Mary of Egypt,* 1733 (no. 1679).

897. *A devotion to the sacred heart of our Saviour Jesus Christ. To which is added the rosary of the blessed name of Jesus.* 3rd ed. Dublin. 1756. 12°. 83, [1] p. Published by: Executors of the late widow Kelly. * ECW.
With one page of adverts for the executors of the late widow Kelly.

898. *A devotion to the sacred heart of our Saviour Jesus Christ. To which is added, The rosary of the blessed name of Jesus.* 4th ed. Dublin. [1790?]. 12°. 73, 1 p. Printed by: Wilkinson, T. Sold by: Wilkinson, T. * MY.
The date 1790 is added in ms note.

899. *Devotion towards the blessed sacrament of the eucharist.* London. 1796. 12°. 24 p. Published by: Coghlan, J.P. * Bevan (1995).

900. *Devotions, for the use of the Liverpool congregation.* Liverpool. 1783. 8°. xiv, [2], xv-xxx, 160, 48 p. Printed by: Woods, G. ESTC t211528. * L.
Includes 'Hymns for Sundays and holidays, throughout the year', with separate pagination.

901. *Devout and instructive reflections on the Lord's Prayer, with penitent sentiments ... Translated from the French. By J. Sharp, D.D.* London. 1748. 12°. x, 115, [1] p. Published by: Marmaduke, J. * Map; Stan; UGL.
Sharp converted to Catholicism in 1715. In the 1750s Marmaduke advertizes this book as written by 'F. Cheminais', i.e. Timoléon Chéminais de Montaigu? Walsh (p. 49) suggests that an English translation of De Montaigu's *Sentiments de piété* came out in 1717. UGL has 4 extra pages of Marmaduke adverts.

902. *The devout Christian's vade mecum; being a summary of select and necessary devotions.* Philadelphia. 1797. 285, [3] p. Printed by: Ustick, S.C. Published by: Carey, M. * CSmH; DLC.
Finotti (p. 249) and Parsons (pp. 21 and 27) suggest that there were eds from 1789 onwards. Sometimes attributed to John Carroll.

903. *Devout ejaculatory prayers.* 12°. 7, [1] p. * Yb.
Bound with no. 2542.

904. *A devout exercise for the time of mass.* [2], 14, [2] p. * Ush.

905. *The devout manual: fitted to the ca-pacities of all Roman Catholicks.* Dublin. 1760. 12°. 72 p. ESTC t165003. * Do (imp.); ECW; IU; Lhe.
The imprint states 'printed at the Cloysters'.

906. *A dialogue between a parishioner and the rector of his parish, concerning the oath required by the national assembly ... Tbanslated [sic] ... by the rev. James Barnard.* London. 1793. 8°. vii, [1], 63, [1] p. Printed by: Coghlan, J.P. Sold by: Debrett, J.; Booker; Keating; Lewis; Robinsons. ESTC t031791. * C; CYc; ECW; L; MY; TxU; Ush.

MY attributes this work to 'abbé Hermès'.

907. *Directorium ad recitandas horas canonicas missasque celebrandas juxta rubricas novissimas breviarii sacri ordinis [Prae]dicatorum in provincia Hiberniae pro anno bissextili M.DCC.XCII.* Dublin. [1792]. 12°. [2], 24, [2] p. Published by: Wogan, P. Sold by: Denmark-street chapel. ESTC t202963. * Dt.

Edited by John Daly.

908. *Directorium Romano-Franciscanum, juxta ritum S.R.E. et nova decreta dispositum ad usum. FF. MM. almae provinciae Angliae pro anno Domini MDCCXCIII.* London. [1793]. 12°. 24, [1], [7], 24. Printed by: Coghlan, J.P. * WDA (imp.).

909. *Directorium sive ordo divini oficii recitandi ... 1750.* [Dublin]. [1749]. Published by: Kelly, I.; Brown, T.; Coldwell, J. (Waterford). * KDA.

910. *Directorium sive ordo divini officii recitandi missaeque celebrandae ... ad usum cleri regni Hiberniae ... pro anno ... 1763.* [Dublin]. 1763. 12°. 47, [1] p. Printed by: [Kelly, E., the executors of the late widow]. * Ush.

With one page of adverts for the executors of the late widow Kelly.

911. *Directorium sive ordo divini officii recitandi missaeque celebrandae ... ad usum cleri regni Hiberniae dispositum ... pro anno ... 1776.* Dublin. [1775]. 8°. 56, [2] p. Published by: Fitzsimons, R. Sold by: Fitzsimons, R. * CME.

912. *Discours prononcé à Guernesey, le 25 Octobre 1795, rar [sic] Mr. Renaudau. Desservant délégué de monseigneur l'Eveque de Coutance, à la benediction du drapeau de la division des émigrés.* Guernesey. 1795. 8°. 14 p. ESTC t121219. * L.

913. *A discourse delivered in one of the Catholic chapels, on the propriety and necessity of taking the oath of allegiance tendered by government.* Durham. 1778. 4°. iv, 14 p. Printed by: Thorne, N. Sold by: Charnley, W. (Newcastle); Crowder, S. (London). ESTC t182849. * C; NCp.

914. *A discourse on catechetical instruction, particularly on the design and use of abbé Fleury's short and larger historical catechisms. Translated from the French by C.C.* Newcastle. 1786. 12°. 44 p. Printed by: Hodgson, S. * Hor.

For Fleury see no. 1052ff. 'C.C.' might be Charles Cordell.

915. *A dispassionate enquiry into the cause of the late riots in London. In which the arcana of popery are candidly disclosed by a Protestant gentleman.* London. 1781. 4°. iv, 103, [1] p. Published by: Almon, J.; Debrett, J. * C; CaOKQ; CoU; E; L; Lfa; Lg; MH-H; O; SHu.

Ms note on tp of Lfa 'disclosed by a pretended Protestant gentleman, but in fact by a Catholick'.

916. *A dissertation, addressed to a friend, on the propriety of admitting the Roman Catholics of Ireland to a share in the elective franchise.* Dublin. 1792. 8°. [2], ii, 41, [1] p. Printed by: Byrne, P. ESTC t034638. * C; CoU; CSmH; D; Dt; Du; KU-S; L; Lse; Mil; MSaE; MY; O; Sto.

Although the author is unknown and might be non-R.C., the book is clearly published in the Catholic interest.

917. *A dissertation upon receiving the body and blood of Jesus Christ under one only kind.* [London?]. [1712]. 12°. 59, [1] p. ESTC t202087. * ECW; Llp; TxU.
> The imprint mistakenly gives '1612'.

918. *Divers church chants, for St. Mark and rogation-days; the proses for Easter, Whitsuntide, and Corpus Christi; six different masses; vespers, matins, lauds and mass for the dead, with the burial office.* London. 1799. 12°. iv, 188 p. Printed by: Coghlan, J.P. ESTC t073161. * E; ECW; L; OClW.

919. Donlevy, Andrew. *The catechism or Christian doctrine by way of question and answer ... An teagasg Chriosduidhe.* Anon. Paris. 1742. 8°. lvi, 518 p. Printed by: Guerin, J. ESTC t097298. * BFq; C; CaQQLa; Ct; CtY-BR; D; Do (imp.); Du; E; FLK; ICR; ICU; IDA; L; LO; Luk; MH-H; Mil; MY; NjR; O; P; PIF; Sal; SIR.
> Tp and text in English and Irish. The work also contains *The elements of the Irish language* by Donlevy and *Abridgement of Christian doctrine* in Irish verse by O'Hussey. See also no. 2047.

920. Donlevy, Andrew. *[The catechism, or Christian doctrine].* 12°. 212 p. * MY (-tp).
> '1742' is written on p. 3, but this might refer to the date of publication of the first ed. (Paris, 1742).

921. Donlevy, Andrew. *The catechism, or Christian doctrine, by way of question and answer; drawn chiefly from the express word of God, and other pure sources.* London. 1791. 8°. xvi, 158 p. Printed by: Connor, J. Published by: Connor, J. ESTC t192026. * D; ECW; LO.

922. Donlevy, Andrew. *The catechism, or Christian doctrine, by way of question and answer; drawn from the express word of God, and other pure sources. Republished by A. Clinton.* Anon. London. 1796. 12°. xvi, 296 p. Printed by: Coghlan, J.P. ESTC t124344. * Do; E; ECB; ECW; FLK; L; Lfa; Lhe; O; Osc; Sco; Ush.
> 'A. Clinton' is Alexander MacKenzie, s.v.

923. Douglass, John. *Instructions and regulations for the fast of Lent, 1791, addressed to the faithful of the southern district.* [London?]. [1791]. fol. 2 p. ESTC t037290. * L; WDA.
> Signed 'John Centurien, V.A.'

924. Douglass, John. *Instructions and regulations for the fast of Lent, 1793. Addressed to the faithful of the London district.* [London?]. [1793]. fol. s.s. ESTC t037291. * L.
> Signed 'John Centurien, V.A.L.'

925. Douglass, John. *Instructions and regulations for the fast of Lent in the present year 1795.* [London]. [1795]. fol. s.s. * WDA.
> Signed and dated 'John Centurien V.A.L. London, January 26, 1795'.

926. Douglass, John. *Instructions and regulations for the fast of Lent in the present year 1796.* [London]. [1796]. fol. s.s. * WDA.
> Signed and dated 'John Centurien V.A.L. London, January 26, 1796'.

927. Douglass, John. *Instructions and regulations for the fast of Lent ... 1797,* and for the observance of Wednesday the 8th of March, as a day of particular humiliation and prayer within the London district. [London]. [1797]. fol. s.s. ESTC t037292. * L.

Signed and dated 'John Centurien, V.A.L., London, Feb. 6, 1797'.

928. Douglass, John. *Instructions and regulations for the fast of Lent, 1798; addressed to the faithful of the London district.* [London]. [1798]. fol. s.s. ESTC t037293. * BAA; L.

Signed and dated 'John Centurien, V.A.L., London, Feb. 5, 1798'.

929. Douglass, John. *Instructions and regulations for the fast of Lent ... 1799, addressed to the faithful of the London district.* [London]. [1799]. fol. s.s. ESTC t037294. * Cli; L.

Dated and signed 'London, Jan. 19th, 1799. John Centurien, V.A.L.'

930. Douglass, John. *Instructions and regulations for the fast of Lent 1800, addressed to the faithful of the London district.* London. [1800]. fol. s.s. Printed by: Coghlan, J.P. ESTC t037295. * BAA; L.

Signed and dated 'John Centurien V.A.L. London: Feb. 13th, 1800'.

931. Douglass, John. *The instructions and regulations for the Lent of 1794. Dearly beloved brethren in Jesus Christ.* [London]. [1794]. 8°. s.s. ESTC t037296. * L; TxU.

Signed 'John, Centurien, V.A.L.'

932. Douglass, John. *John, Bishop of Centuriae, vicar apostolic, to all the faithful, clergy and laity, in the London district.* [London]. [1792]. fol. s.s. ESTC t029106. * DowA; L.

Dated 'London, Oct. 8, 1792'.

933. Douglass, John. *John, Bishop of Centuriae, vicar apostolic, to all the faithful of the London district, clergy and laity.* [London]. [1794]. fol. s.s. ESTC t029107. * L.

Dated 'London, Feb. 10, 1794'.

934. Douglass, John. *John, Bishop of Centuriae, vicar apostolic, to all the faithful, clergy and laity of the London district.* [London]. [1796]. fol. s.s. * WDA.

Signed and dated 'John Centurien, V.A.L. London Feb. 22, 1796'.

935. Douglass, John. *John, Bishop of Centuriae, vicar apostolic, &c. To all the faithful, clergy and laity, of the London district.* [London]. [1797]. fol. s.s. * Ush.

Dated 'London, December 12, 1797'.

936. Douglass, John. *John, Bishop of Centuriae, vicar apostolic, &c. To all the faithful, clergy and laity of the London district.* [London]. [1798]. fol. s.s. ESTC t029108. * L.

Dated 'London Nov. 17th 1798'.

937. Douglass, John. *John, Bishop of Centuriae, vicar apostolic, &c. To all the clergy, secular and regular, of the London district.* [London]. [1799]. fol. s.s. ESTC t029109. * ICN; L; TxU.

Dated 'October 18th, 1799'.

938. Douglass, John. *M. [blank] Voulant concilier le devoir de mon ministère.* [London?]. [1798]. 4°. [2] p. ESTC t038814. * L.

Dated and signed 'A Londres, 24 Mars, 1798, Jean, Evèque de Centurie'.

939. Douglass, John. *Mandates of their lordships John, Bishop of Centuriae ... and of Gregory William, Bishop of Telmessus ... appointing prayers to be sung or said in all the Roman Catholic chapels for his holiness Pope Pius VI. and ... King George III.* London. 1798. 12°. 28, [8] p. Printed by: Coghlan, J.P. ESTC t215148. * Di; TxU.

940. Douglass, John. *Mandates of their lordships John, Bishop of Centuriae ... Gregory William, Bishop of Telmessus ... William, Bishop of Acanthos ... and of Charles, Bishop of Hier. Caes.* London. 1798. 12°. [4], 29, [3] p. Printed by: Coghlan, J.P. ESTC t194892. * Lfa; O; Osc; WDA.

Includes a pastoral letter from Charles Berington, who died this year, and from George Hay 'to the faithful in North Britain'.

941. Douglass, John. *A messieurs les ecclésiastiques Français qui ont obtenu la permission de célébrer la sainte messe dans les chapelles particulieres.* [London?]. [1798]. fol. s.s. ESTC t019058. * L; TxU.

Dated and signed at end 'Donné à Londres ce 24 Mars 1798. Jean Evèque de Centurie ... par Monseigneur Jacques Barnard sécretaire'.

942. Douglass, John. *A new year's gift for the year MDCCXCIII. The grace of our Saviour hath appeared.* [1792]. 8°. 12 p. * ECW.

Signed on p. 12 'J.C.'

943. Douglass, John. *A new year's gift for the year M.D.CC.XCIV. It must needs be that scandals come.* [1793]. 8°. 12 p. * ECW.

Signed on p. 12 'J.C.'

944. Douglass, John. *To all the faithful, clergy and laity, of the London district.* [London]. [1791]. fol. s.s. ESTC t051057. * L; O; Ush.

Signed and dated 'John Centurien, V.A. London, June 14, 1791'; the bishop congratulates his flock on the regained freedom of religion.

945. *The Doway catechism, in English and Irish. For the use of children and ignorant people.* Dublin. 1738. 8°. 99, [1] p. Printed by: Babe, H. ESTC t167488. * D.

The catechism was formulated at the English College at Douai and was used for religious instruction there. According to Fagan (p. 154) Sylvester Lloyd O.F.M., Bishop of Kilaloe was the editor. ESTC states that the imprint may be false, but Munter (p. 18) states that the Dublin printer H. Babe was at work on this Catechism in 1736. The term 'Doway Catechism' was popularly used for Henry Turberville's *An abridgement of Christian doctrine.* See also next item.

946. *The Doway catechism, in English and Irish. For the use of children and ignorant people.* Dublin. 1752. 12°. 128 p. Published by: Kelly, I. ESTC t202192. * D; Eu; MY.

Dedication signed by 'S.L.L.' i.e. Sylvester Louis Lloyd. Pages 126-8 contain 'A few instructions for reading the Irish language'.

947. Dowdall, James. *An appeal to the publick, in relation to an affair that lately pass'd between the rt. rev. B...p Wh...te, head of the Roman Catholick mission in England; and Mr. J...s D...d...ll.* London. [1742?]. 8°. xxiv, 43, [1] p. Printed by: The booksellers of London and Westminster. Sold by: The booksellers of London and Westminster. ESTC t066441. * CLU-C; L; MRu; O.

> 'B...p Wh...te' is Bishop White, i.e. Benjamin Petre. L has ms note giving name of author. According to Gillow (V, 289) edited by Benjamin Petre himself.

948. Driscol, Paddy. *A political address to the Catholics of Ireland.* Dublin. 1792. 8°. 39, [1] p. Printed by: Byrne, P. ESTC t086585. * C; D; Dt; IU; L; Mil; MY; NNUT; Sto.

> The author, although most likely non-R.C. himself, urges his Catholic compatriots to take action.

949. Dryden, John. *The hind and the panther. A poem in three parts.* 1725. 8°. [6], 7-70 p. * SIR.

950. Dryden, John. *The hind and the panther. A poem, in three parts.* [London?]. 1729. 8°. 70, [2] p. ESTC n032878. * CaOHM; Ush.

> Ush has an additional 2 pages of adverts for books to be had 'at the pamphlet-shop in Skinner-Row [Dublin]'.

951. Dryden, John. *The hind and the panther, a poem. In three parts.* London. 1742. 8°. viii, 96 p. ESTC t126026. * CLU-C; Dt; E; ECR; L; MdBJ; Ush.

952. Dryden, John. *The hind and the panther. A poem in three parts.* London. 1764. 12°. [7], 8-71, [1] p. Printed by: Meaghan [sic], T. Sold by: Flyn, W. (Cork). * MY.

> With one page of Flyn adverts. This suggests Cork rather than London as the place of publication; note also the date (after Meighan's death) and the spelling of Meighan's name.

953. Dryden, John. *The hind and the panther. A poem. In three parts.* Dublin. 1783. 12°. 71, [1] p. Printed by: Corcoran, B. ESTC n017610. * D; NSyU.

954. Du Monceau, Alexis. *Exercice tre's-devot envers S. Antoine de Padoue le thaumaturge, de l'ordre séraphique de S. François. Avec un petit recueil de quelques principaux miracles.* Montreal. 1777. 18°. [8], 88 p. Published by: Mesplet, F.; Berger, C. ESTC w016666. * CaOOP; CaOONL; CaQMS.

> This work is said to have been prepared by a Franciscan, Alexis du Monceau, and to have been printed for the first time in 1692.

955. Du Pin, Louis Ellis. *A compendious history of the church, from the beginning of the world to this present time [Histoire de l'église en abrégé].* 4 vols. London. 1713. 12°. Published by: Lintott, B. ESTC t126792. * BMp; C; Ct; L; NjR; NNUT; O; Ol; Osc; Ot; TxU.

> The author is R.C. but the publication is of a general nature. For other eds of this work and other generally Christian works by Du Pin, see ESTC.

956. Dubourg, William. *College of George-Town, (Potomack) in the state of Maryland, United States of America.* [Georgetown]. [1798]. 3, [1] p. * DGU.

> Signed and dated 'George-Town, January 1st, 1798. Wm Du Bourg, President of

the college'. Prospectus of the college.

957. Durand, Laurent. *Cantiques de l'ame dévote. Divisés en xii livres.* Quebec.
1776. 12°. [12], 610, [2] p. Printed by: Mesplet, F.; Berger, C. Sold by:
Mesplet, F.; Berger, C. ESTC w016637. * CaOONL; CaQMBM; CaQMM;
CaQMS; CaQQLa; DLC; NN.

> Despite the imprint, this item was probably printed and actually published in
> Montreal, where Mesplet established his press in May 1776. It is conceivable
> that 'Quebec' refers to the province. This is in fact an ed. of *Cantiques de
> Marseilles*.

958. Durand, Laurent. *Cantiques de Marseilles accommodés à des airs vulgaires,
par M. Laurent Durand, prêtre du diocèse de Toulon.* Quebec. 1800. 16°. 422,
[2] p. ESTC w016638. * CaOOP; CaQMM; CaQQLa.

> This was a popular devotional work first printed in 1678.

959. Dwyer, Joseph John. *The trinitarian manual, being a concise history of the
order of the holy and undivided trinity for the redemption of captives, &c.
Together with prayers at mass ... Translated ... from the Italian.* Dublin. 1795.
12°. 6, iii-vii, [7], 3-210 p. Printed by: Wogan, P. ESTC t209206. * Di; E;
FLK; IDA.

> With a 6-page list of subscribers. Dwyer was the compiler and editor of this
> work.

960. Earle, John. *Remarks on the prefaces prefixed to the first and second
volume of a work entitled The holy bible ... faithfully translated, &c. &c. by the
rev. Alexander Geddes, LL.D. in four letters addressed to him.* London. 1799.
12°. [4], 100 p. Printed by: Coghlan, J.P. Sold by: Booker; Keating; Law;
Robinsons. ESTC t123350. * CAL; DMR; ECW; Gu; L; Ldw; Lfa; Osc; Ush.

> See also no. 1453.

961. Ecclestone, Thomas. *The way to happiness.* Anon. [London?]. 1726. 8°.
[8], viii, 360, [2] p. ESTC t054926. * BB; CLU-C; Do; E; FLK; ICN; L; Lhe;
LO; MdBJ; OrPU; Yb.

962. Ecclestone, Thomas. *The way to happiness.* 2nd ed. London. 1772. 12°.
[2], iv, [4], 314 p. Published by: Coghlan, J.P. ESTC t119392. * Do; Gi; L;
Lhe; Sal; TLP; Ush.

> Lhe has some Coghlan adverts.

963. *Ego N.N. sincere promitto & juro me fidelem futurum & veram fidelitatem
observaturum erga Majestatem suam Regem.* [London]. [1790]. fol. 2 p. Printed
by: [Coghlan, J.P.] . * Cli; Ush.

> Latin oath with a blank space for name of undersigned to promise allegiance to
> the King of England. Cli is attached to a ms letter by Coghlan to Bishop
> Walmesley telling him he is sending a copy.

964. *The eleventh Sunday after Pentecost. On purposes of amendment.* London.
1784. 12°. [4], ii, 25, [1] p. Printed by: Coghlan, J.P. ESTC n050759. * Amp;
MBAt.

965. Elliot, Nathaniel. *Occasional letters on the present affairs of the Jesuits in
France.* Anon. London. [1765?]. 12°. [2], 45, [1] p. Printed by: Balfe, R. ESTC

n012529. * PPL; Ush.

>Attributed to Nathaniel Elliot (ESTC and also ms note in Ush). See also Gillow (II, 159).

966. Elliot, Nathaniel. *Occasional letters on the present affairs of the Jesuits in France.* Anon. London. [1765?]. 12°. xvi, 24, [1], 42-242, iv, 72 p. Printed by: Balfe, R. ESTC t102059. * C; E; InNd; L; LfaA; Lhe; O; Osc; PPL; Sto; Yb.

>In two parts; part 2 has a separate tp *The judgment of the bishops of France* (cf. no. 1537).

967. *Encyclical letter of the Bishops of Rama, Acanthos, and Centuria; to the faithful, clergy and laity, of their respective districts: with a continued commentary for the use of the vulgar.* London. 1791. 8°. viii, 9-28 p. Sold by: Bell, J. ESTC t032646. * BAA; E; L; O; Osc; Ush.

>This parody, dealing with the second Relief Act and attacking the bishops, is sometimes attributed to Alexander Geddes (Fuller, p. 157; Osc and ms note in E).

968. *The end of man display'd.* London. 1746. 8°. viii, 94 p. Published by: Needham, W. Sold by: Needham, W. ESTC n009178. * DUc; Map; NcD; Or; Ush.

969. Englefield, Sir Henry Charles. *A letter to the author of The review of the case of the Protestant dissenters ... To which is added ... some general observations upon the laws now in force against ... Catholic dissenters.* London. 1790. 8°. [4], 66 p. Published by: Elmsly, P. ESTC t012295. * BMp; C; CoU; CtY-BR; CU-BANC; D; DoA; ECW; IISHA; IU; L; Ldw; Lmh; Lu; MBAt; MChB; MnU; MRu; O; Osc; Sto; Ush.

>As an active member of the Catholic Committee Englefield reacted against *The review*, which was attributed to the Bishop of St. David's.

970. *The English College of St. Omer. I. The terms of this college are 24 per annum.* 12°. 2 p. * Ush.

>A prospectus for the college under the secular clergy. A ms letter attached mentions the date '27 January 1787'.

971. *English grammar.* Douai. 1781. 8°. [2], 54, [2] p. Printed by: Derbaix. ESTC t131229. * C; L.

>This grammar was compiled for the use of the English College at Douai.

972. *English grammar compiled for the use of the English College at Douay.* London. 1795. 8°. [2], 54, [2] p. Printed by: Coghlan, J.P. * Cha; DoA.

>Cha bound up with no. 1121.

973. *The entire office, and all the proper masses for the dead.* London. 12°. [3], iv-vi, [1], 8-190 p. Printed by: Keating, P. Sold by: Keating, P. * LO.

>No date but probably late 18th century.

974. *Epistola episcoporum provinciae Dubliniensis, ad SS. D.N. Pium VI. Circa constitutionem, auctorem fidei, condemnatoriam errorum synodi Pistoriensis.* Dublin. 1797. 4°. 5, [1] p. Published by: Fitzpatrick, H. * Cli; WDA.

>A letter by four Irish bishops to the pope and a response from Cardinal Gerdil.

975. *Epistola episcoporum provinciae Dubliniensis, ad SS. D.N. Pium VI. Circa*

constitutionem, auctorem fidei, condemnatoriam errorum synodi Pistoriensis.
Dublin. 1797. 8°. [2], 6 p. Published by: Fitzpatrick, H. * Cli(2).

> The second Cli copy has 6, [4] p. The letter contains the response from Rome to
> the Irish bishops and their answer, in turn, to Rome.

976. *Epitome ritualis Romani, in usum missionum Scotiae. Permissu superiorum.*
London. 1783. 12°. iv, 203, [1] p. Printed by: Coghlan, J.P. Published by:
Coghlan, J.P. * Amp; Cha; E.

977. *Epitome ritualis Romani, in usum missionum Scotiae. Permissu superiorum.*
[Edinburgh?]. 1783. 12°. iv, 190 p. ESTC t202694. * E; PLatS; Sćo.

978. Errington, William. *A letter to Mr. A-d, concerning his motives for
renouncing the popish, and re-embracing the Protestant religion.* Anon. London.
1758. 8°. [4], 42 p. Published by: The widow Needham; Cooper, Mrs. Sold by:
The widow Needham; Cooper, Mrs. ESTC t086892. * C; L; O; Ush.

> 'Mr. A-d' is William Arnold, whose *Motives for renouncing the popish and
> re-embracing the Protestant religion* appeared in 1758. Arnold's name is given
> in Coghlan's *Catalogue* (no. 736), p. 8. For the catalogue of Errington's library
> see no. 738.

979. Erskine, Charles. *Copy of letters.* [London]. fol. 2 p. Published by:
[Coghlan, J.P.]. * DowA; Sto; Ush.

> Copies of letters dated 4 May and 1 May 1798 about the Oath of Allegiance.
> Signed by Charles Erskine and Thomas Hussey.

980. Erskine, Charles. *Funeral oration for his holiness Pope Pius VI. By
Monsignore Erskine, his auditor.* London. 1799. 8°. [2], 72 p. Printed by:
Coghlan, J.P. ESTC t085362. * DoA; L; Lfa; MY; SAN; Ush.

981. *An essay on the church plain chant: part first, containing instructions for
learning the church plain song. With approbation.* London. 1782. 8°. vi, [4], 23,
[1] p. Printed by: Coghlan, J.P. Published by: Coghlan, J.P. ESTC t065388. *
DLC; Do; Dt; L; NRU; O; UshL.

> For the authorship of this work see Bennett Zon, 'Plainchant in the eighteenth-
> century English Catholic church'. See also next 3 items.

982. *An essay on the church plain chant: part second, containing several
anthems, litanies ... as they are sung in the public chapels at London. With
approbation.* London. 1782. 8°. [2], xxxix, [1] p. Printed by: Coghlan, J.P.
Published by: Coghlan, J.P. ESTC t065389. * DLC; Do; L; Lhe; NRU; O;
UshL.

983. *An essay on the church plain chant: part third being a supplement of several
anthems, litanies ... which have been omitted in the second part, yet are sung in
the public chapels at London.* London. 1782. 8°. [2], xvi p. Printed by: Coghlan,
J.P. Published by: Coghlan, J.P. ESTC t065390. * DLC; Do; Dt; L; Lhe; NRU;
O; UshL.

984. *An essay on the church plain chant. 4 parts in 1 vol.* [London]. 1793. 8°.
23, xxxix, xvi, 6 p. Printed by: Coghlan, J.P. * Osc.

985. *An essay on the nature of the church: and a review of the elections of* bishops in the primitive church. Together with some annexed dissertations. Edinburgh. 1728. 8°. v, [1], 19, [1], 246, 177, [1], vii, [1] p. Printed by: Catanach, J. ESTC t056728. * E; IES; L; Lmh.

> R.C. answer to *A view of the elections of bishops in the primitive church* (1728), by James Dundass (ESTC t193363).

986. *An essay or instruction for learning the church plain chant. To which are added, various hymns ... with approbation.* London. 1799. 12°. [8], 92 p. Printed by: Coghlan, J.P. ESTC t121061. * C; E; ECW; ICN; L; Lhe; O; Osc; PPiPT.

> The 'approbation' is signed by James and Thomas Talbot, George Hay and John Geddes.

987. *The establishment of the Royal Catholic College of St. Patrick, at Maynooth, near Dublin. A continuation of the account of British subjects who have suffered by the French Revolution.* London. 1796. 12°. 30 p. Printed by: Coghlan, J.P. ESTC t114517. * FP; L; O; Sto.

> See also *Some account* (no. 2572) and *A continuation* (no. 779). This material also formed part of eds of the *Laity's directory* and the *Ordo*.

988. Eusebius, of Caesarea. *The character of the blessed Emperor Constantine.* [London?]. 1721. 8°. 25 [i.e. 24] p. ESTC n044168. * CLU-C.

989. *Evénemens miraculeux établis par des lettres autentiques d'Italie.* London. 1796. 8°. [2], 28 p. Printed by: Coghlan, J.P. ESTC t194384. * DUc.

> Describes miracles in Ancona, Rome, and other Italian towns in 1796.

Evening office. There are two main series of the evening office of the church. We list them in one chronological sequence.

990. *The evening-office of the church in Latin and English. Containing the vespers, or even-song for all Sundays and festivals of obligation.* [London]. 1710. 12°. Published by: Meighan, T. Gillow IV, 463.

991. *The evening-office of the church in Latin and English. Containing the vespers, or even-song for all Sundays and festivals of obligation ... with the addition of the old hymns.* 2nd ed. [London?]. 1719. 12°. [2], vi, [4], 384, [12] p. Published by: [Meighan, T.?]. ESTC t129572. * E; L.

> With 3 pages of Meighan adverts.

992. *The evening-office of the church in Latin and English. Containing the vespers, or even-song for all Sundays and festivals of obligation.* 3rd ed. London. 1725. 12°. [2], vi, [6], 394, [8] p. Printed by: Meighan, T. * DoA; Gi; Map; Ush.

> With some pages of Meighan adverts.

993. *The evening-office of the church, in Latin and English. Containing the vespers, or even-song, for all Sundays and festivals of obligation ... To which are added, the Bona mors.* 4th. ed. [London]. 1737. 8°. [2], iv, [4], 563, [1] p. ESTC t198223. * DoA; L.

994. *The evening-office of the church, in Latin and English. Containing the vespers, or even-song, for all Sundays and festivals of obligation.* 4th ed.

[London]. 1738. 12°. [2], ix, [1], 484, [8] p. Published by: Meighan, T. ESTC t191136. * LO; NPV; O; SIR.

> This is the second '4th' ed.

995. *The evening-office of the church, according to the Roman breviary: containing the vespers for all Sundays and festivals throughout the year. In Latin and English. To which is added, A pious association.* London. 1748. 12°. 6, [16], 432 p. Published by: Marmaduke, J. ESTC t202974. * DMR; Do; E; Gi; Map.

> This includes 'The true method to learn the church plain-song'. With some pages of Marmaduke adverts.

996. *The evening-office of the church in Latin and English. Containing the vespers, or even-song for all Sundays and festivals of obligation.* 5th ed. [London]. 1748. 12°. xii, 410, [10] p. Published by: Meighan, T. ESTC t191217. * DMR; E; Map; O; Stan; TH.

> With some pages of Meighan adverts. DMR, Map, Stan and TH bound up with no. 97.

997. *The evening-office of the church in Latin and English. Containing the vespers, or even-song for all Sundays and festivals of obligation.* 6th ed. Dublin. 1754. 12°. x, [2], 429, [7] p. Published by: Kelly, E. ESTC t181880. * D (2); FLK; IDA; Lmh.

> IDA and both D copies are bound with *The art of singing* (no. 98).

998. *The evening-office of the church in Latin and English. Containing the vespers, or even-song for all Sundays and festivals of obligation.* 6th ed. [London]. 1759. 12°. xii, 410, [34] p. Published by: Meighan, T. ESTC t181868. * BMp; Gi; Yb.

> This is the second '6th' ed. Page 285 misnumbered 215, page 379 misnumbered 779.

999. *The evening office of the church in Latin and English, containing the vespers or even-song for all Sundays, and festivals of obligation.* [London?]. 1760. 8°. [2], ii, [12], 322, [24] p. ESTC n031157. * AWn; DMR; FMU; Gi; NSPM; Ou; Ush.

1000. *The evening-office of the church, according to the Roman breviary: containing the vespers for all Sundays and festivals ... in Latin and English. To which is added, A pious association.* 2nd ed. London. 1762. 12°. 5, [13], 414 p. Published by: Marmaduke, J. ESTC t202972. * E; Sal; Stan; TLP; Ush.

> Stan has an additional 48 pages containing 'The true method to learn the church plain-song'. See no. 991 for another '2nd' ed.

1001. *The evening-office of the church, according to the Roman breviary: containing the vespers for all Sundays and festivals throughout the year.* 3rd ed. London. 1773. 12°. 5, [11], 412 p. Published by: Marmaduke, J. ESTC t181869. * E; Gi; Hen; NSCH; TxU; Yb.

> See no. 992 for another '3rd' ed.

1002. *The evening-office of the church, in Latin and English, containing the vespers or even-song, for all Sundays, and festivals of obligation throughout the* *year. To which are added, the litanies.* [London?]. 1773. 8°. [2], ii, [14], 360 p. Published by: J. F. W. ESTC t211207. * DMR; ECW; Gi; ICN (imp.); Lfa; Lmh (imp); LO; MY; Stan.

>See Bennett Zon, 'Plainchant in the eighteenth-century' (RH, vol. 21, no. 3, pp. 361-80), who identifies 'J.F.W.' as John Francis Wade.

1003. *The evening-office of the church, according to the Roman breviary: containing the vespers for all Sundays and festivals throughout the year.* 4th ed. London. 1778. 12°. [16], 414 p. Published by: Marmaduke, J. * Do; ECW; Gi; LO; TLP.

>See nos 993 and 994 for other '4th' eds.

1004. *The evening office of the church, according to the Roman breviary: containing the vespers for all Sundays and festivals throughout the year.* 5th ed. London. 1785. 12°. [16], 402 p. Published by: Marmaduke, J. * DMR; Gi.

>See no. 996 for another '5th' ed. DMR has 2½ pages of Marmaduke adverts.

1005. *The evening-office of the church, in Latin and English, containing the vespers or even-song for all Sundays and festivals of obligation.* [London]. 1793. 8°. [2], 11, [15], 361, [1] p. Published by: Clarkson, R. ESTC t181870. * ECW; NSPM.

1006. *The evening-office of the holy week. Which the church performs on Wednesday, Tuesday, and Friday before Easter.* 1760. 8°. iv, 5-216 p. * IDA; LO; Ush.

1007. *Every families assistant, at complin, benediction, night prayers in penitential times and of thanksgiving, etc. in Latin and English. To which is added ... morning, night, and other devotions.* London. 1789. 12°. viii, 167, [1], 72, 20, [6] p. Printed by: Coghlan, J.P. ESTC t202976. * CAL; DAE; E; Gi.

>The second part (without tp) is called 'Morning prayers'; the third part (without tp) is called 'A prayer or offering to the Blessed Virgin Mary'.

1008. *Exercises for the Society of Jesus.* 1712. * ECW.

1009. *An exhortation to be read by all pastors to their congregations on Shrove Sunday, and on the first Sunday of Lent.* 8°. 8 p. * ECW; Ush.

>This is probably a mid-18th century publication.

1010. *An exhortation to be read to the faithful, on Shrove-Sunday, and on the first Sunday of Lent 1769.* [1769]. 8°. 6, [2] p. * ECW.

>Cf. no. 1011.

1011. *An exhortation to be read to the faithful, on Shrove-Sunday, and on the first Sunday of Lent, for the year 1782.* London. [1782?]. 8°. 6, [2] p. Printed by: Coghlan, J.P. * Amp.

>'Lent 1782' on slip pasted over original text reading 'Lent of 1769'. The first page of the last leaf contains 'To all the Catholic clergy' by James Birthan (i.e. James Talbot), dated '30 Jan. 1782'.

1012. *An explication of the ceremonies of the mass, with an exercise to hear it well: and a short treatise of the new-heart. Faithfully translated from the French.* [Dublin?]. 1707. 12°. 118, [2] p. ESTC t124194. * L; Lhe; O; UshL.

>The final leaf contains 'Approbations of the doctors to these treatises' (F.C. de

la Haye, J. Bourgeois, P. Sarrazin and Mauger). See also next item.

1013. *An explication of the ceremonies of the mass, with an exercise to hear it well; and a short treatise of the new-heart. Faithfully translated from the French.* London. 1782. 12°. 129, [1] p. * Amp.

1014. *Extensio universalis jubilaei in urbe celebrati anno Domini millesimo septingentisimo septuagesimo quinto. Ad universum Catholicum orbem.* [Dublin]. 1776. 12°. 12 [i.e. 11], [1] p. Printed by: [Morris, J.]. ESTC t221807. * MY.

1015. *Extarct [sic] from Ross's Dublin Public Register, or Freeman's Journal, of December 29, 1791 ... We, the undernamed his majesty's most dutiful and loyal subjects, Roman Catholics.* [Dublin]. [1792?]. 8°. 8 p. ESTC t193315. * BAA; Lmh; O; Sto; Ush.

  A petition by the Catholics of Ireland declaring their loyalty to the King.

1016. *Extract from the Diary; or Woodfall's Register No. 77 Friday, June 26, 1789. The following are the heads of the bill in favour of ... Catholic dissenters.* [1789]. fol. [2] p. * Sto.

  Clearly a proof with corrections; dated 1789.

1017. *Extract from the proceedings of the board of administration of the district of Douay, on the fourteenth of December, 1791. Relative to the five English, Scotch and Irish houses in that city.* London. [1792?]. 8°. [4], 18, [2] p. Printed by: Coghlan, J.P. Sold by: Booker; Keating; Lewis; Robinsons. ESTC t101013. * L; LEu; LfaA; Osc; Sto; Ush; WDA.

  With some Coghlan adverts.

1018. *Extract of a letter from Douay, dated Feb. 21, 1793. I have sent you a circumstantial and faithful account.* [London?]. [1793]. fol. [2] p. ESTC t033904. * BAA; Cli; L.

  On verso 'Extract of a letter from Paris, dated Feb. 18, 1793'.

1019. *Extract of proceedings respecting the Roman Catholics of the Province of Nova-Scotia. To the honourable Sir Andrew Snape Hamond, Knt. [Halifax]* . [1782]. fol. 3, [1] p. * WDA.

  Signed 'William Meany, John Cody, James Kavanagh, John Mullowny, John Murphy'.

1020. *Extracts from proceedings of the general committee of the Catholics of Ireland, which met on Tuesday April 16, and finally dissolved on Thursday April 25, 1793.* [Dublin?]. [1798?]. 8°. 8 p. Printed by: Fitzpatrick, H. ESTC t121483. * C; D; L; MH.

  There is an additional letter signed 'William Todd Jones', extracted from the *Dublin Evening-Post* of August 25, 1796.

1021. *Extracts from the minutes of a general chapter holden at Birmingham in the month of July, 1798.* [1798]. 4°. [4] p. * BAA; Cli; DowA.

  These extracts are from the English Benedictine Chapter, and dated and signed 'Birmingham, July 17th, Joseph Wilks, George Crook, secretary'.

1022. *Extractum seu summa brevis Benedicti P. XIV. dati die secundo Septembris, anno 1745.* fol. [2] p. * Ush.

  Faculties for (English) missioners; a printed form to be completed with an individual missioner's name in ms.

1023. Eyre, Francis. *A few remarks on The history of the decline and fall of the Roman Empire ... By a gentleman.* London. 1778. 8°. 154 p. Published by: Robson, J. ESTC t035499. * CaOHM; CSmH; E; InNd; IU; L; Lu; MH-H; MRu; NNPM; O; Osc; P; TxU; Ush.

Eyre criticizes Gibbon's *History* from a R.C. perspective.

1024. Eyre, Francis. *A letter to a friend, on the late revolution in France.* Anon. [London?]. 1791. 8°. [4], 80, [2] p. ESTC t063087. * L; O; Ush.

The friend is Mr Bignell of Banbury. Although the work is mainly political, it is written from a R.C. point of view (see also next item and no. 1027).

1025. Eyre, Francis. *A letter to a friend, on the late revolution in France.* Anon. [London?]. [1792]. 8°. [4], 80, [2], 110 p. ESTC t135949. * L; Map.

A reissue of the 1791 ed., with the addition of a further six letters.

1026. Eyre, Francis. *A letter to the rev. Mr. Ralph Churton ... on his Address to his parishioners.* London. 1795. 8°. [4], 104 p. Printed by: Coghlan, J.P. Sold by: Booker; Keating; Lewis; Debrett; Robinsons. ESTC t124229. * Du; DUc; E; ECW; L; Lfa; Lhe; Osc; Ush.

The *Address* was an attack on the doctrines of the Roman Catholic church.

1027. Eyre, Francis. *Letters to a friend, on the late revolution in France.* Anon. [London?]. 1792. 8°. [4], 110 p. ESTC t110397. * CtY; Du; L; Map; O.

Another version of part 2 of no. 1025.

1028. Eyre, Francis. *A reply to the rev. Ralph Churton.* London. 1798. 8°. vi, 494 p. Printed by: Coghlan, J.P. Sold by: Booker; Keating; Lewis; Robinsons. ESTC t124375. * CaOHM; E; L; Lhe.

1029. Eyre, Francis. *A short appeal to the public. By the gentleman, who is particularly addressed in the postscript of the vindication of ... The history of the decline and fall.* Anon. London. 1779. 8°. 41, [1] p. Published by: Robson, J. ESTC t048126. * E; L; MH-H; NNPM; Ush.

See also note to no. 1023.

1030. Eyre, Francis. *A short essay on the Christian religion, descriptive of the advantages which have accrued to society by the establishment of it ... By a sincere friend of mankind.* Anon. London. 1795. 8°. vii, [1], 140 p. Printed by: Coghlan, J.P. Sold by: Booker; Keating; Lewis; Debrett; Robinsons. ESTC t134302. * CaOHM; Du; DUc; E; ECW; L; Lfa; O; Sto; Ush.

1031. Fabry, Raymond. *Méditations sur la révolution Françoise, rédigées en forme de prière.* London [i.e. Brussels?]. 1794. 12°. [8], 280 p. Sold by: Lemaire (Brussels). ESTC t113453. * L; MChB; MiEM; Stan.

1032. Falconer, John. *The life, and miracles, of S. Wenefride; virgin, martyr and abbess; patroness of Wales.* Anon. [London?]. 1712. 12°. [16], 177, [3] p. ESTC t099781. * CLU-C; DFo; L; Lhe; LO; O; Ush.

For the identification of Falconer as the author of this work see ARCR II, no. 268. On the authority of Alban Butler, Kirk states that the book was edited by Philip Metcalfe, S.J., whose real name was Philip Leigh (alias Layton). In 1713 William Fleetwood, Anglican Bishop of St. Asaph, published a reprint of Philip

Leigh's ed. L bound up with no. 1676.

1033. *Familiar instructions about predestination and grace, by way of question and answer. Translated from the French.* London. 1714. 12°. 120, [4] p. Published by: Lewis, W. ESTC t129226. * ECW; L; Lhe; O; Osc; TH; Ush.

The book is a straightforward translation of a French Catholic treatise.

1034. Fell, Charles. *A letter from a Catholic gentleman to his Protestant friend ... By C.V. Christian Catholic.* Anon. London. 1745. fol. 8 p. ESTC n010792. * MH-H.

Defending the loyalty of English Catholics during the Jacobite uprising. The attribution to Charles Fell is made by Kirk (p. 79).

1035. Fell, Charles. *The lives of saints; collected from authentick records, of church history. With a full account of the other festivals throughout the year.* Anon. 4 vols. London. 1729. 4°. [2], xx, 382, [6]; [6], xii, 564, [4]; [6], xii, 436, [2]; [6], xii, 418, [2] p. Published by: Meighan, T. ESTC t112778. * AR; Ct; CtY; DAE; DoA (vols 2, 3, 4); E; ECW; FU; ICN; L; Lhe; LO; Map; NSPM; O; Osc; P; TH; TLP; TxU; UGL (vols 1, 2, 4); Ush.

Published in 1728 and 1729 in 12 numbers, comprising 4 vols, each with a separate tp.

1036. Fell, Charles. *The lives of saints. Collected from authentick records of church history. With a full account of the other festivals throughout the year.* 2nd ed. Anon. 4 vols. London. 1750. 4°. 382, [4] p. (vol. 1); 564, [4] p. (vol. 2). Published by: Osborne, T. ESTC t169671. * C; DoA; Dt; Lhe; NNUT; NSPM; UGL (vol. 3).

1037. Feller, François Xavier de. *The philosophical catechism, or, a collection of observations fit to defend the Christian religion against its enemies ... Translated by the rev. J.P. Mulcaile [Catéchisme philosophique].* 3 vols. Dublin. 1800. 12°. [20], 351, [1]; [6], 399, [1]; [6], 256, [2] p. Printed by: Fitzpatrick, H. Sold by: Keating & Co. London. ESTC t101638. * D; Du; E; IDA; L (vol. 1); Lhe; Mil; MY; NSPM; O; Osc; PPL; SCR; SIR; UGL (vol. 3); UshL (vol. 1).

See no. 1038 for another issue of this work.

1038. Feller, François Xavier de. *The philosophical catechism, or, a collection of observations fit to defend the Christian religion against its enemies ... Translated by the rev. J.P. Mulcaile, from the third edition.* 3 vols. Dublin. 1800. 12°. Printed by: Fitzpatrick, H. ESTC t220422. * FLK; MY; NcD.

With a list of subscribers in vol. 1. Another issue (no. 1037) has the additional imprint 'And sold by Keating and Co., London'.

Fénelon, François de Salignac. See also Blois, Louis de.

1039. Fénelon, François de Salignac. *The Christian pilgrimage: or, a companion for the holy season of Lent: being meditations upon the passion, death, resurrection, and ascension of ... Jesus Christ. Made English by Mrs. Jane Barker.* London. 1718. 12°. [2], vi, [6], 152 p. Published by: Curll, E.; Rivington, C. ESTC t153273. * Do; L.

Do has [4], vi, [6], 152 p., with 3 pages of Curll adverts. Of course, Curll was not R.C., but Jane Barker was a Jacobite, recusant poetess (see Greer, p.355).

1040. Fénelon, François de Salignac. *Pious reflections for every day of the month, by the late Archbishop of Cambray [Manuel de piété].* [London?]. 1717. 24°. [8], 148 p. Published by: [Meighan, T.]. ESTC n020317. * CLU-C; Do; LO; TH.

> The book is listed in adverts in no. 996.

1041. Fénelon, François de Salignac. *Pious reflections for every day in the month. Translated from the French of Fenelon.* Manchester. 1800. 24°. 46, 38, [4] p. Printed by: Dean, R. & W. Published by: Haydock, T. ESTC t093925. * Amp; L; Ush (part 1).

> The 2nd part is formed by Bouhours's *Pious meditations* (no. 343). ESTC lists several more eds published under non-R.C. auspices.

1042. Fénelon, François de Salignac. *Pious thoughts concerning the knowledge and, love of God, and other holy exercises: by the late Archbishop of Cambray.* London. 12°. [2], 210 p. Published by: Cooper, M. * Gi.

> The dates of M. Cooper's business activities are c.1740-c.1770. Other eds of this work were published under non-R.C. auspices.

1043. Fénelon, François de Salignac. *Proper heads of self-examination for a king.* Dublin. 1747. 12°. iv, 5-244 p. Published by: Faulkner, G. * Yb.

> At the end is a list of works by Fénelon.

1044. Ferrers, Joseph. *Discours prononcé par le R.P. Joseph Ferrers ... A discourse pronounced by the R.F.J. Ferrers Provincial of the English Carms, in the chapel of his excellency, the Neapolitan Ambassador.* London. 1793. 4°. 9, [1] p. Printed by: Coghlan, J.P. Sold by: Debrett, J.; Booker; Keating; Lewis; Robinsons; Robins; Gregory. * Ush.

1045. *A few remarks on an address to the Roman Catholics of the United States of America, occasioned by a letter addressed to the Catholics of Worcester by Mr Wharton their late chaplain.* Worcester. [c.1784]. 8°. 24 p. Published by: Author. Sold by: Tymbs, J. * Osc.

> Charles Henry Wharton (1748-1833) was chaplain of the R.C. community at Worcester but became a Protestant in 1784. Osc cat. tentatively ascribes the work to 'J. Hooper'. See also no. 442ff.

1046. *A few thoughts on the reverend Joseph Berington's Examination of events, termed miraculous, as reported in letters from Italy. By a Catholic lady.* London. 1796. 12°. 16 p. Printed by: Coghlan, J.P. * Stan; Sto.

> See no. 240.

1047. Filassier, Marin. *Christian sentiments proper for sick and infirm people ... Translated from the French. To which is added, the doctrine of the holy fathers, on heaven, hell and purgatory [Sentiments chrétiens].* Anon. London. 1747. 12°. [2], xiv, [4], 244, [2] p. Published by: Meighan, T. ESTC t165530. * CAL; CLU-C; Do; E; ECB; ECW; Lhe; MRu; Osc; TxU.

> CAL and Do do not have the final 2 pages. Osc contains 2 pages of Keating adverts.

1048. Fisher, John. *A treatise concerning the fruitful sayings of David, the king and prophet, in the seven penitential psalms ... By the right reverend father in*

God John Fisher. [London]. 1714. 12°. [4], 342 p. ESTC t081045. * CaOTV; COA; Csj; CtY; DMR; Do; DoA; ECW; ICN; L; Lfa; Lhe; LO; MRu; O; TLP; TxU; Yb.

ECW has a 12-page 'Catalogue of books sold by Thomas Meighan' appended.

1049. Fitzherbert, Thomas. *A treatise of policy and religion. Part III.* 3rd ed. London. 1703. 8°. [2], 712 p. Printed by: Hales, T. * ECW.

1050. Fitzherbert, Thomas. *A treatise of policy and religion. Part IIII.* 3rd ed. 1711. 8°. [2], 678, [62] p. * ECW; Lhe.

1051. Fleming, Francis Anthony. *The calumnies of Verus; or, Catholics vindicated, from certain old slanders lately revived; in a series of letters published in different gazettes at Philadelphia, collected and revised by Verax.* Philadelphia. 1792. 12°. v, [2], 8-58 p. Printed by: Johnston and Justice. ESTC w030194. * DGU-W; DLC; PPL; PU.

Chiefly letters written by Francis Fleming (i.e. Verax), Matthew Carey and Robert Annan (i.e. Verus).

1052. Fleury, Claude. *An historical catechism, containing a summary of the sacred history- and Christian doctrine ... Newly translated [Catéchisme historique].* 2 vols. [London?]. 1726. 12°. [4], lxiii, [1], 120, [4]; 297, [11] p. ESTC t115024. * CLU-C; E; Gi; IDA; L; Map; MRu; TLP; TxU.

Translated by William Crathorne. See also the following 'Catechism' items.

1053. Fleury, Claude. *An historical catechism, containing a summary of the sacred history and Christian doctrine. Translated from the French.* 2nd ed. 1740. 12°. 482, [10] p. * Ush.

1054. Fleury, Claude. *An historical catechism, containing a summary of the sacred history and Christian doctrine.* Dublin. 1753. 12°. [4], lx [i.e. xl], 279, [13] p. Published by: Kelly, I. ESTC n001087. * PPL.

1055. Fleury, Claude. *An historical catechism, containing a summary of the sacred history and Christian doctrine. By monsieur Fleury ... Translated from the French.* 2nd ed. [London?]. 1760. 12°. 482, [10] p. Published by: [Needham?]. ESTC t204525. * E; Map.

Monogram on tp suggests Needham as publisher. This is the second '2nd' ed. (Cf. no. 1053).

1056. Fleury, Claude. *An historical catechism, containing a summary of the sacred history and Christian doctrine.* Dublin. 1763. 12°. [4], 279, [13] p. Published by: Gorman, B. ESTC t194053. * D.

With 6 pages of adverts.

1057. Fleury, Claude. *An historical catechism: containing a summary of the sacred history and Christian doctrine.* Dublin. 1765. 12°. [4], 251, [8] p. ESTC t194042. * D.

1058. Fleury, Claude. *An historical catechism. Containing a summary of the sacred history and Christian doctrine. Newly translated from the French.* Dublin. 1776. [4], lx, 279, [14] p. Published by: Wogan, P.; Bean, P. * FLK.

With some pages of Wogan adverts.

112

1059. Fleury, Claude. *An historical catechism, containing a summary of the sacred history and Christian doctrine.* Dublin. 1793. 12°. [4], ix, 279, [13] p. Published by: Wogan, P. * UshL.

> With 5 pages of Wogan adverts.

1060. Fleury, Claude. *An historical catechism, containing a summary of the sacred history and Christian doctrine.* 4th ed. London. 1793. 12°. [4], lxiii, [1], 120, 285, [7] p. Printed by: Coghlan, J.P. Sold by: Booker; Keating; Lewis; Robinsons; Robins (Winchester). ESTC t204527. * E(2); ECW; Sal; Stan.

> One of the E copies is a variant with on tp 'Translated from the Frency'.

1061. Fleury, Claude. *A larger historical catechism: containing an abridgement of sacred history, and of the Christian doctrine [Catéchisme historique. Grand catéchisme].* Newcastle. 1786. 12°. [2], xliii, [1], 202, v, [1] p. Printed by: Hodgson, S. Sold by: Keating, P. and the booksellers in the country. ESTC t124253. * L; NSPM; Ush.

1062. Fleury, Claude. *The manners of the Christians. Translated ... By the reverend Charles Cordell [Les moeurs des Chrestiens].* Newcastle. 1786. 12°. v, [1], 320 p. Printed by: Hodgson, S. Sold by: Keating, P. ESTC t107488. * CAL; E; ECW; L; Lhe; NcD; Osc; Ush.

> Originally translated by William Crathorne, and re-edited by Charles Cordell (Gillow I, 567-8).

1063. Fleury, Claude. *The manners of the Israelites. Wherein is seen the model of a plain and honest policy for the government of states. Translated ... by the rev. Charles Cordell [Les moeurs des Israélites].* Newcastle. 1786. 12°. vi, [2], 210, [2] p. Printed by: Hodgson, S. Sold by: Keating, P., and the booksellers in the country. ESTC t119592. * DoA; E; ECW; FP; FU; Hor; L; Lhe; Ljc; MY; NcD; Osc; Stan; Ush.

1064. Fleury, Claude. *A regular historical account of the first rise of the Reformation, and of its progress during the first eleven years, in Germany ... By W.H. [Histoire ecclésiastique].* Cork. 1764. 8°. [4], 399, [1] p. Published by: Author. ESTC t105027. * CKcl; CKu; D; L; Mil; MY.

> The book is offered as a neutral account, but it is in fact pro-R.C.

1065. Fleury, Claude. *A short historical catechism.* London. 1777. 12°. 71, [1] p. Printed by: Coghlan, J.P. * Amp; DoA; ECW; Stan (imp.)

1066. Fleury, Claude. *Short historical catechism: containing an abridgement of sacred history, and of the Christian doctrine.* Newcastle. 1786. 12°. vii, [1], 94 p. Printed by: Hodgson, S. Sold by: Keating, P. ESTC t123982. * L; Ush.

1067. Fleury, Claude. *A short historical catechism: containing an abridgement of sacred history, and of the Christian doctrine. Taken from the French of abbé Fleury.* Newcastle. 1798. 12°. 108 p. Published by: Coates, F. ESTC t207297. * NCp.

1068. Fleury, Claude. *A short historical catechism.* 5th ed. London. 1800. 12°. [2], xliii, 285, [7] p. Printed by: Keating, Brown & Keating. * CAL.

1069. Flood, Peter. *A letter from the rev. Peter Flood, D.D., president of the*

R.C. Col. Maynooth, to the hon **** *M.P. London, relative to a pamphlet ... by Patrick Duigenan.* London. 1800. 8°. 15, [1] p. Printed by: Coghlan, J.P. Sold by: West; Hughes; Debrett; Keating; Booker. * Ush.

> Signed and dated 'Maynooth, December 15, 1799, Peter Flood'. The pamphlet referred to in the title is Patrick Duigenan's *A fair representation of the present political state of Ireland.*

1070. Flood, Peter. *A letter from the rev. Peter Flood, D.D. president of the R.C. Col. Maynooth, to the hon.* *** **** *M.P. London, relative to a pamphlet, entitled 'A fair representation ...' by Patrick Duigenan.* Dublin. 1800. 8°. 17, [1] p. Printed by: Fitzpatrick, H. ESTC n004903. * C; D; Di; Dk; IU; O; PSt.

1071. Flood, Peter. *A letter from the rev. Peter Flood D.D. president of the R.C. Col. Maynooth, to the hon. ... M.P. London, relative to a pamphlet, entitled 'A fair representation ... of Ireland'.* 2nd ed. Dublin. 1800. 8°. 17, [1] p. Printed by: Fitzpatrick, H. ESTC t177470. * Du; MY; O; UshL.

1072. *La foi couronnée, ou le massacre des pasteurs Catholiques, morts pour la cause de Jesus-Christ, pendant la révolution de France.* London. 1799. 18°. [4], 100, [5], 102-350 p. Published by: Dulau, A. & Co.; l'Homme, L.; Author. ESTC t112032. * L; MH; PU.

> Attributed by ESTC to Pierre Vinson.

1073. *The following account having been sent over by a correspondent ... extract of a letter from Paris, May 30, 1786.* 8°. 4 p. * Ush.

> An account of Miss Pitts's conversion to the Catholic faith.

1074. *The following address of the Roman Catholic peers and commoners of Great Britain has been presented to his majesty by the Earl of Surrey and the right honourable the Lords Linton and Petre.* London. 1778. fol. 2 p. * WDA.

> The address is entitled 'To the King's ...' (cf. no. 2755).

1075. *The following addresses, unanimously voted at a general meeting of the English Catholics, were this day presented to their Majesties.* London. 1789. fol. s.s. Printed by: Coghlan, J.P. * BAA; WDA.

> The addresses are 'To the King's most excellent majesty' and 'To the Queen's most excellent majesty', both signed 'Petre, chairman'.

1076. *The following charge, which was given to the secular and regular clergy on passing of the bill for the relief of the Roman Catholics of England in the year 1778, having been lately much enquired after.* London. 1791. 8°. 15, [1] p. Printed by: Coghlan, J.P. * Ush.

> This work reprints such items as nos 678, 944, 2868, 2897 in an attempt to bring together the whole 'oath debate'.

1077. *The following charge ... given to the ... clergy on passing of the bill for the relief of the Roman Catholics of England, in the year 1778 ... we reprint it, with the psalms and prayers.* [London?]. [1791]. 12°. 15, [1] p. ESTC n061232. * MBAt; WDA.

1078. *The following correct statement of the receipts and expenditures of Saint Patrick's Chapel, from Michaelmas 1792 to Michaelmas 1798, is, by order of the*

board, most respectfully submitted. [London]. [1798]. fol. s.s. * WDA.
> Signed 'Lewis Mansse, secretary'.

1079. *The following is the inscription which the French clergy of the King's House, Winchester, have placed, May 22, 1793 in their chapel.* [London]. [1793]. fol. s.s. Printed by: Coghlan, J.P. ESTC t037275. * L.
> Thanksgiving of the French clergy for having been hospitably received.

1080. *The following letter may certainly be ranked among the toleration edicts, which have lately done so much honour to the Christian world ... Catherine II [of Russia] to Pius VI.* [1782]. 4°. 3, [1] p. * Sto.
> Letter dated '30th Jan, 1782'.

1081. Fontaine, Nicolas. *An abridgment of the history of the old and new testament, interspersed with moral and instructive reflections ... From the French. By J. Reeve [Histoire du vieux et du nouveau testament].* Exeter. 1780. 8°. vii, [1], 390, 178, viii p. Printed by: Thorn, B. Sold by: Thorn, B.; Lewis, T. ESTC t120652. * ECW; L; NIC; NSPM; O; Osc; Stan; TxU.
> Translated and edited by the rev. Joseph Reeve S.J. (see also next 7 items).
> Note that there are many non-R.C. eds of Fontaine's *History*.

1082. Fontaine, Nicolas. *An abridgment of the history of the old and new testament, interspersed with moral and instructive reflections chiefly out of the holy fathers. By the rev. Joseph Reere [sic].* 4th ed. 2 vols. Exeter. 1795. 12°. vii, [1], 478; [2], 160, 276 p. Printed by: Trewman, R. and Son. Sold by: Trewman, R. and Son; Coghlan, J.P. ESTC t150444. * Do; DoA; ICN; LAM; LVu; TxU; Yb (vol. 1).

1083. Fontaine, Nicolas. *A compendious history of the new testament, interspersed with moral reflections, and containing the life of our Lord... Trans. from the French by Mr. Reeves [sic].* Dublin. 1797. 12°. xi, 225, [3] p. Printed by: M'Donnel, T. Sutcliffe, 356.
> Abridged by William Gahan for the use of schools.

1084. Fontaine, Nicolas. *The history of the old and new testament, interspersed with moral and instructive reflections chiefly taken from the holy fathers. From the French by J. Reeve.* Baltimore. [1780]. 476 p. Printed by: Fielding Lucas jun. * DCU; OCH; PPCCH; PV.

1085. Fontaine, Nicolas. *The history of the old and new testament, interspersed with moral and instructive reflections, chiefly taken from the holy fathers. From the French. By J. Reeve.* Dublin repr. [Exeter]. 1782. 8°. viii, 436 p. Printed by: Talbot, C. Published by: Talbot, C. ESTC t204653. * D.
> With a list of subscribers.

1086. Fontaine, Nicolas. *The history of the old and new testament, interspersed with moral and instructive reflections, chiefly taken from the holy fathers.* 3rd ed. Philadelphia. 1784. 8°. vi, [2], 536 [i.e. 436] p. Printed by: Steiner, M. Published by: Talbot, C. ESTC w012743. * DGU-W; DLC; ICN; MdW; MWA; N; PHi; PV.
> According to Parsons (p. 14) edited by the rev. Robert Molyneux S.J.

1087. Fontaine, Nicolas. *The history of the old and new testament, interspersed* *with moral and instructive reflections chiefly taken from the holy fathers.* Dublin. 1799. 8°. vi, 431, [5] p. Printed by: Wogan, P. * FLK.

1088. Fontaine, Nicolas. *A summary, or compendious history of the old testament. Interspersed with moral reflections and instructive lessons. Translated from the French. For the use of schools.* Anon. Dublin. 1795. 12°. 261, [3] p. Printed by: M'Donnel, T. Sutcliffe, 356.

1089. *A form of oath proposed by the Roman Catholic bishops.* fol. s.s. * O.

1090. *Forms of the acts of virtues, necessary for salvation. Published by the approbation of I.P.V.A.* Birmingham. 12°. 8 p. Printed by: Holliwell, T. * Ush.
    Sometimes attributed to John Joseph Hornyold.

1091. *Formulaire de prieres, a l'usage des pensionnaires des religieuses Ursulines.* Montreal. 1778. 12°. [4], 467, [5] p. Published by: Mesplet, F.; Berger, C. * CaNSWA (imp.).

1092. *Formulaire de prieres, a l'usage des pensionnaires des religieuses Ursulines.* Quebec. 1799. 12°. [8], 486 [i.e. 488], [8] p. Printed by: Lelievre, R.; Desbarats, P.E. ESTC w016707. * CaOONL (imp.); CaOTP; CaQMM; CaQMUC; CaQQLa; NN.

1093. *A formulary of instruction and prayers, to be used in the Catholic church, on all Sundays and holidays, either immediately before mass or after the reading of the gospel.* Baltimore. 1789. 6 p. Printed by: Goddard, W. * DCU.

1094. Francis, Bernard. *The decalogue explained, and the creed, theological virtues, seven sacraments, etc. In fifty-one excellent moral discourses.* Dublin. 1778. 12°. 368 p. Printed by: Cross, R. ESTC n028939. * Dt; FLK; MWH.

1095. Francis, Bernard. *Discourses explanatory and moral, on the creed, theological virtues, ten commandments and seven sacraments ... By the rev. F. Bernard Francis, of the order of St. Francis.* Dublin. 1799. 12°. vi, 7-371, [1] p. Printed by: Cross, R. ESTC t183081. * Do; Du; FLK; IDA; Mil; NSCH.
    Edited by Bernard MacMahon.

1096. Francis, Bernard. *Fifty one [explanatory and] moral discourses upon the creed, theological virtues, ten commandments, [and seven] sacraments, &c. Very useful for all pastors [missionaries] and masters of families.* 2nd ed. 12°. Published by: [Kelly, I.]. 340, [4] p. * FLK.
    Tp severely damaged. With list of subscribers and advert for Ignatius Kelly.

1097. Francis de Sales. *An introduction to a devout life ... To which is prefix'd a summary of his life, and adjoyn'd a collection of his choicest maxims [Introduction à la vie dévote].* [Dublin]. 1705. 12°. [18], 408, [26] p. ESTC t194304. * D.
    The frontispiece, which must have been added later, bears the imprint 'sold by Ignatius Kelly in St. Mary's Lane'. Kelly did not enter business until 1738.

1098. Francis de Sales. *An introduction to a devout life ... faithfully render'd into English.* [London?]. 1709. 12°. xxiv, 432, [12] p. ESTC n017034. * CAL; COMC; DMR; FP; Map; O; Yb.
    According to Dr D.M. Rogers (personal communication) printed in the

Netherlands.

1099. Francis de Sales. *An introduction to a devout life. Written originally in French, by S. Francis de Sales ... Faithfully rendered into English.* [1715?]. 12°. [22], 408, [24] p. * DMR.

1100. Francis de Sales. *An introduction to a devout life ... To which is prefixed a summary of his life, and adjoyn'd a collection of his choicest maxims.* [London]. 1726. 12°. 421, [1] p. Published by: Meighan, T. ESTC t117332. * CAL; DMR; Do; DoA; Hen; L; Lhe; O; Osc; Stan.

1101. Francis de Sales. *An introduction to a devout life. Written originally in French by St. Francis de Sales ... faithfully render'd into English. To which is prefix'd a summary of his life.* [London]. 1741. 12°. 386, [8] p. Published by: Meighan, T. ESTC t104453. * DMR; ECW (-tp); L; Lfa; LO; Ush.

1102. Francis de Sales. *An introduction to a devout life ... To which is added his life and a collection of all his maxims. Translated from the French.* 6th ed. Dublin. 1742. 12°. [2], 372, [2] p. Published by: Keating, J. ESTC t195136. * P; Pm.
     With a final advertisement leaf.

1103. Francis de Sales. *An introduction to a devout life ... carefully compared with the original French, and corrected from the errors of former editions, by an eminent divine.* Dublin. 1760. 12°. 348, 3, [11] p. Published by: Executors of E. Kelly; Gorman, B. ESTC t167103. * Du.
     With a list of subscribers.

1104. Francis de Sales. *An introduction to a devout life. Written originally in French by S. Francis de Sales.* Dublin. 1770. 12°. 348, [12] p. Printed by: Fitzsimons, R.; Cross, R. Published by: Fitzsimons, R.; Cross, R. * Do.

1105. Francis de Sales. *An introduction to a devout life. Written originally in French by St. Francis de Sales ... With a collection of his choicest maxims.* Dublin. 1789. 12°. [14], 15-348, [1], 2-3, [9] p. * FLK.

1106. Francis de Sales. *An introduction to a devout life. Written originally in French by St. Francis de Sales.* 16th ed. Dublin. 1795. 12°. 351, [9] p. Printed by: Wogan, P. * SIR.

1107. Francis de Sales. *An introduction to a devout life, written originally in French by St. Francis de Sales ... To which is added, the conversation of Dr Thaulerus with a poor beggar.* 16th ed. Dublin. 1795. 12°. 344, 3, [13] p. Printed by: Cross, R. ESTC t209559. * LANu.
     For another '16th' ed. see no. 1106.

1108. Francis de Sales. *Philothea: or an introduction to a devout life ... Newly translated into English ... By R.C. [Introduction à la vie dévote].* London. 1762. 12°. 403, [7] p. Published by: Needham, W. ESTC t073171. * CLU-C; DMR; Do; ECB; ECW; Hor; L; Lfa; O; TLP.
     'R.C.' is Richard Challoner (see also next 4 items).

1109. Francis de Sales. *Philothea, or an introduction to a devout life ... Newly translated into English from the original French, according to the last edition ...*

By R.C. London. 1767. 12°. 403, [1] p. Published by: Needham, W. * Map.

1110. Francis de Sales. *Philothea: or an introduction to a devout life ... Newly translated into English, from the original French ... By R.C.* 2nd ed. London. 1770. 12°. [2], 311, [5] p. Published by: Coghlan, J.P. ESTC t104734. * DAE; DMR; Do; ECW; L; Lhe; O; Osc; Sal.

1111. Francis de Sales. *Philothea: or an introduction to a devout life. By St. Francis of Sales ... Translated into English by the venerable and most reverend Richard Challoner.* 3rd ed. London. 1787. 12°. [2], xii, 285 [i.e. 287], [1] p. Printed by: Coghlan, J.P. ESTC t199448. * C; DMR; DoA; L; PcA; TLP; Ush.

1112. Francis de Sales. *Philothea, or an introduction to a devout life ... From the French ... Translated into English by ... Richard Challoner.* 4th ed. London. 1794. 12°. [2], xii, 287, [1] p. Printed by: Coghlan, J.P. ESTC t199449. * CAL; Do; LAM; LO; Stan; Ush.
> Page 287 is misnumbered 285 in some copies.

1113. Francis de Sales. *The spiritual directer [sic] of devout and religious souls [Entretiens spirituels.].* [London?]. 1704. 12°. [28], 223, [1] p. ESTC t104175. * DAE; DMR; Do; ECB; ECW; Gi; L; Lhe; LO; Map; Stan; TLP; Ush; Yb.
> Dedication and advertisement to the reader signed 'J.S.', i.e. John Sergeant, the translator (see also next 2 items).

1114. Francis de Sales. *The spiritual director of devout and religious souls.* [Dublin?]. 1704. 16°. [28], 3-225, [1] p. ESTC t160313. * C; CAL; TxU.

1115. Francis de Sales. *The spiritual director, of devout and religious souls.* Dublin. 1777. 12°. 228 p. Printed by: Mehain, J. ESTC t118242. * DMR; L.

1116. Francis-Street Chapel. *Francis-Street Chapel. Thursday - April the ninth. This day, a most numerous and respectable meeting of the Roman Catholics of this city was held in Francis-street chapel.* [Dublin]. [1795]. 8°. 32 p. * MY.
> See also no. 1129.

1117. Frankenberg, Johann Heinrich von. *A letter from his eminence John-Henry of Frankenberg, Count of the Holy Roman Empire, Archbishop of Mechelen ... to the nuns of the convents suppressed in his diocese. With the French original.* London. 1783. 8°. [2], 10 p. Printed by: Coghlan, J.P. ESTC t148352. * Amp; Lu; MY.

1118. Frankenberg, Johann Heinrich von. *A letter from his eminence John Henry of Frankenberg ... to the nuns of the convents suppressed in his diocese.* [London]. [1783] 8°. 4 p. Printed by: [Coghlan, J.P.]. * Sto; Ush.

1119. Frankenberg, John Henry. *A pastoral letter of his eminence the Cardinal Archbishop of Mechlin, for the lent of the year, 1783.* London. 1783. 8°. [2], 35, [1], 4 p. Printed by: Coghlan, J.P. * ECW; MY; Sto; Ush.
> The final 4 pages are *A letter from ... John Henry of Frankenberg ... to the nuns of the convents suppressed in his diocese* (no. 1118).

1120. *French grammar.* Douai. 1783. 8°. 102, [2] p. Printed by: Derbaix. ESTC t131230. * C; L.
> Kirk (p. 98) attributes this grammar to William Gibson, who was president of

Douai from 1781 to 1790. See also next item.

1121. *French grammar, compiled for the use of the English college at Douay.* London. 1795. 12°. [6], 102 p. Printed by: Coghlan, J.P. ESTC t188197. * Cha; D; DoA; O.

> DoA bound with *A short introduction to the Latin tongue* (no. 2549); Cha bound with *English grammar* (no. 972).

1122. French, Nicholas. *The doleful fall of Andrew Sall, a Jesuit of the fourth vow, from the Roman Catholick and apostolick faith.* London. 1749. 12°. [10], 252 p. ESTC t096211. * IDA; L; O; SIR.

> The printer's device and the list of Irish subscribers suggest that the book was in fact printed in Ireland by Philip Bowes. Nicolas French (1604-1678) was president of the Irish College at Louvain.

1123. French, Nicholas. *Iniquity display'd: or, the settlement of the kingdom of Ireland, commonly call'd, the act of settlement, made after the restauration of King Charles II. laid open.* Anon. [London]. 1704. 4°. [2], 70 p. ESTC t027304. * C; D; L.

> Originally published as *A narrative of the Earl of Clarendon's settlement and sale of Ireland* (1668).

1124. Frey de Neuville, Charles. *The funeral oration upon Cardinal de Fleury, minister of state, &c. pronounced ... at Paris, May 25, 1743, by Father Neuville [Oraison funèbre de s.e. monseigneur le Cardinal de Fleury].* London. 1743. 8°. [2], 32, 41-70 p. Published by: Cooper, M. ESTC t067700. * Dt; DUc; L; O; Osc.

1125. Frey de Neuville, Charles. *A new translation of the funeral oration of his eminence the Cardinal de Fleury: pronounced ... May 25, 1743.* London. 1744. 8°. v, [3], 92 p. Published by: Robinson, J. ESTC n022651. * CLU-C; CSmH; MiU.

1126. *The Friday devotion, in honour of the sacred passion of our Saviour, for obtaining a happy death.* 24°. 23, [1] p. * Map (-tp).

> Bound with *The litanies of Jesus*, 1720 (no. 1673) and *Morning and night prayers*, 1726 (no. 1903).

1127. *Friendly advice to C...rs M...n, D.D. concerning the fourth edition of his Letter from Rome, and the prefatory discourse prefix'd to it.* London. 1741. 8°. vi, [2], 48 p. Published by: Needham, F. ESTC n031767. * ECW; MY; NRU; O; Osc.

> For Middleton's *Letter from Rome* see also no. 508. Gillow (V, 153) attributes this pamphlet to Samuel Musson, alias Browne, S.J. (1686-1769).

1128. *A full and accurate report of the debates in the parliament of Ireland, in the session 1793; on the bill for relief of his majesty's Catholic subjects.* Dublin. 1793. 8°. [2], xxvi, [2], 389, [1] p. Published by: Jones, J. ESTC t124516. * BRG; C; CSmH; D; Di; FU; ICR; ICU; IU; PPL.

> With names of members of the General Committee of the Catholics of Ireland.

1129. *A full and correct report of the debates, at the Catholic meeting, held in Francis'-Street Chapel, Dublin, on the ninth of April, 1795; with the resolutions,* *at full length. To which is added, Mr. Teeling's speech, at the late Co. Antrim Catholic meeting.* Belfast. 1795. 8°. 40 p. ESTC t183859. * D; Di; Du.

> See also no. 1116.

1130. Gaddi, Joseph. *Universis patribus, fratribus, ac sororibus ordinis praedicatorum Fr. Pius Joseph Gaddi ... salutem, et mortis recordationem.* [London?]. [1800?]. fol. 6 p. ESTC t131643. * L.

> A funeral oration on Pope Pius VI.

1131. Gahan, William. *A compendious abstract of the history of the church of Christ, from its first foundation to the eighteenth century.* Dublin. 1793. 12°. x, ii, iv, viii, 480 p. Printed by: McDonnel, T. ESTC t212225. * D; DE; FLK; IDA; SIR; Stan.

> With a list of subscribers.

1132. Gahan, William. *A compendious abstract of the history of the church of Christ, from its first foundation to the eighteenth century.* 2nd ed. Dublin. 1795. 12°. xii, 402, [6] p. Printed by: MDonnel, T. ESTC t133500. * CAL; D; Do; Dt; L; Lhe; Sal; TxU.

1133. Gahan, William. *Sermons and moral discourses for all the Sundays and principal festivals of the year.* 2 vols. Dublin. 1799. 8°. [10], 552, [2]; [4], 443, [5] p. Printed by: M'Donnel, T. ESTC t207075. * D; DoA (vol. 1); FLK; IDA; Lhe; Mil (vol. 2); SIR; Ush.

> With a list of subscribers.

1134. Gahan, William. *A short and plain exposition of the small catechism, for the use of grown-up children and other illiterate persons of the Roman Catholic communion.* Dublin. 1797. 12°. 154, [2] p. Printed by: M'Donnel, T. * IDA.

1135. Gahan, William. *Youth instructed in the grounds of the Christian religion. With remarks on the writings of Voltaire, Rousseau, T. Paine.* Dublin. 1798. 12°. xvi, 168 p. Printed by: McDonnel, T. ESTC t133497. * DoA; E; FLK; IDA; L; Lhe; Mil; MY; SIR.

> With a list of subscribers.

1136. Gallagher, James. *Seventeen Irish sermons, in an easy and familiar stile, on useful and necessary subjects. In English characters; as being the more familiar to the generality of our Irish clergy ... By J.G.D.D.* Dublin. 1757. 12°. [2], 210, 4 p. Printed by: Corcoran, B.; Kelly, D. * MY.

> 'J.G.D.D.' is James Gallagher, R.C. Bishop of Kildare (from 1737 to 1751).
> Irish text in English characters, with an English preface (see also next 5 items).
> With 4 pages of adverts.

1137. Gallagher, James. *Seventeen Irish sermons, in an easy and familiar stile, on useful and necessary subjects. In English characters, as being the more familiar to the generality of our Irish clergy ... By J.G.D.D.* Dublin. 1777. 12°. 212, [4] p. Printed by: Corcoran, B. ESTC t178208. * D.

> With 4 pages of adverts.

1138. Gallagher, James. *Seventeen Irish sermons, in an easy and familiar stile, on useful and necessary subjects, in English characters ... In which is included, a sermon on the joys of heaven.* Dublin. 1795. 12°. 212, [4] p. Printed by: Wogan,

P. ESTC t104971. * C; Du; L; O.
> With 4 pages of Wogan adverts.

1139. Gallagher, James. *Seventeen Irish sermons, in an easy and familiar stile, on useful and necessary subjects, in English characters.* Dublin. 1798. 12°. 212, [4] p. Printed by: Wogan, P. ESTC t221280. * D; FLK; Mil.
> With 4 pages of Wogan adverts.

1140. Gallagher, James. *Sixteen Irish sermons, in an easy and familiar stile, on useful and necessary subjects. In English characters; as being the more familiar to the generality of our Irish clergy. By J.G. D.D.* Dublin. 1736. 8°. [2], vi, 244 p. Printed by: Babe, H. ESTC t115028. * FLK; L.

1141. Gallagher, James. *Sixteen Irish sermons, in an easy and familiar stile, on useful and necessary subjects. In English characters ... by J.G. D.D.* Dublin. 1752. 12°. 210, [4] p. Published by: Kelly, I. ESTC t210064. * D; FLK; Mil.
> With 4 pages of Kelly adverts.

1142. Gallagher, Simon Felix. *An oration on the anniversary of the orphan establishment in Charleston, South Carolina. Delivered ... on the 18th October, 1798. Published at the request of the commissioners of the orphan-house.* [Charleston]. [1798]. 8°. 23, [1] p. ESTC w036300. * ScC.
> The Catholic priest Simon Felix Gallagher (1756 or 7-1825) later led the schism against Archbishops Neale and Maréchal.

1143. Gallagher, Simon Felix. *A sermon preached on the ninth day of May, 1798, observed as a day of fasting and prayer ... By the rev. S.F.O'Gallaher [sic] Catholic priest of Charleston.* Charleston. [1798]. [2], 12 p. Printed by: Harrison, W.P. ESTC w036031. * DGU; ScU.

1144. Geddes, Alexander. *An answer to the Bishop of Comana's pastoral letter. By a protesting Catholic.* London. 1790. 8°. [4], 36 p. Published by: Faulder, R.; Coghlan, J.P. ESTC t022043. * BB; C; E; ECW; ICN; L; Lmh; MRu; O; Osc; Sto; Ush.
> A 'protesting Catholic' is Alexander Geddes and the Bishop of Comana is Matthew Gibson. Dated '26 January 1790'. BB bound up with J.F. de la Marche's *The pastoral letter* (no. 1560). For a full bibliography of the works of Alexander Geddes, also listing a number of not specifically R.C. publications omitted from our list, see Fuller, pp. 156-60. Geddes's bible editions occur in our list under *Holy Bible*, nos 1450 and 1453.

1145. Geddes, Alexander. *An apology for slavery; or six cogent arguments against the immediate abolition of the slave-trade.* Anon. London. 1792. 8°. 47, [1] p. Published by: Johnson, J.; Faulder, R. ESTC t022221. * C; CaOHM; E; ECW; GU; L; O.
> An anti-slavery satire.

1146. Geddes, Alexander. *L'avocat du diable: the devil's advocate; or, Satan versus Pictor. Tried before the court of uncommon pleas.* London. 1792. 4°. 19, [1] p. Published by: Johnson, J.; Faulder, R. ESTC t007188. * CSmH; E; GU; L; MiU.

1147. Geddes, Alexander. *The battle of B-ng-r: or the church's triumph; a* *comic-heroic poem, in nine cantos.* Anon. London. 1797. 8°. 74 p. Published by: Johnson, J.; Bell, J. ESTC t021412. * CaOHM; Dt; E; L; MH-H; Osc; PPL; TxU.

>A satire on John Warren, Bishop of Bangor.

1148. Geddes, Alexander. *Critical remarks on the Hebrew scriptures: corresponding with a new translation of the bible.* London. 1800. 4°. viii, 475, [1] p. Printed by: Davis; Wilks; Taylor. Published by: Author. Sold by: Faulder, R.; Johnson, J. ESTC t114136. * ABu; BMp; C; CtY-D; Du; E; GOT; GU; L; LAM; Map; MRp; MRu; NNUT; Osc; PPL.

1149. Geddes, Alexander. *Cursory remarks on a late fanatical publication entitled, A full detection of popery.* Anon. London. 1783. 8°. 53, [1] p. Published by: Author. Sold by: Keating; Faulder; Debrett; Wilkie, etc. etc. ESTC t012323. * BB; E (-tp); ECW; Gu; L; Sto.

>*A full detection of popery* is by John Williams. With one page of adverts.

1150. Geddes, Alexander. *Doctor Geddes's address to the public, on the publication of the first volume of his new translation of the bible.* London. 1793. 4°. [2], 25, [1] p. Published by: Johnon, J. [i.e. Johnson]. ESTC t004174. * C; CSmH; Dt; DUc; L; Lhe; MB; MBAt; MiU; MRu; Osc; PPL; SCA; Ush; WNs.

1151. Geddes, Alexander. *Dr. Geddes's general answer to the queries, counsils, and criticisms that have been communicated to him since the publication of his proposals for printing a new translation of the bible.* London. 1790. 4°. [4], 30 [i.e. 32] p. Printed by: Davis, J. Published by: Author. Sold by: Faulder, R.; Johnson, J. ESTC t125317. * ABu; Dt; Du; E; ET; GOT; ICN; L; MB; MBAt; MiU; O; Or; Osc; SCA; TxU; WNs.

>With a list of subscribers, including several members of the Staffordshire clergy and of the Catholic Committee.

1152. Geddes, Alexander. *Dr. Geddes's general answer to the queries, counsils, and criticisms that have been communicated to him since the publication of his proposals for printing a new translation of the bible.* London. 1790. 4°. [4], 25, [1] p. Printed by: Davis, J. Published by: Author. Sold by: Faulder, R.; Johnson, J. ESTC t162957. * C; E.

1153. Geddes, Alexander. *Idea of a new English edition of the holy bible, for the use of the Roman Catholics of Great Britain and Ireland.* [London?]. [1795?]. 8°. 16 p. ESTC n053750. * CtHT-W; SCA; Ush.

>Ush is interleaved.

1154. Geddes, Alexander. *Letter from the rev. Alexander Geddes, LL.D. to the right rev. John Douglass.* London. 1794. 4°. iv, 55, [1] p. Published by: Author. Sold by: Faulder, R.; Johnson, J. ESTC t125316. * C; E; L; Lfa; MB; MiU; Osc; P; SCA; Sto; TxU; WNs.

>A reply to *A pastoral letter from Charles, Bishop of Rama ... to all the faithful* (no. 2894) which attacked Sir John Throckmorton's two letters to the Catholic clergy (nos 2743-2746).

1155. Geddes, Alexander. *Letter to a Member of Parliament, on the case of the Protestant dissenters.* Anon. London. 1787. 8°. [4], 37, [1] p. Published by:

Faulder, R. ESTC t038059. * C; CaOKQ; CaQMM; CU-SB; E; ECW; L; Ldw; O; Sto; Ush.

1156. Geddes, Alexander. *Letter to the rev. Dr. Priestley; in which the author attempts to prove ... that the divinity of Jesus Christ was a primitive tenet of Christianity.* London. 1787. 8°. [2], 36 p. Published by: Author. Sold by: Faulder, R.; Johnson, J.; Elliot, C. ESTC t038314. * ABu; BMp; CaBVaU; CtHT-W; Dt; E; L; Ldw; Lmh; Lu; MH-AH; Osc; PPL; SCA; Ush (2).

> Dated 'Aug. 14, 1787'. E and one Ushaw copy have 2 additional pages of adverts.

1157. Geddes, Alexander. *A letter to the right reverend the Lord Bishop of London: containing queries, doubts and difficulties, relative to a vernacular version of the holy scriptures.* London. 1787. 4°. [4], 87, [1] p. Printed by: Davis, J. Published by: Faulder, R. ESTC t125315. * BRp; C; Ct; DUc; E; IU; L; Ldw; MB; MiU; O; Osc; SCA; Ush; UshL; WNs.

1158. Geddes, Alexander. *A letter to the rr. the archbishops and bishops of England; pointing out the only sure means of preserving the church from the dangers that now threaten her. By an upper-graduate.* London. 1790. 8°. [2], 25, [1] p. Published by: Johnson, J. ESTC t038444. * CtY; E; ECW; FMU; L; Ldw; O; Omc.

> An 'upper-graduate' is Alexander Geddes.

1159. Geddes, Alexander. *Letter to the vv. apostolic in England. From a Catholic layman. My Lords, I am one of those who lately signed a protestation.* Anon. [London?]. [1790]. 8°. 15, [1] p. ESTC t216011. * O; Osc; Ush.

> According to Milner (ms note in Osc) the 'Catholic layman' is the priest Alexander Geddes, who also signs himself 'a protesting Catholic, but no papist'.

1160. Geddes, Alexander. *A memorial to the public, in behalf of the Roman Catholics of Edinburgh and Glasgow; containing, an account of the late riot against them on the second and following days of February, 1779.* Anon. London. 1779. 8°. [2], 48, [2] p. Printed by: Coghlan, J.P. Sold by: Coghlan, J.P. ESTC t126594. * CLU-C; CSmH; CtY; E; L; Lmh; O; Osc; SCA; Sto.

> For the attribution to Geddes see Fuller's bibliography (pp. 156-160). ESTC attributes the work to George Hay; see also next 2 items. With one page of Coghlan adverts (lacking in SCA and Sto).

1161. Geddes, Alexander. *A memorial to the public, in behalf of the Roman Catholics of Edinburgh and Glasgow; containing, an account of the late riot against them on the second and following days of February, 1779.* 2nd ed. Anon. London. 1779. 8°. [2], 48 p. Printed by: Coghlan, J.P. Sold by: Coghlan, J.P. ESTC t126593. * AWn; C; CLU-C; CtY; CU-BANC; D; Di; E; ECW; InU-Li; L; Lse; MH-H; MH-L; MnU; Ush; Yb.

1162. Geddes, Alexander. *A memorial to the public, in behalf of the Roman Catholics of Edinburgh and Glasgow; containing an account of the late riot against them on the second and following days of Feb., 1779.* 3rd ed. Anon. London. 1779. 8°. [2], 48 p. Printed by: Coghlan, J.P. Sold by: Coghlan, J.P.

ESTC t206075. * BMu; E.

1163. Geddes, Alexander. *A modest apology for the Roman Catholics of Great Britain: addressed to all moderate Protestants; particularly to the members of both Houses of Parliament.* Anon. London. 1800. 8°. xv, [1], 271, [1] p. Printed by: Davis; Taylor; Wilks. Published by: Author. Sold by: Faulder, R.; Booker, T. ESTC t124228. * ABu; C; CaQMM; DLC; DUc; E; ICN; L; Lhe; Lu; MY; Osc; PPL; SIR; StD.

1164. Geddes, Alexander. *A new year's gift to the good people of England, being a sermon, or something like a sermon, in defence of the present war: preached on the day of public thanksgiving, by Polemophilus Brown.* [London?]. 1798. 8°. 43, [1] p. ESTC n011132. * C; E; MnU; MRu; PPL.

    'Polemophilus Brown' is Alexander Geddes. See also no. 1169.

1165. Geddes, Alexander. *Proposals for printing by subscription a new translation of the holy bible, from corrected texts of the originals; with various readings, explanatory notes, and critical observations.* London. 1788. 4°. [32] p. Printed by: Davis, J. Published by: Author. Sold by: Faulder, R.; Johnson, J. ESTC t103907. * E; L; Lu; MiU; O; Osc; P; SCA; WDA.

1166. Geddes, Alexander. *Proposals for printing by subscription a new translation of the holy bible, from corrected texts of the originals; with various readings.* London. 1788. 4°. [22] p. Printed by: Davis, J. Published by: Faulder, R.; Johnson, J. ESTC t168003. * GEU-T; MRu; WNs.

    In this ed. some of the 'specimens of the work' of the 1st ed. are omitted (cf. no. 1165). WNs bound up with *Critical remarks on the Hebrew scriptures* (no. 1148).

1167. Geddes, Alexander. *Prospectus of a new translation of the holy bible from corrected texts of the originals compared with the ancient versions.* Glasgow. 1786. 4°. [8], 151, [1] p. Published by: Author. Sold by: Faulder, R. (London); Eliot, C. (Edinburgh); Cross (Dublin). ESTC t107526. * BRp; Ct; Dt; DUc; E; Gp; ICU; L; Ldw; Leid; Lhe; Lu; Luu; LVu; MB; MBAt; MChB; MiU; MnU; O; Osc; Omc; P; SAN; SCA; ScCR; UshL.

    Parts of Geddes's translation were published in 1790, 1792 and 1797, but the work was never completed. ESTC erroneously has 2 numbers for the same book, t107526 and t194123.

1168. Geddes, Alexander. *A second epistle from Simpkin to his dear brother Simon in Wales.* Anon. [London]. 1791. fol. 7, [1] p. Printed by: Coghlan, J.P. * Osc.

1169. Geddes, Alexander. *A sermon, preached on the day of general fast, February 27, 1799. By Polemophilus Brown, formerly curate, now vicar of P-n.* [London?]. 1799. 8°. 24 p. ESTC t181431. * E; MoU; MRu; O.

    See also no. 1164.

1170. Geddes, John. *A collection of spiritual songs. The following songs, written at different periods ... being now in few hands ... it was thought proper to publish them in this corrected form.* [Aberdeen]. 1791. 12°. 110 p. Printed by: [Chalmers, J.]. ESTC t185024. * E; O.

Compiled by John Geddes (coadjutor of the Lowland district of Scotland and a friend of Robert Burns) and George Hay. Many songs are provided with Catholic notes and comments.

1171. Geddes, John. *The life of Saint Margaret, Queen of Scotland. With some account of her husband Malcolm III, surnamed Kean More, and of their children.* Aberdeen. 1794. 8°. 63, [1] p. Printed by: Chalmers, J. & Co. ESTC t106236. * E; ECB; L; MY; SCA (imp.); Sto; TxU; Ush.

In the preface Geddes apologizes to the Protestant reader for Catholic elements.

1172. Geddes, John. *Watch and pray; or, a method of preparing for dying well.* [London?]. 1797. 8°. 16 p. ESTC t193015. * E; SCA.

1173. *General committee of Roman Catholics, Dublin, 14th January, 1792. The following account of our proceedings was reported, approved of, and ordered to be printed.* [Dublin]. [1792]. fol. 2 p. ESTC n043709. * Lpro.

1174. *General committee of Roman Caholics [sic], January 15, 1792. Edward Byrne, Esq. in the chair. The following resolutions were unanimously agreed to, and ordered to be printed.* [Dublin]. [1792]. fol. 2 p. ESTC n043708. * Lpro.

Signed 'Richard McCormick, sec'.

1175. *General committee of the Catholics of Ireland. Report of the committee of accounts.* [Dublin]. [1793]. 4°. [4] p. ESTC n043674. * Lpro.

Dated and signed 'Dublin, 22nd April, 1793. Luke Teeling, chairman'.

1176. *General instrcutions [sic] for gaining the indulgence, annexed by his holiness the pope to beads, rosaries, crosses, images ... blessed by his holiness.* London. 1788. 12°. 12 p. Published by: Coghlan, J.P. * Ush.

1177. Gerdil, Cardinal. *Responsum per illustres et amplissimi DD. Datas ad sanctissimum D.D.* Dublin. 1797. 8°. 5, [1] p. Printed by: Fitzpatrick, H. * Cli.

An answer to *Epistola episcoporum* (nos 974 and 975) and dated 'Rome, 17th December 1796'.

1178. Gibson, Matthew. *Instructions and regulations for the fast of Lent, 1784; addressed to the faithful of the n. district.* Anon. [Newcastle?]. [1784?]. 8°. 8 p. ESTC n052501. * Amp; ECW; IDA; TxU; Ush.

Matthew Gibson, Bishop of Comana, was vicar apostolic for the northern district from 1780 to 1790. See also next item.

1179. Gibson, Matthew. *Instructions and regulations for the fast of Lent, 1785; addressed to the faithful of the northern district.* Anon. [1785]. 8°. 8 p. * Amp.

1180. Gibson, Matthew. *Instructions and regulations, for the fast of Lent, 1789, addressed to the faithful of the n. district.* [1789]. fol. s.s. * BAA; Cli.

Signed 'Matthew Comanen V.A.'

1181. Gibson, Matthew. *Matthew, Bishop of Comana, to the Catholics at Liverpool, health and benediction from our Lord.* [1783]. 8°. 4 p. * Amp.

1182. Gibson, Matthew. *Our blessed redeemer.* [1790]. 8°. 30, [2] p. * LDA.

Dated '15th January 1790'.

1183. Gibson, Matthew. *A pastoral letter of Matthew, Bishop of Comana, and V.A. addressed to all the clergy, secular and regular; and to all the faithful of* *the northern district.* Newcastle. 1790. 8°. [2], 28 p. Printed by: Hall; Elliot. Sold by: Hall; Elliot; Coghlan, J.P. ESTC t077144. * BAA; BB; ECW; L; O; Osc; Sto; Ush(3).

Dated 'January 15, 1790'. BB, Sto and two Ush copies have [4], 28 p.

1184. Gibson, Matthew. *To all whom it may concern. Whereas Mr C - B - hath formally made known his intention to visit the N - n counties of England.* Anon. fol. s.s. * BAA.

An attack on Charles Butler.

1185. Gibson, William. *The continuation and increase of calamities.* [York?]. [1798]. 4°. 3, [1] p. * Osc.

A pastoral letter dated 'York, May 4, 1798'.

1186. Gibson, William. *Gulielmus, Dei et apostolicae sedis gratia episcopus Acanthensis et in districtu septentrionali Angliae vicarius apostolicus, &c.* s.s. * Ush.

A printed form with a permission to celebrate mass, to be completed with an individual missioner's name in ms. Ush is dated 'December 1794' in ms.

1187. Gibson, William. *In the present circumstances of the middle district, being the senior vicar apostolic in England.* [Durham]. [1799]. 4°. 2 p. * Osc.

Regulations for the fast of Lent, dated 'Durham, Jan. 9, 1799'.

1188. Gibson, William. *Regulations for the fast of Lent, 1792, for the northern district. In consideration of the scarcity of many kinds of provisions.* [York?]. [1792]. 4°. 2 p. * LDA; WDA.

Dated and signed 'York, Jan. the 23rd, 1792. William Acan. vic. ap. of the northern district'.

1189. Gibson, William. *Regulations for the fast of Lent, 1796, for the northern district ... Our duty requires us.* [1796]. 4°. 3, [1] p. * LDA.

Dated '21 Jan. 1796'.

1190. Gibson, William. *Regulations for the fast of Lent in the middle district, for the year 1800.* Newcastle. [1800]. fol. [2] p. Printed by: Walker, E. * BAA; LDA.

Dated '1800, January 31, Durham'.

1191. Gibson, William. *Regulations for the fast of Lent, in the northern district, for the year 1797. Dear brethren, when we consider the calamities that now afflict mankind.* [York?]. [1797]. 4°. 2 p. * WDA.

Dated and signed 'York, February 7th, 1797. William Bishop of Acanthos, & vic. ap. in the northern district'.

1192. Gibson, William. *The undersigned in the name of the Roman Catholic clergy and laity, who are unwilling to assume the title of protesting Catholic dissenters and who have conscientious objections.* [London?]. [1791?]. fol. 3 [i.e. 2] p. ESTC t050397. * L; Sto; WDA.

Signed 'William Gibson' (and by proxy for Charles Walmesley and John Douglass).

1193. Gibson, William. *William, Bishop of Acanthos, vicar apostolic, to all the faithful, clergy and laity, in the northern district. With great joy.* [York?].

[1791]. fol. s.s. ESTC t052516. * Cli; L; LDA; TxU; Ush.
> Dated 'York, June 30, 1791'.

1194. Gibson, William. *William, Bishop of Acanthos, vicar apostolic. To all the faithful, clergy and laity, in the northern district.* York. 1793. fol. s.s. ESTC t052515. * L; LDA; UshA.
> Dated 'York, April the 5th, 1793'.

1195. Gibson, William. *William, Bishop of Acanthos, vicar apostolic, to all the faithful, clergy and laity, in the northern district. Dear brethren, being convinced of your alacrity.* [1794]. 4°. 2 p. * LDA.
> Dated '11 February 1794'.

1196. Gibson, William. *William, Bishop of Acanthos, vicar apostolic, to all the faithful, clergy and laity, in the northern district ... we send this to inform you.* [York]. [1795]. 4°. s.s. * LDA.
> Signed and dated 'William, Bishop of Acanthos, vic. ap. York, Jan the 29th, 1795'.

1197. Gibson, William. *William, Bishop of Acanthos, vicar apostolic, &c. to all the faithful, clergy and laity of the northern district. Regulations for the fast of Lent, 1799, for the northern district. Dearly beloved.* [1799]. 4°. 2, [2] p. * LDA.
> Dated '9 January 1799'.

1198. Gibson, William. *William, Bishop of Acanthos, vicar-apostolic &c. to all the faithful, clergy and laity, of the middle district ... Again our king and country.* [1799]. 4°. 2, [2] p. * LDA.
> Dated '21st February 1799'.

1199. Gibson, William. *William, Bishop of Acanthos, and vicar apostolic, to all the faithful, clergy and laity of the northern district. Regulations for the fast of Lent in the northern district, for the year, 1800.* [1800]. fol. 2, [2] p. * LDA.
> Dated '1800, January 31'.

1200. Gilbert, Nicolas Alain. *A vindication of the doctrine of the Catholic church concerning the eucharist. In two conversations between a Catholic and a Presbyterian.* Anon. London. 1800. 12°. [4], 235, [1] p. Printed by: Coghlan, J.P. ESTC t180608. * Amp; ECW; Lhe; Osc; Sal; Ush.

1201. Gilmore, Robert Paul. *A pious monitor, of the divine presence. Composed by the reverend and learned P.G. preacher of the gospel.* London. 1746. 12°. [3], 6-24 p. Published by: Marmaduke, J. Sold by: Marmaduke, J. ESTC t180258. * O.

1202. Gilmore, Robert Paul. *A pious monitor of the divine presence.* London. 1756. 8°. Published by: Needham, W. *Gillow, II, 493.
> Gillow also mentions a 1773 ed.

1203. Girandeau, Bonaventure. *Histories and parables. Translated from the French of F. Bonaventure. By A.H.* London. 1785. 12°. viii, 196 p. Printed by: Coghlan, J.P. ESTC n051171. * ECW; ICN; Stan.

1204. Gobinet, Charles. *The instruction of youth in Christian piety ... with a very* *profitable treatise for meditation, or mental prayer [Instruction de la jeunesse en la piété Chrétienne].* 3rd ed. 2 vols. London. 1741. 8°. Published by: Needham, F. Sold by: Needham, F. ESTC n028781. * CLU; ECW; Hor; Sal; Stan (vol. 1); TLP; UGL.

> According to Kirk (p. 184) translated by Robert Typper alias Pinckard.

1205. Gobinet, Charles. *The instruction of youth in Christian piety, taken out of the sacred scriptures and holy fathers.* 4th ed. 2 vols. Newcastle. 1783. 8°. Published by: Coates, F.; Coghlan, J.P. Sold by: Coates, F.; Coghlan, J.P. ESTC t097583. * CAL; CLU; DMR; ECW (vol. 1); Gi; ICN; L; Lhe; Nijm; NSCH (vol. 1); Osc; P; TLP; TxU; Ush; Yb.

> Translated by Thomas Eyre.

1206. Gobinet, Charles. *Instruction of youth in Christian piety ... revised and corrected by the rev. B. MacMahon.* 5th ed. 2 vols. Dublin. 1793. 8°. Printed by: Wogan, P. ESTC t097584. * IDA; L.

1207. Gobinet, Charles. *The instruction of youth in Christian piety ... rev. and corr. by the rev. B. MacMahon.* 6th ed. 2 vols. Dublin. 1795. 4°. viii, [1], 10-221; [1], xii, [1], 14-221, [1] p. Printed by: Jones, W. * Stan.

1208. Gobinet, Charles. *A treatise of the imitation of the holy youth of our Lord and Saviour Jesus Christ. Translated from the French original of Mr. Charles Gobinet ... by W.A.M. C.A.D.A. [Instruction de la jeunesse en la piété Chrétienne].* London. 1758. 12°. vi, 7-126, [2] p. Published by: Meighan, T. ESTC t177702. * ECW; Lhe.

> 'W.A.M. C.A.D.A.' is William Maire, Coll. Ang. Duac. Alumn. Maire (1704-1769) was consecrated Bishop of Cinna by Challoner in 1768. With 2 pages of Meighan adverts.

1209. Gobinet, Charles. *A treatise on the two sacraments of penance and the holy eucharist.* [Newcastle]. ix, [1], 325, [1] p. Printed by: Walker, E. Sold by: Cuddon, A. * Do.

1210. Godeau, Antoine. *Scripture penitents. Or, the great efficacy of repentance, in order to a holy life, and a happy death. Illustrated in two and twenty histories, taken from the old and new testament.* 2nd ed. London. 1740. 8°. [54], 184; [18], 264 p. Published by: Meighan, T. ESTC t207293. * Do; E; Hor; Ush.

> Translated by Robert Samber who signs the dedication.

1211. Goetz, Johann Nepomuck. *Predigt von der Heiligkeit christlicher Tempel. Am jährlichen Gedächtniss Tage der feierlichen Eröffnung der allerheiligsten Dreyfaltigkeits-Kirche der teutschen christ-katholischen Gemeinde.* Philadelphia. 1796. 8°. 20 p. Printed by: Schweitzer, H. Sold by: Oeller, J. ESTC w010918. * DP; MWA.

1212. Goetz, Johann Nepomuck. *Rede moral-philosophische bey Veranlassung des allgemeinen Bettages durch die Vereinigten Staaten ... Gehalten am Bet- und Buss-Tage in der College ... den 9ten May, 1798, Philadelphia.* Philadelphia. 1798. 8°. 22 [i.e. 32] p. Printed by: Schweitzer, H. ESTC w000041. * PHi.

1213. Goonan, Silvester. *Sermons on various religious subjects, for different Sundays and festivals of the year. By the late reverend Silvester Goonan.* Dublin.

1798. 8°. [2], xvi, 484 p. Printed by: Wogan, P. ESTC t105003. * D; Dt; Du; FLK; IDA; L; Mil; MRu; SIR.

With a list of subscribers.

1214. Gordon, Alexander. *Memoire de M. Gordon, principal de collège des Ecossois à Paris, pour servir de réponse à l'invective de M. L'Evêque Hay contre les superieurs et élèves du dit collège.* 1785. 4°. [2], 62 p. * E.

1215. Gordon, John. *Pax vobis: or, gospel and liberty, against ancient and modern papists. By E.G. preacher of the word.* 5th ed. Anon. [London?]. 1742. 8°. xv, [1], 112 p. ESTC n020325. * CLU-C; E; ECW; GEU-T; IES; LAM; Lfa; MBAt; O; P; Sal; TH; UGL.

According to ESTC 'E.G.' is John Gordon; Dr D.M. Rogers suggests Ignatius Brown as the author. See further Clancy nos 402-408. See also next item.

1216. Gordon, John. *Pax vobis: or, gospel and liberty: against ancient and modern papists. By E.G. preacher of the word.* 6th ed. Anon. London. 1753. 12°. [10], 118, [2] p. ESTC t118430. * DMR; IU; L.

1217. Gother, John. *Afternoon instructions for the whole year. Tome I. Being practical thoughts for all Sundays and holidays, from Advent to Easter.* Anon. [London?]. 1717. 12°. [6], 391, [5] p. * DoA.

Bound up with tome II (no. 1218). With one page of adverts.

1218. Gother, John. *Afternoon instructions for the whole year. Tome II. Being practical thoughts for all Sundays and holidays, from Easter to Advent.* Anon. [London?]. 1717. 12°. [4], 484, [4] p. ESTC t193104. * DoA; O.

DoA bound up with no. 1217.

1219. Gother, John. *Afternoon instructions for the whole year. Tome I. Being practical thoughts for all Sundays and holidays, from Advent to Easter.* Anon. [London?]. 1730. 12°. [6], 7-380, [4] p. ESTC t193105. * E; Lhe; Map; O; Sal; TH.

1220. Gother, John. *Afternoon instructions for the whole year. Tome II. Being practical thoughts for all Sundays and holidays, from Easter to Advent.* Anon. [London]. 1730. 12°. [2], 3-451, [5] p. * Cha; Lhe; TH; Yb.

1221. Gother, John. *The Catholic year; or, daily lessons on the feasts of the church ... adapted to the present church calendar, by F.S. Husenbeth.* Dublin. 1761. 8°. * Osc.

A compilation taken from other Gother works such as *Instructions for festivals.*

1222. Gother, John. *Christian entertainments: being instructions and practical thoughts on the epistles, lessons and gospels of all the Sundays, festivals and moveable fasts (including Lent) and feasts of the whole year.* 2 vols. Dublin. 1784. 12°. [2]. xix, [1], 379, [1]; [4], 362, [10] p. Published by: Cross, R. ESTC t208578. * D; FLK (vol. 2).

1223. Gother, John. *The collects, epistles and gospels that are read throughout the whole year, according to the use of the holy Roman church. Vol. I from Advent to Easter. Vol. II from Easter to Advent.* 2 vols. London. 1736. 12°. 348, cxxvii, [5]; 268, cxxvii, [1] p. Published by: [Meighan, T.]. ESTC t184348. *

Do (vol. 1); E (vol. 2); Hen (vol. 1); Hor (vol. 2); NSPM (vol. 1); Osc (vol. 2); Pci (vol. 1); Ush (vol. 1); Yb.

With adverts for Thomas Meighan.

1224. Gother, John. *The collects, epistles and gospels, that are read throughout the whole year, according to the use of the holy Roman church. Tome I. From Advent to Easter.* London. 1754. 12°. xxiv, 40, 333, [1], cxxvi, [2] p. Published by: [Meighan, T.]. * E; ECW; Hen.

Hen followed by a 2-page Meighan catalogue, 'The common of the saints' (i-cxxvi) and a 2-page catalogue of Gother's works. E has xxvi, 333, cxxvi, [2], 40 p.

1225. Gother, John. *The collects, epistles and gospels, that are read throughout the whole year according to the use of the holy Roman church. Vol. II of tome II. From Easter to Advent.* London. 1754. 12°. xxiv, 295, 40, cxxvi, [2] p. Published by: [Meighan, T.]. * Do; Lhe; NSPM; Pci.

This contains an English-Latin missal. With 2 pages of Meighan adverts.

1226. Gother, John. *Gother's prayers for Sundays & festivals, adapted to the use of private families or congregations, to which is added an appendix.* Wolverhampton. [1800]. 8°. [2], vii, [2], 4-429, [1] p. Printed by: Smart, J. Sold by: Smart, J.; Booker. ESTC t105223. * BB; CaOHM; DMR; ECW; Gi; L; NSCH; Osc; StD.

See also Chinnici, p. 168). For other versions of this work see *Prayers for Sundays* (no. 1309ff.).

1227. Gother, John. *Instructions and devotions for hearing mass.* Anon. 1705. 12°. 152 p. * Gillow, II, 545.

1228. Gother, John. *Instructions and devotions for hearing mass.* Anon. 1712. 12°. [16], 152 p. * ECW.

1229. Gother, John. *Instructions and devotions for hearing mass.* Anon. [London?]. 1721. 16°. [16], 152 p. ESTC t205200. * Llp.

1230. Gother, John. *Instructions and devotions for hearing mass.* Anon. [London?]. 1725. 24°. [16], 152 p. ESTC n018297. * BB; Du; E; IU; Lhe; O.

1231. Gother, John. *Instructions and devotions for hearing mass; as also instructions for confession, communion, and confirmation.* Anon. London. 1729. 12°. [16], 157, [9] p. Published by: Meighan, T. * DCU; Do.

With 4 pages of Meighan adverts.

1232. Gother, John. *Instructions and devotions for hearing mass.* Anon. [London?]. 1730. 24°. [16], 163, [1] p. ESTC t104730. * ECW; L.

1233. Gother, John. *Instructions and devotions for hearing mass; also for confession, communion, and confirmation.* 2 vols. Anon. [London]. 1740 [1744]. 12°. [16], 150, [2]; [2], 156, [14] p. Published by: [Meighan, T.; Marmaduke, J.] ESTC t198053. * DMR (vol. 1); Do (vol. 1); ECW; L; TxU (vol. 1); Ush (vol. 1).

With a final advertisement leaf to vol. 1. ESTC n046081 (not separately included in our list) is in fact vol. 1 of this ed. L has some pages of Meighan and Marmaduke adverts.

1234. Gother, John. *Instructions and devotions for hearing mass.* [London?]. 1753. 12°. xiv, 118 p. ESTC t205006. * E.

1235. Gother, John. *Instructions and devotions for hearing mass.* Anon. Liverpool. [1755?]. 12°. [16], 150, [2] p. Printed by: Sadler, J. ESTC t188704. * Do; Du; Hen; LVp; Ush.
> Do and Hen lack 2 final pages.

1236. Gother, John. *Instructions and devotions for hearing mass.* Anon. [London?]. 1767. 12°. [16], 150, [2] p. Published by: [Meighan, T.]. ESTC t073180. * BB; COA; DMR; Do; ECW; FLK; ICN; L; Map; O; TxU.
> With 2 pages of Meighan adverts. BB, Do, ECW, and FLK bound up with Pacificus Baker's *Holy altar*, 1768 (no. 154).

1237. Gother, John. *Instructions and devotions for the afflicted and sick, with some help for prisoners, such especially as are to be tried for life.* 1705. 8°. [2], 274 p. * Do.
> Clancy lists a 1697 ed. (no. 538).

1238. Gother, John. *Instructions and devotions for the afflicted and sick, with some help for prisoners such especially as are to be tried for life.* 2nd ed. Anon. 1705. 12°. ii, 284 p. ESTC t139558. * DMR; L.

1239. Gother, John. *Instructions and devotions for the afflicted and sick, with some help for prisoners, such especially as are to be tried for life.* Anon. [London]. 1712. 12°. [4], 300 p. ESTC n018232. * IU.

1240. Gother, John. *Instructions and devotions for the afflicted and sick, with some help for prisoners, such especially as are to be tried for life.* Anon. London. 1725. 12°. 256, [4] p. Published by: Meighan, T. ESTC t060715. * Do; DoA; Du; E; Hen; L; Lhe; NIC; O; Pci.

1241. Gother, John. *Instructions and devotions for the afflicted and sick, with some help for prisoners, such especially as are to be tried for life.* Anon. [London?]. 1730. 18°. 148 [i.e. 248], [4] p. ESTC t078505. * IDA; L; O; Ush.
> Hugh Fenning O.P. (personal communication) suggests Dublin as the place of publication.

1242. Gother, John. *Instructions and devotions for the afflicted and sick, with some help for prisoners, such especially as are to be tried for life.* Anon. 1756. 12°. [4], 256, [4] p. Published by: Meighan, T. * CAL; ECB; LO; Sto; TLP.

1243. Gother, John. *Instructions and prayers for confession, communion and confirmation.* Anon. 1770. 12°. [2], 70 p. * Gi; Ush.
> Both copies stop at p. 70 and appear to be incomplete.

1244. Gother, John. *Instructions concerning an annual spiritual exercise.* Anon. Douai. 1723. 12°. 45, [1] p. Printed by: Derbaix, C.L. * Do.

1245. Gother, John. *Instructions concerning an annual spiritual exercise.* Anon. Douai. 1759. 12°. 95, [1] p. Printed by: Derbaix, C.L. ESTC t083408. * CAL; ECW; L; Osc; Sal; Ush.

1246. Gother, John. *Instructions for apprentices and servants.* Anon. 1718. 12°. 50, [2] p. * Pci.

1247. Gother, John. *Instructions for apprentices and servants.* London. 1786. 12°. 45, [3] p. Printed by: Coghlan, J.P. * Ush.
> With one page of Coghlan adverts.

1248. Gother, John. *Instructions for children.* Anon. [London?]. 1704. 12°. 36 p. ESTC t111550. * DFo; L; SPu.

1249. Gother, John. *Instructions for children.* Anon. [London?]. 1718. 12°. 36 p. ESTC n022880. * Pci; Ush.
> The CLU-C copy listed in ESTC is in fact part of *Instructions for masters, traders, labourers, &c.* (no. 1268).

1250. Gother, John. *Instructions for confession and communion.* Anon. 1702. 12°. 86 p. * CAL (imp.).

1251. Gother, John. *Instructions for confession and communion.* Anon. [London?]. 1720. 24°. [2], 160, [6] p. ESTC n018298. * Du; IU; Llp.
> With 2 pages of Meighan adverts.

1252. Gother, John. *Instructions for confession and communion.* Anon. [London]. 1726. 12°. 124, [4] p. Published by: Meighan, T. ESTC t117351. * DMR; Hen; L; Lhe.

1253. Gother, John. *Instructions for confession and communion.* Anon. [London?]. 1730. 24°. 155, [5] p. ESTC t104719. * L.

1254. Gother, John. *Instructions for confession and communion.* Anon. 1750. viii, 164 p. * Do.

1255. Gother, John. *Instructions for confession and communion.* London. 1779. 12°. 118 p. Printed by: Coghlan, J.P. * P.

1256. Gother, John. *Instructions for confession, communion and confirmation.* Anon. [London?]. 1706. 12°. [2], 70, 75-98, 95-159, [5] p. ESTC n051928. * DFo.
> Approbation dated 'Paris, Feb. 4, 1703'. Partly in catechism form; these *Instructions* later formed vol. 6 of the Newcastle ed. of the *Spiritual works* (no. 1334). See also next 9 items.

1257. Gother, John. *Instructions for confession, communion and confirmation.* Anon. [London]. 1729. 12°. 157, [11] p. Published by: [Meighan, T.]. ESTC t205007. * Do; E; ECB; Lhe.
> With 8 pages of Meighan adverts.

1258. Gother, John. *Instructions for confession, communion and confirmation.* Anon. London. 1736. 8°. 156, [12] p. Published by: Meighan, T. * Osc.
> With 6 pages of Meighan adverts.

1259. Gother, John. *Instructions for confession, communion, and confirmation.* Anon. London. 1744. 12°. 156, [12] p. Published by: Meighan, T. ESTC t188985. * E; ECW; Lhe.
> With some pages of Meighan adverts. Apparently also issued as part of

Instructions and devotions for hearing mass (no. 1233).

1260. Gother, John. *Instructions for confession, communion, and confirmation ...
With approbation.* London. 1752. 12°. [3], 4-114, [4] p. * DMR.

1261. Gother, John. *Instructions for confession, communion and confirmation.*
Liverpool. 1755. 12°. 114, [4] p. Printed by: Sadler, J. ESTC t188734. * C; Gi;
LVp; Ush.
    With 4 pages of Sadler adverts.

1262. Gother, John. *Instructions for confession, communion, and confirmation.*
Anon. London. 1761. 12°. 156, [12] p. Published by: Meighan, T. ESTC
t188732. * C; ECW; Lhe.
    The text of this book is also part of a 1779 publication by Hay (no. 1395).

1263. Gother, John. *Instructions for confession, communion and confirmation.*
London. 1786. 12°. 141, [3] p. Printed by: Coghlan, J.P. * Lhe.
    With 2 pages of Coghlan adverts.

1264. Gother, John. *Instructions for confession, communion, and confirmation.*
Anon. Newcastle. 1792. 12°. 146, [2] p. Published by: Coates, F. ESTC
t205001. * NCp.

1265. Gother, John. *Instructions for confession, communion, and confirmation.*
London. 1796. 12°. 132 p. Printed by: Coghlan, J.P. ESTC t205005. * CYc.

1266. Gother, John. *Instructions for festivals.* 12°. 379, [5] p. * ECW (imp.).
    Tp and prelims missing; starts at page 5.

1267. Gother, John. *Instructions for keeping Sundays.* Dublin. 1793. 8°. 36 p.
Printed by: Byrne, P. ESTC t220158. * Di.

1268. Gother, John. *Instructions for masters, traders, labourers &c. Also for
servants, apprentices, and youth.* Anon. [London?]. 1718. 12°. 56, [2], 50, [2],
53, [3], 36 p. ESTC t109894. * CLU-C; Du; E; L; Map; Pci.
    The *Instructions for apprentices and servants*, *Instructions for youth* and
    Instructions for children have separate tp, pagination and register. Du lacks
    Instructions for youth.

1269. Gother, John. *Instructions for masters, traders, labourers, &c.* London.
1786. 12°. 48 p. Printed by: Coghlan, J.P. ESTC n045955. * MBAt.

1270. Gother, John. *Instructions for particular states and conditions.* [London].
1718. 12°. [2], 3-367, [7] p. Published by: [Meighan, T.]. * ECW.
    With 3 pages of Meighan adverts.

1271. Gother, John. *Instructions for particular states and conditions.* London.
1753. 8°. 331, [5] p. Published by: Meighan, T. * CAL; Do; DoA; Osc; Sal;
Ush.
    The author is given as 'G[-] J[-]'. With 2 pages of Meighan adverts.

1272. Gother, John. *Instructions for the whole year. Part I. For Lent. Being
practical thoughts on the epistles and lessons from Ashwednesday to Tuesday in
Easter-week.* Anon. [London]. 1704. 12°. 344 p. ESTC t139559. * L.

1273. Gother, John. *Instructions for the whole year. Part I, Lent.* 1709. 287, [1]

p. * Lfa.

1274. Gother, John. *Instructions for the whole year. Part III. Tome I. For festivals. Being practical thoughts and directions for all the feasts of obligation and others, from ... Advent to the end of April.* Anon. 1717. 12°. 402, [6] p. * Do.

1275. Gother, John. *Instructions for the whole year. Part I. Tome I. For Sundays ... from Advent to Whitsunday, excepting those of Lent.* Anon. 1718. 12°. [2], xii, [14], 359, [6] p. * ECR.

1276. Gother, John. *Instructions for the whole year. Part I. Tome II. For Sundays, being practical thoughts on the epistles and gospels of all the Sundays and moveable feasts, from Trinity Sunday to Advent.* Anon. [London]. 1718. 12°. 369, [15] p. Published by: [Meighan, T.]. * ECR; ECW; Lhe.
  With 7 pages of Meighan adverts.

1277. Gother, John. *Instructions for the whole year. Part II. For Lent. Being practical thoughts ... and lessons from Ash-Wednesday to Tuesday in Easter-week. In this edition are added the gospels.* Anon. [London?]. 1718. 12°. 424, [8] p. ESTC n008934. * CLU-C.

1278. Gother, John. *Instructions for the whole year. Part II. For Lent. Being practical thoughts on the epistles and lessons, from Ash-Wednesday to Tuesday in Easter-week.* Anon. 1723. 12°. 424, [10] p. ESTC t211680. * Pm; Stan; Ush.
  With 2 pages of adverts for Gother books.

1279. Gother, John. *Instructions for the whole year. Part I. Tome I. For Sundays, being practical thoughts ... from Advent to Whitsunday, excepting those of Lent.* Anon. London. 1726. 12°. [2], xxviii, 359, [9] p. ESTC t217938. * Do; E; ECW; Lfa.
  With an additional tp 'Mr Gother's spiritual works: in sixteen tomes. Tome I. London 1718'.

1280. Gother, John. *Instructions for the whole year. Part I. Tome II. For Sundays, being practical thoughts ... from Trinity Sunday to Advent.* Anon. [London]. 1726. 12°. 369, [15] p. Published by: [Meighan, T.]. * Do; DoA; Lfa; Lhe.
  With 11 pages of Meighan adverts.

1281. Gother, John. *Instructions for the whole year. Part III. Tome I. For festivals. Being practical thoughts and directions for all the feasts of obligation and others, from ... Advent, to the end of April.* Anon. [London]. 1730. 12°. 379, [5] p. ESTC t143532. * DoA; Lu; Pci.

1282. Gother, John. *Instructions for the whole year. Part III. For festivals. Tome II. Being practical thoughts and directions for all the feasts of obligation and others, from the first of May to Advent.* Anon. 1730. 12°. 438, [6] p. * Pci.
  With an additional tp 'Mr Gother's spiritual works Tome V. Instructions on all the feasts from the first of May to Advent. Part II. London, printed in the year 1718'.

1283. Gother, John. *Instructions for the whole year. Part II. Tome III. For Lent.*

Being practical thoughts ... from Ash-Wednesday to Tuesday in Easter-week. In this edition are added the gospels. Anon. [London]. 1736. 12°. 424, [8] p. Published by: Meighan, T. ESTC t193582. * Do; DoA; Lfa; O.

With 2 pages of Meighan adverts, lacking in Lfa.

1284. Gother, John. *Instructions for the whole year. Part I. Tome I. For Sundays, being practical thoughts on the epistles and gospels of all the Sundays and moveable feasts, from Advent to Whitsunday.* Anon. 2 vols. London. 1744. 12°. xxviii, 348, [8] p. (vol. 1). Published by: Meighan, T. ESTC t193248. * Do (vol. 1); ECW; Hen (vol. 1); O; Osc.

1285. Gother, John. *Instructions for the whole year. Part I. Tome II. For Sundays, being practical thoughts on the epistles and gospels of all the Sundays and moveable feasts, from Trinity Sunday to Advent.* Anon. London. 1744. 12°. 363, [9] p. Published by: Meighan, T. * Map.

With several pages of Meighan adverts, and adverts for Gother and Challoner publications.

1286. Gother, John. *Instructions for the whole year. Part II. Tome III. For Lent. Being practical thoughts on the epistles, gospels, and lessons from Ash-Wednesday to Tuesday in Easter-week.* Anon. London. 1752. 12°. 424, [8] p. Published by: Meighan, T. ESTC t204375. * Amp (2); E; ECW; Lfa; Sco.

With one page of Meighan adverts. One Amp copy has xiv preliminary pages.

1287. Gother, John. *Instructions for the whole year. Part I. Tome I. For Sundays, being practical thoughts on the epistles and gospels of all the Sundays and moveable feasts, from Advent to Whitsunday.* Dublin. 1752. 12°. xxv, [1], 306, [4] p. Published by: Kelly, I. * ECW; FLK.

This work also forms a 2-volume set with no. 1288.

1288. Gother, John. *Instructions for the whole year. Part I. Tome II. For Sundays, being practical thoughts on the epistles ... from Trinity Sunday to Advent.* Dublin. 1752. 12°. 324, [4] p. Published by: Kelly, I. ESTC t189014. * D; ECW; FLK.

This work also forms a 2-volume set with no. 1287.

1289. Gother, John. *Instructions for youth.* Anon. [London?]. 1718. 12°. 53, [3] p. ESTC n022879. * Amp; Pci; Ush.

1290. Gother, John. *Instructions upon the sacrament of confirmation.* Anon. Newcastle. 1783. 12°. 44 p. Published by: Coates, F. Sold by: Coates, F. ESTC t205198. * NCp.

1291. Gother, John. *The instructive part of the mass; viz. moral reflections on the introit, prayer, epistle and gospel of all the Sundays in the year.* Anon. [London?]. 1729. 12°. vi, 284 p. ESTC n009077. * BMp; DMR; Do; E; Lhe; MHi; NSPM.

Do attributes this work to Gother. E has 4 extra pages of adverts for P. Keating, the late-18th century publisher.

1292. Gother, John. *Mr. Gother's second method of hearing mass.* London. 1789. 12°. [2], 3-59, [1] p. Printed by: Coghlan, J.P. * ECW.

1293. Gother, John. *A papist misrepresented and represented: or, a two-fold character of popery. To which is prefix'd, the life of the author.* Dublin. 1750. 8°. [10], 132, [4] p. Published by: Bowes, P. ESTC t170358. * D.

    With 4 pages of adverts.

1294. Gother, John. *A papist misrepresented and represented ... By Mr. John Gother. To which is prefix'd, the life of the author.* Waterford. 1750. 8°. [12], 3-132, [4] p. Printed by: Calwell, J. ESTC t170363. * D; Dt; Map.

    With 4 pages of adverts.

1295. Gother, John. *A papist misrepresented, and represented. Or a twofold character of popery ... Abridged from that published by Mr. John Gother, anno 1685.* [London?]. [1752?]. 12°. x, 65, [1] p. ESTC t043608. * E; L; Lhe; Ush.

    Abridged by Richard Challoner. See also next items.

1296. Gother, John. *A papist misrepresented, and represented. Or a twofold character of popery ... Abridged from that published by Mr. John Gother, anno 1685.* [London]. [1760?]. 12°. x, 73, [1] p. Published by: [Needham, W.]. ESTC t043609. * CtY; Do; E; ECW; L; Lfa; Lhe; Lu; NSPM; O; Ush.

    Publisher's name inferred from advert on verso of p. 73. Ush has no adverts. Do cat. gives date [c.1741].

1297. Gother, John. *A papist misrepresented, and represented; or a two-fold character of popery ... Selected from the original of 1683, by the rev. Mr. John Gother, and republished by ... Richard Challoner.* 19th ed. London. 1789. 12°. [2], 66 p. Printed by: Coghlan, J.P. ESTC t170365. * Lfa; LOU; NSPM.

    Lfa has xx, 66 p.

1298. Gother, John. *A papist misrepresented, and represented, or a two-fold character of popery ... Selected from the original of 1683, by the rev. Mr. John Gother, and republished by ... Dr. Richard Challoner.* 20th ed. London. 1792. 12°. xii, 72 p. Printed by: Coghlan, J.P. ESTC t043610. * CtY-BR; ECR; L; Lhe; MH; O.

    With 6 pages of adverts (lacking in ECR).

1299. Gother, John. *A papist misrepresented and represented: or, a two-fold character of popery. To which is pre-fix'd, the life of the author.* Dublin. 1792. 12°. 219, [1] p. Printed by: Hoey, P. ESTC t170359. * C; ICR; IDA; MY.

1300. Gother, John. *A papist misrepresented, and represented, or a two-fold character of popery ... Selected from the original of 1683. By the rev. Mr. John Gother ... Republished by ... Richard Challoner.* 21st ed. London. 1798. 12°. xii, 66 p. Printed by: Coghlan, J.P. ESTC t043611. * Do; E; ECW; L; MY.

1301. Gother, John. *A papist misrepresented and represented or a twofold character of popery. Abridged from that published by Mr John Gother.* [London]. x, 73, [1] p. Printed by: [Coghlan, J.P.]. * Ush (imp.).

    Tp damaged. Printer's name inferred from advert on p. 73.

1302. Gother, John. *A practical catechism in fifty two lessons: one for every Sunday in the year.* Anon. [London]. 1701. 12°. [8], 470, [2] p. ESTC t082733.

* DUc; ECW; Gi; L; Oc; Pm; PRTus; TLP; TxU.

1303. Gother, John. *A practical catechism; in fifty-two lessons: one for every Sunday in the year. With an appendix for particular states.* Anon. 1718. 8°. [8], 456, [4] p. * ECW; Hen; Osc.

  ESTC t211186 seems to be another issue, marketed under non-R.C. auspices (London, printed and sold by Charles Rivington, 1718).

1304. Gother, John. *A practical catechism in fifty-two lessons: one for every Sunday in the year. With an appendix for particular states.* Anon. [London]. 1735. 12°. [8], 442, [6] p. Published by: Meighan, T. ESTC t104250. * Do; E; ECW; FLK; Hen; L; LAM; Lhe; O; Pci; TLP; Ush.

  With 2 pages of adverts. E and Pci are a variant with tp stating 'Mr. Gother's Spiritual works, tome XII'.

1305. Gother, John. *A practical catechism; or, lessons for Sundays.* Dublin. 1786. 8°. 130 p. Published by: White, L. ESTC t215503. * Di.

1306. Gother, John. *Prayers for every day in Lent.* Anon. 1702. 12°. [12], 468 p. ESTC t213659. * DoA; DUc; Lhe; ZDU.

1307. Gother, John. *Prayers for every day in Lent. Tome II.* 1718. Anon. 12°. [12], 456, [4] p. * Lhe.

1308. Gother, John. *Prayers for every day in Lent. By the reverend Mr. John Gother. Part II. Being the 14th vol. of his spiritual works.* London. 1783. 12°. [12], 440, [4] p. Printed by: Coghlan, J.P. ESTC t196491. * Cha (imp.); ECW; Lhe.

1309. Gother, John. *Prayers for Sundays, holidays and other festivals, from Low-Sunday, to the twenty-first Sunday after Pentecost.* Anon. [London?]. 1704. 12°. 574 , [2] p. ESTC t125126. * DFo; DMR; DoA; L; Osc; TH (-tp); Ush.

1310. Gother, John. *Prayers for Sundays, holy-days, and other festivals, from the twenty-first Sunday after Pentecost, to Lent.* Anon. [London]. 1705. 12°. 516 p. ESTC t139560. * DMR; DoA; L; Osc.

1311. Gother, John. *Prayers for Sundays, holy-days, and other festivals. Tome I. Printed in the year 1718.* Anon. 1718. 12°. 521, [7] p. * Gi; Lhe.

  According to Gillow edited by William Crathorne.

1312. Gother, John. *Prayers for Sundays, holy-days, and other festivals from Trinity-Sunday to Advent. Tome III.* Anon. [London]. 1718. 12°. 542, [10] p. Published by: [Meighan, T.]. * ECW; Lhe.

  With 2 pages of Meighan adverts.

1313. Gother, John. *Prayers for Sundays, holy-days and other festivals.* 3 vols. London. 1743. 12°. Published by: Meighan, T. ESTC t175577. * C; E (vol. 1); O (vols 2, 3); TH (vol. 3).

  With some pages of adverts for Gother's works at end of vol. 1.

1314. Gother, John. *Prayers for Sundays, holy-days, and other festivals, from the first Sunday of Advent, to Whitsuntide (Lent excepted). By the rev. Mr. John Gother, part I, being the 13th vol. of his spiritual works.* London. 1782. 12°. [2], 521, [7] p. Printed by: Coghlan, J.P. Published by: Meighan, T. ESTC

t196488. * Lhe.
　　With an additional, undated tp bearing the imprint of T. Meighan.

1315. Gother, John. *Prayers for Sundays, holy-days and other festivals, from the first Sunday of Advent, to Whitsuntide, Lent excepted. Part I. Being the 13th vol. of his spiritual works.* London. 1783. 12°. 521, [7] p. Printed by: Coghlan, J.P. ESTC t196485. * DoA; E; ECW; Lhe; NSPM.
　　A reissue of the 1782 ed., with a cancelled tp.

1316. Gother, John. *Prayers for Sundays, holy-days, and other festivals ... being the 13th, 14th, and 15th vol. of his spiritual works.* 3 vols. London. 1783. 8°. Printed by: Coghlan, J. * Osc; Sal.
　　See also letter Coghlan to John Geddes, 14 June 1783 (SCA, Edinburgh).

1317. Gother, John. *Prayers for Sundays, holy-days, and other festivals, from Trinity Sunday, to Advent. By the rev. Mr. John Gother. Part III. Being the 15th vol. of his spiritual works.* London. 1783. 12°. 542, [6] p. Printed by: Coghlan, J.P. ESTC t196729. * Cha (imp.); E; ECW; Lhe.

1318. Gother, John. *The principles and rules of the gospel, offered for the help of all who desire to live disciples of Jesus Christ. By the rev. Mr. John Gother. Being the eleventh volume of his spiritual works.* London. 1783. 12°. [8], 32 [i.e. 232], [2] p. Printed by: Coghlan, J.P. ESTC t178601. * E; ECW; StD; Ush.
　　Page 232 misnumbered 32.

1319. Gother, John. *The sincere Christian's guide in the choice of religion.* London. 1734. 12°. [8], 196 p. Printed by: Meighan, T. Sold by: Meighan, T. ESTC n023257. * CLU-C; DMR; Lhe; Llp; O.
　　　　Edited by Challoner (see also next 2 items). According to Kirk (p. 102) printed at Peter Giffard's expense.

1320. Gother, John. *The sincere Christian's guide in the choice of religion.* London. 1744. 12°. [6], 198 p. Printed by: Needham, F. Sold by: Needham, F. * Lhe; Map; Sal; Sto.

1321. Gother, John. *The sincere Christian's guide in the choice of religion.* London. 1758. 12°. vi, 197, [1] p. Printed by: Meighan, T. Sold by: Swiney, E. * FLK; MY.

1322. Gother, John. *The sinner's complaints to God: being devout entertainments of the soul with God, fitted for all states and conditions of Christians ... By J.G. author of the Instructions.* London. 1707. 12°. [8], xxxxiv, 514, [6] p. * Do; Ush.

1323. Gother, John. *The sinner's complaint to God: being devout entertainments of the soul with God, fitted for all states and conditions of Christians, whatever their circumstances or necessities be. By J.G.* 1717. 12°. [12], 687, [1] p. * Map.

1324. Gother, John. *The sinner's complaints to God: being devout entertainments of the soul with God, fitted for all states and conditions of Christians ... By J.G. author of the Instructions.* London. 1725. 12°. [8], 587, [5] p. Printed by: Meighan, T. Sold by: Meighan, T. ESTC t174300. * Dt; E; Lhe; P.

1325. Gother, John. *The sinner's complaints to God, being devout entertainments of the soul with God, fitted for all states and conditions of Christians ... By J. G. author of the Instructions.* London. 1737. 12°. 572, [4] p. Printed by: Meighan, T. Sold by: Meighan, T. ESTC t174301. * Do; Hen; O; P; Pci.

1326. Gother, John. *The sinner's complaints to God: being devout entertainments of the soul with God, fitted for all states ... by J. G.* London. 1753. 12°. [3], v-x, [1], 12-572, [4] p. Published by: Meighan, T. ESTC t177200. * DMR; Map; O; StD.

1327. Gother, John. *The sinner's complaints to God: being devout entertainments of the soul with God, fitted for all states and conditions of Christians.* Anon. Birmingham. 1770. 8°. [4], 505, [3] p. Printed by: Holliwell, T. ESTC t104513. * BMp; Do; L.

1328. Gother, John. *The sinner's complaints to God: being devout entertainments of the soul with God, fitted for all states and conditions of Christians.* Dublin. 1774. 12°. xi, [1], 394, [2] p. Printed by: Hoey, J., jun. ESTC t139905. * L.
     With 2 pages of adverts.

1329. Gother, John. *The sinner's complaints to God: being devout entertainments of the soul with God. Fitted for all states and conditions of Christians.* Dublin. 1775. 12°. [2], iv, [10], 13-428 p. Printed by: Ennis, R. ESTC t212624. * Dt (imp.); SIR.
     With a list of subscribers.

1330. Gother, John. *The sinner's complaint to God, being devout entertainments of the soul with God: fitted for all states and conditions of Christians.* Dublin. 1793. 12°. xi, [1], 396 p. Printed by: Wogan, P. ESTC t212613. * Dt; IDA; Yb.

1331. Gother, John. *The spiritual works of the rev. John Gother. Vol. X.* London. 1716. 367, [7] p. * Do; ECW; LO.

1332. Gother, John. *Mr. Gother's spiritual works: in sixteen tomes ... There are added, general indexes and tables to each tome.* 16 vols. London. 1718. 12°. Published by: [Meighan, T.?]. ESTC t186664. * CAL; CaSRU; Do; E; ECW; Lhe; Map; O; P; Pci (imp.); TH; TLP; UGL.
     Edited by William Crathorne, who had been commissioned by Bishop Giffard to edit all the spiritual works of Gother (Kirk, p. 60). CAL, Do, ECW, Map, P, Pci, TLP and UGL are, in varying degrees, incomplete.

1333. Gother, John. *Mr. Gother's spiritual works: in eighteen tomes ... there are added indexes and tables to each tome.* 18 vols. London. [1726?]. 12°. Published by: Meighan, T. ESTC t197900. * C; DoA (- vol. 15); ECW (vols 1, 2, 5, 6, 7); Lhe; P; TxU; Ush.

1334. Gother, John. *The spiritual works of the rev. John Gother.* 16 vols. Newcastle. [1792?]. 12°. Published by: Coates; Keating; Coghlan; Booker (London); Wogan; Cross (Dublin). Sold by: Coates; Keating; Coghlan; Booker (London); Wogan; Cross (Dublin). ESTC t033035. * BB; Cha; Do; DoA; Du; E; ECR; ECW; FU; ICN; ICR; IDA; L; LAM; Lfa; MY; O; Osc; SIR; Stan;

StD; TLP; TxU; UGL; Yb.

> According to Kirk (p. 73) edited by Thomas Eyre. BB, DoA, IDA, L, Stan and Yb are, in varying degrees, incomplete.

1335. Gouvea, Alexandre de. *Relation de l'établissement du Christianisme dans le royaume de Corée, rédigée, en Latin, par Monseigneur de Gouvea Evêque de Pekin ... Traduction sur une copie reçue à Londres le 12 Juillet 1798.* London. 1800. 12°. [2], iii, [1], 37, [1] p. Printed by: le Boussonnier and Co. Sold by: The French booksellers. ESTC t105450. * E; ECW; L.

1336. Grace, George. *A short plea for human nature and common sense. In which it is attempted to state a few general principles for the direction of our judgement of The present state of the Church of Ireland.* Dublin. 1787. 8°. [vi], 2, 56 p. Printed by: Byrne, P. ESTC t077148. * C; Dt; L; Lhl; NNUT; Oc; P.

> *The present state* (Dublin 1787) is by Richard Woodward, Bishop of Cloyne.

1337. Grace, George. *A short plea for human nature and common sense. In which a few general principles are stated to direct the judgement of those who read The present state of the Church of Ireland.* 2nd ed. London. 1787. 8°. viii, 62, [2] p. Printed by: Coughlan [sic], J.P.; Robinsons; Richardson; Faulder; Byrne, P. Sold by: Coughlan [sic], J.P.; Robinsons; Richardson; Faulder; Byrne, P. ESTC n022841. * Lmh; O; Osc; PP; Ush.

> 'Corrected and purged of many errors that had crept into the one published in Dublin: and some additions are made to render it more intelligible to the English reader' (preface, p. 6).

1338. Gracian, Geronymo. *A burning lamp or short compend of Christian perfection [Lámpara encendida.].* Rome. 1731. 16°. xvii, [3], 158, [2] p. Printed by: Peveroni, R. ESTC n015266. * CAL; CaOHM; CLU-C; DAE; Do; ECB; ECR; ECW; Lhe; Sto; TxU.

> In some copies there is a duplicate printing of p. 158 on verso of last leaf.

1339. Gracian, Geronymo. *The burning lamp to enlighten such as truly desire to live a godly life; with meditations, aspirations and other devotions ... By J.W. of the S. of Jesus. Permissu superiorum.* London. 1753. 12°. [16], 164, [2] p. * Amp; ECW.

> 'J.W.' is sometimes identified as John Warner.

1340. Gracian, Geronymo. *The burning lamp to enlighten such as truly desire to live a goldy [sic] life; with meditations, aspirations, and other devotions ... by J.W. of the S. of Jesus.* 2nd ed. London. 1762. 12°. [16], 234 p. * ECW.

1341. Gracian, Geronymo. *The burning lamp to enlighten such as truly desire to live a godly life; with meditations, aspirations and other devotions ... By J.W. of the Society of Jesus.* 3rd ed. Anon. Dublin. 1769. 18°. [16], 164 p. Published by: Walsh, E. ESTC t217763. * Dt (imp).

1342. *Le graduel Romain a l'usage du diocèse de Quebec.* Quebec. 1800. 12°. [12], 431, [1], ccxlv [i.e. ccxliv] p. Printed by: Neilson, J. ESTC w014581. * CaQMBM; CaQMM; CaQQLa; MWA; NN.

> 'Graduel' pp. 1-431; 'Commun des saints' pp. i-cclv. The first example of music printing in Canada.

1343. *Gratitude: a poem on the relief granted to the Roman Catholics of this kingdom. By a member of that communion.* London. 1792. 4°. [4], 11, [1] p. Printed by: Coghlan, J.P. Sold by: Booker; Keating; Lewis; Robinson. * Sto.

1344. Grattan, Henry. *The speech of Henry Grattan, Esq. On the address to his majesty, at the opening of the Irish Parliament, 1792. With an appendix.* London. 1792. 8°. [2], 34, 28 p. Published by: Ridgway, J. ESTC n000198. * BRu; CU-SB; CYc; LU; MB.

> Grattan was not R.C., but this speech was of great importance for the cause of Catholic emancipation in Ireland. The appendix contains declarations and resolutions by the Society of United Irishmen of Dublin, the Catholic Society of Dublin, and the General Committee of Roman Catholics of Ireland. For Grattan see also no. 37ff and no. 2457. For the many other speeches and addresses by Grattan see ESTC.

1345. *The great devotion of the perpetual glorification of the most bd. Trinity upon the verse Glory be to the Father and to the Son, and to the Holy Ghost.* London. 1773. 32°. 32 p. Printed by: Coghlan, J.P. * Ush.

1346. Greene, John Raymond. *To the very reverend most vertuous and most religious sister, mother Anna Busby on her jubily of fifty years in the convent of the English Dominicans, at Brussels, the fifth of June, 1715.* Anon. 1715. 4°. [8] p. * Osc.

> An ode. John Raymond Greene became a Dominican at Bornhem. In 1715 he was at Brussels as confessor to the sisters.

1347. Gregson, Gregory. *The devout miscellany, or the Sunday's companion to the holy mass and vespers; containing the morning and evening service of the Roman Catholic church; the collects, epistles, gospels, &c.* Anon. Leicester. 1790. 8°. vi, 278, [4], lxxvi p. Printed by: Ireland, J. Published by: Booker, T. * CAL; NSPM; Stan.

> For Gregson see Aveling p. 166.

1348. Grostête, Marin. *The truth of the Catholic religion proved from the holy scripture. By Mr des Mahis. Translated from the French.* Newcastle. 1799. 8°. iv, [8], 400 p. Printed by: Walker, E. ESTC t092498. * BB; CLU; Do; E; ECW; Gi; L; LAM; Llp; MChB; NCp; O; Osc; TxU.

> Marin Grostête is Sieur des Mahis. Translated by Bishop William Gibson. Copies have a varying number of preliminary pages.

1349. Grou, Jean-Nicolas. *The characters of real devotion. Translated from the French of l'abbé Grou, by Alexander Clinton [Caractères de la vraie dévotion.].* London. 1791. 8°. [6], 175, [1] p. Printed by: Coghlan, J.P. Sold by: Booker; Keating; Lewis; Robinsons. ESTC t118491. * Do; DoA; E; Gi; L; Lhe; LO; O; OU; Stan; TxU; Ush; WIW.

> 'Alexander Clinton' is Alexander Mackenzie (see also further Grou items).

1350. Grou, Jean-Nicolas. *The characters of real devotion. Translated from the French ... by the rev. Alexander Clinton.* 2nd ed. Dublin. 1795. 12°. [2], viii, [1], 4-158, [2] p. Printed by: Mehain, J.; Cross, R. ESTC t118492. * D; FLK; ICR; IDA; L.

> With a list of subscribers, and final leaf of advertisements.

1351. Grou, Jean-Nicolas. *Méditations en forme de retraite sur l'amour de Dieu: avec un petit ecrit sur le don de soi-même à Dieu.* London. 1796. 12°. [4], 380 p. Printed by: Coghlan, J.P. ESTC t155069. * CAL; DMR; L; Lhe; MoSU-D; O; Stan.

1352. Grou, Jean-Nicolas. *Moral instructions, extracted from the works of the glorious Dr of the church, Saint Augustin. Translated by Alexander Mackenzie [Morale tirée des Confessions de S. Augustin par l'abbé Grou].* 2 vols. Dublin. 1792. 12°. xiv, 150; 167, [1] p. Printed by: Wogan, P. ESTC t180906. * DMR; IDA (vol. 1); LfaA; LOU (2 vols in one); Map; Mil; MnU; NSCH (2 vols in one); O; Ou.

> Mackenzie translated the book while he was chaplain to Thomas Weld at Lulworth Castle. Grou, an old friend and brother Jesuit, joined him there in 1792 after his flight from France (see also next items). With a list of subscribers.

1353. Grou, Jean-Nicolas. *Morality, extracted from the Confessions of Saint Austin. Translated from the French of monsieur l'abbé Grou, by Alexander Clinton.* 2 vols. London. 1791. 8°. xvi, 420; viii, 459, [5] p. Printed by: Coghlan, J.P. Sold by: Booker; Keating; Lewis; Robinsons. ESTC t118944. * CAL; Do; DoA; E; ECB; GEU-T; L; Lhe; LO; Mil; Sto (vol. 1); TxU; Ush (vol. 2); Yb.

1354. Hacket, Andrew. *Catechism or abridgement of Christian doctrine.* [London?]. 1725. 8°. xiv, 167, [1] p. ESTC t192173. * E; Lmh.

> This catechism by Father Andrew Hacket of Drummond Castle near Crieff was condemned by a decree of the Congregation of the Index in 1734 (Anson, p. 199). See also next item.

1355. Hacket, Andrew. *A catechism or abridgment of Christian doctrine for the use of children, and ignorant people.* 2nd ed. 1730. 12°. [2], ii, [4], [1], 127, 15, [1] p. ESTC t192175. * E.

1356. Hamel, Etienne Pierre. *Aux emigrés François discours de consolation extrait de St. Jean Chrysostome, et traduit du Grec; par Estienne Hamel.* London. [1795]. 8°. 43, [1] p. Published by: Author. Sold by: Longman, T. N. ESTC t121284. * C; L.

> Preface dated 'Londres, ee 1er Octa^re, 1795'.

1357. Hamel, Etienne Pierre. *Oraison funèbre de S.E.M. le Cardinal de la Rochefoucauld ... prononcée dans la Chapelle Françoise de St. George's Fields, le 20 novembre.* London. 1800. 8°. 32 p. Printed by: Dulau, A. & Co. * Osc.

1358. Harel, Maximilien-Marie. *The history of the life and writings of Mr Arruet de Voltaire, from a collection published in France, in the year 1781.* Anon. London. 1782. 8°. [2], 74, 41, [1] p. Printed by: Coghlan, J.P. Sold by: Wilkie, G.; Stockdale, J. ESTC t137602. * Amp; ICU; L; MY.

> In two parts with separate pagination. Translation of p. 18-141 of Harel's *Voltaire*, published in 1781.

1359. Harris, Raymund. *An appeal to the public; or, a candid narrative, of the rise and progress of the differences now subsisting in the R...n C...c* *congregation of Liverpool ... with an appendix.* Anon. Liverpool. 1783. 12°. 430 p. ESTC t186001. * C; Gi; LANu; LVp; O; Ush.

> Harris was the assumed name of the Spanish Jesuit Hormasa who settled in England probably in the early 1770s (Gillow III, 392-3).

1360. Harris, Raymund. *Scriptural researches on the licitness of the slave-trade, shewing its conformity with the principles of natural and revealed religion, delineated in the sacred writings of the word of God.* London. 1788. 8°. 77, [1], 14 [i.e. 15], [1] p. Published by: Stockdale, J. ESTC t013518. * C; CaQMM; L; MiU; NHi; NIC; NNC; OClW; OO; P; RP; RPJCB; TxH; ViWC.

> For more eds of this work, which tries to provide a religious justification for the slave trade, see ESTC.

1361. Harris, Raymund. *A sermon on Catholick loyalty to the present government; preached in the Catholick chapel of Liverpool, upon occasion of the late general fast. By Mr. R.H.* [Liverpool]. [1781]. 8°. 16 p. ESTC t197928. * DoA; Lhe; Lu; TLP; Ush.

> Ush suggests [1791]; TLP suggests [c.1773].

1362. Hawarden, Edward. *An answer to Dr. Clark, and Mr. Whiston, concerning the divinity of the Son, and of the Holy Spirit. With a summary account of the chief writers of the three first ages. By H.E.* London. 1729. 8°. [2], xxi, [1], 131, [13] p. Printed by: Roberts, J. Sold by: Roberts, J. ESTC t112968. * BMu; C; Di; E; L; Ldw; Lhe; Lnat; Osc; Ush; Yb.

1363. Hawarden, Edward. *An answer to Dr. Clark, and Mr. Whiston, concerning the divinity of the Son, and of the Holy Spirit. With a summary account of the chief writers of the three first ages. By H.E.* London. 1729. 8°. [2], xxi, [1], 131, [13] p. Published by: Meighan, T. ESTC n005546. * BMu; CLU-C; Do; Dt; ECW; GEU-T; Hen; ICN; LAM; Lhe; MBAt; MdBJ; MRu; NNUT; O; Osc; OKentU; P; Pm; TU; TxU; UGL; Ush; ViU.

> The sheets of the Roberts ed., with a new tp and a larger errata slip.

1364. Hawarden, Edward. *Catholick grounds: or, a summary and rational account of the unchangeable orthodoxy of the Catholick church. By H.E.* [London?]. 1729. 8°. 20 p. ESTC n026731. * BMu; CaOHM; CSmH; Di; Do; E; ECW; ICN; Osc; PP; TxU; Ush.

1365. Hawarden, Edward. *Charity and truth: or, Catholicks not uncharitable in saying, that none are sav'd out of the Catholick communion. Because the rule is not universal. By H.E.* Brussels [London]. 1728. 8°. [2], xviii, 284, [8] p. ESTC t112967. * BB; BMu; C; CLU-C; DMR; Do; DoA; E; FLK; GEU-T; Gi; ICN; InNd; L; Lfa; Lhe; Map; NSPM; O; Osc; P; TH; UGL; Ush.

> The imprint is false; printed in London, probably by J. Roberts. The 'Preface' is dated 'June 28, 1727' (see also next 2 items).

1366. Hawarden, Edward. *Charity and truth: or, Catholicks not uncharitable in saying, that none are sav'd out of the Catholick communion. Because the rule is not universal. By H.E.* [London]. 1728. 8°. [2], xviii, 284, [8] p. Printed by: [Roberts, J.?]. ESTC t199944. * Do; ECB; ECW; L; MiU; Pm; SIR; TLP; TxU; Ush.

With a cancel tp, probably printed by J. Roberts.

1367. Hawarden, Edward. *Charity and truth: or, Catholicks not uncharitable in saying that none are sav'd out of the Catholick communion, because the rule is not universal. By H.E.* 1730. 8°. [2], xviii, 284, [4] p. * Gillow, III, 180.

1368. Hawarden, Edward. *Discourses of religion, between a minister of the Church of England, and a country-gentleman. Wherein the chief points of controversy are briefly discuss'd. By the author of The true church of Christ.* Anon. London. 1716. 12°. xvii, [5], 230 p. ESTC t020919. * ABu; BB; BMu; C; CLU-C; Cm; COA; DAE; DFo; Do; E; ECW; Gi; L; Lfa; Lhe; Lmh; Map; MoSW; O; TH; TLP; TxU; Ush.

1369. Hawarden, Edward. *Four appendixes to the book entitled The true church of Christ &c.* London. 1715. 8°. [5], 328-496, [16] p. ESTC t108650. * Do; DoA; ECW; L; Sto; Ush.
> Sto has pagination [2], 327-496, [16] p. Also published as part of no. 1377 and no. 1378.

1370. Hawarden, Edward. *Postscript: or, a review of the grounds already laid: together with a second and third part of The rule of faith.* Anon. [London]. 1720. 12°. 74, [4], xxiv, [1], 76-344, xxv-xxx, 2 p. ESTC t125392. * ABu; C; CLU-C; Do; Du; E; ECW; L; Lhe; MChB; MY; O; Ou; Sco; Sto; TxDaM-P; TxU; UshL.
> With 2 pages of Meighan adverts. MY lacks the [4] p.

1371. Hawarden, Edward. *The rule of faith briefly consider'd, in a new and easy method, or, a key to controversy.* Anon. 1719. 12°. 65, [1] p. * Osc; UshL.
> UshL has pagination [6], 65, [1] p. An answer to Charles Leslie. See also next 3 items.

1372. Hawarden, Edward. *The rule of faith truly stated, in a new and easy method; or a key to controversy.* Anon. [London]. 1721. 12°. [8], 65, [1] p. Printed by: [Meighan, T.]. ESTC t126203. * ABu; C; CLU-C; Do; Du; E; ECW; L; Lfa; Lhe; MChB; MRu; MY; O; Ou; Sco; Sto; TxU; Ush; UshL.
> Bound up with *Postscript* (no. 1370).

1373. Hawarden, Edward. *The rule of faith truly stated, in a new and easy method; or a key to controversy.* Anon. [London]. 1721. 12°. [4], 344, xxv-xxx, [4] p. Published by: [Meighan, T.]. * DoA; Hen; LO; TH; Yb.
> This is an ed. of the 2nd part of *The rule of faith* (cf. nos 1370 and 1374). With 2 pages of Meighan adverts.

1374. Hawarden, Edward. *The second part of The rule of faith. Wherein the authority of church-guides is stated.* Anon. [London]. [1725?]. 12°. [2], xxiv, 75-344, xxv-xxx, [4] p. Printed by: [Meighan, T.]. ESTC t207613. * E; MY; OKentU; Sco; Sto; Ush.
> With 2 pages of Meighan adverts.

1375. Hawarden, Edward. *Some queries, relating to a book entitled, A compassionate address, to papists, &c in five letters, which the author calls an answer to two popish books.* Anon. [London]. 1717. 8°. 48 p. Published by: Moore, J. ESTC t126246. * BMu; CLU-C; C-S; Dt; E; ECW; InU-Li; L; Lhe;

NNG; O; Osc; Ush.

> A compassionate address is by Francis Hutchinson, Bishop of Down and Connor. The bookseller's name is fictitious. The book is sometimes attributed to Robert Manning. L bound up with Manning's The shortest way (no. 1762).

1376. Hawarden, Edward. *Some remarks on the decree of King Augustus II ... together with an answer to a pamphlet intitled, A faithful and exact narrative of the horrid tragedy lately acted at Thorn ... By H.E.* 1726. 8°. [6], 34 p. Published by: Moore, A. ESTC n022934. * BMu; C-S; Di; E; MWH; Osc.

> According to ESTC the bookseller's name is fictitious. For the eds of A faithful and exact narrative, 1725, see ESTC.

1377. Hawarden, Edward. *The true church of Christ, shewed by concurrent testimonies of scripture, and primitive tradition. In answer to a book, entitled The case stated ... in three parts.* Anon. 2 vols. [London]. 1714-15. 8°. xviii, [12], 293, [9]; xxxv, [21], 496, [14] p. ESTC t108649. * C; Di; Do; Du (vol. 2); E; ECR; ECW; Hor (vol. 1); L; Lfa; Lhe; Map; O (vol. 1); Sal; Sco; Stan (vol. 1); TH; TLP; Ush; UshL.

> The first part is a reply to a book by Charles Leslie (see also next 4 items). Vol. 2 contains the treatises 'Of supremacy' 'Of transubstantiation', and 'Of invocation of the saints', and also Four appendixes (no. 1369).

1378. Hawarden, Edward. *The true church of Christ, shewed by concurrent testimonies of scripture and primitive tradition. Part III.* London. 1715. 8°. xxxv, [11], 323, [1] p. * ECW; Hor.

> Together with Four appendixes (no. 1369) this work was also issued as the 2nd part of no. 1377 and as no. 1380.

1379. Hawarden, Edward. *The true church of Christ, shewed by concurrent testimonies of scripture and primitive tradition. In answer to a book, entitled The case stated, ... in three parts.* 2 vols. London. 1715. 8°. xviii, [12], 293, [9]; xxxv, [12], 247, [1] p. Printed by: Meighan, T. Sold by: Meighan, T. ESTC t108648. * Do; E (vol. 2); ECW (vol. 1); L; O; Osc; UGL; Ush.

> A reissue of part of no. 1377; tp partly reset.

1380. Hawarden, Edward. *The true church of Christ, shewed by concurrent testimonies of scripture and primitive tradition. Part III.* London. 1715. 8°. xxxv, [11], 496, [22] p. Printed by: Meighan, T. Sold by: Meighan, T. * ECW; FLK.

> See notes to nos 1369, 1377 and 1378. FLK has pagination xxxv, [21], 496, [16].

1381. Hawarden, Edward. *The true church of Christ, shewed by concurrent testimonies of scripture and primitive tradition. In answer to a book, entitled The case stated ... In three parts.* 2nd ed. [London]. 1738. 8°. xviii, [8], 293, [9] p. ESTC t105578. * C; Do; Du; E; ECW; Hor; L; Lhe; Sal; TLP; Ush.

> With 2 pages of Meighan adverts.

1382. Hawarden, Edward. *Wit against reason: or, the Protestant champion, the great, the incomparable Chillingworth, not invulnerable. Being a treatise ... By H.E.* Brussels [London]. 1735. 8°. xlvii, [1], 131, [1] p. ESTC t112969. * BB; BMu; CLU-C; Do; DoA; Du; E; ECW; L; LfaA; Lhe; Llp; Map; MY; NNUT;

O; Osc; Sal; StD; TxU; UGL; Ush; UshL.

With one page of adverts for Hawarden books, lacking in MY.

1383. Hawkins, Thomas. *A view of the real power of the pope, and of the power of the priesthood over the laity. With an account how they use it. By T.H. Esq.* London. 1733. 8°. vi, 169, [1], iv, 171-510, [8] p. ESTC t072540. * CLU-C; CYc; Dt; E; EXu; L; Lhe; O.

Hawkins was R.C. but he took up an extremely anti-papal point of view.

1384. Hay, George. *An abridgement of Roman Catholic doctrine, both as to faith and morals, extracted from The sincere and devout Christians: by the author of those works.* Edinburgh. 1795. 12°. 99, [1] p. Printed by: Moir, J. ESTC t188038. * Do; E; ECR; Lhe; O; P; Yb.

Extracted from *The sincere Christian instructed* and *The devout Christian instructed* by George Hay.

1385. Hay, George. *An abridgment of the Christian doctrine. By Bishop Hay.* Philadelphia. 1800. 12°. 152 p. Published by: Carey, M. ESTC w000643. * DGU.

1386. Hay, George. *An answer to Mr W.A.D.'s letter to G.H. in which the conduct of government, in mitigating the penal laws against papists, is justified.* Edinburgh. 1778. 12°. 151, [1] p. Printed by: Ruddiman, W. & T. Sold by: Elliot, C. ESTC n030398. * CLU-S/C; E; ECW (- tp); Lhe; Osc; Ush.

A reply by Hay to William Abernethy Drummond's *The lawfulness of breaking faith with heretics*, 1778 (see also next item). Another ed. of this work was published as *Roman Catholic fidelity* (no. 1416).

1387. Hay, George. *An answer to Mr. W.A.D.'s letter to G.H. in which the conduct of government, in mitigating penal laws against papists, is justified.* 2nd ed. Dublin repr. [Edinburgh]. 1779. 8°. iv, 180 p. Published by: Wogan; Bean & Co. ESTC t127648. * D; Di; Du; L; Lhe; MY; SIR.

1388. Hay, George. *De gravissima villicationis nostrae ratione.* [Aberdeen]. 1794. 4°. 4 p. * Bevan (Advent 1993, no. 192).

An exhortation on the duties of priesthood. The other authors are Hay's colleagues John Geddes and John Chisholm.

1389. Hay, George. *A detection of the dangerous tendency, both for Christianity and Protestancy, of a sermon, said to be preached before an assembly of divines, by G.C.D.D. on the spirit of the gospel.* London. 1771. 8°. [4], 176 p. Published by: Aletheian Club. Sold by: Coghlan, J.P. ESTC t201426. * E; ECW; Lhe; SCA; TH; Ush.

Date is given as 'MDCCLXXI(I)'. Signed 'Staurophilus', i.e. George Hay. An attack on George Campbell's *The spirit of the gospel*. See the Coghlan correspondence in LANre (letter 6 Jan. 1772).

1390. Hay, George. *The devout Christian instructed in the faith of Christ, from the written word.* 2 vols. Dublin. 1795. 12°. x, 422; [2], ii, 351, [1] p. Printed by: Wogan, P. * ECR; ICRL; PV; Sco.

1391. Hay, George. *The devout Christian instructed in the law of Christ from the written word. Being a sequel to The sincere Christian instructed in the faith of*

Christ. 2 vols. London. 1783. 12°. [2], 422; [2], 351, [1] p. Published by: Coghlan, J.P. Sold by: Coghlan, J.P. ESTC t099316. * Do; DoA (vol. 2); E; L; Lhe; Sal; Sco (vol. 1); TxU; Ush; Yb.

1392. Hay, George. *The devout Christian instructed in the law of Christ from the written word. Being a sequel to The sincere Christian instructed in the faith of Christ.* 2 vols. Dublin. 1784. 12°. x, 3-422; [2], 351, [1] p. Printed by: Wogan, P. * FLK; IDA; SCR.

1393. Hay, George. *An explanation of the litanies of the holy name of Jesus, of the Blessed Virgin Mary ... By the right reverend George, Bishop of Daulis, V A N B.* London. 1791. 12°. 12 p. Printed by: Coghlan, J.P. ESTC n047843. * Amp; MoU; Ush.

1394. Hay, George. *Explanatory remarks on the dialogue between Philalethes and Benevolus, against the Appendix to the scripture doctrine of miracles.* Anon. Edinburgh. 1776. 12°. [2], 96 p. Sold by: Elliot, C. ESTC t187572. * DCU; E; O; Sal; SCA.
Written in reply to William Abernethy Drummond (cf. nos 1386 and 1387).

1395. Hay, George. *An explication of the holy sacrifice of the mass; by G.H. ... To which is added, Instructions and devotions for confession, communion, and confirmation. By Mr. John Gother.* London. 1779. 12°. [2], 72, 114, [4] p. Printed by: Coghlan, J.P. ESTC t200648. * Amp; ECW; Gi; Llp; Osc; Sal; TH.
'Instructions and devotions' has separate pagination.

1396. Hay, George. *G.D.V.A. To all the faithfull both clergy and laity ... There is nothing about which the church of Christ has at all times been more solicitous ... with regard to the holy sacrament of marriage.* [1780]. 12°. 11, [1] p. * E (2); SCA (2).
SCA and E each have a variant with the heading in ms.

1397. Hay, George. *G**** by the mercy of God, and the favour of the H*** S** B***** of D*****, and V***** A******* in S*******. To all the clergy under his jurisdiction, both secular and regular, health and benediction.* [Edinburgh?]. [1780]. 8°. 3-96 p. ESTC t203564. * E; SCA.
In SCA Hay signs himself 'G... B... of D..., and V... A... in S...'

1398. Hay, George. *George, Bishop of Daulia, John, Bishop of Oria, & John, Bishop of Morocco, Catholic bishops in Scotland. To all the faithful, clergy and laity, under their charge.* [Edinburgh?]. [1793]. 8°. 3, [1] p. * FK; SCA; WDA.
Dated and signed 'Edin. 12 July 1793. Geo. Daulien V.A., John Orien, V.A., John Morochien V.A.C.'.

1399. Hay, George. *George, Bishop of Daulia, To all the faithful, both clergy and laity, under his charge. Health & benediction from our Lord. Dearly beloved in Christ ... in which all Europe is at present.* [Edinburgh]. [1794]. 8°. 4 p. * SCA.
Dated and signed 'Edin. 15 Feb. 1794. Geo. B. of Daulia'. Request for public prayers in all Catholic chapels.

1400. Hay, George. *George, Bishop of Daulia, vicar-apostolic, &c. John, Bishop of Oria, vicar-apostolic, &c. John, Bishop of Morocco, coadjutor. To all the*

faithful, clergy and laity, under their charge. [Edinburgh]. [1798]. fol. iii, [1] p.
ESTC n045154. * LANre; Lpro; SCA.

> Dated 'Edin. 7 May 1798'. Imploring divine protection against the enemy.

1401. Hay, George. *George, Bishop of Daulis, vic. ap. and John, Bishop of Morocco, his coadjutor. To all the faithful committed to our care, health and benediction. Dearly beloved in Christ.* [1797]. fol. [2] p. * SCA; Sto.

> Signed and dated 'Geo. Bp of Daulis & Jo. Bp. of Morocco. Aberdeen, February 24, 1797'. This concerns the dissolution of the British colleges in France. See also next 2 items.

1402. Hay, George. *George, Bishop of Daulis, vic. ap. and John, Bishop of Morocco, his coadjutor. To all the faithful committed to our care, health and benediction.* [Aberdeen?]. [1797]. 4°. s.s. * WDA.

> Dated 'Aberdeen, February 24, 1797'.

1403. Hay, George. *George, Bishop of Daulis, vic. ap. and John, Bishop of Morocco, his coadjutor. To all the faithful committed to our care, health and benediction. Dearly beloved in Christ, you will all have heard.* [Aberdeen?]. [1797]. 4°. [4] p. * SCA.

> Dated 'Aberdeen, February 24, 1797'.

1404. Hay, George. *Instructiones ad munera apostolica rite obeunda perutiles missionibus S... accommodatae.* Rome. 1782. 12°. 88 p. * E; Sco.

> A revision by the Scottish bishops of Bishop Nicholson's 'Statuta missionis' of 1700; signed and dated '12 July 1781. G. Daulien [G. Hay], A. Polemon [A. MacDonald], J. Maroch [J. Geddes]'.

1405. Hay, George. *Letters on usury, and interest, shewing the advantage of loans for the support of trade & commerce.* London. 1774. 12°. [14], 144 p. Printed by: Coghlan, J.P. Sold by: Snagg, R.; Drummond, W. (Edinburgh). ESTC t063766. * ABu; BMu; C; C-S; CtHT-W; E; KyU; L; Lhe; MdBJ; MH-BA; MRu; NNC; OkU; SCA.

> These 7 letters were originally published separately in the *Edinburgh Weekly Magazine* (see Gordon, pp. 125-6).

1406. Hay, George. *Memorial for the suffering Catholics, in a violent persecution for religion at present carried on in one of the Western Isles of Scotland.* [Edinburgh]. [1771]. 12°. 11, [1] p. ESTC t173996. * CaQMM; E; ECW; Ush; WDA.

> Signed and dated 'Geo. of Doulis [sic], Coadjr. Edinburgh, 27th Nov. 1771'. The island was South Uist and the oppressive landlord Macdonald of Boysdale. According to Burton (II, 154) Challoner had Hay's manuscript printed at his own expense.

1407. Hay, George. *A pastoral address to the Roman Catholics of Scotland.* Edinburgh. 1798. 12°. 12 p. Printed by: Moir, J. Published by: Creech, W; Bell; Bradefute; Hill, P.; Cheyne, S. ESTC t206833. * E; SCA; Sto.

> A warning and an exhortation to guard against the advance of paganism in the wake of the French Revolution.

1408. Hay, George. *Pastoral letter from the Bishop of Daulis to his flock, on occasion of a persecution being raised against them.* [Edinburgh?]. 1779. 12°. 7,

[1] p. ESTC t197511. * E; SCA.

>Dated and signed 'February 8, 1779 Geo. Daulien'. This pastoral letter was reprinted by W. Gray in 1779, together with a Protestant reaction (ESTC t206869).

1409. Hay, George. *A pastoral letter from the Bishop of Daulis to his flock, on occasion of a persecution being raised against them.* [London]. [1779]. fol. 2 p. Printed by: Coghlan, J.P. ESTC t197510. * BAA (imp.); Gu; LANre; SCA; Ush.

>Dated and signed 'February 8, 1779. Geo. Daulien'.

1410. Hay, George. *The pious Christian instructed in the nature and practice of the principal exercises of piety used in the Catholic church: being a third part to The sincere and devout Christians.* Anon. London. 1786. 12°. xii, 474, [2] p. Published by: Coghlan, J.P. Sold by: Coghlan, J.P. ESTC t196528. * E; Lhe; O; TH.

1411. Hay, George. *The pious Christian instructed in the nature and practice of the principal exercises of piety used in the Catholic church, being a third part to The sincere and devout Christian.* Anon. Dublin. 1788. 12°. [6], xii, 512 p. Printed by: Wogan, P. ESTC t206595. * D; Do; FLK(2); IDA.

>Do and one FLK copy have 4, xvi, 512 p.

1412. Hay, George. *The pious Christian instructed in the nature & practice of the principal exercises of piety used in the Catholic church being a third part to The sincere and devout Christian.* Anon. Dublin. 1789. 12°. [2], xvi, 512 p. Printed by: Wogan, P. ESTC t127676. * D; L; NSPM.

1413. Hay, George. *The pious Christian instructed in the nature and practice of the principal exercises of piety used in the Catholic church being a third part to The sincere and devout Christians.* Anon. Edinburgh. 1795. 12°. xii, 367 [i.e. 365], [1] p. Printed by: Moir, J. ESTC t172415. * Do; E; ECR; Lhe; O; P; Sal; Yb.

1414. Hay, George. *The pious Christian instructed, in the nature and practice of the principal exercises of piety, used in the Catholic church.* Philadelphia. 1800. 12°. xii, 299, [1] p. Printed by: Carey, J. Published by: Carey, M. ESTC w027630. * DGU-W; MWA; PU.

>Page 293 misnumbered 193. In imprint 'By James Carey, Nov. 10, 1800'.

1415. Hay, George. *Regulations for the administration of the college of Aquhorties.* Anon. Edinburgh. 1799. 12°. [3], 4-57, [1] p. Printed by: Moir, J. ESTC t168773. * E; Sco.

1416. Hay, George. *Roman Catholic fidelity to Protestants ascertained; or, an answer to Mr. W.A.D.'s letter to G.H. in which the conduct of government, in mitigating the penal laws against papists, is justified.* 2nd ed. London. 1779. 12°. iv, 151, [i.e. 150], [2] p. Printed by: Coghlan, J.P. Published by: Coghlan, J.P. Sold by: Wilkie, J. (Edinburgh); Elliot, C. (Edinburgh). ESTC t128040. * CSt; Do; DoA; E; InU-Li; L; Lfa; Lhe; Map; O; Osc; PcA; PP; SCA; Sto; TxU.

>For the 1st ed. see no. 1386.

1417. Hay, George. *The scripture doctrine of miracles displayed: in which their nature their different kinds, their possibility ... are impartially examined and explained, according to the light of revelation.* 2 vols. London. 1775. 12°. vii, [1], 422; iii, [1], 389, [1] p. Sold by: Coghlan, J.P. ESTC t065963. * C; CaOTU; DAE; DUN (vol. 2); E; ECR; ECW (vol. 1, imp.); Gi; ICR; L; Lhe; MdBJ; P; Pm; Sco; TH; Ush; Yb.

1418. Hay, George. *The scripture doctrine of miracles displayed: in which their nature &c. are impartially examined.* 2 vols. Dublin. 1789. 12°. [2], vi, [2], 345, [1]; [4], 318 p. Printed by: Wogan, P. ESTC t172591. * Do; Dt; Du; DUN; E; ECR; FLK(2); IDA; Mil (vol. 2); MY; RPPC; Sco (vol. 1); SIR.

> Published by subscription. Vol. 1 of one FLK copy has [2], vi, 345, [3] p.; vol. 1 of ECR and the other FLK copy have [12], ii-vi, [2], 345, [1] p. (the preliminary pages include adverts for Wogan).

1419. Hay, George. *The sincere Christian instructed in the faith of Christ from the written word.* Anon. 2 vols. London. 1781. 12°. viii, 405, [1]; iv, 376, [2] p. Published by: Coghlan, J.P. Sold by: Coghlan, J.P. ESTC t207313. * E; ECR (vol. 2); P; Sco.

> The preface states: 'The view I have had in this present work, is to assist the most unlearned; and ... to conduct the reader step by step through the whole body of the truths of revelation' (see also next 4 items).

1420. Hay, George. *The sincere Christian instructed in the faith of Christ from the written word.* Anon. 2 vols. Dublin. 1783. 12°. Published by: Wogan, P. ESTC t199262. * Do (vol. 2); E; O; Osc; Stan; TxU.

1421. Hay, George. *The sincere Christian instructed in the faith of Christ, from the written word.* Anon. 2 vols. Dublin. 1791. 12°. [2], viii, 427, [1]; iv, 396 p. Printed by: Wogan, P. * FLK (2); Lhe.

> Vol. 2 of the second FLK copy has [2], 396 p.

1422. Hay, George. *The sincere Christian instructed in the faith of Christ from the written word.* Anon. 2 vols. Edinburgh. 1793. 12°. xi, [2], 12-402, [2] p. (vol. 1). Printed by: Moir, J. ESTC t174234. * E; Ldw; Lhe; Osc; Sal; TLP (vol. 1); Ush (vol. 1); Yb.

1423. Hay, George. *The sincere Christian instructed in the faith of Christ from the written word.* Anon. 2 vols. Dublin. [1793?]. 12°. [2], viii, 7-368 p. (vol. 1). Published by: Jones, W. * FLK (vol. 1).

1424. Heads. *Heads of a bill for the relief of his majesty's Roman Catholic subjects of the kingdom of Ireland, and for other purposes.* London. [1778]. fol. [2] p. Printed by: Coghlan, J.P. * SCA; Sto; WDA.

1425. Heigham, John. *The touch-stone of the reformed gospel: wherein the principal heads and tenets of the Protestant doctrine ... are briefly refuted.* London. 1737. 12°. 112, 3, [1] p. * Do.

> Usually attributed to Matthew Kellison. On Heigham's authorship see Allison, p. 226ff.

1426. Henry VIII. *Assertio septem sacramentorum; or, a defence of the seven sacraments, against Martin Luther ... To which are adjoined, his epistle to the* *pope. The oration of Mr. John Clark.* 1st Irish ed. Dublin. 1766. 12°. xli, [7], 37-190 p. Printed by: Byrn, J. ESTC t137162. * AzTeS; C; Csj; CSmH; D; DFo; Dt; FLK; ICU; IDA; KU-S; L; Lhl; Mil; MRu; MY.

> Translated from the Latin ed. by Thomas Webster. With a list of subscribers. See no. 1460 for another ed.

1427. Herbert, Lucy. *A method of hearing mass, for the souls in purgatory.* Bruges. 1790. 8°. 88 p. Printed by: Moor, C. de. * ECB; Lhe; Yb.

> ECB bound up with no. 1434.

1428. Herbert, Lucy. *Motives to excite us to the frequent meditation of our saviour's passion.* Bruges. 1742. 8°. 114 p. Printed by: [Cock, J. de]. * Do; Lhe; Ush.

> Also published as part 2 of no. 1433.

1429. Herbert, Lucy. *Motives to excite us to the frequent meditation of our saviour's passion.* [London?]. 1791. 12°. 110 p. * Do; DoA; ECB.

> Also published as part 2 of no. 1435.

1430. Herbert, Lucy. *Several excellent methods of hearing mass ... Several methods and practices of devotion appertaining to a religious life.* Bruges. 1722. 8°. 128, [2], 195, [5] p. Printed by: Cock, J. de. * ECB.

> Part 1 is another issue of no. 1431; part 2 is also found published separately (cf. no. 1437ff).

1431. Herbert, Lucy. *Several excellent methods of hearing mass ... as also several other practises of devotion appertaining to a religious life collected together.* Bruges. 1722. 8°. 128, 40, [2] p. Printed by: Cock, J. de. ESTC t115670. * CLU-C; DMR; ECB; Gi; Hen; L; Lhe (part 1); Map; MH-H; O; TxU; Ush.

> The second part has a drop-head title 'Meditation for each Sunday of the month'.

1432. Herbert, Lucy. *Several excellent methods of hearing mass with fruit and benefit according to the institution of that divine sacrifice and the intention of our holy mother the church.* Bruges. 1732. 8°. Printed by: Cock, J. de. * Osc.

> Part II, 'Motives to excite us to the frequent meditation of our Saviour's passion', has a separate pagination.

1433. Herbert, Lucy. *Several excellent methods of hearing mass with fruit & benefit according to the institution of that divine sacrifice ... with motives to induce all good Christians.* Bruges. 1742. 8°. 140, [2], 114 p. Printed by: Cock, J. de. ESTC t123678. * AWn; CAL; CLU-C; DMR; Do; ICN; L; Lfa; Stan; TH; TxU; Ush.

1434. Herbert, Lucy. *Several excellent methods of hearing mass with fruit & benefit according to the institution of that divine sacrifice and the intention of our holy mother the church.* Bruges. 1790. 8°. 128, [2], 199, [5] p. Printed by: Moor, C. de. ESTC t127655. * E; ECB; L; Lhe; LO; LOU; Stan; TxU; Yb.

> ECB bound with no. 1427.

1435. Herbert, Lucy. *Several excellent methods of hearing mass, with fruit and benefit, according to the institution of that divine sacrifice, and the intention of* *our holy mother the church.* [York?]. 1791. 12°. 140, [2], 110 p. ESTC t127654. * BB; CAL; DAE; Do; DoA; Dt; Du; FK; L; Lhe; Llp; LO; Stan; TLP; TxDaM-P; TxU; Ush; Yb.

> FK bound up with no. 1441. Lhe suggests York as place of publication.

1436. Herbert, Lucy. *Several excellent methods of hearing mass with fruit & benefit according to the institution of that divine sacrifice and the intention of our holy mother the church.* Bruges. 1792. 8°. 237, [5] p. Printed by: Cock, J. de. * DMR.

1437. Herbert, Lucy. *Several methods and practises of devotion: appartaining [sic] to a religious life.* Bruges. 1743. 8°. [2], 237, [5] p. Printed by: de Cock, J. widow of. ESTC t115446. * CAL; Do; ICN; L; Lfa; LO; O; Ush (2).

> The final leaf contains 'A prayer for our King, and countrey', lacking in one Ush copy.

1438. Herbert, Lucy. *Several methods and practises of devotion: appartaining [sic] to a religious life. Collected together by the richt [sic] honourable Lady Lucy Herbert of Powis.* Bruges. 1764. 8°. [2], 237, [3] p. Printed by: Roose, P. ESTC n034954. * CAL; DMR; ECB; Gi; Lhe; Stan (imp.); TxU; Ush; Yb.

1439. Herbert, Lucy. *Several methods and practices of devotion appertaining to a religious life. Collected together by the right honourable Lady Lucy Herbert.* Bruges. 1789. 8°. [2], 233, [5] p. Printed by: de Moor, C. de. ESTC n045853. * Do; ECB; Gi; Lhe; Nijm; TxDaM-P.

1440. Herbert, Lucy. *Several methods and practices of devotion: appertaining to a religious life. Collected together by the right hon. Lady Lucy Herbert.* Bruges. 1790. 8°. 128, [2], 199, [2] p. Printed by: de Moor, C. ESTC t178283. * Lhe.

1441. Herbert, Lucy. *Several methods and practices of devotion: appertaining to a religious life.* [York?]. 1791. 12°. 245, [5] p. ESTC t127656. * AWn; BB; DAE; DMR; Do; DoA; Du; ECB; FK; FU; L; Lfa; Lhe; Llp; Stan; TxU; Ush; Yb.

> Do bound up with first part of no. 1435. FK bound up with no. 1435. Lhe suggests York as place of publication.

1442. Herge, Urbain René de. *Lettre pastorale de monseigneur l'Evèque de Dol, vicaire apostolique de St. Siège.* [London?]. [1795]. 4°. 3, [1] p. ESTC t123894. * L; Lpro.

1443. *Heures Romaines en gros caractère, contenant les offices de la Sainte Vierge et des morts pour l'usage des congréganistes.* Quebec. 1795. 12°. 7, [2]-371, [4] p. Published by: Neilson, J. * CaOTP; CaQQLa.

1444. *High mass, and Sundays vespers, as sung in the parish chapels of the R.C. archdiocess of Cashell.* Dublin. 1799. 12°. iv, 5-96 p. Printed by: Wogan, P. ESTC t204914. * D; FLK; IDA; Ush.

1445. *Histoire abregee des evenemens extraordinaires et miraculeux arrives a Jerusalem a la mort, ou dormition, de la Sainte Vierge, suivant la tradition apostolique.* [Quebec?]. 1797. 8°. 28 p. ESTC w038853. * CaQMBM; CSL.

> The author, who signs himself 'M***, prestre Français', shows that the

misfortunes of France are the inevitable result of the French philosophers' treatment of religion.

1446. Hodgson, Ralph. *A dispassionate narrative of the conduct of the English clergy in receiving from the French king ... the administration of the college of St. Omer ... by a layman.* Anon. London [i.e. Newcastle]. 1768. 8°. viii, 155, [1] p. ESTC t201800. * DAE; E; ECR; ECW; Osc; Ush; WDA.

1447. Hoey, P. *A plain and concise method of learning the Gregorian note: also a collection of church music, selected from the Roman antiphonary and gradual. By the rev. P. Hoey.* Dublin. 1800. 12°. iv, 186, [2] p. Printed by: Wogan, P. ESTC t110789. * D; Dt; L; MY; O.

> R4 is signed A3. Pages 49-60 are a cancel gathering in heavier and dissimilar type. Page 49 misnumbered 4.

1448. *The holy bible translated from the Latin Vulgat ... first published by the English College at Doway, Anno 1609. Newly revised, and corrected, according to the Clementin edition of the scriptures.* 4 vols. [Dublin?]. 1750. 12°. [4], 407 (i.e. 507), [1]; 492; 484; 411 (i.e. 511), [1] p. ESTC t107533. * AR; C; Cha; DAE; Do; DoA; Dt; E; ECB; ECR; FLK (vol. 1); Hen; Hor; L; Lfa; Lhe; LO; O; Osc; Stan; Sto; TLP; TxU; Ush; Yb.

> O.T. and Apocrypha only, as revised by Challoner. Sometimes (e.g. Osc) with an extra vol. 5, being either the 2nd ed. (1750) or the 3rd ed. (1752) of Challoner's N. T. (nos 1948, 1949). D & M 1089.

1449. *The holy bible translated from the Latin Vulgat ... first published by the English College at Doway ... Newly revised, and corrected, according to the Clementin edition of the scriptures.* 5 vols. [Dublin?]. 1763-64. 12°. Sold by: [Fitzsimons, R.] ESTC t093000. * D; Du; IDA (vols 1, 4); L; MRu; O; TLP.

> 2nd ed. of Challoner's revision of the Douai O.T. and 4th ed. of his revision of the Rheims N.T. (no. 0994). Vols 2-5 are dated 1764. With a list of subscribers in vol. 1. Bookseller's name from advert in IDA. D & M 1165. See also Brady, p. 113.

1450. *A new translation of the holy bible ... containing the books of Genesis and Exodus. And part of Leviticus. By the rev. Alexander Geddes. Vol I.* London. 1790. 4°. [2], 200 p. Printed by: Davis, J. Published by: Translator. Sold by: Faulder, R.; Johnson, J.; Author. ESTC t181757. * E; Omc.

> A prospectus had been issued in 1786; two further vols of Alexander Geddes's translation were published in 1792 and 1797 (no. 1453), but the work remained incomplete.

1451. *The holy bible, translated from the Latin Vulgate: diligently compared with the Hebrew, Greek and other editions, in divers languages; and first published by the English College at Doway, anno 1609.* Philadelphia. 1790. 4°. viii, 487, [1], 490 [i.e. 494] p. Printed by: Carey, Stewart, and Co. Sold by: Carey, Stewart, and Co. ESTC w038299. * CtHT-W; CtY; DGU-W; MdE; MWA; NN; NNStJ; PU.

> Two vols bound in one. The first American ed. of the Douai translation. D & M 1343.

1452. *The holy bible translated from the Latin Vulgat: diligently compared with* *the Hebrew, Greek and other editions in divers languages. The old testament first published.* 5th ed. Dublin. 1791. 4°. [14], 998, [2], 272, [12] p. Printed by: Fitzpatrick, H. Published by: Cross, R. ESTC t183577. * DoA; Lhe; MY; NBi; NSPM; O; Ush.

> Two vols bound in one. N.T. has separate tp, pagination and signatures. With a list of subscribers. A reissue of Challoner's revision edited by Bernard MacMahon (see also nos 1455 and 1953) with an approbation by John Thomas Troy.

1453. *The holy bible, or the books accounted sacred by Jews and Christians, otherwise called the books of the old and new covenants; faithfully translated ... by Alexander Geddes.* 2 vols. London. 1792-97. 4°. Printed by: Davis, J. Published by: Geddes, A. Sold by: Faulder, R.; Johnson, J. ESTC t095062. * AWu; BMp; C; Cj; Csj; Dt; Du; DUc; E; GOT; Gu; L; Ldw; Lhe; Ljc; MRp; MRu; ScCR.

> D & M 1416. See also nos 960 and 1450.

1454. *The holy bible, translated from the Latin Vulgat: diligently compared with the Hebrew, Greek and other editions in divers languages, and first published at Doway, 1609.* Manchester. 1793. fol. 954 p. Published by: Radford, R. * Osc.

> D & M 1374.

1455. *The holy bible, translated from the Latin Vulgat ... The old testament, first published ... at Doway, A.D. 1609. And the new testament, first published ... at Rhemes A.D. 1582.* 6th ed. Dublin. 1794. fol. [10], 785, [1], [2], 220, [8] p. Printed by: Reilly, J. Published by: Reilly, J. ESTC t095037. * D; DoA; E; Gu; L; MY.

> Two vols bound in one. With a list of subscribers. D & M 1385. See also no. 1958.

1456. *The holy bible translated from the Latin Vulgate: diligently compared with the Hebrew, Greek and other editions in diverse languages. And first published ... at Douay , anno 1609.* 4 vols. Edinburgh. 1796. 12°. [4], 507, [1]; 492; 484; 511, [1] p. Printed by: Moir, J. ESTC t166044. * DoA; Du; E; ECR (vols 1-3); Gi; Lfa; Lhe; LO; NSPM; NSPN; O; Osc; PcA; TLP; Ush.

> O.T. and Apocrypha only, as revised by Challoner. Lhe and NSPM were issued together with the 1797 N.T. (no. 1960). Published under the inspection of George Hay. D & M 1408.

1457. *The holy mass, in Latin and English.* [London?]. [1730?]. 8°. 40 p. ESTC t214749. * Lmh.

> Lmh bound with *The office for the dead* (no. 2005).

1458. *The holy mass in Latin and English.* Liverpool. 1789. 12°. 38 p. Printed by: Wosencroft, C. Sold by: Wosencroft, C. * UGL.

> Bound up with nos 1530 and 1812.

1459. Hornyold, John Joseph. *Ad animi mei anxietatem.* 1756. 12°. 19, [1] p. * Osc; UshA.

> A pastoral letter, dated '16 Octobris, 1756'.

1460. Hornyold, John Joseph. *The commandments and sacraments explained: in fifty-two discourses. By J.H. To which is added ... K. Henry the VIIIth's defence* *of the seven sacraments ... Faithfully translated ... by T.W.* 2 vols. Dublin. 1770. 12°. [10], 340; [2], viii, 4, 368 p. Published by: Cross, R. ESTC n044556. * FLK; NNUT; Stan (vol. 2).

Published by subscription. See also no. 1426.

1461. Hornyold, John Joseph. *The decalogue explain'd, in thirty-two discourses on the ten commandments. By J- H- C.A-D.S.* London. 1744. 8°. viii, 406, [2] p. Published by: Author. Sold by: Needham, F. ESTC t186675. * Do; ICN; Lfa; Lhe; NcD; TxU.

With 2 pages of Needham adverts.

1462. Hornyold, John Joseph. *The decalogue explain'd, in thirty-two discourses on the ten commandments.* Anon. Dublin. 1746. 12°. [8], 340 p. Published by: Bowes, P. ESTC t184044. * D; FLK.

With some adverts. Published by subscription.

1463. Hornyold, John Joseph. *The decalogue explain'd, in thirty-two discourses on the ten commandments. By J.H., C.A.D.S.* London. 1750. 12°. viii, 9-430, [6] p. Published by: Author. Sold by: Needham, F. ESTC t070370. * BB; Do; DoA; E; L; Lhe; MRu; O; Osc; TxU.

With 4 pages of Needham adverts, lacking in Do.

1464. Hornyold, John Joseph. *The decalogue explain'd in thirty-two discourses on the ten commandments. By J-H-. C.A.D.S.* 3rd ed. Dublin. 1751. 12°. [10], 340 p. Published by: Bowes, P. ESTC t209632. * Di; FLK.

Published by subscription (the subscription list differs from that in no. 1462, the 1746 ed.). Gillow (III, 402) also mentions a London 1770 ed.

1465. Hornyold, John Joseph. *The decalogue explain'd, in thirty-two discourses on the ten commandments. By J. Hornyhold, C.A-D.S.* Liverpool. 1791. 8°. iv, 420 p. Printed by: Johnson, T. ESTC t186677. * Do; ECW; Gi; Lhe; Ush.

1466. Hornyold, John Joseph. *The grounds of the Christian's belief; or the apostles creed explained; in a concise, easy and familiar manner. In twenty-three moral discourses. By J... H..., C.A.D.S.* Birmingham. 1771. 8°. xv, [1], 345, ii, [1] p. Printed by: Holliwell, J.; Coghlan, J.P. Sold by: Holliwell, J.; Coghlan, J.P. ESTC t124685. * BMp; BMu; C; CaQMMD; CLU-C; CSmH; Do; DoA; E; ECW; FU; Hor; L; Lfa; Lhe; O; Osc; Pm; Sal; TLP; Ush.

1467. Hornyold, John Joseph. *A pastoral instruction with regulations for Lent, 1772.* [1772]. 8°. 8 p. * DowA.

Signed in ms at end 'Joannes Philomeliensis'.

1468. Hornyold, John Joseph. *The real principles of Catholicks: or, a catechism for the adult. Explaining the principal points of the doctrine and ceremonies of the Catholick church. By J-H-C.A-D.S.* London. 1749. 8°. [1], viii, [9-15], 16-383, [9] p. Published by: Meighan, T. ESTC t106884. * BB; C; CLU-C; Csj; DAE; Do; DoA; Du; E; ECW; Gi; ICN; L; Lfa; LfaA; Lhe; Llp; Map; MRu; MWH; NcD; O; Sal; Stan; TH; TLP; TxU; Ush.

With 2 pages of Meighan adverts.

1469. Hornyold, John Joseph. *The real principles of Catholicks, or a catechism for the adult.* Dublin. 1750. 12°. x, [8], 11-344, [8] p. Printed by: Bowes, P.

Published by: Bowes, P. ESTC t168335. * D; SIR.
Published by subscription.

1470. Hornyold, John Joseph. *The real principles of Catholicks: or, a catechism for the adult. Explaining the principal points of the doctrine and ceremonies of the Catholick church. By J-H.C.A-D.S.* Dublin. 1773. 12°. [6], 342, [8] p. Published by: Wogan, P. ESTC t070406. * Dt; FLK; L; Mil.

1471. Hornyold, John Joseph. *The sacraments explain'd: in twenty discourses. By J.-H.-C.A.D.S.* London. 1747. 8°. xii, [4], 240 p. Published by: Author. Sold by: Needham, W. ESTC n021431. * CLU-C; Do; ECW; Gi; IU; LfaA; Lhe; LO; MRu; Osc; TLP; TxU; Ush.
'Many, if not most, of these discourses were written by the rev. John Johnson, Bishop Hornyold's predecessor at Longbirch' (Gillow III, 402).

1472. Hornyold, John Joseph. *The sacraments explain'd: in twenty discourses. By J-H-C.A-D.S.* Dublin. 1747. 12°. viii, [8], 223, [1] p. Published by: Bowes, P. ESTC t118328. * Do; Du; FLK; IDA; L.
With a list of about 200 subscribers.

1473. Hornyold, John Joseph. *The sacraments explain'd: in twenty discourses. By J- H- C.A.D.S.* 2nd ed. London. 1770. 12°. [2], v, [1], 236, [6] p. Published by: Coghlan, J.P. ESTC t129872. * Do; DoA; E; ECR; Gi; L; Lhe; O; Stan; TLP; Ush.
With a final advertisement leaf.

1474. Houdet, René. *A treatise on morality: chiefly designed for the instruction of youth.* Philadelphia. 1796. 12°. vi, 120 p. Printed by: Dobson, T. Published by: Author. ESTC w028366. * DB; DGU-W; MWA; MWH; NjR; RPJCB.
Houdet did mission work among French refugees in Philadelphia. Translated by Micheal Fortune.

1475. Howard, Philip. *The scriptural history of the earth and of mankind, compared with the cosmogonies, chronologies, and original traditions of ancient nations.* London. 1797. 4°. [6], 602, [2] p. Published by: Faulder, R. ESTC t114867. * C; DoA; E; L.

1476. Hubert, Jean François. *Lettre circulaire à messieurs les curés de campagne.* [Quebec]. [1787]. fol. [4] p. Printed by: Brown, W. ESTC w016673. * CaOOA; CaOONL; CaOOP; CaQQLa.
This states that 'Applicants for licences to sell liquor must have a letter of recommendation from the parish priest or captain of militia'. Signed and dated 'Jean François Ev. d'Almire, Coadjtr. de Québec. mars, 1787'.

1477. Hubert, Jean François. *Lettre circulaire à messieurs les curés. Monsieur ... Jean Franc Evêque de Quebec.* Quebec. 1789. 4°. [4] p. Printed by: Neilson, S. * CaOOP; CaOOA; CaQQLa.

1478. Hubert, Jean François. *Lettre circulaire à messieurs les curés.* Quebec. 1789. 4°. [4] p. Printed by: Brown, W. * CaOOP; CaQQLa.

1479. Hubert, Jean François. *Lettre circulaire à messieurs les curés.* [Quebec]. [1790]. s.s. * CaQQLa.

1480. Hubert, Jean François. *Mandement de monseigneur l'Eveque de Quebec. Touchant la jurisdiction des prêtres de son diocèse.* [Quebec]. [1788]. 4°. 8 p. Printed by: Brown, W. ESTC w016676. * CaOONL; CaQMM; RPJCB.

> Dated 'le dix décembre, de l'an mil-sept-cent-quatre-vingt-huit'.

1481. Hubert, Jean François. *Mandement de monseigneur l'Eveque de Quebec, qui permet de travailler à certain jours de fêtes.* [Quebec]. [1791]. 4°. 9-15, [1] p. Printed by: Neilson, S. ESTC w016677. * CaOONL; CaOTU; CaQMM; RPJCB.

> Allowing discontinuation of the observance of some of the numerous feast days. Pagination continues that of no. 1480. Dated 'le quinze d'Avril, mil-sept-cent-quatre-vingt-onze'.

1482. Hubert, Jean François. *Mandement du 28 octobre, M.DCC.XCIII.* [Quebec]. [1794]. fol. [2], 13, [1] p. Published by: Neilson, J. ESTC w016678. * CaBVaU; CaOONL; CaQMM; RPJCB.

> This revokes certain provisions of the pastoral letters of Dec. 10, 1788 and April 15, 1791.

1483. Huby, Vincent. *The spiritual retreat of the reverend father Vincent Huby, of the Society of Jesus. Translated from the French.* Philadelphia. 1795. 18°. v, [1], 222, [6] p. Printed by: [Folwell, R.]. Published by: Carey, M. ESTC w022351. * CaOTU; DB; DGU-W; MWA.

> Parsons (p. 35, no. 141) notes: 'Apparently translated from the Paris 1755 ed., which is probably taken from the *Retraite de Vennes* (1778)'. With 6 pages of Carey adverts.

1484. Hugh of S. Victor. *The rule of the great S. Augustin expounded ... Translated into French by the r. father Charles de la Grangé canon regular of S. Victor. And now publish'd in English for the use of the English Augustin nuns.* [Bruges]. [1735]. 12°. [2], 248, 59, [1] p. Printed by: Cock, J. de. * ECB.

> The last part is formed by 'An abridgment of the exposition of the rule of S. Augustin'. A ms note states that it was printed in 1735 and that 'Reverend mother gave to each of the religious one, and 5 to Loven'. ECB has no fewer than 19 copies.

1485. Humberstone, Henry. *A sermon preach'd at Worcester, on the eighteenth of April, 1686, being the Sunday after Easter. By the reverend father Henry Humberstone, priest of the Society of Jesus.* 1741. 8°. [4], 65-86 p. * ECW.

> Also published as part of *A select collection of Catholick sermons*, 1741 (no. 2522).

1486. Humbert, Pierre Hubert. *Instructions Chrétiennes pour les jeunes gens, utiles à toutes sortes de personnes, mêlées de plusieurs traits d'histoires et d'exemples édifians.* Anon. Quebec. 1798 [1799]. 12°. xvi, 448, [4] p. Published by: Neilson, J. ESTC w016711. * CaOOP; CaQMM; CaQQLa.

> 'This publication apparently started printing in 1798, and ... was issued the following year'. (Tremaine 1089).

1487. Humbert, Pierre Hubert. *Instructions Chrétiennes pour les jeunes gens; utiles à toutes sortes de personnes; mêlées de plusieurs traits d'histoire et d'examples édifians.* Anon. 2nd ed. Quebec. 1799. 12°. xvi, 405 [i.e. 406], [6]

p. Published by: Neilson, J. * CaOTP (imp.).

1488. *The humble address of the Roman Catholic peers and commoners of Great Britain.* 1778. s.s. * Map.

> Reprinted from the *London Gazette*, Saturday May 2d, 1778. no. 11870. The address is signed by more than 200 Catholics, headed by several peers (Arundel, Petre) and commoners such as Francis Plowden, Thomas Eyre, Edward Jerningham, Charles Butler and James Butler.

1489. *A humble remonstrance addressed to the mayor, bailiffs, freemen, &c. of the corporation of -- with a few strictures on their religious bigotry, and the impolitic intolerance, in excluding from the benefit of the trade, the citizen as well as the stranger.* Cork. 1789. 8°. 76 p. Printed by: Haly, J. Published by: Author. * MY.

> A plea for Catholic participation in commercial life. The corporation of Cork is said to indulge 'in the favourite idea of making and keeping a pure Protestant town'.

1490. *Humble remonstrance, for the repeal of the laws against the Roman Catholics. With judicious remarks, for the general union of Christians.* Dublin. 1778. 8°. 40, [2] p. Published by: Corcoran, B. ESTC t190876. * C.

1491. Hunter, Thomas. *Apologie du clergé séculier et des Jésuites d'Angleterre, en forme de discours, adressé à M.R.C. aumônier dans les troupes Angloises [A modest defence of the clergy and religious].* Anon. London. 1763. 12°. [4], 104 p. ESTC t189606. * Lfa; LfaA; Lhe.

> The original English version of this book (see next item) was written in reply to *The history of the English college at Doway* (no. 2772) by Hugh Tootell alias Charles Dodd who was at one time chaplain to an English regiment.

1492. Hunter, Thomas. *A modest defence of the clergy and religious, in a discourse directed to R.C. chaplain of an English regiment, about his History of Doway College.* Anon. [London?]. 1714. 8°. [2], 143, [13] p. ESTC t064078. * CLU-C; CSmH; DFo; Do; DoA; E; ECW; ICN; KU-S; L; Lfa; Lhe; LfaA; LO; MChB; Mil; NcD; O; Osc; TxDaM-P; TxU; Ush.

1493. Hussey, Thomas. *A pastoral letter to the Catholic clergy of the united diocesses of Waterford and Lismore.* Waterford. 1797. 8°. [2], 8 p. Printed by: Ramsey, J. jun. ESTC t128495. * D; Dt; ICN; L; Lhl; Lpro; Mil; MY.

> Thomas Hussey (1740-1803), chaplain to the Spanish embassy, became the first president of Maynooth (1795) and in the same year Bishop of Waterford and Lismore. The pastoral letter elicited *Remarks on the rev. Dr. Hussey's pastoral letter* (Dublin, 1797, ESTC t168899). See also next 5 items.

1494. Hussey, Thomas. *A pastoral letter to the Catholic clergy of the united diocesses of Waterford and Lismore.* [Dublin]. [1797]. 8°. 8 p. Printed by: [Fitzpatrick, H.]. ESTC t180503. * D; Di; MY.

1495. Hussey, Thomas. *A pastoral letter to the Catholic clergy of the united diocesses of Waterford and Lismore.* London repr. [Waterford]. 1797. 8°. [2], 8 p. Printed by: Ramsey, J. jun.; Coghlan, J.P. ESTC t196282. * CYc; DUc; O; WDA.

1496. Hussey, Thomas. *A pastoral letter to the Catholic clergy of the united diocesses of Waterford and Lismore.* 6th ed. Dublin. 1797. 8°. 8 p. Printed by: Fitzpatrick, H. ESTC t130630. * D; Dt; L; O; PP.

1497. Hussey, Thomas. *A pastoral letter to the Catholic clergy of the united diocesses of Waterford and Lismore.* 7th ed. London repr. [Waterford]. 1797. 12°. 12 p. Printed by: Ramsey, J. jun.; Coghlan, J.P. ESTC t180153. * C; D; MRu; Yb.

1498. Hussey, Thomas. *A pastoral letter to the Catholic clergy of the united diocesses of Waterford and Lismore.* 8th ed. London repr. [Waterford]. 1797. 12°. 12 p. Printed by: Ramsey, J. jun.; Coghlan, J.P. ESTC t180154. * BMu; D.

1499. Hussey, Thomas. *A sermon preached by the rev. Dr. Hussey, at the opening of the Spanish chapel, on the eighth of December, 1791.* London. 1792. 8°. [4], 22 p. Published by: Ridgway, J. ESTC t017473. * DUc; L; Osc; Ush.

1500. Hussey, Thomas. *A sermon preached by the r. rev. Dr. Hussey, in the chapel in Spanish Place, on the sixth of May, 1798.* London. [1798]. 8°. [2], 27, [1] p. Printed by: Coghlan, J.P. Published by: Coghlan, J.P. Sold by: Booker; Keating; Lewis; Robinsons. ESTC t217234. * Di.
> Another ed. in the same year (no. 1501) includes *A short account of the public prayers in the Spanish chapel, for his holiness Pope Pius VI* (no. 2541).

1501. Hussey, Thomas. *A sermon preached by the r. rev. Dr. Hussey, in the chapel in Spanish Place, on the sixth of May, 1798 ... To which is added a short account of the public prayers in the Spanish chapel.* London. [1798]. 8°. [4], 27, [1], 10 p. Printed by: Coghlan, J.P. Published by: Coghlan, J.P. Sold by: Booker; Keating; Lewis; Robinsons. ESTC t196279. * ECW; O; Osc; Stan; Sto.
> See also no. 2541.

1502. Hussey, Thomas. *A sermon [on John 20, 21] preached in the Spanish chapel, on Sunday the 2d of March, 1800, and taken in shorthand by a gentleman present.* London. 1800. 8°. 24 p. Printed by: Brown, R. Published by: Executors of J.P. Coghlan. Sold by: West; Hughes; Debrett; Keating; Booker. * Osc; Ush.

1503. *I have the honour to inform you, that the protestation of which I send you a copy, was laid before a general meeting of the Catholics, held at the Crown and Anchor tavern, on ... 20th of March.* [London]. [1789]. 8°. s.s. ESTC t146960. * L; Sto.
> Signed and dated 'Charles Butler, secretary. Lincoln's Inn, April 7, 1789'.

1504. Ignatius of Loyola. *The spiritual exercises of S. Ignatius of Loyola. Founder of the Society of Jesus.* St. Omers. 1736. 8°. 156, [4] p. Printed by: Le Febvre, N.J. ESTC t055130. * ICN; L; Lfa; Lhe.

1505. Ignatius of Loyola. *The spiritual exercises of S. Ignatius of Loyola, founder of the Society of Jesus.* St. Omers. [c.1750]. fol. 156, [5] p. Printed by: Le Febvre, N.J. * Sto (T.E. Muir).

1506. *IHS. I thought on the days of old, and I had in my mind the eternal years. Psalm 76, verse 5.* Preston. fol. s.s. Printed by: Sergent, E. * Ush.

A meditation on eternity. E. Sergent was at work in the 1760s.

1507. *The impartial examiner. Or the faithful representer of the various and manifold misrepresentations imposed on the Roman Catholics of Ireland.* Dublin. 1746. 8°. 64 p. ESTC t037024. * CSmH; Dt; L; Lhl; MY (imp.).

> In eight parts, but with continuous pagination. 'Ms attribution in Huntington Library copy to rev. John Jones' (ESTC).

1508. *Impartial remarks on the subject of an union ... In which the sentiments of the Catholic body, are vindicated from the charge of favouring the project.* Dublin. 1799. 8°. [4], 48 p. Published by: Jones, W. ESTC t018090. * CSmH; D; Dt; Du; E; IEN; InU-Li; KU-S; L; MiU; PP.

> A reply to Theobald MacKenna. Also issued as part of *Tracts on the subject of an union*, vol. 3, Dublin, 1799 (ESTC n034538).

1509. *In the letter we had the honour of addressing you on the 31st of last July, we took the liberty to state to you the necessity of rebuilding the Bavarian chapel, and to solicit your subscription to it.* [London?]. [1788]. fol. 3, [1] p. ESTC t037107. * L; Ush.

> The letter is signed 'James Talbot, president, James Moore, secretary' with 21 others. Dated at head of page 1 'London, November 6, 1788'. Page 3 contains regulations governing the committee for rebuilding the chapel, signed 'James Talbot'. For the actual proposal, see no. 2926.

1510. *Instruction Catholique, par demandes et par réponses, sur les droits de l'autel et du trone. Où l'on prouve la verité des principes combattus par les auteurs de la revolution de France.* Winchester. 1795. 12°. vi, 112 p. * Lhe; NIC; Sto.

> 'Par M. D.P.S.D.M. & C.D.P.'

1511. *Instructions concerning the festivals. Chiefly taken from the catechism of Boulogne.* Winchester. [1790?]. 12°. 24 p. * Cj (P.R. Glazebrook).

> Published about 1790, possibly for the use of students of Twyford School. According to the present owner, Mr P.R. Glazebrook of Jesus College Cambridge, the pamphlet is probably by John Milner.

1512. *Instructions for the worthily making and preserving the fruits of the first communion, by way of catechism.* 1778. 12°. 26 p. * O; Ush.

> Contains a reference to Gother's 'Best method of hearing mass'.

1513. *Instructions sur le rosaire.* London. 1797. 12°. [2], 70 p. Printed by: Dulonchamp, J.M. * Ush.

1514. *An introduction to the Latin tongue.* Douai. 1774. 12°. 104 p. Published by: Derbaix, L. ESTC t167410. * C.

> A Latin grammar for the use of the English College at Douai.

1515. *Iontri8aiestsk8a ionskaneks n'aieienterihag gaiatonsera te gari8toraragon ong8e on8e ga8ennontakon.* Montreal. 1777. 8°. 16 p. Published by: Mesplet, F. * WHi.

> A primer with Catholic prayers entirely in the Mohawk dialect.

1516. James II. *The pious sentiments of the late king James II of blessed memory, upon divers subjects of piety.* London. 1704. 8°. [4], 54 p. ESTC t097831. * L;

Ush.

Ush (tp cropped) has [6], 54 p.

1517. Jenkins, Peter. *A commentary on the XLI and XLII psalms, appointed to be sung or said on all Sundays and festivals, in the several Roman Catholic Chapels throughout Great Britain. To which are added, observations and sentiments of the rev. A. O'Leary.* Bury St. Edmund's. 1799. 8°. 36 p. Printed by: Ingram, G. * Lhe.

Gillow (III, 614) gives a 12° London 1799 ed.

1518. Jenkins, Peter. *The doctrine and practice of auricular confession, elucidated and enforced.* Anon. London. 1783. 12°. xii, 203, [1] p. Published by: Author. Sold by: Marmaduke, J. ESTC t092040. * CAL; DMR; Do; DoA; ICN; L; Lfa; Lhe; Osc; UshL.

With one page of Marmaduke adverts.

1519. Jenkins, Peter. *Sunday evening's entertainment: consisting of an explication of the psalms which occur in the evening office of the church, on Sundays and festivals throughout the year.* Anon. London. 1779. 12°. [2], xvi, [2], 172 p. Printed by: Coghlan, J.P. ESTC t126487. * BMu; CtY; Do; E; ECW; L; Lfa; Lhe; Lmh; O; Osc.

1520. Jenks, Silvester. *A contrite and humble heart. With motives and considerations to prepare it.* 5th ed. Anon. [London]. 1719. 12°. 202, [2] p. ESTC t082734. * DoA; E; L; NN; NSCH.

1521. Jenks, Silvester. *A contrite and humble heart, with motives and considerations to prepare it.* 7th ed. Anon. Dublin. 1799. 12°. [3], v-216 p. Printed by: Wogan, P. ESTC t118379. * D; E; Gi; IDA; L; Lfa.

1522. Jenks, Silvester. *An essay upon the art of love, containing an exact anatomy of love and all the other passions which attend it.* Anon. [London?]. 1702. 12°. [8], 9-300 p. ESTC t055647. * CLU-C; CSmH; DFo; DMR; DUc; ECB; Gi; ICU; IU; L; MCR-S; MRu.

1523. Jenks, Silvester. *A short review of the book of Jansenius.* Anon. [London?]. 1710. 12°. [36], 153, [3] p. ESTC n022857. * BB; CLU-C; DFo; Do; DoA; E; ECW; Hen; Lfa; LfaA; Lhe; MRu; O; Osc; Owo; TxU.

1524. Jenks, Silvester. *The whole duty of a Christian in three parts ... the whole being a faithful abstract of the Trent-Catechism; with some additions to it.* Anon. 1706. 12°. [6], 329, [1] p. ESTC t215617. * E; ECW; LO; TLP.

With a final page of adverts for 'Books printed for S.J.' Cf. also Clancy.

1525. Jenks, Silvester. *The whole duty of a Christian. In three parts ... The whole being a faithful abstract of the Trent-Catechism; with some addition to it.* Anon. 1711. 12°. [6], 328 p. * DoA.

Last page incorrectly numbered 399, with a final adverts for 'Books printed for S.J.'

1526. *Jesus, Maria Benedictus. Anno Domini [blank] die [blank] in monasterio Beatae Mariae Virginis de consolatione sanctimonialium ordinis Sancti Benedicti, congregationis Anglicanae Cameraci.* [Cambrai]. s.s. * Lil.

A standardised obit notice used in the monastery of the English Benedictines at Cambrai, to be completed in manuscript.

1527. *Jesus, Maria, Benedictus. Anno Domini 1738 die 3. Julii Bruxellis, in monasterio Sancti-Monialium Anglarum ... domina, D. Elisabeth Chilton.* [Brussels]. [1738]. s.s. * Lil.

Obit notice of Dame Elizabeth Chilton, an English Benedictine nun.

1528. *Jesus, Maria, Benedictus. Anno ... Domini, die 24. Octobris, in conventu nostro Benedictinarum Anglarum de Sanctâ Maria de consolatione Cameraci ... Dominis Thomas Southcott.* [Cambrai]. [1748]. s.s. * Lil.

Obit notice of Thomas Southcott or Southcote, president general of the English Benedictines.

1529. *Jesus, Maria, Benedictus. Anno Domini 1790, die Augusti 20°, in monasterio Beatae Mariae Virginis ... R.D. Thomas Welch.* [Cambrai]. [1790]. s.s. * Lil.

Obit notice of Thomas Welch, an English Benedictine and confessor to the nuns at Cambrai.

1530. *The Jesus psalter.* Liverpool. 1789. 12°. 22 p. Published by: Wosencroft, C. * UGL.

Bound up with nos 1458 and 1812.

1531. *Le Jeudi 3 Septembre dernier, fete du sacerdoce; d'anciens et respectables citoyens de la ville de Quebec, ont presentés la requête suivante.* [Quebec]. [1789]. 4°. [4] p. * CaQQLa.

A petition signed by Pierre Dufau and 27 others begging reinstatement of the priest M. de la Poterie.

1532. Jones, William Todd. *A letter to the Societies of United Irishmen of the town of Belfast, upon the subject of certain apprehensions which have arisen from a proposed restoration of Catholic rights.* Dublin. 1792. 8°. [2], 98 p. Printed by: Chambers, J. ESTC n019643. * BFq; C; Di; Dk; Dt; Lhe; Lhl; LONu; Lse; Om; Sto.

William Todd Jones was a non-R.C. M.P. in favour of Catholic emancipation. For other eds of this work and other publications by Todd Jones see ESTC; but see also nos 1708 and 1711.

1533. *La journée du Chrétien, sanctifiée par la priere et la méditation.* Quebec. 1795. 12°. [6], 176, [2] p. Published by: Germain, L. jun. * CaO (imp.).

1534. *La journée du Chrétien, sanctifiée par la prière et la meditation.* Baltimore. 1796. 12°. [2], 310, [2] p. Printed by: Pechin, W. ESTC w011342. * DB; DGU; ICN; MWA.

Text in French and Latin.

1535. *La journée du Chrétien, sanctifiée par la priere et la méditation.* 2nd ed. Quebec. 1797. 18°. [2], viii, 276, [2] p. Printed by: Vondenvelden, W. Published by: Germain, L. * CaQMBM (imp.).

1536. *La journée du Chrétien, sanctifiée par la priere et la méditation. Nouvelle edition ... augmentée d'un abrégé de la doctrine Chrétienne.* Dublin. 1797. 12°. 249, [3] p. Printed by: Wogan, P. ESTC t206696. * D; FLK; OU.

With 2 pages of Wogan adverts.

1537. *The judgment of the bishops of France, concerning the doctrine, the government, the conduct and usefulness of the French Jesuits.* London. [1765?]. 12°. iv, 72 p. Printed by: Balfe, R.; Lewis, T. ESTC t102058. * L; Lfa; LfaA; Lhe; Mil; Osc; Sto; Ush.

> Part 2 of *Occasional letters on the present affairs of the Jesuits in France*, London [1765?], attributed to Nathaniel Elliot (no. 966).

1538. *The key of paradise, opening the gate to eternal salvation. Part I. Permissu superiorum.* London. 1738. 12°. 608, [4] p. * ECB (-tp); ECW.

1539. *The key of paradise, opening the gate to eternal salvation. With a new and correct calendar.* Dublin. 1782. 18°. 328, [13], 356-623, [3] p. Printed by: Cross, R. * DMR; ECW.

> There are 2 parts. Part II has a separate tp.

1540. *The key of paradise, opening the gate to eternal salvation. This edition is very much amended, and again revised and corrected by the rev. Bernard MacMahon.* Dublin. 1794. 12°. 608, [4] p. Sold by: Booksellers. * DMR; Stan.

> There is a second tp following p. 328 with the imprint 'Dublin: printed and sold by the booksellers. 1795.' This and the next item probably constitute two issues of the same ed.

1541. *The key of paradise, opening the gate to eternal salvation. This edition is very much amended, and again revised and corrected by the rev. Bernard MacMahon. Permissu superiorum.* Dublin. 1794. 12°. 608, [4] p. Printed by: Cross, R. ESTC n033362. * CaOHM; IDA.

1542. *The key of paradise, opening the gate to eternal salvation. To this edition is added, a new calendar. The whole revised and corrected by the reverend B. Mc.M.* Dublin. 1796. 12°. 608, [4] p. Printed by: Wogan, P. ESTC t118709. * L.

> 'B.Mc.M' is Bernard MacMahon.

1543. Kingsley, William. *A vindication of the old Church of England. Or; an answer to Mr. Wainhouse's Novelties of the Church of Rome.* Anon. [London?]. 1731. 8°. 94 p. Printed by: Author. Sold by: Booksellers. ESTC t063953. * L; Lhe.

> Replied to by Richard Wainhouse in *An answer to a popish pamphlet* (1731). The author is identified by Sommervogel (Sup. 534). See also next item.

1544. Kingsley, William. *A further vindication of the old Church of England, or an answer to Mr. Wainhouse's reply.* Anon. 1733. 8°. 104 p. * Ush (imp.).

1545. Kirwan, Walter Blake. *A discourse on religious innovations, pronounced by the rev. Mr. Kirwan, at ... the Neapolitan ambassador's chapel, the 20th March, 1786.* London. [1786?]. 8°. [4], 27, [1] p. Printed by: Coghlan, J.P. ESTC t143538. * Llp; Lu; Osc; Sto; TxU.

1546. Kirwan, Walter Blake. *A discourse on religious innovations ... To which is added, his letter to a friend in Galway, giving his reasons for quitting the Roman Catholic church.* 2nd ed. [Dublin]. 1787. 12°. 39, [1] p. Printed by: Wogan, P. (repr.). ESTC t091066. * D; L.

The edition does not come within the terms of our definition. Kirwan eventually became Anglican Dean of Killala.

1547. L., F., Esq. *The virgin's nosegay, or, the duties of Christian virgins; digested into succinct chapters ... To which is added, Advice to a new married lady.* London. 1744. 12°. [2], ix, [1], 192 p. Published by: Cooper, M. ESTC t118352. * L.

1548. L., F., Esq. *The virgin's nosegay, or, the duties of Christian virgins; digested into succinct chapters ... To which is added, Advice to a new married lady.* London. 1744. 12°. [2], ix, [1], 192 p. Published by: Meighan, T. ESTC t179839. * CAL; O; UshL.

1549. L., F., Esq. *The virgin's nosegay; or, the duties of Christian virgins: digested into succinct chapters ... To which is added, Advice to a new married lady.* Belfast repr. (London). 1744. 12°. [2], ix, [1], 160 p. Printed by: Joy, F. (Belfast). * CtY; DLC; ICU.

1550. L., F., Esq. *A new year's gift; or, the virgin's nosegay, being the duties of Christian virgins: digested into succinct chapters ... To which is added, Advice to a new married lady.* Dublin. 1752. 12°. [2], ix, [1], 176, [4] p. Published by: Kelly, I. ESTC t182104. * D.

Earlier London eds were called *The virgin's nosegay*.

1551. L., F., Esq. *A new year's gift; containing admonitions to young ladies respecting religious duties and moral virtues ... The second edition ... The former being entitled, The virgin's nosegay.* 2nd ed. Dublin. 1792. 12°. [9], 14-220 p. Printed by: Cross, R. ESTC t217131. * Di; IObT.

1552. La Hogue, Louis Egidius de. *Exposé des motifs qui ont determiné le clergé de France à fuir la persecution, et à se retirer en pays étrangers.* Anon. London. 1795. 12°. [4], 88, iv, [2] p. Printed by: Coghlan, J.P. Sold by: Booker, E; Keating; Dulau, A.; Lonchamp. ESTC t111939. * CaQMBN (variant); ICR; L; Lhe; Lu; MY; Nijm; Osc; Ush.

A variant has 'se vend chez' instead of 'se chez vend' in the imprint. Ascribed to La Hogue by Nijm and Ush.

1553. La Hogue, Louis Egidius de. *S. Cyprien consolant les fidèles persécutés de l'eglise de France; convainquant de schisme l'église constitutionnelle; traçant à ceux qui sont tombés des règles de pénitence.* London. 1797. 12°. x, 284, [4] p. Printed by: Spilsbury, W. & C. ESTC t148882. * BMp; CaQQLa; DoA; GOT; MChB; MH.

1554. La Hogue, Louis Egidius de. *S. Cyprien consolant les fidèles persécutés de l'église de France; convainquant de schisme l'église constitutionnelle; traçant à ceux qui sont tombés des règles de penitence.* 2nd ed. London. 1797. 12°. xii, 305, [7] p. Printed by: Spilsbury, W. & C. Published by: Dulau, A. & Co. ESTC t126204. * C; CaQMBN; CYc; E; L; MH; Mil; MY; P.

1555. La Marche, Jean François de. *Conduite à tenir par M.M. les ecclésiastiques François réfugiés en Angleterre.* Anon. [London]. [1798?]. fol. 2 p. Printed by: Coghlan, J.P. ESTC t031165. * L; O.

There is also a French/German ed. of the pamphlet, probably printed in Berlin, with a spurious imprint mentioning Coghlan (see ESTC t031166). See also Bellenger 1986, p. 291.

1556. La Marche, Jean François de. *Letter of the right reverend John Francis de La Marche, Bishop of Leon, addressed to the French clergymen refugees in England [Lettre ... aux ecclésiastiques François].* London. 1793. 8°. [4], 20 p. Printed by: Coghlan, J.P. Published by: Debrett, J.; Booker; Keating; Lewis; Robinsons; Robins (Winchester). ESTC t110150. * C; CLU-S/C; Csj; CSmH; DLC; E; ECW; ICN; KU-S; L; Lhe; MRu; NcD; O; PPAmP; SHp; Ush.

> A letter of gratitude for the hospitality afforded to the French clergy in England, translated by John Milner.

1557. La Marche, Jean François de. *Lettre de M. l'Evêque de Léon aux ecclésiastiques François réfugiés en Angleterre.* London. 1793. 8°. 20 p. Printed by: Coghlan, J.P. ESTC t123892. * C; CSmH; DoA; ECW; FLK; ICN; KU-S; L; LANu; Lhe; Lu; MH; MRu; O; PU; Ush.

1558. La Marche, Jean François de. *Lettre de M. l'Evêque de Léon aux ecclésisatiques [sic] Français réfugiés en Angleterre.* Quebec. 1793. 12°. 18, [2] p. Printed by: Neilson, J. ESTC w016674. * CaOONL; CaQMM; MBAt; P.

1559. La Marche, Jean François de. *Lettre pastorale et ordonnance de M. l'Evêque de Léon, au clergé seculier et regulier, et à tous les fideles de son diocese.* London. [1791]. 8°. [2], 33, [1] p. Printed by: Coghlan, J.P. ESTC t090739. * CaQMBN; DoA; L; Lhe; MY.

> Dated '20 Aoust 1791'.

1560. La Marche, Jean François de. *The pastoral letter and ordinance of the right reverend John Francis de La Marche, Lord Bishop of Leon, addressed to the clergy ... and to all the faithful of his diocese. Translated by ... John Milner.* London. 1791. 8°. [4], xi, [1], 35, [1] p. Printed by: Coghlan, J.P. Sold by: Booker; Keating; Lewis; Robinsons; Ledger (Dover); Cunningham and Co. (Southampton); Lee (Brighthelmstone); Robbins (Winchester). ESTC t174844. * BB; DMR; DoA; Du; DUc; NSPM; O; Osc; RBM; Ush.

> A translation of no. 1559 (see also next item). BB bound up with no. 1144.

1561. La Marche, Jean François de. *The pastoral letter and ordinance of the right reverend John Francis de La Marche, Lord Bishop of Leon, addressed to the clergy ... and to all the faithful of his diocese. Translated by ... John Milner.* Dublin. 1792. 8°. [4], viii, 23, [1] p. Printed by: Wogan, P. ESTC n011970. * C; CaOTU; Dt; MY; PPL; Yb.

1562. La Poterie, Claude F. Bouchard de. *Boston, January 29, 1789. To the publick. The Catholick church of the Holy Cross, in Boston, is, at present, indebted in the sum of one hundred pounds, nearly, to different workmen.* Boston. [1789]. s.s. Printed by: [Hall, S.]. ESTC w030006. * DLC; MB; MH-H; MHi.

> On the financial difficulties of the church, with proposals for opening a school.

1563. La Poterie, Claude F. Bouchard de. *A pastoral letter, from the apostolic vice-prefect, curate of the Holy Cross at Boston.* Anon. [Boston]. [1789]. 4°. 24 p. Printed by: [Thomas & Andrews]. ESTC w027579. * DP; M; MB; MeB;

MH-H; MHi; MWA; RPJCB.

1564. La Poterie, Claude F. Bouchard de. *The resurrection of Laurent Ricci; or, a true and exact history of the Jesuits.* Philadelphia. 1789. 12°. vi, [1], 8-28 p. ESTC w021950. * CtY; DGU; DLC; DP; MH-H; MWA; NIC; NN; RPJCB.

> A bitter arraignment of the Jesuits, dedicated to the new 'Laurent Ricci' (i.e. John Carroll).

1565. La Poterie, Claude F. Bouchard de. *Sir, you will readily discover, in the writing, which M. the abbé de La Poterie has the honour to send you, here inclosed, the spirit and sentiments which animate him.* [Boston]. [1789]. 4°. s.s. ESTC w004082. * MHi (2).

> Dated in ms 'March 3, 1789'. The 'inclosed writing' is La Poterie's *To the publick* (no. 1566).

1566. La Poterie, Claude F. Bouchard de. *To the publick. On the fourth of February ult. 1789, a Frenchman, by the name of Louis Abraham Welch ... being on his death-bed, expressed the greatest desire to receive the last sacrament.* [Boston]. [1789]. 4°. 4 p. ESTC w028142. * DLC; DP; F; MB; MH; MHi; MWA.

> Circular letter by the abbé de La Poterie, defending his character and his ministry.

Laity's directory. Marmaduke commenced publishing the Laity's directory in 1758. In 1764 Coghlan also brought out a Laity's directory. From 1774 Marmaduke styled it the Original laity's directory in order to distinguish it from Coghlan's rival publication. After Marmaduke's death in 1787 Coghlan had the field to himself. We have assumed that a Laity's directory was published in the year before the year of the title. For the obituaries in the Laity's directory from 1773 to 1800 see Hansom.

1567. *The laity's directory; or, the order of the church service ... for the year of our Lord MDCCLIX ... According to the Latin directory.* [London]. [1758]. 12°. 24 p. Printed by: [Marmaduke, J.] Published by: [Marmaduke, J.]. Gillow, IV, 463.

1568. *The laity's directory; or, the order of the church-service ... for the year of our Lord M.D.CC.LXIV. Being bissextile. By permission and with approbation.* [London]. [1763]. 12°. 28 p. Printed by: [Coghlan, J.P.]. Published by: [Coghlan, J.P.]. * Map.

> 'By permission and with approbation' became the trade-mark of J.P. Coghlan.

1569. *The laity's directory; or, the order of the church-service ... for the year of our Lord MDCCLXV ... According to the Latin directory.* [London]. [1764]. 12°. 42, [6] p. Printed by: [Marmaduke, J.]. Published by: [Marmaduke, J.]. * Lhe.

> The 'Directory' is followed by 'Some remarkable words and actions of the holy fathers of the desert'. In this issue Marmaduke complains of Coghlan's rival publication.

1570. *The laity's directory; or, the order of the church service ... for the year of our Lord, M.DCC.LXV. Being the first after leap year. By permission, and with approbation.* [London]. [1764]. 12°. 30 p. Printed by: [Coghlan, J.P.]. Published

by: [Coghlan, J.P.]. * Foley; Map.
> The 'Directory' is followed by a new year's gift for 1765 and 'Rules of a Christian life'.

1571. *The laity's directory; or, the order of the church-service ... For the year of our Lord MDCCLXVII. Being the third after bissextile or leap year.* [London]. [1766]. 12°. 46, [2] p. Printed by: [Marmaduke, J.]. Published by: [Marmaduke, J.]. * Lhe.
> On the final 2 pages the publisher (Marmaduke) makes mention of earlier directories for 1759, 1760, 1761, 1762, 1764, 1765, 1766.

1572. *The laity's directory; or, the order of the church service ... for the year of our Lord MDCCLXVIII. Being leap year, by permission, and with approbation.* [London]. [1767]. 12°. 38 p. Printed by: [Coghlan, J.P.]. Published by: [Coghlan, J.P.]. ESTC t132057. * L.
> The 'Directory' is followed by a new year's gift for 1768.

1573. *The laity's directory; or, the order of the church-service ... according to the Latin directory for the year of our Lord MDCCLXIX. Being the first after bissextile or leap year.* [London]. [1768]. 12°. 48 p. Printed by: [Marmaduke, J.]. Published by: [Marmaduke, J.]. ESTC t132252. * L; WDA.
> The 'Directory' is followed by an attestation of seven Greek archbishops of the East concerning certain points of their belief, and half a page of Marmaduke adverts.

1574. *The laity's directory; or, the order of the church service ... for the year of our Lord M.DCC.LXX. Being the second after leap-year. By permission and with approbation.* [London]. [1769]. 12°. 24, 9, [3] p. Printed by: [Coghlan, J.P.]. Published by: [Coghlan, J.P.]. ESTC t132051. * L.
> The 'Directory' is followed by a new year's gift for 1770 and 3 pages of Coghlan adverts.

1575. *The laity's directory; or, the order of the church service ... for the year of our Lord MDCCLXXI.* [London]. [1770]. 12°. 36 p. Printed by: [Marmaduke, J.]. Published by: [Marmaduke, J.]. * Foley.
> With some pages of Marmaduke adverts.

1576. *The laity's directory; or, the order of the church service ... for the year of our Lord MDCCLXXII.* [London]. [1771]. 12°. 4-47, [1] p. Printed by: [Marmaduke, J.]. Published by: [Marmaduke, J.]. * Foley.

1577. *The laity's directory; or the order of the church service ... for the year of our Lord MDCCLXXIV. Being the second after leap-year. By permission, and with approbation.* [1773]. 12°. 24, 18, 6, [2] p. Printed by: [Coghlan, J.P.]. Published by: [Coghlan, J.P.]. * Foley; Lhe.
> The 'Directory' is followed by a new year's gift for 1774, a 6-page Coghlan catalogue and an advert for stationery.

1578. *The laity's directory; or, the order of the church-service ... according to the Latin directory for the year of our Lord MDCCLXXIV. Being the first after bissextile or leap year.* [London]. [1773]. 12°. 48 p. Printed by: [Marmaduke, J.]. Published by: [Marmaduke, J.]. ESTC t132251. * L.
> With 1½ pages of Marmaduke adverts. In this directory (pp. 46-7) Marmaduke

again complains of the opposition to his directory and urges his claims to priority, adding that 'if he had not thought of it, they perhaps would not have had one to this day'.

1579. *The laity's directory: or the order of the church service ... for the year of our Lord MDCCLXXVI. Being leap year. With approbation.* London. [1775]. 12°. 24, 9, 7 p. Printed by: Coghlan, J.P. Published by: Coghlan, J.P. * Foley; Lhe.

> The 'Directory' is followed by a new year's gift for 1776 and a 7-page Coghlan catalogue. The Foley copy has 3 extra pages with 'Divine history' and a notice on Coghlan's use of Baskerville's types.

1580. *The laity's directory; or the order of the church service ... for the year of our Lord MDCCLXXVIII. With approbation.* London. [1777]. 12°. 24, 13, [1] p. Printed by: Coghlan, J.P. Published by: Coghlan, J.P. * Lhe.

> The 'Directory' is followed by a new year's gift for 1778 and one page of Coghlan adverts.

1581. *The laity's directory; or the order of the church service ... for the year of our Lord MDCCLXXIX. With approbation.* London. [1778]. 12°. 34, [22] p. Printed by: Coghlan, J.P. Published by: Coghlan, J.P. * Lhe.

> The 'Directory' is followed by a new year's gift for 1779, episcopal letters to the Catholic clergy, prayers for the Royal Family, and an 18-page Coghlan catalogue.

1582. *The laity's directory; or, the order of the church service ... for the year of our Lord MDCCLXXX. Being leap year. With approbation.* London. [1779]. 12°. 36, 10, [2] p. Printed by: Coghlan, J.P. Published by: Coghlan, J.P. * Map.

> The 'Directory' is followed by a new year's gift for 1780 and 2 pages of miscellaneous Coghlan adverts.

1583. *The original laity's directory; or, the order of the church-service ... according to the Latin directory. For the year of our Lord MDCCLXXX. Being leap-year.* [London]. [1779]. 12°. 47, [1] p. Printed by: [Marmaduke, J.]. Published by: [Marmaduke, J.]. * Lhe.

> With a final page of Marmaduke adverts.

1584. *The original laity's directory; or, the order of the church-service ... according to the Latin directory. For the year of our Lord, MDCCLXXXI. Being the first after leap-year.* [London]. [1780]. 12°. 48 p. Printed by: [Marmaduke, J.]. Published by: [Marmaduke, J.]. * Lhe.

> With 3 pages of Marmaduke adverts.

1585. *The original laity's directory; or, the order of the church-service ... according to the Latin directory. For the year of our Lord MDCCLXXXII. Being the second after leap-year.* [London]. [1781]. 12°. 48 p. Printed by: [Marmaduke, J.]. Published by: [Marmaduke, J.]. * Lhe.

> With a final page inviting subscriptions to an ed. of Gother's *The sinner's complaints to God*.

1586. *The original laity's directory; or, the order of the church-service ... according to the Latin directory. For the year of our Lord MDCCLXXXIII. Being the third after leap-year.* [London]. [1782]. 12°. 48 p. Printed by: [Marmaduke,

J.]. Published by: [Marmaduke, J.]. * Lhe.

>With half a page advertising *Miscellaneous tracts by the rev. Arthur O'Leary*.

1587. *The original laity's directory; or, the order of the church-service ... according to the Latin directory. For the year of our Lord MDCCLXXXIV. Being leap-year.* [London]. [1783]. 12°. 48 p. Printed by: [Marmaduke, J.]. Published by: [Marmaduke, J.]. * Lhe.

>With 2½ pages of Marmaduke adverts.

1588. *The original laity's directory; or, the order of the church-service ... according to the Latin directory. For the year of our Lord M.DCC.LXXXV. Being the first after leap-year.* [London]. [1784]. 12°. 48 p. Printed by: [Marmaduke, J.]. Published by: [Marmaduke, J.]. ESTC t132250. * L.

>With half a page of Marmaduke adverts.

1589. *The laity's directory; or the order of the church service ... for the year of our Lord MDCCLXXXVI. Being the second after leap year. By permission of the bishop.* London. [1785]. 12°. 24, 2, 28, 6, 12 p. Printed by: Coghlan, J.P. Published by: Coghlan, J.P. * ECW; Lhe; Ush.

>The 'Directory' is followed by a new year's gift for 1786 (a reprint of Challoner's *Pastoral instruction*, no. 615), obituaries, adverts for medicines and travel to the Continent, and a 12-page Coghlan catalogue.

1590. *The original laity's directory; or, the order of the church-service ... according to the Latin directory. For the year of our Lord M.DCC.LXXXVI. Being the second after leap-year.* [London]. [1785]. 12°. 46, [2] p. Printed by: [Marmaduke, J.]. Published by: [Marmaduke, J.]. ESTC t132248. * L.

>With 2 pages of Marmaduke adverts.

1591. *The laity's directory; or, the order of the church service ... for the year of our Lord MDCCLXXXVII. Being the third after leap year. By permission of the bishop.* London. [1786]. 12°. 24, 18, 10 p. Printed by: Coghlan, J.P. Published by: Coghlan, J.P. * Map.

>The 'Directory' is followed by obituaries, adverts for travel to the Continent, and a catalogue of Coghlan's books.

1592. *The original laity's directory; or, the order of the church-service ... according to the Latin directory. For the year of our Lord M.DCC.LXXXVII. Being the third after leap-year.* [London]. [1786]. 12°. 48, [2] p. Printed by: [Marmaduke, J.]. Published by: [Marmaduke, J.]. ESTC t132247. * L; Lhe.

>With 2 pages of Marmaduke adverts.

1593. *The original laity's directory; or, the order of the church-service ... according to the Latin directory. For the year of our Lord M.DCC.LXXXVIII. Being leap-year.* [London]. [1787]. 12°. 48 p. Printed by: [Marmaduke, J.]. Published by: [Marmaduke, J.]. ESTC t132246. * L.

>With 1½ pages of Marmaduke adverts.

1594. *The laity's directory; or the order of the church service ... for the year of our Lord MDCCLXXXVIII. Being leap year. By permission of the bishop.* London. [1787]. 12°. 24, [4], 16, 17, [3] p. Printed by: Coghlan, J.P. Published by: Coghlan, J.P. * Lhe.

The 'Directory' is followed by obituaries, a new year's gift for 1788, and a Coghlan catalogue including adverts for medicines and travel to the Continent.

1595. *The laity's directory; in the church service ... for the year of our Lord M.DCC.LXXXIX. Being the first after leap year ... By permission of the bishop.* London. [1788]. 12°. 31, [1], 12, [3], 32-42, [1], 11-12, [1] p. Printed by: Coghlan, J.P. Published by: Coghlan, J.P. ESTC t132077. * L; Lhe.
The 'Directory' is followed by a new year's gift for 1789, obituaries, an 11-page Coghlan catalogue, and 3 pages of Coghlan adverts.

1596. *The laity's directory; for the church service ... for the year of our Lord MDCCXC. Being the second after leap year ... By permission of the bishop.* London. [1789]. 12°. 32, [4], 11, [5], 12, [4] p. Printed by: Coghlan, J.P. Published by: Coghlan, J.P. ESTC t132076. * L; Lhe; Map.
The 'Directory' is followed by obituaries, a new year's gift for 1790, indulgences, a 12-page Coghlan catalogue, and 4 pages of Coghlan adverts.

1597. *The laity's directory; for the church service ... for the year of our Lord M.DCC.XCI. Being the third after leap year ... By permission.* London. [1790]. 12°. 36, 44 p. Printed by: Coghlan, J.P. Published by: Coghlan, J.P. ESTC t132074. * L; Lhe; Ush.
The 'Directory' is followed by a new year's gift for 1791, obituaries, Catholic educational institutions, survey of Catholic chapels, and a 14-page Coghlan catalogue.

1598. *The laity's directory; for the church service ... for the year of our Lord M.DCC.XCII. Being leap year ... By permission.* London. [1791]. 12°. 24, 12, 28, 12 p. Printed by: Coghlan, J.P. Published by: Coghlan, J.P. ESTC t132073. * L; Lhe; Ush.
The 'Directory' is followed by a new year's gift for 1792, obituaries, a 22-page Coghlan catalogue, encyclical letters concerning the Bill for the relief of English Catholics and prayers for the Royal family. Ush and Lhe have 24, 12, 28, 15, [1] p.

1599. *The laity's directory; for the church service ... for the year of our Lord M.DCC.XCIII. Being the first after leap year ... By permission.* London. [1792]. 12°. 20, [4], 12, 47, [1], 4 p. Printed by: Coghlan, J.P. Published by: Coghlan, J.P. ESTC t132072. * L; Lhe; Map; Ush (imp.); WDA.
The 'Directory' is followed by obituaries, a new year's gift for 1793, indulgences, extract letter Dr Moylan, a survey of Catholic chapels, Catholic educational institutions, sketch of a Bill for the relief of the Roman Catholics, a 24-page Coghlan catalogue and adverts for medicines and travel to the Continent.

1600. *The laity's directory; for the church service ... for the year of our Lord M.DCC.XCIV. Being the second after leap year ... By permission.* London. [1793]. 12°. 20, 12, 24, [4], 22, 3-4 p. Printed by: Coghlan, J.P. Published by: Coghlan, J.P. ESTC t132069. * L; Lhe; UGL; Ush; WDA.
The 'Directory' is followed by a new year's gift for 1794, indulgences, extract letter Dr Moylan, a survey of Catholic chapels, obituaries, Catholic educational institutions, chronology, obituary of the French clergy, and a 24-page Coghlan catalogue. Ush has 20, 12, 6, 24, [4] p. and WDA lacks the last 24 p.

1601. *The laity's directory; for the church service ... for the year of our Lord M.DCC.XCV. Being the third after leap year ... By permission.* London. [1794]. 12°. 20, 11, [1], 33-36, [8], 24, 24 p. Printed by: Coghlan, J.P. Published by: Coghlan, J.P. ESTC t132067. * L; UGL; Ush; WDA.

> The 'Directory' is followed by a new year's gift for 1795, mass in time of war, obituaries, indulgences, extract letter Dr Moylan, a survey of Catholic chapels, Catholic educational institutions, sufferers by the French Revolution, adverts for sacred vessels and the Royal Hotel Inn and a 24-page Coghlan catalogue including adverts for medicines.

1602. *The laity's directory; for the church service ... for the year of our Lord M.DCC.XCVI. Being leap year ... By permission.* London. [1795]. 12°. 19, [1], 12, 52, 24 p. Printed by: Coghlan, J.P. Published by: Coghlan, J.P. ESTC t132047. * L; Lhe; Ush; WDA.

> The 'Directory' is followed by the mass in time of war, new year's gift for 1796, indulgences, extract letter Dr Moylan, a survey of Catholic chapels, sketch of the Bill for the relief of the Roman Catholics, sufferers by the French Revolution, the present state of religion in China, instances of beneficence to Roman Catholics, Catholic educational institutions, obituaries, adverts for medicines and a 24-page Coghlan catalogue including adverts for travel to the Continent. In this and the following items the additional material in the L copies has been misbound.

1603. *The laity's directory; for the church service ... for the year of our Lord M.DCC.XCVII. Being the first after leap year ... By permission.* London. [1796]. 12°. [20], 11, [1], 40, 8, 24 p. Printed by: Coghlan, J.P. Published by: Coghlan, J.P. ESTC t132045. * L; Lhe; UGL; Ush; WDA.

> The 'Directory' is followed by a new year's gift for 1797, indulgences, a survey of Catholic chapels, Catholic educational institutions, an account of the foundation of Maynooth, English convents abroad, the present state of religion in China, obituaries, a 24-page Coghlan catalogue and adverts for sacred vessels, medicines and the Royal Hotel Inn.

1604. *The laity's directory for the church service ... for the year of our Lord M.DCC.XCVIII. Being the second after leap year ... By permission.* London. [1797]. 12°. 20, 12, 28, [8], 29-30, [2], 24 p. Printed by: Coghlan, J.P. Published by: Coghlan, J.P. ESTC t132043. * BHN; L; Lhe; Ush; WDA.

> The 'Directory' is followed by a new year's gift for 1798, indulgences, Catholic educational institutions, sufferers by the French Revolution, letters from Rome, obituaries, pastoral letter by Walmesley (no. 2878), adverts and a 24-page Coghlan catalogue (ESTC t132042). Some copies have a 26-page Coghlan catalogue. Ush has 20, 12, 28, [8], 29-30, [2], 25, [2], 2 p.

1605. *The laity's directory; for the church service ... for the year of our Lord MDCCXCIX. Being the third after leap year ... By permission.* London. [1798]. 12°. 19, [1], 12, 23, [1] p. Printed by: Coghlan, J.P. Published by: Coghlan, J.P. ESTC t132041. * L; Lhe; Osc; Ush; WDA (2).

> The 'Directory' is followed by a new year's gift for 1799, pastoral letters, indulgences, extract letter Dr Moylan, survey of Catholic chapels, Catholic educational institutions, and adverts for sacred vessels. Lhe and one WDA copy have an additional 46, resp. 44, pages. consisting of 'An account of some of the

171

sufferings of Pope Pius VI' (see also no. 19), extracts letters, obituaries, adverts for medicines and travel to the Continent, and a 24-page Coghlan catalogue.

1606. *The laity's directory; for the church service ... for the year of our Lord MDCCC. Being the fourth leap year ... By permission.* London. [1799]. 12°. 20, 12, 40, [10], 24 p. Printed by: Coghlan, J.P. Published by: Coghlan, J.P. ESTC t132039. * L; Lhe; Ush; WDA.

> The 'Directory' is followed by a new year's gift for 1800, a circular letter from the bishops, message for the French priests, indulgences, survey of Catholic chapels, Catholic educational institutions, obituary for 1799, adverts for medicines, portrait of Pius VI and a notice of his death, and a 24-page Coghlan catalogue, including some miscellaneous adverts.

1607. *The laity's directory for the church service, for the year of our Lord MDCCCI. Being the fifth leap year ... By permission.* London. [1800]. 12°. 20, 12, 35, [1], iv, 20 p. Published by: Keating; Brown; Keating. ESTC t132056. * L; Lhe; Ush; WDA.

> The 'Directory' is followed by a new year's gift for 1801, indulgences, Catholic educational institutions, survey of Catholic chapels, portrait of Pius VII, obituaries, and a 20-page Coghlan catalogue including some miscellaneous adverts.

1608. Lambert, Pierre-Thomas. *Lettre de m. l'abbé Lambert à m. l'abbé Barruel.* London. 1800. 12°. 8 p. Printed by: Dulau, A.; Nardini, L. ESTC t082589. * L.

1609. Languet de Villeneuve de Gercy, Jean Joseph. *Catechisme du diocese de Sens. Par monseigneur Jean-Joseph Languet, Archevêque de Sens.* Quebec. [1765]. 177, [3] p. Printed by: Brown & Gilmore. ESTC w016643. * CaQMBM; CaQQLa.

> This catechism, first published at Soissons, 1727, was used in the diocese of Quebec till 1777. It was the first substantial publication brought out by Brown & Gilmore. The English-French war created a market for Catholic devotional works printed in Canada; these formed a considerable part of Brown & Gilmore's printing business (Tremaine, 59). See also next item.

1610. Languet de Villeneuve de Gercy, Jean Joseph. *Catechisme du diocese de Sens. Par monseigneur Jean-Joseph Languet, Archevêque de Sens.* Quebec. [1766]. 148, [4] p. Printed by: Brown & Gilmore. ESTC w016644. * CaOONL; CaQQLa.

1611. Languet de Villeneuve de Gercy, Jean Joseph. *A letter from the Lord Archbishop of Sens, to monsieur ****** counsellor in the parliament of Paris. In answer to the parliament's arret, against the clergy of France, in respect to the certificates of confession, and the Bull Unigenitus [Lettre de M. L'Evêque de Soissons à M***].* London. 1752. 8°. [2], 26 p. Printed by: Jeffery, H. Sold by: Jeffery, H. ESTC n019893. * MoU; PU.

1612. Languet de Villeneuve de Gercy, Jean Joseph. *A short abridgment of Christian doctrine, newly revised for the use of the Catholic church in the United States of America. To which is added a short daily exercise.* 12th ed. Georgetown [D.C.]. [1793]. [44] p. Printed by: Doyle, J. ESTC w009059. * DGU (-tp).

See also 'Short abridgement'.

1613. Languet de Villeneuve de Gercy, Jean Joseph. *A short abridgment of Christian doctrine, newly revised for the use of the Catholic church in the United States of America. To which is added a short daily exercise.* 13th ed. Baltimore. 1795. 54 p. Printed by: Sower, S. Published by: Sower, S. * MdW.

1614. Languet de Villeneuve de Gercy, Jean Joseph. *A short abridgment of Christian doctrine; newly revised for the use of the Catholic church in the United States of America. To which is added a short daily exercise.* 14th ed. Baltimore. [1798]. 18°. 51, [1] p. Printed by: Duffy, M. ESTC w009754. * DGU-W.

1615. Languet de Villeneuve de Gercy, Jean Joseph. *A treatise of confidence in the mercy of God, for the consolation of those souls that are thrown into discouragement by fear [Traité de la confiance en la misericorde de Dieu].* London. 1768. 12°. 276, [4] p. Published by: Marmaduke, J. ESTC t104738. * CAL; CLU; DAE; DMR; Do; DoA; ECB; ECW; Gi (imp.); Hen; Hor; L; LO; NSPM; Osc; Stan; TxU; Yb.

According to Kirk (p. 159) translated by J. Marmaduke.

1616. Languet de Villeneuve de Gercy, Jean Joseph. *A treatise of confidence in the mercy of God, for the consolation of those souls that are thrown into discouragement by fear. From the 6th ed.* Dublin. 1771. 12°. [10], 260 p. Published by: Hoey, P. * IDA; UshA.

With 4 pages of adverts.

1617. Languet de Villeneuve de Gercy, Jean Joseph. *A treatise of confidence in the mercy of God, for the consolation of those souls that are thrown into discouragement by fear. From the 6th ed.* Dublin. 1782. 12°. [8], 260, [4] p. Printed by: Hoey, P. ESTC t176558. * Du; NSPM; Yb.

With 4 pages of adverts.

1618. Lasne d'Aiguebell, M. de. *Sentimental and practical theology, from the French of Le Chevalier de ******* [Sentimens affectueuse de l'âme envers Dieu].* Anon. London. 1777. 8°. viii, 235, [1] p. Printed by: Wilkie, J.; Davies, T.; Leacroft, S. Published by: [Coghlan, J.P.]. ESTC t119352. * C; CAL; E; L; Lhe; O; Osc; Sal; Stan.

Dedicated to the 'right honourable Lady Maria Christina Arundell, countess of the Holy Roman Empire'. Translated by John Jones who signs the dedication. See also letter Coghlan to George Hay, 20 April 1777 (SCA).

1619. Lawson, Thomas. *The devotion to the sacred heart of Jesus, with other pious practices, devout prayers, and instructions for the life and convenience of Christians in general.* Anon. Bruges. 1765. 8°. [2], vi, 287, [5] p. Printed by: Praet, J. van. ESTC t165071. * CAL; DAE; DMR; Do; DoA; ECW; Lfa; LfaA; Lhe; MBAt; Stan; TxU.

Thomas Lawson was rector of the English College at St. Omers but returned home after the suppression of the Jesuits in 1773. He started the Association of the Sacred Heart in England (Gillow IV, 172-3). See also nos 1738 and 1751.

1620. Lawson, Thomas. *The devotion to the sacred heart of Jesus for the use of the association erected under that title in the domestic oratory of the Society of*

Jesus at Bruges. Anon. Bruges. 1767. 8°. [4], 123, [1] p. Printed by: Praet, J. van. ESTC t184424. * Do; DoA; ECB; Lfa; Lhe; O; Osc; Sto (imp.); Ush.

1621. Lawson, Thomas. *The devotion to the sacred heart of Jesus.* 4th ed. London. 1792. 8°. [2], 109, [3] p. Printed by: Keating, P. ESTC t118804. * CAL; ECW; L.

> With one page of Keating adverts.

1622. Lawson, Thomas. *The devotion to the sacred heart of Jesus. With pious practices, devout prayers, and instructions, intended to promote fervour amongst Christians.* [London?]. 1799. 12°. 339, [1] p. ESTC n017681. * CaOHM; Do; ECW; Yb.

> According to Sommervogel (IV, 1579) and Gillow (IV, 171) another Thomas Lawson S.J., who died at Watten in 1750, wrote 'Exhortations of the rules, delivered to the novices at Watten'.

1623. *A lay directory: or a help to find out, and assist at vespers, or evening-office of the church on Sundays and holy days. For the year M.DCC.LXI.* [London]. 1761. 12°. iv, 20 p. ESTC t154609. * L.

> Advertisement on verso of tp dated 'January 1, 1761'.

1624. Le Clerc de Juigné, Antoine Eléonore Léon. *The mandate of his grace, the Archbishop of Paris, ordering the Te Deum to be sung in all the churches of his diocese, in thanksgiving for the re-establishment of peace. Translated from the French.* London. 1784. 8°. [4], 17, [3] p. Printed by: Coghlan, J.P. Sold by: Coghlan, J.P. ESTC n034764. * MBAt; Ush (2).

> One Ush copy has one page of adverts.

1625. Le Courayer, Pierre François. *A defence of the validity of the english ordinations, and of the succession of the bishops in the Church of England ... translated into English by Dan. Williams.* London, 1725. 8°. [22], 405, [3] p. Published by: Innys, W., and J.; Osborne, J.; Rivington, C. ESTC t 113030. * C; CaQMM; CLU-C; CSmH; Csj; CtHT; D; DFo; Dt; E; IES; KU-S; L; Lmh; MnU; MRu; NNUT; O; Oc; Oe; Ol; Omc; On; Owo; PPL; TxU.

> We include one ed. of Le Courayer's chief work because - although clearly not published under R.C. auspices - the author all his life claimed that he was a Catholic and that his work was not unorthodox. For Le Courayer's other publications see ESTC.

1626. Le Gobien, Charles. *Edifying and curious letters of some missioners, of the Society of Jesus from foreign missions.* 1707. 8°. [14], 258, [4] p. Sold by: [Lewis, W.]. * DLC; Hen; InU; MB; Mil; NIC; NN; RPJCB; Ush; Yb.

> A translation (by George Webb S.J. 1653-1724; see Walsh p. 56) of part of Le Gobien's *Lettres édifiantes et curieuses.* This book was later issued as vol. 1 of a 2-vol. ed. See next item.

1627. Le Gobien, Charles. *Edifying and curious letters of some missioners of the Society of Jesus from foreign missions.* 2 vols. [London?]. 1707-09. 8°. [14], 258, [4]; [24], 173, [3] p. Sold by: [Lewis, W.]. ESTC t193627. * CU; DoA; L; LEu; Lfa; LfaA; Lhe; Ush.

> With an advertisement for W. Lewis.

1628. Le Pointe, Thomas. *Dissertation historique sur les libertés de l'église* *gallicane, et l'assemblée du clergé de France de 1682. Adressée à mm. les ecclésiastiques François.* Anon. London. 1799. 8°. [4], 108 p. Printed by: Baylis, T. Sold by: Deboffe. ESTC t098806. * E; L; MH; MY; O; Ush.

1629. Le Pointe, Thomas. *The one only church of Christ, and his divinity pointed out to all by a single fact. From the editions in French. With improvements [La religion prouvée par un seul fait].* London. 1800. 12°. 34 p. Printed by: Baylis, T. Sold by: Keatings [sic] & Brown; Booker. ESTC t105412. * L; Sto.

1630. Le Pointe, Thomas. *La religion prouvée par un seul fait.* London. 1798. 12°. [2], ii, [2], 18 p. Printed by: Baylis, T. ESTC t115269. * L.

1631. Le Pointe, Thomas. *Selecta sanctorum Caroli Borromaei, Francisci Salesii, Ignatii, Xaveriique monita omnibus qui in evangilio [sic] laborant utilia, ad usum cleri Galliarum in patriam remigrantis accommodata.* London. 1800. 12°. 26 p. Printed by: Boussonnier, P. le. Sold by: Keating; Brown; Keating; Booker. ESTC t116508. * L; TxU; Ush.

1632. Le Tourneux, Nicolas. *The history of the life of our Lord Jesus Christ. Newly and faithfully translated from the fifth edition of the French. By W... C... [Histoire de la vie de nostre Seigneur Jésus Christ].* Anon. [London]. 1739. 12°. lxiv, [8], 312, [8] p. Published by: Meighan, T. ESTC n009021. * CLU-C; DAE; Do; DoA; ECB; Map; Sal; Yb.

> 'W... C...' is William Crathorne. See also next item. With advert on last page.

1633. Le Tourneux, Nicolas. *The history of the life of our Lord Jesus Christ. Newly and faithfully translated from the fifth edition of the French. By W... C...* Anon. Dublin. 1763. 12°. xlix, [7], 202 [i.e. 220], [8] p. Printed by: Corcoran, B. Published by: Corcoran, B. ESTC t081493. * IU; L; Sal.

> With one page of Corcoran adverts for books by Francis Blyth and Richard Challoner.

1634. Ledesma, Diego. *The Christian doctrine: in manner of a dialogue between master and scholar ... For the use of children and unlearned Catholics. Also, the manner of serving a priest at mass.* Dublin. 1775. 32°. 32 p. Printed by: Cross, R. * Ush.

1635. *Lessons on the obligation of the paschal communion, and the necessary preparation and dispositions for it. To be read by all pastors to their people on Midlent Sunday.* [London?]. [1800?]. 8°. 8 p. ESTC t037726. * ECW; L; TxU; Ush; WDA.

1636. *Lessons on the obligation of the paschal communion, and the necessary preparation and dispositions for it. To be read by all pastors to their people on Midlent Sunday.* [London?]. [1800?]. 8°. s.s. * Amp.

1637. *A letter addressed to the Catholics of England, by the Catholic Committee.* London. 1792. 4°. [2], 28, iii, [1], 46 p. Printed by: Coghlan, J.P. ESTC t037751. * BAA; C; Hen; L; LfaA; MY; O; Osc; SIR; Sto; TxU; Ush.

> With 10 appendices comprising the documents of the dissolving Catholic Committee. This was also known as 'The Third Blue Book'.

1638. *A letter from a gentleman in Dublin to his friend in Corke ... setting forth*

... *the publication of The case of the Roman-Catholicks of Ireland ... reprinted there from the Dublin edition.* [Dublin]. [1755?]. 4°. 4 p. Published by: Lord, P. Sold by: Lord, P. ESTC t160458. * Du; FLK.

> The letter is dated 'Dublin, 18 July 1755'. For eds of Charles O'Conor's *The case of the Roman-Catholics of Ireland* see nos 1988-1991. According to Hugh Fenning O.P. (personal communication) the present letter was probably written by O'Conor himself.

1639. *A letter from mrs. L***, lady to a president of one of the French parliaments, to the Jesuits of France.* 12°. 34 p. * Sto.

> Clearly in defence of the Jesuits. The letter is followed by 'The act of adherence to the pastoral instruction' by Lewis F. G. d'Orleans de la Motte, Bishop of Amiens, dated 'Amiens, Feb. 1, 1764'.

1640. *A letter from the archbishops and bishops of the province of Dublin to his holiness, Pius VI. On the constitution announcing the condemnation of the errors of the Synod of Pistoia.* London. 1797. 12°. [2], 47, [1] p. Printed by: Coghlan, J.P. ESTC t176547. * DUc; Lhe; O; TxU; Ush(2).

> One Ush copy has 2 pages of adverts.

1641. *Letter of several French bishops residing in England to Pope Pius the VI. With the answer of the sovereign pontiff. Translated from the Latin original by the rev. William Henry Coombes.* London. 1800. 12°. 24 p. Printed by: Coghlan, J.P. * ECW; Lhe.

> The French ed. was entitled *Lettre Latine de plusieurs évêques de France au Pape Pie Six* (no. 1652). See also next 2 items. Lhe bound up with Brancadoro, *Oration*, 1800 (no. 362).

1642. *Letter of several French bishops residing in England to Pope Pius VI. With the answer of the sovereign pontiff. Translated from the Latin original by the rev. William Henry Coombes.* 2nd ed. London. 1800. 12°. [2], 24 p. Printed by: Coghlan, J.P. Sold by: West; Hughes; Debrett; Keating; Booker. ESTC n060638. * ICN.

1643. *Letter of the French bishops residing in England, to the late Pope Pius VI, and the answer of his holiness, together with the Latin originals.* Dublin. 1800. 8°. 29, [1] p. Printed by: Fitzpatrick, H. ESTC t108351. * CU-S; D; L; PP.

1644. *Letter on papal supremacy to the rev. Geo. Bruning.* Manchester. 1799. 12 p. Printed by: Haydock, T. * Amp.

1645. *A letter to a gentleman in the country, on the subject of a late conference, relating to the worship and invocation of angels.* London. 1742. 8°. xii, 50 p. ESTC t170999. * Amp; E; O; Sto.

1646. *A letter to a noble lord, containing a full declaration of the Catholic sentiment on the important question of union. By an Irish Catholic.* Dublin. 1800. 8°. 8 p. Printed by: Folingsby, G. ESTC t179544. * D.

1647. *A letter to John Keogh, Esq. on the subject of a late meeting. By a Roman Catholic.* Dublin. 1795. 8°. 14 p. Published by: Author. ESTC n035046. * TxU.

1648. *A letter to Sir George Saville, Bart. upon the allegiance of a British* *subject: occasioned by his late bill in Parliament in favour of the Roman Catholics.* London. 1778. 8°. 43, [1] p. Published by: Robson, J. ESTC t103678. * E; ICN; L; O; Map; PP; Ush.

> Written by a Roman Catholic, thanking Saville for his enlightened measure.

1649. *A letter to the right revd. Lord Bishop of Down and Connor. Occasioned by a sermon preached by his lordship on the death of Mr Richard Archbold ... who conformed to the ... Church of Ireland.* Dublin. 1760. 8°. [3], 4-20 p. ESTC n019630. * C; Dt; Mil; PP.

> An anonymous attack by a R.C. author on a sermon praising the apostate Jesuit Archibald Bower.

1650. *A letter to the R.R. Thomas Flynn, George Beeston, William Hartley, Joseph Berington, Thomas Stone, John Carter, John Corne ... in answer to their late address to the Catholic clergy of England.* London. [1792]. 8°. 27, [1] p. Published by: Coghlan, J.P.; Keating, P. ; Booker, T. ESTC t169811. * BMp; Ct; Di; ECW; Lhe; Lmh; MY; Osc; Sto; Ush.

> This reply to the Staffordshire clergy is signed by three Jesuits, Alexander Clinton, Joseph Reeve and Charles Plowden, and by some 30 other persons. Sto has 22 p.

1651. *Letters to the Roman Catholic laity, occasioned by doctor Hussey's pastoral letter.* Dublin. 1797. 12°. 24 p. ESTC n034286. * MoU.

> For Thomas Hussey's pastoral letter see nos 1493-1494.

1652. *Lettre Latine de plusieurs évêques de France au Pape Pie Six, et réponse du souverain pontife traduite en François par un prêtre exilé pour la foi.* London. 1799. 8°. [4], 28 p. Printed by: Williams, W. Sold by: Dulau, A.; Marmet, L.; Coghlan, J.P.; Booker, J. ESTC t038592. * CaQMBN; ECW; L; MH-H; Sto.

> Parallel Latin and French texts. For English eds of this *Lettre* see nos 1641-1643.

1653. *Lettres des provinciaux Benedictins, et reponses de messieurs les vicaires apostoliques.* 15, [1] p. * DoA.

> Ten letters, the last one dated '17th December 1753', concerning the apparent encroachment of the English vicars apostolic on the rights of monks and other regulars. Title in French, text in Latin.

1654. *Lettres d'un curé Catholique d'Angleterre à mm. les curés du diocèse de Lisieux, en France, protestant contre les mandemens de leur evêque.* London. 1775. 8°. * Howell, 878.

1655. Leyburn, George. *The memoirs of George Leyburn doctor of divinity, chaplain to Henrietta Maria Queen of England. Being a journal of his agency for Prince Charles in Ireland, in the year 1647.* London. 1722. 8°. [12], xxix, [1], 61, [1] p. Published by: Lewis, W. ESTC t155074. * C; CaOTU; CLU-C; CSmH; DFo; IU; L; NjP; O; Oc; Osc; Owo; Ush; WDA.

> Another edition, possibly by Hugh Tootell, of a posthumous work by the 17th century priest Leyburn. The book addresses the general reader and the interest is largely historical. There was another ed. in 1723 (see ESTC).

1656. Leyburn, John. *A pastoral letter from the four Catholic bishops to the lay-Catholics of England.* London. 1747. 4°. 8 p. ESTC t114270. * L.

177

A pastoral letter on the re-establishment of Roman Catholic episcopal authority in England, originally published in 1688. Signed by John [Leyburn] Bishop of Adramite, Bonaventure [Giffard], Bishop of Madoura; Philip [Ellis], Bishop of Aureliople; James [Smith], Bishop of Callipoli.

1657. Lhomond, Charles François. *Elemens de la langue Latine, a l'ussage [sic] du seminaire des missions etrangeres de Quebec. Imprimé sous la direction de m.m. du seminaire.* Quebec. 1799. 172, 226 [i.e. 126] p. Published by: Neilson, J. ESTC w016663. * CaQMBM; CaQQLa.

1658. Lhomond, Charles François. *Elements de la grammaire Latine.* Quebec. 1799. [2], 76 [i.e. 74], 226, [i.e. 126] p. Printed by: Lelievre, R.; Desbarats, P. E. ESTC w016662. * CaBVaU; CaQMBM; CaQMM.

> We assume that this grammar, like the previous item, was composed for the use of Canadian seminarists .

1659. Lhomond, Charles François. *Pious lectures, explanatory of the principles, obligations and resources, of the Catholic religion; translated ... By the rev. James Appleton [Doctrine Chrétienne].* London repr. [Wolverhampton]. 1794. 8°. [2], xiv, 463, [1] p. Published by: Keating; Brown; Keating. ESTC t101444. * ECW; L.

> A reissue of *Theophilus, or the pupil instructed*, no. 1660.

1660. Lhomond, Charles François. *Theophilus, or the pupil instructed in the principles, the obligations, and the resources of the Roman Catholic religion. By the rev. Mr Appleton. From the French La doctrine Chrétienne.* Wolverhampton. 1794. 8°. xiv, 463, [1] p. Printed by: Smart, J. Published by: Author. Sold by: Coghlan, J.P. ESTC t050047. * Amp; Do; ICN; L; Lhe; MChB; O; Stan; TLP; Ush; WOV.

> Gillow (I, 54) also gives a London 1795 ed.

1661. *Libellus precum et piarum exercitationum in usum piè vivere, et feliciter mori desiderantium. Permissu superiorum.* [St. Omers?]. 1714. 12°. [24], 348 p. * DMR; Ush.

> Apparently this Latin book, published outside England, was popular among English Catholics and it is not unlikely that it was specifically composed for the English market abroad. Sommervogel (Sup. 400) ascribes this book to Thomas Coniers, S.J. (1664-1721). See also next 2 items.

1662. *Libellus precum et piarum exercitationum in usum piè vivere et feliciter mori desiderantium. Permissu superiorum.* [St. Omers?]. 1730. 12°. [24], 336 p. * DMR; ICN; L; Osc; Sto(2); Ush.

> Both Sto copies lack tp. One of them lacks the [24] pages. ICN bound up with no. 6, *Abridgment of the rules of the English sodality*.

1663. *Libellus precum et piarum exercitationum in usum piè vivere et feliciter mori desiderantium. Permissu superiorum.* 1778. 8°. xxiv, 323, [1] p. * Osc; Ush.

> The calendar has a number of English saints. There is a Little Office of Our Lady, and one of St. Joseph. The litanies include St. Francis Xavier, St. Aloysius, and the Three Kings.

1664. *The life of faith. Translated from the French, printed at Lisle.* 1771. 2 p. *

DAE.

Bound up with *A manual* (no. 1804).

1665. *The life of Francis Xavier, apostle of the Indies.* Philadelphia. 1798. 12°. [3], viii-xii, [1], 14-192 p. Printed by: Hogan & M'Elroy. Published by: Brodie, A. ESTC w013616. * CtY; DB; DLC; ICU; MH-AH; MWA; MWH; NcGU; NjR; NN; NNC; PP; PU; RPJCB; WMM.

'The first part of this abstract is taken from two accounts of St. Francis by different men; the rest is from Dominique Bouhours's *Life of St. Francis*, translated by Dryden, London 1688' (preface).

1666. *The life of Saint Mary of Egypt.* [Dublin?]. [1800?]. 8°. 8 p. ESTC t040962. * L.

Popular verse in praise of Mary of Egypt.

1667. *The life of the most eminent and truly illustrious bishop, St. Patrick, the apostle and patron of Ireland. Collected from the most authentick accounts.* Dublin. 1747. 8°. 127, [1] p. Printed by: Bate, E. Published by: Bate, E. ESTC n020000. * CLU-C; ICN.

This is a not specifically R.C., historical work. For other eds by Catholic and non-Catholic publishers, see ESTC.

1668. *A light to the reform'd churches; or, a call and exhortation to consideration, to all who are under any branch of the Reformation.* 1748. 12°. ii, 3-16 p. * DoA.

In verse; the verses begin 'The Holy, Catholic, Apostolic and Roman church is the true way to salvation'.

1669. Limon, Geoffroi, Marquis de. *La vie et le martyre de Louis XVI, Roi de France et de Navarre, immolé le 21 janvier 1793. Avec un examen du décret regicide. Suivi du testament de Louis XVI ... Imprimé au profit du clergé refugié.* London. 1793. 8°. [2], 86 p. Printed by: Coghlan, J.P. Sold by: Debrett, J.; Booker; Keating; Lewis; Robinsons; Robins (Winchester); Gregory (Brighton); Leger (Dover); Watts (Gosport). ESTC t142240. * L; MH; Osc.

1670. *A list of such members of the House of Commons in Ireland as on Tuesday the fourth of August 1778, voted for and against the popery bill, on its return from England without the test clause.* London. [1778]. fol. [2] p. Printed by: Coghlan, J.P. * SCA (2).

One SCA copy has a list of the Lords that voted for and against the popery bill on p. [2].

1671. *The litanies and prayers, in Latin and English recommended to be said in Catholick families.* 3rd ed. London. 1748. 12°. 36 p. Published by: Meighan, T. ESTC t105163. * L.

1672. *Litanies and prayers in Latin and English, recommended to be said in Catholic families.* 4th ed. London. 1755. 8°. 30 p. Printed by: Marmaduke, J. Sold by: Marmaduke, J. * Osc.

1673. *The litanies of Jesus, of the b. Virgin Mary, and of the holy angels. With the short office of the angels.* [London?]. 1720. 24°. 48 p. * Map (2).

One copy bound up with no. 1902; the other with nos 1903 and 1126.

1674. *The litanies of S. Winefrid virgin and martyr.* London. [1703?]. 8°. 8 p. Published by: Nicholas, J. ESTC t202158. * E.

> The publisher's name may be fictitious.

1675. *The litanies of S. Winefrid, virgin and martyr.* [London?]. 1703. 12°. 8 p. ESTC t123698. * L.

1676. *The litanies of S. Wenefride, virgin and martyr.* [London?]. 1712. 12°. 8 p. ESTC t099780. * DFo; L; Lfa; Oe.

1677. *The litanies of St. Winefrid.* [London?]. 1748. 12°. 8 p. * Map.

> Bound up with nos 1853, 595 and 135.

1678. *The litanies of the blessed sacrament: with devout acts and other devotions in honour of that sacred mystery.* [London]. [1790?]. 8°. [2], 14 p. Printed by: Coghlan, J.P. ESTC t105162. * L; MBAt; O.

1679. *Litany of St. Mary of Egypt.* 1733. 12°. 9, [1] p. * CAL.

> Bound up with *A devotion to the sacred heart*, 1733 (no. 1154).

1680. Loop, George. *The queen of heaven's livery: or, a short treatise of the institution, excellency ... of the most famous confraternity of our blessed lady of Mount Carmel ... By G.L. Dis. Carm.* Antwerp. 1709. 12°. [10], 81, [5] p. ESTC t101402. * CSmH; Gi; L; LO; Ush; Yb.

> See also no. 2553ff.

1681. Luis de Granada. *An exhortation to alms-deeds, written originally in Spanish, by the R.F. Lewis, of Granada, and now translated into English.* London. 1775. 32°. [2], v, [1], 128 p. Printed by: Coghlan, J.P. ESTC n045915. * MBAt; O; Ush.

> The preface states that the book was translated into French by F. Simon Martin (1682) and that the English version is based on the French ed. According to Kirk (p. 229) translated by Thomas Talbot. The main text is preceded by one page of errata. See also next item.

1682. Luis de Granada. *An exhortation to alms-deeds. Written originally in Spanish, by the R.F. Lewis, of Granada; and now translated into English.* 2nd ed. London. 1775. 32°. [2], v, [1], 128 p. Printed by: Coghlan, J.P. ESTC n045915. * O; Ush.

> The main text is preceded by one page of Coghlan adverts.

1683. Luis de Granada. *A memorial of a Christian life ... divided into four books [Memorial de la vida Christiana].* Cork. 1756. 8°. [16], 384 p. Printed by: Swiney, E. Sold by: Swiney, E. * IDA.

1684. Luis de Granada. *A memorial of a Christian life ... In four books ... revised and corrected by the rev. B. MacMahon.* 4th ed. Dublin. 1795. 8°. xvi, 371, [5] p. Printed by: Fitzpatrick, H. Published by: Cross, R.; M'Donnel, T.; Fitzpatrick, H. ESTC t122820. * D; DMR; ECW; FLK (imp.); ICN; IDA; L; Lhe; NSchU; TxU.

> With a list of subscribers. FLK is incomplete and might be no. 1683.

1685. Luis de Granada. *The sinners guide, containing a full and ample exhortation to the pursuit of virtue [Guia de peccadores].* [London]. 1702. 8°.

[10], 707, [3] p. Sold by: Metcalfe, T. ESTC t121453. * CaOHM; CLU-C; DFo (imp.); Do; ECB; ECW; Hor; L; Lfa; Lhe; MRu; TH.

1686. Luis de Granada. *The sinners guide, containing a full and ample exhortation to the pursuit of virtue.* [London?]. 1723. 8°. [8], 568, [4] p. ESTC n036292. * D; TxU.

1687. Luis de Granada. *The sinners guide. Containing a full and ample exhortation to the pursuit of virtue.* Dublin. 1740. 8°. [8], 568, [8] p. Published by: Kelly, I. ESTC t174303. * D; FLK.

       With 4 pages of adverts.

1688. Luis de Granada. *The sinners guide, from vice to virtue; giving him instructions and directions how to become virtuous.* 2nd ed. London. 1760. 8°. xii, 554, [2] p. Published by: Gibson, N. ESTC n023305. * BFq; BMu; CLU; Do; ECW; IES; KAS; O; Sal; Sto; TLP.

       'Let the publisher have a share in your good prayers, that may this his labour prove to the glory of God, and the benefit of Christian souls. March 19, 1760. The feast of St. Joseph.' (Preface). TLP has: vii-xii, iii-vi, 554, [2] p.

1689. Luis de Granada. *The sinners guide, from vice to virtue; giving him instructions and directions how to become virtuous.* London. 1761. 8°. [3], vii-xii, 544, [2] p. Published by: Cooper, M. ESTC t122819. * ECW; L; TxU.

1690. Luis de Granada. *The sinners guide. Book the first. Containing a full and ample exhortation to the pursuit of virtue.* Dublin. 1790. 8°. xiv, 450 p. Printed by: Wogan, P. ESTC n023304. * C; FLK; O; OrPU.

       'Book the second' begins on p. [305].

1691. MacCarthy, Florence. *A funeral sermon, preached, at a solemn high mass celebrated in Cork on Wednesday, the sixth of February, for his late most Christian majesty, Louis the Sixteenth. By the rev. F. M'C.* Cork. 1793. 8°. 22 p. Printed by: Haly, J. ESTC t188452. * D; MY; Yb.

1692. MacCarthy, Florence. *A funeral sermon, preached at a solemn high mass, celebrated in Cork, on Tuesday, 12th November, for Marie Antoinette, her late most Christian majesty.* Cork. 1793. 8°. 28 p. Printed by: Haly, J. ESTC t208858. * D; MY.

1693. MacCarthy, Florence. *A funeral sermon, preached at a solemn high mass, celebrated in Cork, on Tuesday, 12th November, for Marie Antoinette, her late most Christian majesty.* 2nd ed. Cork. 1793. 8°. 28 p. Printed by: Haly, J. * CAI; Yb.

1694. MacCary, James Mathew. *The penitent's daily assistant, selected from approved books and records of the Roman Catholic church. By the rev. F.J.M.C.S.O.P and R.F.S.* Belfast. 1795. 12°. [3], viii-x, [3], 4-271, [1] p. Published by: Sheridan, R.F. ESTC t197857. * D.

1695. MacCary, James Mathew. *The sure way to heaven, being a new volume, such never before published in English on the truths of salvation.* Belfast. 1797. 12°. 152, 12 p. ESTC t102953. * D.

       With a list of subscribers.

1696. MacCurtin, Hugh. *The elements of the Irish language, grammatically explained in English. In 14 chapters.* Louvain. 1728. 8°. [15], 12-158, [2] p. Printed by: Overbeke, M. van. ESTC t090681. * C; CLU-C; D; DFo; Du; E; ICN; L; MH-H; Mil; MRu; NjP; NN; O; OCl; P; PV; SCR.

> The last part of the book (pp. 97-158, [2]) consists of a R.C. catechism in Irish 'Suim Bhunudhasach'. It has a separate tp but continuous pagination and register, and the author is identified as John Dowley. The book also contains a religious poem in Irish by Bonaventura O'Hussey (see also nos 2047 and 919).

1697. MacDonald, Archibald Benedict. *A companion to the altar, or, prayers for morning and afternoon service, on Sundays and holidays.* 2nd ed. Liverpool. 1792. 12°. vi, 413, [3] p. * DoA; Gi; Stan; Ush.

> DoA has an additional page of 'Proposals to print ... a set of sermons ... apply to the rev. Mr. McDonald'. The work appeared as *Select discourses on the gospels* in 1801 (Gillow IV, 371). For MacDonald, see Aveling, p. 166.

1698. MacDonald, Archibald Benedict. *The lay-man's afternoon devotion: on all Sundays and holydays throughout the year.* Anon. Preston. 1778. 8°. viii, 173, [3] p. Printed by: Stuart, W. ESTC t088136. * DMR; Do; Gi; L.

1699. MacDonald, Archibald Benedict. *The layman's afternoon devotion, on all Sundays and holidays throughout the year.* Anon. Preston. 1793. 12°. viii, 9-189, [1] p. Printed by: Walker and Kay. Published by: Sharrock, M. * Do; DoA; Gi.

1700. MacDonald, Archibald Benedict. *Moral essays, chiefly collected from different authors, by A.M.* 2 vols. Liverpool. 1796. 12°. vi, 261, [1]; vi, 290 p. Printed by: M'Creery, J. ESTC t170112. * Do; DoA; MdBJ; NSPM (vol. 1); O; Stan.

1701. MacKenna, Theobald. *Address to the Roman Catholics of Ireland, relative to the late proceedings, and on the means and practicability of a tranquil emancipation.* Dublin. 1792. 8°. [4], 52 p. Published by: Rice, J. ESTC t086584. * C; CSmH; D; Di; Dt; FU; L; Lhl; MH; MoSW; MY; Oc.

> Most of MacKenna's publications are in the border area between politics and religion. We have decided to include all of these.

1702. MacKenna, Theobald. *Address to the Roman Catholics of Ireland, relative to the late proceedings, and on the means and practicability of a tranquil emancipation.* 2nd ed. Dublin. 1793. 8°. [2], 52 p. Published by: Rice, J. ESTC t215416. * Di; Sto.

1703. MacKenna, Theobald. *An argument against extermination: occasioned by Doctor Duigenan's "Representation of the present political state of Ireland." By a Catholic and Burkist.* Anon. Dublin. 1800. 8°. [2], 55, [1], 56-57 p. Printed by: Fitzpatrick, H. ESTC t182601. * CSmH; D; Di; ICR; Lhl; MiU; MY.

> Duigenan's *A fair representation of the present political state of Ireland* was published in 1799.

1704. MacKenna, Theobald. *Constitutional objections to the government of Ireland by a separate legislature, in a letter to John Hamilton.* Dublin. 1799. 8°. [2], vi, [1], 4-86 p. Printed by: Fitzpatrick, H. ESTC n003721. * C; CSmH; D;

Di; E; ICN; KU-S; MH-BA; NSbSU; O; Oa; PP.

> Also issued as part of *Tracts on the subject of an union*, vol. 5, Dublin 1799. John Hamilton's *A letter to Theobald M'Kenna, Esq. occasioned by a publication, entitled A memoire* came out in 1799.

1705. MacKenna, Theobald. *Constitutional objections to the government of Ireland by a separate legislature, in a letter to John Hamilton, Esq.* 2nd ed. Dublin. 1799. 8°. [3], iv-viii, [1], 85, [1] p. Printed by: Fitzpatrick, H. ESTC t033127. * CaOTU; CSmH; D; Di; IU; KU-S; L; MH-BA; MoU; MRu; MY; Sto.

1706. MacKenna, Theobald. *Constitutional objections to the government of Ireland by a separate legislature, in a letter to John Hamilton.* 3rd ed. Dublin. 1799. 8°. 85, [1] p. Printed by: Fitzpatrick, H. ESTC t028416. * CSmH; CtY; D; Di; IU; L; MH-BA; MH-H; MiU; MY; NIC; PV.

1707. MacKenna, Theobald. *An essay on parliamentary reform, and on the evils likely to ensue, from a republican constitution, in Ireland.* Dublin. 1793. 8°. [4], 51, [1] p. Published by: Rice, J. ESTC t028417. * C; CoU; D; Di; ICN; InU-Li; KU-S; MoSW; MY; O; PSt; Sto.

1708. MacKenna, Theobald. *A letter to the societies of United Irishmen, of the town of Belfast, upon the subject of certain apprehensions which have arisen from a proposed restoration of Catholic rights, by William Todd Jones. With the declaration of the Catholic Society of Dublin and some thoughts on the present politics of Ireland by Theobald MacKenna.* London repr. [Dublin]. 1792. 8°. [2], 15, [1], 189, [1] p. Published by: Robinson, G.G.J. and J. ESTC t179495. * D; Ldw; OOxM; Sto.

> See also nos 1532 and 1711.

1709. MacKenna, Theobald. *A memoire on some questions respecting the projected union of Great Britain and Ireland.* Dublin. 1799. 8°. [2], 42 p. Printed by: Rice, J. ESTC t056701. * C; CSmH; CtU; CU; D; Dt; Du; E; ICN; IU; KU-S; Lhl; MH; MiU; MRu; MY; NcD; NIC; NN; O; Oc; PP; PPAmP; PV; TxU.

> Also issued as part of *Tracts on the subject of an union*, vol. 2, Dublin, 1799.

1710. MacKenna, Theobald. *Political essays relative to the affairs of Ireland, in 1791, 1792, and 1793; with remarks on the present state of that country.* London. 1794. 8°. lxiii, [3], 226, [4] p. Published by: Debrett, J. ESTC t033128. * C; D; Dt; E; ICR; IU; KU-S; MH; Mil; MY; NN; PV; Sto.

> With 4 pages of adverts.

1711. MacKenna, Theobald. *Reply to an anonymous writer from Belfast, signed Portia. By William Todd Jones, Esq.* Dublin. [1792]. 8°. 2, viii, 77, [1] p. Published by: Carey, W.P.; Rice, J. ESTC t123164. * D; Di; L; MY; OkU.

> The editor's preface 'To the Irish Catholics' is signed by W.P. Carey. The book contains Jones's letter together with MacKenna's answer. See also nos 1532 and 1708.

1712. MacKenna, Theobald. *A review of the Catholic question, in which the constitutional interests of Ireland, with respect to that part of the nation, are* *investigated. To which is annexed the declaration of the Catholic Society of Dublin, and a vindication thereof.* Dublin. 1792. 8°. xvi, 84 p. Printed by: Moore, J. ESTC t088067. * C; CSmH; D; Di; Dt; Du; KU-S; L; Lhl; MH; MY; O; Owo; PU; Sto; TxU.

1713. MacKenna, Theobald. *Some thoughts on the present politics of Ireland. In a letter to Robert Simms, Esq. secretary to the Society of United Irishmen of Belfast, from Theobald M'Kenna, M.D. member of the Royal Irish Academy.* Cork. 1792. 8°. [3], 6-31, [1] p. Printed by: Haly, J. ESTC t155642. * D; MY.

1714. MacKenna, Theobald. *Some thoughts on the present politics of Ireland, in a letter to Robert Simms.* Dublin. 1792. 8°. [4], 27, [1] p. Printed by: Chambers, J. ESTC t033130. * C; CSmH; D; Di; Dt; Du; IU; KU-S; L; Lhe; Lhl; Mil; MY; O.

1715. MacKenna, Theobald. *Substance of the arguments offered by Doctor M'Kenna, to the general meeting of the Roman Catholics, April 22, 1793; with ... papers, written during the discussion of the Catholic affairs.* Dublin. 1793. 8°. [2], vi, 50, [2] p. Printed by: Byrne, P. ESTC t058109. * C; CSt; D; Di; Dt; L; MChB; MY; PU.
> With 2 pages of adverts.

1716. MacKenzie, Alexander. *Frequent communion: or, the advantages and necessity of it, asserted and proved from scripture, authority, and tradition. Compiled by A.C.* London. 1780. 12°. [4], 406, [2] p. Published by: Author. Sold by: Marmaduke, J. ESTC t129416. * DMR; Do; E; ECW; GEU-T (imp); L; Lfa; Lhe; O; Osc; Stan; TxU; Ush; Yb.
> With a letter of dedication to Bishop Challoner. 'A. C.' is Alexander Clinton, i.e. Alexander MacKenzie. See also next 5 items.

1717. MacKenzie, Alexander. *A guide to the altar, or, the advantages of frequent communion in order to obtain everlasting life ... by the rev. A. Clinton, S.J., to which is added, a discourse on the love of God.* [Dublin]. 8°. iv, 431, [9] p. Printed by: Coyne, R. * ECW; Lhe; Osc; Ush.
> With a letter of dedication to Bishop Challoner, and a list of subscribers. The book is undated, but is probably late 18th century. Osc cat. suggests c.1780.

1718. MacKenzie, Alexander. *Hidden treasures, in the hands of the lower classes of Christians.* Anon. Liverpool. 1797. 8°. 52 p. Printed by: M'Creery, J. ESTC t189467. * Lhe; LVp.
> LVp (p. 52) is signed and dated in ms 'Alexander Clinton, Portico near Prescot, July 20th, 1797'.

1719. MacKenzie, Alexander. *A letter to the reverend John Erskine, D.D. one of the ministers of Edinburgh: on the dangerous tendency of his late sketches of church-history.* Anon. Edinburgh. 1798. 8°. 22 p. Published by: Cheyne, S. * Sto.
> Preface signed 'A.C.'

1720. MacKenzie, Alexander. *The poor prisoner's comforter. In a collection of proper instructions and prayers, for Christians in prison ... To which is added, instructions and devout exercises ... according to Mr. Gother.* Anon. London.

1764. 12°. 228 p. Printed by: Balfe, R. ESTC t195790. * O.

1721. MacKenzie, Alexander. *Spiritual guide: containing the chief means which lead to perfection. Extracted from the best authors, by A.C.* London. 1778. 12°. xii, [4], 244, [4] p. Printed by: Marmaduke, J. Sold by: Marmaduke, J. ESTC t160338. * Do; ECW; Gi; Lhe; O; Osc; Sal; Sto; Ush; Yb.

> With 4 pages of Marmaduke adverts.

1722. MacMahon, Hugh. *The charge given by Hugh, Lord Archbishop of Ardmagh [sic] and primate of all Ireland, to his clergy; at the primary visitation of his diocese, begun at Drogheda, July 16.* Dublin. 1725. 4°. 19, [1] p. Printed by: Grierson, G. ESTC n027617. * C; Dt; PPL.

1723. MacMahon, Hugh. *The charge given by Hugh, Lord Archbishop of Ardmagh and primate of all Ireland, at the triennial visitation of the clergy of his province, begun at Trim, June 30, 1730.* Dublin. 1730. 4°. 20 p. Printed by: Grierson, G. * CU-BANC.

1724. MacMahon, Hugh. *The charge given by Hugh, Lord Archbishop of Ardmagh and primate of all Ireland, at the triennial visitation of the clergy of his province, begun at Drogheda, June 15, 1736.* Dublin. 1736. 4°. 19, [1] p. Printed by: Grierson, G. ESTC n027615. * Dt; Llp; PPL.

1725. MacMahon, Hugh. *Jus primatiale Armacanum, in omnes archiepiscopos, episcopos, et universum clerum, totius regni Hiberniae. Assertum per H. A. M. T. H. P.* [Dublin]. 1728. 4°. [2], 8, [2], 222, [36], 125, 11, [6] p. Printed by: [Powell, S.] ESTC t191373. * BIC; Du; FLK; IDA; L; Mil; MRu; MY; O; SCR.

> Hugh MacMahon asserts his primacy over Ireland. The second part, 125 pages, refutes a work by John Hennessy, S.J., of Clonmel.

1726. MacNeven, William James. *An argument for independence, in opposition to an union. Addressed to all his countrymen. By an Irish Catholic.* Dublin. 1799. 8°. [2], 51, [1] p. Printed by: Stockdale, J. ESTC t064629. * C; CaOTU; CSmH; CtY; CU; D; Dt; Du; E; IEN; IMunS; KU-S; L; MH-BA; MH-H; MiU; MoU; O; PP.

> An 'Irish Catholic' is William James MacNeven. Also issued as part of *Tracts on the subject of an union*, vol. 3, Dublin 1799. The book is political rather than religious but is included because the author deliberately presents himself as an Irish Catholic, and because - like MacKenna's publications - the work forms part of Irish Catholic emancipation.

1727. Maillard de Tournon, Charles Thomas. *Memoires for Rome concerning the state of the Christian religion in China, with the decree of ... Pope Clement XI. Concerning the affair of the Chinese worship. And the ordinance of my Lord Card. of Tournon upon the same subject, an. 1710.* London. 1710. 8vo. [8], 271, [1] p. Published by: Tooke, B.; Strahan, G. ESTC t111065. * C; DFo; L; MH-AH; Osc.

> In part a translation of Cardinal Maillard de Tournon's *Mandement sur l'affaire des cultes Chinoises*. Osc suggests Thomas Mainwaring, who was a bitter opponent of the Jesuits, as the translator. Although the imprint suggests that the book was not published under Catholic auspices, it has been included since it

deals with the important controversy of the mission in China. The book elicited a number of reactions published under non-R.C. auspices, such as *The sentiments of the Jesuits*, 1710 (ESTC t175619, t175620) and *True sentiments of the Jesuits*, 1710 (ESTC n051563).

1728. *The manner of baptizing an infant in danger of death.* [London]. [1795?]. 12°. s.s. Printed by: [Coghlan, J.P.]. Published by: [Coghlan, J.P.]. * WDA.
> Found with *The laity's directory* for 1796 (no. 1602). It contains the advice 'Paste this paper on the inside of the cover of your prayer book, that it may be ready on any emergency'.

1729. *The manner of hearing mass, with prayers before confession and communion ... By L.R. D.D. Also Christian reflections for every day of the month. To which is added, The office for the dead.* London. 1754. 18°. vii, [1], 316 p. Published by: Gibson, N. ESTC t118820. * Do; L.

1730. *The manner of performing the novena, or, the nine days devotion to St. Francis Xaverius.* St. Omers. 1702. [1], 21, [4] p. Published by: Farmer, T. * ICN.
> According to Sommervogel (II, 224) translated from the Italian by Levinius Brown S.J. (*vere* Samuel Musson), but Lhe cat. gives Francis Plowden S.J. (1661-1736) as translator.

1731. *The manner of performing the novena: or, the nine days devotion to St. Francis Xaverius ... As also the devotion of the ten Fridays to the same saint.* [London?]. 1741. 12°. 117, [3] p. Printed by: [Hoyles, J.]. ESTC t116029. * Dt; Gi; L; LfaA; Lhe; O; Sto; TxU; Yb.
> With 1½ pages of adverts.

1732. *The manner of performing the novena, or, the nine days devotion to St. Francis Xaverius ... As also the devotion of the ten Fridays to the same saint.* [1741]. 12°. 92 p. * FLK (-tp); Lhe; Osc; Stan.

1733. *The manner of performing the novena, or the nine days devotion to St. Francis Xaverius ... As also the devotion of the ten Fridays to the same saint.* Dublin. 1749. 12°. 88 p. Published by: Kelly, I. * IDA; Yb.

1734. *The manner of performing the novena, or, the nine days devotion to St. Francis Xaverius ... As also the devotion of the ten Fridays to the same saint.* [London?]. [1750?]. 12°. 21, 82, [1] p. ESTC t147951. * L; Lfa (imp.); Yb.

1735. *The manner of performing the novena, or, the nine day's [sic] devotion, to St. Francis Xaverius ... As also the devotion of the ten Friday [sic] to the same saint.* Dublin. 1767. 12°. 88 p. Published by: Wilkinson, T. ESTC t083882. * CtY; L; Map.

1736. *The manner of receiving the Poor Sisters of St. Clare to clothing; and the ceremonies of their professing in the religious order.* Dublin. 1795. 8°. 28 p. Printed by: Barlow, J. * FLK.

1737. Manning, Robert. *The case stated between the Church of Rome and the Church of England in a second conversation betwixt a Roman Catholick lord, and a gentleman of the Church of England.* Anon. 2 vols. [Rouen?]. 1721. 8°. xxiv, 351, [1]; 366 p. ESTC t127907. * CLU-C; DFo; Do; E; ECW; FU; Hen; IaU;

ICN; L; Lfa (vol. 2); Lhe; LO (vol. 1); MiU; MRu; NcD; NN; O; Osc; TH; TxU; Ush; Yb.

In reply to *The case stated* by Charles Leslie.

1738. Manning, Robert. *The Catholic devotion to the Blessed Virgin, with the practice thereof.* 2nd ed. London. 1798. 12°. 36p. Printed by: Coghlan, J.P. ESTC t186199. * Lhe; MBAt; O; Ush.

According to Sommervogel (IV, 1579) Thomas Lawson (1720-1807) edited the two Manning works on the Blessed Virgin Mary (the present item and no. 1751) and distributed them freely.

1739. Manning, Robert. *England's conversion and reformation compared. Or, the young gentleman directed in the choice of his religion.* Anon. Antwerp [i.e. London?]. 1725. 8°. lxiv, [8], 330 p. * AR; Do; DoA; ECW; LO; Map; MY; Sal; Stan.

The book was really printed in London, probably by T. Howlatt for Thomas Meighan (Mitchell, 1984, pp. 38-47). See also next items.

1740. Manning, Robert. *England's conversion and reformation compared. Or, the young gentleman directed in the choice of his religion.* Anon. Antwerp [i.e. London?]. 1725. 8°. lv, [7], 330 p. Published by: C., R.; F., C. ESTC t078046. * AR; CLU-C; CYc; DFo; Do; Dt; Du; E; ECB; ECW; Gi; Hen; InNd; InU-Li; L; Lhe; LOU; LVu; TLP; Ush; Yb.

In this ed. there are no pressfigures. The ornaments are those used by Thomas Howlatt (see also next item).

1741. Manning, Robert. *England's conversion and reformation compared. Or, the young gentleman directed in the choice of his religion.* Anon. Antwerp [i.e. London?]. 1725. 8°. lv, [7], 330 p. Published by: C., R.; F., C. ESTC t078047. * E; L; Lhe; Lu; LU-HLS; MChB.

In this ed. there are some pressfigures.

1742. Manning, Robert. *England's conversion and reformation compared. Or, the young gentleman directed in the choice of his religion ... By the R.F.R.M. of the S.J.* Antwerp. 1736. 8°. [2], xl, [4], 261 [i.e. 260] p. Published by: C., R.; G., C. ESTC t129306. * CLU-C; ECW (imp.); FLK; L; P.

Page 233 is misnumbered, which explains the uneven number of pages.

1743. Manning, Robert. *England's conversion and reformation compared. Or, the young gentleman directed in the choice of his religion.* Anon. Antwerp. 1753. 8°. xlv, [3], 324 p. Published by: C., R.; F., C. ESTC t154380. * C; Llp; Ush.

1744. Manning, Robert. *England's conversion and reformation compared: or, the young gentleman directed in the choice of his religion.* 5th ed. Anon. Dublin. 1792. 12°. xlv, [3], 324 p. Published by: Cross, R. ESTC t102116. * BB; Do; Dt; FLK; IDA; L; Mil.

1745. Manning, Robert. *Modern controversy: or, a plain and rational account of the Catholick faith ... With a preface and appendix, in vindication of Catholick morals, from the old calumnies.* Anon. [London?]. 1720. 8°. [30], 204, lxviii p. ESTC t059201. * C; CLU-C; DCU; Do; DoA; Du; E; ECW; Gi; Hen; L; Lfa;

Lhe; LO; LVu; MRu; MY; O; Owo; PU; StD; TH; Ush; Yb.
For other eds see no. 1752ff.

1746. Manning, Robert. *Moral entertainments on the most important practical truths of the Christian religion.* 3 vols. London. 1742. 12°. [16], 286, [14]; [4], 330, [18]; [4], 293, [31] p. Published by: Meighan, T. ESTC t107067. * CLU-C (vol. 3); Do; E; ECW; GEU-T; Hor; L; Lhe; LO; Map; O; Osc; P; Sal; ScCR; Stan; Sto; TLP; Ush.
Dedicated to Lord Petre, Baron of Writtle.

1747. Manning, Robert. *Moral entertainments on the most important practical truths of the Christian religion.* 2 vols. Dublin. 1749. 12°. [6], 307, [37] p (vol. 2). Published by: Kelly, I. * FLK (vol. 2); ICR.

1748. Manning, Robert. *Moral entertainments on the most important practical truths of the Christian religion.* 2 vols. Dublin. 1764. 12°. [12], 329, [27]; [4], 307, [29] p. Published by: Gorman, B. ESTC t170107. * D; FLK; ICR.

1749. Manning, Robert. *Moral entertainments on the most important practical truths of the Christian religion.* 2 vols. Dublin. 1789. 12°. [10], 11-270, 10 p. (vol. 1). Printed by: Cross, R. * FLK (vol. 1); IDA.

1750. Manning, Robert. *Moral entertainments on the most important practical truths of the Christian religion.* 2 vols. Dublin. 1795. 12°. [12], 346; [5], 6-337, [1] p. Printed by: Wogan, P. ESTC t180951. * FLK; O; PPCCH (vol. 1).

1751. Manning, Robert. *Of devotion to the Blessed Virgin Mary. Extracted from the third volume of the Moral entertainments on the most important practical truths of the Christian religion.* London. 1787. 12°. 36 p. Printed by: Marmaduke, J. Sold by: Marmaduke, J. ESTC t100798. * L; MBAt; Ush.
See note to no. 1738.

1752. Manning, Robert. *A plain and rational account of the Catholick faith, with a preface and appendix in vindication of Catholick morals, from old calumnies [Modern controversy].* 2nd ed. Anon. Rouen [i.e. London?]. 1721. 8°. xxiii, [1], 217, [3] p. ESTC t125370. * DFo; Do; E; Gi; IU; L; Lfa; Lhe; O; Sal; Ush.
The first ed. was entitled *Modern controversy* (no. 1745).

1753. Manning, Robert. *A plain and rational account of the Catholick faith; with a preface and appendix, in vindication of Catholick morals, from old calumnies.* 3rd ed. Anon. Rouen [i.e. London?]. 1721-22. 8°. xvi, 182, [4], xiv, 65, [1] p. ESTC t125371. * CLU-C; DFo; Do; DoA; E; ECR; ECW; Hen; ICR; ICU; L; Lfa; Lhe; LO; MChB; MY; NcD; O; SIR; Sto; TH; TxU; UGL; Ush; Yb.

1754. Manning, Robert. *A plain and rational account of the Catholick faith, with a preface and appendix in vindication of Catholick morals, from old calumnies.* 4th ed. London. 1751. 8°. 338, [2] p. Published by: [Lord, P.]. * ECW.
With an advert for P. Lord on the last page.

1755. Manning, Robert. *A plain and rational account of the Catholic faith: with a preface and appendix in vindication of Catholic morals, from old calumnies.* 5th ed. Dublin. 1794. 12°. vi, xviii, 19-330 p. Printed by: Cross, R. ESTC t206540. * DCU; Dt; FLK; IDA; Llp.

1756. Manning, Robert. *The reform'd churches proved destitute of a lawful ministry. To which is added The antiquity of the doctrine call'd popery. Reprinted from a book entituled, The shortest way ... part 1, ch. 4, 5.* Anon. Rouen. 1722. 8°. xvi, 132 p. ESTC t109186. * DFo; Do; DoA; E; ECW; Gi; IU; L; Lfa; Lhe; Osc; Sto; Ush.

See also nos 1759-1762.

1757. Manning, Robert. *The reform'd churches proved destitute of a lawful ministry.* Anon. Rouen. 1722. 8°. xiv, 65, [1] p. * LO; MBtS.

1758. Manning, Robert. *The rise and fall of the heresy of iconoclasts; or, image-breakers ... collected by R. M.* London. 1731. 8°. [4], 125, [3] p. Published by: Meighan, T. ESTC t010192. * C; CLU-C; CSt; CtHT-W; Do; DoA; E; ECW; Gi; IaU; KBH; L; Lfa; Lhe; Map; MnU; MoU; MY; O; Osc; OU; StD; Ush; Yb.

With 3 pages of Meighan adverts.

1759. Manning, Robert. *The shortest way to end disputes about religion. In two parts. In answer to all objections against infallibility contain'd in a book entitled 'The case stated'.* Anon. Antwerp [i.e. London?] 1716. 8°. [16], 334 p. ESTC n022871. * CLU-C.

The case stated is by Charles Leslie. Part 2 has a separate tp.

1760. Manning, Robert. *The shortest way to end disputes about religion. In two parts.* Anon. Brussels [i.e. London?]. 1716. 8°. [14], 342 p. ESTC n036933. * CAL; CLU-C; CtY; Do; DoA; Dt; ECW; FLK; FU; Gi; ICN; MY; NNUT; TLP; Ush; Yb.

Pages 337, 338 misnumbered 343, 342.

1761. Manning, Robert. *The shortest way to end disputes about religion. In two parts.* Anon. Brussels [i.e. London?]. 1716. 8°. [14], 342 p. ESTC t126237. * CLU-C; DFo; E; ECW; GEU-T; Hen; L; Lhe; MiEM; NNUT; NSPM; Sco; SIR; TLP; TxU; UGL; Ush.

Part 2 has a separate tp with 'Antwerp' in the imprint.

1762. Manning, Robert. *The shortest way to end disputes about religion. In five parts.* Anon. Brussels [i.e. London?]. 1716. 8°. [14], 342 p. ESTC t126238. * Do; ECR; L.

Another ed. of the Brussels 1716 ed., with the errata corrected, although p. 16 is misnumbered 61. L bound up with no. 1375.

1763. Manning, Robert. *The shortest way to end disputes about religion. In two parts.* Dublin. 1754. 12°. 305, [3] p. Published by: Lord, P. ESTC n022872. * DoA; IDA; PPL; TLP.

1764. Manning, Robert. *The shortest way to end disputes about religion. In two parts.* Dublin. 1766. 12°. 309, [1] p. Printed by: Fitzsimons, R. * DCU; P.

DCU has 305, [1] p.

1765. Manning, Robert. *The shortest way to end disputes about religion. In two parts.* Dublin. 1778. 12°. 307, [5] p. Printed by: Fitzsimons, R.; Cross, R. ESTC t131908. * D; FLK; IObT; L.

With 5 pages of adverts.

1766. Manning, Robert. *The shortest way to end disputes about religion. In two parts.* Dublin. 1795. 12°. 305, [7] p. Printed by: Cross, R. ESTC n022873. * CaNSHPH; Gron; MY; PLatS.

1767. Manning, Robert. *A single combat or, personal dispute between Mr. Trapp, and his anonymous antagonist.* Anon. Antwerp [i.e. London?]. 1728. 8°. [2], vi, [2], 182 p. ESTC t126239. * BB; CLU; CLU-C; CSt; CtY-BR; DFo; Do; DoA; E; ECW; FLK; Gi; ICN; ICR; ICU; L; Lfa; Lhe; Map; O; OU; Psg; Sal; Sto; TxU; Ush; Yb.

> A refutation of Trapp's attack on Manning's *England's conversion,* in his *The Church of England defended,* 1727 (see also next item).

1768. Manning, Robert. *A single combat or, personal dispute between Mr. Trapp, and his anonymous antagonist.* Dublin. 1757. 12°. x, [6], 276 p. Published by: Bowes, P. ESTC t129145. * CaOHM; CSmH; D; FLK; L; Lhe; MY; SIR.

> With a list of subscribers.

1769. Mannock, John Anselm. *Christian sacrifice containing a short explication of the chief parts of the mass. With a profitable method how to offer it up according to the four ends of this sacrifice.* Anon. [London]. 1726. 12°. [2], xix [i.e. ix], [1], 95, [1], 91, [5] p. Published by: [Meighan, T.]. ESTC t216393. * Do (imp.); Gi; Llp.

> Two vols bound in one. Imprint mentions 'J. Riddle and Gregory Greenwood O.S.B.' With 5 pages of Meighan adverts.

1770. Mannock, John Anselm. *The poor man's catechism: or, the Christian doctrine explained. With short admonitions.* Anon. 1752. 12°. [4], 316, [4] p. * DMR; DoA; Lhe; TLP; Ush.

> According to Kirk (p. 26) and Gillow (I, 218) edited by George Bishop, priest and grand vicar to Bishop Stonor (d. 1768). See also next item which is another issue with the name of N. Gibson in the imprint.

1771. Mannock, John Anselm. *The poor man's catechism: or, the Christian doctrine explained. With short admonitions.* Anon. [London]. 1752. 12°. [4], 316, [4] p. Published by: Gibson, N. ESTC t072701. * DMR; ECW; L; Lhe; O; TxU; Yb.

1772. Mannock, John Anselm. *The poor man's catechism: or, the Christian doctrine explained. With short admonitions.* [London]. 1762. 12°. [2], 392, [4] p. Published by: Lewis, T. ESTC t100796. * Do; E; ECW; GEU-T; IES; L; TLP.

1773. Mannock, John Anselm. *The poor man's catechism: or, the family instructor ... by the rev. R. C...r. D.D.* 2nd ed. Anon. Dublin. 1767. 12°. iv, 316, [4] p. Published by: Lord, P. * IDA.

> In spite of the variation in the title, this seems to be another ed. of Mannock's catechism, edited by Richard Challoner.

1774. Mannock, John Anselm. *The, poor man's catechism: or the Christian doctrine explained with short admonitions.* 3rd ed. London. 1770. 12°. [4], 380,

190

[4] p. Published by: Coghlan, J.P. * Hen; Sal; TLP.

1775. Mannock, John Anselm. *The poor man's catechism: or the Christian doctrine explained with short admonitions.* 4th ed. London. 1792. 12°. [4], 361, [13] p. Printed by: Coghlan, J.P. * TLP.

1776. Mannock, John Anselm. *The poor man's catechism: or, the Christian doctrine explained. With short admonitions. This edition is newly revised, and much amended by the rev. B. Mc. M.* Anon. Dublin. 1794. 12°. [4], 316, [4] p. Printed by: Cross, R.; Wogan, P. ESTC t072700. * ECW; FLK; ICR; KU-S; L.
> The 'rev. B. Mc. M.' is Bernard MacMahon.

1777. Mannock, John Anselm. *The poor man's catechism: or, the Christian doctrine explained. With short admonitions.* 5th ed. London. 1797. 12°. 356, [4] p. * Do; TLP; Ush.

1778. Mannock, John Anselm. *The poor man's controversy. A posthumous work published by his friends. Permissu superiorum.* [London?]. 1769. 12°. 135, [1] p. ESTC t100797. * BMu; CAL; CLU; CLU-C; CSmH; D; Do; DoA; E; ECW; FK; FLK; L; LAM; Lhe; Map; MH; MRu; Osc; P; Pm; Sal; TLP; UGL; Ush.
> According to Kirk (p. 26) probably edited by George Bishop (see note to no. 1770).

Manual. For a general treatment of the Manual see Blom, chapter 6. For Manual see also under William Clifford and Michael Benedict Pembridge and under 'Approved', 'Catholic', 'Choice collection', 'Complete', 'Devout' and 'New' in the present list.

1779. *A manual of Catholic prayers.* Philadelphia. [1774]. [13], 20-282 p. Printed by: Bell, R. ESTC w022999. * DGU; ICN; RPJCB.
> Includes 'Proposals for printing by subscription, the Catholic Christian instructed'. Probably published by the rev. Robert Molyneux, pastor of St. Joseph's, Philadelphia. Evans (16058) mentions a Philadelphia 1778 ed., printed by Robert Bell.

1780. *A manual of devout prayers, and devotions for every day in the week, morning and evening; fitted for all persons and occasions.* London. 1750. 12°. 524, [4] p. Printed by: Marmaduke, J. Sold by: Marmaduke, J. ESTC t196253. * ECW; Gi; Map; O.
> With 2 pages of Marmaduke adverts.

1781. *A manual of devout prayers and other Christian devotions fitted for all persons & occasions ... Dedicated to her R. Highness the Princess.* St. Geramin [sic] En Laye. 12°. [6], 331, [5] p. Printed by: Weston, W. * ECW.
> William Weston (died 1710) worked as printer for the English court at St. Germain at the end of the 17th and the beginning of the 18th century.

1782. *A manual of devout prayers and other Christian devotions fitted for all persons and occasions.* [London]. 1705. 12°. [10], 306, [8] Printed by: [Metcalfe, T.]. ESTC t171493. * C.
> With some pages of Metcalfe adverts.

1783. *A manual of devout prayers, and other Christian devotions: fitted for all persons and occasions.* 1706. 12°. [21], [1], 2-3, 239, [1] p. * Sto.

1784. *A manual of devout prayers, and other Christian devotions; fitted for all persons and occasions.* [London?]. 1706. 12°. [10], 275, [3] p. ESTC n034797. * TxU.

1785. *A manual of devout prayers and other Christian devotions fitted for all persons and occasions.* London. 1719. 12°. * Amp; Lhe.

> According to Munter (p. 181) the Catholic Dublin publisher James Malone was fined in 1708 for publishing a *Manual of devout prayers*.

1786. *A manual of devout prayers and other Christian devotions.* 1740. 18°. * Howell, no. 2109.

> 'Contains the Jesus Psalter, Prayers of St. Bridget, the Litanies of our Lady of Loretto etc.'.

1787. *A manual of devout prayers and other Christian devotions fitted for all persons & occasions illustrated with cutts.* Dublin. 1742. 12°. [2] p. Sold by: Kelly, I. ESTC t105167. * L (imp.).

> L consists of tp and 10 plates only. Bound up with Challoner's *Garden of the soul*, 1779 (no. 558).

1788. *A manual of devout prayers, and other Christian devotions fitted for all persons and occasions.* London. 1755. 12°. Published by: Meighan, M. * DMR.

> With some pages of adverts for M. Meighan in Drury Lane.

1789. *A manual of devout prayers and other Christian devotions: fitted for all persons and occasions.* London. 1760. 12°. [12], 234, [6] p. Published by: Meighan, T. * Gi.

> With 3 pages of Meighan adverts.

1790. *A manual of devout prayers, and other Christian devotions: fitted for all persons and occasions.* London. 1762-65. 18°. [12], 237, [3], 318, [6] p. Published by: Meighan, T. ESTC t123014. * DAE; Gi; L.

> There is a second part with separate signatures and pagination, dated 1762. It contains the mass and the vespers and is given separately in our list as no. 2508. With 3 pages of Meighan adverts.

1791. *A manual of devout prayers and other Christian devotions: fitted for all persons and occasions.* London. 1766. 12°. [12], 250, [2] p. * Do.

1792. *A manual of devout prayers, and other Christian devotions, fitted for all persons and occasions.* London. 1771. 12°. 234, [2] p. Published by: Meighan, T. * VUA.

1793. *A manual of devout prayers, and other Christian devotions, fitted for all persons and occasions.* 1771. 8°. [4], 252 p. * LOU.

1794. *A manual of devout prayers, and other Christian devotions: fitted for all persons and occasions ... To which are added vespers for Sundays and complin.* Preston. 1777. 12°. [16], 224 p. Printed by: Sergent, W. Sold by: Sergent, W. ESTC t205739. * DoA; P.

1795. *A manual of devout prayers, and other Christian devotions: fitted for all persons and occasions ... To which are added, vespers for Sundays and complin.* Preston. 1780. 12°. [10], 250, [2] p. Printed by: Sergent, W. ESTC t171495. *

Gi; Lhe.
    The table of moveable feasts starts with 1773.

1796. *A manual of devout prayers and other Christian devotions: fitted for all persons and occasions.* Preston. 1785. 8°. [8], 198, [2] p. Printed by: Sergent, E. * O.

1797. *A manual of devout prayers and other Christian devotions: fitted for all persons and occasions. To which are added the vespers and complin, with an account of the indulgences granted to this kingdom.* London. 1786. 12°. 297, [3] p. Printed by: Coghlan, J.P. ESTC t171497. * DMR; Do; Lhe; Stan.
    Do gives Richard Challoner as editor.

1798. *A manual of devout prayers, and other Christian devotions: fitted for all persons and occasions. To which are added, the vespers and complin.* Preston. 1789. 12°. 292, [2] p. Printed by: Binns, N. * Stan.

1799. *A manual of devout prayers, and other Christian devotions, fitted for all persons and occasions.* London. 1793. 12°. [12], 234, [2] p. Published by: Meighan, T. * ECW; Gi; LOU.
    The table of moveable feasts starts with 1774.

1800. *A manual of devout prayers, containing morning and evening prayers; the prayers for confession, and the holy communion; prayers at mass, & other devout prayers.* Prague. 1775. 114, [2] p. Published by: Gerle, W. ESTC t205737. * P.

1801. *A manual of devout prayers for every day in the week, morning and evening; with other devotions and instructions.* London. 1755. 12°. [2], 480, [2] p. * CAL; Do.

1802. *A manual of devout prayers for every day in the week.* London. 1755. 8°. 482 p. Sold by: [Marmaduke, J.]. * Do.
    Do has an additional engraved tp with the imprint 'Sold by J. Marmaduke in May's Buildings, St. Martin's Lane'.

1803. *A manual of devout prayers for every day in the week, morning and evening; with other devotions and instructions.* London. 1765. 8°. 475, [3] p. Printed by: [Marmaduke, J.]. ESTC t205738. * Gi; Hen; Llp; P; TLP.
    With 1½ pages of Marmaduke adverts.

1804. *A manual of devout prayers, for every day in the week, morning and evening; with other devotions and instructions proper for a Christian on all occasions.* London. 1765. 18°. 475, [3] p. ESTC t171425. * DAE; LVu; Ush.
    DAE is bound up with *Acts of faith* (no. 29), and with *The life of faith* (no. 1664).

1805. *A manual of devout prayers for every day in the week, morning and evening: with other devotions and instructions.* London. 1778. 12°. 504 p. Published by: [Marmaduke, J.]. ESTC t118978. * L.
    With some pages of Marmaduke adverts.

1806. *A manual of godly prayers and litanies distributed for every day in the week, with other excellent devotions.* London. 1745. 12°. [12], 234, [6] p.

Printed by: Meighan, T. * ECW.

  With 3 pages of Meighan adverts.

1807. *A manual of godly prayers and litanies. The second part containing the holy mass in Latin and English.* London. 1745. 12°.

  The L copy of this ed. was destroyed during the war. See Blom, p. 184.

1808. *A manual of instructions and prayers useful to a Christian. Translated from the Italian.* London. 1752. 12°. [12], 280 p. Published by: Meighan, T. ESTC t114542. * DoA; E; ECW; L; Stan; TH; Ush.

  Dedication to the Countess of Powess, signed 'P.L.'. See also next item. Ush is a variant lacking 'P.L.' under dedication.

1809. *A manual of instructions and prayers useful to a Christian. Translated from the Italian.* London. 1753. 12°. [13], 2-278 [rest missing] p. Published by: Marmaduke, J. * SIR (imp.).

1810. *A manual of instructions and prayers useful to a Christian. Translated from the Italian.* London. 1767. 12° [10], 280 p. Published by: Meighan, T. ESTC n061367. * Do; TxU.

1811. *A manual of instructions and prayers useful to a Christian. Translated from the Italian.* 2nd ed. London. 1780. [4], 314, [4] p. Printed by: Coghlan, J.P. ESTC t205786. * Do; DoA; E; LO; TLP.

1812. *A manual of instructions and prayers useful to a Christian. Translated from the Italian.* Liverpool. 1789. 12°. [8], 320 p. Printed by: Wosencroft, C. Sold by: Wosencroft, C. * Gi; UGL.

  UGL is bound up with *The holy mass* (no. 1458) and *The Jesus psalter* (no. 1530).

1813. *A manual of prayers and other Christian devotions.* [London?]. 1706. 12°. [26], 463, [3] p. ESTC n034768. * Ct; E.

1814. *A manual of prayers and other Christian devotions, fitted for all persons and occasions.* 1714. 12°. [20], 506, [2] p. * Ush.

1815. *A manual of prayers and other Christian devotions.* 1720. 12°. [30], 552, [2] p. Published by: [Meighan, T.?]. * ECW; FP.

1816. *A manual of prayers, and other Christian devotions.* [Rome]. 1720. 12°. 179, [1] p. ESTC t205782. * E.

  Ms note on fly-leaf 'This little volume was printed at Rome for the use of the English part of the household of King James VIII (the Pretender). I bought it in Rome in September 1820'.

1817. *A manual of prayers and other Christian devotions.* [London?]. 1721. 12°. [26], 475, [3] p. ESTC t205785. * E.

1818. *A manual of prayers and other Christian devotions.* [London?]. 1725. 12°. [26], 475, [3] p. ESTC t171422. * C; Ush.

1819. *A manual of prayers and other Christian devotions.* London. 1728. 12°. vii, [19], 535, [3] p. Sold by: [Meighan, T.]. ESTC t119497. * Amp; Do (-tp); ECW; Gi; L; Opl; TxU; Ush.

A number of copies have an additional engraved tp ('A manual of devout prayers') with the imprint 'sold by Thomas Meighan'.

1820. *A manual of prayers and other Christian devotions.* [London]. 1731. 12°. [2], vi, [20], 475, [3] p. Printed by: Meighan, T. * Do; Gi.
> Do has the additional engraved tp also present in no. 1819.

1821. *A manual of prayers and other Christian devotions.* [Dublin]. 1733. 12°. vii, [19], 3-501, [3] p. ESTC t122613. * Dt; L; O.
> Bound into L are plates printed by the Dublin printer and bookseller R. Cross. Since Cross only started business in 1757 this implies that the plates were added later.

1822. *A manual of prayers and other Christian devotions. Revised ... by R.C. D.D.* London. 1744. 12°. [28], 493, [9] p. Published by: Meighan, T. * Do; Gi; Ush.
> 'R.C. D.D.' is Richard Challoner (see also next 10 items). Do has the additional engraved tp also present in no. 1819; Gi has 6 pages of Meighan adverts.

1823. *A manual of prayers and other Christian devotions. Revised ... by R.C. D.D.* London. 1752. 12°. vi, [20], 493, [7] p. Published by: Meighan, T. * Sco (imp.).
> With 4 pages of Meighan adverts.

1824. *A manual of prayers and other Christian devotions. Revised ... by R.C. D.D.* [London]. 1758. 12°. vi, [18], 440, [6] p. Published by: Meighan, T. ESTC t079987. * DoA; E; L; Nijm; Stan.
> With 3 pp. advertising Gother's works and with a number of Meighan adverts.

1825. *A manual of prayers and other Christian devotions. Revised ... by R.C. D.D.* 1764. vi, [18], 438, [8] p. Published by: Meighan, T. * Lfa; Ush; UshL.
> With some pages of Meighan adverts.

1826. *A manual of prayers and other Christian devotions. Revised ... by R.C. D.D.* London. 1768. 12°. vi, [18], 417, [3] p. Published by: Meighan, T. ESTC t129100. * DoA; Gi; L; Sal; TxU.

1827. *A manual of prayers and other Christian devotions. Revised ... by R. C.* Preston. 1768. 12°. vi, [20], 417, [3] p. Printed by: Stuart, W. ESTC t172638. * Gi; LEu.

1828. *A manual of prayers and other Christian devotions, revised ... by R.C.D.D.* London. 1772. 12°. Printed by: Meighan, T. * P.

1829. *A manual of prayers and other Christian devotions. To which are added the ordinary of the mass in Latin and English, with an explanation... revised by ... Richard Challoner.* London. 1786. 18°. 35, [5], 456 p. Printed by: Coghlan, J.P. ESTC t207602. * Do; E; Gi.

1830. *A manual of prayers and other Christian devotions, to which are added, the ordinary of the mass in Latin and English, with an explanation ... revised by ... Richard Challoner.* London. 1790. 8°. 456 p. Published by: Coghlan, J.P. * Osc.

1831. *A manual of prayers and other Christian devotions. Revised by the late ...*

Richard Chaloner [sic]. London. 1795. 12°. xxxvi, 456 p. Printed by: Coghlan, J.P. * Gi; Stan.

1832. *A manual of prayers and other Christian devotions. Revised by R.C. D.D.* London. 1800. 12°. xxiii, [1], 550 p. Printed by: Low, S. Published by: Booker, E. ESTC t079988. * Do; E; ECW; L; Lfa; Lhe; TxU.

1833. Marconi, Giuseppe Loreto. *The life of the venerable Benedict Joseph Labre ... Translated from the French, by the reverend Mr. James Barnard [Vita del servo di Dio Bento. Guiseppe Labre]*. Anon. London. 1785. 12°. xxv, [1], 231, [1] p. Printed by: Coghlan, J.P. ESTC t129404. * CAL; Do; DoA; E; FLK; Hen; Hor; InNd; L; Lhe; Pm; TxDaM-P; Yb.

> The author is identified in the translator's preface as 'Rev. Mr. Joseph Marconi ... who published his Life in Italian: and an abridgment has been made in French [Vie de Bénoit-Joseph Labre] from which this edition is translated' (see also next 3 items).

1834. Marconi, Giuseppe Loreto. *The life of the venerable Benedict Joseph Labre, who died at Rome ... April, 1783. Translated from the French, by Mr. James Barnard. Together with an appendix.* London. 1785. 12°. [1], xxv, [3], 231, [1] p. Printed by: Coghlan, J.P. ESTC t221992. * O; Osc.

> In this issue the word 'reverend' does not occur in the title. Cf. no. 1833.

1835. Marconi, Giuseppe Loreto. *The life of the venerable Benedict Joseph Labre, who died at Rome, in the odour of sanctity, on the sixteenth of April, 1783. Translated from the French, by the rev. Mr. James Barnard, with an appendix.* Dublin. 1785. 12°. xxv, [1], 230, [8] p. Printed by: Wogan, P. ESTC t205800. * D; Do; Mil.

> Do and Mil have [2], xxv, [1], 230, [4] p.

1836. Marconi, Giuseppe Loreto. *The life of the venerable Benedict Joseph Labre, who died at Rome ... April, 1783. Translated from the French ... Together with an appendix.* Wigan. 1786. 12°. xxvii, [1], 232 p. Printed by: Bancks, W. ESTC t082147. * C; DoA; FP; L; Lhe; O; Stan.

1837. Marin, Michel-Ange. *The perfect religious a work designed for the assistance of those who aspire after perfection ... Written in French by R.F. Michael Angel Marin ... Translated into English by B.F.E.O.S.F.* Douai. 1762. 12°. [12], 482, [10] p. Printed by: Willerval, J.F. ESTC t123005. * DAE; DMR; Do (imp.); ECB; ECW; ICN; L; LOU; Stan; TxU; UGL; Yb.

> Dedicated to all the religious ladies of different orders in the several English monasteries; dedication is signed by the translator, often identified as Bernard Francis Eyston O.S.F., or sometimes as Francis Felix Englefield O.S.F.

1838. Marley, Martin. *The good confessor: or, instructions for the due and worthy administration of the sacrament of penance.* Douai. 1743. 8°. ix, [1], 620, [8] p. ESTC t122505. * C; CLU-C; Dt; Du; ECW; FLK; L; MWH; Sco.

> On p. 537 Marley refers to another work he wrote 'The good pastor'.

1839. Marsollier, Jacques. *The life of St. Francis of Sales, Bishop and Prince of Geneva, founder of the order of visitation. Translated, from the 2nd ed., by William Crathorne [Vie de St. François de Sales]*. 3 vols. London. 1737. 12°.

332, [4]; 358, [10]; 321, [7] p. Published by: Meighan, T. ESTC t142566. *
CtY-BR; DMR; Do; DoA; Du; E; ECW ; Hor (vols 1, 2); ICN; L; LEu; Lfa
(vol. 2); Lhe; Map; NNPM; NSchU; NSPM (vol. 1); O; Sal; TH.

>With some pages of Meighan adverts.

1840. Massillon, Jean Baptiste. *The Bishop of Clermont's discourse to the clergy of his diocese, on the extensive influence of their good and bad conduct. Translated from the French.* London. 1784. 8°. 43, [1] p. Printed by: Marmaduke, J. Sold by: Marmaduke, J. ESTC t199646. * Lmh; MB; MBAt; Osc.

>Probably a translation of one of his *Conférences et discours synodaux sur les principaux devoirs des ecclésiastiques.*

1841. Massillon, Jean Baptiste. *An episcopal charge ... translated into English and addressed to the Catholic clergy of Great Britain and Ireland.* London. 1784. 8°. vi, 25, [1] p. * L; Osc; Ush.

1842. Mattei, Pasquale de. *S. Aloysius Gonzaga proposed as a model of a holy life by particular practices of devotion calculated for keeping six Sundays successively in honour of the same saint. From the Latin edition.* Anon. St. Omers. 1751. 8°. [4], 112 p. Published by: Le Febvre, N. J. ESTC t113074. * C; Do; Dt; ECB; Gi; L; Lfa; Lhe; LVu; Mil; Sto; Yb.

>Dedication signed by the translator 'N.N.' Sommervogel lists this work under Nathaniel Elliot; Sto under Virgilio Cepari. See also Walsh (p. 56) for the tangled bibliographical history of this work. Lfa has [6], 112, [2] p. and is bound with D'Orléans's *The life of Aloysius Gonzaga* (no. 2195).

1843. Mattei, Pasquale de. *Saint Aloysius Gonzaga proposed as a model of a holy life. By considerations prayers, & practices of piety collected together ... By a religious of the Society of Jesus.* [London?]. [1760?]. 8°. 119, [1] p. ESTC t203110. * Lhe.

>According to ESTC translated by 'Nathaniel Ellis' (but see also note to next item). Lhe suggests St. Omers as the place of publication, but title, wording and pagination differ from no. 1842.

1844. Mattei, Pasquale de. *S. Aloysius Gonzaga proposed as a model of a holy life, by particular practices of devotion, calculated for keeping six Sundays successively in honour of the same saint. From the Latin edition.* Anon. [Dublin?]. 1793. 12°. 118, [6] p. ESTC t113358. * CAL; Do; E; ECW; L; MWH; O; TxU.

>The dedication suggests that the translator was a nun of the Irish Benedictine community at Ypres.

1845. Maury, Jean Siffrein. *The speech of the abbé Maury in the National Assembly, upon the civil constitution of the clergy of France.* Cork. 1792. 8°. 53, [1] p. Printed by: Flyn, W. ESTC n024399. * Du; MY; PP; PPL.

>The speech was delivered on 27 Nov. 1790 and was translated by William Coppinger according to a contemporary ms note in MY. Other works by Maury do not come within the terms of our definition.

1846. *Meditations and other devotions for the use of the faithful ... for the time of the jubilee, anno MDCCLXXVI.* London. [1776]. 12°. 84 p. Printed by:

Coghlan, J.P. ESTC t098168. * Do; ECW (tp only); Hen; L; Lhe; O; Ush.

1847. *Meditations and prayers, adapted to the stations of the holy way of the cross.* Cork. 1780. 18°. 36 p. ESTC t172006. * Dt.

1848. *Meditations and prayers adapted to the stations of the holy way of the cross. To which is added, a short catechistical instruction, on the nature and necessity of the three theological virtues.* Dublin. 1787. 12°. 48 p. Printed by: Wogan, P. ESTC t172007. * Du.

1849. *Meditations and prayers, adapted to the stations of the holy way of the cross. To which is added, a short catechistical instruction, on the nature and necessity of the three theological virtues.* Cork. [1790?]. 12°. 72 p. Printed by: Haly, J. Sold by: Haly, J. ESTC n060808. * Dp.
　　Dp has ms date '1790'.

1850. *Meditations and prayers, adapted to the stations of the holy way of the cross. To which is added, a short catechistical instruction, on the nature and necessity of the three theological virtues.* Waterford. 1792. 8°. 44 p. Printed by: Lord, T. Sold by: Lord, T. ESTC t172008. * D.

1851. *Meditations and prayers, adapted to the stations of the holy way of the cross. With additional instructions, extracted from the sermon delivered by the late rev. father Fleming.* 3rd ed. Dublin. 1795. 12°. 48 p. Published by: Editor. Sold by: Cross, R.; Franciscan chapels. ESTC t207544. * D.

1852. *The memory of English saints reviv'd.* 1707. 12°. 24 p. * Stan.
　　Attributed by Gillow (V, 548) to Christopher Tootell. Bound up with no. 2764.

1853. *The memory of English saints reviv'd. Permissu superiorum.* 2nd ed. London. 1746. 12°. 24 p. Published by: Goddard, T. * ECB; ICN; Map; Ush.
　　With half a page of Goddard adverts.

1854. Merlo Horstius, Jacob. *The paradise of the soul of a true Christian, made not only pleasant, but fruitful ... now translated into English for the benefit of the English Catholicks, by T.M. [Paradisus animae Christianae].* London. 1720. 12°. [36], xi, [1], 570, [6] p. ESTC t092138. * CAL; CLU-C; ECW; Hen; L; Lhe; O; Stan.
　　'T.M.' may be Thomas Meighan.

1855. Merlo Horstius, Jacob. *The paradise of the soul of a true Christian, made not only pleasant, but fruitful.* Dublin. 1750. 12°. [16], 29-35, [6], 38-263, 294-365, 396-467, 498-506 p. Published by: Lord, P. Sold by: Lord, P. ESTC n038059. * D (imp.); ECW (imp.); IU (imp.).
　　With a list of subscribers. Text is continuous despite pagination.

1856. Merlo Horstius, Jacob. *The paradise of the soul; containing a great variety of moving instructions and prayers ... Translated in 1720, by T.M. Approved by F.A.V.A.* 2nd ed. Walton. 1771. 12°. xxiv, 493, [7] p. Published by: Sharrock, J. ESTC n025274. * CAL; CaOHM; DAE; DMR; Do; DoA; ECW; FLK; FP; Gi; Hen; L; Lhe; LO; O; Sal; TLP; TxU; Ush; Yb.
　　'F.A.V.A.' is Franciscus Amoriensis Vicarius Apostolicus, i.e. Francis Petre, Bishop of Amoria and V.A. of the northern district.

198

1857. Merlo Horstius, Jacob. *The paradise of the soul of a true Christian: containing the necessary duties of a Christian life ... Revised with the approbation of the ordinary.* 2nd ed. Dublin. 1795. 12°. xxiv, 380 p. Printed by: Wogan, P. ESTC t071383. * FLK; IDA; L.

>IDA has a list of subscribers and xxiv, 9, [1], 1-2, 380, [4] p. This is the second '2nd' ed.

1858. Messingham, Thomas. *A brief history of Saint Patrick's purgatory, and it's pilgrimage. Collected out of ancient historians, written in Latin by the reverend Mr. Thomas Messingham.* Paris. 1718. 8°. [8], 58 p. ESTC t167809. * D; Sto.

>Messingham's *Florilegium insulae sanctorum ... Hiberniae* was published at Paris in 1624. ESTC suggests that this translation may have been printed in Ireland. Brenan (p. 584) suggests C. Nary as editor/translator.

1859. *A method of hearing mass with devotion applied to holy communion. Translated from the French. To which are added pious reflections and acts before and after communion.* Stockton. 1779. 18°. 60 p. * L.

1860. *A method of hearing mass with devotion.* 2nd ed. Yarm. 1783. Printed by: Atkinson, J. * Map.

>With some Atkinson adverts.

1861. *A method of hearing mass with devotion: applied to holy communion. Translated from the French. To which are added pious reflections and acts before and after communion.* 3rd ed. York. 1793. 12°. 67, [1] p. ESTC t172767. * Gi; MRu; Stan.

1862. *A method of hearing mass with devotion: applied to holy communion. Translated from the French. To which are added pious reflections and acts before and after communion.* 5th ed. London. 1800. 12°. [3], 4-48 p. Printed by: Keating; Brown; Keating. * ECW.

1863. *The method of saying the holy rosary, according to the form prescribed by his holiness Pope Pius V. of the holy order of preachers. With some additional reflections on the mysteries.* 12°. 34 p. * Map.

>Bound up with Baker's *A brief essay on the confraternity*, 1752 (no. 135). 'The method of saying the rosary' is also found as part of eds of *Bona mors* and *A choice collection of prayers* with separate tps but continuous signatures and pagination.

1864. Milner, John. *Audi alteram partem.* [London]. [1792]. fol. s.s. ESTC t167644. * BAA; Cli; ECW; FLK; Lhe; Ush.

>Signed 'J.M.' and dated 'May 1, 1792'. A printed letter as part of the oath debate, published in defence of Bp. Walmesley's withdrawal of faculties from Joseph Wilks, O.S.B.

1865. Milner, John. *A brief account of the life of the late r. rev. Richard Challoner, D.D.* London. 1789. 12°. [2], 50, [2] p., plate. Printed by: Coghlan, J.P. ESTC t184338. * DGU; Do; DoA; Lhe (imp.); Osc; P.

>DGU and Lhe tps give date '1798'. Do bound up with Challoner's *Grounds of the old religion* (no. 594).

1866. Milner, John. *Certain considerations on behalf of the Roman Catholics,* who have conscientious objections to changing their name, and to the form of words ... in the oath contained in Mr. Mitford's Bill. [London?]. [1791]. fol. 3, [1] p. ESTC t028994. * BAA; ECW; L; Lhe; O; P; Sto; Ush; WDA.

> Signed and dated 'John Milner, March 7, 1791'.

1867. Milner, John. *The clergyman's answer to the layman's letter, on the appointment of bishops.* London. 1790. 8°. [4], 27, [1] p. Printed by: Coghlan, J.P. ESTC n027241. * C; CLU; CSmH; Do; DUc; ECW; ICR; IEN; L; Lhe; Map; MRu; MY; Osc; SCR; TxU; Ush.

> The 'layman's letter' is *A letter addressed to the Catholic clergy* by Sir John Courtenay Throckmorton (no. 2743). See also no. 2612.

1868. Milner, John. *A discourse delivered at the consecration of the right rev. William Gibson ... in the chapel of Lullworth Castle ... on Sunday, 5th of December, 1790; together with an ... account of the consecration.* London. 1791. 8°. xvi, 28 p. Printed by: Coghlan, J.P. ESTC t065108. * CLU; DUc; ECW; ICR; L; Lfa; Lhe; Lmh; MRu; Osc; P; Sto; Ush.

1869. Milner, John. *A dissertation on the modern style of altering antient cathedrals, as exemplified in the cathedral of Salisbury.* London. 1798. 4°. 54, [2] p. Printed by: Nichols, J. Published by: Nichols, J. Sold by: Pridden, J.; Coghlan, J.P.; Robbins, J. & B. (Winchester). ESTC t064668. * L; O; Osc; Stan; Sto.

> With a final leaf of advertisements.

1870. Milner, John. *The divine right of episcopacy addressed to the Catholic laity of England, in answer to the layman's Second letter to the Catholic clergy of England; with remarks on the oaths of supremacy and allegiance.* London. 1791. 8°. [4], viii, 117, [3] p. Printed by: Coghlan, J.P. Sold by: Booker; Keating; Lewis; Robinsons; Robbins (Winchester); &c. ESTC t132676. * Csj; Do; DUc; E; ECW; ICR; L; Lhe; Lmh; MH; MRu; MY; Osc; Sto; TxDaM-P; TxU; Ush.

> For the layman's *Second letter* see no. 2746. With some pages of Coghlan adverts. ECW has an 'Appendix, no. 11', signed and dated 'Winton, May 21, 1792. J.M.'

1871. Milner, John. *Ecclesiastical democracy detected: being a review of the controversy between the layman and the clergyman concerning the appointment of bishops.* London. 1793. 8°. [4], xv, [1], 185, 188-318 p. Printed by: Coghlan, J.P. Sold by: Debrett, J.; Booker; Keating; Lewis; Robinsons; Robins (Winceester [sic]). ESTC t148221. * BB; CLU; Do; DU; DUc; ECW; ICN; Lfa; Lhe; Lu; MY; Osc; P; StD; TLP.

> Text and register are continuous despite pagination. BB has some adverts for Milner's works. See also notes to nos 1867 and 1870.

1872. Milner, John. *Facts relating to the present contest amongst the Roman Catholics of this kingdom concerning the bill to be introduced into Parliament for their relief.* [Winchester?]. [1791?]. fol. 4 p. ESTC t101135. * BAA; ECW; L; Lhe; LOU; O; P; Sto; Ush; WDA.

> Signed and dated 'John Milner, Winchester, Feb. 24, 1791'. Presented to the Members of the Commons; in it Milner attacks the 'newly assumed name of protesting Catholic dissenters' (Gillow V, 31-2).

1873. Milner, John. *A funeral discourse on the death of the venerable and right reverend Richard Challoner, Bishop of Debra ... who died January 12, 1781. Pronounced January 14, 1781.* Anon. [London]. 1781. 8°. [2], 29, [1] p. Published by: Coghlan, J.P. Sold by: Coghlan, J.P. ESTC t063109. * DoA; DUc; ECW; L; MRu; MY; Ush.

1874. Milner, John. *A funeral discourse on the death of the venerable and right reverend Richard Challoner, Bishop of Debora ... who died Jan 12, 1781, pronounced Jan. 14, 1781.* 1782. 8°. 29, [1] p. * Osc.

1875. Milner, John. *The funeral oration of his late most Christian majesty Louis XVI. Pronounced at the funeral service performed ... April 12, M,DCC,XCIII.* London. [1793?]. 8°. [8], 62 p. Printed by: Coghlan, J.P. Sold by: Debrett, J.; Booker; Keating; Lewis; Robinsons [and 3 others]. ESTC t184195. * CYc; DoA; DUc; E; ECW; Lhe; Osc; Sto; Ush.

1876. Milner, John. *An historical and critical inquiry into the existence and character of Saint George, patron of England.* London. 1792. 8°. [4], 59, [1] p. Published by: Debrett, J.; Robinsons; Collins (Salisbury); Robins (Winchester). ESTC t064669. * C; CLU-C; CSmH; DFo; E; ECW; ICN; IU; L; MH-H; MY; NIC; O; Osc; Ush.

> In part a reaction against Edward Gibbon's *History of the decline and fall*, addressed to George, Earl of Leicester.

1877. Milner, John. *The history, civil and ecclesiastical, & survey of the antiquities, of Winchester.* 2 vols. Winchester. 1798-1801. 4°. Printed by: Robbins, J. Sold by: Robbins; Cadell & Davies (London); Robson; Leigh & Sotheby; Wilkie; Coghlan. ESTC t065099. * C; CaNBFU; CLU; CSt; DFo; DLC; DoA; E; ICU; IU; L; LfaA; Lhe; Lhl; Llp; Lsn; MH; MiU; MY; NcD; NIC; O; OU; SIR; TxU.

> The dedication is dated 1798. Appended to vol. 2 is 'A second appendix to the history &c.'. Kirk (p. 164): 'This work provoked the publication of the rev. J. Sturges's *Reflections on popery*'.

1878. Milner, John. *Letters to a prebendary: being an answer to Reflections on popery, by the rev. J. Sturges ... With remarks on the opposition of Hoadlyism to the doctrines of the Church of England.* [Winchester]. 1800. 4°. 6, [1], 6-300 p. Printed by: Robbins. Sold by: Robbins; Cadell & Davies (London); Robson; Leigh & Sotheby; Nichols; Coghlan; Crosby and Letterman. ESTC t065101. * CaOHM; Dun; E; ICN; KU; KU-S; L; Lhe; MdBP; MY; NIC; NSPM; O; Osc; WNs.

1879. Milner, John. *Oraison funèbre de sa Majesté trés Chrétienne, Louis XVI, Roi de France et de Navarre, prononcée au service funèbre célébré par le clergé François ... traduit par un prêtre François.* London. 1793. 8°. [2], 46 p. Printed by: Coghlan, J.P. Sold by: Debrett; Booker; Keating; Lewis; Robinsons [and 4 others]. * MH; Osc; Sto.

> See no. 1875.

1880. Milner, John. *A reply to the report published by the Cisalpine Club, on the authenticity of the protestation at the Museum: in which the spuriousness of that* *deed is detected.* London. 1795. 8°. [2], ii, 36 p. Printed by: Coghlan, J.P. Sold by: Booker; Keating; Lewis; Debrett; Robinsons. ESTC t190436. * CLU; DUc; ECW; LfaA; Lhe; Osc; Sto; Ush.

> Attacks the authenticity of the copy of the Catholic protestation of 1789 deposited in the British Museum (see also nos 2306 and 2413).

1881. Milner, John. *A serious expostulation with the rev. Joseph Berington, upon his theological errors concerning miracles, and other subjects.* London. 1797. 12°. [4], 137, [3] p. Printed by: Coghlan, J.P. ESTC t118489. * DUc; E; ECW; L; Lfa; Lhe; MY; O; Osc.; P; Ush.

1882. Milner, John. *A sermon preached in the Roman Catholic chapel at Winchester, April 23, 1789. &c. being the general thanksgiving day for his majesty's happy recovery.* London. [1789]. 4°. v, [1], 34 p. Printed by: Coghlan, J.P. Published by: Coghlan, J.P. Sold by: Lewis, T.; Robinsons; Collins (Salisbury); Robins, Blagden (Winchester); and the booksellers at Portsmouth and Southampton. ESTC t059280. * L; Lhe; LVu; NNUT; Osc; STA; Ush.

1883. Milner, John. *A short view of the history and antiquities of Winchester ... Being chiefly extracted from the rev. Mr. Milner's History and survey of Winchester.* Winchester. 1799. 8°. [4], 47, [1] p. Printed by: Robbins. Sold by: Robbins. ESTC t065100. * L; MBNEH.

1884. *Miraculous events established by authentic letters from Italy.* London. 1796. 8°. [4], 35, [1] p. Printed by: Coghlan, J.P. ESTC t146553. * CtY; ECW; IU; L; O.

> Gillow attributes this translation to Benedict Rayment.

1885. *Miraculous events established by authentic letters from Italy, considerably augmented by further details.* 4th ed. London. 1797. 12°. viii, 50 p. Printed by: Coghlan, J.P. ESTC t194303. * CME; DUc.

1886. *Missae propriae ordinis S.P.N. Francisci: quibus interferuntur ... missae novae missalis Romani, cum tabula alphabetica.* London. 1734. 12°. 103, [1], 36 p. * Bevan (1995).

1887. *Missa in festo divini sacerdotii domini nostri J.C. et omnium sanctorum sacerdotum et levitarum.* [Montreal]. [1777] 4°. 4 p. Printed by: [Mesplet, F.]. * CaQQLa.

> Probably printed at Montreal by Fleury Mesplet, 1777, for the Séminaire de St. Sulpice. See also no. 364.

1888. *Missae propriae ordinis S.P.N. Francisci: quibus interferuntur ... missae novae missalis Romani, cum tabula alphabetica.* London. 1766. 12°. [8], 134, [2] p. ESTC t123147. * L; O.

1889. *Missale Romanum, ex decreto sacrosancti concilii Tridentini restitutum, Pii V. pont max. jussu editum, et Clementis VIII. primum, nunc denuo Urbani papae VIII. auctoritate recognitum.* Dublin. 1777. 4°. lii, 528, cvii, [7] p. Printed by: Wogan, P. ESTC t214844. * C; D.

> Pp. 1-212 contain 'Proprium missarum de tempore'; pp. 213-528 'Canon missae'; pp. i-cvii 'Commune sanctorum', and other special services and prayers

for Ireland.

1890. *Missale Romanum ex decreto sacro-sancti concilii Tridentini restitutum. Accedunt festa, quae ... in regno Hiberniae celebrantur.* [Dublin?]. 1777. 4°. 528, cvi, [3] p. Printed by: Morris. * Cha.

'Missae quorundam Hiberniae sanctorum ... approbatae' bound in at end.

1891. *Missale Romanum, ex decreto sacrosancti concilii Tridentini restitutum ... His accedunt festa, quae in regno Hiberniae celebrantur.* Dublin. 1795. 8°. xi, [19], xxiii-lxiv, 558, iii-cvi p. Printed by: Wogan, P. ESTC t207549. * D; Dp; FLK; Op.

1892. *Modus recitandi rosarium beatissimae Virginis Mariae ... sicut recitatur in sodalitate collegii Anglo-Benedictini, S. Gregorii M. Duac.* Douai. 12°. 43, [1] p. Printed by: Willerval, J.F. * DoA.

Cf. Clancy no. 675. The present work might be either late 17th or early 18th c. There is a ms copy of this in DowA, dated 1722.

1893. Molinos, Miguel de. *An abstract of a treatise wrote by Michael de Molinos, intitled, The spiritual guide [Guida spirituale].* London. 1770. 12°. iv, 5-168 p. ESTC t125290. * COCu; ECW (imp.); L; Occ.

In the 18th century De Molinos's publications tended to be generally Christian and were often published under clearly non-R.C. auspices. We include one example of a publication where neither contents nor imprint clearly point in one direction.

1894. Molyneux, Robert. *A funeral sermon, on the death of the rev. Ferdinand Farmer, who departed this life the 17th Aug. 1786, in the 66th year of his age.* Philadelphia. 1786. 12°. 10, [2] p. Printed by: Talbot, C. ESTC w011430. * DGU; ICN; MBtS; MWA; NN; PPL.

Farmer (vere Steinmeyer) was a missionary in Pennsylvania and New York; Molyneux was pastor of St. Joseph's, Philadelphia (see also no. 1779).

1895. Moore, Richard. *Copies of the letters from Bishop White alias Peters to Sir Richard Moore, Bart. With his answers.* London. 1730. 8°. viii, 43, [1] p. ESTC t141066. * L; NIC.

In this tract Sir Richard Moore justifies his character and reacts against the bishop's interference in his marital problems.

1896. More, Cresacre. *The life of Sir Thomas More, Kt. Lord High Chancellour of England under K. Henry the Eighth.* London. 1726. 8°. xxxi, [1], 336, [16] p. Published by: Woodman, J.; Lyon, D. ESTC t086087. * BMs; C; CaAEU; CaOHM; CaOTV; Csj; Ct; CtY; D; DLC; Do; DoA; Dt; DUc; E; ECW; Hen; L; Lhl; Map; MRu; O; Ob; Oc; TxU.

A work by a Roman Catholic originally published in 1627, of a generally historical character.

1897. Morel, Robert. *Devotions to Jesus Christ, in the most holy sacrament of the altar ... Composed in French by Dom Morel [Entretiens].* London. [1756?]. 12°. vii, [1], 435, [1] p. Published by: Meighan, T. ESTC t071044. * CAL; DMR; ECW; ICN; L; LO; Map; O; Osc.

According to Osc cat. Father John Philip Betts, headmaster of Twyford School, may have been the translator.

1898. Morel, Robert. *Devotions to Jesus Christ in the most holy sacrament of the altar ... Composed in French by the rev. father Dominick Morel.* 2nd ed. Dublin. 1795. 12°. [11], 14-358, [2] p. Printed by: Mehain, J.; Cross, R. ESTC t097824. * L.

> With a list of subscribers and a final advertisement leaf. In this issue the subscribers' list starts on sig. A2. There is no dedication leaf.

1899. Morel, Robert. *Devotions to Jesus Christ in the most holy sacrament of the altar ... composed in French by the rev. father Dominick Morel.* 2nd ed. Dublin. 1795. 12°. 358, [2] p. Printed by: Mehain, J.; Cross, R. ESTC t131990. * D; IDA; L; TxU.

> With a list of subscribers and 2 pages of adverts. The subscribers' list starts on sig. A3; there is a dedication to Bishop Francis Moylan of Cork on sig. A2.

1900. *Morning and evening prayers for the use of Catholick families.* 1763. 12°. [4], 20 p. * Gi; TLP; Ush.

> Gi suggests that the work is based on Gother.

1901. *Morning and night prayers.* London. 23, [1] p. Printed by: Meighan, T. Sold by: Meighan, T. * Sto.

> With one page of Meighan adverts.

1902. *Morning and night prayers.* [London]. 1717. 24°. 16 p. Printed by: [Meighan, T.]. Sold by: [Meighan, T.]. * Map (imp.).

> Pages 1-16 only. 'Night prayers' torn out. Bound up with *The litanies of Jesus*, 1720 (no. 1673).

1903. *Morning and night prayers.* London. 1726. 12°. 24 p. Printed by: Meighan, T. Sold by: Meighan, T. * Map.

> Bound up with *The litanies of Jesus*, 1720 (no. 1673), and *The Friday devotion* (no. 1126).

1904. *Morning and night prayers. To which are added, the litanies in Latin and English.* [London?]. 1766. 12°. 118 p. ESTC t181352. * O; Pci.

> See also no. 751.

1905. *Morning and night prayers, &c. To which are added, the prayers for the king and the acts for gaining the indulgence.* 1778. 8°. 49, [1] p. * Yb.

1906. Morony, Joseph. *Sermons, and exhortations for the whole year, on the sacred mysteries and most important truths of the Christian religion. By the late rev. Joseph Morony, S.J.* 2 vols. Dublin. 1796. 12°. xxiii, [1], 260, [4]; [2], 309, [1] p. Printed by: M'Donnell, T. ESTC t195170. * DMR; DoA (vol. 1); Dt; ECW (vol. 1); FLK; IDA; Lfa; Mil; MoSU-D; O; Yb.

> Edited by William Gahan O.S.A. With a list of subscribers.

1907. *Motives for returning to the Catholick church, with a profession of Catholick faith, extracted out of the Council of Trent by Pope Pius IV. and now in use for the reception of converts into the church.* [London?]. 1755. 18°. 70 p. ESTC t090279. * L.

1908. Moylan, Francis. *Doctor Francis Moylan, to his beloved flock, the Roman*

Catholics of the diocese of Cork. [Cork]. [1796]. fol. s.s. ESTC t129284. * L; MY.

> Dated 'Dec. 25, 1796'.

1909. Moylan, Francis. *Doctor Francis Moylan, to his beloved flock, and in particular to the lower order of the Roman Catholic inhabitants of the diocess of Cork.* [Cork]. [1798]. 8°. 7, [1] p. Printed by: Haly, J. ESTC t162835. * D; MRu; MY.

1910. Moylan, Francis. *Doctor Francis Moylan, to the lower order of the Roman Catholic inhabitants of the diocess of Cork.* Cork. 1799. 8°. 15, [1] p. Printed by: Haly, J. ESTC t108345. * L; MY.

1911. Moylan, Francis. *Doctor Moylan's instructions to his beloved flock the Roman Catholics of the diocess of Cork, for the ensuing Lent.* Cork. [1795?]. 8°. 8 p. Printed by: Flyn, W. ESTC t212079. * MY.

1912. Moylan, Francis. *Pastoral instruction to the Roman Catholics of the diocess of Cork.* Dublin. 1798. 8°. 15, [1] p. Printed by: Fitzpatrick, H. ESTC t108346. * Du; FLK; L; Mil; MY.

1913. Moylan, Francis. *Pastoral instruction to the Roman Catholics of the diocess of Cork.* Cork. 1798. 8°. 16 p. Printed by: Haly, J. ESTC t180588. * CSmH; CtY; D; DLC; Dt; Du; Lhl; Lpro.

1914. Moylan, Francis. *A second remonstrance from the r.r. Dr. F. Moylan, the Roman Catholic Bishop of Cork, to the lower order of inhabitants in his diocess. April 16. 1799.* London. 1799. 12°. [3], 2-14 p. Printed by: Coghlan, J.P. * ECW.

1915. Mumford, James. *The Catholick-scripturist: or the plea of the Roman Catholicks.* 3rd. ed. London [St. Omers?]. 1717. 12°. [12], 428, [4] p. ESTC t100481. * BB; Do; ECW (imp.); Gi; L; Lhe; Lmc; MChB; NNUT.

> False imprint, probably printed at the English College Press, St. Omers. The author's name is also spelled 'Montford'. The book was first published in 1662.

1916. Mumford, James. *The Catholic scripturist: or, the plea of the Roman Catholics.* 4th ed. [London?]. 1767. 12°. xxxviii, 335, [1] p. ESTC t092868. * C; CAL; CLU; Do; DoA; E; ECW; FK; L; Lfa; LfaA; Lhe; MBAt; MRu; O; Sal; Sco; StD; TLP; TxU; Ush; UshL.

1917. Mumford, James. *The question of questions; which rightly resolv'd, resolves all our questions in religion.* 3rd ed. London. 1767. 12°. 364 p. ESTC t093749. * CLU; ECW; FLK; Gi; ICR; IDA; L; NNUT; StD.

> IDA contains a list of Irish subscribers, which may suggest that the book was printed in Ireland. The book was first published in 1658.

1918. Muratori, Lodovico Antonio. *A relation of the missions of Paraguay. Wrote originally in Italian, by Mr. Muratori and now done into English from the French translation [Il Cristianismo felice nelle missioni ... nell Paraguay].* London. 1759. 8°. xvi, 294, [2] p. Published by: Marmaduke, J. ESTC t087464. * AzU; BMs; C; CaBVaU; DGU; DLC; Do; E; FU; ICN; L; Lfa; LfaA; Lhe; Lu; Map; NIC; NN; O; PPL; RPJCB; Sto; Ush; ViU; WaPS.

Translated by James Dennett S.J. (1702-1789), provincial of the Society of Jesus in England from 1762 to 1766 (Gillow II, 47). The French translation was made by P. Esprit (Sommervogel II, 1928). ESTC gives a similar work entitled *The Jesuit travels in South-America, Paraguay, Chili &c.* (London, 1788), probably published under non-R.C. auspices.

1919. Muratori, Lodovico Antonio. *The science of rational devotion. From the writings of the learned and celebrated Muratori. By the rev. Alexander Kenny ... To which is prefixed, a preface by the translator.* Dublin. 1789. 12°. xxxvi, 248 p. Printed by: Byrn, J. ESTC t129482. * C; DMR; L.

With a list of subscribers.

1920. Murphy, Cornelius. *A dialogue between Archibald and Timothy; or, some observations upon the dedication and preface to The history of the popes by A... B..., Esquire.* Anon. London. 1748. 8°. vi, 72 p. Printed by: Booksellers of London and Westminster. Sold by: Booksellers of London and Westminster. ESTC t069233. * BRG; CtY; Eu; ICN; L; Lhe; Llp; TxU.

Ascribed to Cornelius Murphy by Sommervogel (Sup. 1911-30, 603). 'A... B...' is the apostate Archibald Bower.

1921. Murphy, Cornelius. *A true and exact relation of the death of two Catholicks, who suffered for their religion at the summer assizes, held at Lancaster in the year 1628.* Anon. London. 1737. 8°. [3], vi-xii, 68 p. ESTC t066468. * BB; C; CSmH; DAE; DFo; Do; DoA; E; ECB; ECW; L; Lfa; LfaA; Lhe; LO; Map; MChB; MRu; NjP; O; Osc; Sto; TxU; Yb.

Generally attributed to Cornelius Murphy.

1922. Musson, Samuel. *A review of the most important controversy concerning miracles ... to which is added a letter, with some remarks on a late performance, called The criterion, or miracles examined.* Anon. London. [1758]. 8°. [4], xii, 456 p. Published by: Needham, M. ESTC t088615. * Do; DoA; ECW (imp.); ICN; L; Lhe; MRu; TLP; Ush.

The author is identified by Walsh (p. 58). 'The letter' is by Cornelius Murphy and is dated 'April 28, 1758'. *The criterion* (1754) was written by John Douglas, Bishop of Salisbury.

1923. *My Lord, we the underwritten clergy of the city in Dublin, pursuant to your Grace's desire, have considered and examined the following oath, contained in a bill for the relief of English Catholics.* [Dublin]. 1791. fol. 4 p. * WDA.

A letter on the oath by 14 Dublin clergymen, addressed to John Thomas Troy, and also a note by Troy to John Douglass, V.A. of the London district.

1924. *A narrative of the misunderstanding between the rev. Arthur O'Leary and the rev. Mr. Hussey.* Dublin. 1791. 8°. 32 p. Published by: Mehain, J. ESTC t173623. * C.

Possibly by Arthur O'Leary himself. Cf. also nos 884 and 2075.

1925. Nary, Cornelius. *An appendix to the letter and rejoinder, in answer to the Charitable address, and reply, of his Grace Edward Lord Archbishop of Tuam, to all, who are of the communion of the Church of Rome.* Dublin. 1738. 8°. 38 p. ESTC t189914. * C; Di; MY.

Dated 'Dublin March the 2nd 1726-7'. An appendix to nos 1927 and 1932. See also next item.

1926. Nary, Cornelius. *An appendix to the letter and rejoinder, in answer to the Charitable address, and reply, of his Grace Edward Lord Archbishop of Tuam, to all, who are of the communion of the Church of Rome.* Dublin. 1738. 8°. 38 p. * MY.

> Dated and signed 'Dublin, July 1737, Cornelius Nary'.

1927. Nary, Cornelius. *A letter to his Grace Edward Lord Arch-bishop of Tuam. In answer to his Charitable address. To all who are of the communion of the Church of Rome.* Dublin. 1728. 8°. 235, [1] p. ESTC t125030. * C; CaOHM; CLU-C; CSmH; D; Di; E; ECW; FLK; ICR; IDA; L; Lhe; Mil; MiU; MWA; MY; Osc; P; SIR; StD; Ush.

> The Archbishop of Tuam, Edward Synge, whose *Charitable address* came out in 1727, answered Nary in 1729 with *The Archbishop of Tuam's defence*, which elicited further rejoinders by Nary (see nos 1925, 1926 and 1932).

1928. Nary, Cornelius. *A letter to the rev'd Mr. Stephen Radcliffe, M.A. vicar of Naas, on the subject of his letter and reply to Mr Synge's sermon and vindication.* Anon. Dublin. 1727. 8°. 56 p. * MY.

> Hugh Fenning O.P. (personal communication) attributes this work to Nary.

1929. Nary, Cornelius. *A modest and true account of the chief points in controversie, between the Roman Catholicks. And the Protestants ... with ... considerations upon the sermons of a divine of the Church of England. By N.C.* Antwerp [i.e. London]. 1705. 8°. [16], 302 p. ESTC n005227. * CLU-C; DCU; DFo; E; ECR; ECW; ICN; Lhe; NjP; NNG; NNUT; Osc; Sco; TH; TxU; Ush.

> Nary acknowledges his authorship in *A rejoinder* (no. 1932). With an initial advertisement leaf, lacking in Ush. 'A divine of the Church of England' is John Tillotson. See also next item.

1930. Nary, Cornelius. *A modest and true account of the chief points in controversy, between the Roman Catholicks and the Protestants ... with ... considerations upon the sermons of a divine of the Church of England. By N. C.* Antwerp [i.e. London]. 1705. 8°. [12], 292 p. Published by: [Metcalfe, T.]. ESTC t041336. * BB; CaQQLa; CLU-C; D; Do; Dt; ECW; GEU; Gi; Hen (imp.); L; Lfa; Lhe; LO; TxU; Ush.

> Lhe and ECW have 4 pages of preface misbound between pp. 290 and 291. ESTC erroneously distinguishes two eds (t041336 and t170053).

1931. Nary, Cornelius. *A new history of the world, containing an historical and chronological account of the times and transactions, from the creation to the birth of our Lord Jesus Christ.* Dublin. 1720. fol. [2], 496 p. Printed by: Waters, E. Published by: Dowling, L. ESTC t109207. * D; DFo; Dp; E; FLK; FMU; IDA; L; MY; PPL.

1932. Nary, Cornelius. *A rejoinder to the reply to the answer to the Charitable address of his Grace Edward, Lord Arch-bishop of Tuam, to all, who are of the communion of the Church of Rome.* Dublin. 1730. 8°. 130 p. ESTC t125031. * C; CSmH; D; Di; E; FLK; GEU-T; ICR; IDA; KU-S; L; Lhe; Mil; MY; Osc; SIR; Ush.

> Brenan (p. 584), gives five more Nary publications that have not been identified,

among them 'A letter of controversy to the vicar of Naas [i.e. Stephen Radcliffe]' (1722).

1933. Nassau, John. *The cause of the Roman Catholics pleaded, in an address to the Protestants of Ireland*. Dublin. 1792. 8°. [4], 60 p. Printed by: Fitzpatrick, H. Published by: Moore, J. ESTC t112227. * C; CSmH; D; Dt; ECW; IU; KU-S; L; MH-H; Mil; MWA; MWH; MY; O; Osc; Ush; WDA.

1934. *The nature, the origin, progress, &c. of the devotion to the adorable heart of Jesus. From the French*. London. 1794. 8°. vii, [1], 118, [2] p. Printed by: Coghlan, J.P. ESTC t128865. * Du; E; L; Lhe; TxU; Yb.

1935. *The nature, origin, progress, &c. of the devotion to the adorable heart of Jesus. From the French*. Dublin. 1800. 18°. viii, 162, [4] p. Printed by: Wogan, P. ESTC t177703. * D; FLK; IDA.

1936. *A net for the fishers of men: and the same which Christ gave to his apostles. Wherein the points controverted betwixt Catholicks and sectaries are briefly vindicated, by way of dilemma. By two gentlemen, late converts*. London. 1723. 24°. [12], 48 p. ESTC t072831. * CLU-C; Do; L.

> The dedication to Mary of Modena is signed 'J.C. J. M'C.' See also next item.
> For a previous ed. see Clancy no. 540.

1937. *A net for the fishers of men: and the same which Christ gave to his apostles. Wherein the points controverted betwixt Catholicks and sectaries are briefly vindicated, by way of dilemma*. London. 1750. 12°. 83, [1] p. ESTC t209286. * Lmh.

1938. *Neuvaine à l'honneur de Saint Francois Xavier, de la Compagnie de Jesus, apôtre des Indes & du Japon*. Montreal. 1778. 147, [1] p. Printed by: Mesplet, F. ESTC w019471. * CaOONL; CaOTP; CaQMM; CaQNicS; CaQQLa.

1939. *Neuvaine à l'honneur de S. François Xavier, de la Compagnie de Jésus, apôtre des Indes et du Japon*. Que[bec]. 1772. 215, [1] p. Printed by: Brown & Gilmore. Sold by: Bargeas, J. * CaNSWA; CaQMM.

> Though the printing probably started in 1772, this work was published in 1773 as the bishop's approbation and the printer's records indicate (Tremaine, 165).

1940. *A new approved manual of Christian devotions*. London. 1760. 12°. 288 p. * Do (imp.).

> Bound up with *The devout manual: fitted to the ca-pacities of all Roman Catholicks* (no. 905). Probably edited by Richard Challoner. See also next item.

1941. *A new approved manual of Christian devotions, adapted to the new-stile*. London. 1776. 12°. 286, [2] p. Printed by: [Coghlan, J.P.?]. ESTC t174640. * ECW; Lhe.

1942. *The new ghospel of the Jesuits, compared with the old one of Jesus Christ. Or a short collection of some choice maxims of these politick casuists against the plain dealing of the prophets*. London. 1708. 8°. [8], 122 p. Published by: Author. ESTC t186630. * C; E; ECW; Lmh; Osc.

> The book is violently anti-Jesuit, but was evidently written by a Catholic.

1943. *A new manual of devout prayers for every day in the week, morning and evening.* Preston. 1780. 12°. [8], 383, [1] p. Printed by: Sergent, W. * DMR (imp.); Gi; Sto; Ush.

1944. *The new testament of our Lord and Saviour Jesus Christ, newly translated out of the Latin Vulgat ... Together with annotations .. By C.N. C.F.P.D.* [Dublin?]. 1718. 8°. ESTC t182027. * D; DAE; ICU; MWH; NN.

> 'C.N. C.F.P.D.' is Cornelius Nary, 'consultissimae facultatis Parisiensis doctor'. See also next item. The book, which was banned in Rome in 1722, was an attempt to provide a simpler version of the Rheims translation. This and the next item are unpaged. Cf. D & M 951 which mentions this 1718 edition.

1945. *The new testament of our Lord and Saviour Jesus Christ, newly translated out of the Latin Vulgat ... Together with annotations ... By C.N. C.F.P.D.* [Dublin?]. 1719. 8°. ESTC t094398. * CLU-C; E; KU-S; L; Lhe; NBu; NcD; NN; O; TH; Ush.

> D & M 951.

1946. *The new testament of Jesus Christ; with arguments of books and chapters: with annotations ... faithfully translated into English ... by the English College then resident in Rhemes.* 5th ed. [London?]. 1738. fol. [2], xix, [1], 646, [32] p. ESTC t094430. * CaAEU; CLU-C; DLC; DoA; Du; GOT; L; Lhe; MRu; NNPM; Occ; Osc; PPL; Sto; TxU; Ush; Yb.

> Gillow (I, 253) and Pope (pp. 374-5) state that it was edited by Francis Blyth in conjunction with Richard Challoner. D & M 1041.

1947. *The new testament of our Lord and Saviour Jesus Christ. Translated out of the Latin Vulgat ... first published by the English College of Rhemes, anno 1582. Newly revised, and corrected.* [Dublin?]. 1749. 12°. [4], 500 p. ESTC t094461. * CAL; CLU-C; L; NN; NNAB; O; TxU; Yb.

> The first ed. of Challoner's revision of the Rheims N.T. See Burton (I, 287) for a discussion of the place of publication. D & M 1086.

1948. *The new testament of our Lord and Saviour Jesus Christ. Translated out of the Latin Vulgat ... Newly revised, and corrected according to the Clementin edition ... With annotations.* [Dublin?]. 1750. 12°. [4], 500 p. ESTC t094439. * C; CAL; Do; E; ECB; ECR; GEU-T; L; Lhe; Llp; Map; O; PcA; Yb.

> The second ed. of Challoner's revision of the Rheims N.T. See also note to no. 1448. D & M 1090.

1949. *The new testament of our Lord and Saviour Jesus Christ. Translated out of the Latin Vulgat ... first published by the English College of Rhemes, anno 1582 ... according to the Clementin edition.* 2 vols. [Dublin?]. 1752. 12°. 296; 239, [1] p. ESTC t094462. * CAL; CLU-C; CYc; E; ECB (vol. 1); Hen; L; Lfa; Lhe; Map; NN; O; Osc; Stan (vol. 1); TxU.

> The third ed. of Challoner's revision of the Rheims N.T. Pope (p. 48) suggests London as place of publication in view of the occurrence of a Coghlan advert in some copies. D & M 1099.

1950. *The new testament of our Lord and Saviour Jesus Christ ... First published by the English College of Rhemes, anno 1582 ... With annotations.* London. 1772. 12°. [6], 533, [1] p. Published by: [Coghlan, J.P.]. ESTC t167047. *

DoA; ECR; MRu; NN; O.

> In this issue of the 1772 ed. of Challoner's revision the imprint does not contain the publisher's name. ECR is part 5 of no. 1448. D & M 1224.

1951. *The new testament of our Lord and Saviour Jesus Christ ... first published by the English College of Rhemes, anno 1582 ... With annotations.* London. 1772. 12°. [6], 533, [1] p. Published by: Coghlan, J.P. ESTC t195689. * DAE; Gi; O; Ush.

> In this issue of the 1772 ed. of Challoner's revision the imprint contains the publisher's name. D & M 1224.

1952. *The new testament of Jesus Christ.* [London]. 1772. fol. [4], xv, [3], 440 p. * Ush.

1953. *The new testament of our Lord and Saviour Jesus Christ.* Dublin. 1783. 12°. Printed by: Graisberry, D. Published by: Cross, R.; Wogan, P. * DGU.

> The fourth ed. of Challoner's revision of the Rheims N.T., revised by Bernard MacMahon. According to Pope (pp. 56-9) this is a debased version of the original Challoner ed. D & M 1292.

1954. *The new testament of Jesus Christ, with arguments of books and chapters: annotations, and other helps ... faithfully translated into English.* 6th ed. Liverpool. 1788. fol. [4], xv, [1], 440 p. Sold by: Ferguson, R. ESTC t094432. * DGU; L; Lhe; NN; NNAB; Osc.

> Challoner's 1749 revision of the Rheims version published in parts with an additional engraved tp, dated 1787. D & M 1330.

1955. *The new testament of Jesus Christ; with arguments of books and chapters; annotations, and other helps ... by the English College then resident in Rhemes in 1582.* 6th ed. Liverpool. 1789. fol. [6], xv, [1], 440 p. Printed by: Wogan, P. Sold by: Wogan, P. ESTC t167084. * Dt; NN.

> Challoner's 1749 revision. With an additional engraved tp. This is another issue of no. 1954, copies of which were disposed of to a bookseller in Dublin, furnished with a new tp, dated 1789, omitting the words 'Permissu superiorum'.

1956. *The new testament, of our Lord and Saviour Jesus Christ ... first published by the English College at Rhemes, A.D. 1582.* 5th ed. Dublin. 1791. 4°. [5], 2-272, [14] p. Printed by: Fitzpatrick, H. Published by: Cross, R. * MY.

> This work is a separate issue of the N.T. part of the *Holy bible*, 1791 (no. 1452). Challoner's revision with an approbation by John Thomas Troy.

1957. *The new testament of our Lord and Saviour Jesus Christ: translated from the Latin Vulgate.* [Edinburgh?]. 1792. 12°. [4], 428 p. ESTC t094405. * Do; L; O; Osc.

> Tp engraved by A. McIntyre. Challoner's revision of the Rheims version, with extensive alterations as far as Romans by James Robertson, O.S.B., and Bishop John Geddes. D & M 1374.

1958. *The new testament, of our Lord and Saviour Jesus Christ, translated from the Latin Vulgat ... first published by the English College at Rhemes, A.D. 1582. With annotations.* 6th ed. Dublin. 1794. fol. [2], 220, [8] p. Printed by: Reilly, J. ESTC t095074. * L.

> This ed. is also found as part of no. 1455. The plates are inscribed 'Reilly's

Doway Bible'.

1959. *The new testament of our Lord and Saviour Jesus Christ, translated from the Latin Vulgat ... first published by the English College at Rhemes, anno 1582. With annotations.* 6th ed. Dublin. 1794. 523, [1] p. Printed by: Cross, R. * DCU.

1960. *The new testament of our Lord and Saviour Jesus Christ, translated out of the Latin Vulgate ... first published by the English College of Rhemes, anno 1582 ... according to the Clementin edition.* Edinburgh. 1797. 12°. 6, [2], 532 p. Printed by: Moir, J. ESTC t094475. * Do; E; ECB; Hor; L; Lhe; O; OMC; Sal; Sco (-tp); Ush.

    See also no. 1456. D & M 1422.

1961. [New testament]. *O novo testamento; isto he, todos os sacrosantos livros e escritos evangelicos e apostolicos do novo concerto de nosso senhor e redemptor Jesu Christo: traduzidos na lingua Portugueza.* Trangambar. 1760-65. 8°. [14], 765, [5] p. Printed by: Real Missao de Dinamarca. ESTC t123201. * L.

1962. [New testament]. *Novum testamentum, vulgatae editionis, juxta exemplum Parisiis editum apud Fratres Barbou. Sumptibus Academiae Oxoniensis in usum cleri Gallicani in Anglia exulantis.* Oxford. 1796. 12°. [2], iv, 473, [3] p. Published by: Clarendon Press. ESTC t131081. * C; CaNBFMM; CtY; E; ICN; L; LAM; O; Oc; Occ; Om; Oma; Osc; TxU.

    Osc cat. states that the book was prepared by French refugee priests and that Oxford University printed 2000 copies of this new testament for free distribution among the French refugee clergy.

1963. *A new year's gift to the people of Ireland, for the year 1750. Being an aera as remarkable, for the present critical state of the kingdom, as for the periodical celebration of the jubilee at Rome.* Dublin. 1750. 12°. 148 p. Published by: Wilson, P. ESTC t085074. * D; Dt; L; O.

Nicole, Pierre, see Arnauld, Antoine.

1964. Nieremberg, Juan Eusebio. *A treatise of the difference betwixt the temporal and eternal ... Translated into English, by Sir Vivian Mullinaux ... And since revised and corrected, according to the last Spanish edition [De la differencia entre lo temporal y eterno].* London. 1732. 8°. [6], 532 p. ESTC t176476. * NSPM; TxU.

1965. Nieremberg, Juan Eusebio. *A treatise of the difference betwixt the temporal and eternal ... Translated into English. By Sir Vivian Mullineaux ... and since revised and corrected, according to the last Spanish edition.* Dublin. 1762. 12°. [6], 532 p. Printed by: Fitzsimons, R. ESTC t176475. * D.

1966. Nieremberg, Juan Eusebio. *A treatise of the difference betwixt the temporal and eternal ... Translated into English, by Sir Vivian Mullineaux ... and since revised and corrected, according to the last Spanish edition.* Dublin. [1775?]. 8°. 483, [5] p. Printed by: Hoey, P. ESTC t131536. * L.

1967. Nieremberg, Juan Eusebio. *A treatise of the difference betwixt the temporal and eternal ... Translated into English, by Sir Vivian Mullineaux ... And since* *revised and corrected, according to the last Spanish edition.* Dublin. 1793. 8°. 483, [5] p. Printed by: Hoey, P.; Cross, R. ESTC n045470. * MiU.

1968. Noailles, Louis Antoine de. *The act of appeal of his eminence the Cardinal de Noailles, Archbishop of Paris, of the third of April MDCCXVII ... from the constitution of our holy father, Pope Clement XI [Acte d'appel].* London. 1717. 8°. 20 p. Published by: Roberts, J. ESTC t135363. * CSmH; L; MH-H; Omc.

1969. Noailles, Louis Antoine de. *The mandate of his eminence the Cardinal de Noailles Archbishop of Paris. On account of the miracle wrought in the parish of St. Margaret on the feast of the Blessed Sacrament the 31st of May [Mandement a l'occasion du miracle].* London. 1725. 8°. [4], 43, [1] p. Printed by: Hughes, J. ESTC t135778. * C; CaOHM; CLU-C; CSmH; L; LEu; MRu; WDA.

> According to Mitchell 1984 (p. 42) the imprint is false. ESTC gives the translator's name as William Gathorne; this is probably a mistake for William Crathorne (Gillow I, 588).

1970. Noailles, Louis Antoine de. *The mandate of his eminence the Lord Cardinal d'Noailles [sic], Arch-bishop of Paris. On the subject of a miracle wrought in the parish of St. Margaret, on the 31st of May, 1725.* [London?]. 1726. 4°. 38 p. ESTC t171513. * Dt.

> There are other de Noailles publications that do not come within the terms of our definition.

1971. *Nouvelles des missions orientales, reçues à Londres, par les directeurs du seminaire des missions etrangères, en 1793, 1794, 1795 & 1796. Pouvant servir de suite aux lettres edifiantes des missionaires.* London. 1797. 12°. [2], xii, [2], 319, [1] p. Printed by: Coghlan, J.P. ESTC n022065. * BMu; InU; LfaA; Lhe; Lras; NIC.

1972. *Nouvelles étrennes spirituelles selon l'usage de Rome.* Philadelphia. 1797. 12°. Printed by: Moreau de St. Mery. * Evans 32777.

> Latin and French.

1973. O., R., Gent. *Reasons why Jews, infidels, Turks and hereticks cannot be saved. And that 'tis impossible the Catholic church can err in faith, or perish ... Permissu superiorum.* Douai [i.e. London?]. 1720. 8°. 38, [2] p. ESTC t046479. * L; Ush.

1974. *The oath contained in the printed bill. I.A.B. do truly and sincerely acknowledge ... that our Sovereign Lord King [blank] is lawful and rightful.* [London?]. [1791?]. fol. 2 p. ESTC t041691. * L; Ush.

> Reprinted from the *Bill for the relief of protesting Catholic dissenters enacted 31 Geo.III.c.32.* Page two contains 'Reasons for the suggested alterations in the oath'.

Obituary. Although obituaries (lists of persons deceased in a given period or year) are occasionally found by themselves, they are not listed separately as they normally form part of compilations such as the Laity's directory and the Ordo recitandi.

1975. O'Brien, [Matthew?]. *A funeral sermon on the late queen of France and Navarre: pronounced, on Sunday, 17th November, in the chapel of the convent of*

St. Ursula. Cork. 1793. 8°. 22 p. Printed by: Haley, J. * CAI.

1976. O'Brien, Matthew. *Sermons on some of the most important subjects of morality and religion.* Cork. 1798. 8°. viii, [2], 229, [1] p. Printed by: Haly, J. ESTC t195718. * Dt; FLK; IDA; RPPC.
> Some copies tend to lack pp. 215-8. With a list of about 300 subscribers.

1977. O'Brien, Timothy. *A brief historical authentic account of the beginning and doctrine of the sects, called Vaudois and Albigeois ... By T.B.* 1743. 4°. 5, [1], 38 p. * Pci.
> O' Brien's R.C. counter version of Pierre Boyer's *History of the Vaudois.* It pretends to be published under Protestant auspices but this is clearly a R.C. ploy. It was attacked by the Protestant Bishop of Cork in a pastoral letter, which - according to Brenan (p. 585) - received an answer from Timothy O'Brien. For further O'Brien contributions to this controversy, see nos 1979 and 1980.

1978. O'Brien, Timothy. *An explication of the jubilee in a sermon preach'd by the reverend doctor T.B. in the year 1721. And publish'd this jubilee year 1745-5. By Mr. S.P.* [1745]. 4°. [4], 32 p. * Pci.
> Brenan (p. 585) mentions a 1725 ed. of this *Explication.*

1979. O'Brien, Timothy. *A rejoynder to the reply made to the answer of the Bishop of Cork's pastoral letter. By T.B.* 1743. 4°. 46 p. * Pci.

1980. O'Brien, Timothy. *Truth triumphant: in the defeat of a book, intitled, A replication to the rejoinder, &c. By T.B.* [Cork]. 1745. 4°. xi, 118, [1], ii p. ESTC t072161. * L; Pci.

1981. *Observanda ab omnibus sacerdotibus ad sacras missiones in nostro districtu admissis.* [London?]. [1775?]. 8°. 8 p. ESTC t131644. * DowA; ECW; Hor; L; UshA.
> UshA is dated in ms '14th Oct. 1775, Durham'; ESTC suggests '1800?'.

1982. *Observations upon some points of doctrin [sic] in the Montpellier catechism intitle'd [sic], General instructions, by way of catechism. Translated into English from the French original.* [London?]. 1724. 12°. [2], 88 p. ESTC n041912. * FLK (imp.); MBAt.
> A R.C. comment on François Aimé Pouget's catechism (nos 2351 and 2352), possibly translated/edited by Peter Manby.

1983. O'Connell, Daniel. *Historical account of the laws against Roman Catholics, and of the laws passed for their relief; with observations on the laws remaining in force against them.* Anon. 1794. 8°. [3], 4-15, [1] p. * ECW.
> This title is often given under Charles Butler due to a reference on the tp to Butler's new ed. of Sir Edward Coke's *Institutes of the laws of England.* Byrns (p. 13) also mentions a 1799 ed. See also next item.

1984. O'Connell, Daniel. *Historical account of the laws respecting Roman Catholics, and of the laws passed for their relief; with observations, on the laws remaining in force against them.* Anon. London. 1795. 8°. [4], 45, [1] p. Printed by: Coghlan, J.P. ESTC t103776. * C; CSmH; CtY-D; CY-c; Di; ICN; L; Lhe; Lmh; MnU; MRu; MY; NcD; O; RP; StD; Sto.

1985. O'Connor, Arthur. *Speech of Arthur O'Connor, Esq. in the House of*

Commons of Ireland, Monday, May 4th, 1795, on the Catholic bill. Dublin. 1795. 8°. [4], 36 p. Printed by: Byrne, P. ESTC t177406. * C; D; KU; Lhl; Mil.

> A short editorial preface makes clear that this speech, by the non-R.C. O'Connor, was published for 'the cause of the Catholics'. There are several other late 18th century eds of this speech.

1986. O'Connor, John. *An essay on the rosary and sodality of the most holy name of Jesus ... By the rev. J----n O C----nn----r.* Dublin. 1772. 12°. [8], iv, 259, [1] p. Published by: Author. Sold by: Cross, R.; Fitzsimons, J. ESTC t105281. * C; Dt; ECW; FLK; IDA; L; MY; SCR; SIR.

> Pages 201-59 contain 'The method of saying the rosary ... and the rosary of the Blessed Virgin' with separate divisional tp. Some copies have 2 pages of Cross adverts.

1987. O'Connor, John. *An essay on the rosary and sodality of the most holy name of Jesus.* 2nd ed. Dublin. 1788. 12°. xii, 339, [1] p. Published by: Wogan, P. ESTC t105280. * FLK; IDA; L; Lhe.

> Pages 196-214 contain 'The method of saying the rosary' with separate divisional tp. Pages 215-339 contain 'An essay or introduction to the rosary ... the third edition' by John Clarkson, O.P. and 'The method of saying the rosary of the Blessed Virgin Mary', both with separate divisional tps.

1988. O'Conor, Charles. *The case of the Roman-Catholics of Ireland. Wherein the principles and conduct of that party are fully explained and vindicated.* Anon. Dublin. 1755. 8°. [2], iii-v, [3], 9-80 p. Published by: Lord, P. ESTC n026876. * CaOHM; CSmH; D; Dt; ICR; Lhl; MChB; Mil; MY; SCR.

1989. O'Conor, Charles. *The case of the Roman-Catholics of Ireland. Wherein the principles and conduct of that party are fully explained and vindicated.* Anon. Cork repr. [Dublin]. 1755. 12°. 55, [1] p. Printed by: Swiney, E. ESTC t189359. * D; Du; SCR.

1990. O'Conor, Charles. *The case of the Roman-Catholics of Ireland. Wherein the principles and conduct of that party are fully explained and vindicated.* 2nd ed. Anon. Dublin. 1755. 8°, viii, 9-80 p. Published by: Lord, P. ESTC t186619. * D; Dt; FLK; MRu; O; PV.

1991. O'Conor, Charles. *The case of the Roman-Catholics of Ireland. Wherein the principles and conduct of that party are fully explained and vindicated.* 3rd ed. Anon. Dublin. 1756. 8°. 70 p. Published by: Lord, P. Sold by: Lord, P. ESTC n026878. * D; KU-S.

1992. O'Conor, Charles. *A cottager's remarks on the farmer's spirit of party.* Dublin. 1754. 8°. 16 p. ESTC t001681. * C; D; Dt; Du; IU; L; PP.

> 'A cottager' is Charles O'Conor. A reply to *The spirit of party* by Henry Brooke.

1993. O'Conor, Charles. *Dissertations on the antient history of Ireland: wherein an account is given of the origine, government, letters, sciences, religion, manners and customs, of the antient inhabitants.* Anon. Dublin. 1753. 8°. [21], vi-xlviii, 248, [20] p. Printed by: Hoey, J. Published by: Reilly, M. ESTC t146898. * CtY; D; DLC; Du; IU; KU-S; L; LOU; MH; P; PV; SIR.

> With a list of subscribers. This work is of a general historical nature. See also next item.

1994. O'Conor, Charles. *Dissertations on the history of Ireland. To which is subjoined, a dissertation on the Irish colonies established in Britain. With some remarks on Mr. Mac Pherson's translation of Fingal and Temora.* Dublin. 1766. 8°. xx, [8], 290, 65, [1] p. Published by: Faulkner, G. ESTC n008915. * C; CtY; DFo; Di; Dt; Du; E; ICN; ICU; IDA; L; MChB; MH; NIC; NN; NNU; O; Oe; Owa; P; PPL; RP; SCR; SWNu; TxU.

1995. O'Conor, Charles. *Seasonable thoughts relating to our civil and ecclesiastical constitution.* Anon. Dublin. 1753. 8°. 51, [1] p. ESTC n021567. * C; CaOHM; CSmH; D; Dt; KU-S; MoU.

1996. O'Conor, Charles. *Seasonable thoughts relating to our civil and ecclesiastical constitution.* Anon. Dublin. 1754. 8°. 51, [1] p. Published by: [Faulkner, G.]. ESTC n021568. * C; CLU-S/C; D; Dt; Mil; PP.

> Mil has one page Faulkner adverts.

1997. O'Conor, Charles. *Some seasonable thoughts, relating to our civil and ecclesiastical constitution: wherein is occasionally consider'd, the case of the professors of popery.* Anon. Dublin. 1751. 8°. 27, [1] p. ESTC t058142. * C; CSmH; D; Dt; InU-Li; L; Lhl; MBAt; MY; O.

> The text consists of a series of questions intended to influence Parliament in favour of Catholic relief.

1998. O'Conor, Charles. *A vindication of the political principles of Roman Catholics. From the Reformation to the present time. Supported by the testimonies of our own most authentic Protestant historians ... By the author of Seasonable thoughts.* Dublin. [1760?]. 8°. 31, [1] p. ESTC t178922. * Du; SCR.

> The author of *Seasonable thoughts* is Charles O'Conor. The imprint has the date '1741' but the author himself gives the date '3 March 1760' in the text.

1999. O'Conor, Charles and John Curry. *Observations on the popery laws.* Anon. Dublin. 1771. 8°. 53, [1] p. Printed by: Ewing, T. ESTC t094012. * C; CaOKQ; CSmH; D; Dt; ICN; IU; L; O.

2000. O'Conor, Charles and John Curry. *Observations on the popery laws.* Anon. London. 1772. 8°. [4], iii, [1], 72 p. Published by: Murray, J.; Ewing, T. (Dublin). ESTC t041838. * CLU-S/C; Dt; L; MH-L; Omc; PP.

2001. O'Conor, Charles and John Curry. *Observations on the popery laws.* 2nd ed. Anon. Dublin. 1774. 8°. 53, [1] p. Printed by: Ewing, T. ESTC t185918. * C; ICU.

2002. O'Conor, Charles (II). *Memoirs of the life and writings of the late Charles O'Conor, of Belanagare, Esq. M.R.I.A.* Dublin. [1796]. 8°. [2], xiv, [2], 450 p. Printed by: Mehain, J. ESTC t174894. * CSmH; IDA; L; NN; O.

> 'Only a small number of copies was printed of vol. 1, which was later suppressed by the author; vol. 2 was never published' (NUC). Dedication dated 'March 11, 1796'.

2003. *Oeconomia clericalis; or the clergyman instructed in housekeeping.* fol.

s.s. * DowA.

> DowA has a ms note stating that this late 18th century broadside was widely circulated among Catholic clergy and laity; its argument was that a priest with a maid could not survive on £50 a year.

2004. *L'office de la semaine sainte, selon le messel & breviaire Romain … Imprimée sur la meilleure edition de Paris.* Montreal. 1778. 12°. 420 p. Printed by: Mesplet, F.; Berger, C. ESTC w016685. * CaBVaU; CaOONL; CaQMM; NN.

2005. *The office for the dead. In Latin and English.* [London]. 1729. 12°. 93, [1] p. Published by: Meighan, T. ESTC t084084. * CLU-C; L; LEu (imp.); Lmh.

> Lmh bound with no. 1457.

2006. *The office for the dead: according to the Roman breviary, missal and ritual. Containing the office entire, with all the proper masses, and the order of burial. In Latin and English.* [London]. 1745. 12°. vi, 186, [2] p. Printed by: Marmaduke, J. ESTC t083409. * L.

> With 2 pages of Marmaduke adverts.

2007. *The office for the dead. In Latin and English.* Dublin. 1747. 12°. 119, [1] p. Published by: Kelly, I. ESTC t173261. * D.

2008. *The office for the dead: according to the Roman breviary, missal and ritual, containing the vespers, mattins, and lauds, with all the proper masses, and the order of burial. In Latin and English.* London. 1748. 12°. vi, 186 p. Printed by: Marmaduke, J. Sold by: Marmaduke, J. ESTC t186269. * E; Map.

2009. *The office for the dead: according to the Roman breviary, missal and ritual. Containing the office entire, with all the proper masses, and the order of burial. In Latin and English.* [London?]. 1761. 12°. vi, 147, [1] p. ESTC t198180. * Do; L.

> According to Gillow (IV, 464) published by J. Marmaduke. L lacks the 6 preliminary pages.

2010. *The office for the dead: according to the Roman breviary, missal and ritual. Containing the office entire, with all the proper masses, and the order of burial. In Latin and English.* London. 1762. 12°. 189, [1] p. Published by: Marmaduke, J. ESTC t181292. * Do; Hen; L; Lhe; Map; O.

> Do has 6 preliminary pages and a final page of Marmaduke adverts.

2011. *The office for the dead: according to the Roman breviary, missal and ritual. Containing the office entire, with all the proper masses, and the order of burial. In Latin and English.* London. 1781. 12°. vi, 190, [2] p. Published by: Marmaduke, J. * Hen; Lhe.

> With 2 pages of Marmaduke adverts.

2012. *The office of the dead: containing the vespers, mattins, lauds, masses, and the order of burial; compiled from the Roman breviary, missal and ritual. In Latin and English.* London. 1790. 12°. viii, [2], 9-214 p. Printed by: Coghlan, J.P. ESTC t186270. * E; Stan; Yb.

2013. *The office for the dead. Translated into English from the Roman breviary.*

London. 1791. 12°. 48 p. Printed by: Coghlan, J.P. * Yb.

2014. *The office for the dead. In Latin and English.* Dublin. 1794. 18°. 161, [1] p. Printed by: Wogan, P. ESTC t186268. * D; MY; Yb.

Office of the B.V. Mary. See also under Primer.

2015. *The office of the B.V. Mary in English. To which is added the vespers, or evensong, in Latin and English, as it is sung in the Catholic church.* London. 1720. 12°. [38], 503, [1] p. Published by: Meighan, T. * Do.

2016. *The office of the B.V. Mary in English. To which is added the ordinary of the holy mass for the dead. With the vespers, or even-song, in Latin and English.* London. 1736. 12°. [36], 216 p. Published by: Meighan, T. * Do.

2017. *The office of the B.V. Mary. To which is added the method of saying the rosary of our blessed lady, and the manner how to serve at mass.* [London?]. 1770. 12°. [20], 102 p. ESTC t206521. * BB; Do; E; ECW; Gi; Llp; UGL.

2018. *The office of the holy week; according to the Roman missal and breviary ... In Latin and English.* [London]. 1723. 12°. xvii, [1], 448 p. ESTC t105411. * Do; E; L; MChB; Stan; Ush.

2019. *The office of the holy week according to the Roman missal and breviary ... In Latin and English.* 2nd ed. [London]. 1729. 12°. xv, [1], 440 p. Published by: Meighan, T. ESTC n042145. * CU-SB; DMR; L; O; TxU.

2020. *The office of the holy week according to the Roman missal, and breviary ... In Latin and English.* 3rd ed. [London]. 1738. 12°. xiv, 452 p. Published by: Meighan, T. ESTC t118050. * DMR; Do; Dt; E; ECW; L; Map; TLP.

2021. *The office of the holy week according to the Roman missal and breviary.* 4th ed. Dublin. 1747. 12°. 292, [4] p. Published by: Kelly, I. ESTC t173260. * C.

With a list of subscribers.

2022. *The office of the holy week according to the Roman missal and breviary ... in Latin and English.* 4th ed. [London]. 1752. 12°. xv, [1], 452 p. Published by: Meighan, T. ESTC t186034. * CAL; DMR; DoA; Lhe; TLP.

This is the second '4th' ed.

2023. *The office of the holy week according to the Roman missal and breviary ... In Latin and English.* 5th ed. [London]. 1759. 12°. xv, [1], 452 p. Published by: Meighan, T. ESTC t107223. * DMR; DoA; E; L; Nijm; PcA.

2024. *The office of the holy week according to the Roman missal and breviary ... In Latin and English.* 6th ed. [London]. 1766. 12°. xv, [1], 452 p. Printed by: Meighan, T. ESTC t198182. * DMR; DoA; ECB; L; Llp; LOU; O.

See also Nixon (p. 35).

2025. *The office of the holy week according to the Roman missal and breviary.* 5th ed. Dublin. 1767. 12°. 292 p. Printed by: Tisdall, I. ESTC t173244. * D; IDA.

This is the second '5th' ed.

2026. *The office of the holy week. With explanation of the ceremonies.* Dublin.

1772. Published by: Kelly, J. * DMR.

2027. *The office of the holy week, according to the Roman missal and breviary ... In Latin and English.* 7th ed. London. 1775. 8°. [4], xv, [1], 452 p. Printed by: Coghlan, J.P. ESTC t199291. * CAL; DMR; Do; Hen; ICN; O.

With a list of subscribers.

2028. *The office of the holy week according to the Roman missal and breviary. Containing the morning and evening-service from Palm-Sunday to Tuesday in Easter-week.* 5th ed. Dublin. 1777. 12°. [2], 292 p. Published by: Kelly, J. ESTC n060717. * Dp.

This is the third '5th' ed.

2029. *The office of the holy week, according to the Roman missal and breviary ... in Latin and English.* 8th ed. London. 1780. 8°. [2], xv, [1], 458 p. Printed by: Coghlan, J.P. ESTC t180971. * BB; DMR; L; Lfa; Lhe; O; TxU.

BB has [4], xv, [5], 458 p.

2030. *The office of the holy week according to the Roman missal and breviary.* 6th ed. Dublin. 1781. 12°. 288 p. Printed by: Cross, R. ESTC t118053. * IU; L; NNUT.

This is the second '6th' ed.

2031. *The office of the holy week, according to the Roman missal and breviary ... in Latin and English.* 9th ed. London. 1788. 4°. [2], xv, [1], 472 p. Printed by: Coghlan, J.P. ESTC t105161. * CAL; DMR; L; Lhe; LO.

2032. *The office of the holy week according to the Roman missal and breviary .... Revised by the rev. B. Mc M.* 7th ed. Dublin. 1793. 12°. 288 p. Printed by: Cross, R. ESTC t186274. * D; Mil.

'B. Mc M.' is Bernard MacMahon. This is the second '7th' ed.

2033. *The office of the holy week, according to the Roman missal and breviary ... In Latin and English.* 10th ed. London. 1796. 12°. [2], xii, 468 p. Printed by: Coghlan, J.P. ESTC t186038. * CAL; DAE; DMR; Do; DoA; ECB; Lhe; MRu; Stan; TLP; TxU.

2034. *The office of the holy week, according to the Roman missal and breviary.* 8th ed. Dublin. 1796. 12°. 288 p. Printed by: Wogan, P. ESTC t186272. * D; FLK; IDA.

This is the second '8th' ed.

2035. *Officia de ss. eucharistiae sacramento, et de conceptione B.V.M. nec non propria sanctorum Societatis Jesu ... Juxta exemplar Neapoli impressum 1696.* London. 1710. 12°. 351, [1] p. ESTC t186091. * C; Gi; LfaA; Lhe (imp.).

2036. *Officia et missae ss. archangelorum Gabrielis et Raphaelis.* Dublin. [1796]. 12°. 34 p. Published by: Cross, R.; Wogan, P. ESTC t186090. * C; IDA.

Page 2 has the decree of 3 July 1796, authorizing the office.

2037. *Officia nova sanctorum. Supplementa ad breviarium Romanum, seu officia sanctorum quorundam recentium in breviario Romano apponenda.* London. 1734. 12°. 134, xiii, [1], 12 p. Published by: Meighan, T. * Cha.

2038. *Officia nova sanctorum de praecepto recitanda, ac in breviario Romano, et missale apponenda. Juxta decreta ss. d.n. Clementis XIV.* [London?]. 1770. 12°. 48 p. ESTC t198185. * L.

2039. *Officia nova sanctorum.* [London?]. [1775?]. 12°. 11, [1] p. ESTC t198187. * L.

2040. *Officia propria quorumdam Hiberniae sanctorum, ex breviariis approbatis, iuxta decreta Benedicti XIV. collecta ... His accedunt officia propria et missae ss. Hiberniae patronorum.* Paris & Dublin. 1769. 12°. [12], 172 p. ESTC t206492. * D; Mil; MY; Pci.

2041. *Officia propria quorumdam Hiberniae sanctorum, ex breviariis approbatis collecta. Additis quibusdam breviarii Romani novis festis. Accedunt officia votiva de ss. sacramento, et immaculatae conceptionis.* Dublin. 1781. 12°. [6], 122, xxxiv p. Published by: Wogan, P.; Cross, R. ESTC t206507. * D; Di.

2042. *Officia propria quorumdam Hiberniae sanctorum, ex breviariis approbatis collecta.* Dublin. [1796]. 12°. [2], 118, xxxiii, [5] p. Printed by: Cross, R.; Wogan, P. ESTC t186222. * C; FLK; IDA; Mil.
> ESTC gives 1792, but the date of publication must be 1796, because the signatures of the IDA copy of this work are continuous from those of the IDA copy of *Officia et missae ss. archangelorum* (no. 2036).

2043. *Officia sanctorum Angliae.* London. 1774. 12°. 20 p. Printed by: Coghlan, J.P. ESTC t198190. * L; Sto; WDA.
> WDA has one page of Coghlan adverts. Sto and WDA bound up with Coghlan's *Ordo* for 1775 (no. 2163).

2044. *Officium defunctorum cum suo cantu, et missa solemnis pro defunctis: quibus adjungitur exequiarum ordo, ex rituali Romano jussu Benedicti XIV. Edito, extractus.* Dublin. 1778. 174 p. Published by: Wogan, P.; Bean, P. * IU.

2045. *Officium defunctorum cum suo cantu, et missa solemnis pro defunctis: quibus adjungitur exequiarum ordo, ex rituali Romano jussu Benedicti XIV, edito, extractus.* Dublin. 1793. 12°. [2], 174, [2] p. Printed by: Wogan, P. ESTC t196328. * FLK; L; Lmh; Mil; MY.

2046. *Officium in honorem domini nostri J.C. summi sacerdotus et omnium sanctorum sacerdotum ac levitarum.* Montreal. 1777. 8°. [2], 11, [3] p. Printed by: Mesplet, F. ESTC w016686. * CaOONL; CaOOP; CaOTP; CaQMBM; CaQMM; CaQQLa; CaSSU; MB; NN; NNPM; RPJCB.
> The first book printed in Latin in Canada (Tremaine, 257). See also no. 364.

2047. O'Hussey, Bonaventure. *An teagasg Criosdaidhe añ so, arna cuma do Bonabenturá ohodasa brátar bos dord San Próinsias accolaisde S. Antoin a Lobain.* 2nd ed. Rome. 1707. 8°. 259 [i.e. 256], [8] p. Published by: Congregatio de Propaganda Fide. ESTC t180574. * C; DMR; Du; FLK; ICN; IDA; L; MH; Mil; MY; NN; SCR (-tp); SIR.
> A catechism first published in Louvain in 1608. Edited by Philip Maguire O.F.M. According to NUC this is really the 3rd ed. Cf. no. 919.

2048. O'Kenny, Nicolaus Antoninus. *The Gallway cathecism. Or Christ. doctrin.*

newly collected and augmented for the use of the three kingdoms. By F.M.N.A.O. Kenny. Paris. 1725. 12°. [12], 146, [10] p. Printed by: Langlois, M. ESTC t185030. * C; DMR.

    DMR has only 8 preliminary pages.

2049. O'Kenny, Nicolaus Antoninus. *[Officia missarum tum in honorem sanctorum patronorum principalium regni Hyberniae tum in honorem novem ordinum coelestium spirituum compilata et edita a R.P. ac domino Nicolao-Antonino ô Kenny.]* Paris. 1734. 4°. * MY (-tp).

    Title supplied from ms note and from preface and approbation. Unpaginated.

2050. O'Leary, Arthur. *An address to the common people of the Roman Catholic religion, concerning the apprehended French invasion.* Cork. 1779. 12°. 16 p. Printed by: Flyn, W. ESTC t215500. * Di.

    The text begins on p. 3 with 'Brethren, countrymen, and fellow-citizens, religion has always considered war as one of the scourges' and is dated 'Cork, August 14, 1779'.

2051. O'Leary, Arthur. *An address to the common people of the Roman Catholic religion, concerning the apprehended French invasion.* 2nd ed. Cork. 1779. 12°. 16 p. Printed by: Flyn, W. ESTC n029210. * D; PP.

2052. O'Leary, Arthur. *An address to the common people of the Roman Catholic religion, concerning the apprehended French invasion.* Dublin repr. [Cork]. [1781?]. 8°. 16 p. Printed by: Wogan; Bean; Pike. ESTC n029212. * C; MiU.

2053. O'Leary, Arthur. *A commentary on the XLII psalms, appointed to be sung or said on all Sundays and festivals.* Bury St. Edmunds. 1799. 8°. 36, [2] p. Printed by: Ingram, G. Sold by: Ingram, G.; Keating; Coghlan; Booker. * Ush.

    With one page of adverts.

2054. O'Leary, Arthur. *A defence of the conduct and writings of the rev. Arthur O'Leary, during the late disturbances in Munster: with a full justification of the Irish Catholics.* London. 1787. 8°. [2], 175, [1] p. Published by: Keating, P. ESTC t135609. * C; CSmH; Ct; D; ECW; GEU-T; ICN; L; Ldw; Lhe; Lmh; MBAt; MH-H; MRu; MY; O; Osc; PP; Ush (2); Yb.

    In part an answer to P. Duigenan's *An address to the nobility and gentry of the Church of Ireland.* With one page of adverts. One Ush copy has [2], viii, [1], 9-175, [1] p. See also *Mr. O'Leary's defence* (no. 2071ff.).

2055. O'Leary, Arthur. *A defence of the conduct and writings of the rev. Arthur O'Leary, during the disturbances in Munster, with a full justification of the Irish Catholics.* London. 1789. 8°. 175, [1] p. Printed by: Keating, P. * P.

2056. O'Leary, Arthur. *An essay on toleration: or, Mr. O'Leary's plea for liberty of conscience.* Philadelphia. 1785. 8°. [11], 4-70, [2] p. Printed by: Kline and Reynolds. Sold by: Kline and Reynolds. ESTC w009078. * DGU-W; MWA; NN; PHC; PHi; PPAmP; PPL; RPJCB.

    With a prospectus for 'a complete American edition of O'Leary's tracts'.

2057. O'Leary, Arthur. *An essay towards the reformation of controversial and recantation sermons. Addressed to the rev. Charles Farrel. By the rev. A-r O'L-y.* Dublin. 1779. 8°. 16 p. Printed by: Wogan; Bean; Pike. ESTC t202768.

* D; Di.

2058. O'Leary, Arthur. *Essays, by the celebrated and much admired R.F. Arthur O'Leary, of the kingdom of Ireland; with notes and observations, critical and explanatory; with the life of the author prefixed.* London. 1782. 8°. [2], viii, 56 p. Printed by: Bladon, S. ESTC t012685. * C; ECW; L.

> This contains *An address to the common people of the Roman Catholic religion, concerning the apprehended French invasion* and *An essay on toleration*, each with its own tp. The title of this work suggests that there was an earlier Dublin ed.

2059. O'Leary, Arthur. *Father O'Leary's address to his countrymen in 1786, presented to the people of Ireland residing in the city of London.* London. 1786. s.s. Printed by: Keating; Brown & Co. * BAA.

> The address is dated '1786, February, 21st. Cork'.

2060. O'Leary, Arthur. *A funeral oration on the late sovereign pontiff Pius the Sixth. By the rev. Arthur O'Leary; to which is prefixed, an account of the solemn obsequies performed to his memory, at Saint Patrick's Chapel.* London. [1799?]. 8°. 56 p. Printed by: Reynell, H. Published by: Keating, P. Sold by: Keating, P.; Coghlan, J.P.; Booker, E.; Lewis, T. ESTC t135551. * C; CSmH; D; Du; ECW; FU; L; MRu; NN; O; Osc; RPB; Sto; TxU; Ush; Yb.

2061. O'Leary, Arthur. *A funeral oration, on the late sovereign pontiff Pius the Sixth. By the rev. Arthur O'Leary, to which is prefixed, an account of the solemn obsequies performed to his memory at Saint Patrick's Chapel.* Dublin. 1800. 8°. 31, [1] p. Printed by: Fitzpatrick, H. ESTC t135552. * D; Dt; Du; L; MY.

2062. O'Leary, Arthur. *Loyalty asserted. Or, the new test oath, vindicated, and proved by the principles of the canon and civil laws, and the authority of the most eminent writers.* Cork. 1776. 8°. [3], 6-107, [1] p. Printed by: Flyn, W. ESTC t205683. * D.

> Brenan (p. 639) mentions a 1777 ed. of this work.

2063. O'Leary, Arthur. *Loyalty asserted; or the new test oath vindicated in a letter to a Protestant gentleman. With an enquiry into the pope's deposing power, and the groundless claims of the Stuarts.* [1779?]. [1], 107 p. * CtY.

> The last 20 pages are *An address to the common people of the Roman Catholic religion*, dated at end 1779 (see also nos 2051 and 2052).

2064. O'Leary, Arthur. *Miscellaneous tracts: by the rev. Arthur O'Leary. Containing, I. A defence of the divinity of Christ ... VI. Essay on toleration ... In which are introduced, the rev. John Wesley's letter and the defence of the Protestant Associations.* Dublin. 1781. 8°. xvi, 87, [3], 107, [1], 101, [1], 24, 81, [3] p. Printed by: M'Donnel, T. ESTC n005164. * C; CLU; CSmH; CU-BANC; Di; DoA; Dt; Du; ECW; FLK; IDA; IObT; KU-S; L; MChB; Mil; MRu; MY; O; PU.

2065. O'Leary, Arthur. *Miscellaneous tracts: by the rev. Arthur O'Leary. Containing, I. A defence of the divinity of Christ ... VI. Essay on toleration ... In which are introduced, the rev. John Wesley's letter and the defence of the Protestant Associations.* 2nd ed. Dublin. 1781. 8°. [2], xvi, 397, [3] p. Printed by: Chambers, J. ESTC n005168. * CAL; CtHT-W; DLC; DMR; FU; ICU; IU; Lhe; MChB; MH; NcD; NN; PPL; PSt; TxDaM-P; TxU.

> With a final advertisement leaf. With an errata slip pasted on verso of tp. See also next item.

2066. O'Leary, Arthur. *Miscellaneous tracts: by the rev. Arthur O'Leary. Containing, I. A defence of the divinity of Christ ... VI. Essay on toleration ... In which are introduced, the rev. John Wesley's letter and the defence of the Protestant Associations.* 2nd ed. Dublin. 1781. 8°. [2], xvi, 397, [3] p. Printed by: Chambers, J. Published by: Keating, P. ESTC t146280. * BB; D; E; L; Lu; NUN.

> With a final advertisement leaf. This is another issue of no. 2065. Probably the sheets printed by Chambers were sent over to England and published by Keating. In BB his name occurs on p. [ii] 'London: published and sold for the author by P. Keating'; in L a similar notice with the text 'London: printed for the author. By P. Keating' has been printed on the verso of the half-title.

2067. O'Leary, Arthur. *Miscellaneous tracts: by the rev. Arthur O'Leary. Containing, I. A defence of the divinity of Christ ... VI. Essay on toleration ... To which is added an apology.* 3rd ed. London. 1782. 8°. xx, 417, [1] p. Printed by: Reynell, H. Published by: Keating, P. ESTC t139583. * BB; C; CaOTV; DoA; E; ECW; ICN; ICU; IDA; L; Lhe; MB; MH; MRu; O; OCl; Osc; P; Ush; Yb.

2068. O'Leary, Arthur. *Miscellaneous tracts: by the rev. Arthur O'Leary. Containing, I. A defence of the divinity of Christ ... VII. An answer to the Bishop of Cloyne's pamphlet.* Dublin. 1791. 12°. viii, 124 [i.e. 424] p. Printed by: M'Donnel, T. ESTC t131789. * C; CaOHM; Du; FLK; IDA; KU-S; L; Lhe; TLP.

2069. O'Leary, Arthur. *Miscellaneous tracts on several interesting subjects, by the rev. Arthur O'Leary.* 3rd ed. London. 1791. 8°. xx, 417, [1] p. Printed by: Keating, P. Published by: Keating, P. ESTC t173289. * CaQMM; CSmH; DAE; ECW; FP; IDA; Lhe; MRu; P; Pci; TxU.

> This is the second '3rd' ed.

2070. O'Leary, Arthur. *Miscellaneous tracts: by the rev. Arthur O'Leary. Containing - I. A defence of the divinity of Christ ... VII. Answer to the Bishop of Cloyne's pamphlet.* 3rd ed. Dublin. 1797. 12°. viii, 124 [i.e. 424] p. Printed by: M'Donnel, T. ESTC t205096. * D.

> This is the third '3rd' ed.

2071. O'Leary, Arthur. *Mr. O'Leary's defence; containing a vindication of his conduct and writings during the late disturbances in Munster.* Dublin. 1787. 8°. 112, 115-175, [3] p. Printed by: Byrne, P. ESTC t033117. * C; CSt; CtHT-W; CtY; CU-SB; D; Di; DLC; Dt; Du; FU; ICN; ICU; IU; L; MB; MdBP; MH; Mil; MRu; O; Oc.

> An answer to P. Duigenan's *An address to the nobility and gentry*. See also next 2 items. With a final advertisement leaf. Some copies have date in imprint spaced 'MDCC.LXXX VII'. See also *A defence* (no. 2055).

2072. O'Leary, Arthur. *Mr. O'Leary's defence: containing a vindication of his* *conduct and writings during the late disturbances in Munster ... In answer to the false accusations of Theophilus, and ... Doctor Woodward.* 2nd ed. Cork. 1787. 8°. 152 p. Printed by: Flyn, W. ESTC t170623. * D; Dt; P.

2073. O'Leary, Arthur. *Mr. O'Leary's defence; containing a vindication of his conduct and writings during the late disturbances in Munster ... In answer to the false accusations of Theophilus, and ... Doctor Woodward.* 2nd ed. Dublin. 1787. 8°. 175, [3] p. Printed by: Byrne, P. ESTC t170622. * D; Dt; Du; FLK; IDA; MY; SCR.

> This is the second '2nd' ed. With a final advertisement leaf.

2074. O'Leary, Arthur. *Mr. O'Leary's letter to the monthly reviewers.* Dublin. 1787. 8°. 15, [1] p. Printed by: Byrne, P. ESTC t170624. * D; Dt; Du; PPL.

2075. O'Leary, Arthur. *Mr. O'Leary's narrative.* [London]. [1791]. fol. 3, [1] p. * WDA.

> Dated 'Aug. 11 1791'; it concerns the row between T. Hussey and O'Leary about the chaplaincy at the Spanish Ambassador's chapel. The narrative was not intended for sale. Cf. also nos 884 and 1924.

2076. O'Leary, Arthur. *Mr. O'Leary's remarks on the rev. John Wesley's letters, in defence of the Protestant associations, in England. To which are prefixed, Mr. Wesley's letters.* Dublin. 1780. 8°. [2], 70 p. Printed by: M'Donnel, T. ESTC t205910. * BRw; CaOHM; D; Di.

2077. O'Leary, Arthur. *Mr. O'Leary's remarks on the rev. Mr. Wesley's letters, in defence of the Protestant associations in England. To which are prefixed, Mr. Wesley's letters.* London repr. [Dublin]. 1780. 12°. [4], 84 p. Published by: Coghlan, J.P. Sold by: Payne, H.; Stockdale, J.; Wilkie, J. ESTC t016666. * BRw; L; Lhe; Osc; PP; Sto; TMM.

2078. O'Leary, Arthur. *Rev. Arthur O'Leary's address to the Lords spiritual and temporal of the Parliament of Great Britain; to which is annexed, an account of Sir Henry Mildmay's bill relative to nuns.* London. 1800. 8°. [4], 66 p. Printed by: Low, S. Published by: Booker, J. ESTC t056436. * C; CU-BANC; DUc; ECW; L; Lhe; PP; Ush; UshL.

> A different impression from that printed for E. Booker (no. 2080).

2079. O'Leary, Arthur. *Rev. Arthur O'Leary's address to the Lords spiritual and temporal of the Parliament of Great Britain; to which is annexed, an account of Sir Henry Mildmay's bill relative to nuns.* Dublin repr. [London]. 1800. 8°. 43, [1] p. Printed by: Fitzpatrick, H. ESTC t108350. * C; L; O; Yb.

> A different and earlier ed. from that in which Fitzpatrick's address is given as 'no. 4, Capel-Street' (no. 2081).

2080. O'Leary, Arthur. *Rev. Arthur O'Leary's address to the Lords spiritual and temporal of the Parliament of Great Britain; to which is annexed, an account of Sir Henry Mildmay's bill relative to nuns.* London. 1800. 8°. [2], 66 p. Printed by: Low, S. Published by: Booker, E. ESTC t143558. * CSmH; ECW; ICN; Lu; MY; Sto.

> A different impression from that printed for J. Booker (no. 2078).

2081. O'Leary, Arthur. *Rev. Arthur O'Leary's address to the Lords spiritual and* *temporal of the Parliament of Great Britain: to which is annexed, an account of Sir Henry Mildmay's bill relative to nuns.* Dublin repr. [London]. 1800. 8°. 44 p. Printed by: Fitzpatrick, H. ESTC t134041. * D; Dt; Du; IU; L; UshL.

> A different and later ed. from that in which Fitzpatrick's address is given as 'no. 2 Up-Ormond-Quay' (no. 2079).

2082. O'Leary, Arthur. *Rev. Arthur O'Leary's address to the Lords spiritual and temporal of the Parliament of Great Britain; to which is annexed, an account of Sir Henry Mildmay's bill relative to nuns.* Cork. 1800. 8°. 24 p. Printed by: Cherry, G. ESTC t171594. * D; MY.

2083. O'Leary, Arthur. *Rev. Arthur O'Leary's address to the Lords spiritual and temporal of the Parliament of Great Britain; to which is annexed, an account of Sir Henry Mildmay's bill relative to nuns.* 2nd ed. Dublin repr. [London]. 1800. 8°. 43, [1] p. Printed by: Fitzpatrick, H. ESTC t171586. * D; Yb.

2084. O'Leary, Arthur. *Rev. Arthur O'Leary's address to the Lords spiritual and temporal in the Parliament of Great Britain, to which is annexed an account of Sir Henry Mildmay's bill relative to nuns.* Edinburgh. 1800. 8°. 43, [1] p. Printed by: Moir, J. Sold by: Macdonald, A. ESTC t171597. * ECR; Lhe; TH; Ush.

2085. O'Leary, Arthur. *The rev. Mr. O'Leary's address to the common people of Ireland; particularly, to such of them as are called Whiteboys. Revised and corrected by himself.* Dublin. 1786. 8°. 30 p. Printed by: Cooney, P. ESTC t218313. * Di; MY.

> Dated 'Cork Feb. 21, 1786'.

2086. O'Leary, Arthur. *The rev. Mr. O'Leary's address to the common people of Ireland; particularly, to such of them as are called Whiteboys. Revised and corrected by himself.* Dublin. 1786. 8°. 30 p. Printed by: Cooney, P. ESTC t215509. * Di.

> According to ESTC this ed. is different from no. 2085.

2087. O'Leary, Arthur. *The reverend Arthur O'Leary's caution to the common people of Ireland, against perjury, so frequent at assizes and elections.* Cork. 1783. 24°. 24 p. Printed by: Sullivan, J. ESTC t198367. * D.

2088. O'Leary, Arthur. *The reverend Arthur O'Leary's caution to the common people of Ireland, against perjury at the ensuing general election.* Cork. 1790. 12°. 23, [1] p. Printed by: Flyn, W. ESTC t193329. * D; Dt; NIC.

2089. O'Leary, Arthur. *A review of the important controversy between Dr. Carroll and the reverend Messrs. Wharton and Hawkins; including a defence of the conduct of Pope Clement XIV. (Ganganelli) in suppressing a late religious order.* London. 1786. 8°. [2], 94, [4] p. Published by: Keating, P. Sold by: Keating, P. ESTC t012324. * AWn; C; CSmH; D; DGU; Dt; ECW; ICN; IDA; L; Lhe; Lmh; MB; MH-H; O; Sto.

> With 2 pages of adverts. Lhe gives J.P. Coghlan as printer.

2090. O'Leary, Arthur. *A review of the important controversy between Dr. Carroll and the reverend Messrs. Wharton and Hawkins. Including a defence of* the conduct of Pope Clement XIV. (Ganganelli) in suppressing a late religious order. 2nd ed. Cork repr. [London]. 1786. 8°. 74 p. Printed by: Flyn, W. ESTC t171316. * C; Dt.

2091. O'Leary, Arthur. *A sermon, preached at Saint Patrick's Chapel, Sutton-street, Soho-Square, on Wednesday, the eighth of March, M.DCC,XCVII.* London. [1797]. 8°. [3], 6-66 p. Printed by: Keating, P. Published by: Keating, P. Sold by: Keating; Coghlan; Booker; Lewis. ESTC t012894. * C; CaQMBN; ECW; Gi; Gu; ICN; L; Lhe; MRu; MY; NjPT; O; Osc; Ush; Yb.

2092. O'Leary, Arthur. *A sermon preached at Saint Patrick's Chapel, Sutton-street, Soho-Square, on Wednesday, March the 8th, 1797: the day of solemn fast, humiliation &c.* Dublin repr. [London]. 1797. 8°. [3], 6-50 p. Printed by: Fitzpatrick, H. ESTC t121864. * C; D; L.

2093. O'Leary, Arthur. *Three letters from the rev. Father Arthur O'Leary to the people of Ireland, particularly to those of the Church of Rome.* Dublin. 1779. 8°. 38 p. Published by: Sheppard and Nugent, Messrs. ESTC n014313. * DLC; PP.

2094. *On the great advantages and happiness of hearing mass.* 4 p. * TLP.
> Late 18th century.

2095. *An opinion concerning the disputed elections of the three doctors and Mr D - y.* [1738]. fol. 4 p. * BAA.
> A circular letter on chapter disputes signed and dated in ms 'Clayton, Simon Berington and Umfreville ... Dec. 9, 1738'. See also nos 2562 and 2566.

2096. *An opinion concerning the disputed elections of the three doctors and Mr. D...y.* [1738]. ii p. * BAA.
> Signed and dated in ms 'Ra. Clayton, S. Berington, Charles Umfreville. Dec. 9, 1738'.

2097. *Oratio ad reginam omnium creaturarum.* 8°. 8 p. * Do; Ush.
> Latin and English; bound up with *Evening office*, 1778 (no. 1003).

2098. *Orations delivered at a numerous and respectable meeting of the Roman Catholics of the city of Dublin, held at Francis-Street Chapel, on Thursday the ninth of April, 1795.* Cork. 1795. 8°. 32 p. Printed by: Haly, J. Sold by: Haly, J. ESTC n020580. * C; CSmH; D; ICR; KU-S; MY.

2099. *The ordinances of the Roman Catholic bishops for the observance of the general fast, on Friday the 20th of February, MDCCXCIV. To which is added, the mass in time of war, and other devotions.* London. [1794]. 8°. [2], xii, 15, [1] p. Printed by: Coghlan, J.P. ESTC t189991. * MRu; Osc; Sto; WDA.
> This prints the five letters of the vicars apostolic concerning the observance of the general fast. The 'prayers in time of war' are in Latin and English.

2100. *The ordinary of the holy mass.* [London]. 12°. 38 p. Published by: [Goddard, M.]. Sold by: [Goddard, M.]. * ICN.
> English and Latin.

2101. *The ordinary of the holy mass.* [London]. [1730?]. 12°. 38 p. Published by: [Gibson, N.]. Sold by: [Gibson, N.]. ESTC t208196. * E; MBAt.

2102. *The ordinary of the mass, vespers and complin, on all Sundays and* *holydays throughout the year. The litany ... with the hymns ... according to the Roman missal and breviary. In Latin and English.* London. 1794. 12°. xxiv, lviii, 635, [1] p. Printed by: Coghlan, J.P. ESTC t181593. * AWn.

　　See no. 2622.

2103. *The ordinary of the mass, vespers and complin, on all Sundays and holydays, throughout the year. The litany ... with the hymns ... according to the Roman missal & breviary. Latin and English.* London. 1799. 12°. xxiv, lviii, 637, [1] p. Printed by: Coghlan, J.P. ESTC n041612. * InNd.

2104. *Ordo administrandi sacramenta, et alia quaedam officia ecclesiastica ritè peragendi in missione Anglicanâ. Ex rituali Romano, jussu Pauli Quinti edito, extractus.* [London]. [1759]. 8°. 86, [2], 47, [1] p. ESTC t155129. * C; CLU; DoA; E; ECW; Hen; ICN; L; Lfa; LO; NNG; TLP; Ush.

　　This was edited by Challoner; see Milner's *Funeral discourse*, p. 15 (no. 1873). Some copies have a second part *Appendix to the ritual* (no. 81).

2105. *Ordo administrandi sacramenta, et alia quaedam officia ecclesiastica rite peragendi ... Pro regno Hiberniae.* Dublin. 1776. 12°. [4], 175, [1] p. Printed by: Wogan, P. * FLK.

2106. *Ordo administrandi sacramenta et alia quædam officia ecclesiastica rite peragendi. Ex rituali Romano, jussu Benedicti XIV edito, extractus.* Dublin. 1777. 12°. [6], 206 p. Printed by: Wogan, P.; Bane. ESTC n060719. * Dp.

2107. *Ordo administrandi sacramenta et alia quaedam officia ecclesiastica rite peragendi. Ex rituali Romana, jussu Pauli edito extractus.* Dublin. 1785. 12°. [6], 208 p. Printed by: Wogan, P. ESTC t131342. * D; L.

　　With an 'Appendix to the ritual' (pp. 147-208). See also no. 81.

2108. *Ordo administrandi sacramenta, et alia quaedam officia ecclesiastica ritè peragendi in missione Anglicanâ, ex rituali Romano, jussu Pauli Quinti edito, extractus.* London. 1788. 8°. 158, [2], 165-230, [6] p. Printed by: Coghlan, J.P. ESTC t181469. * Do; DoA; E; ECW; ICN; KU-S; L; Lfa; Lhe; O; Osc; TLP; UGL; Ush; WDA.

　　With an 'Appendix to the ritual' (pp. 165-230). See also no. 81.

2109. *Ordo baptizandi aliaque sacramenta administrandi, et officia quaedam ecclesiastica. Ritè peragendi. Ex rituali Romano jussu Pauli Quinti edito, extractus. Pro Anglia, Hibernia et Scotia.* Paris [i.e. London]. 1738. 12°. 167, [3] p. ESTC t207189. * D; ECW; MY; Sto; TxU; Ush.

　　Latin and English. The imprint is false; printed in London. Some copies have Marmaduke adverts. There are two appendices: 'The recommendation of a soul departing' (pp. 145-60) and 'A profession of Catholick faith' (pp. 161-7).

2110. *Ordo baptizandi aliaque sacramenta administrandi, et officia quaedam ecclesiastica ritè peragendi. Ex rituali Romano jussu Pauli Quinti edito, extractus. Pro Anglia, Hibernia, & Scotia.* Dublin. 1743. 18°. 143, [1] p. Printed by: Kelly, I. ESTC t181652. * D.

2111. *Ordo baptizandi aliaque sacramenta administrandi, et officia quaedam ecclesiastica ritè peragendi ex rituali Romano jussu Pauli Quinti edito, extractus. Pro Anglia, Hibernia, & Scotia.* Dublin. 1774. 18°. 144 p. Printed by:

Fitzsimons, R. ESTC t181653. * D; ECW.

2112. *Ordo baptizandi aliaque sacramenta administrandi, et officia quaedam ecclesiastica ritè peragendi. Ex rituali Romano jussu Pauli Quinti edito, extractus. Pro Anglia, Hibernia & Scotia.* Dublin. 12°. 144 p. Printed by: Kelly, E. * Sco.

Ordo. Note that with editions of the 'Ordo' relating to a particular year, we have assumed that the actual printing took place in the previous year.

2113. *Ordo divini officii recitandi missaeque celebrandae juxta breviarium et missale Romanum, ad usum ecclesiae totiusque diaecesis Baltimorensis, pro anno domini M,DCC,XCV.* Baltimore. [1794]. 35, [1] p. Printed by: Hayes, J. ESTC w009057. * DLC.

> Parsons and Evans mention other eds for the years 1796, 1797, 1798, 1799 and 1800.

2114. *Ordo divini officii recitandi missaeque celebrandae juxta breviarium et missale Romanum; ad usum ecclesiae totiusque diaecesis Baltimorensis pro anno domini MDCCCI.* Baltimore. [1800]. 16°. [24] p. Printed by: Hayes, J. ESTC w009058. * DGU.

2115. *Ordo recitandi officii divinae & missae celebrandi [sic] stylo vet. conformis ... MDCCXXII.* [London]. [1721]. 12°. [28] p. * WDA (imp.).

> Incomplete, December missing.

2116. *Ordo recitandi officii divini, & missae celebrandae stylo vet. conformis ... Anno bissextili MDCCXXIV.* [London]. [1723]. 12°. [36] p. Printed by: [Meighan, T.]. Published by: [Meighan, T.]. * WDA.

> With a Meighan advert on last page.

2117. *Ordo recitandi officii divini & missae celebrandae stylo vet. conformis ... MDCCXXV.* [London]. [1724]. 12°. [34] p. * WDA (imp.).

> Tp and first 4 pages missing.

2118. *Ordo recitandi officii divini & missae celebrandae stylo vet. conformis ... MDCCXXVI.* [London]. [1725]. 12°. [36] p. * WDA.

2119. *Ordo recitandi officii divini & missae celebrandae stylo vet. conformis ... MDCCXXVII.* [London]. [1726]. 12°. [34] p. * Ush; WDA.

2120. Ordo recitandi. *Ordo officii divinae [sic] & missae celebrandae stylo vet. conformis ... Anno bissextili MDCCXXVIII.* [London]. [1727]. 12°. [36] p. * WDA.

2121. *Ordo recitandi officii divini & missae celebrandae stylo vet. conformis ... MDCCXXX.* [London]. [1729]. 12°. [24] p. Printed by: [Meighan, T.]. Published by: [Meighan, T.]. * WDA (imp.).

> Incomplete, part of June and the whole of July, August, September and October, and part of November missing.

2122. *Ordo recitandi officii divini & missae celebrandae stylo vet. conformis .. anno bissextili MDCCXXXII.* [London]. [1731]. 12°. [36] p. Printed by: [Meighan, T.]. Published by: [Meighan, T.]. * WDA.

2123. *Ordo recitandi officii divini & missae celebrandae, stylo veteri conformis. Pro anno domini MDCCXXXIII.* [London]. [1732]. 12°. [36], iii, [1] p. Printed by: [Meighan, T.]. Published by: [Meighan, T.]. * WDA.
   With one page of Meighan adverts.

2124. *Ordo recitandi officii divini & missae celebrandae stylo vet. conformis. Pro anno domini MDCCXXXIV.* [London]. [1733]. 12°. [40] p. Printed by: [Meighan, T.]. Published by: [Meighan, T.]. * WDA.
   With 3 pages of Meighan adverts.

2125. *Ordo recitandi officii divini & missae celebrandae stylo vet. conformis. Pro anno domini MDCCXXXV.* [London]. [1734]. 12°. [32] p. Printed by: [Meighan, T.]. Published by: [Meighan, T.]. * WDA.
   With 2 pages of Meighan adverts.

2126. *Ordo recitandi officii divini et missae celebrandae stylo veteri conformis. Pro anno MDCCXXXVI. Cum supplemento pro PP Soc. Jesu.* [London]. [1735]. 12°. [32] p. Printed by: [Meighan, T.]. Published by: [Meighan, T.]. * WDA.
   With one page of Meighan adverts.

2127. *Ordo recitandi officii divini et missae celebrandae stylo veteri conformis. Pro anno MDCCXXXVII.* [London]. [1736]. 12°. [32] p. Printed by: [Meighan, T.]. Published by: [Meighan, T.]. * Ush; WDA.
   With one page of Meighan adverts.

2128. *Ordo recitandi officii divini et missae celebrandae stylo veteri conformis. Pro anno MDCCXXXIX.* [London]. [1738]. 12°. [34] p. Printed by: [Meighan, T.]. Published by: [Meighan, T.?]. * Ush (-tp).
   With 4 pages of Meighan adverts.

2129. *Ordo recitandi officii divini et missae celebrandae stylo veteri conformis. Pro anno MDCCXL.* [London]. [1739]. 12°. [36] p. Printed by: [Meighan, T.]. Published by: [Meighan, T.]. * Ush.
   With 5½ pages of Meighan adverts.

2130. *Ordo recitandi officii divini et missae celebrandae pro anno MDCCXLI.* [London]. [1740]. 12°. [32] p. Printed by: [Meighan, T.]. Published by: [Meighan, T.]. * Ush (-tp); WDA.
   Ush has 2½ p. of Meighan adverts. WDA has 4½ p. of Meighan adverts.

2131. *Ordo recitandi officii divini et missae celebrandae pro anno MDCCXLII.* [London]. [1741]. 12°. [36] p. Printed by: [Meighan, T.]. Published by: [Meighan, T.]. * Ush; WDA.
   With 4½ pages of Meighan adverts.

2132. *Ordo recitandi officii divini et missae celebrandae pro anno MDCCXLIII.* [London]. [1742]. 12°. [36] p. Printed by: [Meighan, T.]. Published by: [Meighan, T.]. * Ush; WDA.
   With 4½ pages of Meighan adverts.

2133. *Ordo recitandi officii divini et missae celebrandae pro anno MDCCXLIV.* [London]. [1743]. 12°. [34] p. Printed by: [Meighan, T.]. Published by: [Meighan, T.]. * Ush (-tp).

With 6 pages of Meighan adverts.

2134. *Ordo recitandi officii divini et missae celebrandae stylo veteri conformis pro anno MDCCXLV.* [London]. [1744]. 12°. [36] p. Printed by: [Meighan, T.]. Published by: [Meighan, T.]. * Lfa (imp.); WDA.
With 2 pages of Meighan adverts.

2135. *Ordo recitandi officii divini et missae celebrandae stylo veteri conformis pro anno domini MDCCXLVII.* [London]. [1746]. 12°. [34] p. Printed by: [Meighan, T.]. Published by: [Meighan, T.]. * Ush.
With 2 pages of Meighan adverts.

2136. *Ordo recitandi officii divini et missae celebrandae stylo veteri conformis pro anno domini bissextili MDCCXLVIII.* [London]. [1747]. 12°. [36] p. Printed by: [Meighan, T.?]. Published by: [Meighan, T.?]. * Ush; WDA.
With half a page of adverts.

2137. *Ordo recitandi officii divini et missae celebrandae stylo veteri conformis pro anno domini MDCCXLIX.* [London]. [1748]. 12°. [36] p. Printed by: [Meighan, T.]. Published by: [Meighan, T.]. * Ush; WDA.
With 2 pages of Meighan adverts.

2138. *Ordo recitandi officii divini et missae celebrandae stylo veteri conformis pro anno domini MDCCL.* [London]. [1749]. 12°. [36] p. Printed by: [Meighan, T.]. Published by: [Meighan, T.]. * Ush; WDA.
With 2 pages of Meighan adverts.

2139. *Ordo recitandi officii divini et missae celebrandae stylo veteri conformis pro anno domini MDCCLI.* [London]. [1750]. 12°. [36] p. * Ush.

2140. *Ordo recitandi officii divini et missae celebrandae stylo veteri conformis pro anno domini bissextili MDCCLII.* [London]. [1751]. 12°. [36] p. * Ush.

2141. *Ordo recitandi officii divini et missae celebrandae stylo veteri conformis pro anno domini MDCCLIII.* [London]. [1752]. 12°. [34] p. Printed by: [Meighan, T.]. Published by: [Meighan, T.]. * Ush (-tp).
With 4 pages of Meighan adverts.

2142. *Ordo recitandi officii divini et missae celebrandae stylo veteri conformis pro anno domini MDCCLIV.* [London]. [1753]. 12°. [32] p. * Ush (-tp).

2143. *Ordo recitandi officii divini et missae celebrandae stylo veteri conformis pro anno domini MDCCLV.* [London]. [1754]. 12°. [36] p. Printed by: [Meighan, T.]. Published by: [Meighan, T.]. * Ush (imp.); WDA.
With 1½ pages of Meighan adverts.

2144. *Ordo recitandi officii divini et missae celebrandae stylo veteri conformis pro anno domini MDCCLVI.* [London]. [1755]. 12°. [34] p. Printed by: [Marmaduke, J.]. Published by: [Marmaduke, J.]. * Ush.
With 1½ pages of Marmaduke adverts.

2145. *Ordo recitandi officii divini et missae celebrandae stylo veteri conformis pro anno domini MDCCLVIII.* [London]. [1757]. 12°. [34] p. * Ush.

2146. *Ordo recitandi officii divini et missae celebrandae stylo veteri conformis* *pro anno domini bissextili MDCCLX.* [London]. [1759]. 12°. [36] p. Printed by: [Marmaduke, J.]. Published by: [Marmaduke, J.]. * Ush; WDA.

With 3½ pages of Marmaduke adverts.

2147. *Ordo recitandi officii divini et missae celebrandae pro anno domini MDCCLXI.* [London]. [1760]. 12°. [36] p. Printed by: [Marmaduke, J.]. Published by: [Marmaduke, J.]. * Ush (-tp; imp.); WDA.

With 2 pages of Marmaduke adverts.

2148. *Ordo recitandi officii divini et missae celebrandae pro anno domini MDCCLXII.* [London]. [1761]. 12°. [36] p. Printed by: [Marmaduke, J.]. Published by: [Marmaduke, J.]. * WDA.

With 3½ pages of Marmaduke adverts.

2149. *Ordo recitandi officii divini et missae celebrandae pro anno domini MDCCLXIII.* [London]. [1762]. 12°. [34] p. * WDA.

2150. *Ordo recitandi officii divini et missae celebrandae pro anno domini bissextili MDCCLXIV.* [London]. [1763]. [36] p. Printed by: [Marmaduke, J.]. Published by: [Marmaduke, J.]. * Ush (-tp); WDA.

With 1½ pages of Marmaduke adverts.

2151. *Ordo recitandi officii divini et missae celebrandae, pro anno domini MDCCLXV.* [London]. [1764]. 12°. [34] p. Printed by: [Marmaduke, J.]. Published by: [Marmaduke, J.]. * ECW; Sto; WDA.

With 2 pages of Marmaduke adverts.

2152. *Ordo recitandi officii divini et missae celebrandae, pro anno domini MDCCLXVI.* [London]. [1765]. 12°. [36] p. Printed by: [Marmaduke, J.]. Published by: [Marmaduke, J.] . * Sto; Ush; WDA.

With half a page of Marmaduke adverts.

2153. *Ordo recitandi officii divini et missae celebrandae, pro anno domini MDCCLXVII.* [London]. [1766]. 12°. [36] p. Printed by: [Marmaduke, J.]. Published by: [Marmaduke, J.] . * ECW; Sto; WDA.

With 3½ pages of Marmaduke adverts.

2154. *Ordo recitandi officii divini et missae celebrandae, pro anno domini bissextili MDCCLXVII.* [London]. [1767]. [36] p. Printed by: [Marmaduke, J.]. Published by: [Marmaduke, J.]. * Sto; Ush; WDA.

With 2 pages of Marmaduke adverts. Tp has 'M.DCC.LXVII', but this is in fact the 'Ordo' for 1768. In some copies tp has been corrected in ms.

2155. *Ordo recitandi officii divini et missae celebrandae, pro anno domini MDCCLXIX.* [London]. [1768]. 12°. [36] p. Printed by: [Marmaduke, J.]. Published by: [Marmaduke, J.]. * Ush; WDA.

With 1½ pages of Marmaduke adverts.

2156. *Ordo recitandi officii divini et missae celebrandae, pro anno domini MDCCLXX.* [London]. [1769]. 12°. [36] p. Printed by: [Marmaduke, J.]. Published by: [Marmaduke, J.]. * Ush; WDA (2).

With 2 pages of Marmaduke adverts, lacking in one WDA copy.

2157. *Ordo recitandi officii divini et missae celebrandae, pro anno domini*

MDCCLXXI. [London]. [1770]. 12°. [36] p. Printed by: [Marmaduke, J.]. Published by: [Marmaduke, J.] . * Sto; WDA (2).

    With one page of Marmaduke adverts, lacking in one WDA copy.

2158. *Ordo recitandi officii divini et missae celebrandae pro anno domini MDCCLXXI.* [London]. [1770]. 8°. [36] p. Printed by: [Meighan, T.]. Published by: [Meighan, T.]. * Ush; WDA.

    With one page of Meighan adverts.

2159. *Ordo recitandi officii divini et missae celebrandae, pro anno domini bissextili MDCCLXXII.* [London]. [1771]. 12°. [36] p. Printed by: [Marmaduke, J.]. Published by: [Marmaduke, J.]. * Sto; Ush; WDA (2).

    With 1½ pages of Marmaduke adverts, lacking in one WDA copy.

2160. *Ordo recitandi officii divini et missae celebrandae. Pro anno domini MDCCLXXIII. Perm. sup.* [London]. [1772]. 12°. [44] p. Printed by: [Coghlan, J.P.]. Published by: [Coghlan, J.P.]. * WDA (2).

    One WDA copy includes 'Ex audientia SS D Nri Dni Clem PP XIV' and 'Oratio praemittenda actis fidei, spei, et charitatis'.

2161. *Ordo recitandi officii divini et missae celebrandae, pro anno domini MDCCLXXIII.* [London]. [1772]. 12°. [36] p. Printed by: [Marmaduke, J.]. Published by: [Marmaduke, J.]. ESTC t132249. * L; Sto; Ush; WDA.

    With 1½ pages of Marmaduke adverts.

2162. *Ordo recitandi officii divini et missae celebrandae. Pro anno domini MDCCLXXIV.* [London]. [1773]. 12°. [36] p. Printed by: [Coghlan, J.P.]. Published by: [Coghlan, J.P.]. * Sto; Ush (imp.); WDA.

2163. *Ordo recitandi officii divini et missae celebrandae. Pro anno domini MDCCLXXV.* [London]. [1774]. 12°. [38] p. Printed by: [Coghlan, J.P.]. Published by: [Coghlan, J.P.]. * Sto; Ush; WDA (2).

    Bound up with Sto and one WDA copy is a 20-page *Officia sanctorum Angliae* (no. 2043).

2164. *Ordo recitandi officii et missae celebrandae, pro anno domini MDCCLXXVI.* London. [1775]. 8°. [35], 8, [1] p. Printed by: Coghlan, J.P. Published by: Coghlan, J.P. * Osc; Sto; WDA.

    With Coghlan's 8-page list 'Of prints and books purchased at the sale of the stock-in-trade of Mr. Thomas Meighan, late deceased, by J.P. Coghlan' and a notice that 'the Nobility, Gentry &c. are requested to observe that some time before the death of the late Mr. John Baskerville ... he furnished the office of J.P. Coghlan with his beautiful and much-admired types being the only one in London which has them'. WDA has [44] p.

2165. *Ordo recitandi officii divini et missae celebrandae, pro anno domini MDCCLXXVII.* London. [1776]. 12°. [40], 22 p. Printed by: Coghlan, J.P. Published by: Coghlan, J.P. * BHN; Lhe; Sto; Ush; WDA.

    Using type cast by J. Baskerville. With a 22-page Coghlan catalogue which is given separately in our list (no. 737). Lhe has a 12-page catalogue.

2166. *Ordo recitandi officii divini et missae celebrandae, pro anno domini MDCCLXXVIII.* [London]. [1777]. 12°. [36] p. Printed by: Coghlan, J.P.

Published by: Coghlan, J.P. * Sto; Ush; WDA (2).

> With 3½ pages of Coghlan adverts, lacking in one WDA copy. Using type cast by J. Baskerville.

2167. *Ordo recitandi officii divini et missae celebrandae, pro anno domini MDCCLXXIX ... Permissu superiorum.* [London]. [1778]. [28] p. Printed by: Coghlan, J.P. Published by: Coghlan, J.P. * Ush; WDA.

2168. *Ordo recitandi officii divini et missae celebrandae. Pro anno domini, bissextili, MDCCLXXX ... Permissu superiorum.* London. [1779]. 12°. [34] p. Printed by: Coghlan, J.P. Published by: Coghlan, J.P. * Sto; WDA (2).

> With 6 pages of Coghlan adverts in one WDA copy.

2169. *Ordo recitandi officii divini et missae celebrandae pro anno domini MDCCLXXX ... Permissu superiorum.* London. [1779]. [22] p. Printed by: [Coghlan, J.P.]. Published by: [Coghlan, J.P.]. * Ush; WDA.

2170. *Ordo recitandi officii divini et missae celebrandae anno domini MDCCLXXXI ... Permissu superiorum.* London. [1780]. [28] p. Printed by: Coghlan, J.P. Published by: Coghlan, J.P. * Sto; Ush; WDA (3).

> One of the 3 WDA copies has an additional 24 pages of miscellaneous matter: 'A specimen of type ... for the purpose of printing the church plain song', a 20-page 'Coghlan's catalogue', and adverts for medicines such as 'laxative sulphurated pills prepared under the direction of the real inventor, and sold by J.P. Coghlan'.

2171. *Ordo recitandi officii divini et missae celebrandae anno domini MDCCLXXXII ... Permissu superiorum.* London. [1781]. [28] p. Printed by: Coghlan, J.P. Published by: Coghlan, J.P. * Sto; Ush; WDA (2).

> With a Coghlan advert on last page. One WDA copy has an additional 16-page Coghlan list of 'New publications up to November 1781'.

2172. *Ordo recitandi officii divini et missae celebrandae anno domini MDCCLXXXIII ... Permissu superiorum.* London. [1782]. [28] p. Printed by: Coghlan, J.P. Published by: Coghlan, J.P. * Sto; Ush; WDA (2).

> The last 2 pages contain the requiem calendar for the year 1782. One WDA copy is followed by a 12-page list of 'New publications up to December 6, 1782 ... by J.P. Coghlan', an advert for the Royal Hotel Inn, Dover, and for medicines.

2173. *Ordo recitandi officii divini et missae celebrandae anno domini bissextili MDCCLXXXIV ... Permissu superiorum.* London. [1783]. 12°. [28] p. Printed by: Coghlan, J.P. Published by: Coghlan, J.P. * BHN; Sto; WDA (3).

> The last 4 pages consist of the requiem calendar for the year 1783, and indulgences. The 2nd WDA copy has only [24] pages, BHN and the 3rd WDA copy have an additional 20 pages consisting of a 14-page Coghlan list, adverts for medicines and fares for the journey to Paris.

2174. *Ordo recitandi officii divini et missae celebrandae anno domini MDCCLXXXV ... Permissu superiorum.* London. [1784]. 12°. [28], 12, [2] p. Printed by: Coghlan, J.P. Published by: Coghlan, J.P. * Sto; Ush, WDA (3).

> The last 4 pages consist of the requiem calendar for the year 1784, and indulgences. With a 12-page Coghlan catalogue including 2 pages of proposals

for publishing by subscription sermons by James Archer, and followed by 2 pages of adverts for medicines and the Royal Hotel Inn. Sto has only [28] pages, one WDA copy has only [24] pages.

2175. *Ordo recitandi officii divini et missae celebrandae anno domini MDCCLXXXVI ... Permissu superiorum.* London. [1785]. 12°. [20], 16 p. Printed by: Coghlan, J.P. Published by: Coghlan, J.P. * Sto; WDA (3).

> With a 12-page Coghlan catalogue and 4 pages of miscellaneous adverts. The 2nd WDA copy has [20], the 3rd has [24] pages.

2176. *Ordo recitandi officii divini et missae celebrandae pro anno domini MDCCLXXXVII.* London. [1786]. 12°. [24], 4, 13-20 p. Printed by: Coghlan, J.P. Published by: Coghlan, J.P. * Sto; WDA (3).

> On p. [24] there is half a page of Coghlan adverts. This is followed by 4 pages of 'Oratio' and 'Decretum', and 8 pages of indulgences, obituaries and a Royal Hotel Inn advert. The 2nd WDA copy has an additional 12-page Coglan catalogue; the 3rd WDA copy has only [24] pages.

2177. *Ordo recitandi officii divini et missae celebrandae anno domini bissextili MDCCLXXXVIII ... Permissu superiorum.* London. [1787]. 12°. [32] p. Printed by: Coghlan, J.P. Published by: Coghlan, J.P. * Sto; WDA (2).

> The last 4 pages consist of an obituary for 1787. One WDA copy has 24 pages.

2178. *Ordo recitandi officii divini, et missae celebrandae anno domini MDCCLXXXIX ... Permissu superiorum.* London. [1788]. 12°. [26], 27-42, 10-13, [1] p. Printed by: Coghlan, J.P. Published by: Coghlan, J.P. * Ush; WDA (3).

> The 'Ordo' is followed by indulgences, the obituary for 1788, the announcement of the foundation on 1 Jan. 1788 of a confraternity, a 9-page list of Coghlan books, and adverts for medicines, the Royal Hotel Inn, and Catholic educational institutions. One WDA copy has only [26] pages.

2179. *Ordo recitandi officii divini et missae celebrandae anno domini MDCCXC ... Permissu superiorum.* London. [1789]. 12°. [26], 27-34 p. Printed by: Coghlan, J.P. Published by: Coghlan, J.P. * Sto; WDA (2).

> The 'Ordo' is followed by indulgences, the obituary for 1789, and the announcement of the foundation, on 1 Jan. 1788, of a confraternity. One WDA copy has an additional 16-page Coghlan catalogue.

2180. *Ordo recitandi officii divini et missae celebrandae anno domini MDCCXCI.* London. [1790]. 12°. [32], 25-44 p. Printed by: Coghlan, J.P. Published by: Coghlan, J.P. * Sto; WDA.

> The 'Ordo' is followed by indulgences, a 'Gregorian note', the obituary for 1790, adverts for Catholic educational institutions, a request for donations to the chapel in St. George's Fields, adverts for medicines and the Royal Hotel Inn, and a 12-page Coghlan catalogue. Sto has [32], 25-28 pages.

2181. *Ordo recitandi officii divini et missae celebrandae pro anno domini bissextili MDCCXCII.* London. [1791]. 12°. [24], 25-26, [4], 5-12 p. Printed by: Coghlan, J.P. Published by: Coghlan, J.P. ESTC n041610. * MBAt; Sto; WDA.

> The 'Ordo' is followed by indulgences, the obituary for 1791, and an 8-page Coghlan catalogue. MBAt has only 26 pages.

2182. *Ordo recitandi officii divini et missae celebrandae pro anno domini, MDCCXCIII. Permissu superiorum.* London. [1792]. 12°. [28] p. Printed by: Coghlan, J.P. Published by: Coghlan, J.P. * Lhe; Sto; WDA.

> WDA has only 24 pages; Lhe is bound up with the *Laity's directory* for 1793 (no. 1599).

2183. *Ordo recitandi officii divini et missae celebrandae pro anno domini MDCCXCIV ... Permissu superiorum.* London. [1793]. 8°. [24], 24, [4], 22, 3-4 p. Printed by: Coghlan, J.P. Published by: Coghlan, J.P. * BHN; Sto; Ush; WDA (2).

> The 'Ordo' is followed by indulgences, extract letter Dr Moylan, chapels in and near London, Catholic educational institutions, a chronology, obituary French clergy since 1729, a 20-page Coghlan catalogue, adverts for medicines and the Royal Hotel Inn. One WDA copy has an additional 12-page obituary of the clergy 1779-1793. The other WDA copy and Sto have [24], 24, [4] pages.

2184. *Ordo recitandi officii divini et missae celebrandae. Pro anno domini MDCCXCV ... Permissu superiorum.* London. [1794]. 12°. [32], 24, 24 p. Printed by: Coghlan, J.P. Published by: Coghlan, J.P. * Lhe; Osc; Sto; WDA (3).

> The 'Ordo' is followed by the obituary for 1794, the obituary of the French clergy for 1793 and 1794, indulgences, extract letter Dr Moylan, chapels in and near London, Catholic educational institutions, Milner's 'An account of the communities of British subjects who ... have suffered the confiscation of their houses', adverts for chalices, medicines and the Royal Hotel Inn, and a 22-page Coghlan catalogue. One WDA copy has only [32] pages.

2185. *Ordo recitandi officii divini et missae celebrandae. Anno domini MDCCXCVI ... Permissu superiorum.* London. [1795]. 12°. [24], 52 p. Printed by: Coghlan, J.P. Published by: Coghlan, J.P. * Lhe; Osc; Sto; WDA (3).

> The 'Ordo' is followed by indulgences, extract letter Dr Moylan, survey Catholic chapels, sketch of the Bill for the relief of Roman Catholics, model application for the foundation of a R.C. chapel, sufferings of English communities in France, present state of religion in China, instances of liberality towards Catholics, Catholic educational institutions, obituary of the English clergy in France, adverts for medicines, sacred vessels and the Royal Hotel Inn. One WDA copy has a 24-page Coghlan catalogue.

2186. *Ordo recitandi officii divini et missae celebrandae. Pro anno domini MDCCXCVII ... Permissu superiorum.* London. [1796]. 12°. [28], 40, 8, 24 p. Printed by: Coghlan, J.P. Published by: Coghlan, J.P. * Lhe; Osc; Ush; WDA (3).

> The 'Ordo' is followed by prayers ordered by Bp Walmesley, indulgences, survey Catholic chapels, sketch of the Bill for the relief of Roman Catholics, Catholic educational institutions, an account of the foundation of Maynooth, English convents abroad, present state of religion in China, obituary for 1793-1796, adverts for medicines, sacred vessels, the Royal Hotel Inn and a 20-page Coghlan catalogue. One WDA copy has [28], 8 pages.

2187. *Ordo recitandi officii divini et missae celebrandae. Pro anno domini MDCCXCVIII ... Permissu superiorum.* London. [1797]. 12°. [24], 28, [8], 3, [1] p. Printed by: Coghlan, J.P. Published by: Coghlan. J.P. * Lhe; Sto; WDA (imp).

The 'Ordo' is followed by a plan of education for young gentlemen, letters from Rome, the obituary for 1798 and adverts for sacred vessels. Lhe has 4 additional pages and a 25-page Coghlan catalogue instead of most of the miscellaneous material described above.

2188. *Ordo recitandi officii divini et missae celebrandae. Pro anno domini MDCCXCIX. Post bissextilem tertio ... Permissu superiorum.* London. [1798]. 12°. [24], 24, 12, [8] p. Printed by: Coghlan, J.P. Published by: Coghlan, J.P. * Sto; Ush; WDA (2).

The 'Ordo' is followed by a circular letter from the bishops, a message for the French priests, indulgences, survey Catholic chapels, Catholic educational institutions, the obituary for 1799, adverts for medicines. Ush has [24], 24 pages; one WDA copy has [24], 12, [8] pages, the other one has [24], 24, 12, [8], 24 pages (the final 24 pages are a Coghlan catalogue).

2189. *Ordo recitandi officii divini et missae celebrandae pro anno domini, MDCCC. Post bissextilem quarto ... permissu superiorum.* London. [1799]. 12°. [24], 40, [10], 24 p. Printed by: Coghlan, J.P. * Lhe; WDA (2).

The 'Ordo' is followed by a circular letter from the bishops, a message for the French priests, indulgences, survey Catholic chapels, Catholic educational institutions, the captivity of Pius VI, extracts of letters from Germany, the escape of the rev. Coombes from France, the obituary for 1799, and a 24-page Coghlan catalogue, lacking in one WDA copy.

2190. *Ordo recitandi officii divini et missae celebrandae pro anno domini MDCCI post bissextilem quinto ... permissu superiorum.* London. [1800]. 12°. [24], [4] p. Printed by: Keating; Brown; Keating. Published by: Keating; Brown; Keating. * WDA.

The 'Ordo' is followed by the obituary for 1800.

2191. O'Reilly, Michael. *An teagask creestye, agus paidreagha na mainne agus an tranona.* Anon. Dundalk. 1793. 12°. 48 p. Printed by: Parks, J. ESTC t126493. * L.

Michael O'Reilly was the R.C. Archbishop of Armagh. See also next 2 items.

2192. O'Reilly, Michael. *An teagask creestye, agus paidreagha, na maine, agus an tranona.* Anon. Limerick. [1795?]. 8°. 24 p. Printed by: Googin, W. ESTC t173857. * C.

2193. O'Reilly, Michael. *An teagask creestye, agus paidreagha na mainne agus an tranona.* Dublin. 1800. 12°. 48 p. Printed by: Dunn, J. ESTC t086867. * L.

2194. *Original papers, relative to the present application to the British Parliament for relief of the Roman Catholics in England. Viz: I. A letter to the four vicars apostolic in England ... IX. A list of the controversial publications on the foregoing subjects.* Dublin. 1791. 8°. [2], 77, [1] p. Printed by: Jones, W. ESTC t124225. * C; CLU-C; D; Di; Dk; Dt; ICR; L; Lhl; MChB; MiU; MRu; MY; PU; Sto.

2195. Orléans, Pierre Joseph d'. *The life of S. Aloysius Gonzaga. Of the Society of Jesus [La vie du B. Louis de Gonzague de la Compagnie de Jésus].* St. Omers. 1761. 8°. [2], 156 p. Printed by: Fertel, F.D. ESTC t113075. * Do (?); L; Lfa;

Lhe; Sto; TxU.

> A translation by John Panting S.J., for some time director to the poor Clares at Gravelines, of a French work by Pierre Joseph d'Orléans S.J. written in 1681. Panting died at Stourton, Wiltshire, in 1783 (see also next item). Lfa bound up with no. 1842.

2196. Orléans, Pierre Joseph d'. *The life of S. Aloysius Gonzaga, of the Society of Jesus.* Preston. [1761?]. 8°. 155, [1] p. Printed by: Addison, W. ESTC n055164. * ICN; Lhe.

> With an 'approbatio', dated 1761.

2197. *The outlines of a trial of the Roman Catholics of Great-Britain: with a view to union.* Liverpool. 1788. 4°. [4], 94 p. Printed by: Ferguson, R. Published by: Author. Sold by: Ferguson, R.; Coghlan, J.P. (London). ESTC t074930. * DoA; ICN; L; SCA; Sal; Ush.

2198. Palafox y Mendoza, Juan de. *The new Odyssey, by the Spanish Homer: being the travels of the Christian hero, Ulysses Desiderius Pius [Pastor de noche buena.].* London. 1735. 12°. ix, [3], 154, [2] p. Published by: Gardiner, D.; Baker, S. ESTC n020435. * CLU-C; ICN; MnU; Yb.

> With a final advertisement leaf. The book is a kind of R.C. *Pilgrim's Progress.* See also next 3 items.

2199. Palafox y Mendoza, Juan de. *The new Odyssey, by the Spanish Homer: being the travels of the Christian hero, Ulysses Desiderius Pius ... Translated into English by William Bond, Esquire.* 2nd ed. London. 1736. 12°. ix, [3], 154, [2] p. Published by: Meighan, T.; Batley; Wood, Gardiner D. * ECW; ICN.

> With 2 pages of Baker and Gardiner adverts.

2200. Palafox y Mendoza, Juan de. *The new Odyssey, by the Spanish Homer: being the travels of the Christian hero, Ulysses Desiderius Pius.* Dublin. 1745. 12°. vii, [1], 160 p. Published by: Kelly, I. ESTC t175003. * Dt; ECW; IU; Mil; O.

2201. Palafox y Mendoza, Juan de. *The new Odyssey by the Spanish Homer: being the travels of the Christian hero, Ulysses Desiderius Pius.* Dublin. [1784?]. 12°. xii, 203, [1] p. Printed by: Cross, R. ESTC t094078. * C; CSmH; CtU; Du; ICU; L; OO.

2202. Palafox y Mendoza, Juan de. *Philothea; or, a pilgrimage to the holy Chappel of the Cross. Written originally in Spanish, by the most illustrious and reverend Don Juan of Palafox and Mendoça ... Book 1 [Peregrinacion de Philotea.].* London. 1703. 12°. [12], 297, [1] p. ESTC t075770. * C; CLU-C; DAE (-tp); DFo; ECB; ECW; L; O; Ush.

> Translator's preface signed 'F.H.'

2203. Panisset, François Thérèse. *Declaration et retraction de François Thérèse Panisset Eveque constitutionnel du Mont-Blanc.* [London]. [1796]. 8°. 16 p. ESTC t194329. * L.

2204. Paolucci, Fabrizio. *Epistola secunda.* 4 p. 1715. * OBA.

> Latin and English. A printed copy of Cardinal Paolucci's letter to the president and alumni at Douay, and a printed copy of his two letters to the bishop and

clergy of England and to the College of Douay; dated, respectively, 26 March 1715 and 19 February 1711. See *The Old Brotherhood ... Catalogue*, p. 42, item 115.

2205. Papin, Isaac. *The toleration of the Protestants, and the authority of the church, or, an answer to the libel of monsieur Jurieu. By monsieur Papin, heretofore minister of the Church of England [La tolerance des Protestans et l'autorité de l'Eglise].* London. 1733. 8°. 8, 271, [1] p. ESTC t125824. * CaOHM; L; O; SIR; ViW.

SIR has an additional 4 pages.

2206. *The paradise of the soul: or, a little treatise of vertues. Made by Albert the Great, Bishop of Ratisbon, who died in the year 1280. Translated out of Latin into English. By N.N.* London. 1703. [xiv?], 240 p. * Do (imp.); ECW.

According to Do cat. translated by T. Everard.

2207. *A parallel between the pretended plot in 1762, and the forgery of Titus Oates in 1679 ... In a letter to a noble lord in England.* Cork. 1767. 8°. iv, 5-40 p. ESTC t170420. * D; Di; ECW.

Historical, but clearly pro-Catholic.

2208. *A parallel between transubstantiation and the incarnation; shewing that the objections against transubstantiation are also against incarnation.* London. 1747. 8°. 7, [1] p. Published by: [Marmaduke, J.]. * Ush.

With one page of Marmaduke adverts.

2209. Parkinson, Anthony. *Collectanea Anglo-Minoritica, or, a collection of the antiquities of the English Franciscans, or Friers Minors, commonly call'd Gray Friers. In two parts. With an appendix ... Compil'd and collected by A.P.* London. 1726. 4°. [2], xxviii, [2], 272, viii, 42, [2], 4, [2] p. Printed by: Smith, T. ESTC t093495. * AR; BMp; C; CaOTU; CaQMBN; CLU; CLU-C; CSmH; CtW; CtY; DFo; ECW; FLK; GEU-T; GOT; ICN; L; LU; Map; MH-H; MRu; Osc; Sto; Ush.

Copies show slight variation in the order of binding. A largely antiquarian work intended both for a R.C. and a non-R.C. readership.

2210. Parkinson, Anthony. *Statuta Fratrum Minorum recollectorum almae provinciae Angliae pro missione.* London. 1747. 12°. v, [6]-132 p. Printed by: Hoyles, J. ESTC n046669. * TxU; Ush.

2211. Parsons, Robert. *A Christian directory. Guiding men to their eternal salvation ... There is added also, a method for the use of all. With two fables.* London [i.e. St. Omers]. 1716. 8°. [8], 792, [16] p. Printed by: [English College Press]. ESTC t164427. * Lhe; MY; P.

Printer and place of publication identified by ESTC.

2212. Parsons, Robert. *A Christian directory, guiding men to their eternal salvation. Divided into three books.* London. 1722. 8°. [6], 644, [12] p. ESTC t186533. * O; P.

2213. Parsons, Robert. *A Christian directory, guiding men to their eternal salvation. Divided into three books the first whereof ... is contain'd in this volume.* London. 1739. 8°. x, [6], 660 p. Printed by: Hoyles, J. Sold by:

Meighan, T. ESTC t128157. * C; CLU-C; Do; DoA; ECW; Hen; ICN; ICR; L; Lhe; LO; MWH; NSPM; Osc; TH; TxU; UGL; WaSpG.

2214. Parsons, Robert. *A Christian directory, guiding men to their eternal salvation. Divided into two parts ... And now set forth again with many corrections and additions. There is also added ... the life of the author.* Dublin. 1753. 12°. xxiv, [4], xxv-xxviii, 588, [4] p. Printed by: Lord, P. Sold by: Lord, P. ESTC t164419. * D; FLK.
    With a list of subscribers.

2215. Parsons, Robert. *A Christian directory, guiding men to their eternal salvation. Divided into three books. The first whereof ... is contained in this volume.* Liverpool. 1754. 8°. [2], vi, [6], 660 p. Printed by: Sadler, J. Sold by: Sadler, J. ESTC t095528. * Do; E; ECW; FK; L; Lhe; LVu; MChB; MRu.

2216. Parsons, Robert. *A Christian directory, guiding men to their eternal salvation. Divided into two parts ... also added ... the life of the author.* Dublin. 1767. 12°. xxviii, [4], 588 p. Printed by: Fitzsimons, R.; Cross, R. Published by: Fitzsimons, R.; Cross, R. ESTC t164421. * C; IDA; O.

2217. Parsons, Robert. *A Christian directory, guiding men to their salvation.* London. 1769. 8°. vi, [6], 660 p. Printed by: Marmaduke, J. Sold by: Marmaduke, J. * DoA; UGL.

2218. Parsons, Robert. *A Christian directory, guiding men to their eternal salvation. In two parts ... prefixed the life of the author.* Dublin. 1792. 12°. xxiv, xi-xviii, 588 p. Printed by: Cross, R. Sold by: Cross, R. ESTC t120820. * D; DGU; L.

2219. Parsons, Robert. *A Christian directory, guiding men to their eternal salvation. In two parts ... prefixed the life of the author.* Cork. 1792. 12°. xxiv, xi-xviii, 588 p. Printed by: Haly, J. Sold by: Haly, J. ESTC t164423. * D.

2220. Parsons, Robert. *A Christian directory ... prefixed the life of the author.* Dublin. 1795. 12°. xviii, 588 p. Printed by: Wogan, P. ESTC t164424. * Lhe.

2221. *Part of the trial of Mr. James Webb, June the twenty-fifth, 1768. For exercising the functions of a popish priest, and the trial at large of Mr. James Talbot, February the twenty-seventh, 1771.* London. 1782. 8°. 41, [1] p. Printed by: Coghlan, J.P. * Ush; WDA.
    The two accused priests were both acquitted.

2222. Parvilliers, Adrien. *The devotions of the stations of the passion of Jesus Christ crucified, which are made in Jerusalem. Translated from the French [Stations de N.S. en sa passion à Jerusalem].* [Dublin?]. 1795. 12°. 95, [1] p. * CAL; Do; ECW; Lhe; LO; Ush.

2223. Parvilliers, Adrien. *The devotions of the stations of the passion of Jesus Christ crucify'd, which are made in Jerusalem. Translated from the French.* [Dublin?]. 1796. 12°. 95, [1] p. ESTC t118198. * ECW; Gi; L; O; Stan.

2224. *The passion of our Lord and Saviour Jesus Christ: a sermon on Good-Friday. Preach'd (with some little variation of words) in the year 1738 and* *every year since: this present one included.* 3rd ed. Dublin. 1743. 12°. [2], 96 p. Printed by: Corcoran, B. Published by: Corcoran, B. * Amp.

2225. *The passion of our Lord and Saviour Jesus Christ: a sermon on good Friday. Preach'd (with some little variation of words) in the year 1738, and every year since: this present one included.* 2nd ed. London. 1745. 8°. 242 p. ESTC t217262. * Lhe.

2226. *Pastoral instructions upon the creed, commandments, sacraments, Lord's prayer &c. Collected from the holy scriptures, councils, fathers, and approv'd writers in God's church.* [London?]. 1713. 8°. [16], 440 p. ESTC t061535. * Do; E; ECW; L; Lhe; NSPM; Osc; TH; Ush.

> Gillow (I, 588) attributes this work to William Crathorne.

2227. *Patch work or the comprehension in four canto's semper ego auditor tantum nunquamque reponam? vexatus toties.* [St. Omers?]. [1720?]. 8°. [20], 184 p. ESTC t117403. * CtY; L; NN; O.

> 'Printed by Mark 'em Merry wise for serious Seeker and Company at the sign of the Looking Glass ...' Imprint false; printed abroad, possibly in St. Omers. R.C. satire on the Bangorian controversy. Foxon P120.

2228. *The path to paradise: being the Catholic's companion to the most adorable sacrament of the altar. To which are added, the psalter of the most holy name Jesus; the rosaries; the vespers.* 15th ed. Dublin. [1784?]. 18°. [2], 317, [1] p. Printed by: Wogan, P. * MY.

> The table of moveable feasts starts with 1784. The actual date on tp is illegible.

2229. *Patres Anglo-Benedictini anno M.DCC.XXXIII.* Douai. 1733. s.s. Printed by: Derbaix, C.L. * Lil.

> A list of English Benedictine monks in 1733, probably issued after the general chapter held at Douai from 9-14 August 1733.

2230. *Pax vobis. An epistle to the three churches.* London. 1717. 56 p. Published by: Moore, T. * ICU.

> Sometimes attributed to Thomas Fulford. Gillow (V, 551) attributes it to Hugh Tootell. Published against Bishop Hoadly, and part of the famous Bangorian controversy. See also next item.

2231. *Pax vobis. An epistle to the three churches; with an addition of a preface and postscript.* London. 1721. 8°. [8], 3-144 p. ESTC t131866. * E; ECW; GEU-T; ICN; L; Lhe; O; Omc; Osc; TLP.

2232. Pembridge, Michael Benedict. *The family manual of morning and evening prayers.* Anon. Hereford. 1777. 8°. viii, 61, [11] p. Printed by: Pugh, C. Sold by: Pugh, C.; Marmaduke, J. (London); Booker, T. (London). ESTC t190523. * DoA; ECW; Gi; Lhe.

> For Pembridge see also no. 849.

2233. Pembridge, Michael Benedict. *The family-manual of morning and night prayers ... to which is added A devout exercise preparatory to death.* 3rd ed. London. 1800. 12°. 204 p. Printed by: Coghlan, J.P. * ECW (imp.).

> See also letters Pembridge to Coghlan, Oct. and Nov. 1799 (LANre, RCBu 14/133, 134, 136).

2234. Pembridge, Michael Benedict. *A manual of the daily prayers and duties of a Christian, for the use of infants, with historical lessons abstracted from the old and new testament by M.P.* Hereford. 1799. 12°. Printed by: Pugh, C. Sold by: Pugh, C.; Coghlan, J.P.; Booker, T.; Marmaduke, J.; Sharrock, E. (Preston). * DMR.

2235. Pembridge, Michael Benedict. *The whole duty of a Christian, and a guide to perfection: with directions to parents.* Anon. [London]. 1775. 8°. viii, [8], 410, [14] p. Sold by: Sharrock, E. (Preston). ESTC t099331. * CtY; DMR; Do; DoA; ECW; Hor; L; O; Osc; Sal; Stan; TLP.

> Do suggests Hereford as place of publication. Pembridge was chaplain to the Howard family at Holme Lacy, Herefordshire.

2236. Penswick, Thomas. *A discourse, delivered in the Roman Catholic chapel, at Chester, on Wednesday the seventh of March, 1798 ... by the rev. Thomas Penswick.* Chester. [1798]. 4°. [3], 4-15, [1] p. Printed by: Minshull, W. Sold by: Minshull, W. * Ush.

2237. *The petition of the Catholics of Ireland, to the king's most excellent majesty: presented at St. James's, on Wednesday Jan. 2, 1793, by Messrs. Edward Byrne, John Keogh, James Edward Devereux, Christopher Bellew, and Sir Thomas French, bart.* Dublin. 1793. 8°. 11, [1] p. Printed by: Fitzpatrick, H. ESTC t215328. * Di; MY.

2238. *The petition of the Catholics of Ireland, to the king's most excellent majesty: presented at St. James's, on Wednesday Jan 2, 1793.* Dublin. 1793. 8°. 27, [1] p. Printed by: Fitzpatrick, H. ESTC t087203. * C; CLU-S/C; CoU; CSmH; D; DLC; Du; Gi; L; Lhe; MH; Mil; MiU; MoU; MY; O; PP; PSt; RPB; Sto.

2239. Petition. *The petition of the Catholics of Ireland, to the king's most excellent majesty: presented at St. James's, on Wednesday Jan. 2, 1793 ... To which are annexed notes.* Dublin. 1793. 8°. 45, [3] p. Printed by: Fitzpatrick, H. ESTC t198104. * Dt; ICR; Lhe.

2240. *Petition of the ladies, widows, wives and spinsters ... and other female persons, professing the Roman Catholic religion; to the ... committee appointed to guard and promote the interests of the British Roman Catholics.* [London?]. [1790?]. fol. s.s. ESTC t043923. * L; O.

> A satire concerning the hotly disputed issue of lay democracy in the church.

2241. *Petition of the Roman Catholics of Ireland. Intended to have been presented to Parliament in February 1792. With a preface.* Dublin. 1792. 8°. viii, 9-16 p. Printed by: Byrne, P. ESTC t043924. * BFq; C; D; DLC; Du; FLK; ICR; IU; L; MBAt; MChB; MY; O; PHi; RP; Sto.

2242. *Petition of the Roman Catholics of Ireland. Intended to have been presented to Parliament in February 1792. With a preface.* Dublin. 1792. 8°. [2], x, [1], 4-15, [1] p. Printed by: Byrne, P. ESTC t087204. * C; Dt; KU-S; L; Lhl; MBAt; MY; Owo.

2243. Petre, Benjamin. *Benjamin Dei & s. sedis apostolicae gratiâ Episcopus*

Prusensis, in districtu L. vicarius apostolicus: & Ricardus Episcopus Deborensis in eodem districtu coadjutor; omnibus sacerdotibus missionariis. [London?]. [1753]. 8°. 16 p. ESTC t161129. * ECW; GEU-T; L; TxU.

> Signed and dated 'Datum L. die quinto Octob. anno 1753. Benjamin Prusen. vic. ap. Ricardus Deboren. coadjutor.'

2244. Petre, Benjamin. *Instructions and regulations for the indulgences allowed to the faithful in the L district.* [London]. [1753]. 8°. 15, [1] p. * ECW; Osc; Ush; WDA.

> Dated and signed 'November 21, 1753 B.P. R.D.' i.e. Benjamin Petre V.A. of the London district, and his coadjutor R. Challoner.

2245. Petre, Benjamin. *Instructions and regulations for the indulgences allowed to the faithful in the L- district.* [London]. 1754. 16°. 16, 16 p. ESTC t208252. * DUc; ECR; ECW; Lhe.

> A pastoral letter signed 'B.P., R.D.' Dated 'November 21, 1753'. In fact drawn up by Challoner alone. It includes prayers from his 'Instructions for the time of the jubilee' with separate pagination.

2246. Petre, Benjamin. *Monita quaedam pro sacerdotibus missionariis.* [London?]. [1741]. 8°. 8 p. Published by: [Needham, F.?]. ESTC t123949. * ECW; L; Lhe; Osc; UshA; WDA.

> With a Needham advert on p. 8.

2247. Petre, Francis. *Franciscus Dei & s. sedis apostolicae gratia Episcopus Amoriensis. Communicavimus vobis nuper.* [1753]. 8°. 16 p. * DowA; LDA; Ush.

> Signed 'Franciscus Amorien Vic. Ap.'

2248. Petre, Francis. *Instructions and directions for the jubilee, 1759.* [1759]. 12°. 11, [1] p. * ECW; Ush.

> Signed and dated 'January 14, 1759 F.A.V.A.'

2249. Petre, Francis. *Instructions and directions for the jubilee, 1770.* [1770]. 8°. 8 p. * Ush.

> Signed and dated 'F.A.V.A. June 20, 1770'.

2250. Petre, Francis. *Instructions and regulations for the indulgences allowed to the faithful in the n. district.* 1753. 8°. 15, [1] p. * LDA; Ush.

> Signed 'F.A., December 10, 1753'.

2251. Petre, Francis. *Our holy father Pope Clement XIV. by his brief, dated the 19th of April, 1772.* [1772]. s.s. * UshA.

> Instructions for gaining a plenary indulgence. Signed 'F.A. Vic. Ap'.

2252. Petre, Francis. *There are two whole weeks.* s.s. * UshA.

> Directions for gaining the jubilee.

2253. Petre, Robert Edward. *Letter from the right honourable Lord Petre, to the right reverend doctor Horsley, Bishop of St. David's.* London. 1790. 8°. 44 p. Printed by: Davis, J. Published by: Faulder, R. ESTC t004879. * CaSSU; CLU-S/C; CoU; Csj; CSmH; CtY; DUc; E; ECW; ICN; IU; L; Lfa; Lu; MH-H; MnU; MoU; MRu; NcD; NN; O; Osc; Sto.

> Dated '17 Feb. 1789'. A reply to the remarks on English Roman Catholics in

Bishop Horsley's *Review of the case of the Protestant dissenters*, 1790 (see also next item).

2254. Petre, Robert Edward. *Letter from the right honourable Lord Petre, to the right reverend doctor Horsley, Bishop of St. David's.* Dublin. 1790. 8°. 46 p. Published by: Byrne, P.; Moore, J. ESTC n004222. * Amp; CSmH; CtHT-W; D; Di; Lhl; Mil; MRu; Om; PPL.

2255. Phillips, Thomas. *An appendix to the History of the life of Cardinal Pole: with some remarks on the chief objections which have been made to it.* Anon. London. 1767. 4°. 38 p. Published by: Dodsley, J. ESTC n039667. * DFo; ICN; MH; Oe; Oma.

See note to no. 2257.

2256. Phillips, Thomas. *An appendix to the History of the life of Cardinal Pole. With some remarks on the chief objections which have been made to it.* Anon. Dublin. 1773. 8°. [2], 29, [1] p. ESTC t189916. * Dt.

2257. Phillips, Thomas. *The history of the life of Reginald Pole.* 2 vols. Oxford. 1764. 4°. xxvi, [2], 460; x, 248 p. Printed by: Jackson, W. Sold by: Jackson, W.; Prince, D.; Payne, J.; Marks, J.; Gamidge, S. (Worcester). ESTC t087585. * C; CaOTU; CLU-C; Csj; CU-L; DFo; E; GOT; IaU; ICN; ICU; IES; IEU; InU-Li; L; LEp; Lhe; Llp; Lu; LU; MChB; MH-H; NSPM; O; Osc.

Vol. 2 imprint has 'T. Payne' instead of 'J. Payne'. page 415 of vol. 1 misnumbered 11, and page 248 of vol. 2 misnumbered 288. In view of the clearly R.C. nature of the work, it is included in our list in spite of the fact that it addresses itself to a general readership. See previous 2 and next 3 items.

2258. Phillips, Thomas. *The history of the life of Reginald Pole.* 2 vols. Dublin repr. [Oxford]. 1765. 8°. [4], v-xxxi, [3], 445, [7]; [2], iii-xii, 355, [5]. Printed by: Husband, J.A. ESTC t087417. * C; CSmH; CtY; D; DMR; Dt; Du; ECW (vol. 1); FLK; L; MY; O; OKentU; Sto.

2259. Phillips, Thomas. *The history of the life of Reginald Pole.* 2nd ed. Anon. 2 vols. London. 1767. 8°. xxxi, 495; 340 p. Published by: Payne, T.; Johnston, W.; Bladon, S.; Fletcher, J. and Co.; Nicoll, W.; Flexney, W; Almon, J. ESTC n008604. * BRG; C (vol. 2); CaAEU; CLU (vol. 2); DFo; DoA; ECW; KU-S (vol. 2); L (vol. 1); Lfa; Lhe; PPL (vol. 1); Sal; TxU; Ush; WaPS (vol. 2).

2260. Phillips, Thomas. *The history of the life of Reginald Pole.* 2nd ed. Anon. 2 vols. London. 1767. 8°. xxxi, [3], 495, [1]; xii, 340 p. Sold by: Payne, T.; Johnston, W.; Bladon, S.; Nicoll, W.; Flexney, W. ESTC t129675. * C; CaOHM; CKu (vol. 1); CtHT-W; E; ECB; ECW; InNd; KU-S (vol. 1); L (vol. 1); LAM; MB; MChB; SIR; TH; TLP; VUA; Yb.

This is the second '2nd' ed. with a different imprint.

2261. Phillips, Thomas. *A letter to a student at a foreign university on the study of divinity. By T.P. S.C.T.* London. 1756. 8°. [2], 126 p. Published by: Baldwin, R. ESTC t033020. * CaQMM; Csj; CSmH; CU-SB; E; ECW; ICU; L; Lhe; MoU; O; Sto; TLP; WDA.

'T.P. S.C.T.' is Thomas Phillips, Senior Canon of Tongres. Phillips here gives his 'Thoughts on the several branches of science which make up the study of divinity' (p. 122).

2262. Phillips, Thomas. *Philemon.* [London?]. 1761. 8°. 35, [1] p. Published by: Author. ESTC t117654. * L.

A sketch of his own life.

2263. Phillips, Thomas. *The study of sacred literature fully stated and considered. In a discourse to a student in divinity, at a foreign university. By T.P.S.C.T.* 2nd ed. London. 1758. 8°. xv, [1], 200 p. Published by: Baldwin, R. ESTC t092779. * C; CLU-S/C; CtY; E; GEU-T; L; Lfa; Lhe; Map; NIC; O; Ob; Osc.

See note to no. 2261.

2264. Phillips, Thomas. *The study of sacred literature fully stated and considered, in a discourse to a student in divinity ... To which is added, an answer to the principal objections which have been made to the history of the life of Cardinal Pole.* 3rd ed. London. 1765. 12°. xxiv, 263, [1] p. Published by: Payne, T.; Marks, J.; Jackson, W. (Oxford). ESTC t087418. * AWn; C; DMR; Do; Dt; E; GEU-T; L; LAM; Lfa; Lhe; MRu; MY; NcD; NjP; Ob; Omc.

2265. Phillips, Thomas. *To the right reverend & religious Dame Elizabeth Phillips on her entering the religious order of St. Benet in the convent of English dames of the same order at Gant.* [Ghent?]. [1731]. 4°. [8] p. ESTC t045061. * L; LEu; MH.

Verse. Foxon P259.

2266. Pilling, William Leo. *A caveat addressed to the Catholics of Worcester, against the insinuating letter of Mr. Wharton.* London. 1785. 12°. [2], 109, [1] p. Printed by: Coghlan, J.P. ESTC t129425. * DGU; E; ECW; ICN; InNd; L; MY; Osc; TLP; TxU; Ush.

Gillow (V, 313) states 'In reply to the "Apology" for his apostasy by the late Jesuit missioner at Worcester, Charles Wharton'.

2267. Pilling, William Leo. *A dialogue between a protesting Catholic dissenter and a Catholic on the nature, tendency and import of the oath lately offered to the Catholics of England.* London. 1790. 8°. [2], xi, [1], 60 p. Printed by: Coghlan, J.P. * ECW; ICN; Lfa; Osc; Sto; Ush.

A reply to Sir John Throckmorton. See also next item.

2268. Pilling, William Leo. *A dialogue between an protesting Catholic dissenter, and a Catholic; on the nature, tendency and import of the oath lately offered to the Catholics of England.* London. [1790]. 8°. 4, xi, [1], 60 p. Printed by: Coghlan, J.P. ESTC t121873. * CaOHM; CSmH; Ct; DUc; ICN; L; Lhe; Lmh; MChB; SIR; Sto; TxDaM-P.

2269. Pilling, William Leo. *A letter to the reverend Mr. Joseph Reeves [sic], on his view of the oath, said to be tendered by the legislature, to the Catholics of England.* London. 1790. 8°. [2], 35, [1] p. Printed by: Coghlan, J.P. ESTC t169914. * C; CSmH; CtY-BR; ECW; Hor; ICN; Lfa; Lhe; Lmh; MY (-tp); O; Osc; Sto; Ush.

2270. Pinamonti, Giovanni Pietro. *The cross in its true light; or, the weight of tribulation lessened. Set forth in seven considerations for the seven days in the* *week [Croce alleggerita].* London. 1775. 12°. [12], 161, [1] p. Printed by: Coghlan, J.P. ESTC t076296. * CAL; DLC; DMR; Do; Du; E; ECB; ICN; L; Lhe; Sal; Stan; TxU; Ush; Yb.

> Translator's dedication signed 'Nathaniel Elliot'. Elliot was the provincial of the English Jesuits (1766-1769). Sommervogel gives the alias Sheldon.

2271. Pinamonti, Giovanni Pietro. *Hell opened to Christians; to caution them from entring into it: or considerations of the infernal pains ... Written in Italian by F. Pinamonti [L'inferno aperto al cristiano].* [London?]. 1715. 12°. [10], 84 p. ESTC t115179. * L; Map; NNUT.

2272. Pinamonti, Giovanni Pietro. *Hell opened to Christians; to caution them from entering into it: or, considerations of the infernal pains ... Written in Italian by F. Pinamonti.* [Dublin]. 1753. 12°. xii, 122 [i.e. 123], [1] p. Sold by: Goulding, A. ESTC t204473. * Llp.

2273. Pinamonti, Giovanni Pietro. *Hell opened to Christians; to caution them from entering it; or, considerations of the infernal pains.* London. 1782. 12°. [3], iv-ix, [3], 74 p. Printed by: Coghlan, J.P. * DoA.

2274. Pinamonti, Giovanni Pietro. *Meditations on the four last things, for every day of the month: with directions for a good life.* 4th ed. in English. London. 1796. 12°. 47, [1] p. Printed by: Coghlan, J.P. ESTC n036104. * MoU.

2275. Pinamonti, Giovanni Pietro. *Short meditations upon the four last things, distributed for every day of the month; with directions for a good life at all times.* Douai. 1716. 12°. vii, 8-36 p. Printed by: Derbaix, C.L. * Ush.

2276. Pinamonti, Giovanni Pietro. *Short meditations upon the four last things, distributed for every day of the month; with directions for a good life at all times.* Douai. 1746. 12°. 36 p. Printed by: Derbaix, C.L. * ECW.

> Translated by Thomas Percy Plowden, S.J.

2277. Pinamonti, Giovanni Pietro. *Short meditations upon the four last things, distributed for everyday of the month. With directions for a good life at all times.* 2nd ed. London. 1746. 12°. 36 p. Published by: Needham, W. Sold by: Needham, W. ESTC t175704. * Lhe.

2278. Pinamonti, Giovanni Pietro. *Short meditations upon the four last things, distributed for every day of the month. With directions for a good life at all times.* Anon. 3rd ed. Preston. 1774. 12°. [2], iii-vii, 8-37, [1] p. Printed by: Stuart, W. Sold by: Stuart, W. * DoA.

2279. *A pious association at public meetings once a month. To which is added, the Tantum ergo, Tota pulchra, &c. and the true method to learn the church-plain-song.* London. 1748. 12°. [2], 49, [1] p. Published by: Marmaduke, J. Sold by: Marmaduke, J. ESTC t119561. * L.

> Includes musical notation.

2280. *A pious association of the devout servants of Jesus Christ crucify'd, and of his condoling mother, the Blessed Virgin Mary; for the obtaining a happy death.* 1715. 12°. 107, [1] p. * Do; Map.

2281. *A pious association of the devout servants of Jesus Christ crucify'd and of* his condoling mother the B Virgin Mary. Erected in the English College of the Society of Jesus in S. Omers. [St. Omers?]. 1726. 24°. 48 p. Printed by: Febvre, N.I.L. [sic]. ESTC n037687. * DFo; Do.

2282. *A pious association of the devout servants of Jesus Christ crucify'd, and of his condoling mother the Blessed Virgin Mary; for the obtaining a happy death.* [London?]. 1726. 12°. 107, [1] p. ESTC t179771. * O.

2283. *A pious association of the devout servants of Jesus Christ crucify'd, and of his condoling mother the Blessed Virgin Mary; for the obtaining a happy death.* [London]. 1738. 12°. 67, [5] p. Published by: Meighan, T. ESTC t092694. * DoA; L; NPV.

>	With 5 pages of Meighan adverts.

2284. *The pious guide to prayer and devotion. Containing various practices of piety calculated to answer the various demands of the different devout members of the Roman Catholic church.* George-town. 1792. 12°. iv, [12], 282, [2] p. Printed by: Doyle, J. ESTC w003935. * CSmH; DeU; DGU-W; DGW; PHi.

>	Prepared by the Jesuits of Georgetown College.

2285. *[Pious meditations on the rules of the Society of Jesus].* [1756?]. 8°. 3-81, [1] p. * Ush (-tp).

>	Dated and signed 'Romae 20 Junii 1756 Aloysius Centurionus'. Latin and English.

2286. Pius VI. *Collectio indultorum apostolicorum SS. D. N. Papae Pii VI. Quibus amplissimas & extraordinarias facultates concessit omnibus archiepiscopis, episcopis, & administratoribus dioecesium regni Galliarum.* London. 1797. 8°. [2], 50 p. Printed by: Boussonnier, Ph. le & soc. Sold by: Dulau, A. & soc.; Bené; Keating, P.; Coghlan, J.P.; Booker, E. ESTC t098939. * DUc; ECW; L; MH-H; MY; Osc; Ush; WDA.

2287. Pius VI. *Letters from Rome. With the original Latin.* London. 1794. 8°. [2], 29, [1] p. Printed by: Coghlan, J.P. * Lfa; Sto.

>	Letters from Pius VI to the European hierarchy and superiors. See also next item.

2288. Pius VI. *Letters from Rome. With the original Latin.* London. 1794. 8°. [2], 28 p. ESTC n054833. * ICN.

2289. Pius VI. *The Pope's brief to the Emperor with the Emperor's answer.* London. 1782. 12°. [2], 8 p. Printed by: Coghlan, J.P. ESTC t208867. * L; Ush.

>	A letter from Pius VI to the Emperor Joseph II of Hungary and Bohemia.

2290. Pius VI. *Sanctissimi domini nostri domini Pii divina providentia Papae Sexti damnatio quamplurium propositionum excerptarum ex libro Italico idiomate impresso sub titulo Atti, e decreti del concilio.* London repr. [Rome]. 1794. 8°. [2], 3-39, [1] p. Printed by: Coghlan, J.P. * E; ECW; Osc.

2291. Pius VI. *Two letters from H.H. Pius VI. to the Bishop of Leon, and the prelates of Germany. To which are added a letter from Cardinal Antonelli ... by order of H.H. to the bishops, vicars apostolic, etc.* London. [1795?]. 8°. [2], 29,

[1]; 31, [1] p. ESTC t121130. * CaQMM; CSmH (pt 2); E; L; MY.

Parallel Latin and English texts. With two letters from the pope encouraging the emigré clergy of France and Germany and thanking the British government for their shelter. The 'Bishop of Leon' is J.F. de la Marche. See also next item and no. 70.

2292. Pius VI. *Two letters from H.H. Pius VI. to the Bishop of Leon, and the prelates of Germany. To which are added a letter from Cardinal Antonelli ... by order of H.H. to the bishops, vicars apostolic, etc.* London. [1795?]. 8°. [2], 30, 31, [1] p. ESTC t213430. * MY.

2293. Pius VII. *An encyclical letter of our most holy father Pope Pius VII. to all the Catholic bishops. Translated from the Latin original, by the rev. Benedict Rayment, C.D.A.* London. 1800. 8°. 25, [1] p. Printed by: Keating, Brown & Keating. ESTC t153976. * E; Ush.

For Benedict Rayment (1764-1842) see Gillow (V, 395-397). Cf. also no. 2421.

2294. Pius VII. *Sanctissimi domini nostri Pii divina providentia Papae VII. litterae encyclicae ad omnes Catholicos episcopos.* London. 1800. 8°. 24 p. Printed by: Keating, Brown & Keating. ESTC t172308. * E; ECW; Lhe; O; Ush.

2295. *Plain chant for the chief masses and vespers throughout the year; and for the exposition, salut and benediction of the blessed sacrament, &c. compiled for the use of W-d-r Chapel.* London. 1788. 8°. iv, [8], 216, cxxxiv, [8] p. Printed by: Coghlan, J.P. ESTC t167490. * DoA; L; Sto.

'W-d-r Chapel' is Wardour Chapel. The chants are in Latin; the musical notes are not printed.

2296. *Plan of an association in honor of Jesus Christ, truly and really present in the sacrament of the blessed eucharist.* Baltimore. 1794. 12 p. Printed by: Hayes, J. * MdW.

2297. *Plan of Oscott seminary.* Birmingham. [1794]. 4°. 8 p. Printed by: Swinney; Collins. * BAA.

A prospectus of the seminary at Oscott; on p. 3 the trustees are given as Thomas Talbot, Charles Berington and Charles Dormer. See also no. 2406.

2298. Plessis, Joseph Octave. *Circulaire à messieurs les curés du district de Québec.* [Quebec]. [1800]. 4°. [4] p. Printed by: [Neilson, J.]. * CaOOP; CaQQLa.

2299. Plessis, Joseph Octave. *Discours a l'occasion de la victoire remporte'e par les forces navales de sa majesté Britannique ... le 1 aout 1798 ... Prononcé ... le 10 janvier 1799 ... prrcedé [sic] du mandement de ... Eveque de Quebec.* Quebec. [1799]. 8°. [6], 24, [2] p. Printed by: [Neilson, J.]. ESTC w016657. * CaNSWA; CaOOP; CaOOA; CaOTP; CaQMBM; CaQMJ; CaQMM; CaQMS; CaQQLa; CaSSU; RPJ.

2300. Plowden, Charles. *An answer to the second blue book. Containing a refutation of the principles, charges and arguments advanced by the Catholic Committee against their bishops. Addressed to the Roman Catholics of England.* London. 1791. 8°. vii, [1], 165, [3] p. Printed by: Coghlan, J.P. Sold by:

Booker; Keating; Lewis; Robinsons. ESTC t187473. * BB; C; D; DGU; DUc; ECW; Hen; LfaA; Lhe; Lmh; MY; O; Osc; SCR; StD; Sto; Ush; WDA.

> With a final advertisement leaf. See also no. 2759.

2301. Plowden, Charles. *A candid and impartial sketch of the life and government of Pope Clement XIV containing many interesting anecdotes during that period of church history. In a series of letters from Rome.* Anon. 3 vols. Dublin. 1785-1786. 8°. [4], 156; [2], 155, [1]; 167, [1] p. Printed by: Seymour, I. Published by: Author. Sold by: Booksellers in Great Britain and Ireland (vol. 1); Symonds, H.D. (London, vol. 2). * Lfa; LfaA; Sto; Ush (vol. 2).

> Each letter is signed with the initials J.T., i.e. John Thorpe who assisted Plowden (Kirk, p. 185). The book, written to blacken Clement's character for suppressing the Jesuits, was suppressed itself. See also next item.

2302. Plowden, Charles. *A candid and impartial sketch of the life and government of Pope Clement XIV containing many interesting anecdotes during that period of church history. In a series of letters from Rome.* 2nd ed. Anon. 3 vols. Dublin. 1785-6. 8°. [4], 156; [4], 155, [1]; [4], 167, [1]. Printed by: Seymour, I. Published by: Author. Sold by: Symonds, H.D. (London). ESTC t211955. * D.

> ESTC (which gives the same number to the first and the second eds) suggests that the imprint is false (see also previous item).

2303. Plowden, Charles. *A circumstantial account of the death of abbé Lawrence Ricci, late general of the Society of Jesus. To which is annexed, a copy of the protestation which he left at his death.* Anon. London. 1776. 12°. 23, [1] p. ESTC t105382. * DMR; E; ECW; L; Lhe; TxU; Yb.

> Sutcliffe (337) and Gillow (V, 323) identify Plowden as author.

2304. Plowden, Charles. *Considerations on the modern opinion of the fallibility of the holy see in the decision of dogmatical questions. With an appendix on the appointment of bishops.* London. 1790. 8°. viii, 133, [3] p. Printed by: Coghlan, J.P. Sold by: Robinsons, Messrs. ESTC t165377. * BB; DGU; DoA; DU; DUc; E; ECB; ECW; ICN; Lhe; Llp; O; Osc; P; SCR; Sto; TxDaM-P; Ush; Yb.

2305. Plowden, Charles. *A discourse delivered at the consecration of the right rev. John Douglass ... in the chapel of Lullworth Castle, on Sunday, 19th of December, 1790.* London. 1791. 8°. [4], 5-15, [1] p. Printed by: Coghlan, J.P. ESTC t123166. * BB; DUc; ECW; L; Lfa; Lhe; O; Osc; P; Sto; Ush.

2306. Plowden, Charles. *A letter from the rev. Charles Plowden to C. Butler, W. Cruise, H. Clifford, and W. Throckmorton, Esqrs. and reporters of the Cisalpine Club. In which their reports, on the authenticity of the instrument of Catholic protestation lodged in the British Museum, are examined.* London. 1796. 8°. xvi, 44 p. Printed by: Coghlan, J.P. Sold by: Booker; Keating; Lewis; Debrett; Robinsons. ESTC t012319. * DoA; Du; ECW; L; Lhe; O; Osc; Sto; Ush.

> See also nos 1880 and 2413.

2307. Plowden, Charles. *A letter to the Catholics of England. My lords and gentlemen, in reading the letter of the late Catholic Committee.* [London?]. [1792]. fol. 3, [1] p. ESTC t038225. * BAA; L; Lhe; SIR; Sto; TxU.

Dated 'September 6, 1792'.

2308. Plowden, Charles. *Observations on the oath proposed to the English Roman Catholics.* London. 1791. 8°. [4], 70 p. Printed by: Coghlan, J.P. ESTC t108556. * DGU; DoA; DUc; E; ECW; ICN; L; Lhe; Lmh; O; Osc; SCR; Sto; TxU; Ush.

2309. Plowden, Charles. *Remarks on a book entitled Memoirs of Gregorio Panzani ... Preceded by an address to the rev. Joseph Berington.* Liege. 1794. 8°. [4], v-xvi, 383, [1] p. Sold by: Coghlan, J.P. (London). ESTC t117713. * BB; CU-S; Dt; E; ECR; ECW; L; LfaA; Lhe; LO; Map; MY; O; Osc; P; Pm; Ush.

> With one page of adverts for works by Charles Plowden; the work was printed in Liege and the sheets were sent over 'ready stitched' to Coghlan in London (letter Charles Plowden to Coghlan, 11 Nov. 1793, LANre RCBu 14/29). It is a refutation of Berington's Gallican views regarding Roman authority in the English church. Plowden treated the Panzani Memoirs (no. 249) as a forgery by Berington and Dodd.

2310. Plowden, Charles. *Remarks on the writings of the rev. Joseph Berington, addressed to the Catholic clergy of England.* London. 1792. 8°. xiii, [1], 125, [1] p. Printed by: Coghlan, J.P. Sold by: Debrett; Booker; Keating; Lewis; Robinsons. ESTC t124376. * BB; C; E; ECW; ICN; ICR; InNd; L; Lhe; MRu; MY; NN; Osc; P; SIR; Sto; TxU; Ush.

2311. Plowden, Charles. *A short account of the establishment of the new see of Baltimore in Maryland, and of consecrating the right rev. Dr. John Carroll first bishop thereof ... With a discourse delivered on that occasion.* Anon. London. 1790. 8°. [4], 32 p. Printed by: Coghlan, J.P. ESTC t121894. * DeU; DGU; ECW; L; Lhe; Lmh; LNT; Lu; O; Osc; RPJCB; Stan; Sto; Ush; WDA.

> Finotti (p.17) attributes this to Charles Plowden, who was Carroll's intimate friend and his adviser throughout life. See also next 2 items.

2312. Plowden, Charles. *A short account of the establishment of the new see of Baltimore in Maryland, and of consecrating the right rev. Dr. John Carroll, first bishop thereof ... 1790. With a discourse.* Anon. Dublin. 1790. 8°. 32 p. Printed by: Wogan, P. ESTC t215760. * DGU; Di; NN; WDA.

2313. Plowden, Charles. *A short account of the establishment of the new see of Baltimore, in Maryland, and of the consecrating the right reverend Dr. John Carroll, first bishop thereof, on the Feast of the Assumption, 1790.* Anon. Philadelphia repr. [London]. 1791. 8°. 20 p. Printed by: Carey, Stewart & Co. ESTC w004013. * DCU; DGU-W; MdBJ-G (imp.).

2314. Plowden, Francis. *The case stated, by Francis Plowden, Esq. conveyancer, of the Middle Temple. Occasioned by the Act of Parliament lately passed for the relief of the English Roman Catholics.* London. 1791. 8°. 196 p. Published by: Author. Sold by: Keating, P. ESTC t020313. * C; CaOHM; CSmH; CtY-BR; D; DUc; E; ECW; ICN; L; Ldw; Lfa; Lhe; Llp; Lmh; MRu; MY; NcD; O; Osc; P; SCR; StD; Sto; TxU.

> Lhe cat. gives Coghlan as printer; Lhe is bound up with nos 183 and 2744. Note

that Plowden's strictly legal publications are not included in our list.

2315. Plowden, Francis. *Church and state: being an enquiry into the origin nature and extent of ecclesiastical and civil authority, with reference to the British constitution.* London. 1795. 4°. xix, [1], 620 p. Published by: Robinson, G.G. and J. ESTC t118336. * C; CLU; CLU-S/C; E; ECR; GEU-T; IaU; IES; L; LEu; Lhe; MdBP; NNUT; Oma; P; PPAmP; PPL; TxU.

> Although the author claims to be impartial, he writes from a Catholic point of view.

2316. Plowden, Francis. *Fanaticism and treason: or, a dispassionate history of the rise, progress, and suppression, of the rebellious insurrections in June 1780. By a real friend to religion and to Britain.* London. 1780. 8°. [4], 91, [1] p. Published by: Kearsley, G. ESTC t012684. * BMp; CaOTU; CSmH; Eu; FMU; Gu; InU-Li; L; LEu; MnU; NjP; NN; PPAmP.

> According to DoA the 'real friend to religion and to Britain' is Francis Plowden. See also next 2 items.

2317. Plowden, Francis. *Fanaticism and treason: or, a dispassionate history of the rise, progress, and suppression, of the rebellious insurrections in June 1780. By a real friend to religion and to Britain.* London. 1780. 8°. [4], 120 p. Published by: Kearsley, G. ESTC t138180. * CaQQM; CLU-S/C; CSmH; DoA; IEN-M; L; Lu; MsHaU; O; NN; PPAmP; TxDaM-P.

2318. Plowden, Francis. *Fanaticism and treason: or, a dispassionate history of the rise, progress, and suppression, of the rebellious insurrections in June 1780. By a real friend to religion and to Britain.* 3rd ed. London. 1780. 8°. [4], 120 p. Published by: Kearsley, G. ESTC t138148. * L.

2319. Plowden, Francis. *A short history of the British empire during the last twenty months; viz. from May 1792 to the close of the year 1793.* London. 1794. 8°. [4], 386 p. Published by: Robinson G.G. and J. ESTC t072759. * C; CaMWU; Cj; CKu; DLC; Dt; Du; E; GOT; ICN; ICR; KU-S; KyU; L; Lhe; LVu; MeB; MWA; NjR; O; TxU.

2320. Plowden, Francis. *A short history of the British empire during the last twenty months; viz. from May 1792 to the close of the year 1793.* Dublin. 1794. 8°. [2], 290 p. Printed by: Byrne, P. ESTC n022765. * CSmH; D; DeU; ICU; InLP; IU; MnU; MSaE; MWA; MY; Nj; PPiPT; ViU.

2321. Plowden, Francis. *A short history of the British empire, from May 1792 to the close of the year 1793.* Philadelphia. 1794. 8°. [2], 16, 25-261, [3] p. Published by: Carey, M. ESTC w031442. * CNoS; DB; DLC; ICU; L; MB; MBAt; NN; Vi; ViW; WaU.

> With 2 pages of Carey adverts.

2322. Plowden, Francis. *A short history of the British empire during the year 1794.* London. 1795. 8°. [x], 377, [1] p. Published by: Robinson G.G. and J. ESTC t117117. * C; CaOHM; Du; E; GOT; MChB; MiEM; MoU; NIC; O; OCl; OClW; PPL; PSC; RPJCB; TxU.

2323. Plowden, Robert. *A letter to a Roman Catholic clergyman upon theological inaccuracy.* London. 1795. 8°. [3], vi-viii, 168 p. Printed by: Coghlan, J.P. Sold by: Booker; Keating; Lewis; Debrett; Robinsons. ESTC t124377. * E; ECW; Gi; L; Lfa; LfaA; Lhe; MChB; MY; Osc; Sto.

2324. Plowden, Robert. *A letter to Francis Plowden, Esq. conveyancer, of the Middle Temple. On his work, entitled Jura Anglorum. By a Roman Catholic clergyman.* [London]. [1794]. 8°. [iii], 4-230, [2] p. Printed by: Coghlan, J.P. Sold by: Debrett; Robinsons; Booker; Keating; Lewis; Wogan, P. (Dublin). ESTC n011443. * BB; CoU; C-S; CSmH; FU; InU-Li; KU-S; LfaA; Lhe; Map; MdBJ-P; MY; Osc; Ush; UshL.

> Dated on p. 225 'Feb. 17, 1794'. This is a specifically R.C. comment on Francis Plowden's general discussion of the British Constitution in his *Jura Anglorum* (1792), not included in our list. Robert Plowden frequently used the appellation 'A Roman Catholic clergyman'.

2325. Plowden, Robert. *A review of S.N.'s late publication, entitled, An enquiry into the consistency of Dr. Troy's 'Pastoral Instruction', with the declaration agreed by the committee, 1792, by a Roman Catholic clergyman.* London. 1793. 8°. [4], 70 p. Printed by: Coghlan, J.P. Sold by: Debrett; Robinsons; Booker; Keating; Lewis; Wogan (Dublin). ESTC t215423. * Di; Lfa; MY; Osc; Sto.

> 'S.N.' is Thomas Elrington, Protestant Bishop of Ferns and Leighlin.

2326. Plowden, Robert. *A sermon preached at the opening of the Roman Catholic chapel, Bristol ... June 27, 1790.* Bristol. 1790. 8°. 19, [1] p. Printed by: Bonner, S. ESTC t175163. * Lfa; Lhe; Lmh; O; Osc; Sto; Ush.

2327. Plowden, Robert. *To the gentlemen of the late English province of J--ts.* London. [1796]. fol. 4 p. Published by: Keating; Brown; Keating. * Cli; Lfa (-tp); UshA; UshA.

> Dated 'Bristol, Dec. 12th 1796'.

2328. Plunket, Richard. *A hymn on the life of St. Patrick: extracted from the ancient Scytho-Celtic dialect; into modern Irish. By Richard Plunket, late translator of the new testament into Irish.* Dublin. 1791. 8°. 31, [1] p. * Mil.

> There is a second tp on p. 27 'Short directions for reading Irish ... By Richard Plunket' (Dublin 1791). The final page advertises translations by Plunket into Irish, such as *True wisdom* by Segneri and a translation of the gospels according to the Roman missal.

2329. Poncet de la Rivière, Michel. *The Lord Bishop of Angers his letter to the clergy of his diocess, together with the answer ... on the subject of the Constitution Unigenitus [Lettre de mgr. l'Eveque d' Angers].* [London?]. 1721. 12°. [2], 48 p. ESTC n034474. * Ct; Lhl.

2330. *The poor-man's daily companion: or, a choice collection of prayers, and other spiritual exercises, with the manner of serving at mass, Jesus psalter, examination of conscience.* London. 1787. 24°. 254 p. Printed by: Coghlan, J.P. ESTC t178439. * Lhe.

2331. *The poor man's daily companion.* London. 1791. 8°. 256 p. Printed by: Coghlan, J.P. * Gi.

2332. *The poor man's daily companion: or, a choice collection of prayers and other spiritual exercises; with the addition of Jesus psalter, prayers for* *indulgences*. Preston. [1793?]. 16°. 189, [3] p. Published by: Sergent, E. Sold by: Sergent, E. * Sto.

      Date in ms on tp.

2333. *The poor man's daily companion: or, a choice collection of prayers, and other spiritual exercises: with the manner of serving at mass.* London. 1794. 24°. 256 p. Printed by: Coghlan, J.P. ESTC t178440. * Lhe.

2334. *The poor man's daily companion: or, a choice collection of prayers, and other spiritual exercises.* London. 1799. 8°. 256 p. Printed by: Coghlan, J.P. * Do.

2335. *The poor man's daily companion: or, a choice collection of prayers.* Manchester. 1800. 48°. Published by: Haydock. Gillow IV, 461.

2336. *The poor man's manual of devotions. Or, devout Christian's daily companion. Containing, morning and evening prayers ... To which are added, the vespers in Latin and English.* Dublin. 1790. 12°. 287, [1], 3-72 p. Printed by: Cross, R. * DMR.

2337. *The poor man's manual of devotions: or, devout Christian's daily companion. To which are added the vespers in Latin and English.* Dublin. 1797. 12°. [2], 288 p. Printed by: Wogan, P. * Do.

      With 2 pages of Wogan adverts.

2338. *The poor man's posey of prayers; or the key of heaven. Being a magazine of devotion.* Liverpool. [1755]. 12°. 260, [4] p. Printed by: Sadler. * DoA; Gi.

      Gillow (V, 421) attributes this book to John Rigby S.J. Osc cat. notes: 'This little prayerbook ... was popular among Catholics in England and Scotland for many years. It was one of the standard books clandestinely distributed by Bishop George Hay at a shilling a copy in and after 1793'.

2339. *The poor man's posey of prayers; or the key of heaven: being a magazine of devotion, collected from Catholic authors, and adapted to all persons and occasions.* 2nd ed. Preston. 1768. 12°. 257, [5] p. ESTC t188878. * C.

2340. *The poor man's posey of prayers; or the key of heaven: being a magazine of devotions, collected from Catholic authors, and adapted to all persons and occasions.* 3rd ed. Preston. 1769. 12°. 225, [3] p. Printed by: Stuart, W. ESTC t100744. * Gi; L.

2341. *The poor man's posey of prayers; or the key of heaven, being a magazine of devotion, collected from Catholic authors.* 6th ed. London. 1783. 12°. 355, [5] p. Printed by: Coghlan, J.P. * DoA.

      DoA is followed by 255 pages of ms prayers.

2342. *The poor man's posey of prayers; or the key of heaven. Being a magazine of devotion, collected from Catholic authors.* 7th ed. London. 1786. 12°. 358 p. Printed by: Coghlan, J.P. ESTC t173783. * E; Gi (imp.).

2343. *The poor man's posey of prayers; or the key of heaven: being a magazine of devotion, collected from Catholic authors, and adapted to all persons and occasions.* 6th ed. London. 1788. 12°. vii, 8-445, [5] p. Published by: Booker, T. * BB.

This is the second '6th' ed.

2344. *The poor man's posey of prayers; or the key of heaven; being a magazine of devotion, collected from Catholic authors, and adapted to all persons and occasions.* 8th ed. London. 1793. 12°. 358 p. Printed by: Coghlan, J.P. * DMR; Gi; Hen.

2345. *The poor man's posey of prayers, or the key of heaven: being a magazine of devotion, collected from Catholic authors.* 9th ed. London. 1798. 12°. 360 p. Printed by: Coghlan, J.P. ESTC t173787. * Lhe.

2346. Porter, Jerome. *Edvardus redivivus. The life of St. Edward, king and confessor.* [London]. 1710. 8°. [2], 91, [3] p. ESTC t076179. * BB; BMp; L; Lhe; Map; MoU; NNUT; O; TxU; Yb.

> Extracted from *The flowers of the lives of the most renowned saincts* (ARCR II, 653).

2347. Porter, Jerome. *The life of St. Edward, king and confessor ... Revis'd and corrected.* [London]. 1710. 8°. [2], 91, [3] p. ESTC t076178. * C; DFo; Do; DoA; L; Lfa; O.

> A reissue of no. 2346 with a cancel tp.

2348. *The posey of prayers; or the key of heaven: being a magazine of devotion, collected from Catholic authors, and adapted to all persons and occasions.* 8th ed. London. 1799. 18°. 414, [6] p. Published by: Booker, E. ESTC t118800. * L.

> With a final leaf of advertisements. For other eds see *The poor man's posey of prayers.* This is the second '8th' ed.

2349. Potts, Thomas. *An inquiry into the moral and political tendency of the religion called Roman Catholic.* Anon. London. 1790. 8°. [4], 163, [1] p. Published by: Robinson, G.G.J. and J.; Faulder, R. ESTC t090019. * C; DUc; E; ECW; Hen; ICN; L; Lfa; Lmh; Lu; MB; O; OCU; Osc; Sto; TxDaM-P; Ush.

> ECW, Osc, Sto and Ush give T. Potts as author.

2350. Potts, Thomas. *An inquiry into the moral and political tendency of the religion called Roman Catholic.* Anon. Dublin. 1790. 8°. [4], 123, [1] p. Printed by: Byrne, P.; Jones, W. ESTC t090020. * C; D; Dt; L; O; PP; PU; TxU.

2351. Pouget, François Aimé. *General instructions, by way of catechism, in which the history and tenets of religion ... are briefly explain'd ... translated by S. Ll. [Instructions générales en forme de catechisme].* Anon. London. 1722. 8°. viii, 457, [1], 6 p. * MY.

> The translator is Sylvester Louis Lloyd. Hugh Fenning O.P. (personal communication) suggests that the book was printed in Dublin in view of the fact that Lloyd lived there. It was put on the Index in 1725. See also next item.

2352. Pouget, François Aimé. *General instructions, by way of catechism, in which the history and tenets of religion ... are briefly explain'd, by holy-scripture and tradition.* 2nd ed. Anon. 2 vols. London. 1723. 8°. 8, 425, [1], 6; [4], 275, [1], 155, [7] p. ESTC t184159. * DoA; Dt (vol. 1); Du; (vol. 2); ECW; FLK;

Gi; L (vol. 1); Lhe; NSCH (vol. 2).

2353. Powell, David. *Allwydd y nêf, neu agoriad o'r porth, i'r bywyd tragwyddol: trwy weddiau duwiol, ar amryw achosion; anghenrheidiol, a chyfaddas, i bob christion ffyddlon. O gasgliad D.P. Off.* London. 1776. 12°. xxvii, [1], 439, [1] p. Printed by: Coghlan, J.P. ESTC t091488. * AWu; Do; L; Map.

'D.P.' is David Powell.

2354. Powell, David. *Catechism byrr o'r athrawiaeth ghristnogol; er addysc ysprydol i blant; a'r werinos anwybodus, trwy Gymru oll o Gasgliad Dewi Nantbrân Off. O.S.F.* London. 1764. 12°. vii, [1], 99, [1] p. ESTC t212905. * AWu; Do; E; ECR; Map.

'Dewi Nantbrân' is David Powell.

2355. *Practical instructions on the obligation and manner of keeping Lent.* Dublin. 1771. 12°. 55, [1] p. Printed by: Byrn, J. ESTC t060383. * L.

With a final page of Byrn adverts. The author is given as 'P-st of the D-ss of K-e' (Priest of the Diocese of Kildare).

2356. *The practical penitent: being instructions upon four of the principal duties of Christians: viz. conversion, confession, hearing mass, and holy communion.* London. 1786. 12°. 79, [1] p. Published by: Author. Sold by: Marmaduke, J. ESTC t119865. * Du; L; Lfa; MChB; O; Osc; Ush.

2357. *The practice of the love of God and of our Lord and Saviour Jesus Christ. Done out of French by J.M.D.C. ... highly recommended to all Catholick readers.* 2nd ed. Dublin. 1733. 12°. xxv, [3], 5-191, [1] p. Published by: Hanly, T. Sold by: Hanly, T. * FLK.

2358. *Praxis et oeconomia B. Mariae Virginis ss. rosarii; ad piorum usum, novo methodo et aeneis figuris, ornati. Cui aliqua monita de missa audienda et poenitentia agenda adjiciuntur.* [London?]. 1754. 12°. [2], 32 p. ESTC t207306. * Llp.

With an additional engraved tp 'Beatae Mariae Virginis rosarii mysteria XV, illustrata: anno salutis, 1754'.

2359. *Prayer for our king and country.* 8°. 2 p. * WDA.

Prayer for the Catholic community and King George III.

2360. *A prayer in honour of St. Barbara for a happy death ... An exercise for the morning.* [London?]. [c.1720?]. 12°. * DMR.

2361. *A prayer unto the glorious Virgin Mary, mother of God. With a prayer to our Lord Jesus Christ.* [London?]. 1720. 12°. 12 p. * DLC.

2362. *A prayer unto the glorious Virgin Mary. Mother of God. With a prayer to our Lord Jesus Christ.* London. 1733. 12°. 12 p. Published by: Meighan, T. * Sto.

2363. *A prayer unto the glorious Virgin Mary. Mother of God. With a prayer to our Lord Jesus Christ.* London. 1752. 12°. 12 p. * Ush.

2364. *Prayers and devout instructions for different times & duties of the day.* Liege. 1792. 8°. 245, [3] p. Printed by: Dessain, H. and sisters. ESTC t114571.

* L; NN; Ush.
    English and Latin.

2365. *Prayers, appointed to be said before mass, in all the Roman Catholic chapels in the archdiocess of Dublin, for his holiness Pius VI. and our most gracious sovereign King George III.* Dublin. 1798. 12°. 12 p. Printed by: Fitzpatrick, H. Published by: Wogan, P. ESTC t108342. * L.
    English and Latin (parallel texts).

2366. *Prayers before and after mass. First published for the use of the middle district.* 6th ed. London. 1798. 12°. 24 p. Printed by: Coghlan, J.P. ESTC t194606. * O.
    Taken from John Gother. Bossy (p. 389) mentions a 1792 Wolverhampton ed., WDA has an unidentifiable late 18th century ed. of 22 pages.

2367. *Prayers before and after mass: first published for the use of the middle district.* 8th ed. Birmingham. 1800. 12°. 24 p. Printed by: Grafton & Reddell. ESTC t179746. * BMp.

2368. *Prayers before mass on Sundays.* [London]. 1792. 8°. 24 p. Printed by: Coghlan, J.P. * Ush.

2369. *Prayers for the king, queen and royal family.* [London]. [1778]. fol. 2 p. Printed by: [Coghlan, J.P.]. * BAA; Map; Ush.
    The prayers consist of psalm 19 in English and Latin and by prayers for the pope, King George and Queen Caroline.

2370. *The prayers of all good Christians are humbly desir'd for the soul of Mrs Constantia Holford, who departed this life the 17th day of July, 1758.* [1758]. s.s. * Lil.
    Obit notice.

2371. *The prayers of St. Brigitte.* 12°. 3-22 p. * ECW.
    Bound with *The Christian's guide to heaven*, 1794 (no. 711).

2372. *Prayers proper for the time of an indulgence.* [London?]. [1755?]. 12°. 11, [1] p. ESTC t118937. * L; Ush.

2373. *Prayers to be said before and after mass on Sundays and on Sunday afternoons.* Lancaster. 1799. 12°. 24 p. Printed by: Jackson. * Ush.

2374. *A preparation for death. Done out of French.* London. 1712. 12°. [8], 109, [1] p. * Yb.

2375. *A preparation for death or, the practice of dying well ... by Mr. William Ballantine.* Doway. 1715. 8°. xiii, [1], 90 p. ESTC t208106. * E.
    ESTC suggests that the original French work is by father Jean Suffren. Possibly a translation (by W. Ballantine?) of *L'année Chrestienne, ou le sainct et profitable employ du temps pour gagner l'éternité.*

2376. *A preparation for death. Done out of French.* London. 1716. 24°. [8], 112 p. ESTC t180609. * O.

2377. *A preparation for death. Done out of the French.* London. [1720?]. 12°. viii, 111, [1] p. Printed by: Meighan, T. Sold by: Meighan, T. ESTC t180607. * Do; E.

With one page of adverts.

2378. *A preparation for death. Translated from the French.* Liverpool. [c.1730]. 8°. 77, [1] p. Printed by: Schofield, T. Published by: Schofield, T. Bevan (Advent 1993, no. 345).

Gillow (V, 549) claims that Christopher Tootell was the translator.

2379. *A preparation for death.* Warrington. 1780. 12°. viii, 111, [1] p. Printed by: Eyres, W. * DoA.

2380. *A preparation for death. Done out of French.* Dublin. 1788. 24°. x, 11-128 p. Printed by: Cross, R. * MY.

2381. *A preparation for death. Translated from the French.* London. 1794. 24°. viii, 104 p. Printed by: Coghlan, J.P. ESTC t181353. * FP; O.

2382. Pressy, François Joseph. *Pastoral letter of the late Lord Bishop of Boulogne in France, to establish through his whole diocese the devotion and office of the sacred heart of our Lord Jesus Christ.* London. 1794. 4°. 2, [12] p. Printed by: Coghlan, J.P. * Lfa; Osc.

The Bishop observes that the devotion to the sacred heart had been greatly encouraged by the Queen of France.

2383. Pressy, François Joseph. *The pastoral letter of the late right reverend Lord Bishop of Boulogne in France to establish ... the devotion and office of the sacred heart.* 6th ed. London. 1795. 12°. [2], lvi, 418 p. Printed by: Coghlan, J.P. * CAL; DAE; Sal.

2384. *Prieres de la congregation.* [Montreal] 16 p. Printed by: [Mesplet, F.]. * CaQMC.

Obviously printed at Montreal before 1800, probably by Fleury Mesplet between 1776 and 1794, for the Séminaire de Saint Sulpice.

Primer. See also *Office of the B.V. Mary* and *Short office of the B.V. Mary.* For a general account of the Primer see Blom. The Primers are given here in a chronological sequence, disregarding slight differences in the wording of the title.

2385. *The primer more ample and in a new order, containing the three offices of the B. Virgin Mary, in Latin and English.* Rouen. 1701. 12°. [70], 444, [6] p. Printed by: Turner, N. le. * Do.

Preface signed 'Thomas Fitzsimon, priest'. This ed. was 'revised and corrected by P.R.'. See also nos 2388 and 2389.

2386. *The primer, or, office of the B. Virgin Mary, revis'd: with a new and approv'd version of the church-hymns throughout the year.* [London]. 1706. 12°. [30], 560, [4] p. Published by: [Metcalfe, T.]. ESTC t138656. * DMR; Do (imp.); Gi; Hen; L; Lhe; LO; O.

With a final leaf of Metcalfe adverts.

2387. *The primer, or, office of the B. Virgin Mary, revis'd: with a new and approv'd version of the church-hymns throughout the year: to which are added the remaining hymns of the Roman breviary.* [London]. 1717. 12°. [4], iii-viii, [22], 560, [8] p. Published by: [Meighan, T.]. ESTC t100484. * CSd; DoA; E; ECW; Gi; L; LO; Osc; Stan (imp.); UGL.

With an 8-page 'Catalogue of books sold by Tho. Meighan'; there are two issues (see ESTC under Meighan). Some copies lack the catalogue.

2388. *The primer more ample and in a new order, containing the three offices of the B. Virgin Mary in Latin and English.* Rouen. 1720. 12°. [80], 444, [4] p. Printed by: Turner, N. le, widow of. * C; DMR.

2389. *The primer more ample and in a new order, containing the three offices of the B. Virgin Mary, in Latin and English.* Rouen. 1730. 12°. [80], 444, [4] p. Printed by: Turner, N. le. * FLK (imp.); O.

2390. *The primer; or, office of the B. Virgin Mary, with a new and approv'd version of the church-hymns. To which are added the remaining hymns of the Roman breviary.* [London?]. 1732. 12°. [2], viii, [22], 562, [6] p. Published by: Meighan, T. ESTC t125400. * AR; BB; C; Do; ECW; Gi; L; LO; Map; NNUT; O; UGL; Ush.

2391. *The primer; or, office of the B. Virgin Mary, with a new and approv'd version of the church-hymns. To which are added the remaining hymns of the Roman breviary.* Dublin. 1767. 12°. [38], 572, [4] p. Sold by: Fitzsimons, R. ESTC t105414. * D; L.
> With 4 pages of Fitzsimons adverts.

2392. *The primer; or office of the Blessed Virgin Mary, with a new and approved version of the church-hymns. Translated from the Roman breviary.* London. 1780. 12°. xviii, [8], 560, [4] p. Printed by: Coghlan, J.P. ESTC t147747. * CAL; ECB (imp.); L; O; Stan (imp.); Yb.

2393. *The primer; or office of the Blessed Virgin Mary, with a new and approved version of the church-hymns. Translated from the Roman breviary.* London. 1780. 12°. xviii, [8], 560, [4] p. Printed by: Coghlan, J.P. * Do; Stan (imp.).
> This is an ed. that differs from no. 2392. The present ed. collates: A-Z12, Aa-Bb12; no. 3486 has the collation: π1-π2, A-Zz6, Aaa-Ccc6.

2394. *The primer; or, office of the Blessed Virgin Mary.* Cork. 1789. 12°. 128 p. Printed by: Haly, J. ESTC t176129. * C; D.
> With some pages of Haly adverts.

2395. *The primer or office of the Blessed Virgin Mary, to which are added a new and improved version of the church-hymns, and the remaining hymns of the Roman breviary.* Dublin. [1796]. 12°. [30], 680 p. Published by: Cross, R. * IDA.

2396. *The primer; or, office of the Blessed Virgin Mary.* Dublin. 1799. 8°. 161, [3] p. Printed by: Cross, R. ESTC t216212. * Di.

2397. *Primitiae.* London repr. [Douai]. 1796. 8°. [3], 4-12 p. Printed by: Coghlan, J.P. repr. [Derbaix]. * DMR.
> A thesis by the French refugee Gerard Deleau, prepared under Joseph Berington.

2398. *The principles of the Roman-Catholics exhibited in some useful observations on a pamphlet intituled, Plain matters of fact, humbly recommended to the consideration of the Roman-Catholics of Ireland.* Dublin. 1756. 8°. 104 p.

Published by: Lord, P. Sold by: Lord, P. ESTC t178724. * C; CSmH; D; DFo; Dt; ICR; Mil; MRu.

> A defence of R.C. civil obedience against the pamphlet *A few plain matters of fact* (1756); the latter pamphlet is sometimes attributed to the non-R.C. Bishop Robert Clayton.

2399. *Proceedings at a meeting of the Roman Catholics of Dublin. Reccommended [sic] to the consideration of their fellow subjects in England and Ireland.* London repr. [Dublin]. 1792. 8°. 77, [1] p. Published by: Richardson, W. ESTC t178747. * CSmH; MRu.

2400. *Proceedings at the Catholic meeting of Dublin, duly convened on Wednesday, October 31, 1792, at the Exhibition-Room, Exchequer-Street. With the letter of the corporation of Dublin, to the Protestants of Ireland.* Dublin. 1792. 8°. [4], 72 p. Printed by: Fitzpatrick, H. ESTC t087737. * BFq; C; CaOHM; CLU-S/C; CSmH; D; Dt; Du; Gi; ICR; IU; KU-S; L; Lhe; Lhl; MChB; Mil; MiU; MY; PP; PPL; PSt; RPB.

2401. *The proceedings of a very numerous general meeting of the Roman Catholics assembled at the Exhibition Room, Exchequer-Street, Dublin on Monday, the 31st of October, 1792, together with their declaration.* Cork. 1792. 8°. 55, [1] p. Printed by: Flyn, W. ESTC t208890. * Di; MY.

2402. *Proceedings of the general committee of the Catholics of Ireland, which met on Tuesday April 16, and finally dissolved on Thursday April 25, 1793.* Dublin. 8°. [2], 12 p. Printed by: Fitzpatrick, H. ESTC t087740. * C; CLU-S/C; CSmH; D; Gi; KU-S; L; Mil; MRu; MY; RPB.

2403. *Proofs and a chain of principles of religion.* London. 1798. 8°. [3], 4-23, [1] p. Sold by: Booker, E. * ECW.

2404. *Proposals for opening a subscription in favour of an asylum to receive poor young maids, destitute of places; for preserving their virtue and innocence, 'till proper places can be procured for them.* [1770]. fol. s.s. ESTC t211616. * L; WDA.

> Recommended by Richard Challoner. 'Subscriptions will be taken in by Messrs. Wright and Son, bankers in Covent Garden; or by Mr. James Butler ... or Mrs Carpue'.

2405. *Proposals for printing by subscription; A daily exercise of the devout Christian. Publish'd by T.V. monk of the holy order of St. Benedict.* Wigan. [1786]. 8°. [2] p. Printed by: Bancks, W. * DowA.

> The subscriptions were taken in by William Bancks, printer and bookseller in Wigan. The book does not seem to have been printed. The initials 'T.V.' refer to Thomas Vincent Sadler.

2406. *Prospectus of the plan of education for the Catholic college at Oscott.* Birmingham. [1794]. fol. 4 p. Printed by: Swinney & Collins. * BAA; Cli.

> Signed and dated 'J. Bew, president; T. Potts, vice-president ... October 1794'. The title occurs after three short introductory paragraphs, beginning 'In the month of November last'. See also no. 2297.

2407. *The protest of the English Jesuits, at Saint Omer, upon their being* *deprived of their college.* [London?]. [1762]. fol. s.s. ESTC t085906. * BAA; L; Sto; TxU; UshA; WDA.

>On 7 Sept. 1762 the Jesuits had been expelled from France. The letter is dated September 30, 1762, and signed by Thomas Lawson.

2408. *The psalms of David, tanslated [sic] from the Vulgat.* 2nd ed. [St. Germain en Laye]. 1704. 12°. [10], 357, [1] p. Printed by: [Weston, W.]. ESTC t107532. * Cha; E; L; NN; O; TH; Yb.

>The first ed. was published in 1700 (Clancy nos 809, 18). Translated by J. Caryl. D & M 880 and 881 (D & M distinguish between two states of tp).

2409. *Les psaumes de David, traduction nouvelle, avec des notes tirées des pères ... par un ecclesiastique du diocèse d'Avranches.* 2nd ed. London. 1798. 8°. [1], xix, 654, [2] p. Printed by: Boussonnier, Ph. le. * DoA; Osc.

2410. *Pseautier de David, avec les cantiques à l'usage des ecoles.* Montreal. 1782. 16°. xvi, 304 p. Published by: Mesplet, F. * CaOLU; CaQMS; RPJ.

2411. Pulleine, James. *An teagasg criosdaidhe angoidhleig.* Anon. [Dublin?]. 1748. 12°. 36 p. ESTC t086868. * L.

>Pages 34-6 contain 'Brief rules for reading this little book, which will also serve for any other in the "Irish tongue"'.

2412. Pulleine, James. *An teagasg criosdaidhe angoidhleig.* [Dublin?]. 1782. 12°. 36 p. ESTC t217551. * D.

2413. *Pursuant to a resolution entered into by the Cisalpine Club, at their meeting on the 13th of April last ... respecting the authenticity of the protestation lodged at the Museum.* [London]. [1795]. 4°. 4 p. ESTC t147075. * Cli; L.

>This report was 'presented to the Cisalpine Club, on the 10th of February 1795' (p. 4); the protestation is that presented by the Committee of English Catholics. See also nos 1880 and 2306.

2414. Quesnel, Pasquier. *Moral reflections upon the gospel of St. John ... Translated from the French [Reflexions morales sur l'evangile selon Saint Jean].* [London?]. 1709. 12°. [2], 459, [9] p. ESTC t133132. * ECW; L; O; Osc.

>According to Kirk (p. 215) translated by Thomas Southcote O.S.B., but see also Scott, p. 251, note 457, for a discussion of Southcote's involvement. See also note to no. 2417.

2415. Quesnel, Pasquier. *Moral reflections upon the gospel of St. Luke ... Translated from the French [Reflexions morales sur l'evangile selon Saint Luke].* [London?]. 1707. 12°. 454, [10] p. ESTC t133133. * L; Ldw; O; Osc; Sco; Ush.

>Kirk (p. 235) gives Francis Thwaites as translator/editor. Sco has 16 preliminary pages. See also next items.

2416. Quesnel, Pasquier. *Moral reflections upon the gospel of St. Mark ... Translated from the French. By F.T. [Reflexions morales sur l'evangile selon Saint Marc].* [London]. 1707. 12°. 3-251, [13] p. ESTC t218363. * Amp; NcD; NN; O.

>'F.T.' is Francis Thwaites.

2417. Quesnel, Pasquier. *Moral reflections upon the gospel of St. Matthew ...*

Translated from the French. By T.W. [Reflexions morales sur l'evangile de Saint Matthieu]. London. 1706. 12°. [24], 421, [1] p. ESTC t170142. * Do; Lhe; Ush.

> 'T.W.' is T. Whittenhall, who started the translation of Quesnel's *Moral reflections*. On his death the work was continued by his nephew Francis Thwaites and perhaps by Thomas Southcote. Do is bound in 2 vols.

2418. Quesnel, Pasquier. *Moral reflections upon the gospel of St. Matthew ... Translated from the French. By T.W.* [London]. 1709. 12°. [34], 3-385 [i.e. 421], [1] p. ESTC t118257. * GEU-T; L; O.

2419. *The quintessence of controversy; or a short and compendious treatise concerning the perpetuity, infallibility, unity, and authority of the church ... Written originally in French by G.T.D.M. Permissu superiorum.* London [Dublin?]. 1720. 12°. vi, 180 p. ESTC n021934. * CLU-C; FLK; IDA; MY; O.

> According to M. Pollard (personal communication) almost certainly printed at Dublin.

2420. Ramsay, Andrew Michael. *The life of François de Salignac de la Motte Fenelon [Histoire de la vie de F. de Salignac de la Motte Fénelon].* Dublin. 1771. 12°. 151, [5] p. Printed by: Hoey, J. ESTC t062650. * D; FLK; L.

> With 4 pages of adverts. There are other, non-R.C., 18th century eds from 1723 onwards and Ramsay was the author of many other works, such as the popular *The travels of Cyrus* which are outside the terms of our bibliography.

2421. Rayment, Benedict. *A discourse delivered in the Catholic chapel at Lartington on Wednesday, 12th March, 1800, being the day appointed for the general fast.* London. 1800. 8°. 24 p. Printed by: Brown, R. Sold by: West; Hughes; Debrett; Keating; Booker. ESTC t208663. * MY; Osc; Ush.

> The imprint states 'printed by Brown, for the executors of the late Mr J.P. Coghlan'.

2422. *The real presence as it is held by the Roman Catholicks demonstrated, to be neither contrary to reason, nor the evidence of the senses upon any principles of knowledge, with the notions of Mr. Locke thereon, considered and refuted.* Dublin. 1751. 8°. 31, [1] p. ESTC t179936. * MY; O; SIR.

2423. Redford, Sebastian. *An important enquiry; or, the nature of a church reformation fully considered: wherein is shewn, from scripture, reason and antiquity, that the late pretended reformation was groundless in the attempt, and defective in the execution.* London. 1751. 8°. xxxix, [1], 407, [1] p. ESTC t064625. * CLU-C; Do; DoA; E; ECW (imp.); Gi; KU-S; L; Lfa; Lhe; Osc; Sal; StD; TLP; Ush; Yb.

> Do and Gi have 7 additional pages containing contents. Lhe has 2 extra pages.

2424. Redford, Sebastian. *An important inquiry; or, the nature of a church reformation fully considered.* 2nd ed. Anon. London. 1758. 8°. xxxviii, 412, [4] p. ESTC t064626. * AWn; CLU; CLU-C; Do; E; ECW; ICN; L; Lfa; Lhe; MRu; MWH; O; StD; TLP; UGL; Ush; Yb.

2425. Redford, Sebastian. *The life of St. Mary of Egypt. The example and model of a true penitent.* Anon. Liverpool. 1755. 8°. [2], 74, [4] p. Printed by: Sadler,

J. Published by: Sadler, J. Sold by: Sadler, J. ESTC t096329. * CSmH; DMR; L; Lfa; Lhe; Yb.

> Sommervogel (Sup. 1911-30, p. 733) and Gillow attributed to Sebastian Redford. See also next item. Yb has [12], 74, [10] p.

2426. Redford, Sebastian. *The life of St. Mary of Egypt. The example and model of a true penitent.* Liverpool. 1755. 8°. 68, [2] p. Printed by: Sadler, J. Published by: Sadler, J. Sold by: Sadler, J. ESTC n033591. * Ct; TxU.

2427. Reeve, Joseph. *Practical discourses upon the perfections and wonderful works of God.* Exeter. 1788. 8°. [2], v, [1], 336 p. Printed by: Thorn, E.; Coghlan, J.P. Sold by: Thorn, E.; Coghlan, J.P. ESTC t109765. * EXp; L; Lhe; Yb.

> Reeve's poetical works have not been included since they are not specifically R.C.

2428. Reeve, Joseph. *Practical discourses, upon the perfections and wonderful works of God.* 2nd ed. 2 vols. Exeter. 1793. 12°. [2], v, [1], 358; [4], 362 p. Printed by: Trewman, R. and Son. Sold by: Trewman, R. and Son; Coghlan, J.P. ESTC t109766. * Do; E; L; Lfa; Lhe; O; Osc; Sal; Stan; TxU; Ush.

2429. Reeve, Joseph. *Practical discourses in two volumes. The first, upon the perfections and wonderful works of God: the second, upon the divinity and wonderful works of Jesus Christ.* 2 vols. [Dublin]. 1796. 8°. [2], vi, 262; [4], 265, [1] p. Printed by: Byrne, P. ESTC n020482. * FLK; MChB (vol.1); NjPT; NNUT; PPPrHi; ScCM; SIR; ViU.

2430. Reeve, Joseph. *A view of the oath tendered by the legislature to the Roman Catholics of England.* London. 1790. 8°. vii, [1], 47, [1] p. Printed by: Coghlan, J.P. ESTC t174897. * DUc; ECW; ICN; Lfa; LfaA; Lhe; Lmh; O; Osc; P; Ush.

> See also Milner's *Certain considerations* (no. 1866).

2431. *Reflections on eternity, which may contribute to mutual concord and charity; and to our present and future happiness.* [London?]. [1790?]. 8°. 12 p. ESTC t014218. * L.

> Attributed by Gillow (IV, 344) to Simon Lucas; Gillow gives: '[Newport, 1796]'.

2432. *Reflections on the oaths which are tendered to the subject in this country.* London. 1787. 8°. [4], 87, [1] p. Published by: Debrett, J. * Ush.

2433. *Reflections on the prerogatives, power and protection of Saint Joseph ... with several devotions to the said ... patriarch.* London. 1800. 8°. [4], 100 p. Printed by: Keating; Brown; Keating. ESTC t057188. * DoA; ICN; L; RPJCB.

> Dr D.M. Rogers (personal communication) suggests Paul de Barry as the author. See also under *Some reflections.*

2434. *Reflections on the prerogatives, power and protection of Saint Joseph ... with several devotions to the said ... patriarch.* London. 1800. 24°. 166, [2] p. Printed by: Keating; Brown; Keating. ESTC t107834. * L.

2435. *Réglement de la confrérie de l'adoration perpétuelle du s. sacrement, et de* *la bonne mort. Erigée dans l'eglise paroissiale de Ville-Marie, en l'Isle de Montréal, en Canada. Nouvelle édition revue.* [Montréal]. [1776]. 8°. 40 p. Printed by: Mesplet, F.; Berger, C. ESTC w006067. * CaBVaU; CaNSWA; CaOLU; CaOONL; CaOTU; CaQMBM; CaQMM; CaQMS; CaQQLa; CtY; DLC; MB; MH; MWA; NN; NNC; NNPM; PPRF; RPJCB.

2436. *Regulae observandae in Anglicanis missionibus ab apostolicis vicariis nec nona sacerdotibus missionariis saecularibus ac regularibus.* Rome. 1753. 37, [1] p. Published by: Congregatio de Propaganda Fidei. * DoA; Gi; LfaA; Osc; ScCR; UGL; Ush; UshA.

2437. *Regulae observandae in Anglicanis missionibus ab apostolicis vicariis nec nona sacerdotibus missionariis saecularibus ac regularibus.* Rome. 1753. 8°. 42, [2] p. Published by: Congregatio de Propaganda Fidei. * ECW; Lfa; UshA.
> Signed on page 42 'Cajetanus Amatus'. UshA may be a reprint printed in Durham.

2438. Reilly, Hugh. *The impartial history of Ireland. Containing a summary account, of all the battles, sieges, rebellions, and massacres ... Likewise the case of the Roman Catholics of Ireland ... by the rever'd doctor Nary.* London repr. 1742. 12°. xii, 144 p. * Mil.
> A clearly Catholic view of Irish history, addressed to both R.C. and non-R.C. readers. The eds of *The impartial history* are compilations including such matters as 'The nobility and gentry of Ireland's remonstrance to King Charles II', the dying words of Oliver Plunket, and the civil and military articles of Limerick.

2439. Reilly, Hugh. *The impartial history of Ireland. Containing a summary account, of all the battles ... Ireland's remonstrance ... Likewise the case of the Roman Catholicks of Ireland ... by the rever'd doctor Nary.* London. 1744. 12°. x, 146 p. ESTC t154527. * C; D; Du.

2440. Reilly, Hugh. *The impartial history of Ireland. Containing a summary account, of all the battles ... Ireland's remonstrance ... Likewise the case of the Roman Catholicks of Ireland ... by the rever'd doctor Nary.* London. 1749. 12°. x, 146 p. ESTC n028785. * CSmH; Du.

2441. Reilly, Hugh. *The impartial history of Ireland, containing a summary account, of all the battles, sieges, rebellions and massacres ... In two parts ... To which is annexed ... Ireland's remonstrance.* London. 1754. 12°. viii, 122 p. ESTC t109170. * L.
> Imperfect, only; the text is from another unidentified ed.

2442. Reilly, Hugh. *The impartial history of Ireland, containing a summary account, of all the battles, sieges ... Likewise the case of the Roman Catholicks ... by the revd. doctor Nary.* London. 1762. 12°. 132 p. ESTC t204866. * D; Dp.

2443. Reilly, Hugh. *The impartial history of Ireland, containing a summary account, of all the battles, sieges ... Likewise the case of the Roman Catholicks ... by the revd. doctor Nary.* London. 1768. 12°. 132 p. ESTC t118835. * L.

2444. Reilly, Hugh. *The impartial history of Ireland ... In two parts ... To which are annexed the nobility and gentry of Ireland's remonstrance to King Charles the*

Second ... the celebrated speech of Edmund Burke. Dublin. 1782. 18°. 180 p. Printed by: Wogan, P. ESTC n061138. * Dk.

2445. Reilly, Hugh. *The impartial history of Ireland ... In two parts ... To which are annexed the nobility and gentry of Ireland's remonstrance to King Charles the Second.* Dublin. 1787. 12°. [3], iv-vii, 8-156 p. Printed by: Wogan, P. ESTC t109109. * L.

2446. Reilly, Hugh. *The impartial history of Ireland. Containing a summary account of all the battles ... To which are annexed the nobility and gentry of Ireland's remonstrance to King Charles the Second.* Dublin. 1792. 12°. 170, 75-82 p. Printed by: Wogan, P. ESTC t154528. * Dt (imp.).

2447. Reilly, Hugh. *The impartial history of Ireland, containing a summary account, of all the battles, sieges ... In two parts ... Likewise the case of the Roman Catholics ... The latter by the rev. Dr. Nary.* Limerick. [1800?]. 18°. 143, [1] p. Printed by: Goggin, W. ESTC t204853. * D.

2448. Reilly, Hugh. *The impartial history of Ireland. Containing a summary account of the battles, sieges, rebellions and massacres ... to which is annexed ... the case of the Roman Catholicks ... by doctor Nary.* London. viii, 9, [1], 168 p. * DLC.

2449. Reilly, Hugh. *Ireland's case briefly stated; or, a summary account. Of the most remarkable transactions in that kingdom since the Reformation ... To which is annex'd, the last speech ... of Oliver Plunket.* Anon. [Dublin?]. 1720. 12°. [12], 132, [20] p. ESTC t167001. * C; Di; Lhe; LVu; SCR; Ush.

In fact another ed. of *The impartial history of Ireland.* See also next item.

2450. Reilly, Hugh. *Ireland's case briefly stated; or, a summary account. Of the most remarkable transactions in that kingdom since the Reformation ... To which is annex'd, the last speech ... of Oliver Plunket.* Anon. [London?]. 1720. 12°. [12], 106 [in fact 132], [20] p. ESTC t146964. * CSmH; D; DFo; E; FLK; L; Lhe.

2451. *A relation of a conference before his majesty, and the Earl of Rochester ... concerning the real presence and transubstantiation Nov. 30. 1686. Now publish'd to obviate the false account given thereof by Laurence Echard.* [London?]. 1722. 8°. [12], 60 p. ESTC t103452. * Do; ECW; ICN; L; Lhe; O; Ob; Osc; Ot.

In the conference the Protestant side was represented by William Jane and Simon Patrick, and the Catholic side by Bonaventure Giffard and Thomas Godden. Echard's *History of England* came out in 3 vols between 1707 and 1718.

2452. *Religious solitude. The work of an Italian father of the order of the Capucines. Translated from the Flemish. With some additions, out of other authors.* Bruges. 1792. 12°. 333, [3] p. Printed by: Moor, C. de & Son. ESTC t082755. * CLU-C; ECB; ECW; L; Yb.

2453. *Remarks on a paper lately publish'd, by a gentleman of the law, concerning several claims made to a late deceased gentleman's personal estate.* [London?]. [1745?]. 4°. iv, [1], 6-35, [1] p. ESTC t074427. * CtY; L; Lfa;

LfaA; Lhe; NNU; Sto.

Attributed by ESTC to Philip Carteret. The case concerns the right of religious to inherit estates. It specifically refers to the case of Gilbert Talbot, 13th Earl of Shrewsbury (i.e. Father Talbot or Grey, S.J.). See also other contributions to this debate, such as nos 61-63, 103, 763, 2455 and 2616.

2454. René, Jean. *Translation of the Bishop of Boulogne's pastoral letter on the spiritual authority; and the new civil constitution of the clergy, as decreed by the National Assembly of France.* Dublin. 1791. 8°. [4], 34 p. Printed by: Wogan, P. ESTC t208261. * MY.

Dated 'Boulogne, October 24, 1790'.

2455. *A reply in vindication of Mr. T[albo]t's relations. Reply to a paper lately publish'd, which is called An answer to another.* 4°. 18 p. * Lfa; LfaA.

This work deals with the legal right of religious to inherit estates (see also the note to no. 2453. LfaA suggests Bishop Stonor as author.

2456. *The report of a committee appointed by the Society of United Irishmen of Dublin, 'To enquire and report the popery laws enacted in this realm' ... To which is prefixed an introduction.* 2nd ed. Dublin. 1792. 8°. x, 5-44 p. Published by: Byrne, P. ESTC t044704. * C; C-S; CtY; D; Du; FLK; FU; IU; L; Lhl; MChB; MY; NjR; O; PP; RP; Sto.

One of the aims of this society, founded in 1791, was the propagation of Catholic emancipation. Many of its reports, addresses and proceedings deal with this topic, explicitly or implicitly, yet these have not been included in our list, since - strictly speaking - they do not come within the terms of our definition. We do include the 2nd ed. of the *Report* and the London reprint (no. 1418) because of their explicitly R.C. preliminary material.

2457. *Report of debates in the House of Commons of Ireland, session 1796-7, on the following important topics: Mr. Grattan's amendment on the address to his majesty on opening the session.* Dublin. 1797. 8°. [2], 240 p. Printed by: Fitzpatrick, H. Published by: Byrne, P.; Moore, J.; Fitzpatrick, H. ESTC t072014. * CSmH; D; Du; IU; L; MY; RP.

See the note to no. 1344.

2458. *The report of the committee appointed by the Society of the United Irishmen of Dublin, to enquire into, and report the popery laws in force in that kingdom. To which is prefixed, the declaration of the Roman Catholics of Ireland, with a petition intended to have been presented to Parliament by Mr. O'Hara in February, 1792.* London. 1792. 8°. xv, [1], 88 p. Published by: Debrett, J. ESTC n026421. * BMu; MChB; MRu.

First published in 1792 (see no. 2456).

2459. *A report of the debate which took place at a general meeting of the Roman Catholics of the city of Dublin, held ... Friday, March 23, 1792.* Dublin. 1792. 8°. 23, [1] p. Printed by: Byrne, P. ESTC t044727. * C; CLU-C; CSmH; D; Du; FLK; FU; ICR; IU; L; Lhl; LONu; MChB; MY; NcD; NN; O; PHi; PPL; RP; Sto.

Signed 'Edward Byrne, chairman. Richard McCormick, secretary on behalf of the general committee of the Catholics of Ireland'.

2460. *A report of the debates in both Houses of the Parliament of Ireland, on the Roman Catholic Bill, passed in the session of 1792.* Dublin. 1792. 8°. [2], v, [1], 253, [3] p. Printed by: Fitzpatrick, H. Published by: M'Donnell, T.; Byrne, P.; Moore, J. ESTC n026397. * C; D; Di; Dt; Du; MChB; Mil; MRu; MY; O; SCR.

> The book includes a 2-page list of pamphlets for and against Catholic emancipation. Obviously the debates were of crucial importance to the Catholic community and many reports of these debates were published in the 1790s (for instance the three 1795 *Reports* printed by J. Chambers). We include only the publications with a clearly R.C. involvement. In the present case the editorial preface makes clear that the book was expressly published in the interest of three million R.C. Irishmen. See also no. 2568.

2461. *[Report of the debates on the Roman Catholic bill &c.]* [Dublin?]. [1793?]. [xiii]-xxi, 360 p. * IU (-tp, imp.).

> The R.C. nature of this book is suggested by the fact that on pp. xiii-xxvi the names are given of the members of the general committee of the Catholics of Ireland.

2462. *The resolution of the sacred congregation of bishops and regulars, bearing date Jan. 30th, 1722 N.S.* Anon. [1722]. fol. 5, [1] p. * Sto.

> The authors, who do not mention their names, are a number of English Benedictine monks, who protest against the resolution. Dated 'March 2, 1721, O.S.'. For the background to this resolution see Scott, pp. 51-7.

2463. Reuter, Friedrich Caesar. *Katechetischer Unterricht fur die christl. katholische Jugend.* [Baltimore]. 1797. [6], 112 p. Printed by: Saur, S. Published by: Author. ESTC w015914. * DGU-W; MdW.

> Parsons (no. 184) notes that Reuter was a pastor in Baltimore and that he rebelled against Bishop Carroll.

2464. *A review of the strictures on the declaration of the Catholic Society.* Dublin. 1792. 8°. [2], 37, [1] p. ESTC n013350. * C; CSmH; D; Dt; KU-S; PP; Sto; TxU.

> A reply to the anti-Catholic *Strictures on the declaration of the Society instituted for the purpose of promoting unanimity amongst Irishmen* (1791).

2465. Ribadeneira, Pedro de. *The life, death, and passion of our Lord Jesus Christ.* Paris. 1701. 8°. 288 p. * CAL.

> According to the Approbation given at St. Omers in 1665 this is a translation of a work by Pedro de Ribadeneira, S.J. (cf. Bevan, Summer 1986, no. 20).

2466. Ribadeneira, Pedro de. *The life, death and passion, of our Lord and Saviour Jesus Christ.* Dublin. 1797. 12°. vi, 7-287, [1] p. Printed by: Cross, R. * SIR.

2467. Ribadeneira, Pedro de. *The lives of saints, with other feasts of the year, according to the Roman calendar. Written in Spanish by the rev. Father Peter Ribadeneira [Flos sanctorum o libro de las vidas de los santos].* 2 vols. 2nd ed. London. 1730. fol. [16], 456; [4], 588 p. Printed by: B.S. ESTC t141599. * AR; BMp; CaOTMC; CaOTU; CLU-C; DCU; DFo; DMR; DoA; E; ECR; ECW; GEU-T; ICN; L; Lfa; Lhe; NN; NSPM; Pm; TLP; WIW; Ush; Yb.

Tp states 'Translated into English by W.P. Esq.' Ush has 2 vols in one.

2468. Ribadeneira, Pedro de. *The lives of saints, with other feasts of the year, according to the Roman calendar. Written in Spanish by the rev. Father Peter Ribadeneira.* 3rd ed. 2 vols. Dublin. 1763. fol. Printed by: Gorman, B. Published by: Gorman, B. ESTC t171601. * Pci.

2469. Rivers, William Penketh. *River's manual: or, pastoral instructions upon the creed, commandments, sacraments, Lord's prayer, &c collected from the holy scriptures ... and approved writers.* Wigan. 1782. 8°. xvi, 488 p. Printed by: Ferguson, R. ESTC t169249. * NSPM; Ush.
> Ush has [1], v, 6-12, xiii-xvii, 18-19, xx-xxvi, 488 p.

2470. Rivers, William Penketh. *River's manuel [sic]; or, pastoral instructions upon the creed, commandments, sacraments, Lord's prayer, etc. collected from the holy scriptures ... and approved writers.* Liverpool. 1799. 8°. 24, 506, 6 p. Printed by: Ferguson and Sadler. ESTC t169251. * LVp; Ush.

2471. Robertson, F.J. *The Roman liturgy, and devout Catholic's companion.* 4 vols. Edinburgh. 1792. 12°. Printed by: Mundell & Son. Published by: Author. ESTC t202558. * Cha; DoA; E; Gi.
> Most sets are incomplete. Gi has 2 parts, DoA only one and of the 5 copies in E only 2 are complete.

2472. Romain, M. *L'Evangile médité, donné au peuple en forme d'instructions.* London. 1797. 8°. 194, [4] p. Printed by: Boussonnier, Ph. le. * CAL; Osc.
> Osc notes that 'The author had been a priest of the diocese of Rouen, and was now "Superieur actuel de la maison commune de Paddington Green"'. In the book the author's address is given as '3 Paddington Green'.

2473. *The Roman Catholic primer, to which is added, with approbation, a short abridgment of Christian doctrine, with a short daily exercise ... from the French catechism of John Joseph Languet.* Philadelphia. 1786. Printed by: Spotswood, W. Sold by: Spotswood, W. Evans 19967.

2474. *A Roman Catholic's address to Parliament. With an appendix, containing, the address of the Roman Catholics of Great Britain, to his majesty; and, the act lately passed in the British Parliament.* Dublin repr. [London]. 1778. 8°. [2], 46 p. Published by: Wogan; Bean; Pike. ESTC t209503. * Di; MY.

2475. *A Roman Catholic's address to the Lords and Commons in this present Parliament assembled.* London. 1778. 8°. [2], 48 p. Printed by: Kiernan, C. * ECW; Map; Ush.

2476. *The Roman gradual on the Gregorian notes. Containing the masses for all Sundays throughout the year.* [London?]. 1737. 8°. 117, [1] p. ESTC t181230. * O.

2477. *The Roman liturgy for Sundays and holidays; containing the ordinary, and masses proper for every day of obligation. To which is annexed A short morning and evening exercise.* Edinburgh. 1789. 8°. v, [1], 323, [1] p. Printed by: Mundell & Son. Published by: Downie, D. ESTC t202488. * E.
> With one page of Downie adverts ('orders for this and all other Catholic books

answered by David Downie, Parliament Square, Edinburgh').

2478. *The Roman missal in Latin and English, arranged for the use of the laity.* 4 vols. [London]. 1737-1738. 12°. [8], 170, xxxvi, 86, clxxx; [6], 171-404, xxxvi, 32, clx; [8], 405-625, [1], xxxvi, 56, clxxii; [12], 140, xxxvi, 220, clxxii p. Printed by: [Meighan, T.]. ESTC t202491. * Du; E; Gi (vol. 1); ICN; Osc (vols 1, 2, 4); TH (vol. 4); TxU; Ush (vol. 1).

> Osc suggests William Crathorne as editor. Gillow (I,, 587) suggests Gother and Crathorne as editors.

Roper, William. See Bayly, Thomas.

2479. Roquette, Henri Emmanuel de. *A funeral oration upon the death of the most high, most mighty, most excellent, and most religious prince, James the Second [Oraison funèbre de ... Jacques II., Roy de la Grand' Bretagne].* [London]. 1703. 4°. [2], 40 p. ESTC t071027. * CLU-C; Csj; CSmH; DFo; Do; E; GEU-T; L; MB; MdBJ-P.

2480. Roquette, Henri Emmanuel de. *A funeral oration upon the death of the most high, most mighty, most excellent, and most religious prince, James the Second ... spoken the 19th day of September, 1702.* 2nd ed. [London]. 1703. 4°. [8], 40 p. ESTC t071028. * CAL; CSmH; DFo; DMR; InU-Li; L; MB; O.

> Ten years later this work was republished by the booksellers of London and Westminster as part of the contemporary political controversy (ESTC t167810).

2481. *The royal edict, given at Versailles, in November, 1787. For granting toleration throughout his most Christian majesty's dominions, to dissenters from the established church.* London. 1788. 8°. [2], 26 p. Printed by: Coghlan, J.P. ESTC t175819. * O; Oe.

2482. *The rule of the religious of the immaculate conception of our Blessed Lady.* [1721]. 12°. 80 p. * DoA.

> Bound with the 1721 *Constitutions* (no. 778) of the English nuns of the Immaculate Conception of our Blessed Lady in Paris.

2483. *Rules and orders to be observed by the Baltimore Benevolent Society, established in order to raise a fund for the mutual relief of the members thereof, in case of sickness or infirmity [sic], and for any other charitable purposes, to which the members of the said society may hereafter agree.* Baltimore. 1796. 12°. 15, [1] p. Printed by: Sower, S. ESTC w001515. * DCU; InNd.

> The society was under the patronage of the Bishop of Baltimore and the rector of St. Peter's Church, Baltimore.

2484. *Rules of the charitable society, for educating and cloathing poor Catholic children, in the Wapping district, instituted A.D. 1778 with the approbation, and under the patronage of the late Bishop Talbot.* London. 1799. 12°. 12 p. Printed by: Keating, P. * WDA.

> On page 12, people interested in joining this society are requested to apply 'to any of the clergymen regularly officiating in Virginia-Street Chapel, Ratcliffe Highway'.

2485. *Rules of the charitable society. To the greater glory of God. Society for apprenticing poor girls, established July 26th, 1791.* [London]. [1791]. fol. s.s. *

2486. *Rules of the Society of Jesus.* St. Omers. 1717. 12°. 129, [3] p. Printed by: Beaussart. * DMR; LfaA.

2487. S., A. *The reconciler of religions: or, a brief decider of all controversies in matters of faith ... By A.S.* [London?]. 1711. 12°. 97, [3] p. ESTC t103648. * DoA; E; ECW; Gi; L; Lhe; Sal; TH.

Sadler, T.V. See Crowther, A.

2488. *S. Scholastica's office of devotion or her exercises of divine love ... Presented to the very reverend English Benedictine Dames of Our Blessed Lady's of consolation in Cambray. By Eupoimen.* 1718. 8°. 35, [1] p. * Stan.

2489. Saltmarsh, Edward. *An essay upon indulgences ... by E.S.* [Liège?]. 1714. 8°. [8], 116, [2] p. ESTC t182241. * Amp; CU-L; Dt; ECW; Gi; Lhe; O; UshL.

> 'E.S.' is Edward Saltmarsh, who was at Liège at the time; Gillow attributes the book to Edward Sherbourne. The last leaf is an errata leaf, beginning 'the printer being a stranger to English'.

2490. Sanders, Francis. *An abridgment of the life of James II. King of Great Britain, &c. Extracted from an English manuscript of the reverend Father Francis Sanders ... Done out of the French from the Paris edition, 1703 [Abregé de la vie de Jacques II].* London. 1704. 8°. [8], 192 p. Published by: Wilson, R. Sold by: The booksellers of London and Westminster. ESTC t100280. * C; CaOHM; CaQMM; CLU-C; Csj; CSmH; DFo; E; ECW; KU-S; L; LfaA; Llp; O; Oc; TAUa; TxU; WaPS; Yb.

> R.C. work, though from a neutral publisher. Approbation on p. 192 dated and signed 'Paris, the 13th of December, 1702 ... E. Renaudot'.

2491. *A satyr: shewing, the nature and proceedings of the Church of En......d &c.* [171-?]. 8°. 8 p. * O.

> A R.C. satire. Foxon S69.

2492. Scarisbrick, Edward. *The holy life of Lady Warner, Sister Clare of Jesus. In four books. To which is now added, an abridgement of the pious life of Elizabeth Warner, sister-in-law to Lady Warner ... By a Catholick gentleman.* Dublin. 1769. 12°. xii, 275, [1] p. Printed by: Kiernan, F. Published by: Kiernan, F. ESTC t167610. * C; FLK; Lhe; O; Ush.

> First published in 1691 as *The life of the Lady Warner.* Final page is an advert for Saint Augustine's *City of God* to be published by subscription.

2493. Scarisbrick, Edward. *Rules and instructions for the Sodality of the Immaculate Conception, of the most glorious and ever Virgin Mary, mother of God. With a short appendix, relating to the Second Congregation.* Anon. 1703. 8°. [16], 150p. ESTC t095192. * Do; ECW; Gi; L; Lfa; LO; O; TLP; Ush; UshL.

> UshL (ms note) attributes the book to Edward Scarisbrick, while a ms note in Do gives Francis Scarisbrick. The ESTC suggestion [Dublin?] seems very doubtful.

2494. *Scripture and antiquity in a collection of testimonies, concerning the* *doctrine of the church for the first five hundred years after Christ.* [London?]. 1748. 12°. x, 110, [4] p. ESTC t065898. * CAL; Do; ECW; L; Lhe; MRu; NNMan; O; TxU; Ush; Yb.

2495. Scupoli, Lorenzo. *The spiritual combat. Done into English by J.T. [Combattimento spirituale].* London. 1742. 18°. viii, 261, [1] p. Published by: Needham, F. Sold by: Needham, F. ESTC t103931. * Do; E; ECW; Gi; ICN; L; Stan; TxU; Ush.

>Written by Scupoli and translated into Spanish by Castaniza. According to Gillow 'J.T.' is Robert Pinkard, alias John Typper (see also next items). There are eds under non-R.C. auspices, such as the 1710 Samuel Keble ed.

2496. Scupoli, Lorenzo. *The spiritual combat. To which is added the peace of the soul and the happiness of the heart which dies to itself in order to live to God. Also, twelve advantages arising from the contemplation of death.* Dublin. 1748. 18°. iv, 5-235, [5] p. Published by: Kelly, I. * IDA.
>With 5 pages of Kelly adverts.

2497. Scupoli, Lorenzo. *The spiritual combat. To which is added, the peace of the soul ... Done into English by J.T.* Birmingham. 1769. 12°. [2], ii, 214 p. Printed by: Holliwell, T. ESTC t118997. * BB; BMp; C; DMR; Do; ECW; L; O; OrPU; Pm; SHp; Ush.

2498. Scupoli, Lorenzo. *The spiritual combat. To which is added, the peace of the soul, and the happiness of the heart which dies to itself in order to live to God.* Cork. 1772. 12°. v, [1], 7-285, [3] p. Printed by: Flyn, W. ESTC t082143. * L; SIR.

2499. Scupoli, Lorenzo. *The spiritual combat. To which is added, the peace of the soul, and the happiness of the heart, which dies to itself, in order to live to God.* 3rd ed. Dublin. 1782. 12°. iv, 6-208 p. Printed by: Hoey, P. * Lfa.
>The last 2 pages contain a number of approbations.

2500. Scupoli, Lorenzo. *The spiritual combat. To which is added, the peace of the soul, and the happiness of a heart which dies to itself in order to live to God. Done into English by J.T.* London. 1786. 8°. [4], 214 p. Printed by: Marmaduke, J. Sold by: Marmaduke, J. * DAE.

2501. Scupoli, Lorenzo. *The spiritual combat. To which is added the peace of the soul, thoughts on death, and of penitence.* 4th ed. London. 1788. 12°. vi, 312 p. Printed by: Coghlan, J.P. ESTC t061562. * CAL; DAE; Do (imp.); DoA; L.

2502. Scupoli, Lorenzo. *The spiritual combat. To which is added, the peace of the soul, and the happiness of the heart ... To which is also added. True wisdom: ... Done into English by J.T.* Anon. Waterford. 1792. 8°. 228 p. Printed by: Lord, T. ESTC t160301. * D; Gi.

2503. Scupoli, Lorenzo. *The spiritual combat. To which is added, the peace of the soul and the happines of the haert [sic] ... Also, twelve advantages arising from the contemplation of death.* Anon. Waterford. 1793. 8°. [8], 3-228, [2] p. Printed by: Lord, T. ESTC t160303. * D.
>With a list of subscribers.

2504. Scupoli, Lorenzo. *The spiritual combat. To which is added, the peace of the soul, thoughts on death, and of penitence.* 5th ed. London. 1797. 12°. 312 p. Printed by: Coghlan, J.P. * Do; ECW; Gi; Map; Sco; Vat.

2505. Scupoli, Lorenzo. *The spiritual combat. To which is added, the peace of the soul, and the happiness of the heart, which dies to itself in order to live to God ... Done into English by J.T.* 5th ed. Dublin. 1799. 12°. iv, 248 p. Printed by: Wogan, P. * IDA.

>   This is the second '5th' ed.

2506. *Seasonable reflections, humbly offered to the consideration of the legislature, by some Roman Catholics, of Ireland.* Dublin. [1771?]. 8°. 14, [2] p. Published by: Ewing, T. ESTC n021846. * C; MH-H (imp.).

>   Urging removal of disabilities for Roman Catholics. With a final advertisement leaf.

2507. *A second appeal to his grace the L...d P...e of all I...d, in vindication of the political principles of Roman Catholics, wherein, some matters of fact objected against them, are enquired into.* Dublin. 1758. 8°. 24 p. Printed by: Bowes, P. ESTC t172722. * D.

>   A sequel to nos 76 and 77. See also no. 2699.

2508. *The second part containing the holy mass in Latin and English; as also the mass for the dead in English. The vespers or evensong.* [London]. 1762. 18°. 318, [6] p. Published by: [Meighan, T.]. ESTC t123014. * L.

>   Also published as the second part of the 1765 *Manual* (no. 1790). For a similar case see no. 2847. With 6 pages of Meighan adverts.

2509. *A seekers request. In a letter to Catholick priests, and Protestant ministers, for satisfying his conscience in the truth of what he ought to believe of the Lord's supper.* Dublin. 1736. 8°. 8 p. ESTC t175384. * CtY; D.

>   The author pretends to be impartial, but is in fact an advocate of the R.C. position. See also Clancy nos 878 and 879.

2510. Segneri, Paolo. *The devout client of Mary instructed in the motives and means how to honour and serve her, in the best manner. Written in Italian ... and translated into English by N.N. [Il devoto di Maria].* [Douai?]. 1724. 12°. 340, [4] p. ESTC t105828. * L; LOU; Map; Osc; Yb.

>   According to Sommervogel (VI, 906) the translator was Thomas Percy Plowden S.J. Walsh (p. 53) adds that the 45-page 'Apology for the author' was written by Plowden.

2511. Segneri, Paolo. *The knowledge of ones self: with practical thoughts of humility. Divided into meditations for every day in the week. Written in Italian by ... Paul Segnery ... Now done from the French [Lo specchio che non inganna].* [London?]. 1714. 24°. [14], 105, [1] p. ESTC t192759. * Gi; O.

2512. Segneri, Paolo. *The penitent instructed. Written in Italian by the R.F. Paul Segneri ... Done into English [Il penitente instruito a ben confessarsi].* London. 1703. 8°. [6], 190 p. ESTC n020772. * CLU-C; ECW: Lhe; LO; Map; O; UGL; Ush; Yb.

2513. Segneri, Paolo. *True humility, or the undeceiving mirror, containing the* *theory and practice of self knowledge, divided into seven considerations, for every day of the week ... translated into English by J.R. [Lo specchio che non inganna].* Antwerp. 1711. 12°. iv-xiii, 148 p. * P.

2514. Segneri, Paolo. *The true looking-glass or the theory, and practice of the knowledge of ones self.* St. Omers. 1710. 18°. 122 p. * Lfa.

2515. Segneri, Paolo. *True wisdom: or, considerations for every day of the week. Written in Italian ... with an appendix of what is necessary for a good confession and communion [Vera sapienza].* 1716. 24°. [8], 112 p. * Ush.

2516. Segneri, Paolo. *True wisdom: or, considerations for every day of the week ... With an appendix of what is necessary for a good confession and communion.* [London?]. 1722. 24°. [8], 112 p. ESTC t118472. * L.
  Possibly printed on the Continent.

2517. Segneri, Paolo. *True wisdom: or, considerations for every day of the week.* London. 1753. 24°. x, 11-119, [1] p. Published by: Meighan, T. * ECW.
  With one page of Meighan adverts.

2518. Segneri, Paolo. *True wisdom: or, considerations for every day of the week ... With an appendix of what's necessary for a good confession and communion.* York. 1792. 12°. vi, [3], 10-108 p. * ECB; Ush; Yb.

2519. Segneri, Paolo. *True wisdom: or, considerations for every day of the week ... With an appendix of what is necessary for a good confession and communion.* Cork. 1795. 12°. xx, 178 p. Printed by: Connor, J. ESTC t185878. * D; FLK.
  English tp and Irish tp, 'Eagna fhirinneach'. Parallel text in English and Irish. With a list of subscribers. Cargill Cole, Appendix I, mentions a 1795 Dublin ed. published by subscription; Dix mentions a 1736 English/Irish ed.

2520. Segneri, Paolo. *True wisdom: or, considerations for every day of the week ... with an appendix of what is necessary for a good confession and communion.* Dublin. 1798. 24°. vii, [2], 10-127, [1] p. Printed by: Cross, R. * Stan.

2521. Segneri, Paolo. *True wisdom: or, considerations for every day of the week ... with an appendix of what is necessary for a good confession and communion.* [London]. 24°. 119, [1] p. Printed by: [Meighan, T.]. Published by: [Meighan, T.]. * ECW.
  With one page of Meighan adverts.

2522. *A select collection of Catholick sermons, preach'd before their Majesties King James II. Mary Queen-consort, Catherine Queen-dowager, &c.* 2 vols. London. 1741. 8°. [8], 446; [8], 481, [1] p. ESTC t144507. * C; CLU-C; DFo; Do; DoA; E; ECW; Gi; Hen (vol. 2); Hor (vol. 1); ICN; L; Lfa; Lhe; Map; O; Osc (vol. 1); StD; TLP; TxU; Ush; Yb.
  This contains 28 sermons by various authors, such as Bishops Ellis and Giffard. Gillow (II, 164) also mentions a 2-vol. London 1772 ed.

2523. *A self-examination: with devout prayers, and meditations.* Preston. [1790?]. 12°. 23, [1] p. Printed by: Sergent, E. ESTC n021844. * CLU-S/C.

2524. *Sentimens unanimes de douze évêques réunis à Londres, et plusieurs fois assemblés pour délibérer sur le présent objet.* [London?]. [1796]. 8°. 6 p. ESTC t116510. * L.

Dated 'Septembre 1796'. It deals with the persecution of the Catholics in France. Possibly printed on the Continent.

2525. *Sentiment de m. l'Evêque de Troyes, résidant à Londres, sur la légitimité de la promesse de fidélité, ou réponse à un écrit intitulé: Véritable état de la question de la promesse de fidélité à la constitution, demandée aux prêtres.* London. 1800. 8°. [2], 120, [2] p. Published by: L'Homme, L. Sold by: Le Clere (Paris). ESTC n036376. * MH.

With a final advertisement leaf. A reply to a pamphlet by Henri Benoit Jules de Bethisy de Mézières, Bishop of Uzès. See also no. 177.

2526. Sergeant, John. *An abstract of the transactions relating to the English secular clergy.* [London]. [1706]. 8°. viii, 96 p. * Osc.

This work was based on materials collected by John Ward for a history of the Chapter (Gillow V, 497). Sergeant gives the history of the strife between the regular and the secular clergy.

2527. Sergeant, John. *Of good intentions. By J.S.* London. 1702. 12°. [48], 332, [2] p. ESTC t122842. * CLU-C; Csj; Do; E; ECW; Gi; L; Lfa; Map; Stan; Ush.

2528. Sergeant, John. *Transnatural philosophy, treating of the essences and operations of all beings whatever. Particularly of the essence of man ... By J.S.* 2nd ed. London. 1706. 8°. [4], 25 [i.e. 27], [1] p. Published by: Author. Sold by: Keble, S.; Browne, D.; Roper, A.; Strahan, G. ESTC t027199. * L.

Although the booksellers are neutral, the nature of the book, which sets out to refute the tenets of atheists, deists and socinians, is clearly R.C.

2529. Sergeant, John. *A treatise plainly shewing the only religion that is truly conformable to the express word of God. By J.S.* [London?]. 1702. 8°. 226, [6] p. ESTC n053370. * NjP.

2530. Sergeant, John. *A treatise, which clearly sheweth the only religion; that is truly conformable to the express word of God. By J.S.* 6th ed. London. 1733. 12°. 174, 6 p. ESTC t208865. * Amp; E; L.

2531. *Several religious ladies from France ... propose ... to receive a certain number of children with a view to fulfill those duties to which they have been consecrated.* [London]. [1795]. s.s. Printed by: Coghlan, J.P. * Cli; LANre.

Prospectus of a school proposed to be opened in the London district. LANre has a ms list of subscriptions.

2532. Sharp, John Chrysostom Gregory. *The Catholic church cleared from the charge of corruption and novelty. A sermon occasioned by the late lecture against popery at Salters-Hall ... By the late reverend Mr. John Gunston.* London. 1736. 8°. iv, 22, [2] p. ESTC t120180. * L; Lhe.

John Gunston was an alias of Dr. Sharp, who became a Roman Catholic in 1715; 'the late lecture' refers to *Popery the great corruption of Christianity* by John Barker. Sharp was one of the chief Catholic participants in the debates with Anglicans and dissenters in London in the mid 1730s (see the several eds of *Two conferences held* listed in ESTC). Sharp was probably also the author of *The charter of the kingdom of Christ*, a generally Christian work, sometimes also attributed to the Anglican army chaplain, John Sharp. The *Charter* was part of the Bangorian controversy.

2533. Sharrock, Gregory William. *Gregory William, Bishop of Telmessus, vic. ap. &c. To all the faithful, clergy and laity of the western district. Dearly beloved brethren. Dreadful are the calamities.* [Bath]. [1798]. fol. s.s. * LANre; WDA.

Dated and signed 'Bath, April 26, 1798 Gregory William Telmessen'.

2534. Sharrock, Gregory William. *To all the faithful, clergy and laity, in the western district. We every day hear of the horrors.* [Bath]. [1799]. 3, [1] p. * DowA.

Dated 'Bath, January 18th 1799'.

2535. *A short abridgement of the rules of the gospel. Intended for the benefit of those who are either too much occupied or too slothful to read Mr. Gother's rules at large.* London. 1784. 12°. 43, [1] p. Printed by: Coghlan, J.P. * ECW.

2536. *A short abridgment of Christian doctrine. Publish'd with allowance.* [Glasgow?]. 1728. 12°. 24 p. ESTC t123981. * E; L.

An elementary Catholic catechism. For *Short abridgment* see also Jean Joseph Languet.

2537. *A short abridgment of Christian doctrine; for the instruction of beginners.* 1745. 12°. 16 p. * DoA.

See Pickering for the relationship between this work and Turberville's *An abridgement of Christian doctrine.*

2538. *A short abridgment of Christian doctrine. Newly revised. To which is added, a short daily exercise ... With approbation.* 7th ed. [Norwich]. [1767]. 12°. 24 p. Published by: Loyall, W. ESTC t218989. * ZWTU.

A Roman Catholic catechism. Imprint from colophon, which reads: 'Printed for W. Loyall in the year, 1767'.

2539. *A short abridgement fo [sic] Christian doctrine.* [Mexico]. [1787?]. 8°. 41 p. * NN; RPJCB.

NUC notes that this is the only book known to have been printed in English in Mexico during the Spanish domination. There are 2 preliminary pages in Spanish in which the 'Inquisidores apostolicos' recommend the work.

2540. *A short account of the declaration, given by the Chinese emperour Kam Hi, in the year 1700 [Brevis relatio eorum quae spectant ad declarationem Sinarum imperatoris].* London. 1703. 8°. [28], 71, [1] p. ESTC t139133. * DoA; E; Hen; ICN; ICU; L; Lhe; NCp; NIC; O; Sto; Yb.

This is a defence of the Jesuits in the Chinese rites controversy. The book is signed at the end by Anthony Perkins S.J. and eight others.

2541. *A short account of the public prayers in the Spanish chapel for his holiness Pope Pius VI. on the 14th of May, 1798.* [London?]. [1798]. 8°. 10 p. ESTC t196296. * ECW; O.

2542. *A short and daily exercise for the suffering souls in purgatory: to which is added a prayer for those who are in the agony of death.* London. 1789. 8°. 4 p. Printed by: Coghlan, J.P. * Yb.

Bound with no. 903.

2543. *A short and daily exercise for the suffering souls in purgatory: to which is added a prayer for those who are in the agony of death.* 8°. 4 p. * Ush.

2544. *A short & plain statement of facts.* Wolverhampton. 1798. 8°. 22 p. Printed by: Smart, J. ESTC n036570. * ECW; LfaA; MoU; Osc; Sto; WDA.
> A collection of 6 letters signed by J. Carter, J. Corne, Thomas Southworth, James Tusker, E. Eyre, John Roe and John Kirk, printed at the request of Bishop Berington. The last 2 pages contain extracts of letters by Bishop Berington.

2545. *A short catechism: by way of question and answer. For the use of children & ignorant people.* [London?]. 1709. 8°. 16 p. Printed by: George ... Son. ESTC t219554. * CYc; Ush.
> According to ESTC this catechism was perhaps printed on the Continent.

2546. *A short catechism, or instructions for beginners.* 1730. 12°. 60 p. * Ush.
> The 'Approbation' is signed 'H.E. [Edward Hawarden?] 4th of Dec. 1729'.

2547. *Short directions for those who are of the confraternity of the cord of St. Francis.* [1790?]. s.s. * BAA (imp.)
> Two lists of six directions and rules.

2548. *A short introduction to the Latine tongue.* Douai. 1726. 12°. 92 p. Printed by: Derbaix, C.L. ESTC t020945. * L.
> A grammar intended for the English College at Douai.

2549. *A short introduction to the Latin tongue first compiled for the use of the English College at Doway.* 17th ed. London. 1793. 8°. 90 p. Printed by: Coghlan, J.P. * DoA.
> Page 2 mentions the 2nd ed. of *Rudiments of English grammar* by Lewis Brittain, regent of the English College at Bornhem (ESTC t124558). Since the latter book seems to have been intended for the general market it is not included in our list. DoA bound up with no. 1121.

2550. *The short office of the Blessed Virgin Mary.* London. 1782. 15, [1] p. Published by: Booker, T. ESTC n047012. * CSmH.

2551. *A short, practical and easy method to perform well the ordinary and daily actions of a Christian life. Translated from the Latin.* London. 1764. 12°. 24 p. * NRAB; Ush.

2552. *[Short prayers recommended to be said when you visit the blessed and adorable sacrament].* [c.1790]. 18°. 24 p. * L (-tp).

2553. *A short treatise of the antiquity ... of the famous confraternity of our b. Lady of Mount Carmel. Commonly call'd the Scapular. To which is added, a brief relation of some notable miracles.* [Dublin?]. 1711. 12°. [10], 72, [2] p. Sold by: [Browne, T.]. ESTC t095185. * L.
> An early 19th c. ed. in FLK suggests the Carmelite George Loop as author. Cf. Loop's *The queen of heaven's livery* (no. 1680).

2554. *Short treatise of the antiquity ... of the famous confraternity of our Bl. Lady of Mt. Carmel, commonly called, the Scapular.* Dublin. 1755. 12°. ix,

10-124 p. Published by: Kelly, E. * Do.

2555. *A short treatise of the antiquity ... of the most famous and antient confraternity of our Blessed Lady of Mount Carmel, commonly called the Scapular ... Also, the office of the Blessed Virgin Mary.* London. 1796. 12°. 87, [1] p. Published by: Booker, E. ESTC t180952. * FP; O; Osc.

2556. *A short treatise of the antiquity ... of the famous confraternity of our B. Lady of Mount Carmel. Commonly called, the Scapular.* Dublin. 1799. 18°. [4], vii, [1], 96 p. Printed by: Wogan, P. ESTC t175605. * C; DMR; ECB.

2557. *A short treatise of the antiquity ... of the ... confraternity of our blessed Lady of Mount Carmel; commonly called, the Scapular.* Dublin. 12°. [5], vi-x, [1], 12-108 p. Printed by: Jones, W. * FLK.

2558. *A short treatise on prayer. In which are considered, what prayer is, why our prayers are often fruitless, and the true method of prayer. Translated from the French, by the reverend J. Fd, late p.p. of St. Michael's.* Dublin. 1787. 12°. 12 p. Printed by: Mehain, J. Sold by: Mehain, J. ESTC t215943. * Di.

2559. *A short way with the papists. Shewing, what is the most proper, and most effectual method to extirpate popery, to the satisfaction of all good and moderate men of what party soever.* London. 1706. 4°. [2], 66 p. Published by: Author. ESTC n023051. * CLU-C; MnU; TxU (imp.).

> According to Silvester Jenks (Letter-book of Silvester Jenks, 1703-1707, BL Add. MS 29612, ff. 36-37) a violent attack on the Jesuits by a Roman Catholic. See also Duffy, 1977, 'A rubb-up for old sores' who suggests that the author may be John Sergeant.

2560. *The sincere Catholick's companion. Published with permission, of my Lord John Oliver Briand, Bishop of Quebec.* Quebec. 1778. 18°. 60 p. Printed by: Brown, W. * CaOOA; CaQMS.

> On pp. 57-60 'Profession of the Catholick faith extracted out of the Council of Trent by Pope Pius IV'. Signed 'J. McK'. Issued with no. 14. Produced at the expense of the Bishop of Quebec for Irish Catholic families.

2561. *The sincere Catholick's companion ... printed according to the edition of 1778.* 2nd ed. Quebec. 1800. 18°. 68, 83, [5] p. Printed by: Neilson, J. * CaQQLa.

> The second part is an *Abstract of the Douay catechism.* Approbation dated and signed 'Quebec, 17th Nov. 1800, J. Plessis, vic. gen.'

2562. *Sir, as we are all obliged by our oath to promote the good of the chapter.* [1738]. fol. 3, [1] p. * BAA.

> A printed account of chapter disputes signed and dated in ms 'Ra. Clayton, Simon Berington, Charles Umfreville; 1738 April 13'. See also nos 2095 and 2566 and next item.

2563. *Sir, as we are all obliged by our oath to promote the good of the chapter.* [1738]. s.s. * BAA.

> Signed and dated in ms 'Ra. Clayton, Simon Berington, Charles Umfreville. April 13, 1738'. Printed letter on chapter disputes addressed to Mr Johnson at Longbirch.

2564. *Sir, I have the honour to enclose you the address of the Catholics of Dublin to Mr. Grattan, together, with his answer. The honest zeal and public spirit ... sufficiently recommend it to your attention.* [Dublin]. [1795]. 4°. s.s. ESTC t207260. * D.

>Signed and dated 'John Sweetman, sec. Dublin, March 17, 1795'. The paper enclosed is 'Address of the Catholics of the city of Dublin, to the right honorable Henry Grattan' (cf. e.g. no. 37).

2565. *Sir, I take it for granted that the dissolution of the Society has set us all on a level.* [1773]. 12 p. * UshA.

>Printed circular from an ex-Jesuit on the affairs of the former English Province. The date is supplied by Ush cat.

2566. *Sir, we sent a circular letter a considerable time ago to all the absent capitulars.* [1738]. fol. [2] p. * BAA.

>A printed pamphlet on chapter disputes signed in ms by Clayton, Simon Berington and Umfreville, and dated in ms '1738 September 30'. See also nos 2095 and 2562.

2567. *A sketch of the bill for relieving his majesty's subjects professing the popish religion ... imposed on them by an act of the eleventh and twelfth years of the reign of King William the Third.* [1778]. fol. [2] p. * FLK; Map; Sto.

2568. *A sketch of the debates in both Houses of the Parliament in Ireland, on the Roman Catholic Bill passed in the session of 1792.* Dublin. 1792. 8°. [2], 40 p. Printed by: Byrne, P. ESTC t048417. * D; FLK; FU; IU; L; MBAt; MY; RP.

>Although strictly speaking not a R.C. publication, this sketch has been included in view of its evident importance for the Irish Catholic community. There were other reports of the debate (including no. 2460).

2569. Smith, William Cusack. *Mr William Smith's address to the people of Ireland; being the substance of his speech delivered on Thursday, 24th January, 1799 ... on the subject of a legislative union.* London. 1799. 12°. [2], 105, [1] p. Printed by: Coghlan, J.P. Sold by: Debrett; Booker; Keating; Robinson. ESTC t134247. * E; ICR; L; NcD.

>For a number of not-specifically R.C. eds of this work and other works by Smith, published in Dublin, see ESTC.

2570. Smyth, Patrick. *Mr Smyth's reasons for resuming his station in the parish of Kells, in a letter addressed to the right rev. doctor Plunkett, titular bishop of the diocese of Meath.* Dublin. 1791. 8°. [2], 24 p. Printed by: Chambers, J. * MiU-C.

>MiU-C is bound up with the next item.

2571. Smyth, Patrick. *The present state of the Catholic mission, conducted by the ex-Jesuits in North-America.* Dublin. 1788. 8°. 48 p. Printed by: Byrne, P. ESTC n021195. * D; Lfa; MH-H; MiU-C; MY; NN; NNUT.

>This work contains a denunciation of the policy of John Carroll. For an account and his attack on Carroll see English, p. 570ff.

2572. *Some account of British subjects who have suffered by the French Revolution. 1794.* London. [1794]. 12°. 16 p. Printed by: Coghlan, J.P. ESTC t114519. * L.

See also *A continuation* (no. 779) and *The establishment* (no. 987). This material also formed part of eds of the *Laity's directory* and the *Ordo*.

2573. *Some few of the many reasons which must for ever attach a Roman Catholic to his religion. Set forth in question and answer. In two parts.* Dublin. [1780?]. 12°. 12 p. Printed by: Mehain, J. Published by: Mehain, J. ESTC t160191. * D; ECW.

2574. *Some few of the many reasons which must for ever attach a Roman Catholic to his religion. By way of question and answer; first published in the province of Munster.* 10th ed. London. 1788. 32°. 16 p. Printed by: Coghlan, J.P. * Ush.

2575. *Some of the reasons why a Catholick dare not be a Protestant digested into so plain a method of question and answer, that any Catholick, of an ordinary capacity, may defend his religion by it.* 1718. 12°. [2], 65, [1] p. * Amp.

2576. *Some queries relative to the present state of popery in Ireland.* Dublin. 1756. 8°. 16 p. ESTC t160218. * D; Mil; O.
> A series of questions intended to undermine Protestant objections to Catholic emancipation. We are not sure whether this was published under R.C. or non-R.C. auspices (see also next item).

2577. *Some queries relative to the present state of popery in Ireland.* 2nd ed. Dublin. 1756. 8°. 16 p. ESTC n036872. * ICR; NIC.

2578. *Some reflections on the operation of the popery laws in Ireland.* Dublin. 1777. 8°. 42 p. Printed by: Wogan; Bean; Pike. ESTC t155580. * C; D; Lhl; MoSW; MY.

2579. *Some reflections upon the prerogatives power and protection of St. Joseph ... With several devotions to the said ... patriarch.* [London?]. 1710. 18°. [26], 226 p. ESTC t118180. * Do; ECB; ECW; Gi; L; O.
> Cf. Clancy no. 75ff. Dr D.M. Rogers (personal communication) suggests Paul de Barry as the author. Walsh (p. 51) gives Philip Leigh (1651-1717) as an editor of some early eds of this work. See also next items.

2580. *Some reflections upon the prerogatives, power and protection of St. Joseph ... With several devotions to the said ... patriarch.* 3rd ed. [London?]. 1720. 18°. [24], 226 p. ESTC t118179. * Do; L; Yb.

2581. *Some reflections upon the prerogatives power and protection, of St. Joseph ... With several devotions.* [Louvain?]. 1722. 18°. [24], 204 p. ESTC t124213. * DFo; L; Lhe.

2582. *Some reflections upon the prerogatives power and protection, of St. Joseph ... with several devotions.* [London?]. 1722. 18°. [24], 210 p. ESTC t188626. * Lhe; O.

2583. *Some reflections upon the prerogatives, power, and protection, of St. Joseph ... with several devotions to the said ... patriarch.* Dublin. 1744. 18°. [2], 142 p. Published by: Kelly, I. * FLK.

2584. *Some reflections upon the prerogatives, power, and protection, of St. Joseph ... with several devotions to the said ... patriarch.* Dublin. 1755. 18°.

[2], 142 p. Published by: Kelly, E. ESTC t209845. * Di; FLK.

2585. *Some reflections upon the prerogatives, power, and protection, of St. Joseph ... With several devotions to the said ... patriarch.* Dublin. 1768. 18°. [2], 140 p. Published by: Gorman, B. ESTC t177224. * D.

2586. *Some reflections upon the prerogatives, power and protection of St. Joseph ... with several devotions to that most glorious patriarch.* Dublin. 1787. 12°. 144 p. Printed by: Cross, R. * Do.

2587. *Some reflections upon the prerogatives, power and protection of St. Joseph ... with several devotions to the said ... patriarch.* London. 1791. 12°. 165, [1] p. Printed by: Coghlan, J.P. * Yb.

2588. *Some reflections upon the prerogatives, power, and protection of St. Joseph ... With several devotions to that most glorious patriarch.* Dublin. 1795. 12°. 143, [1] p. Printed by: Cross, R. ESTC t218554. * Di.

2589. *Some reflections upon the prerogatives, power, and protection, of St. Joseph ... With several devotions to that most glorious patriarch.* Dublin. 1796. 12°. 143, [1] p. Printed by: Wogan, P. ESTC t160245. * Dt.

> For two later eds see also *Reflections*.

2590. *The speech of the Bishop of Clermont, in the National Assembly Feb. 11. 1790 on the subject of religious orders. Messieurs, I am bound by promise and by oath.* [London]. fol. s.s. Printed by: Coghlan, J.P. * O; Ush.

2591. Stapleton, Thomas. *A letter, containing some spiritual advice from a gentleman in town to his friend in the country.* Anon. London. 1746. 12°. 48 p. Published by: Author. Sold by: Needham, W. ESTC t155180. * Lmh.

> The author is identified in the Coghlan/Meighan Catalogue of 1776 (no. 737). For Stapleton and his publications see also Mitchell, 'The other Thomas Stapleton'.

2592. Stapleton, Thomas. *Pious considerations on several important practical truths of the Christian religion. Divided into fifty-two chapters. Permissu superiorum.* Anon. London. 1748. 12°. [8], 440, [6] p. Published by: Needham, W. Sold by: Marmaduke, J.; Needham, W. ESTC t125369. * CLU-C; Do; DoA; ECW; Gi; L; Lhe; Map; TH; TLP; TxU.

> With 4 pages of Needham adverts lacking in TLP and DoA.

2593. Stapleton, Thomas. *Prayers and pious considerations for every day in the week, to obtain a happy death.* London. 1745. 12°. 147, [1] p. Printed by: Needham, F. Sold by: Needham, F. * Map; Osc.

> With 3 pages of Needham adverts.

2594. Stapleton, Thomas. *Prayers and pious considerations for every day in the week, to obtain a happy death.* 2nd ed. Anon. London. 1753. 12°. vi, 147, [3] p. Printed by: Needham, W. Sold by: Needham, W. ESTC t125395. * E; ECW; Gi; L; UGL.

> Pages 127-47 contain 'Bona Mors: or a preparation for a happy death' with a tp bearing the imprint 'London printed and sold by F. Needham, 1745'. With 3 pages of adverts for F. Needham.

2595. *The state and case of the Roman Catholicks of Ireland; or reasons why thy [sic] may be allow'd to purchase, take mortgages for their money. Fee-farm, or other leases. Most humbly offer'd to both Houses of Parliament.* Dublin. [1705?]. 8°. 8 p. ESTC t160405. * D.

    See also no. 2600.

2596. *The state of his majesty's subjects in Ireland professing the Roman Catholic religion. Part I. Containing an account of the conduct of the Roman Catholic clergy in Wexford, during the rebellion of 1798; and the refutation of a pamphlet signed Veridicus.* Dublin. 1799. 8°. iv, 72 p. Printed by: Fitzpatrick, H. ESTC t160390. * D; MY.

2597. *The state of his majesty's subjects in Ireland professing the Roman Catholic religion. Part I. Containing an account of the conduct of the Roman Catholic clergy in Wexford.* 2nd ed. Dublin. 1799. 8°. iv, 72 p. Printed by: Fitzpatrick, H. ESTC t160395. * D; IU; Lhl; Mil; MY.

2598. *The state of his majesty's subjects in Ireland professing the Roman Catholic religion. Part II. Containing the refutation of two libels ... both published under the false name of Pat. Duigenan.* Dublin. 1800. 8°. [2], 157, [1] p. Printed by: Fitzpatrick, H. ESTC t180311. * CSmH; D; IU; MY; UshL.

    The two pamphlets (*An answer to ... Henry Grattan* and *A fair representation*) are in fact by Patrick Duigenan.

2599. *The state of his majesty's subjects in Ireland professing the Roman Catholic religion. Part I.* London repr. [Dublin]. 1800. 12°. 4, 94, [2] p. Printed by: Coghlan, J.P. Sold by: Debrett, J. ESTC t160392. * CSmH; E; O.

    With advert on final leaf.

2600. *The state of the Roman Catholicks of Ireland: or, reasons why they may be allowed to purchase, take mortgages for their money, fee-farm and other leases, most humbly offer'd to both Houses of Parliament.* Dublin. [1725?]. fol. s.s. ESTC t087130. * L.

    See also no. 2595.

2601. *Statuta regii collegio seminarii Anglorum Vallisoleti sub invocatione divi Albani erecti.* Madrid. 1770. 8°. 131, [1] p. Published by: Mena, F.E. de. * ECW; Lhe.

    The rules of the English seminary at Valladolid. Written in Latin and Spanish on facing pages.

2602. *Statuta synodalia pro diaecesi Corcagiensi.* Cork. 1768. 12°. 45, [3] p. Printed by: Swiney, E. ESTC t197420. * D.

2603. *Statutes and rules of the congregation established in the parish-chapel of St. Mary-Shandon, of Cork, under the invocation of the Blessed Virgin Mary mother of God.* Cork. 1790. 8°. [4], 5-32 p. Printed by: Cronin, J. * CKu.

2604. *Statutes and rules of the congregation, established in the parish chapel of Saint John's, Limerick, under the invocation of the immaculate conception of the B.V. Mary ... October 1786.* Limerick. 1790. 8°. 48 p. Printed by: Reynolds, J. ESTC t120918. * L.

2605. *The statutes or constitutions of the converse-sisters commonly call'd lay-sisters of the holy order of S. Augustin living in the monastery of the regular canonesses established at Bridges in Flanders.* 1717. 12°. [2], 3-61, [3] p. * ECB.

2606. Stonor, John Talbot. *An exercise of devotion for Sunday and holiday mornings and afternoons; particularly fitted for the use of such ... as have not the opportunity of assisting at church-service.* London. 1742. 12°. [6], 127, [1] p. ESTC t124001. * E; ECW; Gi; L; Lhe; NNUT; Osc; Sal.

The introductory epistle is signed 'J.T.S.'

2607. Stonor, John Talbot. *The indulgence of the jubilee, dear Christians.* [1726]. fol. [2] p. * BAA.

Pastoral letter on jubilee indulgences, dated '1725/6 March 10'.

2608. Stonor, John Talbot. *Instructions and regulations for the indulgences that are allowed to the faithful in the middle district.* Anon. [London?]. 1756. 12°. 12 p. ESTC t118936. * L; Osc; Ush.

John Talbot Stonor was V.A. of the Midland district from 1715 to 1756, in which year he was succeeded by John Joseph Hornyold. Ush has 'Prayers proper for the time of an indulgence' appended.

2609. Stonor, John Talbot. *'Tis now a proper season.* [1731]. 4°. [8] p. * BAA; Osc.

A pastoral letter, proclaiming the jubilee on the accession of Clement XII, dated 'March 12, 1730/1'.

2610. Strahan, Robert. *Serious considerations of a soul that sincerely seeks the way of truth in the sight of God ... Whereunto is added, a soliloquy, or particular reflections upon the irregular passions.* [London?]. 1752. 12°. [2], vii, [1], 101, [1] p. ESTC t083876. * Cha (imp.); DMR; E; ECW; L; Lhe; MChB; Sto; TxU.

2611. Strickland, Joseph. *An apology for not subscribing to the oath, proposed to be taken by the Catholics of England, this present year 1790.* Anon. [1790]. fol. 3, [1] p. * BAA; Cli; Map; O; Ush.

2612. Strickland, Joseph. *Remarks upon a letter, addrssed [sic] by a layman, to the Catholic clergy of England, on the appointment of bishops.* Anon. [1790]. fol. 4 p. * BAA; Map; O; Sto.

Strickland, signs himself 'A clergyman' (see also nos 1867 and 2743-2745). The 'layman' is Sir John Courtenay Throckmorton.

2613. Strickland, Joseph. *A second apology for disapproving of the oath, intended to be taken by the Catholics of England, this present year, 1790.* Anon. [1790]. fol. 4 p. * BAA; Cli; O; Sto; Ush.

2614. Strickland, Joseph. *To the gentlemen of the [blank]. Gentlemen, the catalogue of our deceased brethren.* Anon. London. 1795. fol. [2] p. * Sto.

The blank in the title has been filled in ms: 'late Society of Jesuits'. The name of the author is given in ms. The pamphlet concerns the future management of Jesuit property. A P.S. states that only 25 copies were printed for private circulation. Dated '16th of July, 1795'.

2615. *A summary of the proceedings in the House of Commons, on the petition of the Roman Catholics in Edinburgh and Glasgow, and of the debates which took place on that affair.* London. 1779. 8°. [4], viii, 31, [1] p. Published by: Coghlan, J.P. ESTC t175817. * C; E; O; SCA; Sto; Ush.

2616. *A supplement to the reply in vindication of the kindred of the late Mr. T. With refutations occasionally, of whatever deserves notice, in two pieces since published.* [London?]. [1745]. 4°. 62 p. ESTC t074432. * L; MH-H; STA.

> Dated 'May 25, 1745'. This is part of the 'Talbot controversy'; see also nos 61-63, 103, 763, 2453 and 2454.

2617. *Supplementa ad breviarium Romanum, seu officia sanctorum quorumdam recentium, in breviario Romano apponenda ... Editio novissima.* London. 1734. 12°. 134, xiii, [1] p. Published by: Meighan, T. ESTC t118023. * DMR; E; Hen; L; LVu; O; Ush.

2618. *Supplementa ad breviarium, et missale Romanum in usum missionariorum Anglicorum.* [London?]. 1765. 12°. 72 p. Published by: J.W. Sold by: J.W. ESTC t198183. * DoA; L; Map; TLP.

2619. *Supplementum ad breviarium Romanum, seu officia festorum quorundam nuper in breviario Romano apponenda.* Dublin. 1741. 12°. [4], 31-216 p. Published by: Kelly. I. ESTC t218284. * Di.

2620. *Supplementum ad breviarium Romano-Seraphicum.* Dublin. 1752. 12°. 87, [13], 12 p. Published by: Kelly, I. * FLK.

> The last 12 pages form an appendix to the supplement dated 1753. With a catalogue of books published by Kelly.

2621. *Supplementum novum ad breviarium, et missale Romanum, adjectis officiis sanctorum Angliae.* London. 1778. 12°. [2], ii, 88, [4], 4, 4, [2] p. Printed by: Coghlan, J.P. Published by: Coghlan, J.P. * DMR; ECB; ECW; Hen; Hor; Osc; TLP; UshL.

> Some copies lack one or more of the supplements. For an account of the origins of this English Supplement see Burton (II, 174ff). With 4 pages of Coghlan adverts.

2622. *Supplementum novum ad breviarium, et missale Romanum. Adjectis officiis sanctorum Angliae.* London. 1795. 12°. iv, 90 p. Printed by: Coghlan, J.P. Published by: Coghlan, J.P. ESTC t192854. * ECR; FLK; LAM; O; Ush; UshL.

> A supplement to *The ordinary of the mass, vespers and complin ... according to the Roman missal and breviary. In Latin and English*, published by J.P. Coghlan in 1794 (no. 2102).

2623. Sweetman, John. *A refutation of the charges attempted to be made against the secretary to the sub-committee of the Catholics of Ireland. Particularly that of abetting the defenders.* Dublin. 1793. 8°. [2], 10 p. Printed by: Fitzpatrick, H. ESTC t082065. * CLU-S/C; CoU; CSmH; D; Di; Lhe; Mil; MY; PHi; RPB; Sto.

2624. Taaffe, Nicolaus. *Observations on affairs in Ireland from the settlement in*

1691, to the present time. Dublin. 1766. 43, [1] p. 8°. Printed by: Hoey, J. ESTC t094525. * CaOTU; D; Dt; Du; L; Llp.

> A work by the Catholic Irish nobleman Taaffe, pleading against the anti-Catholic penal laws, addressed to the general public. See also next 6 items.

2625. Taaffe, Nicolaus. *Observations on affairs in Ireland, from the settlement in 1691, to the present time.* Dublin. 1766. 48 p. 8°. Printed by: Hoey, J. ESTC n041595. * IU; Lhl.

2626. Taaffe, Nicolaus. *Observations on affairs in Ireland, from the settlement in 1691, to the present time.* 2nd ed. Dublin. 1766. 48 p. 8°. Printed by: Hoey, J. ESTC t176836. * D; Dt; ICU; MY; SPU.

2627. Taaffe, Nicolaus. *Observations on affairs in Ireland, from the settlement in 1691, to the present time.* London repr. (Dublin). 1766. 43, [1] p. 8°. Printed by: Kiernan, C. Sold by: Cavell, W.; Meighan, T. ESTC t001096. * C; E; L.

2628. Taaffe, Nicolaus. *Observations on affairs in Ireland, from the settlement in 1691, to the present time. With an appendix ... With the addition of the civil articles of Limerick.* 2nd ed. London repr. (Dublin). 1766. 50 p. 8°. Printed by: Kiernan, C. Sold by: Cavell, W.; Meighan, T. ESTC t143358. * CaOHM; CtY; DLC; Ldw; Lu; Map; MeB; MRu; PP.

2629. Taaffe, Nicolaus. *Observations on affairs in Ireland, from the settlement in 1691, to the present time.* London. 1766. 43, [1] p. 8°. Published by: Griffin, W. ESTC t041738. * KU-S; L; Lhl; MH; O; Omc.

2630. Taaffe, Nicolaus. *Observations on affairs in Ireland, from the settlement in 1691, to the present time.* 3rd ed. Dublin. 1767. 48 p. 8°. Printed by: Hoey, J. ESTC n010770. * C; CSmH; D; Dt; InU-Li; IU; KU-S.

2631. Tabula congregationis O.F.M. *Copia vera. In nomine Domini amen. Haec est tabula capituli provincialis almae provinciae Hiberniae fratrum minorum ... Observantiae habiti in loco refugii conventus nostri Dublinienis die 5. Septembris anno 1733.* [1733]. s.s. * FLK.

> Signed 'Fr. Franciscus Stuart commissarius visitator' and 9 others. This and the following documents list all the names of Irish Franciscans in Ireland and abroad, and their functions. There was an unbroken series of 'tabulae' from 1719 onwards, but the years not listed here remained in ms (in FLK). In the following list minor irregularities in spelling have been silently emended. For an extensive survey see Anselm Faulkner.

2632. Tabula congregationis O.F.M. *Copia vera. In nomine Domini amen. Haec est tabula capituli provincialis almae provinciae Hyberniae fratrum minorum strictioris observantiae habiti in loco refugii conventus nostri Dubliniensis die sexta Septembris anni 1736.* [1736]. s.s. * FLK.

> Signed 'F. Patritius Browne, minister provincialis' and 12 others.

2633. Tabula congregationis O.F.M. *Copia vera. In nomine Domini amen. Haec est tabula congregationis intermediae almae provinciae Hiberniae fratrum minorum strictioris observantiae habiti in loco refugii conventus nostri Dubliniensis die sexta Martii an. Dom. 1738.* [1738]. s.s. * FLK.

> Signed 'F. Antonius Mac-Nemarra, provinciae pater' and 9 others.

2634. Tabula congregationis O.F.M. *Copia vera. In nomine Domini amen. Haec est tabula congregationis intermediae almae provinciae Hiberniae fratrum minorum in loco nostri refugii conventus Dubliniensis die 25. Maii anno domini 1741.* [1741]. s.s. * FLK.

Signed 'F. Antonius O'Donnell, primus provinciae pater' and 9 others.

2635. Tabula congregationis O.F.M. *Copia vera. In nomine Domini amen. Haec est tabula capituli provincialis almae provinciae Hiberniae fratrum minorum habiti in loco nostri refugii conventus Dubliniensis hac die 16. Augusti ... 1742.* [1742]. s.s. * FLK.

Signed 'F. Ludovicus O'Donnell, minister provincialis' and 11 others.

2636. Tabula congregationis O.F.M. *Copia vera. In nomine Domini amen. Haec est tabula capituli provincialis almae provinciae Hiberniae fratrum minorum habiti in loco refugii conventus nostri Dubliniensis hac die 18. Augusti ... 1760.* [1760]. s.s. * FLK.

Signed 'Fr. Christophorus French minister provincialis'.

2637. Tabula congregationis O.F.M. *Copia vera. In nomine Domini amen. Haec est tabula congregationis intermediae almae provinciae Hiberniae fratrum minorum strictioris observantiae habitae in loco refugii conventus nostri de Athlone hac die 19. Octobris ... 1761.* [1761]. s.s. * FLK.

Not signed.

2638. Tabula congregationis O.F.M. *Copia vera. In nomine Domini amen. Haec est tabula capituli provincialis almae provinciae Hiberniae fratrum minorum strictioris observantiae habiti in loco refugii conventus nostri Dubliniensis hac die 22. Augusti ... 1763.* [1763]. s.s. * FLK.

Signed 'Fr. Jacobus MacDonnell, minister provincialis' and 10 others.

2639. Tabula congregationis O.F.M. *In nomine Domini amen. Haec est tabula congregationis intermediae provinciae Hiberniae fratrum minorum stricts. Obvae habitae in loco refugii conventus nostri de Athlone hac die 30 Aprilis, A.D. 1778.* [1778]. s.s. * FLK.

Signed 'Fr. Dom McDavett minister provincialis' and 10 others.

2640. Tabula congregationis O.F.M. *In nomine Domini, amen. Haec est tabula capituli provincialis almae provinciae Hiberniae F.F. min. stricts. observantiae, habiti in loco refugii conventus nostri Dubliniensis, hac die 19 Julii, 1779.* [1779]. s.s. * FLK.

Signed 'Fr. Antonius Trench, commissarius visitator' and 10 others.

2641. Tabula congregationis O.F.M. *In nomine Domini. Amen. Haec est tabula congregationis intermediae provinciae Hiberniae fratrum minorum stricts observantiae habitae in loco refugii, conventus nostri de Athlone hac die 29 Maii A.D.* [1781]. s.s. * FLK.

Signed 'Fr. Ludovicus O'Donell, minister provincialis' and 10 others.

2642. Tabula congregationis O.F.M. *In nomine Domini. Amen. Haec est tabula capituli provincialis almae provinciae Hiberniae F.F. min. strict. observantiae habiti in loco refugii conventus nostri Dubliniensis hac 22 Julij, 1782.* [1782]. s.s. * FLK.

Signed 'Fr. Mich. Conry L. Jub. commis. visitator' and 10 others.

2643. Tabula congregationis O.F.M. *In nomine Domini. Amen. Haec est tabula congregationis intermediae almae provinciae Hiberniae F.F. min. strict: observantiae habitae in loco refugii conventus nostri de Athlone. Hac 12 Maij 1784.* [1784]. s.s. * FLK.

Signed 'F. Bernardus Brady, minis. provincialis' and 8 others.

2644. Tabula congregationis O.F.M. *In nomine Domini. Amen. Haec est tabula capituli provincialis almae provinciae Hiberniae F.F. min. strict. observantiae, habiti in loco refugii conventus nostri Dubliniensis hac 25 Julii 1785.* [1785]. s.s. * FLK.

Signed 'F. Christ. Fleming commissarius visitator' and 8 others.

2645. Tabula congregationis O.F.M. *In nomine Domini. Amen. Haec est tabula congregationis intermediae almae provinciae Hiberniae F.F. min. strict. observantiae, habitae in loco refugii conventus nostri de Athlone, hac 9 Maij 1787.* [1787]. s.s. * FLK.

Signed 'F. Joan. Ant. Kennedy, minis. provincialis' and 7 others.

2646. Tabula congregationis O.F.M. *In nomine Domini. Amen. Haec est tabula capituli provincialis almae provinciae Hiberniae fratr. minorum: habiti in loco refugii conventus nostri Dubliniensis hac 14 die Julii 1788.* [1788]. s.s. * FLK.

Signed 'Fr. Laur. Callanan commissarius & praeses capituli' and 10 others.

2647. Tabula congregationis O.F.M. *In nomine Domini. Amen. Haec est tabula congregationis intermediae almae provinciae Hiberniae fratr. minorum: strict. observantiae habitae in loco refugii conventus nostri de Athlone hac 18 Maij 1790.* [1790]. s.s. * FLK.

Signed 'Fr. Jacobus O'Reilly, minister provincialis'. FLK has two states of this broadside, with minor differences.

2648. Tabula congregationis O.F.M. *In nomine Domini. Amen. Haec est tabula capituli provincialis alm. prov. Hib. F.F. minorum; str. obs. habiti in loco refugii conventus nostri Dubliniensis hac 11 â die Julii 1791.* [1791]. s.s. * FLK.

Signed 'Fr Bernard. Brady, prov. pater' and 10 others.

2649. Tabula congregationis O.F.M. *In nomine Domini. Amen. Haec est tabula congregationis intermediae almae provinciae Hiberniae fratrum min. strictioris observae habitae in loco refugii nostri de Athlone hac die 23 a Julii 1793.* [1793]. s.s. * FLK (2).

Signed 'Fr. Franciscus Galagher, S.T.L. jub & custos' and 7 others. This tabula seems to have been set up in type twice and the two FLK copies in fact represent two different eds.

2650. Tabula congregationis O.F.M. *In nomine Domini. Amen. Haec est tabula capituli provincialis almae prov. Hib. FF. minorum, stric. obs. habiti in loco refugii conventus nostri Dubliniensis hac 14 die Julii 1794.* [1794]. s.s. * FLK.

Signed 'Fr. Franciscus Phelan, custos' and 9 others.

2651. Tabula congregationis O.F.M. *In nomine Domini. Amen. Haec est tabula congregationis intermediae almae provinciae Hiberniae fratrum min. strictioris observantiae, habitae in loco refugii nostri de Athlone hac die 6 Junij 1796.*

[Cork]. [1796]. s.s. Printed by: Haly, J. * FLK.
Signed 'Fr. Patritius Lambert, diffinitor' and 6 others.

2652. Tabula congregationis O.F.M. *In nomine Domini. Amen. Haec est tabula congregationis intermediae almae provinciae Hiberniae fratrum min. strictioris observantiae de mandato ... in loco refugii nostri de Athlone hac die 22 Septembris 1800.* [Cork]. [1800]. s.s. Printed by: Haly, J. * FLK.
Signed 'Fr. Patritius Lambert, diffinitor' and 6 others.

2653. Talbot, James. *Orationes dicendae pro salute regis.* [1788]. 4°. 4 p. * Cli.
Signed at end 'J.B.V.G.' (i.e. James Talbot). The date is given in ms in Walmesley's hand. The prayers were ordered because of George III's madness.

2654. Talbot, Thomas. *An address to the faithful of the middle district, concerning the fast of Fridays.* [1781]. fol. 2 p. * BAA.
A pastoral letter dated '1781, Sept. 1'.

2655. Talbot, Thomas. *Entrusted by divine providence with the care of this district, we have seen, with deep concern, the destruction of the English colleges and schools in France.* [1794]. 4°. 2, [2] p. * BAA; Cli; LANre; WDA.
An appeal to finance a new seminary at Oscott. Dated and signed on p. 2 'Longbirch, February 27, 1794. Thomas Talbot, Chas. Berington'. The pamphlet concludes: 'Subscriptions will be gratefully received by Thomas Wright, Esq. and Co. Covent Garden, London; by Thomas Clifford, Esq. Tixall; by the rev. James Archer ... by the rev. Messrs. Kirk and Southworth, Sedgley-Park; and at Longbirch'.

2656. Talbot, Thomas. *Instructions and regulations for the ensuing fast of Lent, 1785. Addressed to the faithful of the middle district.* Anon. [1785]. 8°. 8 p. * ECW.
Thomas Talbot was V.A. of the Midland district from 1778 to 1795.

2657. Talbot, Thomas. *A pastoral instruction on keeping the Sunday. 1785.* Anon. Wolverhampton. 1785. 8°. 24 p. Printed by: Smart, J. ESTC t197489. * DoA; ECW; Lhe; Osc.

2658. Talbot, Thomas. *A short instruction for Lent ... by Thomas Aconen.* 1780. 12°. 12 p. * BAA; Gi.

2659. Talbot, Thomas. *A short instruction for Lent, 1789.* 1789. 12°. 11, [1] p. * Map.
Signed 'T.A. V.A.'.

2660. Talbot, Thomas. *Thomas, Bishop of Acon, vicar apostolic, to all the faithful, clergy and laity, in the middle district. Having by a late act of Parliament, been eased from the heavy load.* [London?]. [1791]. fol. s.s. ESTC t050158. * BAA; L.
Dated 'Longbirch, July 19, 1791'.

2661. Talbot, Thomas. *Thomas Dei et s. sedis apostolicae gratia Episcopus Aconensis, in districtu mediano vicarius apostolicus: venerabilibus et dilectis in Christo fratribus e clero tam saeculari quam regulari.* [1780]. 8°. 11, [1] p. * WDA.
Signed and dated 'Thomas Aconen, V.A. Datum Die 13 Jan. 1780'.

2662. Tempest, Stephen. *Religio leici [sic], &c. I am certain that I have a being in this world.* [London?]. [1764?]. 8°. 149, [1] p. ESTC t046701. * L.

> A work on general morality by a R.C. author clearly aimed at the general reading public. There was a 2nd ed. in 1768 (ESTC t168663).

2663. *The tenebrae: or, evening office for holy week. In Latin and English, according to the Roman breviary.* London. 1792. 12°. [2], 102, [2] p. Printed by: Keating, P. Published by: Keating, P. ESTC t181176. * ECW; Hor; O.

> With a final advertisement. This books belongs to the category of 'Evening office'.

2664. Teresa of Avila. *The exclamations of the soul to God: or the meditations of St. Teresa after communion. Newly translated. Together with an introductory dedication ... By the rev. John Milner [Exclamaciones.].* London. 1790. 8°. [2], xxxiv, 88 p. Printed by: Coghlan, J.P. Sold by: Robinsons. ESTC n016826. * BB; CAL; CLU-C; DAE; Do; DoA; ECB; ECW; Lhe; MH-H; O; Osc; Pci; TLP; TxU; ViU; Ush.

> Based on the French versions of Robert Arnauld d'Andilly and of Father Cyprien de la Nativité de la Vierge, and the English version of Abraham Woodhead. Dedicated to Mary Augustine More, prioress of the English Canonesses at Bruges. In the preface Milner reacts against certain remarks by Joseph Berington in his *State and behaviour of English Catholics* (nos 253 and 254).

2665. Teresa of Avila. *The life of the holy mother St. Teresa ... Together with a short account of the foundations which she made. The whole abridged from her own writings [Las obras de la gloriosa madre Santa Teresa].* London. 1757. 8°. [8], 374, [10] p. Published by: Needham, W. ESTC t105378. * BMu; CSmH; Do; ECB; ECW; HLp; ICN; L; Lfa; Lhe; Llp; LO; Map; Sal; TLP; UGL; Ush; Yb.

> Abridgment by Richard Challoner of Abraham Woodhead's translation.

2666. Teresa of Avila. *The life of the holy mother St. Teresa ... Together with an account of the foundations which she made. The whole abridged from her own writings.* Dublin. 1791. 8°. [16], 374, [10]. Printed by: Mehain, J. ESTC t205803. * D; Do; IDA.

> With a list of subscribers and an advert leaf. IDA gives Alban Butler as the editor.

2667. Teresa of Avila. *The life of the holy mother, St. Teresa ... abridged by the rev. Alban Butler, to which is added her meditations proper for communion, translated from the Spanish original by the rev. John Milner.* Dublin. 1794. 18°. xii, 3-205, [1] p. Printed by: Mehain, J. ESTC t205805. * D.

> With a list of subscribers.

2668. Thanksgiving. *A thanksgiving appointed to be said for the recovery of our most gracious sovereign King George III.* London. 1789. 8°. 11, [1] p. Printed by: Coghlan, J.P. ESTC t116026. * L; Lu; Ush; WDA.

> Parallel Latin and English texts.

2669. Thayer, John. *An account of the conversion of the reverend Mr. John Thayer, lately a Protestant minister, at Boston in North America, who embraced* *the Roman Catholic religion at Rome ... 1783; written by himself.* Manchester. 1787. 12°. 50 p. Printed by: Haydock; Wardle. Sold by: Haydock; Wardle; Booker, E. (London). * Ush.

> Thayer was a congregationalist minister and army chaplain who converted in 1783. The account of his conversion was published frequently between 1787 and 1800.

2670. Thayer, John. *An account of the conversion of the rev. Mr. John Thayer, lately a Protestant minister at Boston ... who embraced the Roman Catholic religion.* Manchester. [1787?]. 12°. 58 p. Printed by: Swindels, G. * MB.

2671. Thayer, John. *An account of the conversion of the reverend Mr. John Thayer, lately a Protestant minister, at Boston in North America, who embraced the Roman Catholic religion at Rome.* 2nd ed. London. 1787. 12°. [2], 66 p. Printed by: Coghlan, J.P. Sold by: Byrne, P. (Dublin) ESTC n002724. * MHi.

2672. Thayer, John. *An account of the conversion of a Protestant minister, written by himself. To which are annexed several extracts from a letter written to his brother ... Also, a letter from a young lady.* Dublin repr. [London]. 1787. 12°. 52 p. Printed by: Boyce, J. ESTC t215920. * Di.

2673. Thayer, John. *An account of the conversion of the reverend Mr. John Thayer, lately a Protestant minister, at Boston in North-America, who embraced the Roman Catholic religion at Rome.* 5th ed. Baltimore. 1788. 8°. 28 p. Sold by: Goddard, W. ESTC w011736. * CSmH; CtY; DCU; DGU-W; DP; MBAt; MeB; MH-H; MHi; MWA; MWH; NN; PPL; PU.

> This is the second '5th' ed.

2674. Thayer, John. *An account of the conversion of the reverend Mr. John Thayer, lately a Protestant minister, at Boston in North America, who embraced the Roman Catholic religion at Rome.* 5th ed. London. 1788. 12°. [4], 78, [2] p. Printed by: Coghlan, J.P. Sold by: Byrne, P. (Dublin). ESTC n043302. * MBAt; Ush.

2675. Thayer, John. *An account of the conversion of the reverend Mr. John Thayer, lately a Protestant Minister, at Boston in North-America, who embraced the Roman Catholic religion at Rome.* 6th ed. Wilmington. 1789. 42 p. Printed by: Bowen & Howard. ESTC w005445. * MHi (imp); NcA-S; NcU.

2676. Thayer, John. *An account of the conversion of the reverend Mr. John Thayer, lately a Protestant minister, at Boston in North America, who embraced the Roman Catholic religion at Rome.* 6th ed. London. 1791. 12°. 72 p. Printed by: Coghlan, J.P. * Ush.

> This is the second '6th' ed.

2677. Thayer, John. *An account of the conversion of the rev. Mr. John Thayer, lately a Protestant minister at Boston in North America.* 4th ed. Dublin. 1797. 12°. 53, [1] p. Printed by: Boyce, J. ESTC t203596. * D.

2678. Thayer, John. *An account of the conversion of the rev. John Thayer, lately a Protestant minister at Boston in North-America, who embraced the Roman Catholic religion at Rome.* 8th ed. London. 1800. 12°. 48 p. Printed by:

Keating, Brown & Keating. ESTC t116863. * E; ECW; L.

2679. Thayer, John. *A collection of prayers; which may serve as morning and evening devotions.* 2nd ed. London. 1789. 32°. 30 p. Printed by: Coghlan, J.P. * Ush.

2680. Thayer, John. *Controversy between the reverend John Thayer, Catholic missionary, of Boston, and the reverend George Lesslie, pastor of a church, in Washington, New-Hampshire.* Georgetown. 1791. 37, [1] p. Printed by: Doyle, A. ESTC w005446. * DGU.

> Three letters written by John Thayer and one by George Lesslie. See Finotti, pp. 241-2.

2681. Thayer, John. *Controversy between the rev. John Thayer, Catholic missionary, of Boston, and the rev. George Lesslie ... To which are added, several other pieces.* [Newburyport]. [1793]. 8°. iv, [1], 6-167, [1] p. Printed by: [Mycall, J.] ESTC w033706. * DCU; DGU; InNd; MB; MBAt; MHi; MWA; RPJCB.

> Preface dated 'Boston, October 5, 1793'.

2682. Thayer, John. *Controversy between the rev. John Thayer, Catholic missionary, of Boston, and the rev. George Lesslie, pastor of a church, in Washington, New-Hampshire.* Philadelphia. 1795. 8°. 32 p. Printed by: Folwell, R. ESTC w014258. * PHi; PU.

2683. Thayer, John. *A discourse, delivered, at the Roman Catholic church in Boston, on the 9th of May, 1798, a day recommended by the president, for humiliation and prayer throughout the United States.* Boston. 1798. 8°. 31, [1] p. Printed by: Hall, S. ESTC w038009. * CLSU; C-S; CSmH; CtHI; CtY; DGU; DLC; DP; InU-Li; MB; MBAt; MeHi; MH-AH; MH-H; MWA; NcD; NjR; PPL; RPJCB.

2684. Thayer, John. *A discourse, delivered, at the Roman Catholic church in Boston, on the 9th day of May, 1798, a day recommended by the president, for humiliation and prayer throughout the United States.* 2nd ed. Boston. 1798. 8°. 31, [1] p. Printed by: Hall, S. ESTC w038008. * CaQMBM; DB; DGU; MB; MWA; MY; NN; RPJCB.

2685. Thayer, John. *A discourse, delivered at the Roman Catholic church, in Boston, on the 9th of May, 1798: a day recommended by the president, for humiliation and prayer. Throughout the United States.* 2nd ed. Baltimore. 1798. 31, [1] p. Printed by: Hanna, A. ESTC w030807. * CSmH; CtY; DGU; DLC; MB; MdBJ-G; MdHi; MH; MWA; RPJCB.

> This is the second '2nd ed.'

2686. Thayer, John. *Relaçaõ de conversaõ do R. Senhor Joaõ Thayer ... Escrita por elle mesmo.* Lisbon. 1788. 8°. 155, [1] p. Printed by: Ameno, F.L. de. ESTC t116861. * CSmH; L; RPJCB.

> Parallel English and Portuguese texts.

2687. Thayer, John. *Relation de la conversion de Mr. Thayer, ministre Protestante, ecrite par lui-meme.* Quebec. [1794?]. 8°. 63, [1] p. Published by:

Germain, L. * CaOTP; CaQMBM; CaQMS; CaQQLa (imp.).
Originally written in English (see no. 2669ff.).

2688. *Theologia universa ... praeside rev. dno. Thoma Eyre ... propugnabunt ... Thomas Penswick ... Richard Thompson ... Thomas Gillow ... quae vero ad religionem revelatam, incarnationem et decalogum spectant, prius tueri conabuntur, Thomas Lupton ... Josephus Swinburn ... Georgius Haydock ... Joannes Rickaby.* Newcastle. 1797. 4°. [2], 75, [1] p. Published by: Walker, E. Sold by: Walker, E. * Amp; ECR; Lhe; MY; Ush; WDA.
Our bibliography only includes strictly theological theses, published in Great Britain. We exclude theses involving Englishmen published abroad.

2689. *Theses theologicae de septem ecclesiae sacramentis, quas ... tueri conabuntur in coll. Cath. (vulgo Crook Hall) in comitatu Dunelmensi. Dom. Tho. Penswick ... Ric. Thompson ... Tho. Gillow ... Car. Saul.* [Durham?]. 1795. 4°. [4]. 43, [1] p. ESTC t124200. * ECR; L; Lhe; TxU; Ush; WDA.

2690. deleted.

2691. *Theses theologicae de revelatione, virtutibus theologicis, gratia actibus humanis, legibus et peccatis, quas Deo juvante. Praeside rev. dno. Thoma Eyre.* Newcastle. 1796. 4°. [2], 24 p. Printed by: Walker, E. * ECR; MY; Ush; WDA.

2692. *Theses theologicae de virtutibus theologicis, actibus humanis, peccatis et legibus, quas, Deo juvante, praeside rev. dno. Gulielmo Poynter ... tueri conabuntur ... Richardus Broderick ... Joannes Clarkson ... Joannes Devereux ... Edvardus Peach.* London. 1796. 4°. 12 p. Printed by: Coghlan, J.P. ESTC t216029. * C.

2693. *Theses theologicae de incarnatione et decalogo, quas Deo juvante, praeside rev. dno. Gulielmo Poynter.* London. 1797. 4°. 12 p. Printed by: Coghlan, J.P. * Lhe (imp).

2694. *Theses theologicae, de Deo uno et trino, de ecclesia, et cultu sanctorum, quas, Deo duce, auspice deiparâ, praeside rev. dno. Guilielmo Henrico Coombes ... in aula Collegii Catholici S. Edmundi ... mag. Thomas Pitchford, mag. Ludovicus Havard.* London. 1798. 4°. 8 p. Printed by: Coghlan, J.P. * Lhe.

2695. *Theses theologicae de Deo, revelatione, ecclesia, &c ... praeside rev. dno. Thoma Eyre ... prius tueri conabuntur ... Thomas Cock ... Thomas Dawson ... Joannes Bradley ... Thomas Lupton ... Josephus Swinburn ... Joannes Rickaby ... propugnabit dom. Georgius Haydock.* Newcastle. 1798. 4°. [2], 33, [1] p. Published by: Walker, E. Sold by: Walker, E. * Amp; ECR; Lhe; MY; Ush; WDA.

2696. *Theses theologicae de septem ecclesiae sacramentis, quas Deo juvante. Praeside rev. dno. Thoma Eyre.* Newcastle. 1799. 4°. [2], 28 p. Printed by: Walker, E. * ECR; MY; Ush; WDA.

2697. *Theses theologicae de virtutibus theologicis, gratia, actibus humanis, legibus et peccatis, quas, Deo juvante. Praeside rev. dno. Thoma Eyre.* Newcastle. 1800. 4°. [2], 19, [1] p. Printed by: Walker, E. * ECR; Ush.

2698. Thiard de Bissy, Henri de. *The mandate of his eminence my Lord Cardinal of Bissy. Bishop of Meaux ... Upon the subject of the constitution Unigenitus, and of the appeal [Lettre circulaire de M. le Cardinal de Bissy].* London. 1718. 8°. 31, [1] p. Printed by: Booksellers of London and Westminster. Sold by: Booksellers of London and Westminster. ESTC t025854. * L.

>According to Sommervogel (Sup. 448) translated by Thomas Ecclestone.

2699. *A third appeal to his grace the Lord Primate of all Ireland. In vindication of the political principles of Roman Catholics. By an honest free-thinker.* Dublin. 1760. 8°. 31, [1] p. Printed by: Chamberlaine, D. ESTC t174765. * C; D; MRu; PP.

>A sequel to no. 2507. See also nos 76 and 77.

2700. *The thirty days prayers. A prayer to the Blessed Virgin Mary, mother of God. With a prayer to our Lord Jesus Christ.* Preston. 1767. 12°. 12 p. Printed by: Stuart, V. Published by: Stuart, V. * Ush.

2701. Thomas Aquinas. *A hymn on the institution of the eucharist, translated by T.P., S.C.T.* [London]. [c.1780]. 8°. 11 , [1] p. Sold by: Marmaduke, J. * Map; Osc; UGL.

>The Latin text of 'Lauda, Sion', with an English translation on the facing page. 'T.P., S.C.T.' is Thomas Phillips, senior canon at Tongres.

2702. Thomas à Kempis. *A collection of sermons and other treatises from the works of the author of the Imitation of Christ. Newly translated. From the edition of Sommalius. S.J. Never before printed in the English tongue.* London. 1765. 12°. 302, [2] p. ESTC t195139. * CAL; DAE; DMR; DoA; ECB; ECW; Hor; Lfa; Lhe; MY; Nijm; Pm; Stan; Yb.

>With a final advertisement leaf.

2703. Thomas à Kempis. *De imitatione Christi, libri quatuor.* Anon. London. Published by: Lewis, T. 1778. 12°. [6], 262 p. ESTC t092385. * Du; E; L; MH.

2704. Thomas à Kempis. *The following of Christ. Written in Latin by Thomas of Kempis ... Reviewed and corrected by W.B. [De imitatione Christi].* Rouen. 1702. 32°. [12], 487, [41] p. Printed by: Turner, N. le. ESTC t092389. * Do; L.

>Dedicated by the printer to King James II. There are numerous non-R.C. versions of the works of Thomas à Kempis, notably in the eds of George Stanhope and George Hickes. These have not been included.

2705. Thomas à Kempis. *The following of Christ. Written in Latin by Thomas of Kempis ... Translated into English, and in this last edition reviewed and compared with several former editions ... with the author's life.* London. 1706. 24°. [6], 474, [2] p. ESTC t092390. * ECB (-tp); L.

>With some adverts for Catholic books.

2706. Thomas à Kempis. *The following of Christ. In four books by Thomas of Kempis. And translated into English, from the Latin.* Dublin. 1733. 12°. [14], 321, [3] p. Published by: Browne, T. ESTC t204825. * D; Du; Gi.

With one page of Browne adverts.

2707. Thomas à Kempis. *The following of Christ. In four books. Written in Latin by Thomas à Kempis. Newly translated into English by R... C... D.D.* London. 1737. 24°. vi, [6], 276 p. Published by: Meighan, T. ESTC t092388. * DoA; ECW; L; MH; Stan.

'R... C... D.D.' is Richard Challoner. See also several of the next items.

2708. Thomas à Kempis. *The following of Christ, in four books. Written in Latin by Thomas à Kempis. Newly translated into English, by R... C... D.D.* 2nd ed. London. 1744. 24°. viii, [8], 272 p. Published by: Meighan, T. ESTC t092630. * CaNSHD; DMR; Do; E; L; MH; NN; TxU.

2709. Thomas à Kempis. *The following of Christ. In four books. Written in Latin by Thomas à Kempis. Newly translated into English, by R... C... D.D.* 3rd ed. Liverpool. 1755. 12°. viii, [8], 272 p. Printed by: Sadler, J. Sold by: Sadler, J. ESTC n007093. * CLU-C; Do; DoA; MH; VUA.

2710. Thomas à Kempis. *The following of Christ, in four books. Written in Latin by Thomas à Kempis. Newly translated into English, by R... C..., D.D.* 3rd ed. London. 1756. 24°. viii, [8], 272 p. Published by: Meighan, T. ESTC n031861. * Csj; Luk; Map; MH; O.

This is the second '3rd ed.'

2711. Thomas à Kempis. *The following of Christ, in four books. Written in Latin by Thomas à Kempis. Newly translated into English, by R... C..., D.D.* 4th ed. London. 1767. viii, [8], 272 p. Published by: Meighan, T. * Do; Lfa; Sal.

2712. Thomas à Kempis. *The following of Christ. In four books. Written in Latin by Thomas a Kempis. Newly translated into English by R... C... D.D.* 5th ed. London. 1779. 12°. ix, [3], 328 p. Printed by: Coghlan, J.P. ESTC t093309. * DoA; L; Lhe; MH; MRu.

2713. Thomas à Kempis. *The following of Christ. In four books. Written in Latin, by Thomas a Kempis. Translated into English, by the rt. rev. father in God, Richard Challoner.* 6th ed. London. 1784. 12°. ix, [1], 358 p. Printed by: Coghlan, J.P. ESTC n031858. * E; ECW; MH; Stan.

2714. Thomas à Kempis. *The following of Christ. In four books. Written in Latin by Thomas à Kempis, translated into English by the rt. rev. father in God, Richard Challoner.* 7th ed. London. 1789. 12°. ix, [1], 358 p. Printed by: Coghlan, J.P. * ECW; Gi.

2715. Thomas à Kempis. *The following of Christ. In four books. Written in Latin by Thomas à Kempis. Translated into English, by the rt. rev. father in God, Richard Challoner.* 8th ed. London. 1793. 24°. ix, [1], 348 p. Printed by: Coghlan, J.P. ESTC t093308. * L.

2716. Thomas à Kempis. *The following of Christ, in four books ... Translated into English, by the rt. rev. father in God, Richard Challoner.* 9th ed. London. 1796. 12°. ix, [1], 349, [1] p. ESTC t204823. * C; DGU; Do; DoA; Gi; Oe.

2717. Thomas à Kempis. *The following of Christ, in four books, by Thomas à Kempis. Translated into English, by the rt. rev. father in God, Richard*

Challoner. 10th ed. London. 1799. 24°. ix, [1], 349, [1] p. Printed by: Coghlan, J.P. ESTC n031860. * MH; Stan; TxDaM-P.

2718. Thomas à Kempis. *The following of Christ. In four books. Written in Latin by Thomas à Kempis. Translated into English by the rt. rev. father in God Richard Challoner, D.D. Bishop of Debra, and V.A.* 9th ed. Philadelphia. 1800. 12°. vii, [1], 9-335, [1] p. Printed by: Carey, J. Published by: Carey, M. ESTC w008883. * DGU; NN.
    This is the second '9th' ed.

2719. Thomas à Kempis. *L'imitation de Jesus-Christ. Nouvelle édition, revue et corrigee par M. L'abbé de la Hogue.* London. 1797. 18°. vii, [1], 402, [22] p. Printed by: Paris, A. Published by: Dulau, A. et Co. Sold by: Dulau; Booker; Keating; Besley. ESTC t092635. * BRG; CAL; L.

2720. Thomas à Kempis. *The imitation of Jesus Christ. In four books. Translated into English from the Latin.* [London?]. 1706. 18°. [12], 346, [2] p. ESTC t092392. * ECB; L; TxU.

2721. Thomas à Kempis. *The imitation of Jesus Christ. In four books. By Thomas of Kempis. And translated into English, from the Latin.* [London?]. 1717. 18°. [12], 346 p. ESTC t197817. * L.

2722. Thomas à Kempis. *Thomas à Kempis of the imitation of Christ. His fourth book of the sacrament. Translated from the original Latin.* London. 1720. 8°. [2], 120 p. ESTC t174485. * Csj; MRu.

2723. Thomas à Kempis. *The imitation of Jesus Christ, in four books ... And translated into English, from the Latin.* London. 1726. 12°. 319, [17] p. Published by: Meighan, T. ESTC t092391. * Csj; DMR; ECW; Gi; ICN; L; Lhe; Stan (imp.); TLP; TxU; Yb.
    With some pages of Meighan adverts.

2724. Thomas à Kempis. *The imitation of Christ in four books. Translated from the late Paris edition, published by the abbé Valart.* Anon. Dublin. 1785. 18°. [2], xxiii, [1], 294, [2] p. Printed by: Boyce, J. * IDA.
    The last 2 pages contain Boyce adverts.

2725. Thomas à Kempis. *The imitation or following of Jesus Christ. In four books. By Thomas of Kempis. Translated into the English from the Latin.* Dublin. 1786. 18°. [4], 314, [6] p. Printed by: Cross, R. ESTC t093922. * L.

2726. Thomas à Kempis. *The imitation of Christ, in four books translated from the Paris edition publish'd by the abbé Valart.* 2nd ed. Anon. Dublin. [1790?]. 18°. [8], xxiii, [3], 294 p. Printed by: Boyce, J. ESTC t093923. * L; MY.
    With a list of subscribers.

2727. Thomas à Kempis. *The imitation, or following of Jesus Christ. In four books. By Thomas of Kempis. Translated into the English from the Latin.* Dublin. 1793. 18°. [2], 311, [7] p. Printed by: Jones, W. ESTC t185350. * C; D (imp.).

2728. Thomas à Kempis. *The imitation or following of Jesus Christ. In four books. By Thomas of Kempis. Translated into the English from the Latin.* Cork.

1795. 18°. [2], 5-394, [6] p. Printed by: Cronin, J. ESTC t185351. * D (imp.).

2729. Thomas à Kempis. *The imitation of Christ. In four books. With practical reflections and prayers at the end of each chapter. Translated from the French by B. M. P. K.* Dublin. 1798. 12°. x, [8], 341, [1] p. Printed by: Chambers, J. Published by: The translators. * Yb.

With a list of subscribers.

2730. Thomas à Kempis. *The imitation of Christ, in four books. Written in Latin by Thomas à Kempis.* Manchester. 1800. 24°. vi, 207, [7] p. Printed by: Dean, R. & W. Published by: Haydock, T. ESTC t093924. * L; Stan; TLP.

Translated by Richard Challoner. This was published as part of a subscription scheme by T. Haydock.

2731. Thomas à Kempis. *Leanmhuin chriosd, ann ceithear leabhraichean: sgriobhta ann Ladoin le Thomais a Cempis: air ur eider-theangacha' gu Gaoilig albannach le R... M... M.A.I.S. [De imitatione Christi. Gaelic].* Dun-Aodain. 1785. 8°. xii, 244 p. ESTC t099332. * Du; E; FLK; L; O; OrPU.

'R... M...' is Robert Menzies (see also no. 2817).

2732. Thomas à Kempis. *Pattrwm y gwir-gristion neu ddilyniad Jesu Grist. A 'scrifenwyd gynta' yn Lladin Gan Thomas â Kempis. Gwedi ei Gyfieithu'n Gymraeg ers talm o Amfer un ô editiwn yr awdur. Gan H.O. Gwenydog ym Môn Esq.* Shrewsbury. [1740]. 12°. [6], 322 p. Printed by: Durston, T. ESTC t204230. * DMR; O; Ush.

The translator of this book was the Welsh convert Hugh Owen (1575-1642). The first ed. was published in 1684 by his Jesuit son, Hugh, who is known also John Hughes. However, during the 18th century Owen's translation was adapted for the protestant market so that this item and the many other 18th century Welsh eds of Thomas à Kempis do not in fact come within the terms of our definition. For these eds see Rees.

2733. Deleted.

2734. Deleted.

2735. Thomé de Jesus. *The sufferings of our Lord Jesus Christ. Written originally in Portuguese by F. Thomas of Jesus ... And newly translated into English [Trabalhos de Jesus].* 3 vols. London. 1753. 12°. [2], iv, [2], 338; [4], 375, [1]; [4], 386 p. Published by: Marmaduke, J. ESTC t105036. * CAL; Cha; CU-A; Do; DoA; E; ECB; ECW; FP (2 vols); Hen (vols 2, 3); ICN; L; Lhe; LO (vols 2, 3); LOU (vols 1, 2); Map; O; Stan; TLP (vol. 1); Ush.

There is a preface by James Marmaduke, describing the dramatic circumstances under which this book was originally composed in the 16th century.

2736. Thomé de Jesus. *The sufferings of our Lord Jesus Christ. Written originally in Portuguese by F. Thomas of Jesus ... To which is added, the third and last part, never before published in English.* 2 vols. Dublin. 1754. 8°. [16], 411, [1]; [8], 399, [1] p. Published by: Kelly, E. * FLK.

With a list of subscribers and one page of Kelly adverts.

2737. Thomé de Jesus. *The sufferings of our Lord Jesus Christ. Written originally in Portuguese by F. Thomas of Jesus ... And newly translated into*

English. To which is added, the third and last part, never before published in English. 2 vols. Dublin. 1794. 8°. vi, 305, [1]; [4], 282 p. Published by: Wogan, P. ESTC t117762. * CAL; Dt; ECW; FLK; L (bound in one vol.); Lhe; MWH; NNUT; NSCH; NSPM; OKentU; Pci. .

2738. Thomé de Jesus. *The sufferings of our Lord Jesus Christ, written originally in Portuguese by F. Thomas of Jesus ... newly translated into English. To which is added, the third and last part, never before published in English.* 2 vols. Dublin. 1794. 8°. vii, [1], 424, [4] p. (vol. 1). Printed by: Hoey, P. * FLK (vol. 1).

2739. Thompson, James. *Reply to Mr. M'Kee's remarks on a pastoral letter, lately written by the rev. doctor Hussey, to the Roman Catholic clergy of the united dioceses of Waterford and Lismore.* Waterford. 1797. 8°. [2], 6 p. Printed by: Ramsey, J. jun. ESTC t175958. * C; MY.
> Hussey was the R.C. bishop of Waterford and Lismore. Robert McKee's *Remarks* was also published at Waterford in 1797.

2740. *Three letters from a gentleman to his brother, explaining the motives of his conversion.* London. 1799. 12°. [2], 70 p. Printed by: Coghlan, J.P. * Do.
> Gillow (V, 396) and Do suggest Benedict Rayment as author. See also next item.

2741. *Three letters from a gentleman to his brother, explaining the motives of his conversion. To which is added a fourth, containing advice that may be useful to a new convert.* 2nd ed. London. 1800. 12°. [2], 96 p. Printed by: Coghlan, J.P. ESTC t176031. * ECW; Hor; Lhe; Ush.

2742. *Three material points of controversie, relating to the rule of faith; to the real presence of Christ's body and blood in the holy eucharist; and to the true Catholick church.* [Paris?]. 1719. 8°. 38 p. ESTC t176041. * Do; Lfa; Lhe; SCA.

2743. Throckmorton, John Courtenay. *A letter addressed to the Catholic clergy of England, on the appointment of bishops. By a layman.* London. 1790. 8°. [2], 22, [2] p. Printed by: Coghlan, J.P. ESTC t155027. * ECW; ICN; Lhe; Lmh; MRu; Sto.
> The letter, arguing for the right of laity and clergy to appoint their own bishops, engaged the author in a controversy with John Milner, Charles Plowden and Joseph Strickland (cf. e.g. nos 2612, 2267 and 2268).

2744. Throckmorton, John Courtenay. *A letter addressed to the Catholic clergy of England. On the appointment of bishops. By a layman.* [London?]. [1790]. 8°. [4], 22 p. ESTC t012300. * DUc; E; L; Lfa; Lhe; Osc; Sto (-tp); TxU.
> Dated at end 'June 12, 1790'. Lhe is bound up with nos 183 and 2314.

2745. Throckmorton, John Courtenay. *A letter addressed to the Catholic clergy of England, on the appointment of bishops ... To which are added further considerations on the same subject, and on the conduct of the English Catholics from the reign of Queen Elizabeth to the present time.* 2nd ed. London. 1792. 8°. xiv, [2], 205, [1] p. Printed by: Coghlan, J.P. Sold by: Booker; Keating; Lewis; Robinsons. ESTC t171528. * D; DCU; Do; ECW; ICN; MH; MY; Osc; Sto;

TxU; Ush.

2746. Throckmorton, John Courtenay. *A second letter addressed to the Catholic clergy of England on the appointment of bishops. In which the objections to the first letter are answered.* London. 1791. 8°. [iv], v-viii, 113, [1], cxi, [3] p. Printed by: Coghlan, J.P. Sold by: Booker; Keating; Lewis; Robinsons. ESTC t012325. * BB; DoA; DUc; E; ECW; ICN; IU; L; Lfa; Lhe; Lmh; MChB; MH; NSPM; O; Osc; SIR; TxU; Ush.

2747. Thunder, Henry. *The enrichment, or pearl of the soul: being a daily oblation ... By H. F. of the Society of Jesus. To which is added, a remembrance ... to pray for the dead. By a father of the same order.* 1756. 32°. [4], 246 p. * FA; Sco (imp.).

> The author is identified in ARCR II (no. 745), which mentions this book as a reprint of an edition now lost, printed in Paris in 1634.

2748. *To the Catholic nobility and gentry of the western district.* [1798]. s.s. * Cli.

> Dated 'London, August 31st, 1798'. It is an appeal to raise money for Bishop Walmesley's successor (Walmesley died 25 Nov. 1797).

2749. *To the Catholic nobility, gentry and others. We the committee, whose names are underwritten, for building the chapel in the borough.* [London]. [1790]. 3, [1 p. * BAA.

> This is an appeal for funds for the building of a chapel in St. George's Fields. The text of the opening of this appeal is reprinted in Ward (I, 194-196). See also no. 2180.

2750. *To the Catholics of England. My lords and gentlemen, I.* [London]. [1789]. 4°. 15, [1] p. ESTC t051174. * BAA; C; Hen; L; MY; P; Sto.

> Signed and dated 'Ch. Berington [and 6 others], 25 Nov. 1789'. There are various eds of this pamphlet in 1789. The present one lacks a final leaf of additions and has a middle paragraph on p. 13, predominantly lower case. This was also known as 'The Blue Book' (see also next 2 items).

2751. *To the Catholics of England. My lords and gentlemen, I.* [London]. [1789]. 4°. 15, [3] p. ESTC t051176. * Hen; L; LO; MRu; SIR; TxU; Ush.

> Signed and dated 'Ch. Berington [and 6 others], 25 Nov. 1789'. With a final leaf of additions (a separate copy of which is at DoA) and a middle paragraph on p. 13 predominantly capitalized.

2752. *To the Catholics of England. My lords and gentlemen, I.* [London]. [1789]. 4°. 15, [1] p. ESTC t051175. * L; Ush.

> Signed and dated 'Ch. Berington [and 6 others], 25 Nov. 1789'. Without a final leaf of additions and with a middle paragraph on p. 13 predominantly capitalized.

2753. *To the English Catholics. Gentlemen, your committee would have felt themselves happy.* London. 1787. fol. 4 p. * BAA; Cli; Ush.

> Signed 'Stourton [and 8 others] London, 10 April 1787'. Report of the Catholic Committee.

2754. *To the honourable Thomas Talbot. My Lord, we, the undersigned Catholic clergy residing in the county of Stafford.* [Stafford?]. [1790]. fol. 2 p. ESTC t067288. * Cli; L; SIR; Sto.

Dated and signed 'Jan. 25, 1790. Anthony Clough, Thomas Flynn [and thirteen others]'. This concerns the revised Catholic oath of allegiance.

2755. *To the King's most excellent majesty, the humble address of the Roman Catholic peers and commoners of Great Britain.* fol. [2] p. Printed by: Coghlan, J.P. * Sto; Ush.

Signed by Norfolk and many others. Reprinted by Coghlan from the *London Gazette*, May 2nd, 1778 and sold by him for 2d. Cf. no. 1074, *The Following address.*

2756. *To the lords and gentlemen of the committee of English Catholics. My lords and gentlemen, we the undersigned.* [London?]. [1790?]. fol. s.s. ESTC t051296. * Hor; L.

This printed petition intended to be signed in ms, refers to the oath of allegiance for English Roman Catholics.

2757. *To the public. As the tenets of Roman Catholics are often mispresented.* 8°. 12 p. * Ush.

A Catholic defence against inveterate prejudices.

2758. *To the right honourable Lord Petre, the right rev. Charles Berington, the rev. Joseph Wilks.* [1790]. 4°. [4] p. * Cli; Sto.

A letter to the Catholic Committee about the oath controversy. There are several ms signatures attached to Sto, the first of which is that of Charles Walmesley. Dated '2 Jan. 1790'.

2759. *To the right reverend father in God, John, Bishop of Centuria, vicar apostolic of the southern district of England ... the right reverend Charles ... William ... John.* [London]. [1791]. 4°. 11, [1], 13-31, 32-33, [1] p. ESTC t051371. * BAA; C; Cli; Hen; L; LO; MRu; MY; O; SIR; Sto; Ush; WDA.

The work contains two letters and the text of the oath of allegiance. Signed and dated 'Ch. Berington [and 7, resp. 9 others] for the committee of English Catholics. Feb. 2, 1791'. This was also known as 'The Second Blue Book'. See also no. 2877 for a reaction by Bishop Walmesley.

2760. *To the vic. ap. of the northern district.* [Manchester?]. [1790?]. 4°. [4] p. ESTC t147133. * Cli; L; Sto; Ush.

A request for a new form of the Catholic oath of loyalty. Signed and dated 'Rev. John Chadwick, V.G. [and 54 others]. Blackbrook, Jan. 1, 1789 [in fact 1790, cf. Ward I, 201]'.

2761. *To vindicate the clergy in England and Doway-College from the aspersions which for some years have been so unjustly cast upon them ... 'tis thought convenient to publish the two following letters.* 12°. [6] p. * Sto.

The letters mentioned were written by Pope Clement XI and dated 1711 and 1715. Latin and English.

2762. Tone, Theobald Wolfe. *An argument on behalf of the Catholics of Ireland.* Anon. [Belfast]. 1791. 8°. 32 p. Published by: Society of United Irishmen of Belfast. ESTC n015917. * CSmH; D; Dt; Du; KU-S; LONu; Osc; PP.

Tone was not R.C. but wrote on their behalf. For more eds of this work and other works by Tone see ESTC.

2763. Tootell, Christopher. *The ceremonies used in the administration of the sacraments, with the blessing of creatures, explain'd by the collections and reflections of C.T.* 1704. 12°. 56 p. * Amp; E; ECW; Stan.

> Some copies are bound up with Christopher Tootell's *The layman's ritual* (no. 2766).

2764. Tootell, Christopher. *Devotions to Jesus, Mary and Joseph, grounded on Gods written word.* Anon. [London]. 1723. 12°. 60 p. * Do; ECW; Gi; Stan.

> Stan bound up with *The memory of English saints reviv'd* (no. 1852).

2765. Tootell, Christopher. *Devotion to Jesus, Mary and Joseph grounded upon God's written word.* Anon. Liverpool. 1754. 12°. 72 p. Published by: Sadler, J. * Bevan (1995).

2766. Tootell, Christopher. *The lay-man's ritual. Part II. Containing explications of the ceremonies us'd at mass, and in the administration of the sacraments.* Anon. [London?]. 1704. 12°. 111, [1] p. ESTC t171244. * Amp; E; ECW; MRu.

2767. Tootell, Hugh. *An apology for the church history of England, from 1500 till 1688 ... Being a reply to ... A specimen of amendments, &c. under the fictitious name of Clerophilus Alethes.* Anon. [London]. 1742. 8°. xv, [1], 208 p. ESTC t086352. * BB; C; CtHT-W; CYc; DFo; DoA; ECR; ECW; Gi; L; Lfa; LfaA; Lhe; LO; Map; MRu; MY; O; Pci; Sal; Sto; TxU; Ush.

> 'Clerophilus Alethes' is John Constable (see no. 774). Tootell is also known as Charles Dodd. Tootell's *Remarks on Bp. Burnet's History of his own time* has not been included because of its general historical nature.

2768. Tootell, Hugh. *Certamen utriusq [sic], ecclesiae: or, a list of all the eminent writers of controversy, Catholicks and Protestants, since the Reformation ... By Charles Dodd.* [London?]. 1724. 4°. [2], 17, [1] p. ESTC t095150. * CLU-C; CSmH; CtY-BR; DFo; Do; ECR; GEU-T; Gi; ICN; InU-Li; L; Lfa; LfaA; Lhe; O; Osc; Sto; Ush.

2769. Tootell, Hugh. *The church history of England, from the year 1500, to the year 1688. Chiefly with regard to Catholicks.* Anon. 3 vols. Brussels [i.e. London]. 1737-42. fol. xx, 579, [1], 9, [1]; [2], 526, 4, [2]; [2], 535, [5] p. Printed by: [Bowyer, W.]. ESTC t090058. * AR; Ce; CLU-C; CtY; D; DAE; DGU; DoA; Dt; Du; Dun; ECR (vol. 1); ECW (vols 1, 2); L; Lhe; LOU; Map; O; Osc; PU; Sto; Ush; VUA.

2770. Tootell, Hugh. *Flores cleri Anglo-Catholici, or, an account of all the eminent clergymen who by their virtue, learning and deaths have supported the cause of the Church of Rome in England since 1500.* Anon. [c.1730]. 4°. 16 p. * Osc.

> This appears to be a pre-publication of some of the material in Tootell's later *Church history*.

2771. Tootell, Hugh. *Histoire du collége de Douay, à laquelle on a joint la politique des Jésuites Anglois. Ouvrages traduits de la langue Angloise.* London. 1762. 12°. [4], 4, 448 p. ESTC n007742. * Ct; Do; DoA; LO; NNC-T.

> This is a translation of *The history of the English College at Doway* (no. 2772),

and *The secret policy of the English Society of Jesus* (no. 2773).

2772. Tootell, Hugh. *The history of the English college at Doway, from its first foundation in 1568, to the present time. As also a particular description of the college, gardens, &c. ... By R.C. chaplain.* London. 1713. 8°. [4], 36 p. Published by: Lintott, B. Sold by: Baldwin, A. ESTC t064085. * C; CLU-C; C-S; Csj; CSmH; CtY; DAE; DFo; Do; DoA; Dt; E; ECR; ECW; Hen; IU; L; Lfa; LfaA; Lhe; O; Ob; Osc; TH; TxU; Ush; WDA.

2773. Tootell, Hugh. *The secret policy of the English Society of Jesus. Discover'd in a series of attempts against the clergy. In eight parts and twenty four letters. Directed to their provincial.* Anon. London. 1715. 8°. [3], 4-331, [9] p. Printed by: Morphew, J. Sold by: Morphew, J. ESTC t147453. * AR; BB; CLU-C; CSmH; CU-SB; DAE; DLC; Do; Dt; E; ECR; ECW; Hen; ICN; L; Lfa; Lhe; MH; MiU; MY; NcD; Osc; TH; TxU; Ush.

> The book was also known as *Dodd's provincial letters.* Part 7 deals with the history of Jansenism and its effect on the English clergy. See also next item.

2774. Tootell, Hugh. *The secret policy of the English Society of Jesus. Discover'd in a series of attempts against the clergy. In eight parts and twenty four letters. Directed to their provincial.* Anon. London. 1717. 8°. 50, [5], 54-132, [5], 136-208, [5], 212-331, [9] p. Printed by: Morphew, J. Sold by: Morphew, J. ESTC t172447. * C; LfaA.

2775. Touchet, George. *Historical collections out of several eminent Protestant historians, concerning the changes of religion.* Anon. Dublin. 1758. 12°. [12], 324 p. Published by: Bowes, P. ESTC t066613. * D; Do; Dt; FLK; ICU; IU; L; Mil; MRu; MY; O.

> Originally published in 1674. With a list of subscribers.

2776. *Tracts on controversy; containing a satisfactory explanation of some of the chief points of the Roman Catholic faith and worship.* Warrington. 1788. 12°. [4], 162 p. Printed by: Eyres, W. ESTC t062239. * BB; Do; DoA; L; Lfa; O.

2777. *Transactions of the General Committee of the Roman Catholics of Ireland, during the year 1791; and some fugitive pieces on that subject.* Dublin. 1792. 8°. [2], 27, [1] p. Printed by: Byrne, P. ESTC t106253. * D; Dt; ICR; IU; L; Lhl; MChB; Mil; MY; PP; PPL; Sto.

> Mil has two extra pages, one of which contains adverts for Byrne.

2778. *Translation of a Latin letter from a German Jesuit to his provincial. Sent by F. Dugaea; a French Jesuit, delivered out of the prison at Lisbon by means of the Queen of France.* [1766]. 12°. 4 p. * Sto.

> Signed and dated 'Laurance, from the prison of St. Julian, on the banks of the Tagus, December 12. 1766'.

2779. *The travels of the Jesuits in Ethiopia: containing 1. The geographical description ... Illustrated with an exact map ... The whole collected, and historically digested by F. Balthazar Tellez.* London. 1710. 4°. [4], 264, [16] p. Published by: Knapton, J.; Bell, A.; Midwinter, D.; Taylor, W. Sold by: Round, J; [and 4 others in London]. ESTC t133244. * GOT; L.

> Compiled by the R.C. editor and translator John Stevens. For several other

accounts of Jesuit travels, intended for the general reading public, see ESTC.

2780. *A treatise of piety, and devotion to Jesus Christ. Translated from the French.* London. 1701. 12°. 71, [1] p. ESTC t127119. * L.

2781. Treuvé, Simon Michel. *The spiritual director for those who have none. Translated out of French [Directeur spirituel].* Anon. [London?]. 1703. 12°. [12], 448 p. ESTC t083100. * DFo; Do; DoA; Du; ECW; L; Lhe; LO; O.

The book has a device on the tp which is very similar to those found on the works of Sylvester Jenks (T.H. Clancy S.J., personal communication).

2782. Troy, John Thomas. *A dialogue between a Protestant and Papist, on the subject of popish absolution, jubilees and indulgences.* [Dublin?]. 1776. 8°. 44 p. ESTC t063610. * L.

2783. Troy, John Thomas. *The excommunication of the rev. Robert M'Evoy priest of the archdiocess of Dublin, for promulgating and upholding principles established by the French Revolution. Published 29th September 1792.* London. 1798. 12°. 12 p. Printed by: Coghlan, J.P. ESTC n016909. * CtY; D.

2784. Troy, John Thomas. *An humble address to our most gracious sovereign King George III. from the Roman Catholic prelates of Ireland, presented on Tuesday, December 17, M,DCC,XCIII, by ... drs John Thomas Troy, Boetius Egan, Thomas Bray and Francis Moylan, to ... John, Earl of Westmorland.* London. 1794. 8°. [5], 8-23, [1] p. Printed by: Coghlan, J.P. Sold by: Debrett, J.; Robinsons; Bookrr [sic]; Keating; Lewis. ESTC t190075. * O.

Signed and dated 'John Thomas Troy. January 14, 1794'.

2785. Troy, John Thomas. *A pastoral address to the Roman Catholicks of the archdiocess of Dublin delivered by the rev. John Thomas Troy ... in the chapel of Francis-street, Dublin, on Thursday, 16th February, M.DCC.XCVII.* Dublin. 1797. 4°. [2], 5-24 p. Printed by: Fitzpatrick, H. Published by: Wogan, P. ESTC t180485. * BAA; D; MY.

2786. Troy, John Thomas. *A pastoral address to the Roman Catholicks of the archdiocess of Dublin delivered ... in the chapel of Francis-Street, Dublin, on Thursday, 16th February, MDCCXCVII.* Dublin. [1797]. 8°. 16 p. Printed by: Wogan, P. * DCU; RPB.

2787. Troy, John Thomas. *A pastoral address to the Roman Catholicks of the archdiocess of Dublin delivered ... in the chapel of Francis-street, Dublin, on Thursday, 16th February M.DCC.XCVII.* London repr. [Dublin]. [1797]. 8°. 16 p. Printed by: Coghlan, J.P. repr. [Wogan, P.]. ESTC t180488. * D; Osc; Sto; WDA.

2788. Troy, John Thomas. *A pastoral instruction on the duties of Christian citizens, addressed to the Roman Catholics of the archdiocese of Dublin.* Dublin. 1793. 8°. [4], 121, [11] p. Printed by: Mills, M. Published by: Wogan, P. Sold by: Moore, J.; Jones, W.; Byrne, P.; McDonnel, T.; Corbet, W. ESTC t112231. * C; CLU-S/C; CSmH; D; Di; Dt; Du; L; LONu; MB; Mil; MiU; MY; TxU.

With two appendices.

2789. Troy, John Thomas. *A pastoral instruction on the duties of Christian citizens, addressed to the Roman Catholics of the archdiocess of Dublin.* 2nd ed. Dublin. 1793. 8°. [4], 133, [11] p. Printed by: Wogan, P. ESTC n019938. * D; E; ECW; ICR; IU; Mil; MoU; Osc; PP; Sto.

2790. Troy, John Thomas. *A pastoral instruction on the duties of Christian citizens, addressed to the Roman Catholics of the archdiocess of Dublin.* 3rd ed. London. 1793. 8°. [4], 147, [1] p. Printed by: Coghlan, J.P. Sold by: Debrett; Robinsons; Booker; Keating; Lewis; Watts (Gosport); Robins (Winchester); Gregory (Brighton); Ledger (Dover); Wogan, P. (Dublin). ESTC t121875. * BB; E; ECW; L; Lfa; Lhe; MRu; NN; O; PP; RPB; Ush.

2791. Troy, John Thomas. *Pastoral instruction to the Roman Catholics of the archdiocess of Dublin.* Dublin. 1798. 8°. 16 p. Printed by: Fitzpatrick, H. Published by: Wogan, P. ESTC t108349. * D; Di; E; L; Lhl; MB; MRu; Sto.

2792. Troy, John Thomas. *Rev. sirs, the following lines are to be distinctly read at each mass.* [Dublin]. [1798]. fol. s.s. Printed by: Fitzpatrick, H. * WDA.
    Dated 'Whit-Sunday, 27th May, 1798'.

2793. Troy, John Thomas. *To the reverend pastors and other Roman Catholic clergy of the archdiocess of Dublin. Please to read the under-written lines from your respective altars, at each mass, on Sunday next.* [Dublin]. [1791]. fol. s.s. ESTC t210322. * Di; WDA.
    Dated 'Dublin, 9th March, 1791'.

2794. Troy, John Thomas. *To the rev. pastors and other Roman Catholic clergy of the arch diocess of Dublin.* [Dublin]. [1795]. fol. [4] p. ESTC n043669. * Lpro.
    Signed and dated 'John Thomas Troy. Dublin, August 6, 1795'.

2795. Troy, John Thomas. *To the rev. pastors and other Roman Catholick clergy of the arch diocess of Dublin.* [Dublin]. [1796]. 4°. s.s. ESTC t108344. * L.
    Dated and signed 'Dublin, 29th February, 1796. J.T.Troy'.

2796. Troy, John Thomas. *To the reverend pastors, and other Roman Catholic clergy, of the archdiocess of Dublin.* [Dublin]. [1798]. 8°. 14 p. Printed by: [Fitzpatrick, H.]. Published by: [Wogan, P.]. ESTC t221693. * MY.
    Signed and dated 'John Thomas Troy. Dublin, 22d June, 1798'.

2797. Troy, John Thomas. *To the reverend pastors, and other Roman Catholic clergy, of the archdiocess of Dublin.* Dublin. 1798. 8°. 16 p. Printed by: Fitzpatrick, H. Published by: Wogan, P. ESTC t108348. * L; MY; Sto.

2798. Troy, John Thomas. *The trustees of the Roman Catholic seminary at Maynooth assembled in Dublin.* [London]. [1799]. fol. 3, [1] p. Printed by: Coghlan, J.P. ESTC n045142. * DoA; LANre; Lpro.
    A statement on behalf of the trustees of the seminary at Maynooth, denying involvement in the late rising. Signed and dated 'J.T. Troy, 23 April 1799'.

2799. *The true motives of the confidence and trust, the faithful ought to put in the protection of the ever glorious Virgin Mary.* London. 1717. 12°. [6], 184, [2] p. * Do; Lfa; LO.

2800. *The true principles of Roman Catholics.* Newport. 1796. 8°. [2], 11, [1] p. Printed by: Albin, J. ESTC t051918. * L.

> The introduction is signed 'Philalbion'. Gillow (IV; 343-4) suggests that this is the priest Simon Lucas (d. 1801).

Turberville, Henry. *An abridgement.* For the intricate relationship between Turberville's *Abridgment* and other popular catechisms such as the *Doway catechism, An abstract of the Douay catechism, Abridgment of Christian doctrine as revised by Challoner,* and *Short abridgment* see Pickering. For practical reasons we list under Turberville all the *Abridgments of Christian doctrine* not clearly attributable to other authors or compilers.

2801. Turberville, Henry. *An abridgment of Christian doctrine; with proofs of scripture for points controverted. Catechistically explain'd, by way of question and answer. Permissu superiorum.* Anon. London. 1708. 12°. [4], 210, [2] p. ESTC t203428. * ECW; Llp.

> The epistle to the reader is signed 'H.T.' The last 2 pages contain 'Dr. Baylie's challenge'. See also the following items.

2802. Turberville, Henry. *An abridgment of Christian doctrine; with proofs of scripture, for points controverted. Catechistically explain'd, by way of question and answer.* Anon. London. 1717. 12°. [4], 210, [2] p. ESTC t118281. * L.

2803. Turberville, Henry. *An abridgment of Christian doctrine; with proofs of scripture, for points controverted. Catechistically explain'd, by way of question and answer.* Anon. London. 1720. 12°. [4], 198, [2] p. ESTC t082746. * L.

2804. Turberville, Henry. *An abridgment of Christian doctrine; with proofs of scripture, for points controverted. Catechistically explain'd by way of question and answer. Permissu superiorum.* Anon. London. 1725. 12°. [4], 210, [2] p. Published by: Meighan, T. * Sco.

2805. Turberville, Henry. *An abridgment of Christian doctrine; with proofs of scripture for points controverted. Catechistically explain'd by way of question and answer ... Permissu superiorum.* London. 1734. 12°. [4], 210, [2] p. Published by: Meighan, T. ESTC t126626. * BB; DoA; ECW; L; Lhe; MChB; Stan; Ush; UshL.

2806. Turberville, Henry. *An abridgment of Christian doctrine; with proofs of scripture for points controverted. Catechistically explain'd by way of question and answer.* London. 1748. 12°. [4], 176 p. Published by: Meighan, T. ESTC t203423. * E; TxU.

> See no. 2807 for another issue without the names of Turberville and Meighan on tp.

2807. Turberville, Henry. *Abridgement of Christian doctrine with proofs of scripture for points controverted ... by way of question and answer.* Anon. London. 1748. 12°. [4], 176 p. Published by: [Meighan, T.]. * Do; DoA; ECW.
> See also no. 2806.

2808. Turberville, Henry. *Abridgement of Christian doctrine with proofs of scripture for points controverted ... by way of question and answer.* Anon.

London. 1756. 180 p. Published by: Meighan, T. * Do; DoA; ECW; TH; TLP; Ush.

2809. Turberville, Henry. *An abridgment of Christian doctrine; with proofs of scripture for points controverted. Catechistically explained by way of question and answer.* [London]. 1782. 12°. 180 p. ESTC t150431. * Lhe.

2810. Turberville, Henry. *An abridgment of Christian doctrine, revised and enlarged by M.G., and published for the use of the n***n district.* Newcastle. 1784. 12°. 48 p. ESTC t215646. * Di; Osc.

> 'M.G.' is Matthew Gibson, Bishop of Comana, V.A. According to Abercrombie 1980 (p. 285) Gibson published this together with Thomas Eyre.

2811. Turberville, Henry. *Abridgement of Christian doctrine with proofs of scripture for points controverted. Catechistically explained by way of question and answer.* London. 1788. 12°. iv, 257, [1] p. Printed by: Coghlan, J.P. ESTC t203424. * Do; E.

2812. Turberville, Henry. *An abridgement of Christian doctrine. Published for the use of the London district.* Anon. London. 1797. 32°. 60 p. Printed by: Coghlan, J.P. * ECW (imp.).

2813. Turberville, Henry. *An abridgement of Christian doctrine. Published for the use of the London district.* London. 1798. 8°. 160 p. Printed by: Coghlan, J.P. * Hen.

> Parallel English and French texts.

2814. Turberville, Henry. *An abridgment of Christian doctrine: with proofs of scripture for points controverted; catechistically explain'd by way of question and answer.* London. 1798. 12°. 256 p. Printed by: Coghlan, J.P. * Gi.

2815. Turberville, Henry. *An abridgment of Christian doctrine. Published for the use of the London district.* Anon. London. 1799. 24°. 64 p. Printed by: Coghlan, J.P. ESTC t203427. * NU.

2816. Turberville, Henry. *Abridgment of Christian doctrine published for the use of the northern district.* Liverpool. 1799. 12°. 32 p. * DoA.

2817. Turberville, Henry. *Aithghearradh n a teagaisg Chriosduidh; le dearbhaidh sgrioptuir, air modh ceisd agus freagair [Abridgment of Christian doctrine. Gaelic].* Anon. [London]. 1781. 12°. xii, 485, [1] p. Printed by: Coghlan, J.P. ESTC t125412. * C; E; ICN; L; MH; Sal; Sco.

> Translated by Robert Menzies (see also no. 2731).

2818. Turberville, Henry. *A manual of controversies: clearly demonstrating the truth of Catholick religion ... To which is added, a poem on the real preesence [sic] and rule of faith ... Collected by J.D.* 5th ed. London. 1744. 12°. [2], iv, [2], 268 p. ESTC n034993. * FLK; Gi; InNd.

> InNd has ii, [2], 268 p.

2819. *Twelve pious meditations on the rules. To which is added Centurioni's letter.* London. 1764. 8°. 81, [1] p. Printed by: Balfe, R. ESTC t200660. * Lhe; Ush.

> Meditations on the rules of the Jesuits. The letter is from Luigi Centurioni, the

Jesuit superior-general. See also next item.

2820. *Twelve pious meditations on the rules. To which is added Centurioni's letter.* London. 1774. 8°. 82 p. Printed by: Balfe, R. * Lfa.

2821. *Two memorials presented by several cardinals, archbishops and bishops; to his Royal Highness the Duke of Orleans, Regent of France … As also a pastoral instruction … Translated into English.* [London?]. 1720. 8°. 155, [1] p. ESTC t178018. * C; CtY.

2822. Ulrick, Anthony. *Fifty reasons or motives why the Roman Catholick apostolick religion ought to be preferr'd to all the sects this day in Christendom [Quinquaginta Romano-Catholicam fidem omnibus aliis praeferendi motiva].* 1712. 12°. x, 108 p. * Lfa.

2823. Ulrick, Anthony. *Fifty reasons or motives why the Roman Catholick apostolick religion ought to be preferr'd to all the sects this day in Christendom.* London. 1715. 12°. [12], 132 p. Printed by: Meighan, T. Sold by: Meighan, T. ESTC t202281. * Hen; Llp; Osc; Ush.

2824. Ulrick, Anthony. *Fifty reasons or motives, why the Roman Catholick apostolick religion ought to be preferr'd to all the sects this day in Christendom … To which are added three valuable papers.* Antwerp. 1715. 12°. [12], 132 p. ESTC n018680. * CLU-C; CtY-BR; Do; ECW; Gi; KU-S; Lhe; Llp; LO; NNUT; O; TxU.

> The 'Three valuable papers' are the decision of the Protestant university of Helmstedt in favour of Catholicism and two papers written by King Charles II and the Duchess of York (Clancy no. 214ff.).

2825. Ulrick, Anthony. *Fifty reasons or motives, why the Roman Catholick apostolick religion ought to be preferr'd to all the sects this day in Christendom … To which are added three valuable papers.* Antwerp. 1715. 12°. [14], 130 p. ESTC n018677. * CaQMM; CLU-C; DLC; Do; NNUT; Osc; TH; Ush; Yb.

2826. Ulrick, Anthony. *Fifty reasons, or motives, why the Roman Catholic, apostolic religion, ought to be preferred to all the sects this day in Christendom.* Antwerp. 1741. 12°. x, 108 p. ESTC t183902. * Lfa; Lhe; Map; O; Sal; TxU; Ush.

> ESTC has also no. t184580 for what seems to be exactly the same book.

2827. Ulrick, Anthony. *Fifty reasons, or, motives, why the Roman Catholick apostolic religion ought to be preferred to all the sects this day in Christendom.* London. 1780. 12°. viii, [10], 141, [5] p. ESTC n060941. * PPAmP; StD.

> The imprint states that the book was sold at Dublin.

2828. Ulrick, Anthony. *Fifty reasons or motives why the Roman Catholic apostolic religion ought to be preferred to all the sects this day in Christendom.* London. 1782. 12°. x, 96 p. * DGU.

2829. Ulrick, Anthony. *Fifty reasons, or motives why the Roman Catholic apostolic religion ought to be preferred to all the sects this day in Christendom.* London. 1792. 12°. viii, 9-96 p. Printed by: Coghlan, J.P. * ECR; Sto.

2830. Ulrick, Anthony. *Fifty reasons or motives, why the Roman Catholic,*

apostolic religion, ought to be preferred to all the sects this day in Christendom.
London. 1793. 12°. [8], 9-96 p. Printed by: Coghlan, J.P. * Gi.

2831. Ulrick, Anthony. *Fifty reasons or motives, why the Roman Catholic, apostolic religion, ought to be preferred to all the sects this day in Christendom.* London. 1798. 12° x, 96, [2] p. * Do; Stan.

2832. Usher, James. *A free examination of the common methods employed to prevent the growth of popery. In which are pointed out their defects and errors, and the advantages they give papists.* Anon. London. 1766. 8°. [2], vii, [1], 186 p. ESTC t063772. * C; CLU; CME; CSt; CtY; CU-SB; Do; E; ECW; GEU-T; ICN; IU; L; Ldw; Lhe; Llp; Lu; MH-H; MRu; O; P; Sal; ScCR; TxU; Ush.

> Several copies lack the postscript. Usher (also spelled 'Ussher') was the author of a number of works that are outside the terms of our definition. The present work is R.C. in spite of its misleading title, and was originally published as a series of letters in the *Public Ledger*, signed 'A Free Thinker'.

2833. Usher, James. *A free examination of the common methods employed to prevent the growth of popery; with their defects and errors, and the advantages they give papists.* Anon. [London]. [1767]. 12°. iii-xii, 252 p. Printed by: [Bladon]. * DLC.

2834. Usher, James. *A free examination of the common methods employed to prevent the growth of popery. Part II.* Anon. London. 1768. 8°. 67, [1] p. ESTC t063773. * C; Do; E; L; Ldw; Lhe; MH-H; MRu; P; ScCR; Sto.

2835. Usher, James. *A free examination of the common methods employed to prevent the growth of popery.* Anon. Dublin. 1774. 12°. xii, 252 p. Printed by: Chamberlaine, D. ESTC n031680. * C; CaQMBN; E; MY; O; Sal; Ush.

2836. Usher, James. *A free examination of the common methods employed to prevent the growth of popery ... To which are added, seasonable reflections ... written before the indulgence granted to Roman Catholics to take long leases.* Cork. 1781. 12°. xii, 252 p. Printed by: Flyn, W. ESTC t112036. * D; Di; Dt; E; L; MY; O; TxU.

2837. *Vade mecum piorum sacerdotum, sive exercitia et preces. Aliaeque selectae devotiones.* Preston. 1774. 8°. 90, [2] p. Published by: Stuart, W. ESTC t123058. * DoA; Gi; L; Lhe; O; Stan; Ush; UshL.

2838. Valsecchi, Antonino. *Of the foundations of religion, and the fountains of impiety ... Translated from the original Italian. By the rev. Thomas Carbry [Dei fondamenti della religione e dei fonti dell' empietà].* 3 vols. Dublin. 1800-1802. 8°. [2], viii, viii, 390; 2, xiv, 567, [1]; 2, xxvi, 576 p. Printed by: Hanvey, E. & J. ESTC t121851. * D (vols 1, 2); Dt; Du; FLK; IDA; L; MY; SIR (vols 1, 2).

> The 3rd vol. bears the imprint 'Printed by W.H. Tyrrell, 1802'.

2839. Vaughan, Arthur. *The triumphs of the cross; or, penitent of Egypt. In eight books.* Anon. Birmingham. 1776. 8°. [2], xvi, 277, [1] p. Published by: Author. Sold by: Coghlan, J.P. ESTC t125800. * BMp; BMu; C; CtY; DMR; ECB; Gi; ICN; L; Map; MH-H; NjP; Osc.

Verse. Kirk (p. 241) identifies the author as Arthur Vaughan and states that he was also the author of 'The ghost of Sansom fields' (on the occasion of the apostasy of Charles Henry Wharton S.J.). NUC notes that there are several variants.

2840. *Le véritable ami, ou, le François Chrétien à ses compatriotes, par Mr. C.A.C.D.V.* London. 1796. 8°. 63, [1] p. Printed by: Boussonnier, Ph. le. * Osc; WDA.

2841. *Vernon Hall school. Deo juvante. In schola Catholica-Romanis ad villam Vernonis, die 28a mensis Decembris, anno 1795. Pro semestri exercitatione.* 1795. 4°. s.s. * Cli.

2842. *Verses on the consecration of the Bishop of Acanthos, by the students in poetry and rhetoric of the English College at Douay.* London. 1791. 8°. [2], iii-vi, 7-16 p. Printed by: Coghlan, J.P. ESTC t175564. * DMR; O; Osc; Ush.
   The Bishop of Acanthos is William Gibson.

2843. *Vesperale novum pro dominicis & festis. In quo continentur antiphonae, psalmi, capitula, hymni, orationes, commemorationes & completorium. Ex antiphonaris et breviario Romanis.* London. [8], 404 p. Printed by: Wade, J.F. * MNS.
   For Wade see Zon.

Vespers. For Vespers see also Evening office.

2844. *The vespers and complin, or evening office of the church for all Sundays and holydays throughout the year, according to the Roman breviary; to which is added the ordinary of the mass.* London. 1790. 12°. xxiii, [1], 696 p. Printed by: Coghlan, J.P. ESTC t181818. * DMR; Gi; O.
   Latin and English.

2845. *The vespers and office for the dead, and its proper mass, together, with the litanies of the Blessed Virgin Mary, and of the saints, in Latin and English.* Dublin. 1791. 8°. 143, [1] p. Printed by: Butler, T. ESTC t207804. * D.
   With a list of subscribers.

2846. *Vespers for Sundays.* [1771]. 12°. 48 p. * Do.
   Bound up with *The paradise of the soul* (no. 1856).

2847. *The vespers, or even-song: with the holy mass. In Latin and English together.* [London?]. 1708. 18°. 282, [12] p. ESTC t120232. * L.
   With 6 final leaves of contents, in which this is called 'The second part, and prayers'. For a similar case see no. 2508.

2848. *Vespers: or the evening-office for every Sunday and festival throughout the year: in Latin and English.* 6th ed. London. 1792. 12°. [2], viii, [1], 18-368 p. Printed by: Keating, P. Published by: Keating, P. ESTC t193418. * AWn (imp.); Hor.

2849. *A view of Mr. White's principles, in his book of The middle state of souls.* London. 1712. 12°. [8], 134 p. Printed by: Howlatt, T. ESTC t082144. * ECW; ICN; L; Lhe.
   Gillow (IV, 334) and ICN attribute this book to Francis Lovel (d. 1716) who

304

worked on the mission in Derbyshire and Leicestershire. For Thomas White, see Clancy.

2850. *A vindication of a pamphlet, lately published, intituled, The case of the Roman-Catholics of Ireland.* Dublin. 1755. 8°. 54 p. Published by: Lord, P. Sold by: Lord, P. ESTC t178626. * C; CSmH; D; Dt; ICR; MRu; O; SCR.

> This work answers *Remarks on a late pamphlet intituled The case of the Roman Catholics* (Dublin 1755), which in its turn was a reply to Charles O'Conor (see no. 1988ff.). The present pamphlet, dated 'Bandon, Aug. 28, 1755', might also be by O'Conor. See also next item.

2851. *A vindication of a pamphlet, lately published, intituled, The case of the Roman-Catholics of Ireland.* Dublin. 1755. 12°. 52 p. Published by: Lord, P. Sold by: Lord, P. ESTC t178627. * Du.

2852. *Vindication of the cause of the Catholics of Ireland, adopted, and ordered to be published by the General Committee, at a meeting held at Taylor's-Hall, Back-Lane, December 7, 1792.* Dublin. 1793. 8°. [2], 38 p. Printed by: Fitzpatrick, H. ESTC t087738. * BFq; C; D; Dt; Gi; IU; L; Lhe; MChB; Mil; MiU; MY; NIC; NN; PPL; PSt; RP; RPB.

2853. *A vindication of the conduct and principles of the Catholics of Ireland from the charges made against them ... with an apppendix of authentic documents ... and ... the petition of 1793.* London. 1793. 8°. [4], 91, [1] p. Published by: Debrett, J. ESTC t178791. * Di; Du; Lmh; MRu; Osc; Ush.

> This publication is discussed in *The Analytical Review*, vol. 15, 1793, p. 318. Osc is Kirk's copy.

2854. *A vindication of the conduct and principles of the Catholics of Ireland, from the charges made against them, by certain late grand juries, and other interested bodies in that country.* 2nd ed. London. 1793. 8°. [4], 108 p. Published by: Debrett, J. ESTC t210610. * Ct; D; MB.

2855. *A vindication of the new oath of allegiance proposed to the Roman Catholics of Ireland. By a steadfast member of the Church of Rome.* Dublin. 1775. [2], 39, [1] p. Published by: Williams, J. * MY; Sto.

2856. *A vindication of the rev. Dr. O'Leary; in reply to an attempted defence of Mr. H.* London. 1791. 8°. 31, [1], p. Published by: Ridgway, J. ESTC t191043. * DUc.

> Signed 'A student of the Middle Temple'. 'Dr. H.' is Thomas Hussey. A reply to *A defence of the character of ... Mr. Hussey* (no. 884), which was itself a reply to *A narrative of the misunderstanding between the rev. Arthur O'Leary and the rev. Mr. Hussey* (no. 1924).

2857. *A vindication of the Roman Catholicks. Being their most solemn declaration of their utter abhorrence of the following tenets.* London. 1743. 12°. 12 p. Published by: Meighan, P. * DoA; Ush.

2858. *Vindiciae Catholicae. A full defence of the declaration of the Catholic Society of Dublin, in reply to an anonymous pamphlet, entitled 'Strictures on the declaration of the Society'.* Dublin. 1792. 8°. [2], 96 p. Published by: Moore, J. ESTC t179004. * D; Dt; InU; MY.

2859. *Vous êtes prié de la part du ministre plenipotentiaire de France, d'assister au Te Deum, qu'il sera chanter dimanche 4 de ce mois, à midi, dans la chapelle Catholique neuve pour celebrer l'anniversaire.* Philadelphia. [1779]. s.s. Printed by: Bailey, F. ESTC w028623. * PPL.

> An invitation by the plenipotentiary of France, Mr. Gerard, to celebrate the Declaration of Independence by a religious service. Dated 'A Philadelphie, le 2 juillet, 1779.

2860. Walenburch, Adriaan van. *De controversiis tractatus generales, contracti.* Dublin. 1796. 12°. [4], vii, [3], 459, [1] p. Printed by: Fitzpatrick, H. ESTC t118972. * D; Dt; FLK; IDA; L; Mil; MY.

> An early Maynooth textbook. Written by Adriaan van Walenburch together with his brother Pieter.

2861. Walker, Augustine. *Cum nobis a capitulo ultimo.* [Paris]. [1783]. 4°. [4] p. * Cli.

> Walker, who was President-General of the English Benedictine Congregation, writes to the Abbot of Lambspring and the provincials, priors, superiors and other members of the congregation to inform them of the permission from Rome to keep Sundays as double major rank. Dated Rome, 22 September 1782, and Paris, 1 October 1783.

2862. Walmesley, Charles. *Answer to a letter, written by the Committee of English Catholics, Nov. 25 1789, to the four apostolic vicars, and signed by the following persons. Char. Berington [and six others].* [Bath?]. 1789. fol. 3, [1] p. * BAA; Cli; Sto; Ush.

> Signed and dated 'Charles Walmesley, V.A. Bath Dec. 24, 1789'.

2863. Walmesley, Charles. *Answer to a letter, written by the Committee of English Catholics, Nov. 25, 1789, to the four apostolic vicars, and signed by the following persons. Char. Berington [and six others].* [Bath?]. [1789]. fol. 2 p. ESTC t021990. * L; O; Ush.

> Signed and dated 'Charles Walmesley, V.A., Bath Dec. 24, 1789'.

2864. Walmesley, Charles. *Carolus Dei & apostolicae sedis gratiâ Episcopus Ramatensis in districtu occidentali vicarius apostolicus.* [1764]. 8°. 4 p. ESTC n061436. * GEU-T; TxU.

> Dated and signed 'Datum Martii 12. 1764. Carolus Ramaten, V.A.'

2865. Walmesley, Charles. *Carolus Dei & apostolicae sedis gratiâ Episcopus Ramatensis in districtu occidentali vicarius apostolicus; omnibus missionariis sacerdotibus tam saecularibus quam regularibus.* [1764]. 8°. 11, [1] p. ESTC n061437. * TxU.

> Dated and signed 'Datum Martii 12. 1764. Carolus Ramaten, V.A.'

2866. Walmesley, Charles. *Carolus Ramaten in districtu occidentali vicarius apostolicus; omnibus missionaribus sacerdotibus tam secularibus quam regularibus, salutem et benedictionem.* [1777]. fol. s.s. * Cli.

> Dated Rome, 9 March 1777, and Bath, 14 May 1777.

2867. Walmesley, Charles. *Charles Bishop of Rama, vicar apostolic, to all the faithful, clergy and laity, in the western district. Our pastoral solicitude for the* *flock.* [Bath]. [1789]. fol. 2 p. * BAA; Cli; DowA; O; Sto; Ush.

Dated 'Bath, November 2, 1789'.

2868. Walmesley, Charles. *Charles, Bishop of Rama, vicar apostolic, to all the faithful, clergy and laity, in the western district. On the present occasion we hasten to congratulate you.* [Bath?]. [1791]. fol. s.s. ESTC t030502. * Cli; Hor; L; P; Ush.

Dated 'June 28, 1791'.

2869. Walmesley, Charles. *Charles, Bishop of Rama, vicar apostolic, to all the faithful of the western district. In compliance with our pastoral charge we announce to you the holy fast of Lent.* [Bath]. [1792]. fol. s.s. * Cli; WDA.

Dated 'Bath, Feb. 8, 1792'.

2870. Walmesley, Charles. *Charles, Bishop of Rama, vicar apostolic, to all the faithful, clergy and laity, in the western district. Dear brethren, the present deplorable state of the refugees from France calls aloud.* [Bath]. [1792]. fol. s.s. * WDA.

Dated 'Bath, Sept 28. 1792'.

2871. Walmesley, Charles. *Charles, Bishop of Rama, vicar apostolic, to all the faithful of the western district.* [Bath]. [1793]. fol. s.s. * Cli.

Dated 'Bath, Jan. 31, 1793'. Regulations for Lent.

2872. Walmesley, Charles. *Charles, Bishop of Rama, vicar apostolic, to all the faithful, clergy and laity, in the western district. Grateful to our august and gracious sovereign and the legislature of his kingdom.* [Bath?]. [1793]. fol. s.s. * WDA.

Dated 'Bath, April 2, 1793'. Ordering a solemn fast on 19 April.

2873. Walmesley, Charles. *Charles, Bishop of Rama, vicar apostolic, to all the faithful, clergy and laity, in the western district.* [Bath]. [1794]. fol. s.s. * Cli.

Dated 'Bath, Feb. 18th 1794'. Regulations for Lent.

2874. Walmesley, Charles. *Charles, Bishop of Rama, vicar apostolic, to all the faithful, clergy and laity, in the western district. Dear brethren, on the general view of the present state of this and the neighbouring nations.* [Bath]. [1795]. fol. s.s. * Cli.

Dated 'Bath Jan. 31st, 1795'.

2875. Walmesley, Charles. *Charles, Bishop of Rama, vicar apostolic, to all the faithful, clergy and laity, in the western district. Dear brethren. We call on your attention.* [Bath]. [1796]. fol. s.s. * Cli; LANre.

Dated and signed 'Bath Jan: 1796 Charles, Bishop of Rama, vicar apostolic'.

2876. Walmesley, Charles. *Charles, Bishop of Rama, vicar apostolic, to all the faithful, clergy and laity, in the western district. Dear brethren, we appeal to you to say, whether in the present state of Europe.* [Bath]. [1797]. fol. 2 p. * BAA; Cli; WDA.

Dated 'Bath, Feb 10, 1797' and 'Bath, Feb 13, 1797'.

2877. Walmesley, Charles. *Charles, Bishop of Rama, vicar apostolic, to the clergy of the western district. Dear brethren, St. Paul by his words, attendate* *vobis*. [Bath]. [1797]. 4°. s.s. * BAA; Cli; LANre; WDA.

> Dated 'Bath, June 3, 1797'. This concerns 'the rebels', who signed the second blue book (see no. 2759). LANre has '25 Sept 1797' added in Walmesley's hand.

2878. Walmesley, Charles. *Charles, Bishop of Rama, vicar apostolic. To the clergy of the western district.* [Bath]. [1797]. 8°. 2 p. * Ush.

> Dated 'Bath, Sept. 25, 1797'.

2879. Walmesley, Charles. *Encyclical letter addressed to all the faithful, both clergy and laity, in the four districts of England, by the four vicars apostolic, Charles Ramaten, James Birthan, Thomas Acon, and Matthew Comanen.* [London]. [1789]. fol. s.s. ESTC t153975. * BAA; Cli; DowA; L; P.

> Dated 'Hammersmith, Oct. 21, 1789'. See also next item.

2880. Walmesley, Charles. *Encyclical letter addressed to all the faithful, both clergy and laity, in the four districts of England, by the four vicars apostolic, Charles Ramaten, James Birthan, Thomas Acon, and Matthew Comanen.* [London]. [1789]. 4°. [4] p. ESTC t081508. * L; Ush.

> Dated 'Hammersmith, Oct. 21, 1789'. The letter is bound up with *Extract from the Diary; or Woodfall's Register no. 77. Friday, June 26. 1789'* (no. 1016).

2881. Walmesley, Charles. *Encyclical letter. Charles, Bishop of Rama, vicar apostolic of the western district; William, Bishop of Acanthos ... and John, Bishop of Centuria ... To all the faithful, clergy and laity ... We think it necessary.* [London]. [1791]. 4°. 2 p. ESTC t032645. * Cli; Hen; L; LO; MdBJ; MRu; O; Sto; TxU; Ush; WDA.

> Dated and signed 'London, Jan. 19, 1791' by Charles Ramaten, William Acanthen and John Centurien. Against the proposed oath of allegiance. See also no. 2882.

2882. Walmesley, Charles. *Encyclical letter. Charles Bishop of Rama, vicar apostolic of the western district; William, Bishop of Acanthos ... and John, Bishop of Centuria ... To all the faithful, clergy and laity ... We think it necessary.* [London]. [1791]. fol. 2 p. ESTC t017850. * BAA; C; DowA; ICN; L; MdBJ; MY; Osc; P; SIR; Sto; Ush.

> Dated and signed 'Jan 19, 1791' by Charles Ramaten, William Acanthen and John Centurien.

2883. Walmesley, Charles. *Exhortations to be used in the administration of the sacraments, etc. in the western district.* 1769. 12°. 28 p. * DoA.

2884. Walmesley, Charles. *Ezechiel's vision explained: or the explication of the vision exhibited to Ezechiel the prophet, and described in the first chapter of his prophecy. By Sig. Pastorini.* London. 1778. 8°. x, vi, 57, [1] p. Printed by: Coghlan, J.P. ESTC n001424. * CsmH; DoA; E; ECW; MY; O; Osc; Sto; Ush.

> 'Sig. Pastorini' is Charles Walmesley. See also next items.

2885. Walmesley, Charles. *The general history of the Christian church, from her birth to her triumphant state in heaven, chiefly deduced from the Apocalypse of St. John the Apostle by Signor Pastorini.* [London]. 1771. 8°. [2], xxvi, 589, [1]

p. Printed by: [Coghlan, J.P.] Published by: [Coghlan, J.P.]. ESTC t117383. *
CaOHM; CLU; Do; DoA; E; ECW; FLK; FP; Gi; ICN; L; Lhe; Map; MdBP;
NN; NNUT; Osc; P; PcA; Sal; Sto; TH; TLP; Ush; Yb.

> For Coghlan's involvement, see letter Coghlan to John Reid, 11 Feb. 1772,
> SCA.

2886. Walmesley, Charles. *The general history of the Christian church, from her
birth to her final triumphant state in heaven. Chiefly deduced from the
Apocalypse of St. John the Apostle. By Sig. Pastorini.* Wigan. 1782. 8°. xxviii,
602 p. Printed by: Ferguson, R. * DoA; UGL.

2887. Walmesley, Charles. *The general history of the Christian church, from her
birth, to her final triumphant state in heaven, chiefly deduced from the
Apocalypse of St. John the Apostle. By Sig. Pastorini.* Dublin. 1790. 8°. xv [i.e.
xvii], [7], 504 p. Printed by: Mehain, J. ESTC t184367. * D; FLK; IDA; MH;
NN.

> With a list of subscribers.

2888. Walmesley, Charles. *The general history of the Christian church, from her
birth, to her final triumphant state in heaven, chiefly deduced from the
Apocalypse of St. John the Apostle. By Sig. Pastorini.* Dublin. 1794. 8°. xv [i.e.
xvii], [7], 504 p. Published by: Wogan, P. ESTC t184085. * Dt; Osc.

2889. Walmesley, Charles. *The general history of the Christian church, from her
birth, to her final triumphant state in heaven, chiefly deduced from the
Apocalypse of St. John the Apostle. By Sig. Pastorini.* Dublin. 1797. 8°. xv, [7],
504 p. Printed by: Wogan, P. * DoA.

> With a list of subscribers.

2890. Walmesley, Charles. *The general history of the Christian church, from her
birth to her final triumphant state in heaven: chiefly deduced from the Apocalypse
of St. John the Apostle ... by ... Sig. Pastorini.* 2nd ed. London. 1798. 8°. [4],
xxvii, [1], 575, [3] p. Printed by: Coghlan, J.P. ESTC t123340. * CAL; DoA;
Du; FP; ICN; L; Stan; TxU; UGL.

2891. Walmesley, Charles. *The general history of the Christian church, from her
birth to her final triumphant state in heaven: chiefly deduced from the Apocalypse
of St. John the Apostle ... by ... Sig. Pastorini.* 3rd ed. Dublin. 1800. 8°. xxiv,
512 p. Printed by: Wogan, P. ESTC n018438. * CAL; FLK; IDA; NN; OAkU.

2892. Walmesley, Charles. *Instructions, regulations and prayers, for the
indulgences in the western district.* [London?]. 1764. 12°. 24 p. ESTC t128236.
* DMR; DoA; L; MChB; O; Osc.

> Signed 'C.R.' i.e. Charles Ramaten. The *Instructions* also form part of
> *Catechism for first communicants* (no. 472).

2893. Walmesley, Charles. *On account of the general decline of religion in these
times.* [1788]. s.s. * Cli; DowA.

> An encyclical letter dated and signed 'January, 8th, 1788. Charles Ramaten'.

2894. Walmesley, Charles. *A pastoral letter from Charles Bishop of Rama,
William Bishop of Acantos, and John Bishop of Centuriae, vicars apostolic, to all
the faithful ... of the western, northern and London districts.* London. 1793. 8°.

[2], 27, [1] p. Printed by: Coghlan, J.P. ESTC t043755. * Amp; CSmH; Di; ECW; ICN; L; Lfa; Lhe; Osc; Sto; TxU; Ush; WDA; Yb.

> Signed and dated 'C. Walmesley, W. Gibson and J. Douglass. December 26, 1792'. Warning against the capital error of denying the authority of the bishops and of introducing innovations in discipline. See note to 1154.

2895. Walmesley, Charles. *Sequentes orationes pro fructibus terrae dicantur quotidie.* 8°. s.s. * Cli.

> Signed 'Charles Ramaten V.A.' Prayers for the harvest to be said daily from May 25 till the end of September. These prayers were probably published in the 1780s.

2896. Walmesley, Charles. *To all the Catholic clergy residing in the western district of England.* [1780]. 4°. 4 p. * Cli.

> Prayers for peace 'in the alarms of the present time', and prayers for the royal family, dated at end 'June 12th, 1780'.

2897. Walmesley, Charles. *To the Catholic clergy, secular and regular residing in the western district of England.* 1778. 8°. [2] p. Published by: [Coghlan, J.P.]. * BAA; Osc; Ush; WDA.

> Dated and signed 'July 3, 1778. Charles Ramaten'. On verso 'To all the Catholic clergy ... residing in the southern district of England'. Dated and signed 'June 4th, 1778 Richard Deboren, James Birthan'. The document is further signed for the middle district by John Philomel and Thomas Acon, and for the northern district by William Trachon. On verso there is also a Coghlan advert.

2898. Walmesley, Charles. *To the honorable the Commons of Great Britain in Parliament assembled; the humble petition of Charles Walmesley, William Gibson, and John Douglass, for and on behalf of themselves.* [London?]. [1790?]. fol. 2 p. ESTC t051229. * L; Ush; WDA.

2899. Walmesley, Charles. *The unhappy events which have taken place in a neighbouring country.* [London]. [1794]. 4°. 4 p. * Cli.

> Signed by Charles Walmesley, William Gibson and John Douglass, and dated 'London, June 20th, 1794'. Launching an appeal for the new school at Tudhoe in county Durham to succeed Douai. See also next item.

2900. Walmesley, Charles. *The unhappy events which have taken place in a neighbouring country.* [London]. [1794]. 4°. [2] p. * UshA.

> Signed by Charles Walmesley, William Gibson and John Douglass, and dated 'London, June, 20th, 1794'.

2901. Walsh, Edward. *A discourse delivered in one of the Catholic chapels, on the day of thanksgiving for his majesty's happy recovery.* London. 1789. 8°. 17, [1] p. Printed by: Coghlan, J.P. Sold by: Coghlan, J.P. ESTC t217228. * STA.

> Dedication signed 'Edward Walsh'. Sometimes wrongly attributed to John Milner.

2902. Walsh, Francis. *Funiculus triplex: or the cord of St. Francis ... Permissu superiorum.* Anon. Antwerp. 1709. 12°. [12], 192 p. * ECW (imp.).

2903. Walsh, Francis. *Funiculus triplex: or, the indulgences of the cord of St. Francis.* London. 1745. 12°. [8], 156, [4] p. Printed by: Meighan, T. ESTC t209846. * Di; FLK.

The final 4 pages (part of the final gathering) are adverts for books printed and sold by I. Kelly of Dublin, which implies either that Meighan printed Kelly's adverts or that Kelly in fact printed the book.

2904. Walsh, Francis. *Funiculus triplex: or the indulgences of the cord of St. Francis.* Dublin. 1790. 12°. vi, 7-141, [3] p. Printed by: Cross, R. Sold by: Cross, R. * FLK.

With some Cross adverts.

2905. Walsh, Francis. *Funiculus triplex: or the indulgences of the cord of St. Francis.* Dublin. 1795. 12°. 141, [3] p. Printed by: Wogan, P. ESTC t218555. * Di.

2906. Walsh, Francis. *Funiculus triplex: or, the indulgences of the cord of St. Francis.* Dublin. 1797. 12°. vi, 7-141, [3] p. Printed by: Wogan, P. ESTC t185283. * C; D; FLK; Lhl.

2907. Walsh, Francis. *Funiculus triplex: or, the indulgences of the cord of St. Francis.* Dublin. 1798. 12°. vi, 7-141, [3] p. Printed by: Cross, R. * ECW; FLK.

2908. Walton, William. *Directions for the faithful of the N.D. touching the future observance of holydays.* Anon. Preston. 1777. 12°. 12 p. Printed by: Stuart, W.; Walton, R.; Sharrock, E. Sold by: Stuart, W.; Walton, R.; Sharrock, E. ESTC t188782. * O.

The identity of the author is established by a ms note in no. 2909 and by Kirk (p. 243).

2909. Walton, William. *Directions for the faithful of the N.D. touching the future observance of holydays.* Anon. [York?]. [1777?]. fol. s.s. ESTC t031877. * BAA; ICN; L; TxU; Ush; UshA.

ESTC suggests 'London?, 1780?'; however, ms notes in BAA and UshA indicate that it was printed at York in 1777. UshA moreover mentions the name of the author.

2910. Walton, William. *The miraculous powers of the church of Christ asserted through each successive century from the apostles down to the present time.* Anon. [London]. 1756. 8°. vi, 301, [11] p. ESTC t127345. * CLU; DAE; Do; E; ECW; FP; GEU-T; Gi; Hen; ICN; L; Lfa; Lhe; Map; MY; NNUT; Osc; RPPC; Sal; TH; TxU; Ush; Yb.

Written in answer to Dr Conyers Middleton's *A free inquiry into the miraculous powers* (1749). In the 1786 ms cat. of St. Edmund's, Paris (at DoA), mention is made of a 1754 ed.

2911. Walton, William. *Miraculous powers of the church of Christ asserted through each successive century from the apostles down to the present time.* London. 8°. vi, 301, [11] p. Printed by: Coghlan, J.P.; Needham, W. Sold by: Coghlan, J.P.; Needham, W. * ECW.

A reprint of the 1756 ed. This ed. must be post 1770 since on tp Walton is called Bishop of Trachon and V.A.; he became bishop in 1770.

2912. Ward, Thomas. *Contradiction authoris'd. By the ecclesiastical canons and* *the thirty nine articles of the Church of England. With some reflections upon the same.* London. 1730. 8°. 16 p. * MY.

> Cf. Ward's *Controversy* (no. 2914) which also prints the text of this work.

2913. Ward, Thomas. *Contradiction authorised, by the ecclesiastical canons and the thirty-nine articles of the Church of England.* Liverpool. [1782]. 4°. 12 p. Printed by: Johnson, T. Published by: Chadwick, J. * Lfa.

> Lfa bound up with Ward's *England's reformation*, 1782 (no. 2922). On tp Chadwick also advertises *England's reformation* and other Catholic books.

2914. Ward, Thomas. *The controversy of ordination truly stated; as far as it concerns the Church of England by law establish'd. Being an exposition of the thirty sixth article ... Also, Contradiction authoris'd.* London. 1719. 8°. [2], ii, 68, 8, [2] p. Printed by: L., J. Published by: L., J. ESTC t132408. * BB; DFo; Do; E; ECW; FLK; KU-S; L; Lhe; MY; NNUT; O; Osc; UPB; Ush.

> The last 8 pages contain 'Contradiction authoris'd'; cf. no. 2912.

2915. Ward, Thomas. *A demonstration of the uninterrupted succession and holy consecration of the first English bishops. Being an extract from Mr. Ward's second canto of his England's reformation.* [London?]. 1766. 8°. 47, [1] p. ESTC n028871. * NcU; PPAmP.

2916. Ward, Thomas. *A demonstration of the uninterrupted succession and holy consecration of the first English bishops. Being an extract from Mr. Ward's second canto of his England's reformation.* [Philadelphia]. [1766]. 8°. 47, [1] p. ESTC w007386. * PPL.

2917. Ward, Thomas. *England's reformation from the time of King Henry the VIIIth to the end of Oates' plot.* Hambourgh [i.e. St. Omers]. 1710. 4°. [4], 136, 72, 73-76, 73-112, 56, 110 p. ESTC t132416. * CaOLU (imp.); CLU-C; CSmH; CtY; DFo; E; ECW; Gi; KU-S; L; LEu; Lfa; Lhe; Llp; NIC; P; TxU; Ush.

> A verse satire in 4 cantos, each with separate pagination and register (see also the 2 previous items and the following ones). The imprint is false. Printed by the English College Press, St. Omers. The satire was also popular among non-R.C. readers and there are a number of eds (with editorial additions) under non-R.C. auspices. See ESTC for 1715, 1716 and 1719 eds.

2918. Ward, Thomas. *England's reformation, from the time of King Henry the Eighth, to the end of Oate's plot. A poem in four cantos.* London. 1731. 4°. 20, 136, 72, 73-76, 73-112, 56, 110, [2] p. ESTC n006951. * CLobS; InNd; LEu; Ush.

> A reissue of the ed. of 1710, with a life of the author and textual notes on the poem. See also next item.

2919. Ward, Thomas. *England's reformation, from the time of King Henry the Eighth, to the end of Oate's plot. A poem in four cantos.* London. 1731. 4°. 20, [2], 136, 112, 56, 110, [2] p. ESTC t193241. * Do; Gi; O.

2920. Ward, Thomas. *England's reformation, from the time of King Henry the Eighth, to the end of Oates's plot. A poem in four cantos.* 5th ed. 2 vols. London. 1742. 12°. 502 [i.e. 492] p. (vol. 1). Printed by: Firstfire, H. Sold by:

Firstfire, H. ESTC t120543. * L; Ldw; MSaE (vol. 1).

This seems to be the only occurrence of the printer's name 'Firstfire'.

2921. Ward, Thomas. *England's reformation, (from the time of K. Henry VIII. to the end of Oates's plot.) A poem in four cantos.* 2 vols. London. 1747. 8°. [6], 336; [4], 207, [1] p. ESTC t132415. * BB (2 vols in one); CAL; CLU; CLU-C; CSmH; DFo; Do; DoA; E; ECW (vol. 2); ICN; ICU; InU-Li; IU; KU-S; L; LEu; Lfa; Lhe; LO (vol. 2); O; Osc; P; TLP; TxU.

2922. Ward, Thomas. *England's reformation, from the time of King Henry the Eighth, to the end of Oates's plot. A poem in four cantos.* 6th ed. Liverpool. 1782. 8°. xv, [1], 456 p. ESTC t132413. * Gi; L; Lfa; LO; LVp; MRu.

Lfa bound up with *Contradiction authoris'd* (no. 2913).

2923. Ward, Thomas. *England's reformation: from the time of King Henry VIII, to the end of Oates's plot, a poem, in four canto's.* Dublin. 1791. 8°. 468 p. Printed by: Hoey, P. ESTC t075348. * D; DMR; L; NjR; PSt; SIR.

2924. Ward, Thomas. *Errata to the Protestant bible: or, the truth of their English translations examined: in a treatise shewing some of the errors that are to be found in the Protestant English translations of the sacred scripture.* London. 1737. 4°. 115, [1] p. Published by: Mead, J. ESTC n031198. * CLU-C; DFo; Do; DoA; E; ECW; FLK; Ldw; Lfa; Lhe; Map; Osc; TxU; UGL; Ush.

The final page is 'A vindication of the Roman Catholicks'. See also next item.

2925. Ward, Thomas. *Errata to the Protestant bible: or, the truth of their English translations examined: in a treatise shewing some of the errors that are to be found in the Protestant English translations of the sacred scripture.* London. 1737. 4°. 115, [1] p. Published by: Meighan, P. ESTC t202708. * Llp.

2926. *We beg leave to inform you, that it is absolutely necessary to take down the Bavarian Chapel in Golden Square.* [London?]. [1788]. fol. 3, [1] p. * Ush.

Signed 'James Moore, secretary' and 22 others. See also no. 1509.

2927. *We whose names are hereunto subscribed, Catholics of England, do freely, voluntarily, and of our own accord, make the following solemn declaration and protestation.* London. 1789. fol. 3, [1] p. * WDA.

2928. *We whose names are hereunto subscribed, Catholics of England, do freely, voluntarily, and of our own accord, make the following solemn declaration and protestation.* [London]. [1789]. s.s. ESTC t147147. * BAA; L; Sto; Ush.

No names subscribed. The protestation was accompanied by a covering letter, dated and signed '7 April, 1789, Charles Butler, secretary'.

2929. *We whose names are hereunto subscribed, Catholics of England, do freely, voluntarily, and of our own accord, make the following solemn declaration and protestation.* [London]. [1791]. fol. 13, [3] p. ESTC t147149. * L.

2930. *We whose names are hereunto subscribed, Catholics of England, do freely, voluntarily, and of our own accord, make the following solemn declaration and protestation.* [London]. [1791]. fol. 15, [1] p. ESTC t147148. * L.

A reissue of no. 2929, with cancel sig. D, pp. 13-15.

2931. Webbe, Samuel. *A collection of masses, with an accompaniment for the organ. Particularly design'd for the use of small choirs by S. Webbe. Published by his permission with others on the same plan by Ricci & Paxton.* [London]. [1792]. 4°. [2], iv, 380 p. Printed by: Jones, T. Sold by: Jones, T.; Keating; Brown. * DuA; L.

> With a list of subscribers; signed and dated 'John Griffiths, John Barkley, George Carney, Peter Tognarelli, London August 1792'.

2932. Webbe, Samuel. *A collection of modern church music consisting of masses &c. Composed by ... Webbe, Paxton, Ricci, and Dr. Arne ... Published by permission of Mr Webbe & under his immediate inspection.* [London]. 1791. 4°. Printed by: Skillern, T. Published by: Proprietors. * L.

2933. Webbe, Samuel. *A collection of motets or antiphons, for 1, 2, 3 & 4 voices or chorus.* London. [1792]. 8°. Published by: Jones, T. Sold by: Keating; Brown. * Stan.

> Unpaginated. The works contains 126 motets. See also next item. Webbe also published many compositions of a non-specifically R.C. nature.

2934. Webbe, Samuel. *A collection of motetts or antiphon[s] for 1, 2, 3 & 4 voices, or chorus. Calculated for the more solemn o[ff] divine worship.* [London]. [1792]. Sold by: Bland, J.; Skillern, T.; Coghlan, J.P. * ICN; IES; L; MB; NRU-Mus; O; RPB.

2935. Weldon, Thomas. *A sermon for the general fast appointed by proclamation, preached to the congregation at Scholes near Prescott. On the tenth of February. 1779. By T.W.* Prescot. 1779. 8°. [2], 22, [2] p. Printed by: Eyres, T. ESTC t059334. * L; Lhe.

> Sutcliffe (464) identifies 'T.W.' as Thomas Weldon (alias or vere Hunter).

2936. Weston, John Baptist. *An abstract of the doctrine of Jesus-Christ, or the rule of the Frier-Minors: literally, morally, and spiritually expounded by brother John Baptist Weston.* Douai. 1718. 4°. [24], 555, [1] p. Printed by: Taverne, J. ESTC t105812. * E; ECW; FLK; ICN; L; O; TxU.

2937. Weston, John Baptist. *A supplement to the abstract being examples of holy men, drawn from the monuments of the order, and apply'd to each text of the rule.* Anon. Douai. 1726. 4°. [4], 176, [18] p. Printed by: Willerval, F. ESTC t207354. * E; FLK.

> The name of the author is supplied from the approbation. It is a supplement to no. 2936.

2938. Weston, John Webbe. *A letter from J. Webbe Weston, Francis Eyre, and William Sheldon, Esqrs. to the gentlemen at whose desire they accepted the office of mediators between the vicars apostolic and the gentlemen of the late Catholic Committee.* London. 1792. 4°. 2, [26] p. Printed by: Coghlan, J.P. ESTC t037893. * L; Lfa; Lhe; MY; Osc; P; SIR; Sto; TxU; Ush.

2939. Weston, John Webbe. *A letter from J. Webbe Weston, Francis Eyre and William Sheldon, Esqrs. to the gentlemen at whose desire they accepted the office of mediators between the vicars apostolic and the gentlemen of the late Catholic*

Committee. London. 1792. fol. [2], 6 p. Printed by: Coghlan, J.P. * WDA.
> Dated 'Bond-Street, May 29, 1792'.

2940. White M'Kenna, J. *The spiritual treasury, or, sacred diary, of the favours ... and perpetual indulgences, granted by the vicars of our Lord Jesus Christ ... to the arch-confraternity of ... St. Augustine, and St. Monica.* Dublin. 1753. 12°. [2], 340 p. Printed by: Byrn, J. Published by: Author. ESTC t215149. * D; IDA.
> IDA gives J. White M'Kenna as translator/author. Ronan (p. 51) makes mention of a 1755 ed. of this work.

2941. Whittingham, John. *An address to Philalethes.* Anon. [Coventry?]. [1780?]. s.s. * O.
> The address is signed 'The old fashion farmer in reply to the old fashion farmer's late address to the public'. O cat. identifies the author as John Whittingham, a Coventry seedsman.

2942. Whittingham, John. *An address to the public.* [Coventry?]. [1780?]. s.s. * O.
> The pamphlet is signed 'The old fashion farmer, on the destruction of Roman Catholic property'.

2943. Whittingham, John. *To Mr. John Wesley. As you have shewn yourself either unable, or unwilling to defend your letter in the Morning Chronicle ... August 23, 1780.* [Coventry?]. [1780]. fol. s.s. * O.

2944. Whittingham, John. *To Mr. Jonathan Evans, greeting.* [Coventry?]. [1780]. s.s. * O.
> Signed 'The old fashion farmer, in reply to Omnia vincit veritas'.

2945. Whittingham, John. *The old fashion farmer's motives for leaving the Church of England, and embracing the Roman Catholic faith; and his reasons for adhering to the same.* Anon. [London?]. 1778. 8°. viii, 206 p. ESTC t148372. * Do; ECW; Lfa; Lhe; LO; LU; MY; NcD; O; Osc; TxU.

2946. Whittingham, John. *To the public.* [Coventry?]. [1780]. s.s. * O.
> Signed 'The old fashion farmer', advocating toleration of Roman Catholicism. There are 2 eds of this pamphlet, the present one is Bodleian Library G.A. Warw. b.1 (119b).

2947. Whittingham, John. *To the public.* [Coventry?]. [1780]. s.s. * O.
> This ed. is Bodleian Library G.A. Warw. b.1 (118).

2948. *Wh----n's ghost: or, lamentations on the loss of a late ch----n.* [Worcester]. [1784]. 8°. 8 p. * Osc.
> A burlesque on the apostate Jesuit Charles Henry Wharton.

2949. Wilks, Joseph. *A copy of a letter from the reverend Mr. Wilks, to Thomas Clifford, Esq. Sir, at the general meeting of the English Catholics, held on the 9th of June last.* [London?]. [1791]. fol. 3, [1] p. ESTC t034109. * BAA; Cli; DowA; L; Lhe; P; Sto; WRW.
> Dated 'Weston, September 28, 1791'.

2950. Wilks, Joseph. *Copy of a letter to the reverend William Cowley.* [Newport?]. [1798]. fol. 3, [1] p. * BAA; Cli; DowA; LANre; WDA.

Dated 'Newport, May 15th, 1798' with a postscript dated 'Newport, November 5th, 1798'.

2951. Witham, Robert. *Annotations on the new testament of Jesus Christ in which I. The literal sense is explained ... II. The false interpretations ... are briefly examined ... III. With an account ... By R.W. D.D.* 2 vols. [Douai?]. 1730. 8°. [24], 506, [6]; [10], 536, [4] p. ESTC t094867. * C; CAL; CLU-C; DAE; Do; DoA; DUu; E; ECB; ECR; ECW; FLK; GEU-T; Gi (vol. 1); L; Lhe; MRu; O; Oc; Osc; Sto; TH; TLP; TxU; UGL; Ush.

> 'R.W.' is Robert Witham, vicar general of the northern district until 1715 when he was appointed president of Douai. D & M 1009.

2952. Witham, Robert. *Annotations on the new testament of Jesus Christ. In which I. The literal sense is explained ... II. The false interpretations ... are briefly examined ... III. With an account ... By R.W. D.D.* 2 vols. [Douai?]. 1733. 8°. ESTC t183473. * DLC; DoA; FLK (vol. 1); L; LO; O; StD; TxU; Ush.

> A reprint of the first ed. (1730). ESTC suggests Douai as place of publication (Witham lived there); Hugh Fenning O.P. (personal communication) notes the occurrence of engravings by Dempsey of Dublin. D & M 1020.

2953. Witham, Robert. *The English translation of the new testament by C.N.C.F.P.D. an. 1719. Examin'd and compar'd with the Latin-vulgat, and the Greek by D.D. anno M.DCC.XXVI.* Anon. Douai. 1727. 4°. 22, [2] p. Printed by: Derbaix, C.L. ESTC n007324. * Dp; NcD; Osc; Ush (-tp).

> This is a comment on Nary's new testament of 1719. In Hyde mention is made of a 1729 ed. of this comment.

2954. Witham, Robert. *Remarks on the four volumes of The lives of saints, publish'd in English, and printed at London anno 1729 ... by Theophilus Eupistinus.* Anon. London. 1732. 4°. [4], 73, [3] p. Published by: Osborne, T. ESTC t147445. * Do; ICN; L; Map; MRu; O; Osc; Ush.

> 'Theophilus Eupistinus' is Robert Witham, who comments on the book by Charles Fell (no. 1035). The preface is by Matthew Prichard (Kirk, 192).

2955. Witham, Thomas. *A short discourse upon the life and death of Mr. Geo. Throckmorton, deceas'd the 5th of April, N.S. 1705, in the 34th year of his age.* Anon. [London?]. 1706. 12°. 120 p. ESTC t098290. * ICN; L.

> Kirk (p. 254) states that Thomas Witham, D.D., is the author.

2956. Woodhead, Abraham. *Ancient church government. Part, III. Of I. Heresy. And II. Schisme, in disceding [sic] from the doctrines ... Reflecting on the later writings of several learned Protestants.* [London]. 1736. 4°. xcv, [1], 232 p. ESTC t110790. * CLU-C; L; Lfa; Lhe; Pci; Ush.

> According to Gillow (I, 198) Simon Berington edited this work and prefixed the life of Abraham Woodhead and a preface.

2957. Worthington, Thomas. *An introduction to the Catholick faith. By an English Dominican.* Anon. L----n. 1709. 8°. [8], 152, [2] p. Printed by: George ---son. ESTC t080388. * C; CKu; CYc; DAE; Do; E; Gi; L; Lhe; Obl; Ush.

> Gillow (I, 345) states that Edward Ambrose Burgis O.P. 'put the finishing hand' to it; see also Kirk, p. 38. The Louvain approbation on final 2 pages suggests

that the book was printed on the Continent.

2958. Wythie, J. *The creed expounded: or, the light of Christian doctrine set up on the candlestick of orthodox interpretation ... being an ample exposition of the twelve articles ... By J.W.M.O.S.B.* London. 1735. 12°. xxiv, [4], 342, [2] p. Published by: Norris, N. ESTC t186701. * Do; Gi; Hor; Lhe; Llp; MRu; NSPM; O; Osc; Sal; Sco.

Also attributed to Wythie's fellow Benedictines John Wilson and Joseph Wyche.

2959. *You are humbly requested to assist at the solemn dirge for the repose of the soul of the right rev. and honorable Dr. James Talbot.* London. 1790. s.s. Printed by: Coghlan, J.P. Ward, 184.

Notice of Requiem Services for Bishop James Talbot. In a footnote Coghlan asks to be kept informed of any changes of address of his clients.

2960. *You are humbly requested to attend the solemn dirge, for the repose of the soul of the venerable and right revd. Dr. Richard Chaloner [sic], V.A. and Bishop of Debra.* [London]. [1781]. s.s. * UshA.

In view of the type, the printer may be J.P. Coghlan.

Index of Titles

Items appearing under their title in the Catalogue are excluded

A l'anonyme. Barruel, Augustin.

Abrégé des mémoires. Barruel, Augustin.

Abridgement of Christian doctrine. Abridgement.

Abridgement of Christian doctrine. Turberville, Henry.

Abridgement of Roman Catholic doctrine. Hay, George.

Abridgement of the Christian doctrine. Hay, George.

Abridgment of the history of the old and new testament. Fontaine, Nicolas.

Abridgment of the life of James II. Sanders, Francis.

Abstract of a treatise. Molinos, Miguel de.

Abstract of the doctrine of Jesus-Christ. Weston, John Baptist.

Abstract of the history of the bible. Challoner, Richard.

Abstract of the history of the clergy. Barruel, Augustin.

Abstract of the history of the new testament. Challoner, Richard.

Abstract of the history of the old and new testament. Challoner, Richard.

Abstract of the transactions. Sergeant, John.

Account of the conversion. Thayer, John.

Account of the life and writings. Butler, Charles.

Account of the miracle. Bertier, Charles.

Act of appeal of his eminence the Cardinal de Noailles. Noailles, Louis Antoine de.

Ad animi mei anxietatem. Hornyold, John Joseph.

Address from the Roman Catholics of America. Carroll, John.

Address to his excellency. Troy, John Thomas.

Address to Philalethes. Whittingham, John.

Address to the common people of the Roman Catholic religion. O'Leary, Arthur.

Address to the faithful of the middle district. Talbot, Thomas.

Address to the inhabitants of Philadelphia. Carroll, John.

Address to the Protestant dissenters. Berington, Joseph.

Address to the public. Whittingham, John.

Address to the Roman Catholics of Ireland. MacKenna, Theobald.

Address to the Roman Catholics of the United States of America. Carroll, John.

Afternoon instructions for the whole year. Gother, John.

Aithghearradh n a teagaisg Chriosduidh. Turberville, Henry.

Allwydd y nêf. Powell, David.

Ancient church government. Part, III. Woodhead, Abraham.

Annals of the church from the death of Christ. Burgis, Edward Ambrose.

Annotations on the new testament of Jesus Christ. Witham, Robert.

Answer to a letter. Walmesley, Charles.

Answer to Dr. Clarke. Hawarden, Edward.

Answer to Mr W.A.D.'s letter to G.H. Hay, George.

Answer to strictures. Carroll, John.

Answer to the Bishop of Comana's pastoral letter. Geddes, Alexander.

Answer to the second bluebook. Plowden, Charles.

Antwort eines Römisch-Catholischen Priesters. Brosius, Francis Xavier.

Apologie du clergé séculier et des Jésuites d'Angleterre. Hunter, Thomas.

319

Apology for Catholic faith. Coghlan, R.B.

Apology for not subscribing to the oath. Strickland, Joseph.

Apology for slavery. Geddes, Alexander.

Apology for the church history of England. Tootell, Hugh.

Appeal to the public, in relation to an affair. Dowdall, James.

Appeal to the public; or, a candid narrative. Harris, Raymund.

Appendix to Butler's lives of the saints. Butler, Alban.

Appendix to the discourses. Blyth, Francis.

Appendix to the history of the life of Cardinal Pole. Phillips, Thomas.

Appendix to the letter. Nary, Cornelius.

Argument against extermination. MacKenna, Theobald.

Argument for independence. MacNeven, William James.

Argument on behalf of the Catholics of Ireland. Tone, Theobald Wolfe.

Audi alteram partem. Milner, John.

Aux emigrés François. Hamel, Etienne Pierre.

Avocat du diable: the devil's advocate. Geddes, Alexander.

Baltimore, December 29, 1799. Carroll, John.

Battle of B-ng-r: or the church's triumph. Geddes, Alexander.

Benjamin Dei & s. sedis apostolicae gratiâ episcopus Prusensis. Petre, Benjamin.

Bishop of Clermont's discourse to the clergy of his diocese. Massillon, Jean Baptiste.

Boston, January 29, 1789. La Poterie, Claude F. Bouchard de.

Bourdaloue's sermon on Ash-Wednesday. Bourdaloue, Louis.

Breve istoria del primo principo. Challoner, Richard.

Breve storia a favore della chiesa cattolica. Challoner, Richard.

Brief abstract of the memorial. Agard de Champs, Etienne.

Brief account from the most authentic Protestant writers. Curry, John.

Brief account of the life of the late r. rev. Richard Challoner. Milner, John.

Brief essay on the confraternity. Baker, Pacificus.

Brief historical authentic account. O'Brien, Timothy.

Brief history of Saint Patrick's purgatory. Messingham, Thomas.

Brief of our holy father. Clement XIII.

Britannia sancta. Challoner, Richard.

Burning lamp. Gracian, Geronymo.

Call to a godly life. Challoner, Richard.

Calumnies of Verus. Fleming, Francis Anthony.

Candid and impartial sketch. Plowden, Charles.

Cantiques de l'ame dévote. Durand, Laurent.

Cantiques de Marseilles. Durand, Laurent.

Carolus Dei & apostolicae sedis gratiâ Episcopus Ramatensis. Walmesley, Charles.

Carolus Ramaten in districtu occidentali. Walmesley, Charles.

Case of the Roman-Catholics of Ireland. O'Conor, Charles.

Case review'd. Darrell, William.

Case stated between the Church of Rome and the Church of England. Manning, Robert.

Case stated, by Francis Plowden, Esq. Plowden, Francis.

Catalogue of a library. Coghlan, James Peter.

Catalogue of all the Catholic books now in print. Coghlan, James Peter.

Catalogue of the several parcels of books. Coghlan, James Peter.

Catechism byrr o'r athrawiaeth ghristnogol. Powell, David.

Catechism moral and controversial. Burke, Thomas Myles.

Catechism or abridgement. Hacket, Andrew (see also under title).

320

Catechism or Christian doctrine. Donlevy, Andrew.

Catechism. Or collection of some points of Christian faith. Barnard, James.

Catechisme du diocese de Sens. Languet, Jean Joseph.

Catholic Christian instructed in the sacraments. Challoner, Richard.

Catholic Church cleared from the charge of corruption. Sharp, John Chrysostom Gregory.

Catholic devotion to the Blessed Virgin. Manning, Robert.

Catholic layman's companion. Cordell, Charles.

Catholic-scripturist. Mumford, James.

Catholic year. Gother, John.

Catholick grounds. Hawarden, Edward.

Catholick layman's companion. Cordell, Charles.

Catholic's resolution shewing his reasons. Crathorne, William.

Cause of the Roman Catholics pleaded. Nassau, John.

Caution against prejudice. Blyth, Francis.

Caveat addressed to the Catholics of Worcester. Pilling, William Leo.

Caveat against the Methodists. Challoner, Richard.

Ceremonies used in the administration of the sacraments. Tootell, Christopher.

Certain considerations on behalf of the Roman Catholics. Milner, John.

Certamen utriusq [sic], ecclesiae. Tootell, Hugh.

Character of the blessed emperor. Eusebius, of Caesarea.

Characters of real devotion. Grou, Jean-Nicolas.

Charge given by Hugh, Lord Archbishop of Armagh. MacMahon, Hugh.

Charity and truth. Hawarden, Edward.

Charles, Bishop of Rama. Walmesley, Charles.

Christian advent. Baker, Pacificus.

Christian directory. Parsons, Robert.

Christian doctrine. Ledesma, Diego.

Christian entertainments. Gother, John.

Christian pilgrimage. Fénelon, François de Salignac.

Christian sacrifice containing a short explication. Mannock, John Anselm.

Christian sentiments proper for sick and infirm people. Filassier, Marin.

Christian thoughts for every day of the month. Bouhours, Dominique.

Chronological index. Butler, Alban.

Church and state. Plowden, Francis.

Church history of England. Tootell, Hugh.

Circulaire à messieurs les curés. Plessis, Joseph Octave.

Circular letter. Clement XIV.

Circumstantial account of the death of Abbé Lawrence Ricci. Plowden, Charles.

City of God of the new testament. Challoner, Richard.

Clergyman's answer to the layman's letter. Milner, John.

Collectanea Anglo-Minoritica. Parkinson, Anthony.

Collectanea sacra. Coyle, Anthony.

Collectio indultorum apostolicorum. Pius VI.

Collection of controversial tracts. Challoner, Richard.

Collection of discourses. Appleton, James.

Collection of masses. Webbe, Samuel.

Collection of modern church music. Webbe, Samuel.

Collection of motets or antiphons. Webbe, Samuel.

Collection of prayers. Thayer, John.

Collection of sermons and other treatises. Thomas à Kempis.

Collection of spiritual songs. Geddes, John.

Collection of the new year's gifts. Challoner, Richard.

Collects, epistles and gospels. Gother, John.

College of George-Town. Dubourg, William.

Commandments and sacraments explained. Hornyold, John Joseph.

Commentary on the XLI and XLII psalms. Jenkins, Peter.

Commentary on the XLII psalms. O'Leary, Arthur.

Companion to the altar. MacDonald, Archibald Benedict.

Compendious abstract. Gahan, William.

Compendious history of the church. Du Pin, Louis Ellis.

Compendious history of the new testament. Fontaine, Nicolas.

Conduite à tenir. La Marche, Jean François de.

Congratulatory poem. Blount, Michael.

Considerations on the declaration against transubstantiation. Berkeley, Robert.

Considerations on the modern opinion. Plowden, Charles.

Considerations on the oath of supremacy. Berkeley, Robert.

Considerations upon Christian truths. Challoner, Richard.

Constant belief of the Catholick Church. Arnauld, Antoine and Pierre Nicole.

Constitution of his holiness Pope Clement XI. Clement XI.

Constitutional objections to the government of Ireland. MacKenna, Theobald.

Continuation and increase of calamities. Gibson, William.

Contradiction authorised. Ward, Thomas.

Contrite and humble heart. Jenks, Silvester.

Controversy. Thayer, John.

Controversy of ordination truly stated. Ward, Thomas.

Copia vera. Tabula congregationis O.F.M.

Copies of the letters from Bishop White. Moore, Richard.

Copy of a letter from Dr Bew at Paris. Bew, John.

Copy of a letter from Rome. Antonelli, Leonardo.

Copy of a letter from the reverend Mr. Wilks. Wilks, Joseph.

Copy of a letter to the reverend William Cowley. Wilks, Joseph.

Copy of a letter to the right reverend Mr. Charles Berington. Clough, Anthony.

Copy of a letter written by express order of his holiness. Antonelli, Leonardo.

Copy of letters. Erskine, Charles.

Cottager's remarks on the farmer's spirit of party. O'Conor, Charles.

Counsels of wisdom. Boutauld, Michel.

Creed expounded. Wythie, J.

Critical remarks on the Hebrew scriptures. Geddes, Alexander.

Cross in its true light. Pinamonti, Giovanni Pietro.

Cum nobis a capitulo ultimo. Walker, Augustine.

Cursory remarks on a late fanatical publication. Geddes, Alexander.

Daily exercise of the devout Christian. Crowther, A. & T.V. Sadler.

De controversiis tractatus generales. Walenburch, Adriaan van.

De gravissima. Hay, George.

De imitatione Christi. Thomas à Kempis.

De sacrificio missae tractatus asceticus. Bona, Giovanni.

Decalogue explained in thirty-two discourses. Hornyold, John Joseph.

Decalogue explained, and the creed, theological virtues. Francis, Bernard.

Declaration et retraction. Panisset, François Thérèse.

Defence of the conduct and writings of the rev. Arthur O'Leary. O'Leary, Arthur.

Defence of the validity of the English ordinations. Le Courayer, Pierre François.

Deism and Christianity fairly consider'd. Constable, John.

Deism self-refuted. Bergier, Nicolas Sylvestre.

Demonstration of the uninterrupted succession. Ward, Thomas.

Détail des raisons péremptoires. Barruel, Augustin.

Detection of the dangerous tendency. Hay, George.

Devotion of Catholicks by the Blessed Virgin. Challoner, Richard.

Devotion to the sacred heart of Jesus. Lawson, Thomas (see also under title).

Devotions in the ancient way of offices. Austin, John.

Devotions of the stations of the passion of Jesus Christ. Parvilliers, Adrien.

Devotions to Jesus Christ. Morel, Robert.

Devotion(s) to Jesus, Mary and Joseph. Tootell, Christopher.

Devout Christian instructed in the faith of Christ. Hay, George.

Devout Christian instructed in the law of Christ. Hay, George.

Devout Christian's companion for holy days. Baker, Pacificus.

Devout client of Mary instructed. Segneri, Paolo.

Devout communicant. Baker, Pacificus.

Devout miscellany. Gregson, Gregory.

Devout paraphrase on the seven penitential psalms. Blyth, Francis.

Dialogue between Archibald and Timothy. Murphy, Cornelius.

Dialogue between a Protestant and Papist. Troy, John Thomas.

Dialogue between a protesting Catholic dissenter and a Catholic. Pilling, William Leo.

Dignity, labours and reward. Barnard, James.

Directions for the faithful of the N.D. Walton, William.

Discours a l'occasion de la victoire. Plessis, Joseph Octave.

Discours pour la bénédiction de la chapelle. Boisgelin de Cucé, Jean de Dieu R.

Discours pour la première communion. Boisgelin de Cucé, Jean de Dieu R.

Discours prononcé. Boisgelin de Cucé, Jean de Dieu R.

Discours prononcé le 4 Juillet. Bandot, Seraphin.

Discours prononcé par le R.P. Joseph Ferrers. Ferrers, Joseph.

Discourse delivered at the consecration of the right rev. William Gibson. Milner, John.

Discourse delivered at the consecration of the right rev. John Douglass. Plowden, Charles.

Discourse, delivered, at the Roman Catholic church in Boston. Thayer, John.

Discourse delivered in one of the Catholic chapels. Walsh, Edward (see also under title).

Discourse delivered in the Catholic chapel at Lartington. Rayment, Benedict.

Discourse delivered in the church of the English dames. Barnardin, Father.

Discourse, delivered in the Roman Catholic chapel, at Chester. Penswick, Thomas.

Discourse on General Washington. Carroll, John.

Discourse on religious innovations. Kirwan, Walter Blake.

Discourses explanatory and moral. Francis, Bernard.

Discourses of Cleander and Eudoxus. Daniel, Gabriel.

Discourses of religion. Hawarden, Edward.

Dispassionate narrative. Hodgson, Ralph.

Dissertation historique sur les libertés de l'église gallicane. Le Pointe, Thomas.

Dissertation on ecclesiastical jurisdiction. Barruel, Augustin.

Dissertation on the modern style of altering antient cathedrals. Milner, John.

Dissertations on the (antient) history of Ireland. O'Conor, Charles.

Dissertations on the Mosaical creation. Berington, Simon.

Divine economy of Christ. Bruning, George.

Divine office for the use of the laity. Cordell, Charles.
Divine right of episcopacy addressed to the Catholic laity. Milner, John.
Divinity of our Lord Jesus Christ. Barnard, James.
Doctor Francis Moylan, to his beloved flock. Moylan, Francis.
Doctor Francis Moylan, to the lower order. Moylan, Francis.
Doctor Geddes's address to the public. Geddes, Alexander.
Doctor Moylan's instructions. Moylan, Francis.
Doctrine and practice of auricular confession. Jenkins, Peter.
Doctrine of antiquity. Constable, John.
Doleful fall of Andrew Sall. French, Nicholas.
Dr. Geddes's general answer to the queries. Geddes, Alexander.
Ecclesiae theoria nova Dodwelliana exposita. Basset, Joshua.
Ecclesiastical democracy detected. Milner, John.
Ecclesiastical history of the English nation. Bede, the Venerable Saint.
Ecclesiastique accompli. Carron, Guy Toussaint Julien.
Edifying and curious letters of some missioners. Le Gobien, Charles.
Edvardus redivivus. Porter, Jerome.
Elemens de la langue Latine. Lhomond, Charles François.
Elements de la grammaire Latine. Lhomond, Charles François.
Elements of French grammar. Cowley, William Gregory.
Elements of the Irish language. MacCurtin, Hugh.
Elevation of the soul to God. Baudrand, Barthélemy.
Encyclical letter addressed to all the faithful. Walmesley, Charles.
Encyclical letter of our most holy father Pope Pius VII. Pius VII.
England's conversion and reformation compared. Manning, Robert.
England's reformation. Ward, Thomas.
English translation of the new testament. Witham, Robert.
Enrichment, or pearl of the soul. Thunder, Henry.
Entertainments for Lent. Caussin, Nicolas.
Entrusted by divine providence. Talbot, Thomas.
Episcopal charge. Massillon, Jean Baptiste.
Errata to the Protestant bible. Ward, Thomas.
Essay on parliamentary reform. MacKenna, Theobald.
Essay on the depravity of the nation. Berington, Joseph.
Essay on the rosary and sodality. O'Connor, John.
Essay on toleration: or, Mr. O'Leary's plea for liberty. O'Leary, Arthur.
Essay towards a proposal for catholic communion. Basset, Joshua.
Essay towards the reformation. O'Leary, Arthur.
Essay upon indulgences. Saltmarsh, Edward.
Essay upon the art of love. Jenks, Silvester.
Essays, by the celebrated and much admired R.F. Arthur O'Leary. O'Leary, Arthur.
Eternal misery. Blyth, Francis.
Evangile et le clergé François. Barruel, Augustin.
Evangile médité. Romain, M.
Examination of events, termed miraculous. Berington, Joseph.
Exclamations of the soul to God. Teresa of Avila.
Excommunication of the rev. Robert M'Evoy. Troy, John Thomas.
Exercice public. Carron, Guy Toussaint Julien.
Exercice tre's-devot. Du Monceau, Alexis.
Exercise of devotion for Sunday and holiday mornings and afternoons. Stonor, John

Talbot.

Exhortation to a thorough conversion from sin to God. Challoner, Richard.

Exhortation to alms-deeds. Luis de Granada.

Exhortations to be used in the administration of sacraments. Walmesley, Charles.

Explanation of the adoration of the holy cross. Blyth, Francis.

Explanation of the litanies. Hay, George.

Explanatory remarks. Hay, George.

Explication of the holy sacrifice. Hay, George.

Explication of the jubilee. O'Brien, Timothy.

Exposé des motifs. La Hogue, Louis Egidius de.

Exposition of the doctrine of the Catholic Church. Bossuet, Jacques Bénigne.

Ezechiel's vision explained. Walmesley, Charles.

Facts relating to the present contest amongst the Roman Catholics. Milner, John.

Family manual of morning and evening prayers. Pembridge, Michael Benedict.

Family manual of morning and night prayers. Pembridge, Michael Benedict.

Fanaticism and treason. Plowden, Francis.

Father O'Leary's address to his countrymen. O'Leary, Arthur.

Few remarks on The history of the decline and fall of the Roman Empire. Eyre, Francis.

Fifty one [explanatory and] moral discourses. Francis, Bernard.

Fifty reasons or motives. Ulrick, Anthony.

First part of the catalogue of a library. Coghlan, James Peter.

Flores cleri Anglo-Catholici. Tootell, Hugh.

Following of Christ. Thomas à Kempis.

Four appendixes to the book entitled The true church of Christ. Hawarden, Edward.

Franciscus Dei. Petre, Francis.

Free examination of the common methods. Usher, James.

Frequent communion. MacKenzie, Alexander.

Funeral discourse on the death of ... Challoner. Milner, John.

Funeral oration for his holiness Pope Pius VI. Erskine, Charles.

Funeral oration of his late most Christian majesty Louis XVI. Milner, John.

Funeral oration on the late sovereign pontiff Pius the Sixth. O'Leary, Arthur.

Funeral oration upon Cardinal de Fleury. Frey de Neuville, Charles.

Funeral oration upon the death of James the Second. Roquette, Henri Emmanuel de.

Funeral sermon ... for ... Louis the Sixteenth. MacCarthy, Florence.

Funeral sermon on the death of the rev. Ferdinand Farmer. Molyneux, Robert.

Funeral sermon on the late Queen of France. O'Brien, [Matthew?].

Funiculus triplex. Walsh, Francis.

Further vindication of the old Church of England. Kingsley, William.

G.D.V.A. To all the faithful. Hay, George.

Gallway catechism. O'Kenny, Nicolaus Antoninus.

Garden of the soul. Challoner, Richard.

General history of the Christian church. Walmesley, Charles.

General instructions, by way of catechism. Pouget, François Aimé.

General view of the arguments for the divinity of Christ. Barnard, James.

George, Bishop of Daulia. Hay, George.

G*** by the mercy of God. Hay, George.

God everywhere present. Boudon, Henry Mary.

Good confessor. Marley, Martin.

Gother's prayers for Sundays & festivals. Gother, John.

Great duties of life. Berington, Simon.

Gregory William, Bishop of Telmessus. Sharrock, Gregory William.
Grounds of the Catholic doctrine. Challoner, Richard.
Grounds of the Christian's belief. Hornyold, John Joseph.
Grounds of the old religion. Challoner, Richard.
Guide to heaven. Bona, Giovanni.
Guide to the altar. MacKenzie, Alexander.
Gulielmus, Dei et apostolicae. Gibson, William.
Hell opened to Christians. Pinamonti, Giovanni Pietro.
Hibernia dominicana. Burke, Thomas Myles.
Hidden treasures. MacKenzie, Alexander.
Hind and the panther. Dryden, John.
His holiness, Pope Clement the XIIIth's constitution. Clement XIII.
Histoire du clergé. Barruel, Augustin.
Histoire du collége de Douay. Tootell, Hugh.
Historical account of the laws against Roman Catholics. O'Connell, Daniel.
Historical account of the laws respecting Roman Catholics. O'Connell, Daniel.
Historical and critical inquiry. Milner, John.
Historical and critical review of the civil wars in Ireland. Curry, John.
Historical catechism. Fleury, Claude.
Historical collections out of several eminent Protestant historians. Touchet, George.
Historical memoirs of the Irish rebellion. Curry, John.
Histories and parables. Girandeau, Bonaventure.
History, civil and ecclesiastical, & survey of the antiquities. Milner, John.
History of the church of Japan. Crasset, Jean.
History of the clergy. Barruel, Augustin.
History of the English college at Doway. Tootell, Hugh.
History of the life and writings of Mr Arruet de Voltaire. Harel, Maximilien-Marie.
History of the life of our lord Jesus Christ. Le Tourneux, Nicolas.
History of the life of Reginald Pole. Phillips, Thomas.
History of the lives of Abeillard and Heloisa. Berington, Joseph.
History of the old and new testament. Fontaine, Nicolas.
History of the reign of Henry the Second. Berington, Joseph.
History of the variations of the Protestant churches. Bossuet, Jacques Bénigne.
Holy altar and sacrifice explained. Baker, Pacificus.
Holy court, in five books. Caussin, Nicolas.
Holy life of Lady Warner. Scarisbrick, Edward.
Homilia sanctiss. domini nostri. Clement XI.
Homily of Pope Clement XI. Clement XI.
Homily spoken by his holyness. Clement XI.
Horae biblicae. Butler, Charles.
Humble address, and petition of the Roman Catholics of Ireland. Burke, Edmund.
Humble address to our most gracious sovereign. Troy, John Thomas.
Hymn on the institution of the eucharist. Thomas Aquinas.
Hymn on the life of St. Patrick. Plunket, Richard.
Hymn to the Blessed Virgin Mary. Bedingfeld, Edward.
Hymn to the Virgin Mary. Benedetti da Todi, Giacopone de'.
Idea of a new English edition of the holy bible. Geddes, Alexander.
Imitation de Jesus-Christ. Thomas à Kempis.
Imitation of Christ. Thomas à Kempis.
Imitation of Jesus Christ. Thomas à Kempis.

Immaterialism delineated. Berington, Joseph.

Impartial history of Ireland. Reilly, Hugh.

Important enquiry. Redford, Sebastian.

In nomine domini amen. Tabula congregationis O.F.M.

In the present circumstances of the middle district. Gibson, William.

Indulgence of the jubilee. Stonor, John Talbot.

Iniquity display'd. French, Nicholas.

Inquiry into the moral and political tendency. Potts, Thomas.

Instruction of youth in Christian piety. Gobinet, Charles.

Instructiones ad munera apostolica. Hay, George.

Instructions and advice to Catholicks. Challoner, Richard.

Instructions and devotions for hearing mass. Gother, John.

Instructions and devotions for the afflicted and sick. Gother, John.

Instructions and directions for gaining the grand jubilee. Challoner, Richard.

Instructions and directions for the jubilee. Challoner, Richard.

Instructions and prayers for children. Carnegy, Ja.

Instructions and prayers for confession. Gother, John.

Instructions and regulations for the ensuing fast of Lent. Talbot, Thomas.

Instructions and regulations for the fast of Lent. Challoner, Richard.

Instructions and regulations for the fast of Lent. Douglass, John.

Instructions and regulations for the fast of Lent. Gibson, Matthew.

Instructions and regulations for the indulgences. Petre, Benjamin.

Instructions and regulations for the indulgences. Stonor, John Talbot.

Instructions and regulations for the Lent of 1794. Douglass, John.

Instructions Chrétiennes pour les jeunes gens. Humbert, Pierre Hubert.

Instructions concerning an annual spiritual exercise. Gother, John.

Instructions for apprentices and servants. Gother, John.

Instructions for children. Gother, John.

Instructions for confession and communion. Gother, John.

Instructions for confession, communion and confirmation. Gother, John.

Instructions for festivals. Gother, John.

Instructions for gaining the jubilee. Benedict XIV.

Instructions for gaining the jubilee. Clement XIV.

Instructions for keeping Sundays. Gother, John.

Instructions for masters, traders, labourers, &c. Gother, John.

Instructions for particular states. Gother, John.

Instructions for the time of the jubilee anno 1751. Challoner, Richard.

Instructions for the time of the jubilee anno 1770. Challoner, Richard.

Instructions for the whole year. Gother, John.

Instructions for youth. Gother, John.

Instructions, regulations and prayers. Walmesley, Charles.

Instructions upon the sacrament of confirmation. Gother, John.

Instructive part of the mass. Gother, John.

Interesting letters. Caraccioli, Louis-Antoine.

Introduction to a devout life. Francis de Sales.

Introduction to the Catholick faith. Worthington, Thomas.

Introduction to the celebrated devotion of the most holy rosary. Clarkson, John.

Ireland's case briefly stated. Reilly, Hugh.

Jean, par la permission de Dieu. Carroll, John.

John, Bishop of Centuriae. Douglass, John.

John, by divine permission. Carroll, John.

John, by the grace of God. Carroll, John.

Jus primatiale Armacanum. MacMahon, Hugh.

Justification of the tenets of the Roman Catholic religion. Butler, James.

Katechetischer Unterricht. Reuter, Friedrich Caesar.

Knowledge of ones self. Segneri, Paolo.

Larger historical catechism. Fleury, Claude.

Layman's afternoon devotion. MacDonald, Archibald Benedict.

Lay-man's ritual. Tootell, Christopher.

Leanmhuin chriosd. Thomas à Kempis.

Lenten monitor to Christians. Baker, Pacificus.

Lessons for Lent. Crathorne, William.

Letter addressed to the Catholic clergy of England. Throckmorton, Sir John Courtenay.

Letter, containing some spiritual advice. Stapleton, Thomas.

Letter from a Catholic gentleman to his Protestant friend. Fell, Charles.

Letter from an English gentleman to a Member of Parliament. Curry, John.

Letter from his eminence. Frankenberg, John Henry.

Letter from the Lord Archbishop of Sens. Languet, Jean Joseph.

Letter from the most reverend doctor Butler. Butler, James.

Letter of July 7th. Carroll, John.

Letter to a friend. Challoner, Richard.

Letter to a friend, on the late revolution in France. Eyre, Francis.

Letter to a Member of Parliament. Geddes, Alexander.

Letter to a Roman Catholic clergyman upon theological inaccuracy. Plowden, Robert.

Letter to a student at a foreign university. Phillips, Thomas.

Letter to Dr. Fordyce. Berington, Joseph.

Letter to Francis Plowden, Esq. Plowden, Robert.

Letter to his grace Edward Lord Arch-bishop of Tuam. Nary, Cornelius.

Letter to Mr. A-d. Errington, William.

Letter to the author of a book. Cordell, Charles.

Letter to the author of The review. Englefield, Sir Henry Charles.

Letter to the Catholics of England. Plowden, Charles.

Letter to the reverend John Erskine. MacKenzie, Alexander.

Letter to the reverend Mr. Joseph Reeves. Pilling, William Leo.

Letter to the rev. Dr. Priestley. Geddes, Alexander.

Letter to the rev. Mr. Ralph Churton. Eyre, Francis.

Letter to the rev'd Mr. Stephen Radcliffe. Nary, Cornelius.

Letter to the right reverend John Douglass. Berington, Joseph.

Letter to the right reverend the Lord Bishop of London. Geddes, Alexander.

Letter to the rr. the archbishops and bishops of England. Geddes, Alexander.

Letter to the societies of United Irishmen. Jones, William Todd.

Letter to the societies of United Irishmen. MacKenna, Theobald.

Letter to the vv. apostolic in England. Geddes, Alexander.

Letters from Rome. Pius VI.

Letters on materialism. Berington, Joseph.

Letters on usury, and interest. Hay, George.

Letters to a friend, on the late revolution in France. Eyre, Francis.

Letters to a prebendary. Milner, John.

Lettre circulaire de Monseigneur l'Evêque. Briand, Jean Olivier.

Lettre circulaire à messieurs les curés. Hubert, Jean François.

Lettre de mgr. l'Evêque de Rennes. Bareau de Girac, François.

Lettre de m. l'Abbé Lambert à m. l'Abbé Barruel. Lambert, Pierre-Thomas.

Lettre de m. l'Evêque de Léon aux ecclésiastiques François. La Marche, Jean François de.

Lettre pastorale de monseigneur l'Evêque de Dol. Herge, Urbain René de.

Lettre pastorale et ordonnance de M. l'Evêque de Léon. La Marche, Jean François de.

Lettres d'un voyageur. Barruel, Augustin.

Life and death of the renowned John Fisher. Bayly, Thomas.

Life, and miracles, of St. Wenefride. Falconer, John.

Life, death and passion, of our Lord (and Saviour) Jesus Christ. Ribadeneira, Pedro de.

Life of Francois de Salignac de la Motte Fenelon. Ramsay, Andrew Michael.

Life of Miss Nano Nagle. Coppinger, William.

Life of our Lord and Saviour Jesus Christ. Bonaventura, Saint.

Life of Pope Clement XIV. Caraccioli, Louis-Antoine.

Life of S. Aloysius Gonzaga. Orléans, Pierre Joseph d'.

Life of Saint Francis Xavier. Bouhours, Dominique.

Life of Saint Margaret, Queen of Scotland. Geddes, John.

Life of Sir Thomas More. More, Cresacre.

Life of Sir Tobie Matthews. Butler, Alban.

Life of St. Edward, King and confessor. Porter, Jerome.

Life of St. Francis of Sales. Marsollier, Jacques.

Life of St. John Francis Regis. Daubenton, William.

Life of St. Mary of Egypt. Redford, Sebastian.

Life of St. Teresa. Butler, Alban.

Life of the holy mother St. Teresa. Teresa of Avila.

Life of the servant of God. Alegani, J.B.

Life of the venerable Benedict Joseph Labre. Marconi, Giuseppe Loreto.

Life of the venerable and right reverend Richard Challoner. Barnard, James.

Little manual of the poor man's daily devotion. Clifford, William.

Lives and deaths of Sir Thomas More ... and of John Fisher. Bayly, Thomas and William Roper.

Lives of saints. Butler, Alban.

Lives of saints; collected from authentick records. Fell, Charles.

Lives of saints, with other feasts of the year. Ribadeneira, Pedro de.

Lives of the fathers, martyrs, and other principal saints. Butler, Alban.

Lives of the primitive fathers. Butler, Alban.

Lives of the principal fathers. Butler, Alban.

London district. Regulations for Lent. Challoner, Richard.

Lord Bishop of Angers his letter to the clergy of his diocess. Poncet de la Rivière, Michel.

Love and charity the basis of religion. Brancas, Henri Ignace de.

Loyalty asserted. O'Leary, Arthur.

M. Voulant concilier. Douglass, John.

Mandate of his eminence my lord Cardinal of Bissy. Thiard de Bissy, Henri de.

Mandate of his eminence the (Lord) Cardinal d'Noailles. Noailles, Louis Antoine.

Mandate of his grace, the Archbishop of Paris. Le Clerc de Juigné, Antoine E. L.

Mandate of the Bishop of Marseilles. Belsunce de Castelmoron, Henri.

Mandate to the clergy. Challoner, Richard.

Mandate of the right reverend father in God the Lord Bishop of Bruges. Caimo, John Robert.

Mandates of their lordships John, Bishop of Centuriae. Douglass, John.

Mandement de Monseigneur l'Evêque de Québec. Denaut, Pierre.

Mandement de Monseigneur l'Eveque de Quebec. Hubert, Jean François.
Mandement du 28 octobre, M.DCC.XCIII. Hubert, Jean François.
Manners of the Christians. Fleury, Claude.
Manners of the Israelites. Fleury, Claude.
Manual of controversies. Turberville, Henry.
Manual of the daily prayers and duties of a Christian. Pembridge, Michael Benedict.
Manual of the glorious doctor St. Augustine. Augustine, Saint.
Matthew, Bishop of Comana, to the Catholics at Liverpool. Gibson, Matthew.
Meditations and discourses. Butler, Alban.
Méditations en forme de retraite sur l'amour de Dieu. Grou, Jean-Nicolas.
Meditations of Saint Augustine. Augustine, Saint.
Meditations on the four last things. Pinamonti, Giovanni Pietro.
Méditations sur la révolution Françoise. Fabry, Raymond.
Memoire de M. Gordon. Gordon, Alexander.
Memoire on some questions. MacKenna, Theobald.
Memoires for Rome. Maillard de Tournon, Charles Thomas.
Mémoires pour servir à l'histoire du Jacobinisme. Barruel, Augustin.
Memoirs, illustrating the antichristian conspiracy. Barruel, Augustin.
Memoirs illustrating the history of Jacobinism. Barruel, Augustin.
Memoirs of George Leyburn. Leyburn, George.
Memoirs of Gregorio Panzani. Berington, Joseph.
Memoirs of Sir Gaudentio di Lucca. Berington, Simon.
Memoirs of missionary priests. Challoner, Richard.
Memoirs of the life and writings of the late Charles O'Conor. O'Conor, Charles (II).
Memorial for the suffering Catholics. Hay, George.
Memorial of a Christian life. Luis de Granada.
Memorial of ancient British piety. Challoner, Richard.
Memorial to the public. Geddes, Alexander.
Memoriale vitae sacerdotalis. Arvisenet, Claude.
Messieurs les ecclésiastiques Français. Douglass, John.
Method of conversing with God. Boutauld, Michel.
Method of hearing mass. Herbert, Lucy.
Miraculous powers of the church of Christ asserted. Walton, William.
Miscellaneous tracts. O'Leary, Arthur.
Modern controversy. Manning, Robert.
Modest and true account of the chief points in controversie. Nary, Cornelius.
Modest apology for the Roman Catholics of Great Britain. Geddes, Alexander.
Modest defence of the clergy and religious. Hunter, Thomas.
Modest enquiry. Berington, Simon.
Monita quaedam pro sacerdotibus missionariis. Petre, Benjamin.
Moral entertainments. Manning, Robert.
Moral essays. MacDonald, Archibald Benedict.
Moral instructions. Grou, Jean-Nicolas.
Moral reflections on the epistles and gospels. Darrell, William.
Moral reflections upon the gospel of St. John. Quesnel, Pasquier.
Moral reflections upon the gospel of St. Luke. Quesnel, Pasquier.
Moral reflections upon the gospel of St. Mark. Quesnel, Pasquier.
Moral reflections upon the gospel of St. Matthew. Quesnel, Pasquier.
Morality, extracted from the confessions of Saint Austin. Grou, Jean-Nicolas.
Morality of the bible. Challoner, Richard.

Motives to excite us to the frequent meditation. Herbert, Lucy.

Moveable feasts, fasts and other (annual) observances. Butler, Alban.

Mr. Gother's second method of hearing mass. Gother, John.

Mr. O'Leary's defence. O'Leary, Arthur.

Mr. O'Leary's letter. O'Leary, Arthur.

Mr. O'Leary's narrative. O'Leary, Arthur.

Mr. O'Leary's remarks on the rev. John Wesley's letters. O'Leary, Arthur.

Mr Smyth's reasons for resuming his station in the parish of Kells. Smyth, Patrick.

Mr William Smith's address to the people of Ireland. Smith, Sir William Cusack.

My dear brethren. Carroll, John.

New history of the world. Nary, Cornelius.

New Odyssey. Palafox y Mendoza, Juan de.

New translation of the funeral oration. Frey de Neuville, Charles.

New translation of the holy bible. Holy bible.

New year's gift to the good people of England. Geddes, Alexander.

New year's gift. Challoner, Richard.

New year's gift. Douglass, John.

New year's gift. L., F.

Novo testamento. New testament.

Novum testamentum. New testament.

Observations on affairs in Ireland. Taaffe, Nicolaus.

Observations on the oath proposed to the English Roman Catholics. Plowden, Charles.

Observations on the popery laws. O'Conor, Charles and John Curry.

Occasional letters on the present affairs of the Jesuits. Elliot, Nathaniel.

Ode to St. Winefride. Daniel, Edward.

Of devotion to the Blessed Virgin Mary. Manning, Robert.

Of good intentions. Sergeant, John.

Of the foundations of religion. Valsecchi, Antonino.

Officia missarum. O'Kenny, Nicolaus Antoninus.

Officia propria sanctorum Hiberniae. Burke, Thomas Myles (see also under title).

Old fashion farmer's motives for leaving the Church of England. Whittingham, John.

On account of the general decline. Walmesley, Charles.

One only church of Christ. Le Pointe, Thomas.

Oraison funèbre. Hamel, Etienne Pierre.

Oraison funèbre of the pontiff Pius VI. Milner, John.

Oration delivered at the funeral obsequies. Brancadoro, Caesar.

Oration on the anniversary of the orphan establishment in Charleston. Gallagher, Simon Felix.

Orationes dicendae pro salute regis. Talbot, James.

Our blessed redeemer. Gibson, Matthew.

Our holy father Pope Clement XIV. Petre, Francis.

Papal brief, dated 2 September, 1745. Benedict XIV.

Papist misrepresented and represented. Gother, John.

Paradise of the soul. Merlo Horstius, Jacob (see also under title).

Passion of our Lord and Saviour Jesus Christ. Blyth, Francis (see also under title).

Pastoral address to the Roman Catholics of Scotland. Hay, George.

Pastoral address to the Roman Catholics. Troy, John Thomas.

Pastoral instruction for the apostolic fast of Lent. Challoner, Richard.

Pastoral instruction on keeping the Sunday. Talbot, Thomas.

Pastoral instruction on the duties of Christian citizens. Troy, John Thomas.

Pastoral instruction to the Roman Catholics. Moylan, Francis.

Pastoral instruction to the Roman Catholics. Troy, John Thomas.

Pastoral instruction with regulations for Lent. Hornyold, John Joseph.

Pastoral instructions proper for penitents as well as confessors. Denhoff, Jan Kazimierz.

Pastoral letter and ordinance. La Marche, Jean François de.

Pastoral letter from Charles Bishop of Rama. Walmesley, Charles.

Pastoral letter from the Bishop of Daulis to his flock. Hay, George.

Pastoral letter from the four Catholic bishops. Leyburn, John.

Pastoral letter of Matthew, Bishop of Comana. Gibson, Matthew.

Pastoral letter to the Catholic clergy of the united dioceses. Hussey, Thomas.

Pastoral letter. Carroll, John.

Pastoral letter addressed to the Catholicks. Challoner, Richard.

Pastoral letter. Frankenberg, John Henry.

Pastoral letter. La Poterie, Claude F. Bouchard de.

Pastoral letter. Pressy, François Joseph.

Pattrum y gwir-gristion. Thomas à Kempis.

Pax vobis: or, gospel and liberty. Gordon, John.

Penitent instructed. Segneri, Paolo.

Penitent: or, entertainments for Lent. Caussin, Nicolas.

Penitent's daily assistant. MacCary, James Mathew.

Pensées ecclésiastiques. Carron, Guy Toussaint Julien.

Perfect religious. Marin, Michel-Ange.

Petit livre de vie. Bonnefons, Amable.

Philadelphia, August 15, 1789. Carey, Mathew.

Philemon. Phillips, Thomas.

Philosophical catechism. Feller, François Xavier de.

Philothea, or an introduction to a devout life. Francis de Sales.

Philothea; or, a pilgrimage to the holy Chappel. Palafox y Mendoza, Juan de.

Pious Christian instructed. Hay, George.

Pious considerations on several important practical truths. Stapleton, Thomas.

Pious lectures, explanatory of the principles. Lhomond, Charles François.

Pious meditations for every day in the month. Bouhours, Dominique.

Pious monitor of the divine presence. Gilmore, Robert Paul.

Pious reflections for every day in (of) the month. Fénelon, François de Salignac.

Pious reflections on patient sufferings. Challoner, Richard.

Pious sentiments of the late king James II. James II.

Pious thoughts concerning the knowledge and, love of God. Fénelon, François de Salignac.

Plain and concise method of learning the Gregorian note. Hoey, P.

Plain and rational account of the Catholic faith. Manning, Robert.

Plain answer to Dr. C-s M-n's letter from Rome. Challoner, Richard.

Plain answer to Dr. Middleton's letter from Rome. Challoner, Richard.

Plaint of the Blessed Virgin. Benedetti da Todi, Giacopone de'.

Political address to the Catholics of Ireland. Driscol, Paddy.

Political essays. MacKenna, Theobald.

Poor man's catechism. Mannock, John Anselm.

Poor man's controversy. Mannock, John Anselm.

Poor man's library. Denhoff, Jan Kazimierz.

Poor prisoner's comforter. MacKenzie, Alexander.

Pope's brief to the Emperor. Pius VI.

Popish pagan the fiction of a Protestant heathen. Berington, Simon.

Postscript: or, a review of the grounds already laid. Hawarden, Edward.

Practical catechism in fifty two lessons. Gother, John.

Practical catechism on the Sundays. Crathorne, William.

Practical catechism; or, lessons for Sundays. Gother, John.

Practical discourses. Reeve, Joseph.

Practical divinity. Bourdaloue, Louis.

Practical methods. Constable, John.

Practical reflections. Bowes, Robert.

Practical theology. Bourdaloue, Louis.

Prayers and pious considerations for every day in the week. Stapleton, Thomas.

Prayers for every day in Lent. Gother, John.

Prayers for Sundays, holidays and other festivals Gother, John.

Précis historique de la vie et du pontificat de Pie VI. Blanchard, Pierre Louis.

Predigt von der Heiligkeit christlicher Tempel. Goetz, Johann Nepomuck.

Present state of the Catholic mission. Smyth, Patrick.

Principles and rules of the gospel. Gother, John.

Principles of the Christian religion. Brittain, Lewis.

Profession of Catholick faith. Challoner, Richard.

Proper heads of self-examination for a king. Fénelon, François de Salignac.

Proposals for a subscription. Carroll, John.

Proposals for printing by subscription. Bell, Robert.

Proposals for printing by subscription. Geddes, Alexander (see also under title).

Prospectus of a new translation of the holy bible. Geddes, Alexander.

Protestant's tryal. Browne, Levinius.

Psalmiste. Boisgelin de Cucé, Jean de Dieu R.

Queen of heaven's livery. Loop, George.

Queries to Dr. Sacheverell. Corker, James Maurus.

Question of questions. Mumford, James.

Real principles of Catholicks. Hornyold, John Joseph.

Reasons why Jews, infidels, Turks and hereticks cannot be saved. R.O., Gent.

Reconciler of religions. S., A.

Rede moral-philosophische bey Veranlassung. Goetz, Johann Nepomuck.

Reflections addressed to the rev. John Hawkins. Berington, Joseph.

Reflections on the appointment of a Catholic bishop. Clifford, Henry.

Reflexions Chretiennes. Carron, Guy Toussaint Julien.

Reform'd churches proved destitute of a lawful ministry. Manning, Robert.

Refutation of the charges. Sweetman, John.

Regular historical account of the first rise of the reformation. Fleury, Claude.

Regulations for Lent. Challoner, Richard.

Regulations for the administration of the College of Aquhorties. Hay, George.

Regulations for the fast of Lent. Challoner, Richard.

Regulations for the fast of Lent. Gibson, William.

Rejoinder to the reply to the answer to the Charitable address. Nary, Cornelius.

Rejoynder to the reply. O'Brien, Timothy.

Relaçao de conversaõ do R. Senhor Joaõ Thayer. Thayer, John.

Relation de la conversion de Mr. Thayer. Thayer, John.

Relation de l'établissement du Christianisme. Gouvea, Alexandre de.

Relation of the missions of Paraguay. Muratori, Lodovico Antonio.

Religio leici [sic], &c. Tempest, Stephen.

Religion prouvée. Le Pointe, Thomas.

Religious soul elevated to perfection. Baudrand, Barthélemy.

Remarks on a book entitled Memoirs of Gregorio Panzani. Plowden, Charles.

Remarks on Bower's Lives of the popes. Butler, Alban.

Remarks on the four volumes of The lives of saints. Witham, Robert.

Remarks on the prefaces. Earle, John.

Remarks on the rev. Joseph Berington's examination. Bruning, George.

Remarks on the two first volumes of the late lives of the popes. Butler, Alban.

Remarks on the writings of the rev. Joseph Berington. Plowden, Charles.

Remarks on two letters against popery. Challoner, Richard.

Remarks upon a letter. Strickland, Joseph.

Remarks upon F. Le Courayer's book. Constable, John.

Remarks upon the introduction to a devout life. Cullin, Michael.

Remonstrance addressed to the lower order of Roman Catholics. Coppinger, William.

Reply of a Roman Catholic priest. Brosius, Francis Xavier.

Reply to an anonymous writer from Belfast. MacKenna, Theobald.

Reply to Mr. M'Kee's remarks on a pastoral letter. Thompson, James.

Reply to the report published by the Cisalpine Club. Milner, John.

Reply to the rev. Ralph Churton. Eyre, Francis.

Réponse à une brocluse intitulée. Barral, Louis Matthias de.

Réponse de M. l'Abbé Barruel. Barruel, Augustin.

Responsum per illustres. Gerdil, Cardinal.

Resurrection of Laurent Ricci. La Poterie, Claude F. Bouchard de.

Rev. Arthur O'Leary's address to the Lords. O'Leary, Arthur.

Rev. Mr. O'Leary's address to the common people of Ireland. O'Leary, Arthur.

Rev. sirs, the following lines. Troy, John Thomas.

Rev. William Coghlan begs leave. Coghlan, William.

Reverend Arthur O'Leary's caution to the common people of Ireland. O'Leary, Arthur.

Reverend Sir. Carey, Mathew.

Review of S.N.'s late publication. Plowden, Robert.

Review of the Catholic question. MacKenna, Theobald.

Review of the important controversy. O'Leary, Arthur.

Review of the most inportant controversy. Musson, Samuel.

Rights of dissenters from the established church. Berington, Joseph.

Rise and fall of the heresy of iconoclasts. Manning, Robert.

River's manual: or, pastoral instructions upon the creed. Rivers, William Penketh.

Roman Catholic fidelity to Protestants ascertained. Hay, George.

Roman Catholic principles in reference to God and the country. Corker, James Maurus.

Roman Catholick's reasons. Challoner, Richard.

Roman liturgy. Robertson, F.J. (see also under title).

Rosary's of the B. Virgin Mary. Burke, Edmund O.P.

Rule of faith briefly consider'd. Hawarden, Edward.

Rule of faith truly stated. Hawarden, Edward.

Rule of S. Augustin, Augustine, Saint.

Rule of the glorious doctor of the church. Augustine, Saint.

Rule of the great S. Augustin expounded. Hugh of S. Victor.

Rules and instructions. Scarisbrick, Edward.

Rules of life for a Christian. Challoner, Richard.

S. Cyprien consolant les fidèles. La Hogue, Louis Egidius de.

Sacraments explain'd. Hornyold, John Joseph.

Sacred eloquence: or discourses selected. Coombes, William Henry.

Sacred hymns, anthems and versicles. Barbandt, Charles.

Sail yr athrawiaeth Gatholic. Challoner, Richard.

Saint Aloysius Gonzaga proposed as a model of a holy life. Mattei, Pasquale de.

Saint Augustine's confessions. Augustine, Saint.

Sanctissimi domini nostri. Pius VII.

Sanctissimi domini nostri. Pius VI.

Sanctus Cyprianus ad martyres. Cyprian, Saint.

Science of rational devotion. Muratori, Lodovico Antonio.

Scriptural history of the earth. Howard, Philip.

Scriptural researches. Harris, Raymund.

Scripture doctrine of miracles displayed. Hay, George.

Scripture doctrine of the church. Challoner, Richard.

Scripture penitents. Godeau, Antoine.

Scripture sentences. Challoner, Richard.

Seasonable thoughts. O'Conor, Charles.

Second address humbly presented. Ben Yizaaker, Abraham.

Second apology for disapproving of the oath. Strickland, Joseph.

Second discourse. Barnardin, Father.

Second epistle from Simpkin. Geddes, Alexander.

Second letter addressed to the Catholic clergy of England. Throckmorton, John Courtenay.

Second part of The rule of faith. Hawarden, Edward.

Second remonstrance. Moylan, Francis.

Secret policy of the English Society of Jesus. Tootell, Hugh.

Secret policy of the Jansenists. Agard de Champs, Etienne.

Selecta sanctorum. Le Pointe, Thomas.

Selection from the new version of psalms. Adams, James B.

Sense prophétique. Caperan, l'Abbé.

Sentimental and practical theology. Lasne d'Aiguebell, M. de.

Sequentes orationes. Walmesley, Charles.

Serious considerations of a soul. Strahan, Robert.

Serious expostulation with the rev. Joseph Berington. Milner, John.

Sermon against popery. Crawley, James.

Sermon for the general fast. Weldon, Thomas.

Sermon on Catholick loyalty. Harris, Raymund.

Sermon on the love of our country. Archer, James.

Sermon on the parable. Baker, Pacificus.

Sermon preached at Saint Patrick's Chapel. Archer, James.

Sermon preached at Saint Patrick's Chapel. O'Leary, Arthur.

Sermon preached at the Catholic Chapel. Adams, James.

Sermon preached at the opening of the Roman Catholic chapel. Plowden, Robert.

Sermon preached by the rev. Dr. Hussey. Hussey, Thomas.

Sermon preached in the Roman Catholic chapel at Winchester. Milner, John.

Sermon preached in the Spanish Chapel. Hussey, Thomas.

Sermon preached, on the day of general fast. Geddes, Alexander.

Sermon preached on the ninth day of May. Gallagher, Simon Francis.

Sermon preach'd at Worcester. Humberstone, Henry.

Sermons, and exhortations for the whole year. Morony, Joseph.

Sermons and moral discourses. Gahan, William.

Sermons for every Sunday in the year. Blyth, Francis.
Sermons on some of the most important subjects. O'Brien, Matthew.
Sermons on various moral and religious subjects. Archer, James.
Sermons on various religious subjects. Goonan, Silvester.
Seventeen Irish sermons. Gallagher, James.
Several excellent methods of hearing mass. Herbert, Lucy.
Several methods and practices of devotion. Herbert, Lucy.
Short abridgment of Christian doctrine. Languet, Jean Joseph (see also under title).
Short account of the establishment of the new see of Baltimore. Plowden, Charles.
Short account of the life and virtues of ... Mary of the Holy Cross. Bedingfield, Anne.
Short and plain exposition. Gahan, William.
Short appeal to the public. Eyre, Francis.
Short daily exercise with devotions for mass. Challoner, Richard.
Short discourse upon the life and death of Mr. Geo. Throckmorton. Witham, Thomas.
Short essay on the Christian religion. Eyre, Francis.
Short explanation of indulgences. Challoner, Richard.
Short historical catechism. Denhoff, Jan Kazimierz.
Short historical catechism. Fleury, Claude.
Short history of the (first) beginning and progress. Challoner, Richard.
Short history of the British empire. Plowden, Francis.
Short instruction for Lent. Talbot, Thomas.
Short meditations upon the four last things. Pinamonti, Giovanni Pietro.
Short plea for human nature and common sense. Grace, George.
Short review of the book of Jansenius. Jenks, Silvester.
Short treatise on the method and advantages. Chrysostome de Saint-Lô, Jean.
Short view of the history and antiquities of Winchester. Milner, John.
Shortest way to end disputes about religion. Manning, Robert.
Sincere Christian instructed in the faith of Christ. Hay, George.
Sincere Christian's guide in the choice of religion. Gother, John.
Single combat or, personal dispute. Manning, Robert.
Sinners guide. Luis de Granada.
Sinner's complaints to God. Gother, John.
Sir, you will readily discover. La Poterie, Claude F. Bouchard de.
Sixteen Irish sermons. Gallagher, James.
Small book intituled England. Coleny, Thomas.
Soliloquies of the glorious doctor. Augustine, Saint.
Some queries. Hawarden, Edward.
Some remarks on the decree of King Augustus II. Hawarden, Edward.
Some seasonable thoughts. O'Conor, Charles.
Some thoughts on the present politics of Ireland. MacKenna, Theobald.
Specimen of amendments candidly proposed. Constable, John.
Specimen of the spirit of the dissenting teachers. Challoner, Richard.
Speech of Arthur O'Connor. O'Connor, Arthur.
Speech of Henry Grattan. Grattan, Henry.
Speech of the Abbé Maury. Maury, Jean Siffrein.
Spiritual combat. Scupoli, Lorenzo.
Spiritual director for those who have none. Treuvé, Simon Michel.
Spiritual director of devout and religious souls. Francis de Sales.
Spiritual exercises of S. Ignatius of Loyola. Ignatius of Loyola.
Spiritual guide. MacKenzie, Alexander.

Spiritual retreat for one day in every month. Croiset, Jean.

Spiritual retreat. Huby, Vincent.

Spiritual treasury. White M'Kenna, J.

Spiritual works. Gother, John.

State and behaviour of English Catholics. Berington, Joseph.

Statuta Fratrum Minorum. Parkinson, Anthony.

Streams of eternity. Blyth, Francis.

Study of sacred literature. Phillips, Thomas.

Substance of the arguments. MacKenna, Theobald.

Sufferings of our Lord Jesus Christ. Thomé de Jesus.

Suim athgar an teagasg criosduighe. Butler, James.

Summary, or compendious history of the old testament. Fontaine, Nicolas.

Sunday evening's entertainment. Jenkins, Peter.

Sundays kept holy. Baker, Pacificus.

Supplement to the abstract. Weston, John Baptist.

Supplementum Hiberniae Dominicanae. Burke, Thomas Myles.

Sure way to heaven. MacCary, James Mathew.

Tabula congregationis 1733-1800. Tabula congregationis O.F.M.

Teagasg Criosdaidhe. O'Hussey, Bonaventure.

Teagasg Criosdaidhe. Pulleine, James.

Teagasg Criosduidhe. Butler, James.

Teagask Creestye. O'Reilly, Michael.

Teagusg Crèesdéegh. Butler, James.

Theophilus, or the pupil instructed. Lhomond, Charles François.

There are two whole weeks. Petre, Francis.

Think well on't. Challoner, Richard.

Third discourse. Barnardin, Father.

Thirty meditations. Challoner, Richard.

Thomas, Bishop of Acon, vicar apostolic. Talbot, Thomas.

Thomas Dei et s. sedis apostolicae. Talbot, Thomas.

Three letters from the rev. Father Arthur O'Leary. O'Leary, Arthur.

'Tis now a proper season. Stonor, John Talbot.

To all the Catholic clergy. Challoner, Richard.

To all the Catholic clergy. Walmesley, Charles.

To all the faithful of the midland district. Berington, Charles.

To all the faithful, clergy and laity, in the western district. Sharrock, Gregory William.

To all the faithful, clergy and laity, of the London district. Douglass, John.

To all whom it may concern. Gibson, Matthew.

To his beloved children. Clement XII.

To his most excellent majesty James III. Berington, Simon.

To Mr. John Wesley. Whittingham, John.

To Mr. Jonathan Evans, greeting. Whittingham, John.

To the Catholic clergy. Walmesley, Charles.

To the Catholic nobility, gentry and others. Griffiths, John (see also under title).

To the clergy of the London district. Berington, Charles.

To the faithful of the L... district. Challoner, Richard.

To the gentlemen. Plowden, Robert.

To the gentlemen. Strickland, Joseph.

To the honorable the Commons of Great Britain. Walmesley, Charles.

To the honourable Thomas Talbot. Clough, Anthony.

To the public. Whittingham, John (see also under title).

To the publick. La Poterie, Claude F. Bouchard de.

To the rev(erend) pastors and other Roman Catholic clergy. Troy, John Thomas.

To the right reverend & religious Dame Elizabeth Phillips. Phillips, Thomas.

To the very reverend ... Anna Busby. Greene, John Raymond.

To the vic. ap. of the northern district. Chadwick, John.

Toleration of the Protestants. Papin, Isaac.

Touchstone of the new religion. Challoner, Richard.

Touch-stone of the reformed gospel. Heigham, John.

Translation of the Bishop of Boulogne's pastoral letter. René, Jean.

Transnatural philosophy, treating of the essences and operations. Sergeant, John.

Treatise concerning the fruitful sayings of David. Fisher, John.

Treatise of confidence in the mercy of God. Languet, Jean Joseph.

Treatise of policy and religion. Fitzherbert, Thomas.

Treatise of the difference betwixt the temporal and eternal. Nieremberg, Juan Eusebio.

Treatise of the imitation of the holy youth. Gobinet, Charles.

Treatise on morality. Houdet, René.

Treatise of the real presence. Darrell, William.

Treatise on the two sacraments. Gobinet, Charles.

Treatise plainly shewing the only religion. Sergeant, John.

Treatise, which clearly sheweth the only religion. Sergeant, John.

Trinitarian manual. Dwyer, Joseph John.

Triumphs of the cross. Vaughan, Arthur.

True and exact relation of the death of two Catholicks. Murphy, Cornelius.

True church of Christ. Hawarden, Edward.

True humility, or the undeceiving mirror. Segneri, Paolo.

True looking-glass. Segneri, Paolo.

True principles of a Catholic. Challoner, Richard.

True wisdom: or, considerations for every day of the week. Segneri, Paolo.

Trustees of the Roman Catholic seminary at Maynooth. Troy, John Thomas.

Truth of the Catholic religion proved from the holy scripture. Grostête, Marin.

Truth triumphant. O'Brien, Timothy.

Tryal of the cause of the Roman Catholics. Brooke, Henry.

Two letters from H.H. Pius VI. Pius VI.

Undersigned in the name of the Roman Catholic clergy. Gibson, William.

Unerring authority of the Catholick church. Challoner, Richard.

Unhappy events which have taken place in a neighbouring country. Walmesley, Charles.

Universis patribus, fratribus, ac sororibus. Gaddi, Joseph.

Vie et le martyre de Louis XVI. Limon, Geoffroi, Marquis de.

View of the oath. Reeve, Joseph.

View of the real power of the pope. Hawkins, Thomas.

Vindication of the doctrine of the Catholic Church. Gilbert, Nicolas Alain.

Vindication of the old Church of England. Kingsley, William.

Vindication of the political principles of Roman Catholics. O'Conor, Charles.

Vindication of the Roman Catholic clergy of the town of Wexford. Clinch, J. B.

Virgin's nosegay. L., F., Esq.

Watch and pray. Geddes, John.

Way to happiness. Ecclestone, Thomas.

Whole duty of a Christian. Jenks, Silvester.

Whole duty of a Christian. Pembridge, Michael Benedict.

William, Bishop of Acanthos. Gibson, William.
Wit against reason. Hawarden, Edward.
Wonders of God in the wilderness. Challoner, Richard.
Works of the reverend father Pacificus Baker. Baker, Pacificus.
Young gentleman instructed. Challoner, Richard.
Youth instructed in the grounds of the Christian religion. Gahan, William.

Index of Printers, Publishers
and
Booksellers

Boyce, J. 425, 431, 2672, 2677, 2724, 2726
Brabham, H. 650, 651
Bradefute 1407
Brigonci, P. 719
Broderick 743
Brodie, A. 1665
Brompton Chapel 32
Brown 393, 413, 463, 574, 1068, 1607, 1609, 1610, 1629, 1631, 1659, 1862, 1939, 2059, 2190, 2292, 2294, 2327, 2433, 2434, 2678, 2931, 2933
Brown, G. 475
Brown, R. 361, 362, 1502, 2421
Brown, T. 909
Brown, W. 14, 1476, 1478, 1480, 2560
Browne, D. 2528
Browne, T. 699, 2553, 2706
Buck, J. 295
Burnet, G. 827
Burton, T. 199, 200
Butler, T. 2845
Byrn, J. 610, 1426, 1919, 2355, 2940
Byrne, P. 33, 49, 91, 94, 243, 252, 384, 385, 418, 420, 728, 916, 1267, 1336, 1337, 1715, 1985, 2071, 2073, 2074, 2241, 2242, 2254, 2320, 2350, 2429, 2456, 2457, 2459, 2460, 2568, 2571, 2671, 2674, 2777, 2788
C., R. 1740, 1741-1743
Cadell 1877, 1878
Calwell, J. 776, 1294
Camera Apostolica, printing-house of 718
Carey 50, 674, 1451, 2313
Carey, J. 1414, 2718
Carey, M. 437, 438, 563, 676, 691, 902, 1385, 1414, 1483, 2321, 2718
Carey, W.P. 1711
Carli, P. 504
Carpenter, H. 363
Catanach, J. 272, 985
Cavell, W. 2627, 2628
Chadwick, J. 2913
Chalmers, J. 1170, 1171
Chamberlaine, D. 2699, 2835
Chambers, J. 401, 402, 808, 809, 1532, 1714, 2065, 2066, 2570, 2729
Charnley, W. 913
Chavepeyre, J. 8
Cherry, G. 2082

Cheyne, S. 1407, 1719
Clarendon Press 1962
Clarke, C. 100
Clarke, J. 572
Clarkson, R. 1005
Clere, Le 2525
Coates 780, 1334
Coates, F. 231, 393, 404, 413, 414, 786, 1067, 1205, 1264, 1290
Cock, J. de 1428, 1430-1433, 1436, 1484
Cock, J. de, his widow 1437
Coghlan, J.P. 15, 19, 22-26, 28, 35, 36, 45, 51, 69, 70, 82, 88, 90, 92, 120, 121, 133, 138, 139, 141-143, 146-148, 154, 155, 158, 159, 162-164, 168-172, 183, 185, 186, 192, 207, 208, 211, 283, 284, 311, 313, 315, 316, 318, 330, 337, 338, 344, 360, 361, 366, 367, 373, 374, 382, 383, 395, 404, 406, 412, 414, 419, 422, 435, 436, 440, 456, 457, 472, 501, 502, 507, 516-518, 521, 522, 524, 525, 528, 535, 539, 559, 560, 562, 565, 566, 568, 570, 571, 574, 583, 585, 587, 592-594, 597, 598, 615-18, 627, 640, 642, 658-660, 670, 672, 673, 675, 678, 687-690, 703, 713, 731, 736-740, 767, 768, 779, 780, 837, 854, 882, 899, 906, 908, 918, 922, 930, 939, 940, 960, 962-964, 972, 976, 979-984, 986, 987, 989, 1007, 1011, 1017, 1026, 1028, 1030, 1044, 1046, 1060, 1065, 1069, 1075, 1076, 1079, 1082, 1110-1112, 1117-1119, 1121, 1144, 1160-1162, 1168, 1176, 1183, 1203, 1205, 1247, 1255, 1263, 1265, 1269, 1292, 1297, 1298, 1300, 1301, 1308, 1314-1318, 1334, 1337, 1343, 1345, 1349, 1351, 1353, 1358, 1389, 1391, 1395, 1405, 1409, 1410, 1416, 1419, 1424, 1466, 1473, 1500, 1501, 1502, 1519, 1545, 1552, 1555-1557, 1559, 1560, 1568, 1570, 1572, 1574, 1577, 1579-1582, 1589, 1591, 1594-1606, 1618, 1624, 1637, 1640-1642, 1650, 1652, 1660, 1669, 1670, 1678, 1681, 1682, 1728, 1738, 1774, 1775, 1797, 1811, 1829-1831, 1833, 1834, 1846, 1865, 1867-1871, 1873, 1875, 1877-1882, 1884,

Hall 473, 561, 1183
Hall, S. 2683, 2684
Hal(e)y, J. 151, 781, 813, 874, 1489, 1691-1693, 1713, 1849, 1910, 1913, 1975, 1976, 2098, 2219, 2394, 2651, 2652
Hanly, T. 2357
Hanna 448
Hanna, A. 2685
Hanvey, E. 2838
Hanvey, J. 2838
Harris 782
Harris, M. 423
Harrison, G. 759
Harrison, W.P. 1143
Haydock 2335, 2669
Haydock, T. 343, 572, 1041, 1644, 2728
Hayes, J. 380, 432, 2113, 1214, 2296
Hill, P. 1407
Hill, T. 836
Hodgson, S. 914, 1061, 1061-1063, 1066
Hoey, J. 122, 123, 227, 400, 699, 827, 834, 1993, 2420, 2624-2626, 2630
Hoey, J. jun. 1328
Hoey, P. 821-823, 879, 1299, 1616, 1617, 1966, 1967, 2499, 2738, 2923
Hogan 1665
Holliwell, J. 1466
Holliwell, T. 1090, 1327, 2497
L'Homme 196, 291
L'Homme, L. 51, 1072, 2525
Howard 2675
Howlatt, T. 1739, 2849
Hoyles, J. 277, 286, 649, 770, 774, 873, 1731, 2210, 2213
Huard 291
Huard, P. 459, 462
Hudson 201
Huggonson, J. 622
Hughes 1069, 1502, 1642, 2421
Hughes, J. 1969
Huot, F. 323, 479
Hurst, T. 483
Husband, J.A. 2258
Ingram, G. 1517, 2053
Innys 256
Innys, J. 1625
Innys, W. 1625
Ireland, J. 1347

Jackson 2373
Jackson, W. 2257, 2264
Jeffery, H. 1611
Johnson, J. 435, 436, 1145-1148, 1150-1152, 1154, 1156, 1158, 1165, 1166, 1450, 1453
Johnson, T. 1465, 2913
Johnston 1051
Johnston, W. 2259, 2260
Jones, J. 1128
Jones, T. 2931, 2933
Jones, W. 243, 252, 538, 824, 1207, 1423, 1508, 2194, 2350, 2557, 2727, 2788
Joy, F. 1549
Justice 1051
Kammerer, H. 193
Kay 1699
Kearsley, G. 2316-2318
Keating 23, 24, 70, 183, 373, 393, 413, 463, 574, 711, 780, 906, 960, 1017, 1026, 1028, 1030, 1037, 1044, 1060, 1068, 1069, 1149, 1334, 1343, 1549, 1353, 1500-1502, 1552, 1556, 1560, 1607, 1629, 1631, 1650, 1659, 1669, 1862, 1870, 1871, 1875, 1879, 1880, 2053, 2059, 2091, 2190, 2293, 2294, 2300, 2310, 2323-2325, 2327, 2421, 2433, 2434, 2569, 2678, 2719, 2745, 2746, 2784, 2790, 2931, 2933
Keating, J. 213, 1102
Keating, P. 31, 36, 48, 87, 88, 90, 92, 231, 404, 414, 444, 745, 746, 801, 973, 1061-1063, 1066, 1621, 2054, 2055, 2060, 2066, 2067, 2069, 2089, 2091, 2286, 2314, 2484, 2663, 2848
Keble, S. 2528
Kelly, D. 215, 491, 610, 1136
Kelly, E. 98, 997, 2112, 2554, 2584, 2736
Kelly, E., executors of 553, 816, 897, 910, 1103
Kelly, I. 228, 334, 341, 390, 667, 868, 909, 946, 1054, 1096, 1141, 1287, 1288, 1550, 1687, 1733, 1747, 1787, 2007, 2021, 2110, 2200, 2496, 2583, 2619, 2620, 2903
Kelly, J. 2026, 2028
Kiernan, C. 407, 738, 2475, 2627, 2628
Kiernan, F. 129, 2492

Kline 2056
Knapton, J. 2779
Kylly, D. 216
L., J. 2914
Lamb, J. 131, 278
Lambert, M. 775
Langlois, M. 2048
Law 960
Leacroft, S. 1618
Le(d)ger 183, 186, 192, 1560, 1669, 2790
Lee 1560
Leigh 1877, 1878
Lelievre, R. 886, 1092, 1658
Lemaire 185, 1031
Letterman 1878
'Levi, Ephraim' 225
Lewis 23, 24, 70, 88, 183, 256, 373, 780, 906, 1017, 1026, 1028, 1030, 1044, 1060, 1343, 1349, 1353, 1500, 1501, 1556, 1560, 1669, 1870, 1871, 1875, 1879, 1880, 2091, 2300, 2310, 2323-2325, 2745, 2746, 2784, 2790
Lewis, T. 90, 92, 146, 154, 158, 407, 751, 833, 835, 1081, 1537, 1772, 1882, 2060
Lewis, W. 378, 865, 1033, 1626, 1627, 1655
Lintot(t), B. 955, 2772
Lloyd, T. 694
Lonchamp 1552
Longman 743
Longman, T.N. 1356
Lord, P. 77, 215-217, 1638, 1754, 1763, 1773, 1855, 1988, 1990, 1991, 2214, 2398, 2850, 2851
Lord, T. 1850, 2502, 2503
Loring 66
Low, S. 87, 93, 483, 1832
Loyall, W. 2538
Lucas, F. jun. 1084
Lyon, D. 1896
Mc'Allister 243
Macdonald, A. 2084
Mairesse, M. 10, 850
Manby 256
Manning 66
Marks, J. 2257, 2264
Marmaduke, J. 55, 135-137, 140, 146, 154, 156-158, 160, 161, 346, 702, 901, 995, 1000, 1001, 1003, 1004,

1201, 1233, 1518, 1567, 1569, 1571, 1573, 1575, 1576, 1578, 1583-1588, 1590, 1592, 1593, 1615, 1672, 1716, 1721, 1751, 1780, 1802, 1803, 1805, 1809, 1840, 1918, 2006, 2008-2011, 2146-2148, 2150-2157, 2159, 2161, 2208, 2217, 2232, 2234, 2279, 2356, 2500, 2592, 2701, 2735
Marmet, L. 1652
M'Creery 806
M'Creery, J. 795, 1700, 1718
M'Donald, R. 405
M'Donnell (M Donnel, M'Donnel, Mc Donnel), T. 149, 150, 152, 747, 786, 1083, 1088, 1131-1135, 1906, 2064, 2068, 2070, 2076, 2460, 2788
Mead, J. 2924
Meadows 256
Mehain, J. 231, 347, 786, 1115, 1350, 1898, 1899, 1924, 2002, 2558, 2573, 2666, 2667, 2887
Meighan 256, 264
Meighan, M. 1788
Meighan, P. 212, 214, 891, 2857, 2925
Meighan, T. 96, 97, 127, 138, 141, 146, 154, 158, 218, 219, 257, 267, 275, 304-306, 317, 335, 336, 349, 356, 357, 378, 379, 489, 500, 505, 506, 508, 511, 514, 526, 527, 544-549, 552, 554, 577, 624, 637, 641, 647, 653-656, 661-666, 669, 692, 693, 697, 698, 704, 706-708, 712, 716, 717, 788, 800, 803, 804, 815, 838-841, 844, 846, 863, 864, 866, 873, 890, 892, 952, 990-992, 994, 996, 998, 1035, 1040, 1047, 1100, 1101, 1208, 1210, 1223-1225, 1231, 1233, 1236, 1240, 1242, 1252, 1257-1259, 1262, 1270, 1271, 1276, 1280, 1283-1286, 1304, 1312-1314, 1319, 1321, 1324-1326, 1332, 1333, 1363, 1372-1374, 1379, 1380, 1468, 1548, 1632, 1671, 1739, 1746, 1758, 1769, 1789, 1792, 1799, 1806, 1808, 1810, 1819, 1820, 1822-1826, 1828, 1839, 1897, 1901-1903, 2005, 2015, 2016, 2019, 2020, 2022-2024, 2037, 2116, 2121-2138, 2141, 2143, 2158, 2199, 2213, 2283, 2362, 2377, 2387, 2390, 2478, 2508, 2517, 2521, 2617, 2627, 2628, 2707, 2708, 2710, 2711, 2723,

Robbins, J. 1869, 1877
Roberts, J. 265, 266, 1362, 1365, 1366, 1968
Robertson, J. 272
Robinson 36, 1343, 2569
Robinson, G. 181, 237, 238, 239, 241, 242, 245, 246, 248, 249, 251, 829, 1708, 2315, 2319, 2322, 2349
Robinson, J. 181, 237, 238, 239, 241, 242, 249, 251, 829, 1125, 1708, 2315, 2319, 2322, 2349
Robinsons 23, 24, 70, 170, 171, 183, 192, 225, 330, 373, 419, 440, 727, 780, 906, 960, 1017, 1026, 1028, 1030, 1044, 1060, 1337, 1349, 1353, 1500, 1501, 1556, 1669, 1870, 1871, 1875, 1876, 1879, 1880, 1882, 2300, 2304, 2310, 2323-2325, 2664, 2745, 2746, 2784, 2790
Robson 1877, 1878
Robson, J. 1023, 1029, 1648
Roose, P. 852, 1438
Roper, A. 2528
Round, J. 2779
Ruddiman, T. 1386
Ruddiman, W. 1386
S., B. 2467
Sadler 2338, 2470
Sadler, J. 307, 490, 668, 842, 1235, 1261, 2215, 2425, 2426, 2709, 2765
Sammer, R. 710
Saur, S., (Sower) 480, 488, 1613, 2463, 2483
Schofield, T. 2378
Schweitzer, H. 1211, 1212
Sergent, E. 314, 1506, 1794-1796, 2332, 2533
Sergent, W. 16, 1943
Seymour, I. 2301, 2302
Sharrock 780
Sharrock, E. 2234, 2235, 2908
Sharrock, J. 1856
Sheppard 2093
Sheridan, R.F. 1694
Skillern, T. 2932, 2934
Smart 780
Smart, A.M. 82
Smart, J. 78, 573, 1226, 1660, 2544, 2657
Smith, T. 2209
Snagg, R. 319, 1405

Society of United Irishmen of Belfast 2762
Sotheby 1877, 1878
Sower, S., see Saur
Spilsbury, C. 1553, 1554
Spilsbury, W. 1553, 1554
Spotswood, W. 2473
Steiner 165
Steiner, M. 1086
Stewart 50, 674, 1451, 2313
Stewart, W. 555
Stockdale, J. 207, 1358, 1360, 1726, 2077
Strahan, G. 1727, 2528
Stuart, V. 2700
Stuart, W. 308, 359, 492, 582, 1698, 1827, 2278, 2340, 2836, 2908
Sullivan, J. 2087
Swindel(l)s, G. 696, 2670
Swiney, E. 75, 495, 817-819, 1321, 1683, 1989, 2602
Swinney 45, 249, 2297, 2406
Swinney, M. 237, 238, 239, 241, 242, 248, 250, 251
Symonds, H.D. 2301, 2302
Talbot, C. 410, 515, 1085, 1086, 1894
Taverne, J. 2936
Taylor 1148, 1163
Taylor, W. 2779
Tessyman 780
Thomas 1563
Thorn, B. 208, 1081
Thorn, E. 2427
Thorne, N. 913
Tisdall, I. 2025
Todd 780
Tooke, B. 1727
Tourneisen, J.J. 244
Trewman, R. 1082, 2428
Turner, M. 814
Turner, N. le 2385, 2389, 2704
Turner, N. le, widow of 2388
Tymbs, J. 443, 1045
Tyrrell, W.H. 2838
Ustick, S.C. 902
Vesey 436
Voldenvelden (Vondenvelden), W. 478, 1535
Vos, C.H. de 187
W., J. 2618
Wade, J.F. 1002, 2843

Walker 45, 249, 1699

Walker, E. 398, 1190, 1209, 1348, 2688, 2691, 2695, 2697

Walker, T. 206

Walsh, E. 869, 1341

Walton, R. 2908

Wardle 2669

Warner 448

Warner, T. 720

Waters, E. 1931

Waterworth, J. 758

Watson, W. 198

Watts 183, 186, 192, 1669, 2790

West 1069, 1502, 1642, 2421

Weston, W. 1781, 2408

White, J. 416, 433

White, L. 243, 828, 1305

White, R. 243, 876-878

White, T. 424, 820

Whitfield 436

Wilford, J. 697

Wilkie 1149, 1877

Wilkie, G. 207, 1358

Wilkie, J. 740, 1416, 1618, 2077

Wilkinson, T. 898, 1735

Wilks 1148

Willerval, F. 2937

Willerval, J.F. 851, 1837, 1892

Williams, J. 833, 835, 2855

Williams, W. 1652

Wilson 780

Wilson, A. 433

Wilson, P. 1963

Wilson, R. 2490

Wogan 1334, 1387, 2057, 2325, 2474, 2578

Wogan, P. 83, 130, 132, 194, 195, 206, 210, 348, 351, 409, 445, 536, 780, 786, 830, 848, 870, 907, 959, 1058, 1059, 1087, 1106, 1138, 1139, 1206, 1213, 1330, 1352, 1390, 1392, 1411, 1412, 1418, 1420, 1421, 1444, 1447, 1470, 1521, 1536, 1542, 1546, 1561, 1690, 1750, 1776, 1835, 1848, 1857, 1889, 1891, 1935, 1953, 1955, 1987, 2014, 2034, 2036, 2041, 2042, 2044, 2045, 2052, 2105-2107, 2220, 2228, 2312, 2324, 2337, 2365, 2444-2446, 2454, 2505, 2556, 2589, 2737, 2785-2791, 2797, 2888, 2889, 2891, 2905, 2906

Wood 2199

Woodman, J. 1896

Woods, G. 900

Wosencroft, C. 1458, 1530, 1812

Index of proper names in titles and notes

Note that we also include entries on Catholic Committee (England), Catholic Committee (Ireland) and Cisalpine Club

Abeillard, 241.
Acanthos, Bishop of, see William Gibson.
Acon, Thomas, see Thomas Talbot.
Adanen, 68-9.
Aitken, John, 748.
Albert the Great, 2206.
Alethes, Clerophilus, see John Constable.
Aloysius Gonzaga, Saint, 1842-4.
Annan, Robert, 1051.
Antonelli, Cardinal, 2291-2.
Appleton, James, 1659-60.
Archbold, Richard, 1649.
Archer, James, 2174, 2655.
Arne, Dr, 2932.
Arnold, William, 978.
Arundel, Lord, 1488.
Arundell, Lady Maria Christina, 1618.
Ashby, 53.
Baker, Pacificus, 1236, 1863.
Ballantine, William, 2375.
Bancks, William, 2405.
Barbara, Saint, 2360.
Barker, Jane, 1039.
Barker, John, 661-2, 2532.
Barkley, John, 2931.
Barnard, James, 69, 906, 941, 1833-5.
Barrett, Mr, 485.
Basil the Great, Saint, 780.
Baskerville, John, 1579, 2164-6.
Baylie, Dr, 2801.
Beeston, George, 784, 1650.
Beeston, Robert, 895.
Bellew, Christopher, 2237.
Bell, John, 398.
Benedict XIV, Pope, 229, 606, 1022, 2044-5, 2106.
Berington, Charles, 784, 940, 2297, 2544, 2655, 2750-2, 2758-9, 2862-3.
Berington, Joseph, 46, 78, 374, 784,
1046, 1650, 1881, 2309-10, 2397, 2664.
Berington, Simon, 72, 2095, 2096, 2562-3, 2566, 2956.
Bethisy, Henri B.J. de, 177-8, 2525.
Betts, John Philip, 1897.
Bew, John, 2406.
Bignell, Mr, 1024.
Birthan, James, see James Talbot.
Bishop, George, 1770-1, 1778.
Blyth, Francis, 318, 1633, 1946.
Bond, William, 2199.
Borromeus, Carolus, 1631.
Bouhours, Dominique, 1041, 1665.
Bourgeois, J., 1012.
Bower, Archibald, 410, 1649, 1920.
Bowes, Philip, 1122.
Boyer, Pierre, 1977.
Bradley, Joannes, 2695.
Brady, Bernard, 2643, 2648.
Braughall, Thomas, 482.
Bray, Thomas, 2784.
Brewer, John, 785.
Briand, Jean Olivier, 474-9, 1887, 2560.
Brigitte, Saint, 2371.
Brittain, Lewis, 367, 2549.
Broderick, Richard, 2692.
Brook, Basil, 489-94, 497.
Brooke, Henry, 1992.
Brown, Ignatius, 1215.
Brown, Levinius, see Samuel Musson.
Brown, Polemophilus, see Alexander Geddes.
Browne, Patritius, 2632.
Bruning, George, 240, 1644.
Burgis, Edward Ambrose, 2957.
Burke, Edmund, 383.
Burke, James, 882.
Burke, Thomas Myles, 381.
Burnet, Gilbert, 2767.

Burns, Robert, 1170.
Butler, Alban, 222, 412-4, 621, 1032, 2666-7.
Butler, Charles, 78, 105, 406, 715, 765, 1184, 1488, 1503, 1983, 2306, 2928.
Butler, James, 1488, 2404.
Byrne, Edward, 113-7, 134, 386, 1174, 2237, 2459.
Cajetanus Amatus, 2437.
Callanan, Laur., 2646.
Callipoli, Bishop of, see James Smith.
Campbell, George, 1389.
Carbry, Thomas, 2838.
Carey, Matthew, 1051.
Carey, W.P., 1711.
Carney, George, 2931.
Caroline, Queen, 2369.
Carpue, Mr, 701.
Carpue, Mrs, 2404.
Carr, Mr, 441.
Carroll, Anthony, 346-8.
Carroll, John, 346, 902, 1093, 2089, 2090, 2311-13, 2463, 2571.
Carter, John, 1650, 2544.
Carteret, Philip, 61, 2453.
Caryl, J., 2408.
Castaniza, Juan de, 2495.
Catherine II, 1080.
Catholic Committee (England), 104-7, 109, 119, 1503, 1637, 2300, 2307, 2750-3, 2759, 2927-30.
Catholic Committee (Ireland), 3-5, 79, 112, 114-7, 365, 885, 1020, 1173-5, 1344, 2069, 2238-9, 2241-2, 2399, 2400, 2461, 2623, 2777, 2852-4.
Centuria, Bishop of (Centurionis), see Douglass, John.
Centurioni, Luigi, 2285, 2819.
Cepari, Virgilio, 1842.
Chadwick, 2760.
Challoner, Richard, 1-4, 172-3, 223, 335, 338, 407, 545, 681, 712-3, 752, 1108-12, 1285, 1295, 1297-8, 1300, 1319, 1406, 1448-9, 1452, 1456, 1589, 1633, 1716-7, 1773, 1797, 1822ff, 1832, 1865, 1872, 1874, 1940, 1946-51, 1953-7, 1960, 2104, 2243, 2245, 2404, 2665, 2707-2718, 2730, 2897, 2960.
Champeaux, Abbé de, 35, 51.

Chandler, Samuel, 661.
Charles II, King, 2825.
Chéminais de Montaigu, Timoléon, 901.
Chilton, Elizabeth, 1527.
Chisholm, John, 1388, 1398, 1400.
Churton, Ralph, 1026, 1028.
Cisalpine Club, 714-5, 1157, 2306, 2413.
Clark, Dr, 1362-3.
Clark, John, 1426.
Clarke, Samuel, 631, 1362.
Clarkson, John, 1987.
Clarkson, John (1773-1823), 2692.
Clayton, Ra., 2095-6, 2562-3, 2566.
Clayton, Robert, 2398.
Cleander, 856-8.
Clement VIII, Pope, 1889.
Clement XI, Pope, 80, 1043, 2491, 2761.
Clement XII, Pope, 2609.
Clement XIV (Ganganelli), 434-6, 791-2, 2089-90, 2160, 2251, 2301-2.
Clifford, Henry, 104, 111, 714-5, 2306.
Clifford, Robert, 198.
Clifford, Thomas, 2655, 2949.
Clifford, Walter, 757-8.
Clinton, Alexander (Alexander Mackenzie), 922, 1349-50, 1352-3, 1650, 1716-9, 1721.
Clough, Anthony, 784, 2754.
Cloyne, Bishop of, see Richard Woodward.
Cock, Thomas, 2695.
Cody, John, 1019.
Coghlan, Anne, 176.
Coghlan, Elizabeth, 174-5.
Coke, Edward, 1983.
Comanen, Matthew, see Matthew Gibson.
Coniers, Thomas, 1661.
Conry, Mich., 2642.
Constable, John (Clerophilus Alethes), 773-4, 2767.
Constantine, Emperor, 988.
Coombes, William Henry, 361-2, 1641-2, 2189, 2694.
Coppinger, William, 329, 331, 1845.
Cordell, Charles, 230, 435, 473, 750, 1062, 1063.
Corker, James Maurus, 250.

Corne, John, 1650, 2544.

Cowley, William, 2950.

Coxeter, T., 212.

Coxon, Thomas, 52.

Crathorne, William, 264, 357, 838, 1052, 1062, 1311, 1332, 1632, 1839, 1969, 2226, 2478.

Crispe, Mary, 273.

Crook, George, 1021.

Cruise, William, 715, 2306.

Cyprien de la Nativité de la Vierge, Father, 2664.

C.A.C.D.V., 2840.

Daly, John, 907.

D'Andilly, Robert Arnauld, 2664.

Daniel, Edward, 373.

Darrell, William, 856.

D'Astorga, Baron, 226.

Dawson, Thomas, 2695.

De Barry, Paul, 2579.

Deboren, Richard (Bishop of Debra), see Richard Challoner.

Deleau, Gerard, 2397.

Dennett, James, 1918.

Dermot, Anthony, 383.

Devereux, James Edward, 426, 2237.

Devereux, John, 2692.

Dicconson, Edward (Bishop of Malla), 229

Dodd, Charles (Hugh Tootell), 774, 1491, 1655, 2230, 2309, 2767-8, 2773.

Dormer, Charles, 2297.

D'Orleans de la Motte, Lewis F.G., 1639.

Douglass, John, 247, 756, 967, 1154, 1192, 1923, 2305, 2898-2900.

Douglas, John, 2759, 2881-2, 2894.

Douglas, John, Bishop of Salisbury, 1922.

Dowley, John, 1696.

Drummond, William Abernethy, 1386-7, 1394, 1416.

Dryden, John, 341, 1665.

Du Monceau, Alexis, 954.

Ducin, Louis, 52.

Dufau, Pierre, 1531.

Dugaea, F., 2778.

Duigenan, Patrick, 38, 1069-70, 1703, 2054, 2071, 2598.

Dun, Gul., 120.

Dundass, James, 985.

E.G., 1215.

Echard, Laurence, 2451.

Edward, King, 2346-7.

Egan, Boetius, 2784.

Elliott, Nathaniel, 1537, 1842, 2270.

Ellis, Michael (Philip), 1656, 2522.

Ellis, Nathaniel, 1843.

Elrington, Thomas, 2325.

Englefield, Francis Felix, 1837.

Errington, William, 738.

Esprit, P., 1918.

Eucherius, Saint, 780.

Eudoxus, 856-8.

Eupistinus, Theophilus, see Robert Witham.

Evans, Jonathan, 2944.

Everard, T., 2206.

Eyre, Edward, 784, 2544.

Eyre, Francis, 2938-9.

Eyre, Thomas, 1205, 1334, 1488, 2688, 2691, 2695-7, 2810.

Eyston, Bernard Francis, 1837.

F.H., 2202.

Fairfax, Thomas, 53, 465.

Farmer, Ferdinand, 1894.

Farrel, Charles, 2057.

Fell, Charles, 2954.

Fenelon, François de Salignac de la Motte, 272, 2420.

Fingal, Earl of, 383.

Fisher, John, 212-7.

Fisher, S. Th. Gul., 120.

Fitzsimon, Thomas, 2385.

Fleming, Christ., 1851, 2644.

Fleury, Cardinal de, 1124.

Fleury, Claude, 914.

Flynn, Thomas, 44, 784, 1650, 2754.

Fordyce, Dr., 246.

Francis Xavier, Saint, 341-2, 1631, 1665, 1730-5, 1938-9.

Francis de Sales, Saint, 825, 1631, 1839.

French, Christophorus, 2636.

French, Thomas, 2237.

Fulford, Thomas, 2230.

Gahan, William, 149-52, 711, 1083, 1906.

Galagher, Franciscus, 2649.

Ganganelli, see Clement XIV.

Gaudentio di Lucca, 258.

Geddes, Alexander (Polemophilus Brown), 225, 960, 967, 1164, 1169, 1450.

Geddes, John, 516, 986, 1316-7, 1388, 1398, 1400-4, 1957, 2759.

George III, King, 939, 2359, 2364-5, 2369, 2653, 2668, 2784.

George, Earl of Leicester, 1876.

George, Saint, 1876.

Gerard, Mr, 2859.

Gerdill, Cardinal, 974.

Gibbon, Edward, 1023, 1876.

Gibson, Matthew, 783, 1144, 2810, 2879.

Gibson, William, 588, 940, 967, 1120, 1868, 2842, 2880-2, 2894, 2898, 2899-2900.

Giffard, Bonaventure, 1565, 2451, 2522.

Giffard, Peter, 1319, 1332.

Gillow, Thomas, 2688, 2689.

Gobinet, Charles, 347.

Godden, Thomas, 2451.

Goetz, Johann Nepomuck, 452.

Gordon, George, 46.

Gother, John, 154, 554, 752, 849, 1395, 1512, 1585, 1720, 2366, 2478, 2535.

Grascome, Samuel, 204.

Grattan, Henry, 37-9, 41, 49, 482, 874, 2457, 2564, 2598.

Green, William, 59.

Greenwood, Gregory, 1769.

Griffiths, John, 2931.

Gunston, John, 2532.

Halford, Mr, 701.

Hamilton, John, 1704-6.

Hamond, Andrew Snape, 1019.

Harris, Walter, 831-5.

Hartley, 248.

Hartley, William, 1650.

Havard, Lewis, 2694.

Havers, William, 109, 119.

Hawarden, Edward, 2546.

Hawkins, John, 250, 2089-90.

Hawkins, Thomas, 495.

Haydock, George Leo, 2688, 2695.

Hay, George, 7, 17, 736, 752, 940, 986, 1160, 1170, 1214, 1456, 1618, 2338.

Heloisa, 241.

Hennessy, John, 1725.

Henry VIII, King, 1460.

Hermès, Abbé, 906.

Hickes, George, 2704.

Hier. Caes. (Charles, Bishop of), see Charles Berington.

Hoadly, Benjamin (Bishop), 2230.

Hodgson, Teresa, 22.

Holford, Constantia, 2370.

Hooper, J., 1045.

Hormosa (Harris, E.), 1359.

Hornyold, John Joseph, 678, 1090, 2608, 2897.

Horsley, Samuel (Bishop of St. Davids), 969, 2253-4.

Howard, Charles, 766.

Howard, family, 2235.

Hughes, John, 2732.

Hunter, see Thomas Weldon.

Huntington, Countess Dowager, 740.

Husenbeth, F.S., 1221.

Hussey, Baron, of Galtrin, 134.

Hussey, Thomas, 884, 979, 1651, 1924, 2075, 2739, 2856.

Hutchinson, Francis (Bishop of Down and Connor), 1375.

Hutchinson, Mr, 701.

Ignatius of Loyola, Saint, 1631.

Innocent XI, Pope, 328, 330.

J.C. J. M'C., 1936, 1937.

J. Fd, 2558.

J.M., 761, 762.

J.M.D.C., 2357.

J.R., 2513.

J.R., Mr, 692.

James II, King, 2479-80, 2490, 2704.

James VIII (III), King, 261, 1816.

Jane, William, 2451.

Jansenius, 1523.

Jenks, Silvester, 465, 2559, 2781.

Jerningham, Edward, 1488.

John Chrysostom, Saint, 780, 1356.

Johnson, John, 771, 1471.

Johnson, Mr, 2563.

Jones, John, 1618, 2816.

Jones, Philip, 406.

Jones, William Todd, 1020, 1708, 1711.

Joseph II, Emperor, 207, 2289.

Jurieu Mr, 2205.

Kam Hi, Chinese emperor, 2540.

Kavanagh, James, 1019.
Keating, Edmond, 375.
Kellison, Matthew, 1425.
Kenmare, Lord Viscount, 420-2, 876-8.
Kennedy, Joan. Ant., 2645.
Kenny, Alexander, 1919.
Keogh, Bryan, 134.
Keogh, John, 1647, 2237.
Kirk, John, 2544, 2655, 2853.
L.R.D.D., 1729.
La Grangé, Charles de, 1484.
La Haye, F.C. de, 1012.
La Hogue, Louis Egidius de, 2719.
La Marche, Jean François de, 1144, 2291.
La Poterie, M. de, 1531.
La Rochefoucauld, Cardinal de, 1357.
Labre, Benedict Joseph, 55, 1833-36.
Lambert, Abbé de, 202.
Lambert, Patritius, 2651-2.
Lane, 354.
Langrishe, Sir Hercules, 384.
Languet, Jean Joseph, 1528, 2536.
Lartique, J.J., 888.
Lawson, Thomas, 1622, 1679, 1738, 2407.
Layton, 1032.
Le Courayer, Pierre François, 773.
Leigh, Philip, 1032, 2579.
Leslie, Charles, 859-60, 871, 1372, 1377, 1737.
Lesslie, George, 2680-2.
Lincoln, Richard, 777.
Linton, Lord, 1074.
Lloyd, Sylvester, 945-6, 2351.
Locke, John, 2422.
Loes, Nicholas, 126.
Loop, George, 2553.
Lorraine, Philip, 260.
Louis XVI, King of France, 1669, 1691, 1875, 1879.
Lovel, Francis, 2849.
Lucas, Simon, 2431, 2800.
Luis de Granada, 621.
Lupton, Thomas, 2688, 2695.
Lyttleton, George, 242.
MacDonald, Alexander (Polemon), 1404.
Macdonald of Boysdale, 1406.
MacDonnell, Jacobus, 2638.
MacKenna, Theobald, 879, 881, 1508,

1669, 1726.
MacKenzie, Alexander, see Alexander Clinton.
MacMahon, Bernard, 347-8, 1095, 1206-7, 1452, 1540-2, 1684, 1776, 1953, 2032.
Mac-Nemarra, Antonius, 2633.
MacPherson, James, 1994.
Maguire, Philip, 2047.
Mainwaring, Thomas, 1727.
Maire, William, 1208.
Malcolm III, 1171.
Mallen, Edwardus, see Edward Dicconson.
Malone, James, 1785.
Manby, Peter, 1982.
Manning, Robert, 1375.
Mannock, John, 695.
Mansse, Lewis, 1078.
Maréchal, Archbishop, 1143.
Margaret, Saint, Queen of Scotland, 1171.
Marie Antoinette, Queen of France, 1692-3, 1975.
Martin, J. 124.
Martin, Simon, 1681.
Mary of Egypt, Saint, 896, 1666, 1679, 2425-6.
Mary of Modena, 684.
Mary of the Holy Cross, 222.
Mary-Anne-Joseph of Jesus, sister, see Anne Coghlan.
Mary-Elizabeth of Jesus, sister, see Elizabeth Coghlan.
Mason, Richard, 153, 709.
Matthews, Tobie, 395.
Mauger, 1012.
McCarthy, Justin, 108.
McCormick, Richard, 116, 1174, 2459.
McDavett, Dom, 2639.
McDermot, 365.
McIntyre, A., 1957.
McK., J., 2560.
McNeven, (William James), 365.
Meany, William, 1019.
Meindarts, Johannes Petrus, 722.
Melsheimer, Frederick Valentine, 369.
Menzies, Robert, 2731, 2817.
Metcalfe, Philip, 1032.
M'Evoy, Robert, 36, 2783.
Middleton, Conyers, 260, 508-9, 526,

622-3, 1127, 2910.

Mildmay, Henry, 2078-84.

Milner, John, 593-594, 780, 791, 1159, 1511, 1556, 1560-1, 2104, 2430, 2664, 2743, 2901.

Mitford, Mr, 1866.

M'Kee, Robert, 2739.

Molyneux, Robert, 515, 1086, 1779.

Montford, James, 1915.

Moore, James, 1509, 2926.

More, Mary Augustine, 2664.

More, Thomas, 215-7, 1896.

Morgan, Thomas, 770.

Morocco (Maroch), Bishop of, see John Geddes.

Moylan, Francis, 1599-1602, 1605, 1899, 2183-5, 2784.

Mulcaile, J.P., 1037-8.

Mullinaux, Sir Vivian, 1964-67.

Mullowny, John, 1019.

Murphy, Cornelius, 872, 1922.

Murphy, John, 1019.

Musson, Samuel, 333, 1127, 1730.

Nagle, J., 593.

Nagle, Nano, 781.

Nary, Cornelius, 1858, 1944-5, 2438-40, 2442-3, 2447-8, 2953.

Neale, Archbishop, 1143.

Oates, Titus, 2207.

O'Conor, Charles, 828, 1638, 2850.

O'Donnell, Antonius, 2634.

O'Donnell, Ludovicus, 2635, 2641.

O'Dunn, Chev., 796.

O'Hara, Mr, 2458.

O'Hussey, Bonaventura, 919, 1696.

O'Leary, Arthur, 48, 884, 1586, 1924, 2856.

O'Reilly, Jacobus, 2647.

Orien (Bishop of), see John Chisholm.

Orleans, Pierre d', 1842.

Owen, Hugh, 2732.

P.L., 1808.

P.R., 2385.

Paine, Thomas, 1135.

Panting, John, 2195.

Panzani, Gregorio, 249, 2309.

Pastorini, see Charles Walmesley.

Patrick, Saint, 1667, 1858, 2328.

Patrick, Simon, 2451.

Patsall, Mrs, 72.

Paul V, Pope, 2107-12.

Paxton, 2931-2.

Peach, Edward, 2692.

Peckwell, Rev., 766.

Penswick, Thomas, 2688-9.

Pergolesi, 227.

Perkins, Anthony, 2540.

Peters, see Benjamin Petre.

Petre, Benjamin, 229, 595, 600, 947, 1895.

Petre, Francis, 60, 1856.

Petre, Robert Edward (Lord Petre), 105, 1074-5, 1488, 1746, 2758.

Phelan, Franciscus, 2650.

Phelan, James, 218, 877, 878-80.

Philalbion, 2800.

Philip, Bishop of Aureliople, see Michael (Philip) Ellis.

Phillips, Elizabeth, 2265.

Phillips, Thomas, 2701.

Philomel, John, see John Joseph Hornyold.

Pinkard, Robert (J.T.), 1204, 2495, 2502, 2505.

Pitchford, Thomas, 2694.

Pitt, Miss, 1073.

Pius IV, Pope, 575-87, 624-5, 1907, 2560.

Pius V, Pope, 716-7, 1863, 1889.

Pius VI, Pope, 19, 20, 270-1, 361-2, 597, 893, 939, 974-5, 980, 1080, 1130, 1204, 1500, 1605-6, 1640, 1642-3, 1652, 2060-1, 2189, 2286-7, 2289-90, 2365, 2541.

Pius VII, Pope, 1607, 2293-94.

Plessis, J. O., 887, 2561.

Plowden, Charles, 249, 1650, 2743.

Plowden, Francis, 1488, 1730, 2324.

Plowden, Robert, 208.

Plowden, Thomas Percy, 18, 772, 2277, 2510.

Plunket, Oliver, 2449-50.

Plunkett, Dr., 2570.

Podmore, Mr, 64.

Pole, Reginald, 2255-60, 2264.

Polemon, see Alexander MacDonald.

Potts, T., 2406

Pouget, François Aimé, 1982.

Powell, David, 643, 2353-4.

Powess, Countess of, 1808.

Poynter, William, 2692-3.

Preston, James, 383.

Price, James, 295.
Prichard, Matthew, 2954.
Priestley, Joseph, 170, 238, 248, 1156.
Prusen, Benjamin, see Benjamin Petre.
Questall, John, 212.
Radcliffe, Stephen (Vicar of Naas), 1928, 1932.
Rama, Bishop of (Ramaten), see Charles Walmesley.
Rayment, Benedict, 1884, 2293, 2740.
Reeve, Joseph, 1081-5, 1650, 2269.
Regis, John Francis, Saint, 5, 873.
Reid, John, 2885.
Renaudau, Mr, 912.
Renaudot, E., 2490.
Ricci, Laurent, 1564, 2303.
Ricci, 1177, 2932.
Rickaby, John, 2688, 2695.
Riddell, William, 797.
Riddle, J., 1769.
Rigby, John, 2338.
Robertson, James, 1957.
Roe, John, 2544.
Roper, Thomas, 216.
Rousseau, Jean-Jacques, 230-1, 1135.
Sabran, Lewis, 5.
Sacheverell, Henry, 793.
Sall, Andrew, 1122.
Samber, Robert, 1210.
Sarrazin, P., 1012.
Saul, Charles, 2689.
Saville, George, 1648.
Scarisbrick, Francis, 2493.
Segneri, Paolo, 2328.
Sergeant, John, 1113, 2559.
Sharp, John, 901, 2532.
Sharrock, Gregory William (Bishop of Telmessus), 939, 940.
Sheldon (Nathaniel Elliot), 2270.
Sheldon, Edward, 339, 349.
Sheldon, William, 2938-9.
Shepherd, John, 801.
Sherbourne, Edward, 2489.
Simms, Robert, 1713-4.
Smith, Dr., 218.
Smith, James, 1656.
Sobieski, Clementina, Princess, 21.
Soldini, Francesco Maria, 503.
Sommalius, 2702.
Southcote (Southcott), Thomas, 1528, 2414, 2417.

Southworth, Thomas, 2544, 2655.
Spinckes, Nathaniel, 204.
Stanhope, George, 2704.
Stanislaus, King of Poland, 1484.
Staurophilus (George Hay), 1389.
Steinmeyer, 1894.
Stephens, Edward, 204.
Stevens, John, 218-9, 2779.
Stone, George, 76-7.
Stone, Thomas, 1650.
Stonor, John, 229.
Stonor, John Talbot, 763, 1771, 2455.
Stourton, Lord, 109, 2753.
Strickland, Joseph, 2743.
Stuart, Franciscus, 2631.
Sturges, J., 1877-8.
Suffren, Jean, 2375.
Surrey, Earl of, 1074.
Sweetman, John, 482, 2564.
Swinburn, Joseph, 2688, 2695.
Synge, Edward, 1925-8, 1932.
T.M., 5519, 1856.
T.P.S.C.T. see Thomas Phillips.
T.V. (Thomas Vincent Sadler), 2405.
Talbot, Gilbert, 61-3, 103, 763, 2453, 2455, 2616.
Talbot, James, 268, 338, 627, 678-80, 986, 1011, 1509, 2221, 2484, 2879-80, 2897, 2959.
Talbot, Thomas, 678, 986, 1681, 2297, 2754, 2879-80.
Tandy, James Napper, 876.
Teeling, Luke, 1129, 1175.
Tellez, Balthazar, 2779.
Telmessus, Bishop of, see William Gregory Sharrock.
Teresa of Jesus, Saint, 396.
Theophilus, 2072-3.
Thespiensis, Joannis, see John Stonor.
Thimelby, Richard, 53.
Thomas a Becket, 242-4.
Thompson, Richard, 2688-9.
Thorpe, John, 2301.
Throckmorton, George, 2955.
Throckmorton, John Courtenay, 107, 415, 1154, 1867, 2267, 2612.
Throckmorton, William, 715, 2306.
Thwaites, Francis, 2415-7.
Tillotson, John, 1929.
Tognarelli, Peter, 2931.
Tootell, Christopher, see Charles Dodd.

Tootell, Hugh, 774, 1491, 1655, 2230.
Trachon, William, see William Walton.
Trapp, Joseph, 1768, 1776.
Trench, Antonius, 2640.
Troy, John Thomas, 36, 42, 1452, 1923, 1956, 2325.
Turberville, Henry, 1, 8, 945, 2537.
Turner, M., 814.
Tusker, James, 2544.
Typper, John, see Robert Pinkard.
Ulysses Desiderius Pius, 2198-2201.
Umfreville, Charles, 2095-6, 2562-3, 2566.
Urban VIII, Pope, 1889.
Vailiant, John, 363.
Valart, Abbé, 2724, 2726.
Valerian, 780.
Verax (Francis Fleming), 1051.
Verax, 731-5.
Veridicus, 2596.
Veritas, 731-5.
Verus (Robert Annan), 1051.
Voltaire, Arruet de, 1135, 1358.
W. H., 1064.
W. P., 2467.
Wade, John Francis, 1002.
Wainhouse, Richard, 1543-4.
Walenburch, Pieter van, 2860.
Walmesley, Charles, 472, 678, 780, 963, 967, 1154, 1192, 1604, 1864, 2186, 2748, 2758, 2759, 2884, 2886-9.
Walton, William, 678, 756, 2897.
Ward, John, 2526.
Warner, Elizabeth, 2492.
Warner, John, 350, 1339-40.
Warner, Lady, 2492.

Warren, John, 1147.
Washington, George, 440, 447-8.
Weardon, Jane, 22.
Webbe, Samuel, 2931.
Webb, George, 1626.
Webb, James, 2221.
Webster, Thomas, 1426.
Welch, Louis Abraham, 1566.
Welch, Thomas, 1529.
Weld, Thomas, 1352.
Weldon, Thomas, (Hunter), 2935.
Wenefride, Saint, see Winefrid.
Wesley, John, 2064-66, 2076-7, 2943.
Westmorland, John Earl of, 42, 2784.
Wharton, Charles Henry, 250, 442, 444-5, 1045, 1362, 2089-90, 2266, 2839, 2948.
Whiston, William, 280, 1362, 1363.
White, Bishop, (Benjamin Petre), 947, 1895.
White, Thomas, 2849.
Whittenhall, T., 2417.
Witham, Robert (Eupistinus Theophilus), 2954.
Wilks, Joseph, 44, 785, 1021, 1864, 2758.
Williams, John, 1149.
Wilson, John, 2958.
Winefrid, Saint, 855, 1032, 1674-7.
Woodhead, Abraham, 2664-5.
Woodward, Richard, Bishop of Cloyne, 418-20, 422, 808-9, 2068, 2070-3.
Wright Messrs, 2404.
Wright, Thomas, 2655.
Wyche, Joseph, 2958.
Yates, Edward, 317-20.
York, Duchess of, 2824.